VICE PRESIDENTS OF THE UNITED STATES
1789–1993

President Gerald R. Ford congratulating Vice President Nelson
Rockefeller after his swearing in on December 19, 1974

VICE PRESIDENTS
OF THE UNITED STATES
1789–1993

Mark O. Hatfield
United States Senator

Donald A. Ritchie
Jo Anne McCormick Quatannens
Richard A. Baker
William T. Hull
U.S. Senate Historical Office

Edited by
Wendy Wolff
U.S. Senate Historical Office

U.S. Government Printing Office
Washington

[iii]

104th Congress, 2d Session
S. Con. Res. 34

Senate Document 104–26
U.S. Government Printing Office
Washington: 1997

Supt. of Docs. No.: 052–071–01227–3

Cover illustration: Vice President Henry A. Wallace (*center*); Senator Harry S. Truman (*right*), who had recently won the Democratic nomination for vice president; and Senate Majority Leader Alben W. Barkley (*left*) in August 1944.

Library of Congress Cataloging-in-Publication Data

Vice Presidents of the United States, 1789–1993 / Mark O. Hatfield . . .
    [et al.] ; edited by Wendy Wolff.
        p. cm.
    Includes bibliographical references and index.
    1. Vice-Presidents—United States—Biography. I. Hatfield, Mark O.,
1922– . II. Wolff, Wendy.
E176.49.V53   1997
973′ .09′9
[B]—DC21   96–51492
                                   CIP

For sale by the U.S. Government Printing Office, Superintendent of Documents,
Mail Stop; SSOP, Washington, DC 20402–9328

To Gerald W. Frank

An exemplary citizen and leader in many civic causes.
A longtime friend, chief of staff, and confidant.

MOH

CONTENTS

VICE PRESIDENTS

(Alphabetical)

INTRODUCTION

Holding the least understood, most ridiculed, and most often ignored constitutional office in the federal government, American vice presidents have included some remarkable individuals. Fourteen of the forty-four former vice presidents became president of the United States—more than half of them after a president had died. One defeated the sitting president with whom he served. One murdered a man and became a fugitive. One joined the Confederate army and led an invasion of Washington, D.C. One was the wealthiest banker of his era. One received the Nobel Peace Prize and composed a popular melody. One served as a corporal in the Coast Guard while vice president. One had cities in Oregon and Texas named after him. Two resigned the office. Two were never elected by the people. One was the target of a failed assassination plot. One was mobbed in his car while on a goodwill mission. Seven died in office—one in his room in the U.S. Capitol and two fatally stricken while on their way to preside over the Senate. And one piano-playing vice president suffered political repercussions from a photograph showing him playing that instrument while famous movie actress Lauren Bacall posed seductively on top of it.

I have encountered these and many other stories over the past four years in the course of my inquiry into the history of the American vice-presidency. As is apparent from such examples, the men who served as vice president of the United States varied greatly in their talents and aptitude for the post. What they generally had in common was political ambition and experience in public office. Most hoped the position would prove a stepping stone to the presidency, but some—old and tired near the close of their careers—simply hoped that it would offer a quiet refuge from political pressures and turmoil.

The stories of these diverse individuals attempt to sketch the development of the vice presidency itself—that colorful, important, and routinely disparaged American political institution.

I. Constitutional Origins and Structural Changes

Electoral system

Our Constitution's framers created the vice-presidency almost as an afterthought. In setting up a system for electing presidents, they devised an electoral college and provided that each of its members was to vote for two persons, "of whom one at least shall not be an Inhabitant of the same State with themselves." In those days when loyalty to one's state was stronger than to the new nation, the framers recognized that individual electors might be inclined to choose a leader from their own immediate political circle, creating the danger of a crippling deadlock, as no one candidate would win a plurality of all votes cast. By being required to select one candidate from outside their own states, electors would be compelled to look for individuals of national stature. Under the system the framers created, the candidate receiving the most electoral votes would be president. The one coming in second would be vice president.

In the election of 1800, however, the constitutional system for electing presidents broke down, as both Jefferson and Aaron Burr received the same number of electoral votes. This impasse threw the contest into the House of Representatives, where for thirty-five separate ballots, neither candidate was able to gain a majority. When the stalemate was finally broken, the House elected Jefferson president, thus making Aaron Burr our third vice president. Within four years of this deadlocked election, Congress had passed, and the necessary number of states had ratified, the Twelfth Amendment to the Constitution, instituting the present system wherein electors cast separate ballots for president and for vice president.

Presidential succession

Although the office of vice president did not exist under the Continental congresses or the Articles of Confederation, the concept of a concurrently elected successor to the executive was not without precedent for the framers of the Constitution in 1787. Prior to the Revolution, lieutenant governors presided over the governors' councils of the royal colonies—which, in their legislative capacities, functioned as upper houses. John Adams was certainly familiar with this arrangement, since the lieutenant governor presided over the upper house in his own state of Massachusetts. After the states declared their independence, they adopted new constitutions, retaining, in some instances, earlier forms recast to meet current needs. As Alexander Hamilton noted in *The Federalist* No. 68, New York's 1777 constitution provided for "a Lieutenant Governor chosen by the people at large, who presides in the senate, and is the constitutional substitute for the Governor in casualties similar to those, which would authorise the vice-president to exercise the authorities and discharge the duties of the president." The Constitution established the office of vice president primarily to provide a successor in the event of the president's death, disability, or resignation.

The document, however, was vague about the way the presidential succession would work, stating only that, in cases of presidential death or disability, the "Powers and Duties of the said Office . . . shall devolve on the Vice President" (Article II, section 1). What did "devolve" mean? Would the vice president become acting president until another was chosen, or would he become president in his own right? A half-century would pass before the nation would have to address that murky constitutional language. Although the Constitution's framers kept their intentions about presidential succession shrouded in ambiguity, they left no doubt about vice-presidential succession. There was to be none. "[I]n the absence of the Vice President, or when he shall exercise the Office of the President of the United States" the Senate would simply choose a president pro tempore.

The framers' failure to provide a method for filling a vice-presidential vacancy continued to plague the nation. In 1792 Congress made a first stab at addressing the problem by adopting the Presidential Succession Act, providing that, if a president should die when there was no vice president, the Senate president pro tempore and the Speaker of the House of Representatives, in that order, would succeed to the office. In 1886, responding to a concern that few presidents pro tempore had executive branch experience, Congress altered the line of succession to substitute for the congressional officials cabinet officers in order of rank, starting with the secretary of state. In 1947, after the vice-presidency had been vacant for most of a presidential term, Congress again changed the line of succession. Concerned that cabinet officers had not been elected, it named the House Speaker as the first official to succeed if a president died during a vacancy in the vice-presidency, followed by the president pro tempore.

Finally, after the death of President John F. Kennedy in 1963 and the resulting vice-presidential vacancy, Congress debated what became the second constitutional amendment related to the structure of the vice-presidency. In 1967, the Twenty-fifth Amendment, addressing presidential vacancy and disability, became part of our Constitution. The absence of any provision for filling a vice-presidential vacancy had become intolerable in the nuclear age. Added impetus for the change came from a growing public concern at the time about the advanced ages of President pro tempore Carl Hayden, who was eighty, and House Speaker John W. McCormack, who was seventy-six. The amendment states that the president may appoint a vice president to fill a vacancy in that office, subject to approval by both houses of Congress. Before a decade had passed, the provision was used twice, first in 1973 when President Nixon appointed Gerald R. Ford to replace Spiro Agnew, who had resigned, and again in 1974, with the appointment of Nelson Rockefeller after Nixon himself resigned and Ford became president. The amendment also sets forth very specifically the steps that would permit the vice president to serve as acting president if a president becomes "unable to discharge the powers and duties of his office." Each of these changes further reflected the increased importance of the office.

Vice-presidential duties

The framers also devoted scant attention to the vice president's duties, providing only that he "shall be President of the Senate, but shall have no Vote, unless they be evenly divided" (Article I, section 3). In practice, the number of times vice presidents have exercised this right has varied greatly. More than half the total number of 233 tie-breaking votes occurred before 1850, with John Adams holding the record at 29 votes, followed closely by John C. Calhoun with 28. Since the 1870s, no vice president has cast as many as 10 tie-breaking votes. While vice presidents have used their votes chiefly on legislative issues, they have also broken ties on the election of Senate officers, as well as on the appointment of committees in 1881 when the parties were evenly represented in the Senate.

The vice president's other constitutionally mandated duty was to receive from the states the tally of electoral ballots cast for president and vice president and to open the certificates "in the Presence of the Senate and House of Representatives," so that the total votes could be counted (Article II, section 1). Only a few happy vice presidents—John Adams, Thomas Jefferson, Martin Van Buren, and George Bush—had the pleasure of announcing their own election as president. Many more were chagrined to announce the choice of some rival for the office.

Several framers ultimately refused to sign the Constitution, in part because they viewed the vice president's legislative role as a violation of the separation of powers doctrine. Elbridge Gerry, who would later serve as vice president, declared that the framers "might as well put the President himself as head of the legislature." Others thought the office unnecessary but agreed with Connecticut delegate Roger Sherman that "if the vice-President were not to be President of the Senate, he would be without employment, and some member [of the Senate, acting as presiding officer] must be deprived of his vote."

Under the original code of Senate rules, the presiding officer exercised great power over the conduct of the body's proceedings. Rule XVI provided that "every question of order shall be decided by the President [of the Senate], without debate; but if there be a doubt in his mind, he may call for a sense of the Senate." Thus, contrary to later practice, the presiding officer was the sole judge of proper procedure and his rulings could not be turned aside by the full Senate without his assent.

The first two vice presidents, Adams and Jefferson, did much to shape the nature of the office, setting precedents that were followed by others. During most of the nineteenth century, the degree of influence and the role played within the Senate depended chiefly on the personality and inclinations of the individual involved. Some had great parliamentary skill and presided well, while others found the task boring, were incapable of maintaining order, or chose to spend most of their time away from Washington, leaving the duty to a president pro tempore. Some made an effort to preside fairly, while others used their position to promote the political agenda of the administration.

During the twentieth century, the role of the vice president has evolved into more of an executive branch position. Now, the vice president is usually seen as an integral part of a president's administration and presides over the Senate only on ceremonial occasions or when a tie-breaking vote may be needed. Yet, even though the nature of the job has changed, it is still greatly affected by the personality and skills of the individual incumbent.

II. The Individuals

Political Experience

Most of our former vice presidents have brought to that office significant public service experience. Thirty-one of the forty-four served in Congress, and fifteen had been state or territorial governors. Five—Schuyler Colfax, Charles Curtis, John Garner, Alben Barkley, and Lyndon Johnson—gave up powerful congressional leadership posts to run for that much-derided office. Another, House Minority Leader Gerald Ford, observed that he had been trying for twenty-five years to become Speaker of the House. "Suddenly, I am a candidate for the President of the Senate, where I can hardly ever vote, and where I will never get a chance to speak."

Nineteen former vice presidents came to their role as president of the Senate already familiar with the body, having served as U.S. senators. Several vice presidents later returned to serve again in the Senate, among them former President Andrew Johnson. Nine vice presidents won renomination and election to a second term. Two of these, George Clinton and John C. Calhoun, held the office under two different presidents.

Of the fourteen vice presidents who fulfilled their ambition by achieving the presidency, eight succeeded to the office on the death of a president. Three of these and six other former vice presidents were later elected president. Four former vice presidents ran unsuccessfully for president. Two unlucky vice presidents, Hannibal Hamlin and Henry Wallace, were dropped from the ticket after their first term, only to see their successors become president months after taking office, when the assassination of Abraham Lincoln made Andrew Johnson president and the death of Franklin D. Roosevelt raised Harry Truman to the presidency. Similarly, when Spiro Agnew resigned, he was replaced under the Twenty-fifth Amendment by Gerald R. Ford, who became president when Richard M. Nixon resigned less than a year later.

The vice-presidency was generally held by men of mature years—thirty-two of them were in their fifties or sixties when they took office—but ten were in their forties, and the youngest, John C. Breckinridge of Kentucky, was thirty-six at the beginning of his term. At seventy-two, Alben Barkley, another Kentuckian, was the oldest when his term began.

The earliest vice presidents: Adams and Jefferson

The nation's first vice presidents were men of extraordinary ability. Both John Adams and Thomas Jefferson gained the office as runners-up in presidential contests, with the support of those who believed they were amply qualified to hold the top office. Each recognized, in assuming this new and as yet loosely defined position, that his actions would set precedents for future vice presidents. But one precedent established by Adams and Jefferson would not be repeated for over three decades; although both men won election as president immediately following their terms as vice president, no sitting vice president would repeat this pattern until 1836, when Martin Van Buren succeeded Andrew Jackson. (The gap thereafter was even longer. More than 150 years elapsed before George Bush won the presidency in 1988 at the conclusion of his eight years as Ronald Reagan's vice president.)

During his two vice-presidential terms, Adams maintained a cordial, but distant, relationship with the president, who sought his advice only occasionally. In the Senate, Adams played a more active role, particularly during his first term. On at least one occasion, he persuaded senators to vote against legislation he opposed, and he frequently lectured the body on procedural and policy matters. He supported Washington's policies by casting the twenty-nine tie-breaking votes that no successor has equalled.

Thomas Jefferson, learning in 1797 that he had been elected vice president, and always happy to return to his beloved Monticello, expressed his pleasure. "A more tranquil and unoffending station could not have been found for me. It will give me philosophical evenings in the winter [while at the Senate] and rural days in the summer [at Monticello]." Unlike Adams, who shared the political beliefs of the president with whom he served, Jefferson and his president belonged to different political parties. Although two later vice presidents, George Clinton and John C. Calhoun, joined with anti-administration forces in their efforts to prevent the reelection of the presidents with whom they served, Jefferson's situation would prove to be unique in all the nation's history. No one expected Jefferson to be President Adams' principal assistant. Instead he devoted his four-year term to preparing himself for the next presidential election and to drafting a guidebook on legislative procedure. Jefferson hoped that his *Manual of Parliamentary Practice* would allow him and his successors to preside over the Senate with fairness, intelligence, and consistency. That classic guide has retained its usefulness to both the Senate and the House of Representatives through the intervening two centuries.

Nineteenth-century vice presidents

Adoption of the Twelfth Amendment, together with the strategy employed by the Republicans in their successful effort to capture the presidency in 1800—and to retain it for the next quarter century—proved to have a serious impact on the overall quality of individuals drawn to the vice-presidency.

Aaron Burr, whose refusal to defer to Jefferson had precipitated the electoral crisis of 1800, became one of the most maligned and mistrusted figures of his era and, without question, the most controversial vice president of the early republic. He was also a man of extraordinary ability, and a key player in New York politics—a consideration of overriding importance for Republicans, given the fact that New York's electoral votes accounted for over 15 percent of the total needed to achieve an electoral majority. Burr was the first of a series of vice presidents who hailed from the northern states, chosen more for their ability to bring geographical balance to presidential tickets headed by Virginia Republicans than for their capacity to serve as president. During the quarter century that the "Virginia dynasty" presidents (Jefferson, James Madison, and James Monroe) held sway, the vice-presidency was the province of men widely regarded as party hacks or men in the twilight of illustrious careers. Much of the scholarship on the vice-presidency makes but passing mention of these individuals, or focuses on their obvious shortcomings. But these vice presidents (Burr, George Clinton, Elbridge Gerry, and Daniel D. Tompkins)—all of them New Yorkers, with the single exception of Elbridge Gerry, a Massachusetts man—helped cement the "Virginia-New York" alliance that enabled the Republicans to control the presidency for six consecutive terms. Their ties to local and state party organizations, which they maintained during their vice-presidential terms, helped ensure the continued allegiance of northern Republicans. For the most part, these vice presidents presided over the Senate with an easy or indifferent hand, while a series of presidents pro tempore attended to administrative matters at the beginning and end of each legislative session.

John C. Calhoun's vice-presidency stands in vivid contrast to the experience of his immediate predecessors. He accepted the second office, under John Quincy Adams, after his 1824 presidential bid failed, offering himself as Andrew Jackson's running mate four years later in hopes of eventually succeeding Jackson. A man of formidable intellect and energy, Calhoun approached his legislative duties with a gravity, dedication, and concern for maintaining order not seen since the time of Adams and Jefferson. A scrupulous guardian of the Senate's written rules, he disdained its unwritten customs and practices. After a quarter century of ineffective or incapacitated vice presidents, the Senate chafed under Calhoun's tutelage and began a lengthy examination of the role of its presiding officer. Calhoun's endorsement of nullification effectively killed his chances of becoming president. In 1836, his successor and rival, Martin Van Buren, became the first vice president since Jefferson to win the presidency.

Richard Mentor Johnson, Martin Van Buren's vice president, came to the office along a unique path not yet followed by any subsequent vice president. The Twelfth Amendment provides that if no vice-presidential candidate receives a majority, the Senate shall decide between the two highest vote getters. A controversial figure who had openly acknowledged his slave mistress and mulatto daughters and devoted himself more to the customers of his tavern than to his Senate duties, Johnson received one electoral vote less than the majority needed to elect. The Senate therefore met on February 8, 1837, and elected Johnson by a vote of 33 to 16 over the runner-up.

Johnson's successor, John Tyler, wrote an important chapter in American presidential and vice-presidential history in 1841 when William Henry Harrison became the first president to die in office. Interpreting the Constitution in a way that might have surprised its framers, Vice President Tyler refused to consider himself as acting president. What "devolved" on him at Harrison's death were not the "powers and duties" of the presidential office, he contended, but the office itself. Tyler boldly claimed the presidency, its full $25,000 salary (vice presidents were paid 20 percent of that amount—$5,000), and all its prerogatives. Congressional leaders and members of Harrison's cabinet who were inclined to challenge Tyler eventually set aside their concerns in the face of the accomplished fact. Nine years later, when Vice President Millard Fillmore succeeded to the presidency after Zachary Taylor's death, no serious question was raised about the propriety of such a move.

During the nineteenth century, the vice-presidency remained essentially a legislative position. Those who held it rarely attended cabinet meetings or otherwise involved themselves in executive branch business. Their usefulness to the president generally ended with the election. While those who had served in Congress might offer helpful political information and connections to a presidential candidate, or might attract electoral votes in marginal states, their status and value evaporated after inauguration day. In fact, as political circumstances altered during their first term, some presidents began considering a new running mate for the reelection campaign. Abraham Lincoln, for example, had no need of Vice President Hannibal Hamlin of Maine for a second term, since his state was certain to vote to reelect Lincoln in 1864. Success being less assured in the border state of Tennessee, party leaders chose Senator Andrew Johnson to replace Hamlin in the second position.

Relegated to presiding over the Senate, a few nineteenth-century vice presidents took that task seriously. Men such as George Dallas, Levi Morton, and Garret Hobart studied the Senate's rules and precedents and presided most effectively. Others, such as Henry Wilson—Grant's second vice president—spent their time as they pleased. As vice president, Wilson wrote a three-volume history of slavery before dying in his Capitol office.

The vice-presidency in the nineteenth century seldom led to the White House, because vice presidents of the era were rarely men of presidential stature. Of the twenty-one individuals who held that office from 1805 to 1899, only Martin Van Buren managed to be elected president. Four others achieved the presidency only because the incumbent died, and none of those four accidental presidents subsequently won election in his own right.

Twentieth-century vice presidents

The twentieth century opened without a vice president. Vice President Garret Augustus Hobart had died in November 1899, leaving the office vacant, as it had been on ten previous occasions for periods ranging from a few months to nearly four years. The nation had gotten along just fine. No one much noticed.

People noticed the next vice president. Cowboy, scholar, naturalist, impetuous enthusiast for numerous ideas and causes, Theodore Roosevelt owed his nomination to the desire of New York state political bosses to get him out of the state's politics. The former Rough Rider held presidential ambitions and worried that the job could be "a steppingstone to . . . oblivion." He also felt that he lacked the financial resources needed to entertain on the grand scale expected of his immediate predecessors. Roosevelt argued in vain that the party should find someone else, but Republican leaders wanted him, believing he would bring a new kind of glamour and excitement to President McKinley's candidacy. When his magnetic presence at the national convention fired the enthusiasm of his partisans, the nomination was his. Roosevelt then defied conventional practice by waging an active national campaign for the ticket, publicizing the Republican cause in a way that President McKinley could not. Had not an assassin's bullet in September 1901 propelled Roosevelt to the White House, his impact on the vice-presidency during a four-year term would most likely have been profound. In 1904, Theodore Roosevelt became the first vice president who succeeded to the presidency to be elected president in his own right.

For the next forty years, the role of the office grew slowly but perceptibly. Party leaders rather than presidential candidates continued to make vice-presidential selections to balance the ticket, often choosing someone from a different party faction who was not personally close to the presidential nominee. In fact, Presidents Theodore Roosevelt, William Howard Taft, and Herbert Hoover protested the individuals selected to be their running mates. The feeling was often mutual. When Charles Curtis gave the customary vice-presidential inaugural address in the Senate chamber, he omitted any reference to his running mate, President Hoover. A few minutes later, Hoover returned the favor by neglecting to mention Curtis in his official remarks on the Capitol's east portico.

The principal twentieth-century growth in the vice president's role occurred when the national government assumed a greater presence in American life, beginning with the New Deal era and extending through the cold war years. That era brought to the vice-presidency such major political leaders as House Speaker John "Cactus Jack" Garner and Senate Majority Leaders Alben Barkley and Lyndon Johnson. This distinguished cast of elected vice presidents also included Senators Harry Truman, Richard Nixon, Hubert Humphrey, Walter Mondale, and Al Gore (who is serving as vice president at this writing and is therefore not included in this book). The group also includes George Bush, whose previous experience ranged from the House of Representatives to the Central Intelligence Agency. With the exception of Garner and possibly Truman, these men were selected not by party wheelhorses but by the presidential candidates themselves. Competence and compatibility became the most sought-after qualities in a running mate. These characteristics were especially evident in the Truman-Barkley and Clinton-Gore tickets, both of which set aside the traditional selection considerations of geographical and ideological balance.

During the twentieth century, the focus of the vice-presidency has shifted dramatically from being mainly a legislative position to a predominately executive post. As modern-era presidents began playing an increasing role as legislative agenda setters, their vice presidents regularly attended cabinet meetings and received executive assignments. Vice presidents represented their presidents' administrations on Capitol Hill, served on the National Security Council, chaired special commissions, acted as high level representatives of the government to foreign heads of state, and assumed countless other chores—great and trivial—at the president's direction. Beginning with Richard Nixon, they have occupied spacious quarters in the Executive Office Building and assembled staffs of specialists to extend their reach and influence. From fewer than 20 staff members at the end of Nixon's vice-presidency, the number increased to 60 during the 1970s, with the addition of not only political and support staff but advisers on domestic policy and national security. Walter Mondale expanded the vice president's role as presidential adviser, establishing the tradition of weekly lunches with the president, and subsequent vice presidents have continued to be active participants in their administrations.

Expansion of the office did not come without a cost, however. In assuming substantive policy responsibilities, vice presidents often ran afoul of cabinet secretaries whose territories they invaded. As administration lobbyists, they also irritated members of Congress. My favorite example of this problem occurred in 1969. President Nixon had pledged to give his vice president a significant policy-making role and—for the first time—an office in the White House itself. Spiro Agnew was determined to make the most of that role and to expand his legislative functions as well. Since he lacked previous legislative experience, he had the Senate parliamentarian tutor him on the intricacies of Senate floor procedure. Soon he began to inject himself into the course of Senate proceedings, contrary to the well-worn practice that constrained his predecessors. During the debate over the Anti-Ballistic-Missile Treaty, Agnew approached Idaho Republican Senator Len Jordan and asked how he was going to vote. "You can't tell me how to vote!" said the shocked senator. "You can't twist my arm!" At the next regular luncheon of Republican senators, Jordan accused Agnew of breaking the separation of powers by lobbying on the Senate floor, and announced the "Jordan Rule." Under his rule, if the vice president tried to lobby him on anything, the senator would automatically vote the other way. Agnew concluded from this experience, "after trying for a while to get along with the Senate, I decided I would go down to the other end of Pennsylvania Avenue and try playing the executive game."

In 1886 the Senate initiated the practice of honoring former vice presidents by acquiring marble busts of those who had held the office, with the expenses paid from the contingent fund of the Senate. The previous year, in 1885, the Senate had placed in the Vice President's Room a bust of Henry Wilson, who had died in that room a decade earlier. Under the 1886 resolution, busts of former vice presidents, beginning with those of John Adams and Thomas Jefferson, were placed in the niches around the gallery level of the Senate chamber. Once those twenty spaces were filled, the Senate adopted an amended resolution in 1898 to place future vice-presidential busts elsewhere in the Senate wing of the Capitol. The practice continues today.

III. Goals and Execution of the Project

During the commemoration of the bicentennials of the U.S. Constitution and the U.S. Congress in the late 1980s, I realized that the vice-presidency and those who have held the office were largely neglected in the various two-hundred-year celebrations. Clearly, there was a need to look more closely at both the institution and the individuals. Although the debate over the Twenty-fifth Amendment in the 1960s had inspired a number of books on the history and operations of the vice-presidency, most of those works were narrowly drawn, serving only to make a case for or against the amendment. The ones that took a biographical approach focused on just the most "significant" vice presidents.

Yet, obscure as many of those who have held this office may be today, most were active in public service at both the state and federal levels, often reaching the vice-presidency after long and valuable careers in both Congress and the executive branch. Studying the lives of even the men of less than presidential stature and the reasons they were selected for the post—as well as the reasons they failed to reach the White House—provides useful insights into the history of our nation's political process. Examining the successive stories of the former vice presidents in chronological order illuminates the way in which their strengths and personalities helped to shape the evolution of this office that was so vaguely defined by the framers. The changes in the vice-presidency, in turn, shed light on the nation's political development; for example, the growing importance of the office in the decades since World War II mirrors the expansion of the role of the federal government during that period.

Having conceived the idea for this project, I met in the summer of 1991 with the director of the Senate Historical Office. We discussed a plan that would focus on the role of all our former vice presidents within the institutional context of the United States Senate. We agreed that the resulting book should include for each vice president: brief biographical background, the circumstances surrounding his selection, a summary of the major issues confronting the nation during his service, the nature of his relations with the president, his broader national and international role, and his contributions to the office and the nation. Such a study had never before been undertaken. In the course of our work, we conducted a major search for source materials and consulted all significant book- and article-length biographies of these forty-four men, as well as appropriate Senate records.

Acknowledgements

When I proposed this book to Dr. Richard A. Baker, the Senate historian, he expressed great interest, sharing my view that this topic had received too little attention. The staff of the Senate Historical Office prepared the forty-four chapters discussing each of the former vice presidents, under the direction of Secretary of the Senate Kelly D. Johnston and his predecessors, Walter J. Stewart, Martha Pope, and Sheila Burke. I carefully reviewed and critiqued each of these chapters in draft and have reviewed them again in proofs. I believe that, collectively, these essays make the case that the institution of the vice-presidency and those who have held the office have made a substantial contribution to our nation.

I would particularly like to thank Dr. Baker for his crucial role in shaping the concept and content of this book. He and his colleagues, Dr. Donald A. Ritchie and Dr. Jo Anne McCormick Quatannens, wrote the bulk of the chapters, drawing upon their deep understanding of the nation's political history, as well as the extensive professional expertise that each has in a particular period of the Senate's history. Others who participated by writing one or more chapters were Mark Clifford, Richard Hill, Jonathan Marcus, and the late William T. Hull. Mr. Hull, a gifted historian whose promising career was tragically cut short by cancer in the fall of 1995, contributed the chapters on Theodore Roosevelt, Charles Fairbanks, and Richard Nixon, as well as offering insights into his particular interest, the Republican party in the period between the New Deal and the Eisenhower administration.

Others in the Senate Historical Office who contributed to this project were Wendy Wolff, who prepared the appendix and index and edited the text for publication, and Matthew T. Cook, who researched and assisted me in selecting the illustrations.

As one who has greatly enjoyed and profited from the study of American presidential history, I relish this project and trust that it will add new color to the rich mosaic of our nation's political development. Statesmen and murderers; scholars and scoundrels; piano players and composers; military heroes and invading generals—what a fascinating lot!

MARK O. HATFIELD

Chapter 1

JOHN ADAMS
1789–1797

JOHN ADAMS

Chapter 1

JOHN ADAMS

1st Vice President: 1789–1797

It is not for me to interrupt your deliberations by any general observations on the state of the nation, or by recommending, or proposing any particular measures.

—JOHN ADAMS

On April 21, 1789, John Adams, the first vice president of the United States, began his duties as president of the Senate.

Adams' role in the administration of George Washington was sharply constrained by the constitutional limits on the vice-presidency and his own reluctance to encroach upon executive prerogative. He enjoyed a cordial but distant relationship with President Washington, who sought his advice on occasion but relied primarily on the cabinet. Adams played a more active role in the Senate, however, particularly during his first term.

As president of the Senate, Adams cast twenty-nine tie-breaking votes—a record that no successor has ever threatened.[1] His votes protected the president's sole authority over the removal of appointees, influenced the location of the national capital, and prevented war with Great Britain. On at least one occasion he persuaded senators to vote against legislation that he opposed, and he frequently lectured the Senate on procedural and policy matters. Adams' political views and his active role in the Senate made him a natural target for critics of the Washington administration. Toward the end of his first term, he began to exercise more restraint in the hope of realizing the goal shared by many of his successors: election in his own right as president of the United States.

A Family Tradition of Public Service

John Adams was born in Braintree, Massachusetts, on October 19, 1735, into a family with an established tradition of public service. As a child, he attended town meetings with his father, who was at various times a militia officer, a deacon and tithe collector of the local congregation, and selectman for the town of Braintree. Determined that his namesake attend Harvard College, the elder Adams sent young John to a local "dame" school and later to Joseph Cleverly's Latin school. Adams was an indifferent student until the age of fourteen, when he withdrew from the Latin school to prepare for college with a private tutor, "Mr. Marsh."[2] Adams entered Harvard College in 1751, and plunged into a rigorous course of study. After his graduation in 1755, he accepted a position as Latin master of the Worcester, Massachusetts, Grammar School. The following year, finding himself "irresistibly impelled" toward a legal career, Adams apprenticed himself to James Putnam, a local attorney. He continued to teach school while reading law at night until his admission to the Boston Superior Court bar on November 6, 1758.[3]

His legal studies completed, Adams returned to Braintree to establish his legal practice, which grew slowly. In the spring of 1761, on the death of his father, Adams inherited the family farm— a bequest that enabled him, as a "freeholder" with a tangible interest in the community, to take an active part in town meetings. He served on several local committees and led a crusade to require professional certification of practitioners before the local courts. In February 1761, on one of his regular trips to Boston to attend the Court of Common Pleas, Adams observed James Otis' arguments against the writs of assistance before the Massachusetts Supreme Court. Adams recalled in later years that Otis' impassioned oratory against these general search and seizure warrants convinced Adams that England and the colonies had been "brought to a Collision," and left him "ready to take arms" against the writs. However, Adams' political career remained limited to local concerns for several more years until 1765, when he played a crucial role in formulating Massachusetts' response to the Stamp Act.[4]

A Lawyer and a Legislator

As a member of the town meeting, Adams drafted instructions for the Braintree delegate to the Massachusetts provincial assembly, known as the General Court, which met in October 1765 to formulate the colony's response to the Stamp Act. Adams' rationale, that the colonies could not be taxed by a parliament in which they were not represented, and that the stamp tax was "inconsistent with the spirit of the common law and of the essential fundamental principles of the British constitution," soon appeared in the *Massachusetts Gazette and Boston News Letter*. His cousin, Samuel Adams, incorporated John's argument in the instructions that he drafted for the Boston delegates, and other towns adopted the same stance.[5]

With the repeal of the Stamp Act, Adams focused his energies on building his law practice and attending to the demands of the growing family that followed from his marriage to Abigail Smith in 1764. Finding few opportunities for a struggling young attorney in Braintree, the young family moved in 1768 to Boston, where John's practice flourished. Adams soon found himself an active participant in the local resistance to British authority as a consequence of his defense of John Hancock before the vice admiralty court for customs duty violations. He argued in Hancock's defense that the Parliament could not tax the colonies without their express consent and added the charge, soon to become a part of the revolutionary rhetoric, that the vice-admiralty courts violated the colonists' rights as Englishmen to trial by jury. Although the crown eventually withdrew the charges against Hancock, Adams continued his assault on the vice-admiralty courts in the instructions he wrote for the Boston general court representatives in 1768 and 1769.[6]

Adams subsequently agreed to defend the British soldiers who fired upon the Boston mob during the spring of 1770. His able and dispassionate argument on behalf of the defendants in the Boston massacre case won his clients' acquittal, as well as his election to a brief term in the Massachusetts assembly, where he was one of Governor Thomas Hutchinson's most vocal opponents. The enmity was mutual; when the general court elected Adams to the Massachusetts council, or upper house, in 1773, the governor denied Adams his seat. The general court reelected Adams the following year, but Hutchinson's successor, Thomas Gage, again prevented him from serving on the council. The general court subsequently elected Adams to the first and second Continental congresses. Although initially reluctant to press for immediate armed resistance, Adams consistently denied Parliament's right to regulate the internal affairs of the colonies, a position he elaborated in a series of thirteen newspaper essays published under the name "Novanglus" during the winter and spring of 1775. Like Adams' other political writings, the *Novanglus* essays set forth his tenets in rambling and disjointed fashion, but their primary focus—the fundamental rights of the colonists—was clear.[7]

An Architect of Independence

An avowed supporter of independence in the second Continental Congress, Adams was a member of the committee that prepared the Declaration of Independence. Although Thomas Jefferson of Virginia composed the committee draft, Adams' contribution was no less important. As Jefferson later acknowledged, Adams was the Declaration's "pillar of support on the floor of Congress, its ablest advocate and defender."

New Jersey delegate Richard Stockton and others styled Adams "the 'Atlas' of independence." [8] Adams further served the cause of independence as chairman of the Board of War and Ordnance. Congress assigned to the board the onerous tasks of recruiting, provisioning, and dispatching a continental army; as chairman, Adams coordinated this Herculean effort until the winter of 1777, when Congress appointed him to replace Silas Deane as commissioner to the Court of Paris.[9]

Adams served as commissioner until the spring of 1779. On his return to Massachusetts, he represented Braintree in the state constitutional convention. The convention asked him to draft a model constitution, which it adopted with amendments in 1780. Adams' model provided for the three branches of government—executive, legislative, and judicial—that were ultimately incorporated into the United States Constitution, and it vested strong powers in the executive. "His Excellency," as the governor was to be addressed, was given an absolute veto over the legislature and sole power to appoint officers of the militia.[10] Throughout his life, Adams was an advocate of a strong executive. He believed that only a stable government could preserve social order and protect the liberties of the people. His studies of classical antiquity convinced him that republican government was inherently vulnerable to corruption and inevitably harbored "a never-failing passion for tyranny" unless balanced by a stabilizing force.[11] In 1780, Adams considered a strong executive sufficient to achieve this end. In later years, he grew so fearful of the "corruption" he discerned in popular elections that he suggested more drastic alternatives—a hereditary senate and a hereditary executive—which his opponents saw as evidence of his antidemocratic, "monarchist" intent.

Before the Massachusetts convention began its deliberations over Adams' draft, Congress appointed him minister plenipotentiary to negotiate peace and commerce treaties with Great Britain and subsequently authorized him to negotiate an alliance with the Netherlands, as well. Although Adams' attempts to negotiate treaties with the British proved unavailing, in 1782 he finally persuaded the Netherlands to recognize American independence—"the happiest event and the greatest action of my life, past or future."[12] Adams remained abroad as a member of the peace commission and ambassador to the Court of St. James until 1788. On his return to the United States, he found to his surprise that he was widely mentioned as a possible candidate for the office of vice president of the United States.[13]

1788 Election

Although George Washington was the inevitable and unanimous choice for president, there were several contenders for the second office. At the time of the first federal elections, political sentiment was divided between the "Federalists," who supported a strong central government and toward that end had worked to secure the ratification of the Constitution, and the "Antifederalist" advocates of a more limited national government. Adams was the leading Federalist candidate for vice president. The New England Federalists strongly supported him, and he also commanded the allegiance of a few key Antifederalists, including Arthur Lee and Richard Henry Lee of Virginia. Benjamin Rush and William Maclay of Pennsylvania also backed Adams, hinting that he could assure his election by supporting their efforts to locate the national capital in Philadelphia. Other contenders were John Hancock of Massachusetts, whose support for the new Constitution was predicated on his assumption that he would assume the second office, and George Clinton, a New York Antifederalist who later served as vice president under Thomas Jefferson and James Madison.[14]

As much as he coveted the vice-presidency, Adams did not actively campaign for the office, refusing the deal proffered by Rush and Maclay. Maclay later explained that the Pennsylvanians played to Adams' "Vanity, and hoped by laying hold of it to render him Useful." They failed to take into account the strong Puritan sense of moral rectitude that prevented Adams from striking such a bargain, even to achieve an office to which he clearly felt entitled. Maclay, who served in the Senate for the first two years of Adams' initial vice-presidential term, never forgave Adams and petulantly noted in his diary that the vice president's "Pride Obstinacy And Folly" were "equal to his Vanity."[15]

The principal threat to Adams came from Federalist leader Alexander Hamilton, who perceived in the New Englander's popularity and uncompromising nature a threat to his own career aspirations. Acting secretly at Hamilton's behest, General Henry Knox tried but failed to persuade Adams that he was too prominent a figure in his own right to serve as Washington's subordinate. When Hamilton realized that Adams commanded the overwhelming support of the New England Federalists and could not be dissuaded, he grudgingly backed his rival but resolved that Adams would not enjoy an overwhelming electoral victory.[16]

Hamilton exploited to his advantage the constitutional provision governing the election of the president and vice president. Article II, section 1 of the Constitution authorized each presidential elector to cast votes "for two Persons, of whom one at least shall not be an Inhabitant of the same State with themselves." The candidate with the greatest number of electoral votes would become president and the candidate with the next-highest number would become vice president. The Constitution's framers created the vice-presidency, in part, to keep presidential electors from voting only for state or regional favorites, thus ensuring deadlocks with no candidate receiving a majority vote. By giving each presidential elector two ballots, the framers made it possible to vote for a favorite-son candidate as well as for a more nationally acceptable individual. In the event that no candidate received a majority, as some expected would be the case after George Washington passed from the national stage, the House of Representatives would decide the election from among the five largest vote getters, with each state casting one vote.

The framers, however, had not foreseen the potential complications inherent in this "double-balloting" scheme. Hamilton realized that if each Federalist elector cast one vote for Washington and one for Adams, the resulting tied vote would throw the election into the House of Representatives. Hamilton persuaded several electors to withhold their votes from Adams, ostensibly to ensure Washington a unanimous electoral victory. Adams was bitterly disappointed when he learned that he had received only thirty-four electoral votes to Washington's sixty-nine, and called his election, "in the scurvy manner in which it was done, a curse rather than a blessing."[17]

Hamilton's duplicity had a more lasting effect on the new vice president's political fortunes: the election confirmed his fear that popular elections in "a populous, oppulent, and commercial nation" would eventually lead to "corruption Sedition and civil war." The remedies he suggested—a hereditary senate and an executive appointed for life[18]—prompted charges by his opponents that the vice president was the "monarchist" enemy of republican government and popular liberties.

The First Vice President

Adams took office as vice president on April 21, 1789.[19] Apart from his legislative and ceremonial responsibilities, he did not assume an active role in the Washington administration. Although relations between the two men were cordial, if somewhat restrained, a combination of personality, circumstance, and principle limited Adams' influence. Adams attended few cabinet meetings, and the president sought his counsel only infrequently.[20] Hesitant to take any action that might be construed as usurping the president's prerogative, he generally forwarded applications for offices in the new government to Washington. As president of the Senate, Adams had no reservations about recommending his friend Samuel Allyne Otis for the position of secretary of the Senate, but declined to assist Otis' brother-in-law, General Joseph Warren, and Abigail's brother-in-law, Richard Cranch, in obtaining much-needed sinecures. Adams was similarly hesitant when Washington solicited his advice regarding Supreme Court nominations.[21]

Although Washington rarely consulted Adams on domestic or foreign policy matters, the two men, according to Adams' most recent biographer, John Ferling, "jointly executed many more of the executive branch's ceremonial undertakings than would be likely for a contemporary president and vice-president."[22] Washington invited the vice president to accompany him on his fall 1789 tour of New England—an invitation that Adams declined, although he met the president in Boston—and to several official dinners. The Washingtons routinely extended their hospitality to John, and to Abigail when she was in the capital, and Adams frequently accompanied the president to the theater.[23]

For his own part, Adams professed a narrow interpretation of the vice president's role in the new government. Shortly after taking office, he wrote to his friend and supporter Benjamin Lincoln, "The Constitution has instituted two great offices . . . and the nation at large has created two officers: one who is the first of the two . . . is placed at the Head of the Executive, the other at the Head of the Legislative." The following year, he informed another correspondent that the office of vice president "is totally detached from the executive authority and confined to the legislative."[24]

But Adams never *really* considered himself "totally detached" from the executive branch, as the Senate discovered when he began signing legislative documents as "John Adams, Vice President of the United States." Speaking for a majority of the senators, William Maclay of Pennsylvania quickly called Adams to account. "[A]s President of the Senate only can [y]ou sign or authenticate any Act of that body," he lectured the vice president. Uneasy as some senators were at the prospect of having a member of the executive branch preside over their deliberations, they would permit Adams to certify legislation as *president of the Senate, but not as vice president.* Never one to acquiesce cheerfully when he believed that important principles were at stake, Adams struck an awkward compromise, signing Senate documents as "John Adams, Vice President of the United States and President of the Senate."[25]

To the extent that Adams remained aloof from the administration, his stance was as much the result of personality and prudence as of principle. He held the president in high personal esteem and generally deferred to the more forceful Washington as a matter of course.[26] Also, as his biographer Page Smith has explained, the vice president always feared that he would become

a "scapegoat for all of Washington's unpopular decisions." During the furor over Washington's 1793 proclamation of American neutrality, a weary Adams confided to his wife that he had "held the office of Libellee General long enough."[27]

In the Senate, Adams brought energy and dedication to the presiding officer's chair, but found the task "not quite adapted to my character."[28] Addressing the Senate for the first time on April 21, 1789, he offered the caveat that although "not wholly without experience in public assemblies," he was "more accustomed to take a share in their debates, than to preside in their deliberations." Notwithstanding his lack of experience as a presiding officer, Adams had definite notions regarding the limitations of his office. "It is not for me," he assured the Senate, "to interrupt your deliberations by any general observations on the state of the nation, or by recommending, or proposing any particular measures."[29]

President of the Senate

Adams' resolve was short-lived. His first incursion into the legislative realm occurred shortly after he assumed office, during the Senate debates over titles for the president and executive officers of the new government. Although the House of Representatives agreed in short order that the president should be addressed simply as "George Washington, President of the United States," the Senate debated the issue at some length. Adams repeatedly lectured the Senate that titles were necessary to ensure proper respect for the new government and its officers. Pennsylvania Senator William Maclay complained that when the Senate considered the matter on May 8, 1789, the vice president "repeatedly helped the speakers for Titles." The following day, Adams "harangued" the Senate for forty minutes. "What will the common people of foreign countries, what will the sailors and soldiers say," he argued, "George Washington president of the United States, they will despise him to all eternity." The Senate ultimately deferred to the House on the question of titles, but not before Adams incurred the lasting enmity of the Antifederalists, who saw in his support for titles and ceremony distressing evidence of his "monarchist" leanings.[30]

Adams was more successful in preventing the Senate from asserting a role in the removal of presidential appointees. In the July 14, 1789, debates over the organization of executive departments, several senators agreed with William Maclay that removals of cabinet officers by the president, as well as appointments, should be subject to the advice and consent of the Senate. Adams and his Federalist allies viewed the proposal as an attempt by Antifederalists to enhance the Senate's powers at the expense of the executive. After a series of meetings with individual senators, Adams finally convinced Tristram Dalton of Massachusetts to withdraw his support for Maclay's proposal. Richard Bassett of Delaware followed suit. When the Senate decided the question on July 18 in a 9-to-9 vote, Adams performed his sole legislative function by casting a tie-breaking vote against Maclay's proposal.[31] His action was purely symbolic in this instance, however, as a tie vote automatically defeats a measure.

During the protracted debates over the Residence bill to determine the location of the capital, Adams thwarted another initiative dear to Maclay's heart: a provision to establish the permanent capital "along the banks of the Susquehannah" in convenient proximity to the Pennsylvania senator's extensive landholdings. The disgruntled speculator attributed his defeat to the vice president's tie-breaking votes and the "barefaced partiality" of Adams' rulings from the chair. Maclay was enraged that Adams allowed frequent delays in the September 24, 1789, debates, which permitted Pennsylvania Senator Robert Morris, whose sympathies lay with Philadelphia, to lobby other senators against the Susquehannah site. After Morris' motion to strike the provision failed, Adams granted his motion to reconsider over Maclay's strenuous objection that "no business ever could have a decision, if minority members, were permitted to move reconsiderations under every pretense of new argument." Adams ultimately cast the deciding vote in favor of Morris' motion.[32]

The vice president's frequent and pedantic lectures from the chair earned him the resentment of other senators, as well. Shortly after the second session of the First Congress convened in January 1790, John Trumbull warned his friend that he faced growing opposition in the Senate, particularly among the southern senators. Adams' enemies resented his propensity for joining in Senate debates and suspected him of "monarchist" sentiments. Trumbull cautioned that "he who mingles in debate subjects himself to frequent retorts from his opposers, places himself on the same ground with his inferiors in rank, appears too much like the leader of a party, and renders it more difficult for him to support the dignity of the chair and preserve order and regularity in the debate." Although Adams denied that he had ever exceeded the limits of his authority in the Senate, he must have seen the truth in Trumbull's observations, for he assured his confidant that he had "no desire ever to open my mouth again upon any question." Acutely aware of the controversy over his views and behavior, Adams became less an active participant and more an impartial moderator of Senate debates.[33]

Although stung by Trumbull's comments and the censure of less tactful critics, Adams continued to devote a considerable portion of his time and energy to presiding over the Senate; Abigail Adams observed that her husband's schedule "five hours constant sitting in a day for six months together (for he cannot leave his Chair) is pretty tight service."[34]

In the absence of a manual governing Senate debates, Adams looked to British parliamentary procedures for guidance in deciding questions of order.[35] Despite complaints by some senators that Adams demonstrated inconsistency in his rulings, Delaware Senator George Read in 1792 praised his "attentive, upright, fair, and unexceptionable" performance as presiding officer, and his "uncommonly exact" attendance in the Senate.[36]

Still, as a national figure and Washington's probable successor, Adams remained controversial, particularly as legislative political parties emerged in the 1790s. Although sectional differences had in large part shaped the debates of the First Congress, two distinct parties began to develop during the Second Congress in 1791 to

1793. The Federalists, adopting the name earlier used by supporters of the Constitution, were the conservative, prosperous advocates of a strong central government. They supported Treasury Secretary Alexander Hamilton's proposals to assume and fund the states' revolutionary debts, encourage manufactures, and establish a Bank of the United States. Hamilton's fiscal program appealed to the mercantile, financial, and artisan segments of the population but sparked the growth of an agrarian-based opposition party—initially known as Antifederalists and later as "Republicans"—led by Secretary of State Thomas Jefferson.[37] Adams supported Hamilton's fiscal proposals and, with the Federalists still firmly in command of the Senate and the controversy over public finance largely confined to the House of Representatives,[38] he emerged unscathed from the partisan battles over fiscal policy.

The outbreak of the French Revolution prompted a more divisive debate. Republicans greeted the overthrow of the French monarchy with enthusiasm while the Federalists heard in the revolutionaries' egalitarian rhetoric a threat to the order and stability of Europe and America. France's 1793 declaration of war on Great Britain further polarized the argument, with the Republicans celebrating each British defeat, the Federalists dreading the consequences of a French victory, and both belligerents preying on American shipping at will. While Washington attempted to hold the United States to a neutral course, his vice president—who considered political parties "the greatest political evil under our Constitution," and whose greatest fear was "a division of the republic into two great parties, each arranged under its leader, and concerting measures in opposition to each other"—became, as he had anticipated, the target of concerted Republican opposition.[39]

Adams articulated his thoughts on the French Revolution and its implications for the United States in a series of newspaper essays, the *Discourses on Davila*. He predicted that the revolution, having abolished the aristocratic institutions necessary to preserve stability and order, was doomed to failure. He warned that the United States would share a similar fate if it failed to honor and encourage with titles and appro-

priate ceremony its own "natural aristocracy" of talented and propertied public men. Adams even went so far as to predict that a hereditary American aristocracy would be necessary in the event that the "natural" variety failed to emerge. The *Davila* essays were consistent with Adams' long-standing belief that a strong stabilizing force—a strong executive, a hereditary senate, or a natural aristocracy—was an essential bulwark of popular liberties. They also reflected his recent humiliation at the hands of Alexander Hamilton. Still smarting from his low electoral count in the 1788 presidential election, Adams observed in the thirty-second essay that "hereditary succession was attended with fewer evils than frequent elections." As Peter Shaw has noted in his study of Adams' character, "it would be difficult to imagine . . . a more impolitic act." The *Discourses on Davila*, together with Adams' earlier support for titles and ceremony, convinced his Republican opponents that he was an enemy of republican government. Rumors that Washington would resign his office once the government was established on a secure footing, and his near death from influenza in the spring of 1790, added to the Republicans' anxiety. In response, they mounted an intense but unsuccessful campaign to unseat Adams in the 1792 presidential election.[40]

Second Term

Persuaded by Hamilton, Jefferson, and Madison to run for a second term, George Washington was again the obvious and unanimous choice for president. Adams was still the preferred vice-presidential candidate of the New England Federalists, but he faced a serious challenge from Republican candidate George Clinton of New York. Although many of his earlier supporters, including Benjamin Rush, joined the opposition in support of Clinton, Adams won reelection with 77 electoral votes to 50 for Clinton.[41] On March 4, 1793, in the Senate chamber, Washington took the oath of office for a second time. Adams, as always, followed Washington's example but waited until the Third Congress convened on December 2, 1793, to take his second oath of office. No one, apparently, gave much thought to the question of whether or not the nation had a vice president—and a successor to Washington, should he die in office or become incapacitated—during the nine-month interval between these two inaugurations.[42]

Early in Adams' second vice-presidential term, France declared war on Great Britain. Washington's cabinet supported the president's policy of neutrality, but its members disagreed over the implementation of that policy. Hamilton urged the president to issue an immediate proclamation of American neutrality; Jefferson warned that only Congress could issue such a declaration and counseled that delaying the proclamation would force concessions from France and England. Recognizing the United States' commercial dependence on Great Britain, Hamilton proposed that the nation conditionally suspend the treaties that granted France access to U. S. ports and guaranteed French possession of the West Indies. Secretary of State Jefferson insisted that the United States honor its treaty obligations. The secretaries similarly disagreed over extending recognition to the emissary of the French republic, "Citizen" Edmond Genêt.

Adams considered absolute neutrality the only prudent course. As a Federalist, he was no supporter of France, but his reluctance to offend a former ally led him to take a more cautious stance than Hamilton. Although Washington sought his advice, Adams scrupulously avoided public comment; he had "no constitutional vote" in the matter and no intention of "taking any side in it or having my name or opinion quoted about it."[43] After the president decided to recognize Genêt, Adams reluctantly received the controversial Frenchman but predicted that "a little more of this indelicacy and indecency may involve us in a war with all the world."[44]

Although Adams, as vice president, had "no constitutional vote" in the administration's foreign policy, he cast two important tie-breaking foreign policy votes in the Senate, where Republican gains in the 1792 elections had eroded the Federalist majority. In both cases, Adams voted to prevent war with Great Britain and its allies. On March 12, 1794, he voted in favor of an embargo on the domestic sale of vessels and goods seized from friendly nations. The following month, he voted against a bill to suspend American trade with Great Britain.[45] Despite these votes, Adams made every effort to stay aloof from the bitter controversy over foreign policy, remaining silent during the Senate's 1795 debates over the controversial Jay Treaty. Privately, Adams considered the Jay Treaty essential to avert war with Great Britain, but the Federalists still commanded sufficient votes to ratify the treaty without the vice president's assistance.[46]

1796 Election

The popular outcry against the Jay Treaty strengthened Washington's resolve to retire at the end of his second term, and he announced his intentions in September 1796. Although the majority of the Federalists considered Adams the logical choice to succeed Washington, Hamilton preferred their more pliant vice-presidential candidate, former minister to Great Britain Thomas Pinckney. The Republican candidates were Thomas Jefferson and Aaron Burr. Once again Hamilton proved a greater threat to Adams than the opposition candidates. The Federalists lost the vice-presidency because of Hamilton's scheming and came dangerously close to losing the presidency as well. Repeating the tactics he had used to diminish Adams' electoral count in the 1788 election, Hamilton tried to persuade South Carolina's Federalist electors to withhold enough votes from Adams to ensure Thomas Pinckney's election to the presidency. This time, however, the New England Federalist electors learned of Hamilton's plot and withheld sufficient votes from Pinckney to compensate for the lost South Carolina votes. These intrigues resulted in the election of a president and vice president from opposing parties, with president-elect Adams receiving 71 electoral votes to 68 for Thomas Jefferson.[47]

Vice president Adams addressed the Senate for the last time on February 15, 1797. He thanked current and former members for the "candor and favor" they had extended to him during his eight years as presiding officer. Despite the frustrations and difficulties he had experienced as vice president, Adams left the presiding officer's chair with a genuine regard for the Senate that was in large part mutual. He expressed gratitude to the body for the "uniform politeness" accorded him "from every quarter," and declared that he had "never had the smallest misunderstanding with any member of the Senate." Notwithstanding his earlier pronouncements in favor of a hereditary Senate, Adams assured the members that the "eloquence, patriotism, and independence" that he had witnessed had convinced him that "no council more permanent than this . . . will be necessary, to defend the rights, liberties, and properties of the people, and to protect the Constitution of the United States." The Senate's February 22 message expressing "gratitude and affection" and praising his "abilities and undeviating impartiality" evoked a frank and emotional response from Adams the following day. The Senate's "generous approbation" of his "undeviating impartiality" had served to "soften asperities, and conciliate animosities, wherever such may unhappily exist," for which the departing vice president offered his "sincere thanks." [48]

President

Adams served as president from 1797 to 1801. He failed to win a second term due to the popular outcry against the repressive Alien and Sedition Acts, which he had reluctantly approved as necessary wartime measures, as well as the rupture in the Federalist party over the end of hostilities with France. Hamilton was determined to defeat Adams after the president responded favorably to French overtures for peace in 1799, and he was further outraged when Adams purged two of his sympathizers from the cabinet in May 1800. In a letter to Federalist leaders, Hamilton detailed his charges that Adams' "ungovernable indiscretion" and "distempered jealousy" made him unfit for office. With the Federalist party split between the Hamilton and Adams factions, Adams lost the election. After thirty-five ballots, the House of Representatives broke the tied vote between Republican presidential candidate Thomas Jefferson and vice-presidential candidate Aaron Burr in Jefferson's favor. [49]

Adams spent the remainder of his life in retirement at his farm in Quincy, Massachusetts. In an attempt to vindicate himself from past charges that he was an enemy of American liberties, Adams in 1804 began his *Autobiography*, which he never finished. He also wrote voluminous letters to friends and former colleagues toward the same end. In 1811, Adams resumed his friendship with Jefferson, and the two old patriots began a lively correspondence that continued for fifteen years. Although largely content to observe political events from the seclusion of Quincy and to follow the promising career of his eldest son, John Quincy, Adams briefly resumed his own public career in 1820, when he represented the town of Quincy in the Massachusetts constitutional convention. Adams died at Quincy on July 4, 1826, the fiftieth anniversary of American independence. [50]

NOTES

[1] Linda Dudik Guerrero, in her study of Adams' vice presidency, found that Adams cast "at least" thirty-one votes, a figure accepted by Adams' most recent biographer. The Senate Historical Office has been able to verify only twenty-nine tie-breaking votes by Adams—still a record, although George Dallas claimed that he cast thirty tie-breaking votes during his vice-presidency (See Chapter 11, page 158 and note 35). Linda Dudik Guerrero, *John Adams' Vice Presidency, 1789–1797: The Neglected Man in the Forgotten Office* (New York, 1982), p. 128; U.S., Congress, Senate, *The Senate 1789–1989*, by Robert C. Byrd, S. Doc. 100–20, 100th Cong., 1st sess., vol. 4, *Historical Statistics, 1789–1992*, 1993, p. 640; John Ferling, *John Adams: A Life* (Knoxville, 1992), p. 311.

[2] Peter Shaw, *The Character of John Adams* (Chapel Hill, 1976), pp.1–6; Page Smith, *John Adams* (Westport, CT, 1969, reprint of 1962–1963 ed.), 1:1–14.

[3] *Diary and Autobiography of John Adams*, ed. L.H. Butterfield, The Adams Papers, Series I (Cambridge, 1962), pp. 263–64; Smith, 1:27–43.

[4] Shaw, pp. 43–46; Smith, 1:54–80; Theodore Draper, *A Struggle for Power: The American Revolution* (New York, 1996), pp. 184–89.

[5] Smith, 1:80–81.

[6] Shaw, p. 57; Smith, 1:94–104.

[7] Shaw, pp. 58–85; Smith, 1:121–26.

[8] Shaw, pp. 94–98; Ferling, pp. 149–50.

[9] Shaw, pp. 106–7; Smith, 1:266–67, 285–350.

[10] Shaw, pp. 128–30; Smith, 1:438–44.

[11] Shaw, pp. 218–22.

[12] Ibid., pp. 131–63; Smith, 1:444–535.

[13] Shaw, pp. 157–225.

[14] Kenneth R. Bowling and Helen E. Veit, eds., *The Diary of William Maclay and Other Notes On Senate Debates, Documentary History of the First Federal Congress of the United States of America*, vol. 9 (Baltimore, 1988), pp. 85–86; Smith, 2:734–37.

[15] *Diary of William Maclay*, pp. 85–86; Shaw, p. 225, Smith, 2:737–39.

[16] Smith, 2:739–41.

[17] Ibid., 2:739–42.

[18] Shaw, pp. 231–32.

[19] Linda Grant De Pauw, Charlene Bangs Bickford, and LaVonne Marlene Siegel, eds., *Senate Legislative Journal, Documentary History of the First Federal Congress of the United States of America*, vol. 1 (Baltimore, 1972), pp. 21–23.

[20] Shaw, p. 226; Guerrero, pp. 169–83.

[21] John R. Howe, Jr., *The Changing Political Thought of John Adams* (Princeton, 1966), pp. 212–13; Shaw, p. 288; Smith, 2:761–63; "Biographical Sketches of the Twenty-Two Secretaries of the United States Senate," undated report prepared by the U.S. Senate Historical Office. In 1789, Adams asked Washington to appoint his improvident son-in-law, Colonel William Smith, federal marshal for New York—a request that the president obliged. In 1791, Adams sought Smith's appointment as minister to Great Britain. Although the president did not send Smith to the Court of St. James, he subsequently named Smith supervisor of revenue for New York. Adams' concern for his daughter "Nabby" and her children prompted these rare departures from his customary practice. Ferling, pp. 323–24; Guerrero, p. 82, fn. 41.

[22] Ferling, p. 310.

[23] Ibid.; Guerrero, pp. 166–69.

[24] John Adams to Lincoln, May 26, 1789, and John Adams to Hurd, April 5, 1790, quoted in Guerrero, p. 185.

[25] David P. Currie, "The Constitution in Congress: The First Congress and the Structure of Government, 1789–1791," *University of Chicago Law School Roundtable* 2 (1995): 161.

[26] Howe, p. 212; Ferling, p. 310.

[27] Smith, 2:763, 842–43.

[28] Ibid., 2:769.

[29] *Senate Legislative Journal*, pp. 21–23.

[30] *Senate Legislative Journal*, pp. 44–45; Howe, 176–79; *Diary of William Maclay*, pp. 27–32; Shaw, pp. 227–30.

[31] *Senate Legislative Journal*, pp. 83–87; Smith, 2:774–76; *Diary of William Maclay*, pp. 109–19.

[32] *Diary of William Maclay*, pp. 132–35, 152–64.

[33] Smith, 2:788–91.

[34] Quoted in U.S., Congress, Senate, *The United States Senate, 1787–1801: A Dissertation on the First Fourteen Years of the Upper Legislative Body*, by Roy Swanstrom, S. Doc. 100–31, 100th Cong., 1st sess., 1988, p. 254.

[35] Richard Allan Baker, "The Senate of the United States: 'Supreme Executive Council of the Nation,' 1787–1800," in *The Congress of the United States, 1789–1989*, vol. 1, ed. Joel Silbey (Brooklyn, NY, 1991), p. 148, originally published in *Prologue* 21 (Winter 1989): 299–313; *Diary of William Maclay*, p. 36.

[36] George Read to Gunning Bedford, quoted in Swanstrom, p. 254.

[37] John C. Miller, *The Federalist Era, 1789–1801* (New York, 1963; reprint of 1960 ed.), pp. 99–125.

[38] Howe, p. 197; Swanstrom, pp. 274–76.

[39] Howe, 193–97; Miller, pp. 126–54.

[40] Howe, pp. 133–49; Shaw, pp. 229–37; Smith, 2:794, 826–33.

[41] Miller, p. 96; Smith, 2:826–33.

[42] Stephen W. Stathis and Ronald C. Moe, "America's Other Inauguration," *Presidential Studies Quarterly* 10 (Fall 1980): 552.

[43] Miller, pp. 128–30; Smith, 2:838–44.

[44] Smith, 2:845.

[45] Miller, p. 154; Smith, 2:853; U.S., Congress, Senate, *Annals of Congress,* 3d Cong., 1st sess., pp. 66, 90.

[46] Smith, 2:873–75; Swanstrom, pp. 120–23.

[47] Miller, pp. 198–202; Smith, 2:898–910.

[48] U.S., Congress, Senate, *Annals of Congress,* 4th Cong., 2d sess., pp. 1549–58.

[49] Miller, pp. 251–77; Smith, 2:1056–62.

[50] Smith, 2:1067–1138.

Chapter 2

THOMAS JEFFERSON
1797–1801

THOMAS JEFFERSON

Chapter 2

THOMAS JEFFERSON

2nd Vice President: 1797–1801

. . . a more tranquil & unoffending station could not have been found for me. . . . It will give me philosophical evenings in the winter, & rural days in the summer.
—THOMAS JEFFERSON TO BENJAMIN RUSH, JANUARY 22, 1797 [1]

Thomas Jefferson entered an ill-defined vice-presidency on March 4, 1797. For guidance on how to conduct himself, he had to rely on a brief reference in the U.S. Constitution, the eight-year experience of John Adams, and his own common sense. Of a profoundly different political and personal temperament from his predecessor, Jefferson knew his performance in that relatively new office would influence its operations well into the future. Unlike Adams, who shared the political beliefs of the president with whom he served, Jefferson and his president belonged to different political parties—a situation that would prove to be unique in all the nation's history. No one who knew the two men expected that Vice President Jefferson would be inclined to serve as President Adams' principal assistant. More likely, he would confine his duties to presiding over the Senate and offering leadership to his anti-administration Republican party in quiet preparation for the election of 1800.[2]

Scholar and Legislator

Thomas Jefferson was born on April 13, 1743, in what is now Albemarle County, Virginia. He was the third child of Peter Jefferson, a surveyor, and Jane Randolph, daughter of a distinguished Virginia family. Classical languages formed the base of his early formal education. A thorough and diligent student, inspired by the Enlightenment's belief in the power of reason to govern human behavior, Jefferson graduated from the College of William and Mary after only two years, at the age of nineteen. Dr. William Small, the chair of mathematics at the college, helped cultivate Jefferson's intellectual interests, especially in science. In addition to his academic pursuits, young Thomas excelled as a horseman and violinist. He studied law under George Wythe, Virginia's most eminent legal scholar of that era. Admitted to the Virginia bar in 1767, Jefferson maintained a successful practice until abandoning the legal profession at the start of the American Revolution.[3]

Jefferson's political career began in May 1769 when he became a member of the Virginia house of burgesses. He served there until the body was dissolved in 1775. While not considered an effective public speaker, Jefferson gained a reputation as a gifted writer. Unable to attend the Virginia convention of 1774, he sent instructions for the Virginia delegates to the first Continental Congress. These proposals, eventually published as *A Summary View of the Rights of British America*, asserted that the American colonies' only legitimate political connection to Great Britain was through the king, to whom they had submitted voluntarily, and not to Parliament.

In 1775, the thirty-two-year-old Jefferson gained a seat in the Continental Congress, where he was appointed to a committee to draft a declaration of independence from the mother country. He became the declaration's principal author and later counted it, along with establishment of the University of Virginia and creation of the Virginia statute for Religious Freedom, among his three proudest lifetime accomplishments. The Declaration of Independence and the *Summary View* ensured Jefferson's standing in the mid-1770s as the American Revolution's most significant literary theorist.

After spending less than a year in the Continental Congress, Jefferson resigned that post and entered the Virginia house of delegates. While he produced an admirable legislative record during his service from October 1776 to June 1779, his tenure as Virginia's governor from 1779 to mid-1781 was less successful. Although the Virginia assembly had made sizeable contributions to the Continental effort, it failed to make adequate provision for local defenses, and the state offered only token resistance to the British invasion in early 1781. Jefferson narrowly escaped capture, fleeing on horseback as Lt. Col. Banastre Tarleton's forces ascended Carter's Mountain toward Monticello, two days after his gubernatorial term expired but before the Virginia legislature could designate a successor. Jefferson had already decided not to seek reelection to a third term, but his perceived abdication at this critical juncture earned him considerable scorn. The Virginia house of delegates immediately ordered an investigation of his conduct, only to join with the state Senate in exonerating the former governor after he appeared before both houses six months later to explain his actions. Deeply mortified by the public scrutiny and increasingly alarmed by his wife's serious illness, Jefferson retreated to Monticello.[4]

In what proved to be a temporary retirement from public life, Jefferson turned his attention to farming and scientific endeavors—pursuits that he found more enjoyable. During this time, he organized and published his *Notes on the State of Virginia*, which his preeminent biographer, Dumas Malone, believed "laid the foundations of Jefferson's high contemporary reputation as a universal scholar and of his enduring fame as a pioneer American scientist."[5]

On the death of his wife Martha in September 1782, Jefferson returned to public life. In June of the following year he became a delegate to the Congress under the Articles of Confederation and served on several major committees. During his service, he prepared various influential committee papers, including a report of March 22, 1784, calling for prohibition of slavery in the western territory after the year 1800. The report also declared illegal any western regional secession. Although Congress did not adopt the report as presented, Jefferson's language subsequently influenced the drafting of the 1787 Northwest Ordinance with its highly significant slavery restrictions.

Diplomacy and the Cabinet

Jefferson prepared a report in December 1783 on the procedure for negotiating commercial treaties. His recommendations became general practice, and in May 1784 Congress appointed him to assist Benjamin Franklin in arranging commercial agreements with France. Within a year he succeeded Franklin as minister to that country. While Jefferson would later make light of his accomplishments during his ministerial tenure, he proved to be a talented diplomat. Following his own pro-French leanings, and his belief that France could serve to counter Britain's threat to American interests, Jefferson worked hard for improved relations.

On returning home in December 1789, Jefferson accepted President George Washington's appointment to be the nation's first secretary of state. Progressively harsher disputes with Treasury Secretary Alexander Hamilton troubled his tenure in that office. Their differences extended from financial policy to foreign affairs and grew out of fundamentally conflicting interpretations of the Constitution and the scope of federal power.

The rise of two rudimentary political groupings during the early 1790s reflected Hamilton's and Jefferson's differing philosophical views. Formed generally along sectional lines, these early parties were known as Federalists (with strong support in the North and East) and Republicans (with a southern base). In later years the Republicans would come to be called "Democrats," but in the 1790s, that term carried a negative connotation associated with mob rule.[6]

In May 1790, Pennsylvania Senator William Maclay, with his customarily acerbic pen, recorded the following physical description of the secretary of state:

> When I came to the Hall Jefferson and the rest of the Committee were there. Jefferson is a slender Man [and] has rather the Air of Stiffness in his Manner. His cloaths seem too small for him. He sits in a lounging Manner on One hip, commonly, and with one of his shoulders elevated much above the other. His face has a scrany aspect. His Whole figure has a loose shackling Air. He had a rambling Vacant look & nothing of that firm collected deportment which I expected would dignify the presence of a Secretary or Minister. I looked for gravity, but a laxity of Manner, seemed shed about him. He spoke almost without ceasing, but even his discourse partook of his personal demeanor. It was lax & rambling and Yet he scattered information wherever he went, and some even brilliant sentiments sparkled from him.[7]

Worn out from his battles with Hamilton, Jefferson resigned as secretary of state at the end of 1793 and handed leadership of the emerging Republican party to his fellow Virginian James Madison. For the next three years, Madison worked to strengthen the party in Congress, transforming it from a reactive faction to a positive political force with its own distinctive programs and, by April 1796, a congressional party caucus to establish legislative priorities.[8]

The 1796 Election

When President Washington announced in September 1796 that he would not run for a third term, a caucus of Federalists in Congress selected Vice President Adams as their presidential candidate. Congressional Republicans turned to Jefferson as the only person capable of defeating Adams, who enjoyed a strong following in New England and was closely associated with the success of the American Revolution.[9] Jefferson had told friends in 1793 that his "retirement from office had meant from all office, high or low, without exception."[10] While he continued to hold those views in 1796, he reluctantly allowed Republican leader Madison to advance his candidacy—in part to block the ambitions of his archrival, Alexander Hamilton. Jefferson confided to Madison that he hoped he would receive either the second- or third-largest number of electoral votes. A third-place finish would allow him to remain home the entire year, while a second-place result—making him the vice president—would permit him to stay home two-thirds of the year.[11] Jefferson made no effort to influence the outcome. He believed that Madison, as an active party leader, would have been a more suitable candidate. But even though Jefferson had left the political stage more than two years earlier, he remained the symbol of Republican values—in no small part due to Hamilton's unremitting attacks.

In devising the constitutional system that obligated each presidential elector to cast two ballots, the framers intended to produce a winning candidate for president who enjoyed a broad national consensus and, in second place, a vice president with at least strong regional support. They assumed that electors would give one vote to a home state favorite, reserving the second for a person of national reputation, but this view failed to anticipate the development of political parties. Thus the framers apparently gave little consideration to the potential for competing slates of candidates—seen for the first time in the 1796 presidential contest.

As part of a strategy to erode Jefferson's southern support, the Federalists selected as Adams' running mate Thomas Pinckney of South Carolina, author of the popular 1795 treaty with Spain.[12] Hamilton, Adams' bitter rival within the Federalist party, encouraged Federalist electors in the North to give both their votes to Adams and Pinckney. On the safe assumption that Pinckney would draw more votes than Adams from the other regions, and recognizing that Jefferson lacked support north and east of the Delaware River, Hamilton mistakenly concluded this tactic would assure Pinckney's election.[13] Adams' supporters countered Hamilton's plan by convincing a number of their party's electors to vote for someone other than Pinckney. As a result, Adams won the presidency with 71 of a possible 138 electoral votes. But Jefferson with 68 votes, rather than Pinckney with 59 votes, became vice president. Aaron Burr, the Republican vice-presidential contender, received only 30 votes, while 48 other votes were scattered among nine minor candidates.[14] This election produced the first and only mixed-party presidential team in the nation's history.

Not looking forward to reentering the political fray and feeling unprepared to assume presidential responsibilities for foreign policy at a time when relations with European nations were strained, Jefferson may have been the only person in the history of American politics to celebrate the fact that he lost a presidential election. He preferred the quietness of the vice-presidency. He wrote Benjamin Rush, "a more tranquil & unoffending station could not have been found for me." And he told James Madison, "I think they [foreign affairs] never wore so gloomy an aspect since the year 83. Let those come to the helm who think they can steer clear of the difficulties. I have no confidence in myself for the undertaking."[15] In a classic assessment of the presidency's thankless nature, Jefferson wrote Edward Rutledge, "I know well that no man will ever bring out of that office the reputation which carries him into it. The honey moon would be as short in that case as in any other, & its moments of extasy would be ransomed by years of torment & hatred."[16]

Vice President

On February 8, 1797, Vice President Adams, as one of his final official duties, presided over a joint session of Congress in the Senate chamber to tally electoral votes for the nation's two highest offices. To his obvious satisfaction, he announced his own victory for the first office and that of Thomas Jefferson for the second.[17] When the confirming news of his election reached Jefferson in Virginia, he initially hoped to avoid the trip to Philadelphia by seeking a senator who would administer the oath of office at his home.[18] But rumors were beginning to spread that Jefferson considered the vice-presidency beneath his dignity. To quash that mistaken notion, the Virginian decided to attend the inauguration; but he requested that local officials downplay his arrival at the capital. Despite these wishes, an artillery company and a sixteen-gun salute greeted Jefferson on March 2 at the completion of his arduous ten-day journey by horseback and stage

coach. He stayed the first night with James Madison and then moved to a nearby hotel for the remainder of his week-and-a-half visit.

The Senate convened at 10 a.m. on Saturday, March 4, in its ornate chamber on the second floor of Congress Hall at the corner of Sixth and Chestnut Streets. As the first order of business, Senate President Pro Tempore William Bingham administered the brief oath to the new vice president. Over six feet tall, with reddish hair and hazel eyes, and attired in a single-breasted long blue frock coat, Jefferson established a commanding presence as he in turn swore in the eight newly elected members among the twenty-seven senators who were present that day. He then read a brief inaugural address.

In that address Jefferson apologized in advance for any shortcomings members might perceive in the conduct of his duties. Anticipating the role that would most define his vice-presidential legacy, Jefferson promised that he would approach his duties as presiding officer with "more confidence because it will depend on my will and not my capacity." He continued:

> The rules which are to govern the proceedings of this House, so far as they shall depend on me for their application, shall be applied with the most rigorous and inflexible impartiality, regarding neither persons, their views, nor principles, and seeing only the abstract proposition subject to my decision. If in forming that decision, I concur with some and differ from others, as must of necessity happen, I shall rely on the liberality and candor of those from whom I differ, to believe that I do it on pure motives.

Having devoted half of his less than three-minute speech to his role as presiding officer, Jefferson briefly referred to the Constitution and its defense. But he quickly returned to his own more limited station, supposing that "these declarations [are] not pertinent to the occasion of entering into an office whose primary business is merely to preside over the forms of this House."[19] Concluding his remarks, Jefferson led the Senate downstairs to the House of Representatives' chamber to attend President-elect Adams' inaugural address and subsequent oath-taking.

Three potential roles awaited the new vice president in his as yet only marginally defined office. He could serve as an assistant to the president; he could concentrate on his constitutional duties as the Senate's presiding officer; or he could become an active leader of the Republican party. Jefferson had no interest in being an assistant to the chief executive. He told Elbridge Gerry that he considered his office "constitutionally confined to legislative functions,"[20] and he hoped those functions would not keep him away from his cherished Monticello. In any event, the job provided a comfortable and needed regular salary—$5,000 paid in quarterly installments.[21]

Adams and Jefferson started off cordially. The Virginian, having enjoyed Adams' friendship in the second Continental Congress and while in retirement at Monticello, set out to forge a good public relationship with him as his vice president. Although he realized that they would probably disagree on many issues, Jefferson deeply respected Adams' prior service to the nation.[22]

On the eve of their inaugurations, Adams and Jefferson met briefly to discuss the possibility of sending Jefferson to France as part of a three-member delegation to calm the increasingly turbulent relations between the two countries. When the two men concluded that this would be an improper role for the vice president, they agreed on substituting Jefferson's political ally, James Madison. The bond between president and vice president seemed—for the moment—particularly close.

Several days after the inauguration, Jefferson encountered the president at a dinner party. He took the opportunity to report that Madison was not interested in the diplomatic mission to France. Adams replied that, in any event, he would not have been able to select Madison because of pressure from within his cabinet to appoint a Federalist. This confirmed Jefferson's view that the new president lacked his own political compass and was too easily swayed by partisan advisers. Thereafter, Adams never consulted Jefferson on an issue of national significance.[23] For his part, the vice president turned exclusively to his political role as leader of the Republicans and to his governmental duty as the Senate's presiding officer.

While in Philadelphia to commence his vice-presidential duties, Jefferson acceded to a second leadership position—the presidency of the American Philosophical Society. Conveniently located near Congress Hall, this august scientific and philosophical body counted among its previous leaders Benjamin Franklin and mathematician David Rittenhouse. Jefferson attained the post on the strength of his *Notes on the State of Virginia* (first English edition, 1787), which secured his reputation as a preeminent scholar and scientist and is today considered "the most important scientific work published in America in the eighteenth century."[24] Within days of his inaugural address to the Senate, Jefferson delivered his presidential address to the society—a task that he found considerably more gratifying. His subject: the recently discovered fossil remains of a large animal, found in western Virginia, that he called the "Megalonyx" or "Great Claw."[25] Jefferson would preside over the society until 1815. He considered his contributions to its proceedings among his proudest endeavors.

A Republican Leader

After his inauguration, Jefferson had written to Aaron Burr (the former New York senator and intended vice-presidential candidate on the Republican ticket) to complain about the partisan direction of the new Federalist administration and seek his aid in building Republican support in the northeast. This move signalled Jefferson's intention to play an active political role during his vice-presidency. With James Madison retired from the House of Representatives and the new House leader, Albert Gallatin, preoccupied with the nation's financial problems, Jefferson stood as the country's preeminent Republican leader. Considering himself separate from the executive branch, he felt free to criticize the Adams administration. Yet, to avoid public controversy, he limited his criticism to private communications with political allies, particularly after the distortion of a letter he had written in April 1796 to the Italian intellectual Philip Mazzei.

In that letter, composed as Federalists and Republicans battled over the pro-British Jay Treaty, Jefferson had complained about the Federalists

THOMAS JEFFERSON

as "an Anglican monarchical, and aristocratical party" whose intention was to impose the substance of British government, as well as its forms, on the United States. Federalists in high government posts were "timid men who prefer the calm of despotism to the boisterous sea of liberty." [26] A translated version of his strongly worded communication appeared in several European newspapers and in a May 1797 edition of the New York *Minerva*. Liberties taken in translation served only to increase the letter's tone of partisan intemperance. Federalists offered the letter as evidence of the vice president's demagoguery, and the affair increased animosity between the political parties. Unhappy with the consequences of the Mazzei letter, Jefferson cautioned all future correspondents to "[t]ake care that nothing from my letters gets into the newspapers." [27]

Although Jefferson greatly respected the institution of the Senate, he had little affection for the Federalist senators over whom he presided. The Federalists enjoyed a 22-to-10 majority in 1797 and Jefferson expected the worst. Fearing that the majority might routinely employ the Senate's power to try impeachments to quiet senators who harbored contrary views, Jefferson took more than a passing interest in the impeachment proceedings against his fellow Republican, former Tennessee senator William Blount, whose trial he presided over in December 1798. Almost a year earlier, as the Senate worked to establish rules and procedures for the first impeachment trial, the vice president had secretly reinforced Virginia Senator Henry Tazewell's argument that Blount had a Sixth Amendment right to a jury trial, providing precedents he extracted from the parliamentary writings of William Blackstone and Richard Woddeson. "The object in supporting this engraftment into impeachments," he wrote Tazewell on January 27, 1798, "is to lessen the dangers of the court of impeachment under its present form & to induce dispositions in all parties in favor of a better constituted court of impeachment, which I own I consider as an useful thing, if so composed as to be clear of the spirit of faction." Anxious to conceal his role in the Republican effort to circumscribe the impeachment power, he cautioned Tazewell,

"Do not let the enclosed paper be seen in my handwriting." [28] A month later, after Tazewell's effort failed, Jefferson confided to Madison that the Federalists "consider themselves as the bulwarks of the government, and will be rendering that the more secure, in proportion as they can assume greater powers." [29]

Alien and Sedition Acts

Deteriorating relations with France preoccupied the government during Jefferson's vice-presidency and fostered anti-French sentiment at home. No one event caused the conflict, but a decree of the ruling Directory and a series of French proposals fueled the spreading fire. The decree declared that neutral ships with English merchandise or commodities could be seized. Congress, in turn, sought to protect American commerce by authorizing the arming of private vessels.

In what proved to be a futile attempt to improve relations, President Adams sent three envoys to France. When they reached Paris in October 1797, however, the French government refused to receive them until they satisfied requirements that the Americans considered insulting. Minor French officials—publicly labeled "X, Y, and Z"—met with the envoys and presented proposals that included a request for a $12 million loan and a $250,000 bribe in exchange for recognition of the United States and the establishment of formal ties. Despite his sympathies for France, Jefferson viewed the proposals as a supreme insult, yet he understood that a war could undermine the nation's newly set constitutional foundations and strengthen the pro-British Federalist leadership.

The publication in April 1798 of what became known as the "XYZ papers" produced widespread anger and created a frenzied atmosphere in which overzealous patriotism flourished. In an effort to restore their party's popularity, Federalist legislators—recently the targets of public scorn for their support of the unpopular Jay treaty with England—seized on the anti-French hostility that the XYZ affair had generated. Federalists in Congress, their numbers expanded in response to public anger against France, quickly passed a series of tough measures to set the nation on a war footing. Most notorious of these statutes were the Sedition Act, the Naturalization Act, and the Alien Act, all viewed by their Republican opponents as distinctly partisan measures to curtail individual rights.[30]

The Senate approved the Sedition Act on July 4, 1798, in the final days of the Fifth Congress after Jefferson had left for Virginia. The statute curtailed the rights of Americans to criticize their government and provided punishment for any person writing, uttering, or publishing "any false, scandalous and malicious writing" against the president or Congress with the intent of inflaming public passions against them.[31] The Federalists immediately invoked the law's provisions to suppress Republican criticism.

The Naturalization Act was also a decidedly partisan measure in that it targeted immigrants, who tended to support the Republican party, by lengthening the residency requirements for U.S. citizenship from five to fourteen years.[32] Finally, President Adams, on June 25, 1798, signed a third repressive law passed by the Federalist Congress. The Alien Act, which Jefferson called "a most detestable thing," authorized the president, acting unilaterally, to deport any noncitizen whom he viewed as "dangerous to the peace and safety of the United States."[33] Adams never exercised this power, but the Act inflamed the dispute over the scope of presidential power in the young nation.

Jefferson recognized that these measures raised fundamental questions regarding the division of sovereignty between the national and state governments and the means for settling disputes between the two levels of government. As vice president and head of the party that this legislation was designed to restrain, Jefferson found himself powerless at the national level to combat these measures that he believed were "so palpably in the teeth of the Constitution as to shew they mean to pay no respect to it."[34]

Looking to the states to provide an arena for constructive action, Jefferson drafted a set of resolutions assailing these acts as unconstitutional violations of human rights.[35] He sent them to Wilson Nicholas, a member of the Virginia assembly, with a request that he arrange for their introduction in the North Carolina legislature.

By chance, Nicholas encountered John Breckinridge, a member of the Kentucky house of representatives, many of whose members strongly opposed these repressive laws. Breckinridge agreed to introduce Jefferson's resolutions in his legislature while keeping their author's identity secret.

The first sentence of Jefferson's "Kentucky Resolutions" asserted:

> That the several states composing the United States of America are not united on the principle of unlimited submission to their general government, but that, by a compact under the style and title of a Constitution for the United States, and of amendments thereto, they constituted a general government for special purposes,—delegated to that government certain definite powers, reserving, each State to itself, the residuary mass of right to their own self-government; and that whensoever the general government assumes undelegated powers, its acts are unauthoritative, void, and of no force.[36]

Although the vice president had no desire to subvert the Union, his suggestion that any state had the power to nullify a federal law if it determined the legislation to be unconstitutional harbored grave consequences for the nation's stability. He also argued that the federal judiciary should not decide issues of constitutionality because it was a partisan arm of the federal government. Jefferson did not specifically call for the nullification of the Alien and Sedition acts, but he did use the word "nullify," which was subsequently dropped from the version of the resolution that the Kentucky legislature adopted in November 1798.

The Virginia legislature passed similar measures prepared in a less strident form by James Madison who, like Jefferson, found the Sedition and Alien laws to be constitutionally flawed and dangerous to individual freedom. To Jefferson's chagrin, no other states joined in this action, as most legislatures thought Jefferson's ideas too extreme. The resolutions as passed in Kentucky and Virginia simply called on states to seek repeal of the odious statutes through their representatives at the next session of Congress.[37] The Kentucky legislature passed additional resolutions in 1799—specifically calling for nullification of objectionable laws. Although Jefferson sympathized with their aim, he had no part in their drafting. Congress did not renew the Alien and Sedition acts in 1801 when they expired.

Thomas Jefferson's involvement with the Kentucky Resolutions reflected his passion for protecting civil liberties from repressive measures by omnipotent government. He favored a governmental system that would resist tyranny and corruption. He found republicanism to be closest to his ideal of a balanced and strong yet non-intrusive form of government. "The legitimate powers of government," he wrote, "extend to such acts only as are injurious to others." [38] Yet his philosophy did allow for a distinction between the relative powers of the state and federal governments.

Conditioned by his overriding fear of centralized power, Jefferson argued that the federal government could not infringe on the freedom of the press. He vehemently opposed the Sedition Act, but he believed the states had the right to restrict the press to some degree. The possibility that states might abuse this power did not concern Jefferson. On the contrary, he saw the states as the bulwarks of freedom, as his involvement with the Kentucky Resolutions demonstrated. Years later, he would write, "the true barriers of our liberty in this country are our State governments; and the wisest conservative power ever contrived by man, is that of which our Revolution and present government found us possessed." [39]

Jefferson sought to enhance the authority of the states only to further the cause of individual rights. But when a foreign nation posed a threat to the country, Jefferson was quick to underscore the importance of the Union, which he described as "the last anchor of our hope." Though he would eschew war at all costs, Jefferson believed the states had an obligation to support the Union, even if it blundered into war.

Jefferson's *Manual*

Thomas Jefferson's *Manual of Parliamentary Practice* is, without question, the distinguishing feature of his vice-presidency. The single greatest contribution to the Senate by any person to serve as vice president, it is as relevant to the Senate of the late twentieth century as it was to the Senate of the late eighteenth century. Reflecting the *Manual*'s continuing value, the Senate in 1993 provided for its publication in a special edition to commemorate the 250th anniversary of Jefferson's birth.

Jefferson had conceived the idea of a parliamentary manual as he prepared to assume the duties of the vice-presidency early in 1797. John Adams offered an inadequate model for the role of presiding officer, for he had earned a reputation for officious behavior in the Senate president's chair. To avoid the criticism that attended Adams' performance, Jefferson believed the Senate's presiding officer needed to follow "some known system of rules, that he may neither leave himself free to indulge caprice or passion, nor open to the imputation of them." [40] The lack of carefully delineated rules, he feared, would make the Senate prone to the extremes of chaos and tyranny. He was particularly concerned about the operation of Senate Rule 16, which provided that the presiding officer was to be solely responsible for deciding all questions of order, "without debate and without appeal." [41]

Before leaving Virginia to take up his new duties, Jefferson had contacted his old mentor, George Wythe. Acknowledging that he had not concerned himself about legislative matters for many years, Jefferson asked Wythe to help refresh his memory by loaning him notes on parliamentary procedure that Wythe had made years earlier. To Jefferson's disappointment, the eminent jurist reported that he had lost track of his notes and that his memory no longer served him well. Jefferson then consulted his "Parliamentary Pocketbook," which included notes on parliamentary procedure he had taken when he studied under Wythe and during his service as a member of the Virginia house of burgesses. Although he considered these notes his "pillar," he realized they would be of little direct assistance in resolving Senate procedural disputes.

The new vice president admired the British House of Commons' rules of procedure because, in the words of a former Speaker, they provided "a shelter and protection to the minority, against the attempts of power." [42] "Its rules are probably as wisely constructed for governing the debates of a deliberative body, and obtaining its true sense, as any which can become known to us."[43] A Senate in which the Federalists had a two-to-one majority over the Republicans accentuated Jefferson's fears and made him particularly sensitive to the preservation of minority rights. Distrusting the process in which small committees under majority party control made key decisions, the vice president wished to protect minority interests by emphasizing those procedures that permitted each senator to have a say in important matters.

Jefferson compiled his *Manual of Parliamentary Practice* during the course of his four-year vice-presidency. He designed it to contain guidance for the Senate drawn from "the precepts of the Constitution, the regulations of the Senate, and where these are silent, the rules of Parliament." To broaden his understanding of legislative procedure, Jefferson studied noteworthy works on the British Parliament such as John Hatsell's three-volume *Precedents of Proceedings in the House of Commons* (1785), Anchitell Grey's ten-volume edition of *Debates in the House of Commons* (1769), and Richard Wooddeson's three-volume *A Systematical View of the Laws of England* (1792, 1794). The resulting *Manual*, loaded with references to these British parliamentary authorities, contained fifty-three sections devoted to such topics as privileges, petitions, motions, resolutions, bills, treaties, conferences, and impeachments.

Jefferson's *Manual* was first published in 1801, shortly after he became president. A second edition followed in 1812, and in 1837 the House of Representatives established that the rules listed in the *Manual* would "govern the House in all cases to which they are applicable and in which they are not inconsistent with the standing rules and orders of the House and the joint rules of the Senate."[44] Although the *Manual* has not been treated as "a direct authority on parliamentary procedure in the Senate,"[45] it is the Senate that today more closely captures Jefferson's ideal of a genuinely deliberative body. His emphasis on order and decorum changed the way the Senate of his day operated. In the assessment of Dumas Malone, Jefferson "exercised his limited functions [as presiding officer] with greater care than

his predecessor and left every successor his debtor."[46]

President

On February 17, 1801, after thirty-six ballots, the House of Representatives elected Thomas Jefferson president of the United States.[47] Following the precedent that Vice President Adams set in February 1797, Jefferson delivered a brief farewell address to the Senate on February 28, 1801. He thanked members for their indulgence of his weaknesses.

> In the discharge of my functions here, it has been my conscientious endeavor to observe impartial justice without regard to persons or subjects; and if I have failed of impressing this on the mind of the Senate, it will be to me a circumstance of the deepest regret. . . . I owe to truth and justice, at the same time, to declare, that the habits of order and decorum, which so strongly characterize the proceedings of the Senate, have rendered the umpirage of their President an office of little difficulty; that, in times and on questions which have severely tried the sensibilities of the House, calm and temperate discussion has rarely been disturbed by departures from order.[48]

After completing these remarks, Jefferson followed another Adams precedent by stepping aside a few days prior to the end of the session. This action allowed the Senate to appoint a president pro tempore, a post filled only when the vice president was absent from the capital. Next to the vice president in the line of presidential succession at that time, the president pro tempore would serve until the swearing in of a new vice president at the start of the next session.

On March 4, 1801, Jefferson took the oath of office as president of the United States, thereby successfully accomplishing the nation's first transfer of presidential power between the two major political parties. He served two terms as president, retiring at last from public life in 1809. He renewed his friendship with John Adams, and the two men corresponded regularly until their deaths—both dying on July 4, 1826, the fiftieth anniversary of Jefferson's Declaration of Independence.

Jefferson's Contributions

Thomas Jefferson infused the vice-presidency with his genius through the contribution of his *Manual of Parliamentary Practice*—a magisterial guide to legislative procedure that has retained its broad utility through two centuries. He also contributed to the office his example of skillful behind-the-scenes legislative leadership, and he offered a philosophical compass on the issues of constitutionalism and individual rights. Biographer Dumas Malone provides a final analysis of Jefferson's style as party leader during his vice-presidential tenure:

His popular success was due in considerable part to his identification of himself with causes for which time was fighting—notably the broadening of the political base—and to his remarkable sensitivity to fluctuations in public opinion. As a practical politician, he worked through other men, whom he energized and who gave him to an extraordinary degree their devoted cooperation. His leadership was due not to self-assertiveness and imperiousness of will but to the fact that circumstances had made him a symbolic figure and that to an acute intelligence and unceasing industry he joined a dauntless and contagious faith. [48]

NOTES

[1] Paul Leicester Ford, *The Writings of Thomas Jefferson* (New York, 1892–1899), vol. 7, p. 114.

[2] Biographical accounts of Jefferson's life are plentiful and rich. The definitive modern study is Dumas Malone, *Jefferson and His Time*, 6 vols. (Boston, 1948–1981). The volume in that series that covers the years of his vice-presidency is *Jefferson and the Ordeal of Liberty* (Boston, 1962). A first-rate single-volume biography is Noble E. Cunningham, Jr., *In Pursuit of Reason: The Life of Thomas Jefferson* (Baton Rouge, 1987). For the period of Jefferson's vice-presidency, see Noble E. Cunningham, Jr., *The Jeffersonian Republicans: The Formation of Party Organization, 1789–1801* (Chapel Hill, 1957). For a series of twenty-five excellent essays that focus on each of Jefferson's "extraordinary collection of talents," see Merrill D. Peterson, ed., *Thomas Jefferson: A Reference Biography* (New York, 1986). This work also contains a comprehensive bibliography. There are several major collections of Jefferson's writings, including Paul Leicester Ford, *The Writings of Thomas Jefferson*, 10 vols. (New York, 1892–1899) and the more comprehensive, but as yet incomplete, Julian P. Boyd, et al., eds., *The Papers of Thomas Jefferson* (1950–). The latter work has appeared to date only to the mid-1790s and thus is of no assistance for the vice-presidential period. One volume associated with this massive project, however, is of direct value; appearing as part of the project's "Second Series" is Wilbur Samuel Howell, ed., *Jefferson's Parliamentary Writings: 'Parliamentary Pocket-Book' and A Manual of Parliamentary Practice* (Princeton, 1988).

[3] For a thorough study of Jefferson's early years see Marie Kimball, *Jefferson: The Road to Glory, 1743 to 1776* (New York, 1943) and Dumas Malone, *Jefferson the Virginian* (Boston, 1948).

[4] Cunningham, *In Pursuit of Reason*, pp. 64–75.

[5] Dumas Malone, "The Life of Thomas Jefferson," in Peterson, ed., p. 7.

[6] Noble E. Cunningham, Jr., "The Jeffersonian Republican Party," in *History of U.S. Political Parties*, ed. Arthur M. Schlesinger, Jr. (New York, 1973), 1:240.

[7] Kenneth R. Bowling and Helen E. Veit, eds., *The Diary of William Maclay and Other Notes on Senate Debates, Documentary History of the First Federal Congress of the United States of America*, vol. 9 (Baltimore, 1988), p. 275.

[8] Cunningham, "The Jeffersonian Republican Party," pp. 246–47.

[9] Malone, *Jefferson and the Ordeal of Liberty*, pp. 274–75.

[10] Quoted in Cunningham, "The Jeffersonian Republican Party," p. 249.

[11] Malone, *Jefferson and the Ordeal of Liberty*, p. 291.

[12] Ibid., p. 274.

[13] Ibid., p. 278.

[14] *Congressional Quarterly's Guide to U.S. Elections*, 3d ed. (Washington, 1994), p. 361.

[15] Jefferson to Rush, January 22, 1797, in Ford, 7:114; Malone, *Jefferson and the Ordeal of Liberty*, p. 292.

[16] Ford, 7:93–94.

[17] Only two other vice presidents subsequently shared Adams' pleasant task: Martin Van Buren in 1837 and George Bush in 1989.

[18] Malone, *Jefferson and the Ordeal of Liberty*, p. 295.

[19] U.S., Congress, *Annals of Congress*, March 4, 1797, pp. 1580–82.

[20] Jefferson to Gerry, May 13, 1797, in Ford, 7:120.

[21] Malone, *Jefferson and the Ordeal of Liberty*, p. 300.

[22] Ibid., p. 293; Cunningham, *In Pursuit of Reason*, pp. 206–7; John Ferling, *John Adams: A Life* (Knoxville, 1992), pp. 332–34.

[23] Malone, *Jefferson and the Ordeal of Liberty*, p. 299.

[24] Silvio A. Bedini, "Man of Science," in Peterson, ed., p. 257.

[25] Cunningham, *In Pursuit of Reason*, 206–7; Malone, *Jefferson and the Ordeal of Liberty*, chapter XXII; Bedini, in Peterson, ed., pp. 253–76.

[26] Ford, 7: 76; Cunningham, *The Jeffersonian Republicans*, p. 119.

[27] Jefferson to Colonel Bell, May 18, 1797, in Andrew A. Lipscomb and Albert Ellery Bergh, ed., *The Writings of Thomas Jefferson* (Washington, 1903), 9:387; Cunningham, *The Jeffersonian Republicans*, pp. 118–19.

[28] Thomas Jefferson to Henry Tazewell, January 27, 1798, in Ford, 7:194–95.

[29] Thomas Jefferson to James Madison, February 22, 1798, in Ford, 7:206–8.

[30] Malone, *Jefferson and the Ordeal of Liberty*, chapter XXIV.

[31] 1 *Stat.* 596–597.

[32] 1 *Stat.* 566–569.

[33] 1 *Stat.* 570–572.

[34] Jefferson to James Madison, June 7, 1798, in Ford, 7:267.

[35] This issue is treated in full detail in Malone, *Jefferson and the Ordeal of Liberty*, chapter XXV.

[36] Ford, 8:458–61.

[37] Cunningham, *In Pursuit of Reason*, pp. 217–18.

[38] Quoted in Malone, *Jefferson and the Ordeal of Liberty*, p. 393.

[39] Jefferson to Destutt de Tracy, January 16, 1888, in Ford, 9:308–10; Malone, *Jefferson and the Ordeal of Liberty*, p. 394.

[40] Thomas Jefferson, *A Manual of Parliamentary Practice for the Use of the Senate of the United States*, in The Papers of Thomas Jefferson, Second Series, *Jefferson's Parliamentary Writings*, Wilbur Samuel Howell, ed., p. 355. Howell has produced the definitive scholarly edition of Jefferson's *Manual* (pp. 339–444).

[41] U.S., Congress, Senate, *History of the Committee on Rules and Administration, United States Senate*, S. Doc. 96–27, 96th Cong., 1st sess., p. 6.

42 Speaker Arthur Onslow quoted in Section I of Jefferson's *Manual of Parliamentary Practice*, Howell ed., p. 357.

43 Howell, ed., p. 355.

44 The Senate has regularly published that work as a companion to the body's formal rules. The *Manual* was included as a section within the *Senate Manual* from 1886 to 1975 and was republished in 1993, on the occasion of the 250th anniversary of Jefferson's birth, in the original 1801 edition. Some practices discussed in Jefferson's *Manual* set core precedents that the Senate has followed ever since, although the work is not considered a direct authority on procedure. The *Manual*'s influence quickly extended beyond domestic legislatures, as editors translated the work into other languages. At least 143 editions have been printed. The work has abetted self-government in countries as far away as the Philippines, where over one-hundred years later it was adopted as a supplementary guide in that nation's senate and house of representatives.

45 U.S., Congress, Senate, *Riddick's Senate Procedure: Precedents and Practices*, by Floyd M. Riddick and Alan S. Frumin, S. Doc. 101–28, 101st Cong., 1st sess., p. 754.

46 Malone, *Jefferson and the Ordeal of Liberty*, pp. 452–53.

47 A description of this election and the resulting Twelfth Amendment to the Constitution appears in Chapter 3 of this volume, "Aaron Burr."

48 *Annals of Congress*, 6th Cong., 1st sess., pp. 753–54.

48 Malone, "The Life of Thomas Jefferson," in Peterson, ed., p. 15.

Chapter 3

AARON BURR
1801–1805

AARON BURR

Chapter 3

AARON BURR

3rd Vice President: 1801–1805

Was there in Greece or Rome a man of virtue and independence, and supposed to possess great talents, who was not the subject of vindictive and unrelenting persecution?

—AARON BURR TO THEODOSIA BURR ALSTON [1]

I never, indeed thought him an honest, frank-dealing man, but considered him as a crooked gun, or other perverted machine, whose aim or stroke you could never be sure of.

—THOMAS JEFFERSON [2]

Col. Burr . . . [is] Not by any means a model man . . . but not so bad as it is the fashion to paint him.

—GEORGE W. JOHNSON [3]

Congressional Republicans were in a festive mood on January 24, 1804, as they gathered at Stelle's Hotel on Capitol Hill for a banquet celebrating the transfer of the Louisiana Territory to the United States. The festivities began at noon with the discharge of "three pieces of cannon." President Thomas Jefferson and Vice President Aaron Burr were among the honored guests; they departed after the banquet, but the revelry continued until nightfall. "A number of the guests drank so many toasts that in the night they returned to their houses without their hats," one contemporary reported. But when one celebrant offered a toast to Vice President Burr, the effect was pronounced and chilling: "few cheered him," the chronicler observed, "& many declined drinking it." [4]

None of Aaron Burr's contemporaries knew quite what to make of this complex and fascinating individual. As Senator Robert C. Byrd observed in his November 13, 1987, address on the life and career of this controversial vice president, "there is much that we will never know about the man." Much of Burr's early cor-

respondence, entrusted to his daughter for safekeeping, was lost in 1812, when the ship carrying Theodosia Burr Alston from South Carolina to New York for a long-awaited reunion with her father disappeared off the North Carolina Coast. [5]

Burr was one of the most maligned and mistrusted public figures of his era—and, without question, the most controversial vice president of the early republic—but he never attempted to justify or explain his actions to his friends or to his enemies. One editor of Burr's papers has lamented, "Almost alone among the men who held high office in the early decades of this nation, Burr left behind no lengthy recriminations against his enemies . . . no explanations and justifications for his actions." He seems to have cared very little what his contemporaries thought of him, or how historians would judge him. [6] Few figures in American history have been as vilified, or as romanticized, by modern writers. [7] Urbane and charming, generous beyond prudence, proud, shrewd, and ambitious, he stood apart from other public figures of his day.

An anomaly in an era when public office was a duty to be gravely and solemnly accepted but never pursued with unseemly enthusiasm, Burr enjoyed the ''game'' of politics. His zest for politics enabled him to endure the setbacks and defeats he experienced throughout his checkered career, but, as Mary-Jo Kline, the editor of Burr's papers suggests, it also gave him the ''spectacular ability to inspire suspicion—even fear—among the more conventional Founding Fathers.'' [8]

Early Years

Aaron Burr was born at Newark, New Jersey, on February 6, 1756. His father, Aaron Burr, Sr., was a highly respected clerical scholar who served as pastor of the Newark First Presbyterian Church and as president of the College of New Jersey (now Princeton University). His mother, Esther Edwards Burr, was the daughter of the noted Puritan theologian and scholar, Jonathan Edwards, who is most often remembered for his passionate and fiery sermons. The family moved to Princeton when the college relocated there soon after the future vice president's birth, but Burr did not remain there long. His father contracted a fever and died when young Aaron was only a year-and-a-half old. His mother and her parents died soon thereafter. An orphan by the age of two, Burr and his older sister, Sally, moved to Philadelphia, where they lived with family friends until 1759, when their uncle, Timothy Edwards of Stockbridge, Massachusetts, became their legal guardian.

Edwards and his young wards moved to Elizabeth Town, New Jersey, the following year. Uncle Timothy soon discovered that Esther's ''Little dirty Noisy Boy'' had inherited much of the Edwards family's renowned intellect but little of their piety. High-spirited, independent, precocious and self-confident, young Aaron at first studied with a private tutor. In 1769 he began his studies at the College of New Jersey, graduating in 1772. In 1773, he enrolled in the Reverend Joseph Bellamy's school at Bethlehem, Connecticut, to prepare for the ministry but soon realized that he could neither wholly accept the Calvinist discipline of his forebears nor forgo the distractions of the town.[9] He had, his authorized

biographer relates, ''come to the conclusion that the road to Heaven was open to all alike.'' [10] In May 1774, he moved to Litchfield, Connecticut, to study law under his brother-in-law, Tapping Reeve, but the outbreak of the American Revolution interrupted his studies.

Burr joined the march on Quebec as an uncompensated ''gentleman volunteer'' in the summer of 1775. His bravery under fire during the ill-fated assault on that heavily fortified city on December 31, 1775, won him a coveted appointment as an aide to the American commander in chief, General George Washington, but he was almost immediately reassigned to General Israel Putnam. Burr served as Putnam's aide until 1777, when he finally received a commission as a lieutenant colonel and command of his own regiment. Washington seems to have taken an immediate dislike to his ambitious young aide, and Burr appears to have reciprocated this sentiment. When Washington ordered the court-martial of General Charles Lee for dilatory conduct at the battle of Monmouth Courthouse, New Jersey, in June 1778, Burr sided with Lee. His own regiment had suffered heavy losses during the engagement after Washington ordered Burr to hold an exposed position in the blazing ninety-six-degree heat. But notwithstanding his dislike for Colonel Burr, Washington respected his abilities, assigning him the difficult but crucial task of determining the future movements of the British forces in New York. Burr later commanded the troops stationed at Westchester, New York, imposing a rigid but effective discipline that brought order to the frontier outpost where unruly soldiers and footloose marauders had formerly terrorized the nearby settlers. Burr resigned his commission in early 1779, his health broken by the accumulated stresses of several exhausting campaigns. He always took pride in his military record, and for the remainder of his long life, admirers referred to him as ''Colonel Burr.'' [11] Of his many accomplishments, only two are memorialized on the stone that marks his grave: Colonel in the Army of the Revolution, and Vice President of the United States.[12]

Aaron Burr lived an unsettled existence after leaving the army, travelling about the countryside, visiting friends and family, and studying law as his health permitted. In 1782, he began his legal practice and married Theodosia Bartow Prevost, the widow of a British army officer. In November 1783, the Burr family—which included his wife's two sons by her first husband and an infant daughter, named Theodosia for her mother—moved to New York after British forces evacuated the city. Burr lavished special attention on his only child, carefully supervising her education and cultivating her intellect. Young "Theo," in turn, idolized her father, and she became his closest confidante after her mother died in 1794.[13]

Early Political Career

Burr was an able lawyer. A New York law barring non-Whigs from the legal profession worked to his advantage as he rose to prominence in that calling. At this stage in his career, he was not, apparently, an adherent of any particular political persuasion. Despite his alacrity in responding to the call for volunteers at the outbreak of the Revolution, he seems to have been curiously detached from the political ferment that brought it about. Once Burr began his political career, he served a single term in the New York assembly during the 1784–1785 session,[14] not returning to public life until 1788. Then, as the editors of his papers suggest, he "appears to have played a minor and equivocal role" in the New York debate over ratification of the proposed federal constitution. The radical Sons of Liberty touted Burr as a possible delegate to the ratification convention, but, for reasons he never elaborated, he declined to serve.[15] Before long, however, he abandoned whatever reservations he may have had with respect to the new Constitution. "After adoption by ten states," he advised one correspondent, "I think it became both politic and necessary to adopt it."[16]

Burr was soon actively involved in New York politics. Joining forces with his future rival, Alexander Hamilton, he supported Richard Yates—a moderate Antifederalist and a longstanding friend who had helped him win admission to the bar—in the 1789 gubernatorial election. Yates lost to George Clinton, a more ardent Antifederalist who had served as governor of New York since 1777. Governor Clinton, either willing

to forgive Burr or shrewd enough to realize that the brilliant young newcomer would soon emerge as a key player in New York politics, appointed him attorney general in 1789. In 1791, Clinton helped orchestrate Burr's election to the U. S. Senate, unseating Senator Philip Schuyler and making a lifelong enemy of Schuyler's son-in-law, Alexander Hamilton.[17]

Senator Burr had acquired a taste for politics—a profession that, he would later advise an aspiring candidate, he found "a great deal of fun."[18] In 1792, he entered the New York gubernatorial race but soon withdrew in Clinton's favor. Northern Republicans mentioned him as a prospective vice-presidential candidate in 1792, but Burr deferred to Clinton again after southern Republicans refused to support the ambitious young senator. Better to select "a person of more advanced life and longer standing in publick trust," James Monroe of Virginia cautioned, "particularly one who in consequence of such service had given unequivocal proofs of what his principles really were."[19]

Burr was a vehement partisan in the Senate, siding with the anti-administration forces who opposed Hamilton's financial system and Washington's foreign policy. He mounted a spirited, though unsuccessful, defense of Pennsylvania Senator Albert Gallatin, the Swiss-born Republican who was unseated in 1794 after the Federalist majority determined that he did not meet the Constitution's nine-year citizenship requirement for senators. He voted against Washington's nomination of John Jay as an envoy to Great Britain in 1794, on the grounds that it would be "mischievous and impolitic" to appoint Jay, the chief justice of the United States, to "any other office or employment emanating from, and holden at the pleasure of, the executive." Burr was also one of the most outspoken opponents of the unpopular "Jay Treaty," which the Federalist-dominated Senate approved in 1795.[20]

In 1796, the determined senator again set his sights on the vice-presidency, and—in a striking departure from eighteenth-century electoral etiquette—began an energetic campaign to secure the support of his fellow Republicans. On June 26, 1796, the Republican caucus endorsed him as their vice-presidential candidate, although, as

Burr's biographers have noted, "For their party's vice-presidential nomination, the Republicans were less unified than in their determination that [Thomas Jefferson] was the man to head their party's drive to oust the 'aristocrats.'" Republicans concentrated on capturing the presidency but succeeded only in electing Thomas Jefferson vice president. Over half of the electors who voted for Jefferson failed to cast their second votes for Burr, who finished a disappointing fourth with only thirty electoral votes.[21]

Burr retired from the Senate in 1797. The following year, he returned to the New York assembly, making several enemies during his brief and troubled term. He advocated defensive measures to protect New York harbor as relations with France worsened in the wake of the "X,Y,Z affair"—a prudent stance, given New York's strategic importance and vulnerable location, but one that prompted accusations from more doctrinaire Republicans that Burr had joined the Federalist camp. He became vulnerable to charges that he had abused the public trust for his personal benefit when he participated in a private land speculation venture in western New York and then sought to enact legislation removing restrictions on land ownership by noncitizens—a measure that would increase the value of his western lands. Working in concert with Hamilton, Burr helped secure a charter and raise subscriptions for a private company to improve the water supply of pestilence-ridden Manhattan, but New Yorkers were shocked to learn that the surplus capital from the venture had been used to establish the Bank of Manhattan. Although Federalists were heavily involved in the enterprise, the bank was controlled by Republicans. New York voters, suspicious as they were of banks, deserted the party in droves in the 1799 state election, and Burr was turned out of office.[22] One observer commented in disgust that the Republicans "had such a damn'd ticket that no decent man could hold up his head to support it."[23]

But although some Republicans were increasingly uncomfortable with Burr's questionable financial dealings and his willingness to cooperate with Federalists to achieve his ends, he remained a valuable asset. He had, one Federalist admitted, "by his arts & intrigues . . . done a great deal towards revolutionizing the State,"[24] building a political base that would help launch his national career. Burr's vehement opposition to the Alien and Sedition Acts in the New York assembly had won Republicans the support of New York's large and rapidly growing immigrant community. In a feat one admirer attributed to "the intervention of a Supreme Power and our friend Burr the agent," he ensured that New York City elected a Republican delegation to the state legislature in 1800, laying the groundwork for a Republican victory in the presidential contest later that year. New York was one of the states in which the legislature selected presidential electors, and its 12 electors comprised over 15 percent of the 70 votes necessary to achieve an electoral majority. Republican control of the New York legislature was crucial, and New York City's thirteen-member delegation gave the party a majority.[25]

The Election of 1800

In 1800, Republican strategists hoped to cement their fledgling coalition by seeking, for geographical balance, a New Yorker as their vice-presidential candidate. One obvious choice was New York's elder statesman, George Clinton, but his reluctance to enter the race[26] cleared the way for Burr's unanimous nomination by the Republican caucus on May 11, 1800. Although Jefferson would later claim—after Burr discredited himself by his behavior during the election and in office—that he had harbored reservations about his New York lieutenant from the time of their first meeting in 1791 or 1792, contemporary correspondence suggests that their relationship was cordial during the 1790s. If Jefferson had reservations about Burr in 1800, he laid them aside to secure a Republican victory, using his influence to ensure that all of Virginia's twenty-one electors would cast their second votes for his running mate.[27]

Jefferson waged a behind-the-scenes campaign, writing letters to his political lieutenants and encouraging the preparation and dissemination of pamphlets and press accounts critical of John Adams' administration, which had supported the Alien and Sedition Acts and increased the military establishment. Burr was an active campaigner, visiting Rhode Island and Connecticut in late August to shore up Republican support. "The Matter of V.P—is of very little comparative Consequence," he informed one correspondent as he speculated that the election might result in the election of Jefferson as president and Adams as vice president, "and any Sacrifice on that head ought to be made to obtain a single vote for J———." [28] Surprising as it might appear to modern observers, Burr's clearly successful political prowess in the 1800 election only raised suspicions among his rivals and allies that he was not to be trusted. He did not fit the mold of the dispassionate statesmen who remained aloof from the fray of politics while their supporters worked to secure their election. But "the creation of nationwide, popularly based political parties," one Burr scholar explains, "demanded men who were willing to . . . bargain regional alliances, men able to climb the ladder of popular support and to convey their own enjoyment of the 'fun' of politics." In this respect, she suggests, Burr was "The Ghost of Politics Yet to Come." [29]

Jefferson soon had ample reason to distrust Burr. In 1800, as in the three previous presidential elections, each elector cast two votes without distinguishing between presidential and vice-presidential candidates. Republican strategists expected that all of their electors would cast one vote for Jefferson and that most—enough to guarantee that Burr would receive the second highest number of votes but not enough to jeopardize Jefferson's margin—would cast their second votes for Burr. Jefferson and his lieutenants left the implementation of this scheme to chance, never asking even a single elector to withhold a vote from Burr, although Jefferson's friend and adviser, James Madison, would later allege that Republicans had been lulled by "false assurances dispatched at the critical moment to the electors of one state, that the votes of another would be different from what they proved to be."

Increasingly confident of victory as the news of the election filtered in from the states, Republicans were stunned to learn by mid-December that, although they had clearly defeated Adams and his running mate, Charles Cotesworth

Pinckney of South Carolina, they had failed to elect a president. Jefferson and Burr, whether by neglect or miscalculation, would each receive 73 electoral votes. The election would be decided by the House of Representatives, as provided in Article II, section 1, of the Constitution, which directed that "if there be more that one [candidate] who have such a majority, and have an equal Number of Votes, then the House of Representatives shall immediately chuse by Ballot one of them for President," with "each State having one Vote." [30] The representatives from each state would poll their delegation to determine how their state would cast its single vote, with deadlocked states abstaining.

As soon as the outcome of the election became apparent, but before Congress met to count the electoral votes on February 11, 1801, the Federalists began a last-ditch effort to defeat Jefferson. Some, while resigned to a Republican victory, believed that the less partisan and more flexible Burr was by far the lesser of two evils. Others supported Burr in the hope that, if a deadlock could be prolonged indefinitely, the Federalist-dominated Congress could resolve the impasse with legislation authorizing the Senate to elect a Federalist president—a hope that had no constitutional basis but demonstrated the uncertain temper of the times. Alexander Hamilton, a prominent New York Federalist, actively opposed Burr, repeatedly attempting to convince his colleagues that Burr was a man whose "public principles have no other spring or aim than his own aggrandisement." [31]

Burr never explained his role in the drama that subsequently unfolded in the House of Representatives, which cast thirty-six ballots before finally declaring Jefferson the winner on February 17, 1801. The few comments he ventured at the time were guarded, evasive, and contradictory. Professing indignation at rumors that he was soliciting Federalist support in an attempt to wrest the presidency from Jefferson, Burr initially denied "that I could submit to be instrumental in counteracting the wishes & expectations of the U. S.," instructing his friend Samuel Smith "to declare these sentiments if the occasion shall require." One prominent Federalist, Robert Goodloe Harper of South Carolina, advised Burr against withdrawing from the presidential contest, urging that he "take no step whatsoever, by which the choice of the House of Representatives can be impeded or embarassed," and instead "keep the game perfectly in your own hand." Burr appears to have followed Harper's advice to the letter during the tense and confused days that followed. He never actively solicited Federalist votes but seemed willing enough to accept them. In late December, he informed Samuel Smith that, if the House elected him president, he would not step aside for Jefferson.[32]

Rumors of Burr's change of heart soon appeared in the press. Tempers flared and reports of impending armed conflict spread, but Burr remained silent. When the House cast the first ballot on February 11, eight of the sixteen states—one less than the simple majority required to elect the president—voted for Jefferson. Six states voted for Burr, with two states divided and not voting. This ratio remained constant through thirty-four subsequent ballots taken over the course of a week. The deadlock was not resolved until February 17, when Jefferson received the votes of ten states on the thirty-sixth ballot. Representative James A. Bayard (F-DE) and Burr himself finally resolved the impasse. As Delaware's only representative, Bayard controlled his state's vote. He voted for Burr on the first several ballots, but was under considerable pressure from Hamilton to change his vote and resolve the contest in Jefferson's favor. (In thus throwing his support to Jefferson, Hamilton rose above partisan interests and helped to save the nation.) Concluding that Burr could not muster enough Republican support to win the election (and having received assurances with respect to Jefferson's fiscal and appointments policies), Bayard finally informed his fellow Federalists that he could not "exclude Jefferson at the expense of the Constitution."[33] Correspondence from Burr, who was awaiting the outcome of the election in New York, had arrived on February 15; these letters, now lost, revealed that he had abandoned any hope of winning the presidency.[34] His supporters finally agreed that, when the state delegations were polled before

the House cast its thirty-sixth ballot on February 17, Vermont and Maryland Federalists would withhold their votes, a move that freed their previously deadlocked delegations to vote for Jefferson. Bayard and the South Carolina representatives would cast blank ballots, further eroding Burr's margin. Jefferson, with ten votes, would become president, while Burr, with four, would become vice president.[35]

The election, and the confusion that followed, exposed a critical flaw in the constitutional provision governing the election of the president and the vice president. The Twelfth Amendment, which passed both houses during the fall of 1803 and was ratified by the requisite number of states in time for the 1804 election, changed the method of election by requiring electors to designate one vote for a presidential candidate and the other for a vice-presidential candidate. Intended to prevent an unscrupulous vice-presidential candidate (or his supporters) from subverting the electoral process, the amendment was a Republican initiative, sponsored in the House of Representatives by John Dawson (R-VA) and in the Senate by Burr's rival De Witt Clinton (R-NY).[36]

Vice President Aaron Burr

If Burr was at all chagrined by the outcome of the election, or by the taint he had acquired from not emphatically renouncing his widely rumored presidential aspirations, he gave no sign of it. "I join my hearty Congratulations on the Auspicious events of the 17th:," he wrote to Albert Gallatin while en route to Washington for the March 4 inauguration; "as to the infamous slanders which have been so industriously circulated—they are now of little Consequence & those who believed them will doubtless blush at their own Weakness."[37] Burr arrived in Washington three days before the inauguration and found accommodations in nearby Georgetown.

On March 4, 1801, Senate President pro tempore James Hillhouse (F-CT) administered the oath of office to Burr in the Senate chamber on the ground floor of the new Capitol in Washington. The new vice president offered a brief extemporaneous address of "about three sentences," which the press ignored in favor of Jefferson's elegant and conciliatory inaugural address. Burr assumed the president's chair and administered the oath of office to the newly elected senators who presented their credentials. When Jefferson and the presidential party arrived in the Senate chamber, Burr left the Senate president's seat and joined Chief Justice John Marshall to listen to Jefferson's inaugural address. He later described the day as "serene & temperate—The Concourse of people immense—all passed off handsomely—great joy but no riot."[38]

The new vice president soon received a flood of letters from friends, political allies and relatives, seeking appointments in the new administration or demanding the removal of Adams' Federalist appointees. Burr, who could never refuse a friend and considered patronage a means of cementing alliances and paying political debts, passed a number of these requests along to Jefferson. The president, however, became increasingly uncomfortable with each new recommendation. Most damning, as historian Mary-Jo Kline has explained, were the "repeated requests for consideration of the claims of the 'faithful' from other states and territories." Jefferson was perfectly willing to replace Adams' "midnight appointments" with marshals and court officers who were loyal Republicans, as well as to remove Federalists who displayed "malversation or inherent disqualification" for office, appointing Republicans to the vacant posts. Still, mindful of the charges of nepotism and cronyism he had levelled against the Adams administration, he hesitated to dismiss civil servants solely for political reasons. Nor did he think it appropriate for the ambitious New Yorker to concern himself with appointments to federal offices in other states. The final insult appears to have occurred in the fall of 1801 with Burr's campaign to secure an appointment for his ally, Matthew L. Davis, to a naval post in New York. The president, already suspicious of the enterprising vice president who had jeopardized his election, soon began to distance himself from Burr.[39] Thereafter, in making federal appointments in New York, he relied on George Clinton or Clinton's nephew De Witt.

After the Clintons replaced Burr as the administration's liaison to the New York Republican

party, De Witt spared no effort to discredit the vice president in his home state. Assisted by [New York] *American Citizen* editor James Cheetham, he waged a savage war against the vice president in the local press.[40] "The handbills were numerous, of various descriptions, uniform however in Virulent and indecent abuse," Burr reported. "[T]o Vilify A.B. was deemed of so much consequence, that packages of them were sent to Various parts of the country." It was becoming painfully apparent, one of his allies observed, that the vice president's "influence and weight with the Administration is in my opinion not such as I could wish."[41] Bereft of the political base that had made him a formidable force in New York politics and an attractive vice-presidential prospect, he was now a liability to the administration. During Burr's single term in office, whatever influence or status he enjoyed would derive solely from his position as president of the Senate.[42]

President of the Senate

Burr was one of the most skilled parliamentarians to serve as president of the Senate, a striking contrast to Adams and a worthy successor to Jefferson. "Mr. Burr, the Vice President, presides in the Senate with great ease, dignity & propriety," Senator William Plumer (F-NH) observed. "He preserves good order, silence—& decorum in debate—he confines the speaker to the point. He has excluded all spectators from the area of the Senate chamber, except the members from the other House. A measure which contributes much to good order."[43]

But, although Burr was universally respected for his parliamentary skills and his impartial rulings, Senate Republicans noted with mounting concern his easy familiarity with his many Federalist friends. Alienated from his own party, pragmatic at the expense of principle, and beset by the chronic financial difficulties that dogged him throughout his career, Burr was increasingly regarded by his fellow Republicans as an unprincipled opportunist who would stop at nothing to rebuild his shattered political and personal fortunes.[44] They found ample evidence of the vice president's apostasy on January 27, 1802, when Burr cast a tie-breaking vote that undercut the

Republican effort to repeal the Judiciary Act of 1801.

That act, signed into law less than a week before Jefferson's election, enacted badly needed reforms, providing circuit court judges to relieve the Supreme Court justices from the burdensome and exhausting chore of riding circuit, and reducing the number of justices from six to five, effective with the next vacancy. The act became effective in time to allow John Adams to appoint Federalist judges to the new circuit courts, a development that heightened Republican fears of a Federalist-controlled judiciary. And, with one less Supreme Court justice, it appeared unlikely that Jefferson would ever have an opportunity to appoint a Republican nominee to the Supreme Court. On January 6, 1802, Senator John Breckinridge (R-KY) introduced a bill to repeal the Judiciary Act. Burr's vote would prove crucial in the Senate, where the absence of one Republican and the resignation of another had eroded the administration's already slim majority. Republicans were greatly relieved when the Senate deadlocked on a vote to proceed to a third reading of the repeal bill on January 26, and Burr resolved the tie in favor of the repealers. But he had secretly informed Federalists that he would support their attempts to block repeal by adding amendments that would make the Judiciary Act acceptable to moderate Republicans. Thus, the next day, when his friend Jonathan Dayton (F-NJ) moved to refer the bill to "a select committee, with instructions to consider and report the alterations which may be proper in the Judiciary system of the United States," Burr resolved the tie in favor of the Federalists.[45] Burr explained that he had voted for referral in hopes of reaching a compromise:

> I am for the affirmative, because I never can resist the reference of a measure where the senate is so nicely balanced, when the object is to effect amendment, that may accommodate it to the opinions of a larger majority; and particularly when I can believe that gentlemen are sincere in wishing a reference for this purpose. Should it, however, at any time appear that delay only is intended, my conduct will be different.[46]

Republicans who resented Burr's treachery were outraged when he announced the members of the select committee. During the early 1800s, senators voted to choose members of these temporary committees, which normally consisted of three members, but on this occasion two senators tied for first place and three for second place. The committee would therefore, Burr announced, be comprised of five members: two Republicans who favored repeal; two Federalists who had voted against repeal and subsequently voted to refer the bill to committee in hopes of effecting a compromise; and one Republican moderate, John Ewing Colhoun (R-SC), who had sided with the Federalists.[47] An account of the proceedings in the New York *Evening Post* reveals that Burr answered Republican challenges to this unexpected development with his customary ease and composure:

> . . . The Democratic [Republican] members appeared extremely discontented at the apparent result; and before the vote was finally declared by the Vice President, General [James] Jackson [R-GA] rose and proposed, that the Senate should ballot again for the committee. This dashing proposition did not materially interrupt the regularity of the scrutiny.

> The Vice President was very deliberate. He took the ballots of the respective Senators, examined them attentively, stated the number of them, and holding them up in his hand, mentioned that gentlemen, if they chose, might come and examine them. Mr. G[ouverneur] Morris [F-NY] hoped never to see, in the Senate a proceeding implying so much distrust.

> After a pause, the Vice President declared his opinion, that the ballots were truly counted. Of course, the committee was composed as stated above, to the no small chagrin of some of the Democratic members of Congress, in both Houses.[48]

Although Burr had substantive objections to the repeal bill,[49] and told one correspondent that he was troubled at the prospect "of depriving the twenty-six judges of office and pay,"[50] his growing estrangement from the administration was also a factor. He may, as one scholar of the early judiciary suggests, have hoped to "enhance his stature not only with moderates of his own party but also with Federalists, and perhaps even pave the way for the eventual formation of a third party under his leadership,"[51] but the immediate result of Burr's abortive attempt to reach a compromise was his further isolation from his party. He had, as Jefferson's biographer has noted, "offended one side without satisfying the other."[52] Among the advisers who comprised Jefferson's inner circle, only Treasury Secretary Albert Gallatin continued to support the increasingly troublesome vice president.[53]

Burr soon abandoned any hope of winning renomination to a second term. In early 1804, he called on Jefferson to inform him that he recognized "it would be for the interest of the republican cause for him to retire; that a disadvantageous schism would otherwise take place," but he was concerned that "were he to retire, it would be said that he shrunk from the public sentence." He would need, Burr suggested, "some mark of favor . . . which would declare to the world that he retired with [Jefferson's] confidence." Jefferson replied that he had not attempted to influence the 1800 election on his own or Burr's behalf, nor would he do so in the next election—a cool rejoinder that masked his now considerable resentment of the man whom, he claimed, he had "habitually cautioned Mr. Madison against trusting too much."[54]

The Republicans ultimately settled on George Clinton as their new vice-presidential candidate. Burr retired from national politics, without Jefferson's "mark of favor," entering the 1804 New York gubernatorial race in a desperate attempt to restore his rapidly failing career.

The Burr-Hamilton Duel

Burr no longer commanded the respect and support from New York Republicans that he had once enjoyed. He entered the gubernatorial race as an independent and actively sought Federalist support when it became apparent that the Federalists would not offer a candidate of their own. But Alexander Hamilton was soon "intriguing for any candidate who can have a chance of success against A.B." Burr plunged enthusiastically into the campaign, delivering speeches and distributing campaign literature, but he could not overcome the liabilities he had acquired since

1800. He lost the election by an overwhelming 8,000-vote margin.[55]

Burr's defeat left him bitter and disillusioned. He blamed Hamilton for his predicament, and when he learned that his rival and former ally had referred to him, at a private dinner party, as a "dangerous man, and who ought not to be trusted," he demanded an explanation. The conflict escalated, as Burr and Hamilton exchanged a series of letters, and finally came to a head on June 27, 1804, when Burr challenged Hamilton to a duel. The grim engagement took place on July 11 at Weehawken, New Jersey, and resulted in Hamilton's death the following day.[56]

Burr's opponents called for his arrest, but the outcry against him was by no means universal. Duelling was expressly prohibited by law in most states, and murder was a crime in every state. But encounters on the "field of honor" still took place during the early nineteenth century, particularly in the southern states. Burr had previously challenged Hamilton's brother-in-law, John Church, to a duel—a bloodless encounter that enabled them to confront and then forget their differences—and Hamilton's son, Philip, had incurred a mortal wound on the duelling ground the previous year. Henry Clay, Andrew Jackson, and others of similar stature subscribed to the *Code Duello*, but few suffered the stigma that Burr carried after that fatal morning at Weehawken. He left New York a month after Hamilton's death to allow "public opinion" to "take its proper course," travelling south in hopes of a reunion with his daughter Theodosia, now the wife of Joseph Alston, a South Carolina planter with impeccable Republican credentials, and his young grandson, Aaron Burr Alston. He was eventually indicted in New York and New Jersey, but never stood trial in either jurisdiction.[57]

Burr returned to the Senate in early November, in time for the second session of the Eighth Congress. It was, as Senator Plumer noted, an awkward occasion:

Nov. 7, 1804

This day the Senate made a quorum for the first time this session [which began two days earlier]. Mr. Burr, the Vice President, appeared and took his seat in the Senate the very first day of the session. It has been unusual for the Vice President to take his seat the first day of the session. But this man, though indicted in New York & New Jersey for the murder of the illustrious Hamilton, is determined to brave public opinion. What a humiliating circumstance that a man Who for months has fled from Justice—& who by the legal authorities is now accused of murder, should preside over the first branch of the National Legislature!

I have avoided him—his presence to me is odious—I have merely bowed & spoken to him—Federalists appear to despise neglect & abhor him. The democrats [Republicans], at least many of them, appear attentive to him—& he is very familiar with them—What line of conduct they will generally observe to him is yet uncertain.[58]

Republicans had indeed become "more attentive" to Burr; even Jefferson seemed anxious to mend fences with his errant vice president. "Mr. Jefferson has shewn more attention & invited Mr. Burr oftener to his house within this three weeks than ever he did in the course of the same time before," Plumer marvelled. "Mr. Gallatin, the Secy of the Treasury, has waited upon him often at his (Burr's) lodging—& on one day was closeted with him more than two hours. The Secretary of State, Mr. Madison, formerly the intimate friend of Genl. Hamilton, had taken his murderer into his carriage rode with him—accompanied him on a visit to M. Terreau the French Minister."[59] United States Attorney Alexander Dallas wrote to New Jersey Governor Joseph Bloomfield, urging him to grant clemency to the vice president.[60]

Republicans in Congress, particularly in the Senate, were equally solicitous of Burr. "The proceedings in New York in consequence of the duel are deemed by a number of the Senators to be harsh and unprecedented," Senator Samuel L. Mitchill (R-NY) explained to his wife. "They believe it very unfair and partial to make him the victim of justice, while several other persons who have killed their opponents in duels at Hoboken are suffered to go at large without molestation. Under these impressions an address has been drawn up to Governor Bloomfield for the purpose of inducing him to quash or suspend the proceedings against the Vice President."[61] Fed-

eralists were stunned by the Republicans' new-found respect for Burr, which Plumer attributed to "their joy for the death of Hamilton."[62] But the real reason for Republicans' apparent change of heart, as Burr's biographers Herbert Parmet and Marie Hecht have suggested, was the impending impeachment trial of Supreme Court Justice Samuel Chase.[63]

The Impeachment Trials of John Pickering and Samuel Chase

Burr had earlier presided over the impeachment trial of New Hampshire Judge John Pickering, a revered patriot and the author of his state's 1784 constitution, who by 1803 had become insane and an alcoholic. The House of Representatives impeached Pickering on March 2, 1803, for conduct "contrary to his trust and duty as judge," and the trial in the Senate was held a year later. Even the judge's Federalist supporters were embarrassed by his ravings from the bench, but they saw in the charges against him the opening salvo in the Republicans' assault on the federal judiciary. They would defend him at all costs, maintaining throughout his trial that insanity did not constitute grounds for removal. Republicans were forced to counter that the judge was perfectly sane, but guilty of misconduct that justified his removal from office, although Jefferson and some moderate Republicans were uneasy at the thought of subjecting a man so obviously tormented to the ordeal of an impeachment trial.[64]

The trial was a highly partisan proceeding, and on March 12, 1804, the final vote that removed Pickering from office split along party lines. The vice president made "very formal arrangements" for the trial, Representative Manasseh Cutler, a Federalist from Massachusetts, informed a correspondent, "and the court was opened with a dignified solemnity."[65] Burr presided over the preliminary proceedings and most of the trial with his customary tact and skill, deferring to the Senate to resolve the difficult procedural issues that arose after Pickering failed to appear and his son's attorney, Robert Goodloe Harper, informed the court that the judge, "being in a state of absolute and long continued insanity," could "neither appear nor authorize another to appear for him." But on March 10, Burr, concerned about his gubernatorial campaign in New York, "abruptly left the Senate," departing in the midst of a heated debate over Connecticut Federalist Uriah Tracy's motion to postpone the trial until the following session. President pro tempore Jesse Franklin, a North Carolina Republican, presided for the remainder of the trial, and Burr's unexpected departure made no apparent difference in the outcome of the proceedings.[66] Pickering's trial, as Jefferson's biographer has stressed, was a "confused and tragic episode."[67] The participants in this sorry spectacle all realized that Pickering was a deeply disturbed man and were greatly relieved when the trial ended with his removal from office.

But the impending trial of Associate Supreme Court Justice Samuel Chase, impeached for judicial misconduct by the House of Representatives on March 12, 1804—the day Pickering's trial ended—was another matter. Appointed to the court by President Washington and confirmed by a narrow margin, Chase was an inveterate Federalist, known for his intemperate and partisan harangues from the bench and for his flagrant prejudice against defendants accused of violating the Sedition Act. For many Republicans, Chase personified all the evils inherent in the Federalist-controlled judiciary. As his impeachment trial approached, these Republicans were painfully aware that they could ill afford to offend the man whose rulings would govern the proceedings, and they thus treated Burr with studied deference.[68]

But it was an uneasy truce, at best. Burr was noticeably uncomfortable in the Senate chamber. "After the minutes of the preceding day have been read—the little business before us dispatched," Plumer observed, the vice president would "leave the chair—come to some one Senator, & intimate in strong terms that it was best to adjourn—& sometimes request a senator to move an adjournment—& in a few minutes he was gone." He seemed to have "lost those easy graceful manners that beguiled the hours away the last session—He is now uneasy, discontented, & hurried."[69] Plumer also sensed "an unusual concern & anxiety in the leading democratic members of the senate," who feared "the

talents of Burr." The vice president appeared "friendly to them," he reflected, but "[s]ome office must be given him—what office can that be, that he will accept, & not injure them?"[70]

Burr imposed a rigid discipline on the conduct of the Chase impeachment trial, conducting the proceedings, as one reporter observed, "with the dignity and impartiality of an angel, but with the rigor of a devil."[71] Manasseh Cutler reported that the trial was "conducted with a propriety and solemnity throughout which reflects honor upon the Senate. It must be acknowledged that Burr has displayed much ability, and since the first day I have seen nothing of partiality."[72] Although the managers appointed by the House of Representatives and led by Republican Representative John Randolph of Virginia were responsible for trying the case, Burr would occasionally intervene, posing questions of his own to a witness when the irrational and ineffective Randolph (or another interrogator) failed to pursue a particular line of questioning, or seeking clarification of an incomplete or ambiguous response. When either side objected to a question posed by the other, Burr took careful note of the objection, ordering that the offending question be "reduced to writing" and put to the Senate for a determination.[73]

But at times Burr's rigid insistence on absolute decorum only increased the tensions that simmered in the Senate chamber, elaborately redecorated for the occasion under his careful supervision. Although Senator Plumer would conclude by the end of the trial that Burr had "certainly, on the whole, done himself, the Senate & the nation honor by the dignified manner in which he has presided over this high & numerous Court," he was outraged at Burr's treatment of Chase on January 2, 1805, when the judge appeared before the Senate to enter his plea. Before the court opened, Plumer had overheard the vice president's caustic comment as he ordered Sergeant at Arms James Mathers to remove the chair set aside for the aged justice: "Let the Judge take care to find a seat for himself." Mathers replaced the chair, after Chase "moved that a seat be assigned him," and the vice president "in a very cold formal insolent manner replied he presumed the Court would not object to taking a seat," but Burr would not permit Mathers to provide a table for the judge's convenience. Burr repeatedly interrupted the aged and frail judge as Chase, at times breaking into tears, requested additional time to prepare his answer to the impeachment.[74]

Burr's "peevishness" continued as the proceedings unfolded; on one occasion, he notified one of Chase's attorneys, Philip Barton Key, "that he must not appear as counsel in his loose coat" ["greatcoat," or overcoat], a proviso that senators criticized and Key ignored. By the first week of February, the Senate's now "remarkably testy" president was "in a rage because we do not sit longer."[75] Unruly senators on both sides of the aisle bristled, Plumer observed, when Burr lectured them on judicial etiquette after the high court of impeachment had adjourned for the day on February 12:

> Just as the time for adjourning to tomorrow was to be put in the Secretary's office—Mr. Burr said he wished to inform the Senate of some irregularities that he had observed in the Court. Some of the senators as he said during the trial & while a witness was under examination walked between him & the Managers—Others eat apples—& some eat cake in their seats.
>
> Mr. [Timothy] Pickering [F-MA] said he [did] eat an apple—but it was at a time when the President had retired from the chair. Burr replied he did not mean him—he did not see him.
>
> Mr. [Robert] Wright [R-MD] said he did eat cake—he had a just right so to do—he was faint—but he disturbed nobody—He never would submit to be schooled & catechised in this manner.
>
> At this instance a motion was made by Mr. [Stephen Row] Bradley [R-VT], who also had eaten cake, for an adjournment—Burr told Wright he was not in order—sit down—The Senate adjourned—& I left Wright & Burr scolding.[76]

Although rightfully concerned about maintaining an atmosphere of judicial decorum, Burr had obviously lost much of the "easy grace" and consummate tact that had made him such an effective presiding officer. The ordeal ended on March 1, when Burr announced, after a separate vote on each article of impeachment, "that there is not a Constitutional majority of votes finding Samuel Chase, Esq., guilty, on any one article."[77]

Burr's Final Days in the Senate

Burr's final days in the Senate would have been unpleasant even without the strain of presiding over a taxing and bitterly contested impeachment trial. He presided over the February 13, 1805 joint session of Congress, counting the electoral returns. In that capacity, he announced that Jefferson had been reelected and that his old rival, George Clinton, would succeed him as vice president. Senator Samuel Mitchill reported that Burr performed this "painful duty" with "so much regularity and composure that you would not have seen the least deviation from his common manner, or heard the smallest departure from his usual tone." But, Mitchill observed, the always impeccably attired vice president "appeared rather more carefully dressed than usual" for the occasion.[78]

A week later, Republican Senator John Smith of New York introduced a bill "freeing from postage all letters and packets to and from Aaron Burr," and Burr found himself in the unenviable position of listening as senators questioned the propriety of granting him the franking privilege. Although surviving accounts of the debate do not indicate that the issue of Burr's character was ever raised in his presence, it was certainly an unspoken consideration. The debate was particularly intense on February 27. Senator John Quincy Adams, a Massachusetts Federalist, proposed an amendment to extend the frank to all former vice presidents (omitting the explicit reference to Burr), and Republican James Jackson of Georgia cautioned in response that "We might hereafter have a Vice President to whom it would be improper to grant the privilege." After Federalist Senators Timothy Pickering of Massachusetts and James Hillhouse of Connecticut finally "advocated the indelicacy of the situation of having Mr. Burr in the chair," the vice president volunteered that "he was apprehensive that tomorrow he should be afflicted with pain in the head & should be unable to attend." With Burr absent from the chamber, his opponents were free to speak their minds. The debate was bitter and intense; Senator Hillhouse was resolutely opposed to giving Burr such a dangerous privilege. "The Vice President is an ambitious man," he warned his colleagues. "[H]e aspired to the Presidency—disappointed ambition will be restless. You put arms into his hands to attack your government—He may disseminate seditious pamphlets, news papers & letters at the expence of the very government he is destroying." Senator Pickering feared that Burr would "sell the right of franking to commercial houses—And in the city of New York alone it might give him a fortune." But Burr's supporters countered, "The reason why gentlemen oppose this bill is because Mr. Burr has fought a duel and killed a man." Although the bill passed by a vote of 18 to 13, with all but three of the New England senators voting against it, the House subsequently postponed the measure.[79]

Burr's Farewell Address

Burr left the Senate the day after the Chase trial concluded and just two days before George Clinton took office as the nation's fourth vice president. Federalists and Republicans alike were deeply moved by his March 2, 1805, farewell address, still one of the most celebrated speeches in the history of the early Republic. His remarks were intended for the senators alone, unexpectedly delivered at the conclusion of a closed-door executive session.

Burr began his twenty-minute address with an acknowledgement that "he must at times have wounded the feelings of individual members." But he had "avoided entering into explanations at the time," he explained, "because a moment of irritation was not a moment for explanation; because his position (being in the chair) rendered it impossible to enter into explanations without obvious danger of consequences which must injure the dignity of the Senate, or prove disagreeable and injurious in more than one point of view." Only "the ignorant and unthinking," he continued, "affected to treat as unnecessary and fastidious a rigid attention to rules and decorum." But Burr "thought nothing trivial which touched, however remotely, the dignity" of the Senate, and he cautioned senators "to avoid the smallest relaxation of the habits which he had endeavored to inculcate and establish." Likening the Senate to "a sanctuary, a citadel of law, of order, and of liberty," Burr predicted that "if the

Constitution be destined ever to perish by the sacrilegious hands of the demagogue or the usurper, which God avert, its expiring agonies will be witnessed on this floor."

Concluding his remarks with the customary expressions of respect and good will, Burr left the Senate chamber, closing the door behind him, Senator Mitchill noted, "with some force." "[A] solemn and silent weeping" filled the Senate chamber "for perhaps five minutes." Mitchill, for one, had "never experienced any thing of the kind so affecting," and New York Republican John Smith, "stout and manly as he is . . . laid his head upon his table and did not recover from his emotion for a quarter of an hour or more."[80] But De Witt Clinton's ally, [New York] *American Citizen* editor James Cheetham, and others who suspected that Burr's "melodio, harmonico pathos" was merely an effort to restore his political fortunes, doubted that "the flowing tear" could "wash away the dingy stains" of Burr's "political degeneracy."[81]

The "Burr Conspiracy"

The forty-nine-year-old former vice president was heavily in debt at the time of his forced retirement from politics. He had been involved in a number of speculative ventures throughout his career, many of which had resulted in substantial losses. Generous beyond prudence, Burr could never refuse a relative or a friend in need, even if it meant going further into debt. He had assumed responsibility for a number of young wards throughout the years—some of them the children of clients, others rumored to have been his own offspring—and his generosity to his charges further strained his always precarious finances. Burr had always lived, dressed and entertained well, even when he could ill afford to do so.[82] Surveying his limited prospects, the optimistic and always enterprising former vice president now looked to the West.

The full extent of Burr's business and other ventures in the West will probably never be known, but his first undertaking appears to have been the Indiana Canal Company. Burr and his fellow investors intended to construct a canal to circumvent the Ohio River rapids at Louisville, but, as his biographers have explained, the resourceful vice president had "more than one plan for the future but several alternate ones depending on change and history." His most ambitious scheme was contingent upon the outbreak of war with Spain, which was still in possession of West Florida and Mexico and increasingly hostile toward the burgeoning new nation that pressed along its eastern border. Burr planned an assault on Mexico and anticipated that the western states would leave the Union to join in a southeastern confederacy under his leadership. One of Burr's accomplices, Louisiana Governor James Wilkinson, betrayed the conspiracy before Burr could begin his expedition, and the former vice president was arrested on charges of treason. Chief Justice John Marshall presided over Burr's trial, which opened on August 3, 1807, in Richmond, Virginia. The jury, guided by Marshall's written opinion that two witnesses must testify to a specific, overt act to establish treason—a standard that the prosecution failed to meet—ultimately found "that Aaron Burr is not proved to be guilty under this indictment." Pressed by debts and fearful of further prosecution, Burr departed for Europe under an assumed name in June 1808.[83]

Burr's Later Years

Burr spent the next four years in self-imposed exile. He travelled throughout England and the continent, sightseeing, reading, entertaining the ladies, who found him an attractive companion, and seeking support for another southwestern expedition. His overtures to the British and French courts failed miserably. In the spring of 1812, convinced that a war between the United States and Great Britain was imminent, Burr returned home under the alias, "M. Arnot." He took a room near the Boston waterfront—a far cry from the handsome and well-furnished New York mansion, Richmond Hill, that he maintained in better times—while testing the waters to determine whether he could safely return to New York.[84]

Burr reappeared in New York in June 1812, ready to resume his legal career. He eagerly looked forward to a reunion with his beloved "Theo" and his grandson Aaron Burr Alston but soon learned that young "Gampy," as Burr called his namesake, had died. In late December 1812, the grief-stricken Theo set out from her home in Georgetown, South Carolina, to visit her father in New York and was never seen again. The schooner that carried Theodosia Burr Alston and her escort probably sank in a storm off Cape Hatteras, North Carolina, but the mysterious circumstances of her disappearance, and the controversy and mystery that always dogged Burr's career, spawned legends that the unfortunate Mrs. Alston had been forced to walk the plank by pirates or mutineers, or was still alive as a prisoner in the West Indies.[85]

Although devastated by his daughter's death, Burr continued to practice law and to supervise the education of his young wards. Snubbed by many of his former acquaintances and wholly removed from the "game of politics" that had once been his joy and delight, Burr followed the independence movements that were changing the face of Latin America with a lively but cautious interest. In 1829, he petitioned the government for a pension based on his military service during the Revolution, a crusade that continued until his plea was finally granted in 1834. He became progressively more eccentric and impoverished as the years passed. In 1831, William Seward found him living in a dirty garret, shabbily dressed but optimistic as ever.

In 1833, Aaron Burr married a second time. His new bride, a wealthy widow with a past almost as controversial as his own, soon became disenchanted with her husband when she discovered that he had mismanaged her assets, and she divorced him the following year. Incapacitated by a series of strokes in 1834, Burr lived on the charity of friends and relatives until his death at Port Richmond, Staten Island, on September 14, 1836. During his final hours, a clergyman inquired about his prospects for salvation. Evasive and cryptic to the end, Burr only replied, "On that subject I am coy." Aaron Burr was buried with military honors at Princeton, New Jersey, on September 16, 1836.[86]

NOTES

[1] Herbert S. Parmet and Marie B. Hecht, *Aaron Burr: Portrait of an Ambitious Man* (New York, 1967), p. 285.

[2] Paul L. Ford, ed., *The Writings of Thomas Jefferson* (New York, 1905) 10:387, quoted in Parmet and Hecht, p. 287.

[3] Milton Lomask, *Aaron Burr*, vol. 2 (New York, 1982), pp. 372–73.

[4] Everett Somerville Brown, ed., *William Plumer's Memorandum of Proceedings in the United States Senate, 1803–1807* (New York, 1923), p. 123.

[5] Remarks of Senator Robert C. Byrd, "Profile of 'That Great Enigma': Aaron Burr," U.S., Congress, Senate, *Congressional Record*, 100th Cong., 1st sess., p. 31910.

[6] Mary-Jo Kline, "Aaron Burr as a Symbol of Corruption in the New Republic," in *Before Watergate: Problems of Corruption in American Society*, ed. Abraham S. Eisenstadt, Ari Hoogenboom and Hans L. Trefousse (Brooklyn, NY, 1978), p. 74. Mary-Jo Kline and Joanne Wood Ryan's two-volume letterpress edition of Burr's public papers, published by Princeton University Press in 1983, is an invaluable resource for scholars.

[7] See, for example, Samuel H. Wandell, *Aaron Burr in Literature: Books, Pamphlets, Periodicals, and Miscellany Relating to Aaron Burr and His Leading Political Contemporaries* (Port Washington, NY, 1972; reprint of 1936 edition).

[8] Kline, "Aaron Burr as a Symbol of Corruption in the New Republic," p. 70.

[9] Parmet and Hecht, pp. 1–16.

[10] Matthew L. Davis, *Memoirs of Aaron Burr* (Freeport, NY, 1970; reprint of 1836 edition), 1:45.

[11] Parmet and Hecht, pp. 17–51.

[12] Byrd, p. 31910.

[13] Parmet and Hecht, pp. 52–58, 64–65. A second daughter, Sally Reeve Burr, was born in 1785 and died in February 1789.

[14] Parmet and Hecht, pp. 58–62.

[15] Kline, Mary-Jo, and Joanne Wood Ryan, eds., *Political Correspondence and Public Papers of Aaron Burr*, vol. 1 (Princeton, 1983), p. 46.

[16] Aaron Burr to Richard Oliver, July 29, 1788, in Kline and Ryan, 1:33.

[17] Parmet and Hecht, pp. 65–66.

[18] Kline, "Aaron Burr as a Symbol of Corruption in the New Republic," p. 74.

[19] Parmet and Hecht, p. 84.

[20] Ibid., pp. 68–110.

[21] Ibid., pp. 108–10.

[22] Ibid., pp. 112–43.

[23] [New York] *Commercial Advertiser*, May 4, 1799, quoted in Kline and Ryan, 1:402.

[24] Robert Troup to Rufus King, May 6, 1799, quoted in Kline and Ryan, 1:420.

[25] Noble E. Cunningham, Jr., "Election of 1800," in *History of American Presidential Elections, 1789–1968*, vol. 1, ed. Arthur M. Schlesinger, Jr., and Fred L. Israel (New York, 1985), pp. 108–10; Dumas Malone, *Jefferson and the Ordeal of Liberty* (Boston, 1962), pp. 473–74; Parmet and Hecht, pp. 131–48.

[26] See Chapter 4 of this volume, "George Clinton," p. 53.

[27] Malone, *Jefferson and the Ordeal of Liberty*, p. 474; Kline and Ryan, 1:389–90, 430–34; Kline, "Aaron Burr as a Symbol of Corruption in the New Republic, p. 70; Cunningham, "Election of 1800," p. 110.

[28] Cunningham, "Election of 1800," pp. 104, 113–15; Kline and Ryan, 1:443–49; Malone, *Jefferson and the Ordeal of Liberty*, pp. 473–83.

[29] Kline, "Aaron Burr as a Symbol of Corruption in the New Republic," p. 75.

[30] Malone, *Jefferson and the Ordeal of Liberty*, pp. 489–94; Thomas Jefferson to Aaron Burr, December 15, 1800, in Kline and Ryan, 1:469–70.

[31] Malone, *Jefferson and the Ordeal of Liberty*, pp. 489–96; Parmet and Hecht, pp. 158–60; Cunningham, "Election of 1800," pp. 131–32.

[32] Kline and Ryan, 1:469–87, see especially Aaron Burr to Samuel Smith, December 16, 1800, p. 471, and Aaron Burr to Samuel Smith, December 29, 1800, pp. 478–79; Malone, *Jefferson and the Ordeal of Liberty*, pp. 499–505; Parmet and Hecht, pp. 144–67.

[33] Kline and Ryan, 1:486–87; Malone, *Jefferson and the Ordeal of Liberty*, pp. 502–5; Cunningham, "Election of 1800," pp. 131–34; Parmet and Hecht, pp. 162–67; Richard E. Ellis, *The Jeffersonian Crisis: Courts and Politics in the Young Republic* (New York, 1974; reprint of 1971 edition), p. 28; Forrest McDonald, *Alexander Hamilton: A Biography* (New York, 1979), pp. 352–53.

[34] Kline and Ryan, 1:486.

[35] Ibid., 1:486–87; Malone, *Jefferson and the Ordeal of Liberty*, pp. 502–5; Cunningham, "Election of 1800," pp. 131–34; Parmet and Hecht, pp. 162–67; Ellis, p. 28.

[36] U.S., Congress, House, *Annals of Congress*, 8th Cong., 1st sess., pp. 372–77; U.S., Congress, Senate, *Annals of Congress*, 8th Cong., 1st sess., pp. 21–25, 81–210; Dennis J. Mahoney, "Twelfth Amendment," *Encyclopedia of the American Constitution*, vol. 4 (New York, 1986), p. 1927; Tadahisa Kuroda, *The Origins of the Twelfth Amendment: The Electoral College in the Early Republic, 1787–1804* (Westport, CT, 1994).

[37] Aaron Burr to Albert Gallatin, February 25, 1801, in Kline and Ryan, 1:509.

[38] Aaron Burr to Caesar A. Rodney, March 3, 1801 (with March 4 postscript), in Kline and Ryan, 1:517–19; *Annals of Congress*, 6th Cong., 2d sess., pp. 762–63.

[39] Kline and Ryan, 1:519–45; Dumas Malone, *Jefferson the President: First Term, 1801–1805* (Boston, 1970), pp. 69–89;

Kline, "Aaron Burr as a Symbol of Corruption in the New Republic," pp. 70–71; Noble E. Cunningham, Jr., *The Jeffersonian Republicans in Power* (Chapel Hill, NC, 1963), pp. 38–44.

40 Kline and Ryan, 2:641–46, 724–28.

41 Cunningham, *Jeffersonian Republicans in Power*, pp. 38–44; Parmet and Hecht, pp. 172–77.

42 Noble E. Cunningham, Jr., *The Process of Government Under Jefferson* (Princeton, 1978), p. 16.

43 Brown, pp. 74–75.

44 Kline, "Aaron Burr as a Symbol of Corruption in the New Republic," pp. 69–76; Parmet and Hecht, pp. 168–93.

45 Parmet and Hecht, p. 184; Ellis, pp. 15–16, 36–52; Kline and Ryan, 2:653–73; Malone, *Jefferson the President, First Term*, 121–30.

46 Aaron Burr, "Comment on a Motion to Repeal the Judiciary Act," [New York] *American Citizen*, February 3, 1802, in Kline and Ryan, 2:656. According to Kline and Ryan, this version of Burr's remarks, which differs slightly from the version printed in the *Annals* (*Annals of Congress*, 7th Cong., 1st sess., p. 150), is "the version closest to a direct quotation that survives among contemporary accounts." Ibid., p. 655.

47 *Annals of Congress*, 7th Cong., 1st sess., p. 150.

48 New York *Evening Post*, February 2, 1801; Kline and Ryan, 2:655.

49 Parmet and Hecht, p. 179.

50 Ibid., p. 179.

51 Ellis, p. 48.

52 Malone, *Jefferson the President, First Term*, pp. 123–24.

53 Ibid., pp. 395–98.

54 Thomas Jefferson, Memorandum of a Conversation with Burr, January 26, 1804, Kline and Ryan, 2:819–22.

55 Parmet and Hecht, pp. 194–201; Kline, "Aaron Burr as a Symbol of Corruption in the New Republic," pp. 72–73.

56 Parmet and Hecht, pp. 194–215.

57 Ibid., pp. 210–23; Samuel L. Mitchill to Mrs. Mitchill, November 20, 1804, "Dr. Mitchill's Letters from Washington: 1801–1813," *Harper's New Monthly Magazine* 58 (April 1879): 748; W.J. Rorabaugh, "The Political Duel in the Early Republic: Burr v. Hamilton," *Journal of the Early Republic* 15 (Spring 1995): 14.

58 Brown, p. 185.

59 Ibid., pp. 203–4.

60 Parmet and Hecht, p. 224.

61 Samuel L. Mitchill to Mrs. Mitchill, November 30, 1804, "Dr. Mitchill's Letters from Washington," p. 748.

62 Brown, p. 203.

63 Parmet and Hecht, p. 224.

64 Ellis, pp. 69–75; Malone, *Jefferson the President, First Term*, pp. 460–64, 469; *Annals of Congress*, 8th Cong., 1st sess., pp. 315–68.

65 Manasseh Cutler to the Rev. Dr. Dana, March 3, 1804, in *Life, Journals and Correspondence of Rev. Manasseh Cutler, LL.D.*, by William Parker Cutler and Julia Perkins Cutler, vol. 2 (Cincinnati, 1888), pp. 164–66.

66 Brown, pp. 97–177; Ellis, pp., 69–75; Manasseh Cutler to Dr. Torrey, March 13, 1804, *Life, Journals and Correspondence of Rev. Manasseh Cutler* 2:166–68; *Annals of Congress*, 8th Cong., 1st sess., pp. 315–68; Peter Charles Hoffer and N.E.H. Hull, *Impeachment in America, 1635–1805* (New Haven, 1984), pp. 206–20.

67 Malone, *Jefferson the President, First Term*, p. 464.

68 Parmet and Hecht, p. 224; Malone, *Jefferson the President, First Term*, pp. 464–69; Ellis, pp. 76–79.

69 Brown, p. 213.

70 Ibid., pp. 218–19.

71 Quoted in Byrd, p. 31914.

72 Manasseh Cutler to Dr. Torrey, March 1, 1805, *Life, Journals and Correspondence of Manasseh Cutler* 2:192–94.

73 Report of the Trial of Samuel Chase, *Annals of Congress*, 8th Cong., 2d sess., pp. 81–676.

74 Ibid., pp. 92–98; Brown, pp. 235–39; Ellis, p. 96; Hoffer and Hull, p. 238.

75 Brown, pp. 239–311.

76 Ibid., p. 285.

77 *Annals of Congress*, 8th Cong., 2d sess., p. 669.

78 Ibid., pp. 55–57; Samuel L. Mitchill to Mrs. Mitchill, February 14, 1805, "Dr. Mitchill's Letters from Washington," p. 749.

79 Brown, pp. 302–7; *Annals of Congress*, 8th Cong., 2d sess., pp. 63–66; Kline and Ryan, 2:910.

80 *Annals of Congress*, 8th Cong., 2d sess., pp. 71–72; Dr. Mitchill to Mrs. Mitchill, March 2, 1805, "Dr. Mitchill's Letters from Washington," p. 750; Kline and Ryan, 2:909–17.

81 Kline and Ryan, 2:911–12.

82 Parmet and Hecht, passim; Lomask, vols. 1 and 2, passim; Kline and Ryan, vols. 1 and 2, passim.

83 Parmet and Hecht, pp. 233–310.

84 Ibid., pp. 305–26.

85 Ibid., pp. 326–31.

86 Ibid., pp. 332–41; Kline and Ryan, 2:1169–1229.

Chapter 4

GEORGE CLINTON
1805–1812

GEORGE CLINTON

Chapter 4

GEORGE CLINTON

4th Vice President: 1805–1812

George Clinton the Vice President . . . is an feeble old man . . . What a vast difference between him & Aaron Burr! One would think that the office was made for Clinton, & not he for the office.
—SENATOR WILLIAM PLUMER (F-NH), DECEMBER 16, 1805.[1]

George Clinton took office as the nation's fourth vice president on March 4, 1805. He was the second vice president to serve under Thomas Jefferson, having replaced fellow New Yorker Aaron Burr whose intransigence in 1800 had nearly cost Jefferson the presidency. A Revolutionary War hero who had served as governor of New York for two decades, Clinton seemed an ideal choice to supplant Burr while preserving the New York-Virginia alliance that formed the backbone of the Republican coalition.

Even though Republican senators may have been relieved to be rid of Burr, the contrast between their new presiding officer and his urbane, elegant predecessor must have been painfully apparent when Chief Justice John Marshall administered the oath of office to Jefferson and Clinton in the Senate chamber. Jefferson offered a lengthy inaugural speech celebrating the accomplishments of his first term, but Clinton declined to address the members of Congress and the "large concourse of citizens" present.[2] Two days earlier, on March 2, 1805, Burr had regaled the Senate with a "correct and elegant" farewell oration so laden with emotion that even Clinton's friend, Senator Samuel L. Mitchill (R-NY), pronounced the scene "one of the most affecting . . . of my life."[3] But when Clinton assumed the presiding officer's chair on December 16, 1805, two weeks into the first session of the Ninth Congress, he was so "weak & feeble" of voice that, according to Senator William Plumer (F-NH), the

senators could not "hear the one half of what he says."[4]

Clinton's age and infirmity had, if anything, enhanced his value to the president, because Jefferson intended to pass his party's mantle to Secretary of State James Madison when he retired after his second term, yet he needed an honest, "plain" Republican vice president in the meantime. Clinton would be sixty-nine in 1808, too old, Jefferson anticipated, to challenge Madison for the Republican presidential nomination. Clinton had already retired once from public life, in 1795, pleading ill health.[5] But, for all Clinton's apparent frailty, he was still a force to be reckoned with. His earlier decision to retire owed as much to the political climate in New York, and to his own political misfortunes, as to his chronic rheumatism. He had been an actual or prospective vice-presidential candidate in every election since the first one in 1788, and later capped his elective career with a successful run for the office in 1808.

Clinton was, in the words of a recent biographer, "an enigma." The British forces that torched Kingston, New York, during the Revolution, as well as the 1911 conflagration that destroyed most of Clinton's papers at the New York Public Library, have deprived modern researchers of sources that might have illuminated his personality and explained his motives.[6] Much of the surviving evidence, however, coupled with the observations of Clinton's contemporaries, support historian Alan Taylor's assessment that "Clinton crafted a masterful, compelling public persona . . . [T]hat . . . masked and permitted an array of contradictions that would have ruined a lesser, more transparent politician."[7] He was, in Taylor's view, "The astutest politician in Revolutionary New York," a man who "understood the power of symbolism and the new popularity of a plain style especially when practiced by a man with the means and accomplishments to set himself above the common people."[8]

War and Politics

George Clinton's parents were Presbyterian immigrants who left Longford County, Ireland, in 1729 to escape an intolerant Anglican regime that imposed severe disabilities on religious dissenters. Charles and Elizabeth Denniston Clinton settled in Ulster County, New York, where the future vice president was born on July 26, 1739. Charles Clinton was a farmer, surveyor, and land speculator, whose survey of the New York frontier so impressed the governor that he was offered a position as sheriff of New York City and the surrounding county in 1748. After the elder Clinton declined the honor, the governor designated young George as successor to the clerk of the Ulster County Court of Common Pleas, a position he would assume in 1759 and hold for the rest of his life.

George Clinton studied under a Scottish clergyman to prepare for his future responsibilities, interrupting his education at the age of eighteen in 1757 to serve in the French and Indian War. After the war, he read law in New York City under the renowned attorney William Smith. He began his legal practice in 1764 and became district attorney the following year. Clinton's aptitude for surveying and his penchant for land speculation eventually made him one of the wealthier residents of Ulster County,[9] but, despite his considerable fortune, he was a man of frugal habits and congenial, unassuming manners. Even in later life, when chronic ill health made it difficult for him to perform his public duties, observers remarked on his "pleasing cheerfulness" and "flow of good humor."[10] Large-boned and coarse-featured,[11] he was, one

scholar relates, "a man of powerful physique, whose mere presence commanded respect."[12]

In 1768, the twenty-nine-year-old Clinton was elected to the New York assembly, where he supported the "Livingston" faction, an alliance that he cemented two years later with his marriage to Cornelia Tappan, a Livingston relative. The Livingstons and their allies, who represented the wealthy, predominantly Presbyterian landowners of the Hudson Valley, assumed a vehemently anti-British posture as relations between England and her North American colonies deteriorated during the early 1770s. Clinton emerged as their leader in 1770, when he defended a member of the Sons of Liberty imprisoned for "seditious libel" by the royalist majority that still controlled the New York assembly. He was a delegate to the second Continental Congress in 1775, where a fellow delegate observed that "Clinton has Abilities but is silent in general, and wants (when he does speak) that Influence to which he is intitled." Clinton disliked legislative service, because, as he explained, "the duty of looking out for danger makes men cowards," and he soon resigned his seat to accept an appointment as a brigadier general in the New York militia. He was assigned to protect the New York frontier, where his efforts to prevent the British from gaining control of the Hudson River and splitting New England from the rest of the struggling confederacy earned him a brigadier general's commission in the Continental army and made him a hero among the farmers of the western counties.[13]

The social and political changes that the Revolution precipitated worked to Clinton's advantage, and he made the most of his opportunities. As Edward Countryman so forcefully demonstrated in his study of revolutionary New York, "the independence crisis . . . shattered old New York, both politically and socially."[14] The state's new constitution greatly expanded the suffrage and increased the size of the state legislature. The "yeoman" farmers of small and middling means, who had previously deferred to the Livingstons and their royalist rivals, the DeLanceys, emerged as a powerful political entity in their own right, and George Clinton became their champion and spokesman. Their support proved crucial in the 1777 gubernatorial election, when Clinton defeated Edward Livingston in a stunning upset that "signalled the dismemberment of the old Livingston party."[15] The election also signalled Clinton's emergence as a dominant figure in New York politics; he served as governor from 1777 until 1795 and again from 1801 until 1804, exercising considerable influence over the state legislature.[16]

Before leaving the battlefield to assume his new responsibilities, Clinton promised his commander in chief, General George Washington, that he would resume his military duties "sh'd the Business of my new appointm't admit of it." True to his word, he soon returned to the field to help defend the New York frontier. There, American troops under his command prevented Sir Henry Clinton (said to have been a "distant cousin") from relieving the main British force under General John Burgoyne, precipitating Burgoyne's surrender at Saratoga on October 17, 1777.[17] The Saratoga victory, which helped convince the French that the struggling colonies were worthy of the aid that proved so crucial to the revolutionary effort, marked a turning point in the war.

Governor Clinton's civilian labors were equally impressive. Like other wartime governors, he was responsible for coordinating his state's war effort. New York's strategic importance and large Loyalist population, coupled with Vermont's secession in 1777, posed special problems for the beleaguered governor, but he proved an able administrator. He was increasingly frustrated, however, as war expenses mounted, and as the Continental Congress, which lacked the power to raise revenues and relied on state contributions, looked to New York to make up the shortfall that resulted when other states failed to meet their quotas. He supported Alexander Hamilton's call for a stronger Congress with independent revenue-raising powers, warning Continental Congress President John Hanson in 1781 that "we shall not be able without a Change in our Circumstances, long to maintain our civil Government."[18]

Clinton's perspective changed in 1783, after Congress asked the states to approve a national tariff that would deprive New York of its most lucrative source of income. He had long believed that Congress should facilitate and protect the foreign commerce that was so important to New York. Toward that end, he had supported Hamilton's efforts to strengthen the Articles of Confederation during the war. But the specter of a national tariff helped convince him that a national government with vastly enlarged powers might overwhelm the states and subvert individual liberties. "[W]hen stronger powers for Congress would benefit New York," his biographer explains, "Clinton would endorse such measures. In purely domestic matters, the governor would put New York concerns above all others."[19] The governor's primary concern, according to another scholar, "was to avoid any measure which might burden his agrarian constituents with taxes." The tariff had supplied nearly a third of New York's revenue during the 1780s, and Clinton feared that if this critical source of income was diverted to national coffers, the state legislature would be forced to raise real estate and personal property taxes.[20]

A Perennial Candidate for Vice President

Clinton emerged as one of the most prominent opponents of the new Constitution. He was a delegate to the New York ratification convention, where an Antifederalist majority elected him presiding officer. But with the establishment of the federal union almost a foregone conclusion by the time the convention assembled at Poughkeepsie on June 17, 1788 (eight states had already ratified, with the enabling ninth expected to follow) Clinton's options were sharply limited. He had initially hoped to secure a conditional ratification, contingent upon the adoption of "amendments calculated to abridge and limit" federal power, but after the Antifederalists failed to agree on a common strategy and popular sentiment shifted in favor of unconditional ratification, there was little he could do to accomplish even this limited objective. Bowing to the inevitable, he finally signalled his allies that, if their constituents had come to favor unconditional ratification, they should vote accordingly. He did so, as biographer John Kaminski suggests, because he "sensed that he might make the perfect vice presidential candidate. . . . Once elected,

Vice President Clinton could advise Washington, support constitutional amendments as he presided over the first United States Senate, and perhaps be heir apparent when Washington decided to retire."[21]

Friends of the new Constitution were much alarmed when New York and Virginia Antifederalists proposed Clinton as a vice-presidential candidate in 1788.[22] James Madison was horrified that "the enemies to the Government . . . are laying a train for the election of Governor Clinton,"[23] and Alexander Hamilton worked to unite Federalists behind John Adams.[24] Well-placed rumors tainted Clinton's candidacy by indicating that Antifederalist electors intended to cast one of their two electoral votes for Richard Henry Lee or Patrick Henry for president and the other vote for the New York governor. Prior to the ratification of the Twelfth Amendment in 1804, electors cast two votes in presidential elections without distinguishing between presidential and vice-presidential candidates, and the runner-up in the presidential race simply became vice president. Each elector, however, voted with the clear intent of electing one individual as president and the other as vice president. In the charged and expectant atmosphere surrounding the first election under the new Constitution, Federalists who learned of the rumored conspiracy to elect Lee or Henry president feared that a vote for Clinton would be tantamount to a vote against George Washington. Popular enthusiasm for the new government and Clinton's well-known opposition to the Constitution also worked against him. John Adams won the vice-presidency with 34 electoral votes; Clinton received 3 of the 35 remaining electoral votes that were distributed among a field of ten "favorite son" candidates.[25]

Clinton fared better in the 1792 election. By the end of Washington's first term, the cabinet was seriously divided over Treasury Secretary Alexander Hamilton's financial system, and all parties agreed that Washington's reelection was essential to the survival of the infant republic. In spite of their earlier reservations about Clinton, Secretary of State Thomas Jefferson and his Virginia allies, Madison and James Monroe, were determined to replace the "monarchist" and ab-

rasive Vice President Adams. They considered the "yeoman politician" from New York the candidate most likely to unseat him.[26]

Clinton's candidacy faced several obstacles. He was still widely suspect as an opponent of the Constitution, and the circumstances of his reelection as governor earlier in the year had aroused the consternation of even his most steadfast supporters. John Jay, the Federalist candidate, had received a majority of the votes in the gubernatorial race, but the destruction of ballots from Federalist-dominated Otsego County on highly suspicious technical grounds by Antifederalist canvassers had tipped the balance in Clinton's favor. Jefferson worried that the New York election would jeopardize "the cause of republicanism," and Madison went so far as to suggest that Clinton should resign the governorship if he believed that he had been fraudulently elected.[27] Even though Adams was reelected vice president with 77 electoral votes, Clinton managed to garner a respectable 50 votes, carrying Virginia, Georgia, New York, and North Carolina.[28] The election provided a limited measure of comfort to Jefferson and Madison, who saw in the returns a portent of future success for the emerging Republican coalition.[29]

Despite his strong showing in the national election, Governor Clinton found it increasingly difficult to maintain his power base in New York. Pleading exhaustion and poor health, he announced his retirement in 1795. Although his rheumatism was by that time so severe that he could no longer travel to Albany to convene the state legislature, other factors influenced his decision. The circumstances of his 1792 reelection remained a serious liability, and his effectiveness had been greatly diminished when the Federalists gained control of the state legislature in 1793. Clinton was further compromised when his daughter Cornelia married the flamboyant and highly suspect French emissary, "Citizen" Edmond Genêt, in 1794.[30]

Clinton remained an attractive vice-presidential prospect for Republican leaders hoping to preserve the Virginia-New York nexus so crucial to their strategy, although he was never entirely comfortable with the southern wing of the party. Party strategists tried to enlist Clinton as their vice-presidential candidate to balance the ticket headed by Thomas Jefferson in 1796, but he refused to run. He soon found himself at odds with Jefferson, who became vice president in 1797 after receiving the second highest number of electoral votes. In his March 4, 1797, inaugural address to the Senate, Jefferson praised his predecessor, President John Adams, as a man of "talents and integrity." Clinton was quick to voice his outrage at this apparent "public contradiction of the Objections offered by his Friends against Mr. Adams's Election." In 1800, however, when approached by an emissary from Representative Albert Gallatin (R-PA), Clinton did agree to become Jefferson's running mate, although he seemed noticeably relieved when Republicans finally chose his fellow New Yorker, Aaron Burr, to balance the ticket.[31]

Governor Once More

Clinton ended his retirement in 1800, when he was elected to a seat in the New York legislature. He had entered the contest at Burr's urging, to ensure the selection of Republican presidential electors, and probably intended to retire when his term expired. But when New York Republicans, anticipating Jefferson's victory in the national election and hoping to consolidate their gains on the local level, asked him to enter the 1801 gubernatorial election, he agreed. He was at first reluctant to seek the nomination—his acceptance was subject to the caveat that he would resign the governorship if the office proved too much for him—but Burr soon provided him with a compelling reason to remain in the contest.[32]

Eleven years earlier, Governor Clinton had appointed Aaron Burr attorney general of New York. In 1789, with Federalists in control of the state legislature, he had been anxious to add Burr and his allies to the Clinton coalition. But he never completely trusted Burr, and his suspicions were confirmed when Burr refused to defer to Thomas Jefferson after the two candidates received an equal number of electoral votes in the 1800 presidential contest. After the furor subsided, and after the House of Representatives finally declared Jefferson the winner on the thirty-sixth ballot, Clinton's nephew and political heir, De Witt Clinton, predicted that

Burr would resign the vice-presidency and try to recoup his shattered fortunes by running for governor of New York. De Witt apparently persuaded his uncle that he was the only prospective candidate who could prevent Burr from taking control of the state Republican party. George Clinton was elected governor by an overwhelming margin, carrying traditionally Federalist New York City and all but six counties.[33]

During his last term as governor, Clinton was overshadowed by his increasingly powerful and ambitious nephew. Still, although De Witt was now "the real power in New York politics," George Clinton was much revered by New York voters. Anxious to preserve the Virginia-New York coalition, but determined to limit Burr's role in his administration, Jefferson turned to Clinton for advice in making federal appointments in New York. "[T]here is no one," he assured Clinton, "whose opinion would command me with greater respect than yours, if you would be so good as to advise me."[34] Jefferson was, in practical effect, repudiating Burr, although he never publicly disavowed or openly criticized his errant vice president.[35] One Federalist observer soon noted that "Burr is completely an insulated man in Washington."[36] As the 1804 election approached, De Witt wrote to members of the Republican caucus suggesting his uncle George as a replacement for Burr.[37]

Vice President at Last

Widely respected for his heroism during the war and for his devotion to Republican principles, George Clinton was a candidate who could replace Burr without alienating New York voters. His age and precarious health were important considerations for Jefferson, who calculated that in 1808 the sixty-five-year-old hero would be too old to challenge his intended successor, Secretary of State James Madison, for the Republican presidential nomination.[38] But Clinton had no intention of deferring to Madison in 1808. As Madison's biographer, Ralph Ketcham, has explained, New York Republicans were deeply jealous of the Virginians who had dominated their party's councils since 1792. "George Clinton's replacement of Burr as Vice President in 1804 was not so much a reconciliation with the

Virginians," he suggests, "as a play for better leverage to oust [the Virginians] in 1808."[39]

After the election, Clinton was all but shunted aside by a president who had no wish to enhance his vice president's stature in the administration or encourage his presidential ambitions. Jefferson no longer asked Clinton's advice in making political appointments in New York or elsewhere, or on any other matter of substance,[40] relying instead on the counsel of Madison and Treasury Secretary Albert Gallatin. When he felt it necessary to consult Republican legislators, he did so in person[41] or through Gallatin, whose Capitol Hill residence served as the meeting place for the Republican caucus.[42] (Now known as the Sewell-Belmont House, this building still stands, adjacent to the Hart Senate Office Building.)

Clinton also took little part in the social life of the administration.[43] Washington society had a distinctly southern flavor, and, as the vice president confided to Senator Plumer, he found the "habits, manners, costoms, laws & country" of New England "much preferable to the southern States."[44] A widower for four years at the time of his election, Clinton and his daughter Maria lived frugally with House of Representatives Clerk John Beckley and seldom entertained.[45] Even in an administration that consciously avoided ceremony and ostentatious display in favor of the simple, republican style that shocked foreign visitors and scandalized Federalists, Clinton's parsimony was legend. "Mr. Clinton, always comes to the city in his own carriage," Plumer noted. "He is immensely rich—but lives out at board like a common member—keeps no table—or invites anybody to dine. A style of living unworthy of the 2d officer in our government."[46] Another senator observed that "Mr. Clinton . . . lives snug at his lodgings, and keeps aloof from . . . exhibitions."[47] Clinton's sole function was to preside over the Senate.

An Ineffectual Presiding Officer

Nor was he an effective presiding officer. Senator Plumer observed, when Clinton assumed the presiding officer's chair on December 16, 1805, that he seemed "altogether unacquainted" with the Senate's rules, had a "clumsey awkward way of putting a question," and "Preserves little or no order."[48] Senator John Quincy Adams (F-MA) shared Plumer's concern. The Senate's new president was "totally ignorant of all the most common forms of proceeding in the Senate," he wrote in his diary. "His judgement is neither quick nor strong: so there is no more dependence upon the correctness of his determination from his understanding than from his experience . . . a worse choice than Mr. Clinton could scarcely have been made."[49] Clinton's parliamentary skills failed to improve with experience, as Plumer observed a year later:

> The Vice President preserves very little order in the Senate. If he ever had, he certainly has not now, the requisite qualifications of a presiding officer. Age has impaired his mental powers. The conversation & noise to day in our lobby was greater than I ever suffered when moderator of a town meeting. It prevented us from hearing the arguments of the Speaker. He frequently, at least he has more than once, declared bills at the *third* reading when they had been read but once—Puts questions without any motion being made—Sometimes declares it a vote before any vote has been taken. And sometimes before one bill is decided proceeds to another. From want of authority, & attention to order he has prostrated the dignity of the Senate. His disposition appears good,—but he wants mind & nerve.[50]

Although Plumer and others attributed the vice president's ineptitude to his advanced age and feeble health, Clinton's longstanding "aversion to councils"[51] probably compounded his difficulties. He had little patience with long-winded senators, as a chagrined John Quincy Adams discovered after an extended discourse that was, by his own admission, "a very tedious one to all my hearers." "The Vice-President," he concluded, "does not love long speeches." Clinton could do little to alleviate his discomfort, given the fact that the Senate's rules permitted extended debate, but on at least one occasion he asked a special favor: "that when we were about to make such we should give him notice; that he might take the opportunity to warm himself at the fire."[52]

Clinton was frequently absent from the Senate, but he apparently summoned the strength to attend when he found a compelling reason to do so. A case in point was his tie-breaking vote to approve the nomination of John Armstrong, Jr., a childhood friend and political ally, as a commissioner to Spain. Federalist senators, and many of their Republican colleagues, vehemently opposed Armstrong's nomination, alleging that he had mishandled claims relating to the ship *New Jersey* while serving as minister to France. At issue was Armstrong's finding that the 1800 convention with France indemnified only the original owners of captured vessels, a position he abandoned after Jefferson insisted that insurers should also receive compensation. Senator Samuel Smith (R-MD), a member of Jefferson's own party and the brother of Navy Secretary Robert Smith, so effectively mustered the opposition forces that, by Adams' account, no senator spoke on Armstrong's behalf when the Senate debated his nomination on March 17, 1806. After Senator John Adair (R-KY) "left his seat to avoid voting," the vice president, who had earlier informed Plumer "that he had intended not to take his seat in the Senate this session," resolved the resulting 15-to-15 tied vote in Armstrong's favor. "I apprehended," Plumer surmised, that "they found it necessary & prevailed on him to attend." Clinton was absent for the remainder of the session.[53]

Clinton's only known attempt to influence legislation as vice president occurred in early 1807, when he asked John Quincy Adams to sponsor a bill to compensate settlers who had purchased western Georgia lands from the Yazoo land companies. In 1795, the Georgia legislature had sold thirty-five million acres of land to four land speculation companies, which resold the properties to other land jobbers and to individual investors before the legislature canceled the sale and ceded the lands to the United States. A commission appointed to effect the transfer to the United States proposed that five million acres be earmarked to indemnify innocent parties, but Representative John Randolph (R-VA) charged that congressional approval of the arrangement would "countenance the fraud a little further" and blocked a final settlement. In March 1806, the Senate passed a bill to compensate the Yazoo set-

tlers, but the House rejected the measure.[54] With sentiment against compensation steadily mounting, the Senate on February 11, 1807, enacted a bill "to prevent settlements on lands ceded to the United States unless authorized by law." The following day, Adams recorded in his diary that "The Vice-President this morning took [Adams] apart and advised [him] to ask leave to bring in a bill on behalf of the Yazoo claimants, like that which passed the Senate at the last session, to remove the effect of the bill passed yesterday." Clinton apparently abandoned the effort after Adams responded that he did "not think it would answer any such purpose."[55]

Clinton's always tenuous relationship with Jefferson became increasingly strained as the president responded to English and French assaults on American shipping with a strategy of diplomatic maneuvering and economic coercion. Clinton viewed the escalating conflict between England and France with alarm. He believed that war with one or both nations was inevitable and became increasingly frustrated with Jefferson's seeming reluctance to arm the nation for battle. The vice president's own state was particularly vulnerable, because New York shippers and merchants suffered heavily from British raids, yet Jefferson's proposed solution of an embargo on foreign trade would have a devastating impact on the state's economy. New York's limited coastal defenses, Clinton feared, would prove painfully inadequate in the event that the president's strategy failed to prevent war.[56]

The Election of 1808

Congress approved the Embargo Act, closing United States ports to foreign trade, in December 1807. When the Republican congressional caucus met the following month to select the party's 1808 presidential candidate, the vice president's supporters were conspicuously absent. Clinton knew that the caucus would choose Madison, the architect of Jefferson's foreign policy, as their presidential candidate but apparently believed that he could win the presidency without the support of the caucus. "[O]ur venerable friend the Vice-President," Senator Mitchill observed, "considers himself as fully entitled to the first place in the nation." Clinton was so "self-complacent," Mitchill marvelled, that he failed to "discern what was as plain as daylight to any body else," that there was not "the remotest probability of his success as President." But Clinton still commanded a substantial following among disaffected Republicans from the Middle Atlantic states. Because New Yorkers, in particular, resented Virginia's near-monopoly of the presidency since 1789, Madison's campaign managers considered Clinton enough of a threat to suggest him as a possible running mate.[57]

Much to Clinton's chagrin, the caucus renominated him to a second term as vice president. His only public response was a letter to De Witt—subsequently edited for maximum effect and released to the press by the calculating nephew—denying that he had "been directly or indirectly consulted on the subject" or "apprised of the meeting held for the purpose, otherwise, than by having accidentally seen a notice."[58] George Clinton neither accepted nor expressly refused the vice-presidential nomination, a posture that caused considerable consternation among Republican strategists. When caucus representatives called on him to discuss the matter, his "tart, severe, and puzzling reply" left them "as much in a quandary as ever what to do with their nomination of him." He was, Senator Mitchill theorized, "as much a candidate for the Presidency . . . as for the Vice Presidency."[59]

As far as Clinton was concerned, he remained a presidential candidate. While he affected the disinterested posture that early nineteenth-century electoral etiquette demanded of candidates for elective office, his supporters mounted a vigorous attack on Jefferson's foreign policy, warning that Madison, the president's "mere organ or mouth piece," would continue along the same perilous course. But Clinton, one pamphleteer promised voters, would "protect you from foreign and domestic foes."[60] Writing under the pseudonym, "A Citizen of New-York," the vice president's son-in-law, Edmond Genêt, promised that Clinton would substitute "a dignified plan of neutrality" for the hated embargo.[61] Turning their candidate's most obvious liability to their advantage, Clintonians portrayed the vice president as a seasoned elder statesman, "a repository of experimental knowledge."[62]

The tension between Jefferson and his refractory vice president flared into open hostility after Clinton read confidential diplomatic dispatches from London and Paris before an open session of the Senate on February 26, 1808. The president had transmitted the reports to the Senate with a letter expressly warning that "the publication of papers of this description would restrain injuriously the freedom of our foreign correspondence." But, as John Quincy Adams recorded, "The Vice-President, not remarking that the first message was marked on the cover, confidential, suffered all the papers to be read without closing the doors." Clinton claimed that the disclosure was inadvertent, but the dispatches *had* seemed to affirm his own conviction that "war with Great Britain appears inevitable."[63] Much to his embarrassment, the blunder was widely reported in the press. Entering the Senate chamber "rather late than usual" one morning, Adams witnessed an unusual display of temper:

> The Vice President had been formally complaining of the President for a mistake which was really his own. The message of the twenty-sixth of February was read in public because the Vice-President on receiving it had not noticed the word "confidential" written on the outside cover. This had been told in the newspapers, and commented on as evidence of Mr. Clinton's *declining years*. He thinks it was designedly done by the President to ensnare him and expose him to derision. This morning he asked [Secretary of the Senate Samuel] Otis for a certificate that the message was received in Senate without the word "confidential;" which Otis declining to do, he was much incensed with him, and spoke to the Senate in anger, concluding by saying that he thought the *Executive* would have had more magnanimity than to have treated him thus.[64]

Support for Clinton's presidential bid steadily eroded as the election approached and even the most ardent Clintonians realized that their candidate had no chance of winning. Some bowed to the will of the caucus as a matter of course,[65] while the prospect of a Federalist victory eventually drove others into the Madison camp.[66] New England Federalists, energized by their opposition to the embargo, briefly considered endorsing Clinton as their presidential candidate but ultimately nominated Charles Cotesworth Pinckney of South Carolina after intelligence reports from New York indicated that Republicans there "were disposed to unite in the abandonment of Clinton."[67] Madison won an easy victory with 122 electoral votes; Clinton finished a distant third with only six electoral votes—a face-saving gesture by sympathetic New York Republicans, who cast the state's thirteen remaining votes for Madison.[68]

The vice-presidential contest posed a unique problem for Republican electors.[69] Clinton was still the Republican vice-presidential candidate, notwithstanding the fact that, as Senator Wilson Cary Nicholas (R-VA) observed, his conduct had "alienated [him] from the republicans." Although painfully aware that "among the warm friends of Mr. Clinton are to be found the bitterest enemies of the administration," they ultimately elected him vice president because they feared that repudiating the caucus nomination would set a dangerous precedent. "[I]f he is not elected," Nicholas argued, "there will not in future be any reliance upon such nominations, all confidence will be lost and there can not be the necessary concert."[70] As Virginia Republican General Committee Chairman Philip Norborne Nicholas stressed, it would be impossible to reject Clinton "without injury to the Republican cause."[71]

The Final Term

Clinton left for New York before Congress assembled in the House of Representatives chamber to count the electoral votes on February 8, 1809, thus avoiding the unpleasant task of proclaiming Madison's election as president and his own reelection as vice president. He did not return in time to witness Madison's inauguration on March 4 (and surviving records do not indicate where or when he took his own oath).[72] In the meantime, his supporters had already joined forces with disaffected Republican Senators Samuel Smith of Maryland, William B. Giles of Virginia, and Michael Leib of Pennsylvania in a successful attempt to prevent Madison from nominating Albert Gallatin as secretary of state.[73]

Clinton opposed Madison's foreign and domestic policies throughout his second vice-presi-

dential term, but he lacked the support and the vitality to muster an effective opposition. Still, he dealt the administration a severe blow when he cast the deciding vote in favor of a measure to prevent the recharter of the Bank of the United States. Madison had once opposed Hamilton's proposal to establish a national bank, but by 1811, "twenty years of usefulness and public approval" had mooted his objections. Treasury Secretary Gallatin considered the bank an essential component of the nation's financial and credit system, but Clinton and other "Old Republicans" still considered the institution an unconstitutional aggrandizement of federal power. The Senate debated Republican Senator William H. Crawford of Georgia's recharter bill at great length before voting on a motion to kill it on February 20, 1811. Clinton voted in favor of the motion after the Senate deadlocked by a vote of 17 to 17. His vote did not in itself defeat the bank, since the recharter bill had already failed in the House of Representatives,[74] but this last act of defiance dealt a humiliating blow to the administration and particularly to Gallatin, who observed many years later that "nothing can be more injurious to an Administration than to have in that office a man in hostility with that Administration, as he will always become the most formidable rallying point for the opposition."[75]

In a brief and dignified address to the Senate, Clinton explained his vote, declaring his long-standing conviction that "Government is not to be strengthened by an assumption of doubtful powers." Could Congress, he asked, "create a body politic and corporate, not constituting a part of the Government, nor otherwise responsible to it by forfeiture of charter, and bestow on its members privileges, immunities, and exemptions not recognised by the laws of the States, nor enjoyed by the citizens generally? . . . The power to create corporations is not expressly granted [by the Constitution]," he reasoned, but "[i]f . . . the powers vested in the Government shall be found incompetent to the attainment of the objects for which it was instituted, the Constitution happily furnishes the means for remedying the evil by amendment."[76] Then-Senator Henry Clay, a Kentucky Republican, later claimed that he was the author of the vice president's remarks. Long after Clinton's death, but before Clay reversed his own position to become one of the bank's leading advocates during the 1830s, the ever-boastful Clay asserted that the speech "was perhaps the thing that had gained the old man more credit than anything else that he ever did." Clay, however, admitted that "he had written it . . . under Mr. Clinton's dictation, and he never should think of claiming it as his composition." [77]

Clinton's February 20, 1811, speech was his first and last formal address to the Senate. Two days later, he notified the senators that he would be absent for the remainder of the session.[78] He returned for the opening session of the Twelfth Congress on November 4, 1811, and faithfully presided over the Senate throughout the winter, but by the end of March 1812 he was too ill to continue. President pro tempore William Crawford presided for the remainder of the session, while Clinton's would-be successors engaged in "[e]lectioneering . . . beyond description" for the 1812 vice-presidential nomination. On April 20, 1812, Crawford informed the Senate of "the death of our venerable fellow-citizen, GEORGE CLINTON, Vice President of the United States." [79]

The following afternoon, a joint delegation from the Senate and the House of Representatives accompanied Clinton's body to the Senate chamber. He was the first person to lie in state in the Capitol, for a brief two-hour period, before the funeral procession escorted his remains to nearby Congressional Cemetery. President Madison was among the official mourners, although he and the first lady held their customary reception at the Executive Mansion the following day. In the Senate chamber, black crepe adorned the presiding officer's chair for the remainder of the session, and each senator wore a black arm band for thirty days "from an unfeigned respect" for their departed president.[80] Clinton's former rival, Gouverneur Morris, later offered a moving—if brutally frank—tribute to the fallen "soldier of the Revolution." Clinton had rendered a lifetime of service to New York and the nation, Morris reminded his audience, but "to share in the measures of the administration was not his part. To influence them was not in his power." [81]

NOTES

[1] Everett Somerville Brown, ed., *William Plumer's Memorandum of Proceedings in the United States Senate, 1803–1807* (New York, 1923), pp. 352–53.

[2] U.S., Congress, Senate, *Annals of Congress*, 8th Cong., 2d sess., pp. 77–80; Stephen W. Stathis and Ronald C. Moe, "America's Other Inauguration," *Presidential Studies Quarterly* 10 (Fall 1980): 561.

[3] Brown, pp. 312–13; Samuel L. Mitchill to Mrs. Mitchill, March 2, 1805, "Dr. Mitchill's Letters from Washington: 1801–1818," *Harper's New Monthly Magazine* 58 (April 1879): 749.

[4] Brown, pp. 353–53.

[5] John Kaminski, *George Clinton: Yeoman Politician of the New Republic* (Madison, WI, 1993), pp. 247, 255–56, 274.

[6] Kaminski, p. 1.

[7] Alan Taylor, review of Kaminski, George Clinton, in *Journal of the Early Republic* 13 (Fall 1993): 414–15.

[8] Alan Taylor, *William Cooper's Town: Power and Persuasion on the Frontier of the Early American Republic* (New York, 1995), p. 156.

[9] Kaminski, pp. 11–14; U.S., Congress, Senate, *Biographical Directory of the United States Congress, 1774–1989*, S. Doc. 100–34, 100th Cong., 2d sess., 1989, p. 795.

[10] Brown, pp. 450, 635.

[11] Several portraits of Clinton, at various stages of his career, are reproduced in Kaminski, pp. 22, 58, 112, 190, 228.

[12] Manning Dauer, "Election of 1804," in *History of American Presidential Elections, 1789–1968*, ed. Arthur M. Schlesinger, Jr., and Fred L. Israel, vol. 1 (New York, 1971), p. 161.

[13] Kaminski, pp. 14–25, 251, 293.

[14] Edward Countryman, *A People in Revolution: The American Revolution and Political Society in New York, 1760–1790* (New York, 1989; reprint of 1981 edition), p. 162.

[15] Kaminski, pp. 19–25; Countryman, pp. 161–202.

[16] As Countryman has noted, during the Confederation period alone, "some 170 laws were passed and 40 other actions taken . . . in response to the governor's suggestions." Countryman, p. 210.

[17] Kaminski, pp. 26–36; Robert Middlekauff, *The Glorious Cause: The American Revolution, 1763–1789* (New York, 1982), pp. 382–84; Countryman, p. 211.

[18] Kaminski, pp. 23–57.

[19] Ibid., pp. 60–63, 85–96, 115–21.

[20] Alfred F. Young, *The Democratic Republicans of New York: The Origins, 1763–1791* (Chapel Hill, NC, 1967), pp. 56–57.

[21] Kaminski, pp. 113–69.

[22] Marcus Cunliffe, "The Elections of 1789 and 1792," in Schlesinger and Israel, ed., 1:15.

[23] Kaminski, p. 171.

[24] As noted in Chapter 1 of this volume, "John Adams," p. 6, Hamilton perceived Adams as a threat to his own ambitions and schemed—successfully—to erode his electoral count in 1788. Yet, even though, as Kaminski acknowledges, "Hamilton did not particularly care for Adams," Adams' support for the Constitution made him infinitely preferable, in Hamilton's estimation, to Clinton. Kaminski, pp. 173–74.

[25] Cunliffe, p. 18; *Annals of Congress*, 1st Cong., 1st sess., p. 17.

[26] Kaminski, p. 231.

[27] Ibid., pp. 211–27; Stanley Elkins and Eric McKitrick, *The Age of Federalism* (New York, 1993), p. 288.

[28] Clinton also received one of Pennsylvania's 15 electoral votes.

[29] Ralph Ketcham, *James Madison: A Biography* (Charlottesville, VA, 1992; reprint of 1971 edition), p. 336.

[30] Young, p. 430; Kaminski, p. 237–49.

[31] Kaminski, pp. 249–55; *Annals of Congress*, 5th Cong., special sess., March 4, 1797, pp. 1581–82.

[32] Kaminski, pp. 249–56; *Annals of Congress*, 5th Cong., special sess., March 4, 1797, pp. 1581–82.

[33] Kaminski, pp. 192, 256–60.

[34] Noble E. Cunningham, Jr., *The Jeffersonian Republicans in Power: Party Operations, 1801–1809* (Chapel Hill, NC, 1963), p. 39; Dumas Malone, *Jefferson the President: First Term, 1801–1805* (Boston, 1970), p. 88; Noble E. Cunningham, Jr., *The Process of Government under Jefferson* (Princeton, NJ, 1978), p. 16; Kaminski, p. 261.

[35] Cunningham, *Jeffersonian Republicans in Power*, pp. 42–43, 205–13; Noble E. Cunningham, Jr., *In Pursuit of Reason: The Life of Thomas Jefferson* (Baton Rouge, LA, 1987), p. 271; Malone, *Jefferson the President: First Term*, pp. 123–24, 141, 432; Kaminski, pp. 261–64.

[36] Cunningham, *Jeffersonian Republicans in Power*, p. 205.

[37] Kaminski, pp. 262–73.

[38] Dauer, pp. 159–69; Kaminski, p. 274.

[39] Ketcham, p. 466.

[40] Kaminski, p. 279; Cunningham, *The Process of Government Under Jefferson*, p. 16; Cunningham, *Jeffersonian Republicans in Power*, passim; and Dumas Malone, *Jefferson the President: Second Term, 1805–1809* (Boston, 1974), passim.

[41] Cunningham, *The Process of Government Under Jefferson*, pp. 188–93; Alexander B. Lacy, Jr., "Jefferson and Congress: Congressional Method and Politics, 1801–1809," Ph.D. dissertation (University of Virginia, 1964), pp. 97–101.

[42] Lacy, p. 102; Leonard D. White, *The Jeffersonians: A Study in Administrative History, 1801–1809* (New York, 1951), p. 50.

[43] Kaminski, pp. 274–75.

[44] Brown, pp. 348–49.

[45] Kaminski, p. 275.

[46] Brown, pp. 634–35.

[47] Samuel L. Mitchill to Mrs. Mitchill, November 23, 1807, "Dr. Mitchill's Letters from Washington," p. 748.

[48] Brown, pp. 352–53.

[49] Adams' criticism followed his account of a debate in which Clinton ruled his motion to amend a resolution out of order. Charles F. Adams, ed., *Memoirs of John Quincy Adams* (12 vols., Philadelphia, 1874–1877), 1:382–85.

[50] Brown, p. 593.

[51] Kaminski, p. 292.

[52] Adams, 1:400.

[53] Ibid., 1:421; Brown, pp. 452, 455–57; Malone, *Jefferson the President: Second Term*, pp. 88–89.

[54] Cunningham, *In Pursuit of Reason*, pp. 281–82; *Annals of Congress*, 9th Cong., 1st sess., p. 208; U.S., Congress, House, *Annals of Congress*, 9th Cong., 1st sess., pp. 906–21.

[55] Adams, 1:452–53. The controversy was eventually settled by the Supreme Court's 1810 ruling in *Fletcher* v. *Peck*.

[56] Kaminski, pp. 278–79; Malone, *Jefferson the President: Second Term*, pp. 469–506.

[57] Samuel L. Mitchill to Mrs. Mitchill, January 25, 1808, "Dr. Mitchill's Letters to Washington," p. 752; Irving Brant, "Election of 1808," in Schlesinger and Israel, 1:185–221; Ketcham, pp. 466–67.

[58] "Letter from Vice-President George Clinton to De Witt Clinton, March 5, 1808," in Schlesinger and Israel, 1:228; Brant, 1:202; Kaminski, pp. 280–81, 332n.

[59] Samuel L. Mitchell to Mrs. Mitchell, April 1, 1808, "Dr. Mitchell's Letters from Washington," p. 753.

[60] Kaminski, pp. 285–86.

[61] "A Citizen of New-York," quoted in Kaminski, pp. 286–87.

[62] Kaminski, p. 284.

[63] Adams, 1:516; *Annals of Congress*, 10th Cong., 1st sess., p. 150.

[64] Adams, 1:529.

[65] Cunningham, *Jeffersonian Republicans in Power*, pp. 118–21.

[66] Brant, 1:218.

[67] Kaminski, p. 283.

[68] Ibid., p. 288; Brant, 1:202; Ketcham, pp. 466–69. Pinckney carried the New England states with 76 electoral votes.

[69] The Twelfth Amendment, which provides that electors "shall name in their ballots the person voted for as President, and in distinct ballots the person voted for as Vice-President," was ratified on June 15, 1804. This procedure—designed to prevent a recurrence of the situation that occurred in 1800, when the Republican presidential and vice-presidential candidates received an equal number of electoral votes—was first employed during the 1804 election.

[70] Cunningham, *Jeffersonian Republicans in Power*, pp. 122–23.

[71] Ibid., p. 123.

[72] *Annals of Congress*, 10th Cong., 2d sess., pp. 337, 344–45; U.S., Congress, Senate, *Journal*, 10th Cong., special session, March 4–March 7, 1809, pp. 365–68; and *Journal*, 11th Cong., 1st sess., pp. 373–74; Stathis and Moe, pp. 561, 566n. Neither the *Annals* nor the Senate *Journal* indicates where, or on what date, Clinton took his oath of office. He was not present for the special session of March 4–March 7, 1809. The Senate *Journal* notes that "[t]he Honorable George Clinton, Vice President of the United States and President of the Senate," was present when the Eleventh Congress convened on May 22, 1809, but does not indicate that he took the oath of office at that time.

[73] Ketcham, pp. 481–82. Gallatin continued to serve as secretary of the treasury until 1814.

[74] Ketcham, pp. 506; *Annals of Congress*, 11th Cong., 3d sess., pp. 121–347; Kaminski, pp. 289–90; Chase C. Mooney, *William H. Crawford, 1772–1834* (Lexington, KY, 1974), pp. 17–26; Robert V. Remini, *Henry Clay: Statesman for the Union* (New York, 1991), pp. 68–71.

[75] Kaminski, p. 289.

[76] *Annals of Congress*, 11th Cong., 3d sess., pp. 346–47.

[77] Adams, 7:64; Remini, pp. 68–71, 379, and passim.

[78] *Annals of Congress*, 11th Cong., 3d sess., pp. 350–70.

[79] Ibid., pp. 9, 177, 205–6. The "electioneering" for Clinton's office was mentioned in correspondence from First Lady Dolley Madison to Anna Cutts, quoted in Ketcham, p. 521.

[80] Kaminski, p. 291; *Annals of Congress*, 12th Cong., 1st sess., p. 206; Ketcham, p. 520.

[81] Kaminski, pp. 292–93.

Chapter 5

ELBRIDGE GERRY
1813–1814

Eng⁴ by H. & C. Koevoets. N.Y.

ELBRIDGE GERRY

Chapter 5

ELBRIDGE GERRY

5th Vice President: 1813–1814

It is the duty of every man, though he may have but one day to live, to devote that day to the good of his country.

—ELBRIDGE GERRY [1]

The vice-presidency had been vacant for nearly a year by the time Elbridge Gerry took office as the nation's fifth vice president on March 4, 1813. His predecessor, George Clinton, an uncompromising "Old Republican" with frustrated presidential ambitions, had died in office on April 20, 1812. Clinton's constant carping about President James Madison's foreign policy had put him at odds with the administration. Gerry, who replaced Clinton as the Republican vice-presidential nominee in the 1812 election, was a vice president more to Madison's liking. An enthusiastic supporter of Jefferson's embargo and Madison's foreign policy, he offered a welcome contrast to the independent-minded and cantankerous New Yorker who had proved so troublesome during the president's first term. But, like Clinton, Gerry would die in office before the end of his term, leaving Madison—and the nation— once again without a vice president.

Early Career

Elbridge Gerry was born in Marblehead, Massachusetts, on July 17, 1744, one of Thomas and Elizabeth Greenleaf Gerry's eleven children. A former ship's captain who emigrated from England in 1730, Thomas Gerry was a pillar of the Marblehead community, serving as a justice of the peace and selectman and as moderator of the town meeting. The family was prosperous, thanks to a thriving mercantile and shipping business and an inheritance from Elizabeth

Gerry's side of the family. The Gerrys were also pious, faithfully attending the First Congregational Church and avoiding ostentatious display. Young Elbridge was probably educated by a private tutor before his admission to Harvard College in 1758. Like many of his fellow scholars, he paid careful attention to the imperial crisis that would eventually precipitate the American Revolution, arguing in his master's thesis that the colonists were justified in their resistance to "the new Prohibitory Duties, which make it useless for the People to engage in Commerce." [2]

Gerry returned home after graduation to join the family business. A thriving port and commercial center, Marblehead was a hotbed of anti-British activity during the 1760s and 1770s. The future vice president played a limited role in the resistance movement until the spring of 1770, when he served on a local committee to enforce the ban on the sale and consumption of tea. He was elected to the Massachusetts legislature in 1772, and later to its successor body, the Provincial Congress, serving as chairman of the committee on supplies during the fall and winter of 1774–1775.[3] The historian Mercy Otis Warren— a contemporary—later recalled that Gerry coordinated the procurement and distribution of arms and provisions with "punctuality and indefatigable industry," [4] an effort he would continue while serving in the Continental Congress. Following a practice that was neither unusual nor illegal at the time, Gerry awarded several supply contracts to his family's business. But, unlike many of his fellow merchants, he refused to take excessive profits from wartime commerce, explaining that he would "prefer any Loss to the least Misunderstanding with the public relative of Interest." [5]

Gerry was elected to the second Continental Congress in December 1775, serving until 1780 and again from 1783 to 1785. If he was, as his biographer George Athan Billias admits, a "second rank figure" in a body that included such luminaries as Thomas Jefferson and John and Samuel Adams, he was also a diligent legislator. His efforts to persuade wavering middle colony delegates to support independence during the summer of 1776 evoked paeans of praise from John Adams. "If every Man here was a Gerry," Adams claimed, "the Liberties of America would be safe against the Gates of Earth and Hell." [6]

But, like Adams, Gerry could also be trying and impractical—even Adams despaired of his friend's "obstinacy that will risk great things to secure small ones." [7] He was "of so peculiar a cast of mind," Continental Congress Secretary Charles Thomson marvelled, "that his pleasure seems proportioned to the absurdity of his schemes." [8] Modern scholars agree that "his work in Congress was remembered most for its capriciousness and contrariness," citing the "phobias against sword, purse, and centralized power" that "drove him to oppose any kind of peacetime army and any taxing scheme to raise revenue for the central government." [9] But Gerry's biographer discerns a fundamental logic in his seemingly erratic career. The Revolution was Gerry's defining moment, Billias emphasizes, and the future vice president considered "the signing of the Declaration of Independence . . . the greatest single act of his entire life." [10] All of his subsequent actions, inconsistent and idiosyncratic as they may have appeared to others, were driven by his single-minded goal of preserving the hard-won gains of the Revolution.

For all his commitment to Revolutionary principles, however, Gerry was no egalitarian. He believed that a "natural elite" of able and talented individuals should govern the new nation. As a member of that favored class, he considered public service a responsibility, not an opportunity for personal or financial gain. Like many of his contemporaries, he believed that the ideal form of government was a "mixed" constitution, incorporating in a delicately balanced equilibrium the best features of a monarchy, an aristocracy, and a democracy. A constitution that inclined too much toward any of the three would, Gerry feared, threaten the stability of the government or jeopardize the liberties of the people. This stance accounts for his seemingly inconsistent behavior during the Constitutional Convention and the ensuing ratification debate. [11]

Constitutional Convention

One of four delegates chosen by the Massachusetts legislature to attend the 1787 Constitutional Convention, Gerry was, in his biographer's words, "one of the most active participants in the entire Convention." [12] A member of the moderate bloc—he was neither an extreme nationalist nor a committed states' rights advocate—he acted as a conciliator during the first phases of the convention. As chair of the committee that resolved the impasse between the large and small states over representation in the national legislature, Gerry made several impassioned speeches in support of the "Great Compromise," which provided for equal representation of the states in the Senate and proportional representation in the House of Representatives. [13]

Soon after the convention adopted the compromise, Gerry began to worry that the constitution that was slowly emerging during those hot and tense days in Philadelphia would create a powerful national legislature capable of jeopardizing the people's liberties and overshadowing the states. Although the convention adopted several of his proposals to limit congressional power, including the prohibition against bills of attainder and ex post facto laws, these provisions failed to satisfy his apprehensions. Struggling to save a document that he now considered seriously flawed, Gerry offered a motion to include a bill of rights and several specific proposals to safeguard popular liberties. The convention's majority disagreed with this approach and defeated each of these initiatives. On September 15, 1787, a dispirited Gerry stated "the objections which determined him to withhold his name from the Constitution," concluding that "the best that could be done . . . was to provide for a second general Convention." Two days later, as his more optimistic colleagues prepared to sign the new Constitution, Gerry explained his change of heart. James Madison, whose notes of the convention provide the only authoritative account of its proceedings, recorded the awkward scene:

> Mr. Gerry described the painful feelings of his situation, and the embarrassment under which he rose to offer any further observations on the subject which had finally been decided. Whilst the plan was depending, he had treated it with all the freedom he thought it deserved. He now felt himself bound as he was disposed to treat it with the respect due to the Act of the Convention. He hoped he should not violate that respect in declaring on this occasion his fears that a Civil war may result from the present crisis of the U.S.[14]

Gerry objected to several provisions in the new Constitution, including the language in Article I, section 3, specifying that "The Vice President of the United States shall be President of the Senate." During the September 7 debate over the "mode of constituting the Executive," he had voiced his reservations about assigning legislative responsibilities to the vice president. "We might as well put the President himself at the head of the Legislature," he had argued. "The close intimacy that must subsist between the President & vice-president makes it absolutely improper." But, he now admitted, he could have accepted this provision and others that he found troubling had the Constitution not granted Congress such sweeping powers.[15]

Fearful as he was about the new Constitution, Gerry was equally worried that "anarchy may ensue" if the states failed to ratify it. He did not, therefore, reject it outright during the ratification struggle. Abandoning his earlier call for a second convention, he worked to build support for amendments "adapted to the 'exigencies of Government' & the preservation of Liberty." Reviled as a traitor to his class by elites who strongly favored ratification, Gerry suffered an overwhelming defeat in the 1788 Massachusetts gubernatorial election. Still, he noted with some satisfaction that his state and four others ratified the

Constitution with recommendations for amendments.[16]

The New Nation

Gerry served in the United States House of Representatives during the First and Second congresses (1789–1793). A conciliatory and moderate legislator, he supported Treasury Secretary Alexander Hamilton's proposals to fund the Revolutionary War debt and to establish a national bank. Disillusioned by the increasingly partisan nature of the debate that Hamilton's proposals generated, Gerry retired at the end of his second term, returning to Elmwood, his Cambridge, Massachusetts, estate, to attend to his business affairs and to care for his large and growing family. He had remained a bachelor until the age of forty-one, marrying Ann Thompson, the European-educated daughter of a wealthy New York merchant, in 1786. Ann Gerry's frequent pregnancies—ten children arrived between 1787 and 1801—placed a severe strain on her health, and Elbridge was needed at home.[17]

Gerry's brief retirement ended in 1796, when he served as a presidential elector, supporting his friend and former colleague, John Adams. In 1797, with relations between the United States and France steadily worsening after the adoption of the Jay Treaty, President Adams appointed Gerry an envoy to France. The mission failed after representatives of the French government demanded a bribe before they would begin negotiations. Gerry's fellow commissioners left Paris, but Gerry, who had been meeting privately with the French in an effort to facilitate negotiations, remained behind, believing that accommodation was possible. Eventually, he left France empty-handed but convinced that his efforts had averted war. Attacks on American shipping continued, however, and Gerry was widely criticized for the failure of the mission.[18]

Maligned by Federalists who believed him partial to France, and courted by Republicans for the same reason, Gerry tried to remain aloof from the partisan warfare of the late 1790s. Then, in 1800, energized by President John Adams' warning that Hamilton would use the army to gain control of the government, he aligned himself with the moderate wing of the Jeffersonian coalition, eventually emerging as the leader of the Massachusetts Republicans. After a brief second retirement from politics between 1804 and 1809, Gerry was elected governor of Massachusetts in 1810. The success of his efforts to reconcile Federalists and Republicans, who were bitterly divided over foreign policy issues, led to his reelection the following year. During his second term, however, Governor Gerry adopted a more "hard-line" approach, as Massachusetts Federalists became increasingly outspoken in their opposition to Madison's foreign policy. He prosecuted Federalist editors for libel, appointed family members to state office, and approved a controversial redistricting plan crafted to give Republicans an advantage in the state senatorial elections. The Federalist press responded to this plan with cartoon figures of a salamander-shaped election district—the "Gerrymander"—adding to the American political lexicon a term that is still used to connote an irregularly shaped district created by legislative fiat to benefit a particular party, politician, or other group. Governor Gerry's highly partisan agenda led to his defeat in the April 1812 gubernatorial election. Heavily in debt after cosigning a note for a brother who defaulted on his obligation, and saddled with the expenses of a large family, Gerry asked President James Madison to appoint him collector of customs at Boston.[19]

Vice-Presidential Career

Madison had other plans for Gerry. With the 1812 presidential election fast approaching and the vice-presidency vacant since George Clinton's death in April, Madison was more anxious to find a suitable running mate than to fill a customs post. He preferred a candidate who would attract votes in the New England states yet would not threaten the succession of the "Virginia dynasty" in the 1816 election. Former Senator John Langdon of New Hampshire, the party's first choice, was too old and too ill to accept the nomination. After he declined, the Republican caucus turned to the sixty-seven-year-old Gerry, a choice that Madison approved despite Albert Gallatin's prediction that the Massachusetts patriot "would give us as much trouble as our late Vice-President."[20] Gerry had supported Jefferson's embargo and Madison's foreign policy, remaining steadfast after the United States declared war against Great Britain in June 1812. Like Madison, he believed that the war was necessary to protect the liberties that both men had labored so hard to secure during the Revolution.[21]

Although Gerry was certainly no liability, he turned out not to be as valuable an asset as the Republicans had hoped. Of Massachusetts' 22 electors, only 2 voted for Gerry and none voted for Madison. In an election that was, as one scholar has observed, "a virtual referendum" on the War of 1812, editors and electioneers paid relatively little attention to the vice-presidential candidates. By a margin of 39 electoral votes, Madison defeated opposition candidate De Witt Clinton, and Gerry triumphed over Jared Ingersoll of Pennsylvania.[22]

Gerry remained at home in Massachusetts on inauguration day, March 4, 1813, taking his oath of office there from U.S. District Judge John Davis.[23] When the Senate convened at the beginning of the Thirteenth Congress on May 24, 1813, he appeared in the chamber with a certificate attesting to the fact that he had taken the oath of office. Gerry's inaugural address, an extended oration condemning the British and praising Madison, was unusual in content and length. He explained that "to have concealed" his "political principles and opinions" during "a crisis like this might have savored too much of a deficiency of candor."[24] He was now on record as a supporter of the war effort and a loyal ally of the president.

Gerry's early hopes that "unanimity should prevail" in the Senate[25] soon faded, as the war deepened the divisions between the parties and threatened to split the Republican coalition. Republicans far outnumbered Federalists in the Senate, but mounting opposition to the war effort among disaffected Republicans steadily eroded the administration's 28-to-8 majority. The president was such an inept commander in chief that even his loyal ally, House Speaker Henry Clay of Kentucky, considered him "wholly unfit for the storms of War."[26] As anti-administration sentiment reached a fever pitch after American forces suffered humiliating defeats in Canada

ELBRIDGE GERRY

and at sea, [27] several members of the president's party balked at the nomination of Treasury Secretary Albert Gallatin as envoy to Great Britain and Russia. Instead, they supported a resolution ordering Madison to inform the Senate whether Gallatin would retain his cabinet post (and, if so, who would serve in his absence). Ultimately, these Republicans joined with Federalists to defeat the nomination by a vote of 18 to 17.[28]

Elbridge Gerry found it increasingly difficult to remain impartial in such a highly charged atmosphere, especially after Madison became seriously ill in mid-June 1813. Gerry, himself, was in poor health. He had recently suffered a "stroke," and old age had so withered his slight physique that one observer likened his appearance to that of a "scant-patterned old skeleton of a French Barber." The March 1, 1792, act which at that time governed the presidential succession provided that if the president and the vice president died in office—a development that many considered possible, if not imminent, during the summer of 1813—the president pro tempore of the Senate would serve as president. And if Gerry left the Senate before Congress adjourned, as all of his predecessors had done to allow election of a president pro tempore, anti-administration forces might combine to elect an individual hostile to Madison's agenda. One Federalist editor had already suggested New York Federalist Senator Rufus King as a possible successor, while Secretary of State James Monroe warned that disaffected Senate Republicans had "begun to make calculations, and plans, founded on the presumed death of the President and Vice-President, and it has been suggested to me that [Virginia Senator William Branch] Giles is thought of to take the place of the President of the Senate." [29]

But if Gerry remained in the chair, and if he survived until the end of the session, the person next in the line of succession would be Speaker of the House Henry Clay, an outspoken "warhawk." Breaking with the precedent established by John Adams, Gerry therefore refused to vacate the chair, presiding over the Senate until the first session of the Thirteenth Congress adjourned on August 2, 1813. "[S]everal gentlemen of the Senate had intimated a wish that he

would retire from the Chair two or three weeks before the time of adjournment, and would thus give to the Senate an opportunity for choosing a President *pro tempore*," he later explained, but "other gentlemen expressed a contrary desire, and thought that the President should remain in the Chair, and adjourn the Senate." Gerry ultimately decided that, as "a war existed and had produced a special session of Congress," he was "differently circumstanced from any of his predecessors, and was under an obligation to remain in the Chair until the important business of the session was finished." [30] (Decades later, in March 1890, the Senate established the current practice of having presidents pro tempore hold office continuously until the election of another president pro tempore, rather than serving only during the absence of a vice president.)

With the presidential succession safe and Madison's physical condition much improved by the time the Senate adjourned, Gerry was free to return home. He was absent when the second session of the Thirteenth Congress convened in December and did not return to Washington until early February 1814.[31] Partisan sentiments remained strong in the Senate, he soon discovered. By one observer's count, the administration's opponents outnumbered its supporters by a margin of 20 to 16. The vice president suspected that a Senate stenographer was the source of recent anti-administration articles in the local press, but with opposition forces now in the majority he was reluctant to "meddle with serpents," and he let the matter drop.[32]

Unpleasant as his Senate duties had become, Gerry still enjoyed the endless round of dinners, receptions, and entertainments that crowded his calendar. With his elegant manners and personal charm, the vice president was a favorite guest of Washington's Republican hostesses, including first lady Dolley Madison. He maintained an active social schedule that belied his advanced years and failing health, visiting friends from his earlier days, who were now serving as members of Congress or administration appointees, and paying special attention to Betsy Patterson Bonaparte, the American-born sister-in-law of Napoleon, whose revealing attire caused a stir wherever she went.[33]

Gerry remained in Washington until the second session of the Thirteenth Congress adjourned on April 18, 1814, leaving the Senate chamber only a few moments before adjournment to permit the election of South Carolina Republican John Gaillard as president pro tempore. Mindful that the war had "increased his responsibility," and apprehensive of "the tendency of contrary conduct to prostrate the laws and Government," however, he had refused to relinquish the chair "whilst any important bill or measure was pending, and was to be finished at that session."[34]

Gerry spent the summer of 1814 in Massachusetts, awaiting news of the war effort from Madison.[35] He found the capital much changed when he returned in the fall; British troops had burned most of the city's public buildings, including the Capitol, and the Senate would meet in temporary quarters for the remainder of his term. He was outraged to learn that Massachusetts Federalists had called for a convention of the New England states to consider defensive measures and to propose constitutional amendments. In the fall of 1814, the Hartford Convention, which would not issue its recommendations until after Gerry's death, was widely rumored to be a secessionist initiative. The vice president therefore urged Madison to counter with a "spirited manifesto" against the proceedings.[36]

Gerry was still an energetic defender of the administration and of the war, but, by that autumn, his public responsibilities, coupled with his relentless socializing, had sapped his strength. He became seriously ill in late November 1814, retiring early on the evening of November 22 and complaining of chest pains the next morning. De-termined to perform his public responsibilities, he arrived at the temporary capitol in the Patent Office Building later that morning. Then, realizing that he was in no condition to preside over the Senate, he returned to his boardinghouse. Members of the Senate, assembling in the chamber at their customary hour and hearing reports of Gerry's death, sent Massachusetts Senators Joseph Varnum and Christopher Gore to the vice president's lodgings "to ascertain the fact." When they returned with confirmation that the reports were true, the Senate appointed five senators to a joint committee "to consider and report measures most proper to manifest the public respect for the memory of the deceased." The body then adjourned as a mark of respect to its departed president. On the following day, the Senate ordered that the president's chair "be shrouded with black during the present session; and as a further testimony of respect for the deceased, the members of the Senate will go into mourning, and wear black crape round the left arm for thirty days."[37] Although the Senate passed legislation providing for payment of Gerry's vice-presidential salary to his financially strapped widow for the remainder of his term, the House rejected the plan.

Not long after Gerry's interment at Congressional Cemetery, the United States claimed victory over Great Britain. The young nation received few tangible concessions from the British under the Treaty of Ghent,[38] but a new generation of leaders viewed America's "victory" in the War of 1812 as a reaffirmation of the ideals that had animated and sustained Elbridge Gerry since the summer of 1776.

NOTES

[1] Inscription on the Elbridge Gerry monument, Congressional Cemetery, Washington, D.C., reproduced in James T. Austin, *The Life of Elbridge Gerry*, vol. 2 (New York, 1970; reprint of 1829 edition), p. 403.

[2] George Athan Billias, *Elbridge Gerry, Founding Father and Republican Statesman* (New York, 1976), pp. 1–7.

[3] Ibid., pp. 7–54.

[4] Quoted in ibid., p. 53.

[5] Ibid., pp. 73–75.

[6] Quoted in ibid., p. 70.

[7] Quoted in Samuel Eliot Morison, "Elbridge Gerry, Gentleman-Democrat," *New England Quarterly* 2 (1929), reprinted in *By Land and By Sea: Essays and Addresses* (New York, 1953), p. 190.

[8] Quoted in Stanley Elkins and Eric McKitrick, *The Age of Federalism: The Early American Republic, 1788–1800* (New York, 1993), p. 557.

[9] Elkins and McKitrick, p. 557.

[10] Billias, p. 70.

[11] Ibid., pp. xiii–xvii and *passim*; Jackson Turner Main, *The Antifederalists: Critics of the Constitution, 1781–1788* (Chapel Hill, NC, 1961). p. 171.

[12] Billias, p. 158; Ralph Ketcham, *James Madison: A Biography* (Charlottesville, VA, 1992; reprint of 1971 edition), p. 194.

[13] Billias, pp. 153–84.

[14] Ibid., pp. 185–205; *Notes of Debates in the Federal Convention of 1787 Reported By James Madison* (New York, 1987; reprint of 1966 edition), pp. 652–58.

[15] *Notes of Debates in the Federal Convention*, pp. 594–97, 652.

[16] Billias, pp. 206–17.

[17] Ibid., pp. 147, 218–35.

[18] Ibid., pp. 245–86.

[19] Ibid., pp. 287–325.

[20] Ketcham, p. 523; Norman K. Risjord, "Election of 1812," in *History of American Presidential Elections, 1789–1968*, edited by Arthur M. Schlesinger, Jr. and Fred L. Israel, vol. 1 (New York, 1971). p. 252.

[21] According to Madison scholar Robert Allen Rutland, the president believed that "war with Britain would reaffirm the commitment of 1776." Robert Allen Rutland, *The Presidency of James Madison* (Lawrence, KS, 1990), p. 97. Gerry elaborated his sentiments in his May 24, 1813, inaugural address. U.S., Congress, Senate, *Annals of Congress*, 13th Cong., 2d sess., pp. 10–13.

[22] Risjord, "Election of 1812," pp. 249–72; Norman K. Risjord, "1812," in *Running for President: The Candidates and Their Images*, ed. Arthur M. Schlesinger, Jr., vol. 1, *1789–1896* (New York, 1994), pp. 67–72.

[23] Stephen W. Stathis and Ronald C. Moe, "America's Other Inauguration," *Presidential Studies Quarterly* 10 (Fall 1980), p. 561. Gerry's legislative duties would not commence until the Thirteenth Congress convened two months later, which may account for his decision to remain in Cambridge until that time. Samuel Eliot Morison speculates that Ann Gerry's illness may have prevented her from accompanying her husband to Washington in 1813; her condition might also have delayed her husband's departure. Morison, "Elbridge Gerry," pp. 197–98.

[24] *Annals of Congress*, 13th Cong., 1st sess., pp. 9–13.

[25] Ibid., p. 10.

[26] Robert V. Remini, *Henry Clay: Statesman for the Union* (New York, 1991), p. 97.

[27] Ibid., pp. 94–97.

[28] Ketcham, p. 560; Robert Ernst, *Rufus King: American Federalist* (Chapel Hill, NC, 1968), pp. 324–25; *Annals of Congress*, 13th Cong., 1st sess., pp. 84–90.

[29] The vice president's social life is chronicled in the diary of his son, Elbridge Gerry, Jr., who visited his father in Washington during the summer of 1813. Elbridge, Jr.'s diary makes no mention of his father's health, but the vice president's most recent biographer notes that the elder Gerry suffered a "stroke" while Madison was ill. Claude Bowers, ed., *The Diary of Elbridge Gerry, Jr.* (New York, 1927), passim; Ketcham, pp. 560–62; Billias, pp. 326–29.

[30] *Annals of Congress*, 13th Cong., 2d sess., pp. 776–78.

[31] Ketcham, p. 562; *Annals of Congress*, 13th Cong., 2d sess., pp. 537–622.

[32] Billias, p. 327.

[33] Ibid., pp. 327–28.

[34] *Annals of Congress*, 13th Cong., 2d sess., pp. 622–778.

[35] Rutland, p. 151.

[36] Billias, p. 326; Marshall Smelser, *The Democratic Republic, 1801–1815* (New York, 1968), pp. 296–99.

[37] Billias, pp. 328–29; *Annals of Congress*, 13th Cong., 3d sess., pp. 109–110.

[38] Smelser, pp. 308–11.

Chapter 6

DANIEL D. TOMPKINS
1817–1825

DANIEL D. TOMPKINS

Chapter 6

DANIEL D. TOMPKINS

6th Vice President: 1817–1825

The name of Daniel Tompkins deserves to be more kindly remembered than it has been.
—*New York Herald-Tribune* EDITORIAL, JUNE 21, 1932 [1]

Daniel D. Tompkins was by all accounts an exceptionally handsome individual. He had a "face of singular masculine beauty," one essayist noted, and a "gentle, polished and unpretentious" demeanor. Tompkins' biographer discovered that "almost every noted American artist" of the time painted the handsome New York Republican, [2] and the images reproduced in Raymond Irwin's study of Tompkins' career depict an attractive and obviously self-confident young politician. John Trumbull's 1809 portrait, for example, shows Tompkins as he appeared during his first term as governor of New York: a carefully dressed, poised, and seemingly contented public man, his dark hair framing an even-featured and not-yet-careworn face. [3]

But had Trumbull painted Tompkins in 1825, the year he retired from public life after two terms as vice president during James Monroe's administration, he would have captured a vastly different likeness. A decade of financial privation and heavy drinking, coupled with accusations that he had mishandled state and federal funds while serving as governor of New York during the War of 1812, had prematurely aged Tompkins. He was, at the age of fifty, an embittered and tortured old man, his once-promising career brought to an untimely end. "There was a time when no man in the state dared compete with him for any office in the gift of the people," a contemporary reflected after Tompkins' death on June 11, 1825, "and his habits of intemperance alone prevented him from becoming President of the United States." [4]

Tompkins' Early Years

Daniel D. Tompkins was born in Westchester County, New York, on June 21, 1774, one of eleven children of Jonathan Griffin Tompkins and Sarah Ann Hyatt Tompkins. His parents were tenant farmers, who acquired middle-class status only shortly before his birth when they purchased a farm near Scarsdale. Jonathan Griffin Tompkins joined several local resistance committees during the Revolution, serving as an adjutant in the county militia. After the war, he served several years as a town supervisor and as a delegate to the state legislature. A self-educated man, the elder Tompkins was determined to provide young Daniel with a classical education.

The future vice president began his education at a New York City grammar school, later transferring to the Academy of North Salem and entering Columbia University in 1792. An exceptional scholar and a gifted essayist, Tompkins graduated first in his class in 1795, intent on pursuing a political career. In 1797, he was admitted to the New York bar and married Hannah Minthorne, the daughter of a well-connected Republican merchant. Tompkins' father-in-law was a prominent member of the Tammany Society, a militant, unabashedly democratic political organization that would one day challenge the Clinton dynasty for control of the New York Republican party. Also known as "Bucktails," after the distinctive plumes worn at official and ceremonial gatherings, the Tammanyites were a diverse lot. As Tompkins' biographer has noted, the society was comprised of "laborers . . . Revolutionary War veterans . . . who admired republican France and hated monarchical England; more than a sprinkling of immigrants . . . befriended by the Society . . . and, of course, hopeful politicians."[5]

Tompkins began his political career in 1800, canvassing his father-in-law's precinct on behalf of candidates for the state legislature who would, if elected, choose Republican electors in the forthcoming presidential contest. He was a skilled and personable campaigner, never forgetting a name or a face; by the time the election was over, he knew nearly every voter in the Seventh Ward. Resourceful and energetic, he managed to circumvent New York's highly restrictive voter-qualification laws by pooling resources with other young men of modest means to purchase enough property to qualify for the franchise. The engaging and tactful Tompkins never allowed politics to interfere with personal friendships—an enormous asset for a New York politician, given the proliferation of factions in the Empire State during the early 1800s. Tompkins served as a New York City delegate to the 1801 state constitutional convention and was elected to the New York assembly in 1803. In 1804 he won a seat in the United States House of Representatives, but he resigned before Congress convened to accept an appointment as an associate justice of the New York Supreme Court.[6]

War Governor

Tompkins was a popular and fair-minded jurist, well respected by members of the several factions that were struggling for control of the state Republican party during the early 1800s. He was also a close associate of De Witt Clinton, who supported him in the 1807 gubernatorial race in an effort to unseat Morgan Lewis. Lewis was a "Livingston" Republican, supported by the landed aristocracy who sided with the Livingston clan, wealthy landlords whose extensive holdings had assured them of a prominent role in New York politics. In contrast, the Clintonians

stressed their candidate's humble origins—Tompkins was the "the Farmer's Boy," with not a drop of "aristocratical or oligarchical blood" in his veins—and won a solid victory. During his first months in office, the new governor apparently took his marching orders from Clinton, sending him advance copies of his official addresses for review and comment. But he soon asserted his independence by supporting President Thomas Jefferson's foreign policy and backing Clinton's rival, James Madison, in the 1808 presidential election.[7]

Reelected governor in 1810, Tompkins was a loyal supporter of the Madison administration. He advised Treasury Secretary Albert Gallatin about patronage appointments in New York and, after the United States declared war on Great Britain in the summer of 1812, did his best to comply with War Department directives and requisitions. With Federalists in control of the state legislature and the Clintonians resolutely opposed to the war, Tompkins was hard pressed to comply with the constant stream of requests for men and materiel. He used his own funds to pay and arm the militia and personally endorsed a series of loans from local banks in a desperate effort to buttress the state's defenses. It was a risk Tompkins could ill afford to take; he had already made substantial contributions to the war effort and had borrowed heavily to finance several large purchases of land on Staten Island. When President Madison offered him a cabinet appointment in the fall of 1814, Tompkins protested that he would be more useful to the administration as governor of New York. But, he later confessed, "One of the reasons was the inadequacy of my circumstances to remove to Washington & support so large and expensive family as mine is, on the salary of that office."[8]

The Election of 1816

Tompkins' able and energetic leadership during the war made him one of the best-loved men in his state. One of his aides, novelist Washington Irving, pronounced him "absolutely one of the worthiest men I ever knew . . . honest, candid, prompt, indefatigable,"[9] a sentiment that many shared. The editor of the *Albany Argus* suggested in January 1816 that "if private worth—

if public service—if fervent patriotism and practical talents are to be regarded in selecting a President then Governor Tompkins stands forth to the nation with unrivalled pretensions." [10] Republicans in the state legislature endorsed him as their presidential candidate on February 14, 1816, and a week later he was renominated as the party's gubernatorial candidate. Tompkins defeated Federalist Rufus King by a comfortable margin in the gubernatorial race after an intensely partisan campaign focusing on the candidates' wartime records. But the victory was marred by Federalist accusations that Governor Tompkins had misused public monies during the war, charges that would haunt him for the remainder of his life. [11]

Encouraged by Tompkins' victory, his supporters redoubled their efforts to secure his presidential nomination. Outside of New York, however, few Americans had ever heard of Tompkins, and few Republicans believed him capable of winning the presidency. Not even all New York Republicans backed Tompkins; some, like Albany Postmaster Samuel Southwick, a Madison appointee and the editor of the *Albany Register*, declared for Republican "heir apparent" James Monroe, who received the Republican presidential nomination on March 16, 1816. In a concession to New York Republicans, who were crucial to the party's national strategy, Daniel Tompkins did receive the vice-presidential nomination. Tompkins, like many New Yorkers, believed that Virginians had monopolized the presidency long enough, but, he assured one supporter, he had "no objection to being vice President under Mr. Munro." He declared, however, that he could not accept a cabinet post in the Monroe administration because "the emoluments . . . would not save his private fortune from encroachment . . . the vice Presidency in that respect would be more eligible to him—as he could discharge the Duties of that office and suffer his family to remain at home & probably save something for the support of his family."

The end of the war, by then popularly acclaimed as an American triumph, brought a resurgence in popularity for the Republicans and marked the beginning of the end for the Federalists, who had become suspect because of their opposition to the war. In this euphoric atmosphere, Monroe and Tompkins won an easy victory over Federalist presidential candidate Rufus King and an array of vice-presidential candidates. [12]

Absentee Vice President

Tompkins' first term began auspiciously. He returned to his Staten Island home soon after taking the oath of office on March 4, 1817. There he welcomed President Monroe, who began the term with a tour of the northern states in the summer of 1817. A gesture reminiscent of President Washington's 1789 New England tour, the trip was intended to quell the partisan resentments that had so bitterly divided the country during the Jefferson and Madison administrations. After the president's brief visit to Staten Island, Tompkins accompanied him to Manhattan, where they attended a military review and a reception at City Hall and toured New York's military installations. When Monroe was made an honorary member of the Society for Encouragement of American Manufactures on June 13, 1817, Tompkins, the society's president, chaired the proceedings. [13]

But Tompkins paid only sporadic attention to his vice-presidential duties after Monroe left New York to continue his tour. The vice president was in poor health, the result of a fall from his horse during an inspection tour of Fort Greene in 1814. By the fall of 1817, Tompkins was complaining that his injuries had "increased upon me for several years until finally, for the last six weeks, they have confined me to my house and . . . sometimes to my bed. . . . My present prospect is that kind of affliction and confinement for the residue of my life." The problem was so severe that he expected to "resign the office of Vice President at the next session, if not sooner, as there is very little hope of my ever being able to perform its duties hereafter." [14]

Tompkins' health eventually improved enough to permit his return to public life, but his financial affairs were in such a chaotic state by 1817 that he found little time to attend the Senate. In his haste to raise and spend the huge sums required for New York's wartime defense, he had failed to document his transactions, commingling his own monies with state and federal funds. An 1816 audit by the New York comptroller had revealed a $120,000 shortfall in the state treasury, the rough equivalent of $1.2 million 1991 dollars.[15] A state commission appointed to investigate the matter indicated that Tompkins had apparently used the funds to make interest payments on an 1814 loan incurred "on the pledge of the United States stock and Treasury notes, and on his personal responsibility, for defraying the expenses of carrying on the war." In 1819 the New York legislature awarded him a premium of $120,000, but currency values had plummeted since 1814. Tompkins maintained that the state now owed him $130,000, setting the stage for a long and bitter battle that continued through his first term as vice president.[16]

Tompkins' efforts to settle accounts with the federal treasury proved equally frustrating. Perplexed by the intricacies of the government's rudimentary accounting system and lacking adequate documentation of his claims, he received no acknowledgement of the government's indebtedness to him until late 1822 and no actual compensation until 1824. In the meantime, Tompkins could neither make mortgage payments on his properties nor satisfy the judgments that several creditors, including his father-in-law and a former law tutor, obtained against him. Tompkins slid deeper into debt and began to drink heavily.[17]

The vice president's financial troubles, and his continuing involvement in New York politics, kept him away from Washington for extended periods. He spent much of his first term in New York, trying to develop his Staten Island properties and negotiating with Comptroller Archibald McIntyre to settle his wartime accounts—a nearly impossible task, given the political climate in the state. De Witt Clinton had succeeded Tompkins as governor, and Comptroller McIntyre was Clinton's staunch ally. Governor Clinton's resentment of the "Virginia dynasty" knew no bounds, and with Tompkins now on record as a supporter of the Monroe administration, the long-simmering rivalry between the vice president and his former mentor finally came to a head. "[B]oth parties thought they could make

political capital" out of Tompkins' financial embarrassments, one contemporary observed, "and each party thought it could make more than the other."[18] In the spring of 1820, the New York Senate voted to award Tompkins $11,870.50 to settle his accounts, but Clinton's allies in the state assembly blocked a final settlement and affirmed the comptroller's contention that Tompkins was still in arrears.[19]

Tompkins grew increasingly bitter with each new assault on his integrity, but many New Yorkers, having themselves suffered severe financial reverses during the panic of 1819, sympathized with his plight, and continued to hold him in high regard. In 1820, the Bucktails nominated Tompkins as their candidate to oppose Clinton in the gubernatorial race—a move that heightened public scrutiny of the charges against him while foreclosing any possibility of reaching a settlement before the election. Some questioned the wisdom of nominating Tompkins. Republican strategist Martin Van Buren tried, without success, to replace him with a less controversial candidate. But Tompkins, fearful that his withdrawal would only lend credence to the charges against him, refused to step aside. Although Clinton ultimately won reelection by a narrow margin, Tompkins achieved a personal victory when the state legislature finally approved a compromise settlement of his accounts in November 1820.[20]

When Tompkins did find time to attend the Senate, he was an inept presiding officer. His shortcomings were painfully apparent during the debates over the admission of Missouri into the Union, a critically important contest that became, in the words of historian Glover Moore, "a struggle for political power between the North and South."[21] New York Representative James Tallmadge, Jr. had sparked the debate when he offered an amendment to the Missouri statehood bill prohibiting "the further introduction of slavery or involuntary servitude" in the prospective state and requiring the emancipation, at the age of twenty-five, of all slave children born after Missouri's admission into the Union. The Senate took up the Missouri question in February 1819, with Senator Rufus King of New York leading the restrictionist charge and southern Republicans opposing the effort to restrict the spread of slavery. The debates continued through the spring of 1820, when Congress finally approved the Missouri Compromise.[22]

In this contentious atmosphere, Tompkins found it difficult to maintain order. Mrs. William A. Seaton, who followed the debate with avid interest from the Senate gallery, recounted one particularly chaotic session that took place in January 1820:

. . . There have been not less than a hundred ladies on the floor of the Senate every day on which it was anticipated that Mr. Pinckney[23] would speak . . . Governor Tompkins, a very gallant man, had invited a party of ladies who he met at Senator Brown's,[24] to take seats on the floor of the Senate, having, as President of the Senate, unlimited power, and thinking proper to use it, contrary to all former precedent. I was one of the select, and gladly availed myself of the invitation, with my good friend Mrs. Lowndes, of South Carolina, and half a dozen others. The company in the gallery seeing a *few* ladies very comfortably seated on the sofas, with warm footstools and other luxuries, did as they had a right to do,—deserted the gallery; and every one, old and young, flocked into the Senate. 'Twas then that our Vice-President began to look alarmed, and did not attend strictly to the member addressing the chair. The Senators (some of them) frowned indignantly, and were heard to mutter audibly, 'Too many women here for business to be transacted properly!' Governor Tompkins found it necessary the next morning to affix a note to the door, excluding all ladies not introduced by one of the Senators.[25]

Tompkins left for New York shortly after this embarrassing incident, turning his attention to the gubernatorial race while the Missouri debate dragged on. His abrupt departure angered antislavery senators, who were thus deprived of the vice president's tie-breaking vote in the event of a deadlock between the free states and the slave states. There is little evidence to suggest that Tompkins' absence had any effect on the ultimate outcome of the Missouri debate, since his vote was never needed to resolve an impasse, but restrictionists reviled him as a "miserable Sycophant who betrayed us to the lords of the South . . . that smallest of small men Daniel D. Tompkins." In one his last official acts as governor, Tompkins had petitioned the New York legislature to set a date certain for emancipation, and northern senators apparently expected some type of support from his quarter during the Missouri debate. They were bitterly disappointed. Rufus King, for one, lamented that Tompkins had "fled the field on the day of battle."[26]

The vice president was, admittedly, distracted by the New York election and obsessed with clearing his name, but in "fleeing the field," he had also avoided taking a public stand that would certainly have alienated the president, an important consideration since Tompkins had every intention of remaining on the ticket as Monroe's running mate in 1820. Monroe never commented publicly on the Missouri controversy, although he privately informed some advisers that he would veto any statehood bill incorporating a restrictionist proviso. Because his overriding concern had been to resolve the crisis before the 1820 election, he had worked quietly behind the scenes to help fashion a compromise acceptable to northern and southern Republicans. Monroe's biographer has suggested that, given the controversy over his unsettled accounts, Tompkins knew that he had little chance of winning the New York gubernatorial election and "intended to protect his career by remaining on the national ticket as Vice-President."[27]

Whatever his motives, the vice president was by 1820 a bitter and desperate man, his judgment and once-considerable abilities severely impaired both by the strain of his ordeal and by his heavy drinking. Still, even though some Republicans attempted to block his renomination, most remained faithful to "the Farmer's Boy." The 1820 presidential contest generated surprisingly little interest, given the problems then facing the nation. The country was suffering from a severe depression, and the American occupation of Spanish Florida had unleashed a torrent of anti-administration criticism from House Speaker Henry Clay of Kentucky. Although the Missouri controversy had been resolved for the moment, the truce between North and South was still perilously fragile. Historian Lynn W. Turner has suggested that the reelection of Monroe and Tompkins in 1820 can perhaps be attributed to "the nineteenth-century time-lapse between the perception of political pain and the physical reaction to it." Monroe ran virtually unopposed, winning all but one of the electoral votes cast— a "unanimity of indifference, not of approbation," according to John Randolph of Roanoke.[28]

Some of the electors who were willing to grant Monroe another term balked at casting their second votes for Tompkins. Among these was Federalist elector Daniel Webster of Massachusetts, who predicted that "[t]here will be a number of us . . . in this state, who will not vote for Mr. Tompkins, and we must therefore look up somebody to vote for." Federalist elector and former Senator William Plumer of New Hampshire felt "compelled to withhold my vote from . . . Tompkins . . . because he grossly neglected his duty."[29] The vice president's only official function, Plumer maintained, was to preside over the Senate, "for which he receives annually a salary of five thousand dollars." But "during the last three years he was absent from the Senate nearly three fourths of the time, & thereby occasioned an extra expense to the nation of nearly twenty five hundred dollars. He has not that weight of character which his office requires—the fact is he is grossly intemperate."[30] But Tompkins, like Monroe, ran virtually unopposed. He was easily reelected with 218 electoral votes.

Vindication

Tompkins' second term was, in his biographer's words, a time of "intensifying personal trial, and even of crushing misfortune."[31] In 1821, he attended the New York constitutional convention and was deeply honored when his fellow delegates chose him to chair the proceedings. But his detractors complained that "Mr. Tompkins"—now "a degraded sot"—owed his election only to "the madness of party."[32]

Tompkins missed the opening session of the Seventeenth Congress on December 3, 1821, but he was back in the Senate by December 28. He attended regularly until January 25, 1822, when the Senate was forced to adjourn until the following day, "the Vice President being absent, from indisposition." Less than a week later, Senator King arrived with a letter from Tompkins informing the Senate that, his health having "suf-fered so much on my journey" and since his arrival in town, he intended, "as soon as the weather and the state of the roads permit, to return to my family."[33]

Tompkins was clearly losing control. During his brief stay in Washington, he had managed to alienate Monroe, having severely criticized the president during a meeting with Postmaster General Return J. Meigs and others.[34] Not long after his departure, one observer ventured that Tompkins had never been "perfectly sober during his stay here. He was several times so drunk in the chair," Dr. James Bronaugh informed Andrew Jackson, "that he could with difficulty put the question."[35] Tompkins would spend the next several months trying to settle his accounts with the federal treasury. Before leaving Washington, he assigned what property he still owned, including his Staten Island home, to a group of trustees, and on his return to New York he moved into a run-down boardinghouse in Manhattan.[36]

Tompkins' absence spared him the humiliation of presiding over the Senate as it considered a provision in the 1822 General Appropriation bill to withhold the salaries of government officials who owned money to, or had failed to settle their accounts with, the Treasury. The provision, part of a continuing effort to reform the government's auditing process and to insure greater accountability in public administration, prompted extensive debate.[37] The April 19 session would have been particularly difficult for Tompkins, with New York Senator Martin Van Buren asking whether "gallant and heroic men, who had sustained the honor of their country in the hour of danger, should be kept out of their just dues"— an oblique reference, perhaps, to the vice president's plight—and South Carolina Senator William Smith exhibiting "voluminous lists of those who had been reported public debtors of more than three years' standing," lists that included the name of Daniel Tompkins.[38]

The General Appropriation Act became law on April 30, 1822, depriving Tompkins of his last remaining source of funds.[39] In a desperate attempt to settle his accounts, Tompkins petitioned the United States District Court for the District of New York to bring suit against him for the "supposed balance for which I have been reported among the defaulters." His trial began on June 3, 1822, with the U.S. district attorney seeking a judgment of over $11,000 and the defendant coordinating his own defense. For three days, the jurors heard accounts of Tompkins' wartime sacrifices: bankers who had lent him funds to pay and arm the militia testified in his behalf, and Senator Rufus King recounted that he had urged his friend to take out personal loans for the common defense. Another witness gave a detailed accounting of Tompkins' transactions. But the high point of the trial was Tompkins' highly emotional summation to the jury, a detailed chronicle of "long ten years' . . . accumulated and protracted wrongs." After deliberating for several hours, the jury finally decided in favor of Tompkins. Although the court could by law deliver only a general verdict, the jurors proclaimed that "there is moreover due from the United States of America to the Defendant Daniel D. Tompkins the sum of One hundred and thirty six thousand seven hundred and ninety nine dollars and ninety seven cents." [40]

Tompkins returned to Washington by December 3, 1822, to resume his duties in the Senate. Finally exonerated after a decade-long struggle, Tompkins seemed a changed man. "[T]he verdict . . . had an evident effect on his spirits," *Niles' Weekly Register* reported. "His mind appeared to resume all its former strength, and, during the last session, in his attention to the duties of his office as president of the senate, it is the opinion of many of the older members, that no one ever conducted himself more satisfactorily, or with greater dignity filled the chair." He remained until February 18, 1823; two days later, the Senate approved a bill to "adjust and settle the accounts and claims of Daniel D. Tompkins" and to restore his salary. [41]

Tompkins received no actual remuneration until much later, however. Government accountants ultimately recommended a settlement of just over $35,000, a finding that Monroe, convinced that "a larger sum ought to be allowed him," delayed transmitting to Congress. But Tompkins and his family were in dire straits, although rumors of his confinement to a New York debtors' prison ultimately proved false. On December 7, 1823, Monroe asked Congress for a $35,000 interim appropriation to provide the vice president with "an essential accommodation." Congress approved the request in late December. [42]

On January 21, 1824, Tompkins returned to the Senate. He was "determined to take no part in the approaching election," he informed John Quincy Adams, "and wished for nothing thereafter but quiet and retirement." He still suffered from bouts of insomnia but was finally "relieved of all his embarrassments." He remained in Washington until the end of the session, taking his final leave from the Senate on May 20 with "a few brief remarks" expressing "his sense of the kind and courteous treatment he had experienced from the members, collectively and individually." On May 26, the Senate approved Monroe's request for an additional appropriation of just over $60,000 "for the payment of the claims of Daniel D. Tompkins." [43]

The 1823 and 1824 appropriations came too late to be of much use to the impoverished vice president. He continued to drink heavily, and after years of indebtedness his business affairs were convoluted beyond resolution. Daniel Tompkins died intestate on June 11, 1825, and was interred in St. Mark's Church in New York City. After his death, his creditors squabbled over his once-magnificent Staten Island estate, until it was finally disposed of in a series of sheriff's sales. In 1847, Congress approved a payment of close to $50,000 to Tompkins's heirs. [44] But even this amount, one scholar noted long after the fact, "was only part of what was due him as generally admitted." [45]

NOTES

1 Quoted in Ray W. Irwin, *Daniel D. Tompkins: Governor of New York and Vice President of the United States* (New York, 1968), p. 309, n. 55.

2 Irwin, pp. 59, 227.

3 Reproduced in ibid., facing p. 66.

4 Philip Hone, quoted in ibid., p. 309.

5 Ibid., pp. 1–36.

6 Ibid., pp. 25–50.

7 Ibid., pp. 51–75.

8 Ibid., pp. 83–84, 145–213; Harry Ammon, *James Monroe: The Quest for National Identity* (Charlottesville, Va., 1990; reprint of 1971 edition), pp. 314–37.

9 Washington Irving to William Irving, October 14, 1814, quoted in Pierre M. Irving, ed., *The Life and Letters of Washington Irving*, vol. 1 (Detroit, 1967; reprint of 1863 edition), pp. 320–21.

10 Quoted in Irwin, pp. 197–98.

11 Ibid., pp. 197–205.

12 Donald B. Cole, *Martin Van Buren and the American Political System* (Princeton, NJ, 1984), pp. 46–47; Irwin, pp. 206–11; Lynn W. Turner, "Elections of 1816 and 1820," in *History of American Presidential Elections, 1789–1968*, ed., Arthur M. Schlesinger, Jr., and Fred L. Israel, vol. 1 (New York, 1985), pp. 299–321.

13 Irwin, pp. 221–23; Ammon, pp. 371–79.

14 Irwin, pp. 185, 223.

15 Based on 1860 Composite Consumer Price Index, in John J. McCusker, *How Much Is That in Real Money? A Historical Price Index for Use as a Deflator of Money Values in the Economy of the United States* (Worcester, MA, 1992; reprint of 1991 edition), pp. 326–32.

16 Irwin, pp. 231–32, and *passim*.

17 Ibid., pp. 279–305, and *passim*.

18 Jabez Hammond, quoted in ibid., p. 234.

19 Ibid., pp. 220–63.

20 Ibid., pp. 243–63; Cole, *Martin Van Buren and the American Political System*, pp. 61–62.

21 Glover Moore, *The Missouri Controversy, 1819–1821* (Gloucester, MA, 1967; reprint of 1953 edition), p. 126.

22 Moore, passim; Robert Ernst, *Rufus King: American Federalist* (Chapel Hill, NC, 1968), pp. 369–74; Ammon, pp. 449–57.

23 Maryland Senator William Pinkney.

24 Louisiana Senator James Brown.

25 Josephine Seaton, *William Winston Seaton of The "National Intelligencer"* (New York, 1970; reprint of 1871 edition), pp. 146–47.

26 Irwin, pp. 211–12, 249–50; Moore, p. 182 and *passim*.

27 Ammon, pp. 450–58.

28 Turner, pp. 312–21.

29 Ibid., pp. 312–18.

30 Irwin, p. 262.

31 Ibid., p. 279.

32 Ibid., pp. 264–80.

33 U.S., Congress, Senate, *Annals of Congress*, 17th Cong., 1st sess., pp. 9–43, 157, 174.

34 Irwin, p. 282.

35 Dr. James Bronaugh to Andrew Jackson, February 8, 1822, quoted in Irwin, p. 283, n. 9.

36 Irwin, pp. 280–84.

37 Leonard D. White, *The Jeffersonians: A Study in Administrative History*, 1801–1829 (New York, 1961), pp. 162–79.

38 *Annals of Congress*, 17th Cong., 1st sess., pp. 391–408.

39 Irwin, p. 284; White, p. 179.

40 Irwin, pp. 286–94.

41 *Niles' Weekly Register*, quoted in Irwin, p. 295; *Annals of Congress*, 17th Cong., 2d sess., pp. 10–260.

42 *Annals of Congress*, 18th Cong., 1st sess., p. 26; Irwin, pp. 297–99.

43 *Annals of Congress*, 18th Cong., 1st sess., pp. 127, 766, 788; Irwin, pp. 273, 300.

44 Irwin, pp. 300–311.

45 Henry A. Holmes, quoted in ibid., p. 301, n.43.

Chapter 7

JOHN C. CALHOUN
1825–1832

JOHN C. CALHOUN

Chapter 7

JOHN C. CALHOUN

7th Vice President: 1825–1832

. . . There are no two events in my life, in which I take greater pride, than those to which you have so kindly alluded. My first public act was to contribute . . . to the maintenance of our national rights against foreign aggressions, and my last had been to preserve in their integrity, as far as it depended on men, those principles of presiding in the Senate, which are essentially the most vital of political rights, the freedom of debate . . . it will ever to me be a proud reflection, that I have been thought worthy of suffering in a great cause, . . . the freedom of debate, a cause more sacred than even the liberty of the press.

—JOHN C. CALHOUN, SEPTEMBER 7, 1826 [1]

John C. Calhoun assumed office as the nation's seventh vice president on March 4, 1825, during a period of extraordinary political ferment. The demise of the Federalist party after the War of 1812 had not, as former President James Monroe had hoped, ushered in an "Era of Good Feelings," free from party divisions. Contrary to Monroe's expectations, the partisan strife of earlier years had not abated during his two terms as president but had, instead, infected the Republican party, which had declined into a broad-based but rapidly disintegrating coalition of disparate elements. Five individuals, all of them Republicans, had entered the 1824 presidential contest, one of the most controversial and bitterly contested races in the nation's history. The "National Republicans," a group that included Calhoun, House Speaker Henry Clay, and Secretary of State John Quincy Adams, supported an expansive, nationalist agenda; the "Radicals," allies of Treasury Secretary William Crawford, were strict constructionists and advocates of limited government. Other Republicans had rallied to the standard of Andrew Jackson, a former Tennessee senator and the military hero whose stunning victory at the Battle of New Orleans had salvaged the nation's pride during the War of 1812.

In this momentous contest, John Quincy Adams had emerged the winner, but his victory came at great cost to his administration and to the nation. The election was decided in the House of Representatives, where Clay had used his influence as leader of the western bloc and as Speaker to secure Adams' election. Adams, in turn, had appointed Clay secretary of state, a nomination that stunned Jackson supporters, strict constructionists, and particularly Vice President Calhoun. The "corrupt bargain" deeply offended Calhoun's strict sense of honor and propriety, pushing him toward the opposition camp, a fragmented assortment of Radicals, southern agriculturalists, and men of conscience who shared the vice president's conviction that Adams and Clay had subverted the popular will. These diverse elements, which were frequently at odds with one another, would eventually coalesce to form the Democratic party. But the nation would first pass through a chaotic and turbulent period of political realignment, which Calhoun described for his friend and mentor, Monroe, in the summer of 1826:

. . . Never in any country . . . was there in so short a period, so complete an anarchy of political relations. Every prominent publick man feels, that he has been thrown into a new attitude, and has to reexamine his position, and reapply principles to the situation, into which he was so unexpectedly and suddenly thrown, as if by some might[y] political revolution . . . Was he of the old Republican party? He finds his prominent political companions, who claim and take the lead, to be the very men, against who, he had been violently arrayed till the close of the late war; and sees in the opposite rank, as enemies, those with whom he was proud to rank . . .

Taking it altogether, a new and dangerous state of things has suddenly occurred, of which no one can see the result. It is, in my opinion, more critical and perilous, than any I have ever seen.[2]

Congress was changing, as well. The Senate, as Senator Robert C. Byrd has noted in his authoritative history, was "beginning to challenge the House as the principal legislative forum of the nation." Before the 1820s, the press and public had paid relatively little attention to the Senate's deliberations, being drawn instead to the livelier and more entertaining theater in the House of Representatives. By 1825, the House had become too large to permit the lengthy speeches and extended debates that had drawn observers to its galleries, while in the Senate, growth had brought increased influence. "At the formation of the Government," Calhoun observed in his inaugural remarks, "the members of the Senate were, probably, too small to attract the full confidence of the people, and thereby give to it that weight in the system which the Constitution intended. This defect has, however, been happily removed by an extraordinary growth"—eleven new states, and twenty-two senators, in a thirty-six-year period. The 1819–1820 debate over the extension of slavery into the Missouri territory signalled that an era of increasingly virulent sectional discord had arrived. The Senate, with its equality of representation among states and rules permitting extended debate, would become the forum where sectional concerns were aired, debated, and reconciled during the next quarter century, a momentous era known to scholars as "The Golden Age of the Senate."[3]

Calhoun, who presided over the Senate at the dawning of its Golden Age, had reached the height of his career. Given his meteoritic rise to national prominence as a talented young congressman during the War of 1812 and his solid record of accomplishment as secretary of war during Monroe's administration, he had every reason to assume that he would one day become president.

Calhoun's Early Life and Career

John Caldwell Calhoun was born on March 18, 1782, near Long Canes Creek, an area later known as the Abbeville District, located in present-day McCormick County, South Carolina. His parents, Patrick and Martha Caldwell Calhoun, were of Scotch-Irish ancestry. The Calhouns had immigrated to Pennsylvania during the 1730s and moved steadily southward until 1756, when Patrick reached the South Carolina backcountry.[4] One of the most prosperous planters (and one of the largest slaveowners) in his district, Patrick Calhoun was a leader in local politics; he served in the South Carolina legislature from 1768 to 1774. During the late 1760s, he was a Regulator, one of the self-appointed vigilantes whose well-intentioned but rough efforts to impose justice on a crime-racked frontier wholly lacking in judicial institutions finally prompted the South Carolina legislature to establish circuit courts in the backcountry. During the Revolution, he sided with the patriot cause.[5]

Young John received only a sporadic education during his early years, attending a "field school" for a few months each year. In 1795, he entered a private academy in Appling, Georgia, but the school closed after a few months. The boy plunged into an exhausting course of self-study, but his father's death soon forced him to return to Abbeville to manage the family farm. The disappointed young scholar remained at home until 1800, when his mother and brothers, having recognized his formidable intellectual abilities, returned him to the academy, which had since reopened. He was a diligent student, qualifying for admission to Yale College in 1802.

Calhoun completed his studies at Yale in 1804. After graduation, he spent a month at the Newport, Rhode Island, summer retreat of Floride

Bonneau Colhoun.[6] Mrs. Colhoun was the widow of the future vice president's cousin, Senator John Ewing Colhoun; her daughter, also named Floride, was attractive, well-connected in South Carolina lowcountry circles, and socially accomplished. John C. Calhoun married his young cousin in 1811. The union conferred wealth and social prestige on the earnest young upcountry lawyer, but Calhoun was also attracted to Floride's "beauty of mind . . . soft and sweet disposition," and "amiable and lovable character."[7] Not until later would he experience her stubborn will and unwavering sense of moral rectitude, so like his own.

Calhoun began his legal education in 1804 soon after leaving Newport, studying first in Charleston and later at the Litchfield, Connecticut, school of Tapping Reeve, a distinguished scholar who counted among his former students such notables as James Madison and Aaron Burr. He returned to South Carolina in 1806 and served brief apprenticeships at Charleston and Abbeville. Admitted to the bar in Abbeville in 1807, Calhoun soon found another calling. In the summer of 1807, he helped organize a town meeting to protest the British attack on the American vessel *Chesapeake* off the Virginia coast. His speech recommending an embargo and an enhanced defense posture electrified the militantly nationalistic crowd assembled at the Abbeville courthouse, winning him immediate acclaim. He was elected to the South Carolina legislature, where he served two terms, and in 1810 he won a seat in the United States House of Representatives.[8]

Congressman Calhoun

Calhoun arrived in Washington shortly after the Twelfth Congress convened on November 4, 1811, taking quarters in a boardinghouse soon to be known as the "War Mess." The nation's capital boasted few amenities during the early nineteenth century, and members of Congress rarely brought their families to town. They lodged instead with colleagues from their own states or regions and, as one student of early Washington discovered, "the members who lived together, took their meals together, and spent most of their leisure hours together also voted together with

a very high degree of regularity."[9] Calhoun's mess mates included two members of the South Carolina delegation, Langdon Cheves and William Lowndes; Felix Grundy of Tennessee; and the newly elected Speaker of the House of Representatives, Henry Clay of Kentucky.[10] They, and other like-minded young congressmen known as the "warhawks," believed that nothing short of war would stop British raids on American shipping and restore the young nation's honor.

Calhoun, who had been appointed to the Foreign Affairs Committee[11] at the beginning of his first term and became its chairman in the spring of 1812, played a leading role in the effort, supporting legislation to strengthen the nation's defenses. Working in concert with Secretary of State James Monroe, he introduced the war bill that Congress approved in June 1812.[12] Although Calhoun soon realized that Madison was "wholly unfit for the storms of war," he labored so diligently to defend the administration and to assist in the war effort that he became known as "the young Hercules who carried the war on his shoulders." He was, as a historian of the period has noted, "an administration leader second only to Clay."[13]

Calhoun served in the House until 1817. Sobered by the nation's near-defeat during the War of 1812, he continued his interest in military affairs, opposing troop reductions and advocating the establishment of two additional service academies. As his modern biographer has observed, Calhoun "equated defense with national self-sufficiency." Toward that end, he accepted protective tariffs and helped draft legislation to establish the Second Bank of the United States in 1816. Concerned that the nation's interior settlements lacked the roads and other improvements that he believed essential to economic development and national security, he proposed legislation to earmark for internal improvements the $1.5 million charter fee the bank paid to the federal government, as well as the yields of government-owned bank stocks.[14]

Secretary of War

Calhoun resigned from the House in November 1817 to accept an appointment as secretary of war in President James Monroe's cabinet, a post he would hold for more than seven years. Calhoun was not the president's first choice; Monroe had approached several others, but all had declined. With the nation's military establishment in complete disarray after the war, reforming a badly managed department with over $45 million in outstanding accounts (at a time when the government's annual budget amounted to less than $26 million) seemed to most a near-impossible task. But Calhoun believed that a strong defense establishment was essential to maintaining the nation's honor and security, and he welcomed the chance to reform the troubled department. The thirty-two-year-old cabinet officer was also ambitious and well aware that, as another biographer has noted, "no man had yet held the presidency . . . who had not proved his worth in some executive capacity."[15]

President Monroe relied heavily on his cabinet and submitted all matters of consequence to his department heads before deciding upon a course of action, a practice that assured the gifted young war secretary a prominent role in the new administration.[16] Monroe seems to have felt a special fondness for Calhoun—and for Floride, who moved to Washington and soon became one of the capital's most popular hostesses. Official protocol during the early nineteenth century dictated that the president refrain from "going abroad into any private companies," but when the Calhouns' infant daughter contracted a fatal illness in the spring of 1820, Monroe visited their residence every day to check on her condition.[17]

Calhoun began his first term as secretary of war with an exhaustive review and audit of the department's operations and accounts.[18] Acting on his recommendations, Congress reorganized the army's command and general staff structure, revamped the accounting and procurement systems, and voted annual appropriations to construct fortifications and pay down the war debt. By the end of Calhoun's second term as secretary, outstanding accounts had been reduced from $45 to $3 million.[19] Congress, however, refused to approve Calhoun's proposals for a network of coastal and frontier fortifications and military roads, imposing steep cuts in the defense budget after Treasury Secretary William

Crawford's 1819 annual report projected a budget deficit for 1820 of $7 million (later adjusted to $5 million). Postwar economic expansion had given way to a depression of unprecedented severity, and the panic of 1819 had left hundreds of speculators impoverished and in debt. These conditions, and Crawford's dire forecast, prompted calls for sharp reductions in government expenditures. The war department came under immediate attack, which intensified when the press reported that one of Calhoun's pet projects, an expedition to plant a military outpost on the Yellowstone River, had run significantly over budget.[20]

Some scholars have suggested that Crawford timed the release of his report both to embarrass Monroe and Calhoun and to enhance his own presidential prospects. Shortly afterwards, the president received an anonymous letter alleging that Calhoun's chief secretary had realized substantial profits from an interest in a materials contract. The transaction was not illegal, for war department officials enjoyed considerable latitude in awarding government contracts, and the primary contractor had submitted the lowest bid, but the appearance of impropriety gave Crawford additional ammunition. Congress began an exhaustive review of the war department, with the "Radicals" taking the lead. Although the investigation found no evidence of malfeasance on Calhoun's part, Republicans were inherently suspicious of standing armies, and even the National Republicans were reluctant to fund a peacetime army on the scale envisioned by Calhoun. Congress ultimately reduced the war department budget by close to 50 percent.[21]

The 1824 Presidential Election

Calhoun declared himself a candidate for the presidency in December 1821, much to the surprise of Secretary of State John Quincy Adams, widely considered to be Monroe's heir apparent by virtue of his office. Calhoun and Adams were friends; both avid nationalists, they had also been political allies until the Missouri crisis in 1820 exposed their profound disagreement over slavery. Calhoun, however, became convinced that Adams was too weak a candidate to defeat

Crawford, who enjoyed a significant following within the congressional nominating caucus. The South Carolinian, determined to prevent Crawford's election at any cost, therefore decided to become a candidate himself.

In addition to Calhoun, Adams, and Crawford, the crowded field of prospective candidates for 1824 soon included House Speaker Henry Clay and the revered hero of New Orleans, Andrew Jackson—all Republicans. Calhoun believed that he was the only candidate who could command a national following; he had been warmly received during a visit to the northern and middle states in 1820, and his efforts to strengthen the nation's defenses had won him a following in the West, as well. His quest, however, lost momentum after the South Carolina legislature voted to endorse another favorite son, William Lowndes. Not only did Calhoun face formidable opposition from Crawford's supporters, now ably led by New York Senator Martin Van Buren, but, to the amazement of many, Jackson soon emerged as a leading contender. Calhoun's Pennsylvania supporters eventually declared for Jackson, endorsing Calhoun as their vice-presidential candidate. As other states followed suit, the ambitious young secretary of war was, in one scholar's words, "everybody's 'second choice.'" Thus, in the general election, Calhoun was overwhelmingly elected vice president, with support from both the Jackson and Adams camps.

None of the presidential candidates, however, achieved an electoral majority—although Jackson received a plurality. The election was therefore thrown into the House of Representatives, where each state delegation had a single vote. Having come in fourth in the general election, Clay was not a contender in the House balloting, but he played a pivotal part in determining the outcome by persuading the delegations of the three states he had carried (Ohio, Kentucky and Missouri) to vote for Adams. These three western states, as well as New York, after heavy lobbying by Clay and Massachusetts Representative Daniel Webster, gave Adams the margin he needed to defeat Jackson.

Clay's maneuvering and his subsequent appointment as Adams' secretary of state deeply offended Calhoun, nudging him toward the Jackson camp.[22] He "would probably have coalesced with the Jacksonians in any event," one scholar of the period has surmised, since South Carolina and Pennsylvania, the two states crucial to Calhoun's abortive presidential strategy, had gone for Jackson.[23] But politics alone could not fully account for Calhoun's shift. He knew that the Kentucky legislature had expressly instructed its delegation to vote for Jackson, who had run second to Clay in the general election. Yet, at Clay's urging, the Kentuckians had cast their state's vote for Adams, who had received few, if any, popular votes in the state. "Mr. Clay has made the Prest [President] against the voice of his constituents," Calhoun confided to a friend, "and has been rewarded by the man elevated by him by the first office in his gift, the most dangerous stab, which the liberty of this country has ever received."[24]

The Senate Examines the Role of the Presiding Officer

Wholly lacking in experience as a presiding officer, Calhoun prepared himself for his new responsibilities by studying Jefferson's *Manual of Parliamentary Practice* and other parliamentary authorities.[25] But even this rigorous course of study could not adequately prepare him for the challenges he would face. The Senate, experiencing "growing pains" as it completed its transformation from the "chamber of revision" envisioned by the Constitution's framers to a full-fledged legislative body in its own right, was beginning to reconsider rules and procedures that seemed outdated or impractical. As the Senate's debates became increasingly contentious, the body began rethinking the role of its presiding officer, as well.

Calhoun's difficulties began shortly after the Nineteenth Congress convened in December 1825, when he announced appointments to the Senate's standing committees. Prior to 1823, the Senate had elected committee members by ballot, an awkward and time-consuming process. The rule was revised during the Eighteenth Congress to provide that "all committees shall be appointed by the presiding officer of this House, unless specially ordered otherwise by the Senate." Before Calhoun became vice president, the new procedure had been used only once, on December 9, 1823, the day the Senate adopted the revised rule. On that occasion, Vice President Daniel Tompkins was absent, a frequent occurrence during his troubled tenure, and President pro tempore John Gaillard of South Carolina had appointed the chairmen and members of the Senate's standing committees.

As one scholar of the period has noted, Calhoun made "an honest effort to divide control of the committees between friends and enemies of the administration."[26] An analysis of his appointments suggests that he took into account a senator's experience. He reappointed nine of the fifteen standing committee chairmen whom Gaillard had chosen two years earlier. The two chairmen who had left the Senate he replaced with individuals who had previously served on their respective committees. Of the four remaining committees, three were chaired by senators friendly to the administration. After Military Affairs Committee Chairman Andrew Jackson resigned his seat in October 1825, Calhoun chose as his replacement the only member of the Senate whose military record could match Jackson's—Senator William Henry Harrison, the hero of the Battle of Tippecanoe.[27]

As a result of Calhoun's appointments, senators hostile to the administration retained or gained control of several important committees: Maryland Senator Samuel Smith, a Crawford Republican who would eventually join the Jackson camp, remained in charge of the influential Finance Committee, while New York Senator Martin Van Buren, who would soon unite the opposition forces behind Andrew Jackson, continued to chair the Judiciary Committee. Administration supporters were outraged to learn that the Foreign Relations Committee included only one Adams-Clay man and that its new chairman was Nathaniel Macon of North Carolina, who had voted against confirming Clay as secretary of state.[28] Bitter divisions between administration supporters and the opposition forces were beginning to infect the Senate, and Calhoun, in his attempt to please everyone, had satisfied no one. The pro-administration Philadelphia *Democratic Press* and several other papers vehemently criticized Calhoun, publishing unfounded allega-

tions that he had made the offending appointments after Adams ignored Calhoun's demand to dissociate himself from Henry Clay.[29]

In the meantime, Senator Van Buren had enlisted Calhoun's support for a concerted challenge to the expansive agenda that President Adams outlined in his December 6, 1825, annual message to Congress. Adams had proposed a national university, a national observatory, and a network of internal improvements unprecedented in the nation's history, as well as foreign policy initiatives. In particular, Calhoun, not yet the strict constructionist he would later become, was concerned that Adams' plan to send observers to a conference of South and Central American ministers scheduled to meet in Panama the following year would reinvigorate the sectional tensions that had emerged during the Missouri crisis. Calhoun saw United States participation in the Panama Congress as a perilous first step toward extending diplomatic recognition to Haiti, a nation of former slaves. He had cautioned Adams, through an intermediary, that the initiative would "in the present tone of feelings in the south lead to great mischief." But Clay, an early and enthusiastic supporter of the Latin American independence movements, had prevailed.[30]

The president sent the names of prospective delegates to Panama to the Senate for approval in late December 1825, touching off a protracted and contentious debate that continued through March 14, 1826, when the Senate approved the mission by a narrow margin. Missouri Senator Thomas Hart Benton later reflected that "no question, in its day, excited more heat and intemperate discussion, or more feeling between a President and Senate, than this proposed mission." Although the vice president had "no vote, the constitutional contingency to authorize it not having occurred," Benton recalled, Calhoun had been "full and free in the expression of his opinion against the mission."[31] It was a costly victory for the administration. The United States delegation arrived too late to have any impact on the deliberations, and all but one of the Latin American republics failed to ratify the accords approved at the convention. The president had wasted a great deal of political capital in a confrontation that hardened the party divisions in the Senate, and Calhoun and Van Buren had taken the first tentative steps toward an alliance that would drive Adams from office in the next election.

Calhoun also endorsed the opposition's efforts to curtail the powers of the executive, through constitutional amendments to abolish the electoral college and to limit the president to two terms. Although the Senate had considered similar amendments in previous sessions, the move acquired a new urgency after the 1824 election. Thomas Hart Benton renewed the initiative on December 15, 1825, with a resolution to appoint a select committee "to inquire into the expediency" of choosing the president and vice president "by a direct vote of the People, in districts." Other senators suggested amendments to provide for the election of the president and vice president "without the intervention of the Senate or House of Representatives" and to "prohibit the appointment of any Member of Congress to any office of honor or trust under the United States during the term for which such Senator or Representative should have been elected." The latter proposal represented an obvious slap at Secretary of State Henry Clay, who had resigned from the House to take the executive post.

Calhoun appointed Benton chairman of the select committee, which the Senate directed to determine "the best, most preferable, and safest mode in regard to such elections." Benton was pleased that the other members of the nine-man select committee "were . . . carefully selected, both geographically as coming from different sections of the Union, and personally and politically as being friendly to the object." Only one, Senator John Holmes of Maine, was an Adams man. Calhoun had appointed the administration's most vocal critics to the committee, which reported to the Senate on January 19, 1826, a constitutional amendment calling for the direct election of the president and vice president. Calhoun confided to a correspondent that he expected the administration to resist "all attempts that can limit or counteract the effects of patronage. They will in particular resist any amendment of the Constitution," he predicted, "which will place the Presl [Presidential] election in the hands of the voters, where patronage can have little, or no

effect." As for Calhoun, he promised that "no one who knows me, can doubt where I will be found."[32]

The constitutional debate over the select committee's report took an unexpected turn on March 30, 1826, when Virginia Senator John Randolph rose to address the Senate after North Carolina Senator John Branch offered a resolution protesting the president's appointment of ministers to the Panama Congress "without the advice and consent of the Senate." Randolph was a diehard "Old Republican," a strict constructionist and a resolute opponent of change in any form. Stubbornly clinging to the customs, attire, and rhetoric of a bygone era, he regarded any departure from the dicta of the Founding Fathers as tantamount to heresy. Calhoun thought him "highly talented, eloquent, severe and eccentric," while others, alternately amused and offended by his rambling and caustic speeches, his eighteenth-century dress and manners, and his bizarre behavior, dismissed him as thoroughly insane. His March 30 address was vintage Randolph: a disjointed litany of personal grievances interspersed with his objections to the administration, the Panama Congress, and the "practice . . . that the Secretary of State shall succeed the President." Calhoun remained silent as the agitated Virginian took Adams to task for elevating patronage above patriotism—"buying us up with our own money"—and suggested that Clay had "manufactured" the invitation to the Panama Congress. Even Randolph's likening of Adams and Clay to "Bliful and Black George," two unsavory characters from the popular novel, *Tom Jones*, brought no rebuke from the chair.[33]

After Randolph ended his harangue, the Senate turned to the select committee report. Randolph, trumpeting his opposition "to all amendments to the Constitution," moved to table the report. New Jersey Senator Mahlon Dickerson, who had spoken at great length the previous day in support of his own proposal to limit the president to two terms in office, prepared to speak in opposition to Randolph's motion. He had just started to explain his position when Calhoun cut him short, ruling him out of order on the grounds that "the motion now pending . . . did not admit of debate." Randolph added that "it is unreasonable, after having spoken an hour and thirty-five minutes [the previous day], to speak again to-day'' and explained that he would oppose any effort to amend the Constitution. When Dickerson attempted to respond to Randolph's remarks, Calhoun ruled him out of order a second time. Randolph finally agreed to Dickerson's request to postpone the discussion until the next day, bringing the awkward exchange to an end. On April 3, 1826, the Senate approved the select committee's amendment providing for the direct election of the president and vice president.[34]

Fallout from the explosive session of March 30, 1826, would haunt Calhoun for the remainder of his term. Deeply offended at Randolph's charges, Clay demanded a duel with the Virginian. The resulting nerve-wracking but bloodless encounter ended with a handshake after two exchanges of fire. Those who had expressed amusement at Randolph's March 30 performance, or agreed with him in principle, were suddenly sobered at the thought that the vice president's failure to restrain an intemperate senator had resulted in a near-tragedy.[35] Calhoun's enemies criticized him for twice calling the sedate and congenial Dickerson to order while permitting Randolph to vent his spleen at will. In the following weeks the Senate, for the first time in its history, attempted to define the vice president's legislative duties and responsibilities.

In the decade prior to 1826, the Senate had paid increasing attention to organizational matters, a clear indication of its increased workload, enlarged membership, and heightened importance as a national forum. It had established standing committees in 1816, revised its rules in 1820, and required the publication of regular financial reports by the secretary of the Senate after 1823. The body also enhanced the powers of the chair. Not only had it authorized the presiding officer in 1823 to appoint members of standing and select committees, but in 1824 it also directed the presiding officer to ''examine and correct the Journals, before they are read,'' and to ''have the regulation of such parts of the Capitol . . . as are . . . set apart for the use of the Senate and its officers.''[36] These changes reflect an institution in transition, conscious of its changing role in a rapidly altering political environment. After the

March 30, 1826, spectacle, however, any discussion of Senate rules inevitably invited comment on the vice president's legislative duties and on Calhoun's conduct as president of the Senate.

On April 13, 1826, John Randolph offered a motion to rescind ''so much of the new rules of this House, which give to the presiding officer of this body the appointment of its committees, and the control over the Journal of its proceedings.'' The debate continued on April 15, as several Calhoun supporters, including Van Buren, reviewed ''the considerations that had led the Senate'' to change its rules in 1823 and 1824. The fragmentary published accounts in the *Register of Debates* suggest that, when the Senate vested in the presiding officer the power to appoint committees, it had done so assuming that the president pro tempore would actually make the selections—a reasonable assumption when the debilitated Daniel D. Tompkins served as vice president. Randolph's cryptic remarks on April 12, when he notified the Senate that he would propose the rules changes on the following day, also hint that the Senate had given the presiding officer the responsibility of supervising the *Journal* because the secretary of the Senate had been negligent in performing this important task.

The reporter who followed the April 15 debate was careful to note that ''the gentlemen who favored the present motion, as well as the one who offered it, disclaimed the remotest intention to impute to the Vice President an improper exercise of the duties devolved on him by the rules.'' But the debate took a personal turn after Randolph, sensitive to mounting and widespread criticism of Calhoun for failing to stifle his recent outburst, asserted that ''it is not the duty, nor the right, of the President of the Senate to call a member to order.'' That right, Randolph argued, was reserved to members of the Senate. At the conclusion of the debate, the Senate voted, by overwhelming margins, to resume its former practice of selecting committee members by ballot, and ''to take from the President of the Senate, the control over the Journal of the Proceedings.''[37]

Some contemporary observers, as well as modern day scholars, have interpreted the April 15 vote as a pointed rebuke of a vice president who had exceeded his authority and offended the Senate. On the other hand, the caveats of Van Buren and opposition senators suggest that, although some senators may well have intended to curtail Calhoun's authority, others were animated by concern for maintaining the Senate's institutional prerogatives. Calhoun, edging toward the strict constructionist stance he would champion in later years, seems to have approved of the changes, or at least to have accepted them with his customary grace. "[N]o power ought to be delegated which can be fairly exercised by the constituent body," he agreed shortly after the vote, "and . . . none ought ever to be delegated, but to responsible agents . . . and I should be inconsistent with myself, if I did not give my entire assent to the principles on which the rules in question have been rescinded." Calhoun did bristle, however, at the suggestion that he had been negligent in not calling Randolph to order. He had diligently studied the Senate's rules, he informed the senators, and had concluded that, although the chair could issue rulings on procedural matters, "the right to call to order, on questions touching the latitude or freedom of debate, belongs exclusively to the members of this body, and not to the Chair. The power of the presiding officer . . . is an appellate power only; and . . . the duties of the Chair commence when a Senator is called to order by a Senator." He had been elected vice president by "the People," he reminded the Senate, and "he had laid it down as an invariable rule, to assume no power in the least degree doubtful." [38]

The debate over the vice president's role in the Senate continued a month later on May 18. A select committee chaired by Randolph that had been appointed "to take into consideration the present arrangement of the Senate chamber," reported a resolution that would make access to the Senate floor by anyone other than past and current members of Congress and certain members of the executive and judicial branches contingent upon written authorization by the vice president. The resolution also specified that the officers of the Senate would be responsible to the vice president and that all, except for the secretary of the Senate, would be subject to immediate removal "for any neglect of duty." The Senate chamber would "be arranged under the direction of the Vice President, . . . so as to keep order more effectually in the lobby and the gallery," a change intended to regulate the crowds who were flocking to the Senate galleries in increasing numbers.

As this first session of the Nineteenth Congress neared its end, Senator John Holmes submitted a resolution, for consideration in the next session, to appoint a committee that would consider rules to clarify and enhance the powers of the chair. Randolph moved to take up the Holmes resolution immediately, but Calhoun ruled him out of order on the grounds that "when a member offered a resolution, if he did not desire its consideration, it would lie one day on the table." Undaunted, Randolph moved to instruct the committee that it would be "inconsistent with the rights and privileges of the States" to authorize the chair to call a member. He then proceeded to castigate a Massachusetts editor for his alleged misconduct in the chamber. The debate degenerated into a shouting match after Massachusetts Senator James Lloyd rose to defend his constituent, but Calhoun remained impassive until Alabama Senator William R. King intervened with a call to order. Rigidly adhering to the Senate's rule governing the conduct of debate, Calhoun instructed King "to reduce the exceptionable words to writing." King responded that "it was not necessary to reduce the words to writing," since he had merely intended to "check the gentlemen when they were giving way to effervescence of feeling." Calhoun explained that he had "no power beyond the rules of the Senate;" if King would not comply, Randolph was free to continue. After Randolph finished his diatribe, Calhoun again reminded the Senate that "The Chair . . . would never assume any power not vested in it." [39]

A weary Calhoun left the chair on May 20, 1826, two days before the Nineteenth Congress adjourned, in order to allow for the election of a president pro tempore, but the controversy over his conduct in the Senate continued throughout the spring and summer and into fall. On April 24, the *National Intelligencer* had published a letter from Senator Dickerson, who maintained that Calhoun had treated him with appropriate courtesy and respect during the March 30 debate,[40] as well as a submission from an anonymous "Western Senator" defending the vice president. On May 1, the pro-administration *National Journal* published the first in a series of five articles by "Patrick Henry," an anonymous writer friendly to the administration, charging that Calhoun had abused his office. These essays, which continued through August 8, cited an impressive array of parliamentary scholarship to support the author's contention that Calhoun had been negligent in permitting the "irrelative rhapsodies of a once powerful mind" to disturb the Senate "without one effort of authority, or one hint of disapprobation from its president." The vice president had also allowed "selfish considerations" to influence his committee appointments, "Henry" charged. "From the commencement of the Government until the last session of Congress," the essayist scolded Calhoun in his August 4 installment:

> order had been preserved in the Senate under every Vice-President, and decorum, almost rising to solemnity, had been a distinctive feature of its proceedings. But no sooner were you sent to preside over it, than its hall became, as if by some magic agency, transformed into an arena where political disappointment rioted in its madness.

Modern scholars have never conclusively established the identity of "Patrick Henry," although Calhoun and many others believed him to be President Adams. The vice president responded in his own series of essays, published in the *National Intelligencer* between May 20 and October 12, 1826, under the pseudonym "Onslow," in honor of a distinguished eighteenth-century Speaker of the British House of Commons. Echoing Calhoun's pronouncements in the Senate, the writer's opening salvo offered a forceful defense of the vice president's refusal to restrain "the latitude or freedom of debate." The decision to rule Dickerson out of order had involved a procedural matter, well within the scope of the vice president's authority; silencing Randolph's outburst would have required "a despotic Power, worse than the sedition law." As for the vice president's committee appointments,

"Onslow" maintained in his October 12 epistle, "The only correct rule is, to appoint the able, experienced, and independent, without regard to their feelings towards the Executive." To appoint only pro-administration partisans, he argued, would have drastically expanded the power of an executive who already had "the whole patronage of the Government" at his disposal.[41] These arguments, the modern-era editors of Calhoun's papers have stressed, reveal "the ground principles of all Calhoun's later thinking," and mark "the 'turning point' in Calhoun's career from nationalist and latitudinarian to sectionalist and strict constructionist."[42]

Not until 1828 did the Senate finally revise the rule governing debate to authorize the presiding officer, or any senator, to call a member to order. After this revision was adopted, Calhoun stubbornly remarked that "it was not for him" to comment on the change, assuring the Senate "that he should always endeavor to exercise it with strict impartiality." He did heartily approve of another change adopted in 1828, a revision that made rulings of the chair subject to appeal. "It was not only according to strict principle," he informed the Senate, "but would relieve the Chair from a most delicate duty."[43]

The Calhoun-Jackson Alliance

On June 4, 1826, Calhoun notified Andrew Jackson that he would support his 1828 presidential bid. Calhoun, with his disciplined intellect and rigid sense of propriety, presented a striking contrast to the popular and dashing military hero. The two were never close, and Calhoun never completely trusted Jackson. In fact, several years earlier, while serving in Monroe's cabinet, the South Carolinian had urged the president to discipline Jackson for his unauthorized invasion of Spanish Florida during the Seminole War.[44] But Calhoun needed time to recoup his political fortunes, and Jackson had vowed to serve but a single term if elected president. The old hero welcomed Calhoun's support, assuring him that they would "march hand in hand in their [the people's] cause," cementing one of the most ill-starred partnerships in the history of the vice-presidency.[45]

When Calhoun returned to the Senate for the second session of the Nineteenth Congress in early December, he was relieved to find that he was not "the object of the malignant attack of those in power." He did observe, however, that in the Senate "the line of separation is better drawn, and the feelings on both sides higher than in the last session."[46] Calhoun's respite came to an abrupt halt on December 28, when the Alexandria, Virginia, *Phoenix Gazette*, an administration mouthpiece, resurrected the old charges that Calhoun's chief secretary at the War Department had improperly profited from his interest in a materials contract.[47] On the following day, Calhoun notified Secretary of the Senate Walter Lowrie that he had asked the House of Representatives to investigate the charges and would not preside over the Senate until the matter was resolved. "[A] sense of propriety forbids me from resuming my station till the House has disposed of this subject," he explained.[48]

On January 2, 1827, the Senate chose Nathaniel Macon of North Carolina to preside over its deliberations while a House select committee pursued the allegations. Henry Clay, who still commanded enormous influence in the House of Representatives, played a silent role in the appointment of the House select committee, which was heavily weighted against Calhoun. Even though the committee cleared Calhoun after six weeks of hearings, press accounts of the investigation, combined with the muddled language that Clay had persuaded his allies to insert in the select committee's February 13, 1827, report, contributed to the widespread perception that the vice president had done *something* wrong while serving as secretary of war.[49] Some Jacksonians would have gladly withdrawn their support for Calhoun's vice-presidential bid at that point. But Jackson's chief strategist, Martin Van Buren, insisted that Calhoun was essential to his strategy of forging a coalition of "planters of the South and the plain Republicans of the North" to drive Adams from the White House.[50]

The vice president, for his part, was increasingly disturbed at the concessions that Van Buren seemed willing to make to secure Jackson's election, particularly with respect to the tariff. Van Buren and New York Senator Silas Wright had finessed a protective tariff through the Senate in the spring of 1828. This so-called "Tariff of Abominations" included no concessions to southern agricultural interests, as had previous tariffs, and imposed severe hardships on the region. Still, Calhoun convinced the South Carolina delegation to hold its fire, fearing that the backlash might cost Jackson the election and hoping that Jackson would, if elected, reform the tariff schedules.[51] "[T]he Tariff of the last session excites much feelings in this and the other Southern atlantick states," he wrote to Jackson from South Carolina in July, continuing,

> The belief that those now in power will be displaced shortly, and that under an administration formed under your auspices, a better order will commence, in which an equal distribution of the burden and benefit of government . . . and finally the removal of oppressive duties will be the primary objects of policy is what mainly consoles this quarter of the Union under existing embarrassment.[52]

Jackson and Calhoun won 56 percent of the popular vote in 1828—a sweeping victory widely acclaimed as a triumph for "the common man." The "Jacksonians" boasted an organization vastly more efficient than that of Adams' National Republicans, a factor that had helped them gain control of both houses in the 1827 congressional elections. The presidential campaign was one of the most bitterly contested in the nation's history. Adams' supporters charged Jackson and his wife with immoral conduct (the two had married before Rachel's divorce from her first husband) and Jacksonians countered by reminding the electorate of the "corrupt bargain." Calhoun and the National Republican vice-presidential candidate Richard Rush were barely noticed in the fray.[53]

Candidate Calhoun had spent most of the election year at "Fort Hill," his Pendleton, South Carolina estate, supervising farm operations and, at the request of the South Carolina legislature, preparing a critique of the tariff. His point of departure for the resulting South Carolina "Exposition" was an argument that Jefferson had marshalled three decades earlier in his crusade against the Alien and Sedition Acts: that the

Union was a compact between states, which retained certain rights under the Constitution. But Calhoun carried the argument several steps farther, asserting that a state could veto, or "nullify," any act by the federal government that encroached on its sovereignty or otherwise violated the Constitution. The "Exposition" and an accompanying set of "Protest" resolutions were widely circulated by the South Carolina legislature. Calhoun, wary of jeopardizing his national standing, was careful not to claim authorship, but Jackson and Van Buren soon suspected that the vice president had written the controversial tract.[54]

The Senate Debates Nullification

Calhoun's second vice-presidential term was even more of an ordeal than his first. His suspicions that Jackson might pose as great a threat to popular liberties as his predecessor were soon confirmed. The president failed to repudiate the tariff—clear evidence that he had fallen under Van Buren's spell—and his appointment of the "Little Magician" as secretary of state boded ill for Calhoun. The vice president was soon isolated within an administration where Van Buren and his protectionist allies appeared to be gaining the upper hand.[55]

Calhoun's novel theory came under attack in the Senate early in his second term, during a debate over the disposition of western lands, a lengthy exchange that one historian has termed "the greatest debate in the history of the Senate."[56] The debate began on December 29, when Connecticut Senator Samuel Foot offered a resolution to curtail the sale of public lands in the West. South Carolina Senator Robert Y. Hayne changed the tone of the debate on January 19, 1830, when he argued that the federal government should leave land policy to the states and that individual states could nullify federal legislation. The remainder of the debate, which lasted through January 27, consisted of a spirited exchange between Hayne and Massachusetts Senator Daniel Webster, who summoned all of his formidable oratorical talents in a passionate defense of the Union.

But the Webster-Hayne debate was, in fact, a confrontation between Webster and Calhoun.

Hayne received a steady stream of handwritten notes from the chair as he articulated Calhoun's doctrines for several hours on January 21, and Webster clearly directed at the vice president his second reply to Hayne of January 26–27. His charge that "leading and distinguished gentlemen from South Carolina" had reversed their stand on internal improvements brought an immediate and pointed inquiry from the vice president: "Does the chair understand the gentleman from Massachusetts to say that the person now occupying the chair of the Senate had changed his opinions on the subject of internal improvements?" Webster responded: "If such change has taken place, I regret it. I speak generally of the State of South Carolina."[57]

The president, although not directly involved in the debate, was clearly interested in the outcome. Jackson sympathized with advocates of states' rights, but, as a passionate defender of the Union, he regarded nullification as tantamount to treason. When his friend and adviser, William B. Lewis, having witnessed the sparring between Hayne and Webster from the Senate gallery, reported that Webster was "demolishing our friend Hayne," the president responded with a succinct "I expected it."[58] An open confrontation between Jackson and Calhoun soon followed, at the April 13, 1830, banquet commemorating Jefferson's birthday. The event was a longstanding tradition among congressional Republicans, but the recent use of Jefferson's writings to justify nullification imbued the 1830 celebration with particular significance. Warned in advance by Van Buren that several "nullifiers" were expected to attend, the president and his advisers carefully scripted his remarks. After the meal, and an interminable series of toasts, Jackson rose to offer his own: "Our Union. It must be preserved." Calhoun was well prepared with an explosive rejoinder: "The Union. Next to our liberty, the most dear." Jackson had the last word a few days later, when he asked a South Carolina congressman about to depart for home to "give my compliments to my friends in your State, and say to them, that if a single drop of blood shall be shed there in opposition to the laws of the United States, I will hang the first man I can lay my hand on engaged in such treasonable conduct, upon the first tree I can reach." [59]

Jackson Repudiates Calhoun

Even without Calhoun's intransigence on the tariff and nullification, Jackson had ample reason to dislike his vice president. In May 1830, the president finally received incontrovertible proof that Calhoun, as he had long suspected, had urged Monroe's cabinet to censure him for his invasion of Spanish Florida during the Seminole War. Demanding an explanation from Calhoun, Jackson was stunned when the vice president responded that he could not "recognize the right on your part to call in question my conduct." Calhoun went on to explain that neither he, as secretary of war, nor President Monroe had authorized the occupation of the Spanish posts in Florida, and that "when orders were transcended, investigation, as a matter of course, ought to follow." His opponents had resurrected a long-forgotten incident to discredit him in Jackson's eyes, the vice president warned. "I should be blind not to see, that this whole affair is a political manoeuvre." Thus began a lengthy and strident correspondence, which concluded only after Jackson wrote from his Tennessee home in mid-July that "I feel no interest in this altercation . . . and now close this correspondence forever," and Calhoun concurred that the correspondence "is far from being agreeable at this critical juncture of our affairs." Anxious to contradict inaccurate press accounts of his quarrel with the president, Calhoun published the correspondence in the *United States' Telegraph* of February 17 and 25, 1831, prefaced with a lengthy explanation addressed "To the People of the United States." His break with Jackson, so long in the making, was now complete. [60]

Calhoun soon found himself completely eclipsed by Van Buren. After a longstanding dispute over official protocol had culminated in the resignation of the entire cabinet in April 1831, all of Jackson's new secretaries were Van Buren men. Calhoun had his wife Floride to thank for this unfortunate development. Mrs. Calhoun, the unofficial arbiter of Washington society, had thrown the capital into turmoil with her deliberate snub of Secretary of War John Eaton and his wife, Peggy. Peggy Eaton was a lively and attractive woman of dubious reputation and a special favorite of the president. The daughter of an innkeeper, she was clearly not the social equal of the haughty and highly critical Floride. She had married Eaton, a boarder at her father's hotel, soon after her first husband had died at sea—Washington scandalmongers hinted that he had taken his life in despair after learning of Peggy's affair with Eaton. Floride's reputation as an accomplished hostess, her husband's position, and the fact that both the president and Van Buren were widowers gave her enormous influence in Washington society. When she refused to return Peggy Eaton's calls, several of the cabinet wives followed suit.

Floride's actions put her husband in an awkward position, but he acquiesced in her decision because he regarded social protocol as her rightful sphere of authority and because he knew that nothing he did or said would shake her resolve. The president, who considered Eaton "more like a son to me than anything else"—and later pronounced Peggy "chaste as a virgin"—was sorely offended. His outrage was compounded by memories of his late wife, Rachel, who had suffered a fatal heart attack after hearing the vicious attacks on her character that the Adams camp had circulated during the presidential campaign.

The "Petticoat War" split the cabinet for well over a year, with Van Buren emerging the winner. The shrewd and gallant widower had conspicuously entertained the Eatons and orchestrated the cabinet's resignation to resolve the impasse. Jackson was profoundly grateful to Van Buren for the opportunity to purge his cabinet of Calhoun's supporters, and rewarded him with an appointment as ambassador to Great Britain. [61]

Nullification Leader

Calhoun initially believed that his break with Jackson would only enhance his chances of winning the presidency in 1832. He still enjoyed considerable support in the South and believed he might be able to reconcile southern agriculturalists and northern manufacturers with selective modifications in the tariff schedules. But events in South Carolina soon forced him to make public his position on the tariff and nullification, a move that effectively killed his chances of ever becoming president. In the summer of 1831, Calhoun protégé George McDuffie electrified a Charleston, South Carolina, audience with a fiery declamation advocating nullification *and* secession. Calhoun was horrified at this development, as well as by accounts that South Carolina merchants were refusing to pay duties that they considered unconstitutional. Calhoun had advanced the doctrine of nullification to provide southern states with a peaceful mechanism for obtaining redress of their grievances, never contemplating the possibility of disunion. He had not endorsed secession in his 1828 "Exposition," arguing that a state could veto and refuse to enforce any law it considered unconstitutional, but, if three fourths of the states subsequently affirmed the law, the nullifying state must defer to the collective will.

Until this point, Calhoun had never publicly claimed authorship of his controversial doctrine, but now he felt compelled to assume control of the nullification movement to minimize its destructive potential. He published in the July 26, 1831, issue of the Pendleton, South Carolina, *Messenger* his first public statement on nullification, the "Rock Hill Address," a forceful restatement of the principles first articulated in the South Carolina "Exposition." Calhoun was well aware of the risk he had assumed. "I can scarcely dare hope," he conceded shortly after the "Rock Hill Address" appeared in print, "that my friends to the North will sustain me in the positions I have taken, tho' I have the most thorough conviction that the doctrines I advanced, must ultimately become those of the Union; or that it will be impossible to preserve the Union." Once the most ardent of nationalists, Calhoun would henceforth be known as the South's advocate and, by Jackson supporters, as a traitor.[62]

Calhoun "Elects" a Vice President

Calhoun returned to Washington after a lengthy absence in time for the opening of the Twenty-second Congress in December 1831. He had devoted the time since the Twenty-first Congress had adjourned on March 3 to nullification and to his anticipated presidential campaign.

One of the first items on the Senate's agenda was the confirmation of Jackson's reconstituted cabinet. The Senate approved these nominations without incident, but Jackson's appointment of former Secretary of State Martin Van Buren as ambassador to Great Britain aroused a firestorm of controversy. Henry Clay, leading the anti-Jackson forces in the Senate, blamed Van Buren for the "pernicious system of party politics adopted by the present administration,"[63] a sentiment shared by many disaffected Jacksonians and Calhoun supporters, as well.

Tempers flared as the Senate debated the controversial nomination on January 24 and 25, 1832, with several senators venting their anger at the administration. Massachusetts Senator Daniel Webster took Van Buren to task for his trade policies, while his southern colleagues, Senators Stephen Miller of South Carolina and George Poindexter of Mississippi, took aim at Van Buren's personal life. When Missouri's Alexander Buckner rose to Van Buren's defense, asserting that only a "liar" would accuse Van Buren of malfeasance or misconduct, Vice President Calhoun ruled him out of order. Georgia Senator John Forsyth, a staunch Jackson man, pointedly reminded the vice president, "[I]f you remember your own decisions you must know that you are grossly out of order for this interference." Forsyth clearly intended to taunt Calhoun, not to raise a substantive objection, since the Senate had, four years earlier, revised its rules to authorize the presiding officer to call a member to order.

The debate over Van Buren's appointment ended in a tied vote—orchestrated, one scholar suggests, to give the vice president the "distinction and honor of defeating Van Buren's nomination." Calhoun, as expected, cast his vote against the nomination, a decision that, Missouri Senator Thomas Hart Benton predicted, "elected a Vice President."[64] But Benton was only partially correct. Rigid in defense of his principles, but wholly lacking the abundant political skills of the "Little Magician," Calhoun had played into Van Buren's hands throughout his second term as vice president. His decision to assume control of the South Carolina nullification movement had already killed his presidential prospects. Van

Buren would become the Democratic vice-presidential candidate in 1832 and would succeed Jackson as president four years later.

Calhoun spent the remainder of the year in the Senate disheartened by the enactment of the 1832 tariff. That measure was intended to reconcile northern manufacturers and all but the most diehard free traders, but, in one scholar's assessment, it "satisfied neither protectionists nor free traders." [65] "It is, in truth," Calhoun wrote to a kinsman as the Senate labored over the tariff in early March 1832, "hard to find a midle [sic] position, where the principle of protection is asserted to be essential on one side, and fatal on the other. It involves not the question of concession, but surrender." [66] In early July, a despairing Calhoun offered a gloomy précis of the Senate's action on the tariff:

> We have spent a long & fruitless season. The Tariff Bill was late last evening ordered to the 3d. reading in the senate with many amendments all going to increase the burden on us. Every southern member voted against it including the South West, with the exception of the Senators from Louisiana. The question is no longer one of free trade, but liberty and despotism. The hope of the country now rests on our gallant little State. Let every Carolinian do his duty. Those who do not join us now intend unqualified submission. [67]

Senator Calhoun

In South Carolina, where antitariff sentiments had reached a fever pitch, Calhoun found it increasingly difficult to contain the deadly forces that he had unwittingly unleashed. Nullifiers gained control of the state legislature in the fall 1832 election. The new legislature promptly called for a nullification convention, which passed an ordinance declaring the 1828 and 1832 tariffs void as of February 1, 1833. The Ordinance of Nullification also warned that, if the administration resorted to coercion to collect the offensive duties, South Carolina would "proceed to organize a separate government." An irate Jackson ordered reinforcements to the federal installations surrounding Charleston Harbor but soon announced his support for a revised tariff. On December 10, he proclaimed nullification "incompatible with the existence of the Union."

Calhoun would help defuse this explosive situation, but not as vice president. Elected to the Senate to replace Robert Hayne, he resigned the vice-presidency on December 28, 1832, more than two months before his term was up. Except for a brief stint as secretary of state during John Tyler's administration, he spent the rest of his life in the Senate, valiantly defending his state and attempting to reconcile its interests with those of the nation at large. Undaunted by rumors that Jackson intended to try him for treason if the impasse over nullification resulted in an armed confrontation, Calhoun joined forces with Henry Clay to help guide through the Senate a revised tariff, acceptable to the southern states. The nullifiers, encouraged by the prospect of a more equitable tariff, and counseled by coolheaded emissaries from Virginia to show restraint, postponed the effective date of the ordinance until March 4. Jackson's supporters had, in the meantime, introduced a measure to force South Carolina's compliance with the old tariff, which passed the Senate by overwhelming margins. Calhoun and eight of his fellow senators stalked out of the chamber in protest when the Senate adopted the "Force bill," but Jackson never had occasion to employ its provisions against the nullifiers. The crisis passed after Congress approved both the revised tariff and the Force bill shortly before adjourning on March 3, 1833. Calhoun returned to South Carolina firmly convinced that nullification had "dealt the fatal blow" to the tariff. [68]

For the next several years, Calhoun remained aloof from the Jacksonian coalition, which had become known as the Democratic party. But during Van Buren's administration, from 1837 to 1841, he set aside his longstanding aversion to "the Little Magician" and risked the wrath of his fellow South Carolinians to support the independent treasury plan, Van Buren's solution to the credit and currency problems that he and Calhoun believed responsible for the 1837 depression. Alarmed at the prospect that Whig presidential candidate William Henry Harrison would back tariff concessions for special interests, Calhoun rejoined the Democrats in 1840 and began making plans to enter the 1844 presidential race.[69]

Hoping to present himself as an independent candidate with no institutional affiliation, Calhoun resigned from the Senate on March 3, 1843. His campaign faltered, however, when several prominent Virginia Democrats backed Van Buren and the New York City convention followed suit. Calhoun consoled himself by focusing his attention on his farm, badly in debt after several years of depressed cotton prices, and his family, torn by a protracted financial disputes between Calhoun's son, Andrew Pickens Calhoun, and his son-in-law, Thomas Green Clemson. In mid-March 1844, he accepted President John Tyler's offer of an appointment to succeed Secretary of State Abel Upshur, who had been killed by an exploding cannon during an outing on the ship *Princeton*. Calhoun remained at the State Department until Tyler's term ended on March 3, 1845, participating in the final stages of the negotiations for the Texas Annexation Treaty.[70]

Calhoun returned to the Senate in November 1845 and remained there for the rest of his life. Increasingly defensive about the institution of slavery as the abolition movement gained momentum, and agitated at the growing discord between the slaveholding and free states, he spoke, as he informed the Senate in 1847, as "a Southern man and a slaveholder." As secretary of state Calhoun had strongly supported the annexation of Texas. After Pennsylvania Representative David Wilmot offered his famous proviso as an amendment to an administration war bill, however, the South Carolina senator realized that the acquisition of additional territory would inevitably heighten the sectional conflict over slavery. The Wilmot Proviso, which would have barred slavery from all lands acquired from Mexico, pushed Calhoun into the anti-administration camp. He vehemently opposed the war policy of President James K. Polk, warning that the acquisition of Mexican territory, with its population of "pure Indians and by far the larger portion of the residue mixed blood," would corrupt the nation's culture and institutions.[71]

By 1850, the precarious balance between the slaveholding and free states was again at risk.

California's petition to enter the Union as a free state threatened to upset the delicate equilibrium. Other unresolved issues, too, including slavery in the District of Columbia and the enforcement of fugitive slave laws, loomed large on the horizon during the final weeks of Calhoun's life. To resolve the impasse, Calhoun's old friend and rival, Henry Clay, on January 29, 1850, offered a series of proposals, collectively known as the Compromise of 1850. Clay proposed that California enter the Union as a free state and that Congress agree to impose no restrictions on slavery in the New Mexico and Utah territories. The compromise also provided that Congress would not prohibit or regulate slavery in the District of Columbia, would abolish the slave trade in the District, and would require northern states to comply with fugitive slave laws. Massachusetts Senator Daniel Webster sought Calhoun's support for the compromise, but the South Carolinian, vehemently opposed to abolishing the slave trade in the nation's capital and admitting California as a free state, refused to endorse the plan.

On March 4, a dispirited and emaciated Calhoun, his body so ravaged by tuberculosis that he could no longer walk unassisted and his once penetrating voice so weak that he could no longer speak, presented his final address to the Senate. Virginia Senator James Mason spoke for Calhoun, who sat nearby, his pitiful frame huddled in his chair. Only an immediate halt to antislavery agitation and a constitutional amendment to preserve the balance between North and South would save the Union, Calhoun warned. Even senators who had long considered Calhoun a disunionist were shocked when Mason pronounced his ultimatum: if the northern states were unwilling to reconcile their differences with the South "on the broad principle of justice and duty, say so; and let the States we both represent agree to separate and part in peace." Three days later, Senator Webster delivered his famous "Seventh of March" speech, a ringing plea for compromise and Union that Calhoun interrupted with a resolute, "No sir! the Union can be broken"—one of his last utterances in the Senate.[72]

The Senate ultimately approved Clay's compromise, not as a package, but as separate items. Calhoun died on March 31, 1850, convinced that his beloved South would one day withdraw from the Union he had labored so long and hard to strengthen and preserve. Even in death, he was a controversial figure. Senator Thomas Hart Benton refused to speak at the April 5 memorial service in the Senate chamber; Calhoun was "not dead," he maintained. "There may be no vitality in his body, but there is in his doctrines." Senator Daniel Webster, one of the official mourners chosen by the Senate to accompany Calhoun's body to South Carolina, could not bring himself to perform this awkward and painful task. He took his leave from Calhoun at the Virginia landing as the funeral party departed for the South. Calhoun was buried in Charleston, in a crypt in St. Philip's churchyard.[73]

NOTES

[1] Clyde N. Wilson and W. Edwin Hemphill, eds., *The Papers of John C. Calhoun*, vol. 10 (Columbia, SC, 1977), pp. 199–203.

[2] John C. Calhoun to James Monroe, June 23, 1826, *Calhoun Papers*, 10:132–35.

[3] U.S., Congress, Senate, *The Senate, 1789–1989: Addresses on the History of the United States Senate*, by Robert C. Byrd, S. Doc. 100–20, 100th Cong., 1st sess., vol. 1, 1988, p. 88; U.S., Congress, Senate, *Journal*, 18th Cong., special session of March 4, 1825, pp. 271–74.

[4] John Niven, *John C. Calhoun and the Price of Union* (Baton Rouge, LA, 1988), p. 10.

[5] Niven, pp. 1–12; for an account of the Regulator movement, see Richard Maxwell Brown, *The South Carolina Regulators* (Cambridge, 1963).

[6] By the eighteenth century, the family had changed the spelling of their name, originally "Colquhoun" (after the Scottish clan of that name), with one branch of the family adopting the most commonly known spelling, "Calhoun," and the other spelling the name "Colhoun." Charles M. Wiltse, *John C. Calhoun*, vol. 1, *Nationalist, 1782–1828* (New York, 1968; reprint of 1944 ed.), p. 12; Niven, p. 20.

[7] Wiltse, *John C. Calhoun: Nationalist*, p. 50.

[8] Niven, pp. 21–34; Merrill D. Peterson, *The Great Triumvirate: Webster, Clay, and Calhoun* (New York, 1987), pp. 23–27.

[9] James Sterling Young, *The Washington Community, 1800–1828* (New York, 1966), pp. 97–102.

[10] Niven, pp. 34–35; Peterson, p. 23.

[11] The Committee on Foreign Affairs did not become a standing committee of the House of Representatives until 1822. U.S., Congress, House of Representatives, *Guide to the Records of the United States House of Representatives at the National Archives, 1789–1989*, 100th Cong., 2d sess. (Washington, 1989), p. 135.

[12] Peterson, p. 18; Niven, pp. 41–52; Harry Ammon, *James Monroe: The Quest for National Identity* (Charlottesville, VA, 1990; reprint of 1971 edition), p. 309; James F. Hopkins, "Election of 1824," in History of American Presidential Elections, 1789–1968, ed. Arthur M. Schlesinger, Jr., and Fred L. Israel, vol. 1 (New York, 1971), p. 354.

[13] Peterson, pp. 18, 39.

[14] Charles Sellers, The Market Revolution: Jacksonian America, 1815–1846 (New York, 1991), pp. 76–79; Peterson, p. 49; Niven, pp. 51–57. President James Madison vetoed the "Bonus Bill" on Constitutional grounds.

[15] Niven, pp. 58–60; Ammon, pp. 357–60, 470; Richard W. Barsness, "John C. Calhoun and the Military Establishment, 1817–1825," *Wisconsin Magazine of History* 50 (Autumn 1966), pp. 43–53; Wiltse, *John C. Calhoun: Nationalist*, p. 140.

[16] Young, pp. 230–31.

[17] Allan Nevins, ed., *The Diary of John Quincy Adams, 1794–1845* (New York, 1951), p. 354; Wiltse, *John C. Calhoun: Nationalist*, pp. 208–209.

[18] Peterson, pp. 87–88.

[19] Barsness, pp. 43–53; Ammon, p. 470.

[20] Ammon, pp. 470–72; Peterson, pp. 88–89, 93; Niven, pp. 78–79. See also Chapter 9 of this volume, "Richard Mentor Johnson," pp. 123–24.

[21] Barsness, pp. 43–53; Niven, pp. 86–93.

[22] Peterson, pp. 116–31; Hopkins, pp. 349–81; Niven, pp. 93–109.

[23] Peterson, p. 130.

[24] John C. Calhoun to J.G. Swift, in *Calhoun Papers*, 10:9–10.

[25] Niven, p. 116; for Calhoun's caveat that he was "without experience, which only can give the requisite skill in presiding," see his March 4, 1825, inaugural address, U.S., Congress, Senate, *Journal*, 18th Cong., special sess. of March 4, 1825, pp. 272–73.

[26] Peterson, p. 136.

[27] For a list of committee chairmen during the 18th Congress, see U.S., Congress, Senate, *Annals of Congress*, 18th Cong., 1st sess., p. 27; a comprehensive list of committee chairs from 1789 through 1992 appears in Byrd, *The Senate, 1789–1989*, vol. 4, *Historical Statistics, 1789–1992* (Washington, 1993), pp. 522–81.

[28] Peterson, p. 136; Niven, p. 114. Macon had served as a member of the Foreign Relations Committee in the 18th Congress; Virginia Senator James Barbour, a Crawford Republican who served as the committee's chairman during that Congress, had resigned in March 1825, to accept an appointment as secretary of war. *Annals of Congress*, 18th Cong., 1st sess., p. 27; U.S., Congress, Senate, *Biographical Directory of the United States Congress, 1771–1989*, S. Doc. 100–34, 100th Cong., 2d sess., 1989, pp. 574–75.

[29] Peterson, p. 136.

[30] Niven, pp. 113–15; Peterson, pp. 136–40; Robert V. Remini, *Martin Van Buren and the Making of the Democratic Party* (New York, 1959), pp. 105–13.

[31] Thomas Hart Benton, *Thirty Years View; or, A History of the Working of the American Government for Thirty Years, from 1820 to 1850* (New York, 1871; reprint of 1854 edition), vol. 1, pp. 65–69; Remini, *Martin Van Buren and the Making of the Democratic Party*, pp. 105–13. The Senate confirmed the appointments of John Sergeant and Richard Clark Adams as delegates to the Panama Congress by a vote of 24 to 20.

[32] U.S., Congress, *Register of Debates in Congress*, 19th Cong., 1st sess., pp. 384–406; Benton, 1:78; John C. Calhoun to Micah Sterling, February 4, 1826, in *Calhoun Papers*, 10:72–73.

[33] Robert V. Remini, *Henry Clay: Statesman for the Union* (New York, 1991), pp. 292–93; Niven, pp. 114–16; Peterson, pp. 140–41; *Register of Debates in Congress*, 19th Cong., 1st sess., pp. 384–406.

[34] *Register of Debates in Congress*, 19th Cong., 1st sess., pp. 384–407. The amendment was sent to the House of Representatives, where it died in committee.

[35] Remini, *Henry Clay*, pp. 293–95; Peterson, pp. 140–42.

[36] *Annals of Congress*, 18th Cong., 1st sess., pp. 114–17; U.S., Congress, Senate, *Journal*, 18th Cong., 1st sess., pp. 106, 114, 125.

[37] *Register of Debates in Congress*, 19th Cong., 1st sess., pp. 525–26, 571–73.

[38] Senator John Holmes of Maine noted, in his April 15, 1826 remarks, that proposed rules changes "had proceeded from an intimate personal friend of the Vice President, which will itself contradict the presumption that any conduct" of Calhoun's "had induced the proposition." His remarks brought an immediate disclaimer from the ever-erratic Randolph that he had "offered the resolution in no such character . . . of the personal friend or enemy of any gentleman on this floor with one exception." *Register of Debates in Congress*, 19th Cong., 1st sess., pp. 571–74.

[39] *Register of Debates in Congress*, pp. 754–59.

[40] Editorial note and summary, *Calhoun Papers*, 10:91.

[41] The essays of "Patrick Henry" appear in *Calhoun Papers*, 10:91–96; 113–27; 165–75; 175–87; 188–97; for the "Onslow" essays, see pp. 99–104; 135–47; 147–155; 208–215; 215–21; 223–33. See also the editors' introduction, xix-xxx.

[42] *Calhoun Papers*, 10:xxi.

[43] *Register of Debates in Congress*, 20th Cong., 1st sess., pp. 278–341 ("Powers of the Vice President").

[44] John C. Calhoun to Andrew Jackson, June 4, 1826, *Calhoun Papers*, 10:110–11; Peterson, pp. 151–52; Niven, pp. 68–71, 119–21.

[45] Harry L. Watson, *Liberty and Power: The Politics of Jacksonian America* (New York, 1990), pp. 73–74.

[46] John C. Calhoun to Lt. James Edward Colhoun, December 24, 1826, *Calhoun Papers*, 10:238–40.

[47] Alexandria *Phoenix Gazette*, December 28, 1826, *Calhoun Papers*, 10:241–42.

[48] John C. Calhoun to the secretary of the Senate, December 29, 1826, *Calhoun Papers*, 10:243.

[49] Niven, pp. 124–26; editorial note, *Calhoun Papers*, 10:246.

[50] John C. Calhoun to the Rev. Moses Waddel, February 24, 1827, *Calhoun Papers*, 10: 266–67; Niven, pp. 125–26.

[51] Niven, pp. 131–37; Peterson, pp. 159–61.

[52] John C. Calhoun to Andrew Jackson, July 10, 1828, *Calhoun Papers*, 10:395–97.

[53] Robert V. Remini, "Election of 1828," in Schlesinger and Israel, eds., pp. 413–33.

[54] Niven, pp. 154–78; Peterson, pp. 169–70.

[55] Niven, pp. 165–69.

[56] Peterson, p. 170.

[57] Byrd, *The Senate, 1789–1989*, vol. 3, *Classic Speeches, 1830–1993* (Washington, 1994), pp. 1–77; Robert V. Remini, *Andrew Jackson and the Course of American Freedom, 1822–1832* (New York, 1981), pp. 232–33; Peterson, pp. 170–83; Niven, pp. 169–72.

[58] Remini, *Jackson and the Course of American Freedom*, p. 233.

[59] Ibid., pp. 185–86; Peterson, pp. 233–37.

[60] Remini, *Jackson and the Course of American Freedom*, pp. 240–47; Peterson, pp. 187–89; Niven, pp. 174–75. For the Calhoun-Jackson correspondence regarding the Seminole War investigation, and an account of Calhoun's subsequent publication of the exchange, see Clyde N. Wilson, ed., *The Papers of John C. Calhoun*, vol. 11 (Columbia, SC, 1978), pp. 94–96, 159–225, 285, 334–38.

[61] Remini, *Jackson and the Course of American Freedom*, pp. 161–63, 320–21; Peterson, pp. 183–85; Niven, pp. 167–69, 174. For further discussion of this incident, see Chapter 8 of this volume, "Martin Van Buren," p. 108.

[62] Niven, pp. 180–84; Charles M. Wiltse, *John C. Calhoun*, vol. 2, *Nullifier, 1829–1839* (New York, 1968; reprint of 1949 ed.), pp. 110–20; John C. Calhoun to Samuel D. Ingham, July 31, 1831, *Calhoun Papers*, 11:441–45.

[63] Remini, *Jackson and the Course of American Democracy*, p. 347.

[64] Ibid., pp. 347–49; Niven, pp. 185–87; Peterson, p. 203; *Register of Debates in Congress*, 20th Cong., 1st sess., pp. 278–341.

[65] Peterson, pp. 203–9.

[66] John C. Calhoun to Francis W. Pickens, March 2, 1832, *Calhoun Papers*, 11:558–59.

[67] John C. Calhoun to Samuel D. Ingham, July 8, 1832, *Calhoun Papers*, 11:602–3.

[68] Niven, pp. 189–99; Richard E. Ellis, *The Union at Risk: Jacksonian Democracy, States' Rights, and the Nullification Crisis* (New York, 1987), pp. 74–91, and *passim*.

[69] Niven, pp. 200–58.

[70] Ibid., pp. 259–82.

[71] Ibid., pp. 295–313.

[72] Ibid., pp. 339–45; Peterson, pp. 449–66.

[73] Peterson, pp. 467–68; Niven, pp. 343–45.

Chapter 8

MARTIN VAN BUREN
1833–1837

MARTIN VAN BUREN

Chapter 8

MARTIN VAN BUREN

8th Vice President: 1833–1837

a true man with no guile

—Andrew Jackson on Martin Van Buren [1]

you were a great intriguer—the author of sundry plots

—William L. Marcy to Martin Van Buren [2]

Few people ever *really* knew Martin Van Buren. The impeccable attire, ready wit, and unfailing tact that set him apart from his contemporaries masked a nagging sense of insecurity that dogged him throughout his political career. His father, a tavern keeper of modest means, had been able to provide him with only a rudimentary education. One of Van Buren's better-educated associates observed that his "knowledge of books outside of his profession was more limited than that of any other public man" he had ever known and that Van Buren never prepared a state paper without asking a friend to "revise and correct that document."

Van Buren received his real education in the turbulent and factious world of New York politics, and he was an apt pupil. He learned to hold his counsel as others debated the hotly contested issues of the day, carefully observing the course of a debate and weighing all of the issues before staking out a position of his own. "Even after deciding on a course of action," one scholar has observed, "Van Buren might move with an air of evasiveness." Circumspect to a fault, he "enjoyed a name for noncommittalism that survived when most other things about him were forgotten." [3]

Reviled as a "schemer" and a master "manipulator" by contemporaries who lacked (and prob-

ably envied) his uncanny political acumen, he was known throughout his career by an unparalleled assortment of nicknames, none of them entirely favorable. But "the Little Magician" (also known as "the American Talleyrand," "the Red Fox of Kinderhook," the "Mistletoe Politician," and by a variety of other sobriquets) [4] left a solid record of accomplishment that few of his better-known fellows could rival. More than any other individual of his time, Van Buren realized the importance of party organization, discipline, and political patronage. He engineered Andrew Jackson's victory in the 1828 presidential election and later became a trusted confidant and adviser to "Old Hickory," a relationship that continued after Van Buren became vice president in 1833. No previous vice president enjoyed a greater measure of influence than Van Buren, and no vice president, in over three decades, had assumed that office as the "heir apparent."

Van Buren's Early Years

Martin Van Buren was born on December 5, 1782, in the predominantly Dutch community of Kinderhook, New York. His father, Abraham, was a tavern keeper and farmer of modest means; his mother, Maria Goes [5] Van Alen, was a widow with two sons from her first marriage. Both were of undiluted Dutch ancestry, a fact that Van Buren took care to note in his *Autobiog-*

raphy. One of the six children born to Abraham and Maria, Martin grew up in a crowded household, lodged above his father's tavern. From his father, a resolute opponent of Federalism, he inherited his genial manners and political creed but very little else. Dilatory about collecting his debts and generous beyond his means, Abraham barely supported his large family. Young Martin inherited his ambition from his mother, who insisted that her sons receive the best education possible, given their limited resources. He attended a local school until the age of fifteen, then served as an apprentice to Francis Sylvester, a local lawyer. During his apprenticeship, Van Buren became involved in local politics, attending his district's 1800 Republican convention and helping to elect John Peter Van Ness to the United States House of Representatives in 1801. These activities strained his relationship with Sylvester, a prominent Federalist, and Van Buren terminated their arrangement after the election. Van Ness, grateful for Van Buren's efforts on his behalf, paid his young supporter's travel and expenses while he finished his legal studies in New York City, clerking for the congressman's brother, William.

New York City politics fascinated Van Buren, but he returned to Kinderhook shortly after his admission to the bar in 1803 to establish a legal practice with his half brother, James Van Alen. In leaving the city he also sought to distance himself from the intraparty warfare that infected the New York Republican coalition after the 1800 presidential election. In Kinderhook, much of Van Buren's time was spent defending tenants and small landholders in suits against the powerful Livingston clan. The Livingstons, landed gentry whose control of the New York legislature had helped them expand their extensive holdings by questionable means, had retained the best legal minds in the state. Rigorous and careful preparation on Van Buren's part helped him prevail against these notable attorneys and won him the respect of De Witt Clinton, Governor George Clinton's nephew and political heir. Van Buren backed Clinton's candidate, future Vice President Daniel D. Tompkins, in the 1807 gubernatorial race and received for his efforts an appointment as Columbia County surrogate on March 20, 1808.[6]

In 1808, Van Buren married Hannah Hoes, a distant relative, and settled in Hudson, the Columbia County seat. The marriage was a happy one, notwithstanding the frequent absences imposed by the demands of Martin's career, but by the time their fifth son was born in 1817, Hannah had contracted a fatal case of tuberculosis. Van Buren was profoundly affected by her death in 1819; although much in demand as an escort and dinner companion, particularly during the years that he lived in Washington, he never remarried.[7]

Van Buren served as Columbia County surrogate from 1808 until 1812, when he was elected to the New York senate. During the War of 1812, he was an avid supporter of the administration's war effort, offering legislation to facilitate mobilization of the state's defenses. He opposed the Federalists' antiwar stance and broke with his mentor, De Witt Clinton, after learning that Clinton had solicited Federalist support for his 1812 presidential bid. In 1815, Van Buren became state attorney general and moved his family to Albany. He held that office until 1819 and continued to serve in the state senate until 1820, delegating his growing legal practice to his junior partner, Benjamin F. Butler.[8]

Van Buren soon emerged as the guiding force of the "Bucktail" faction, one of several groups jockeying for control of the New York Republican party. The Bucktails, opponents of De Witt Clinton who took their name from the distinctive plumes they affixed to their hats, rapidly gained in influence under Van Buren's tutelage. A Bucktail-controlled convention made major revisions in New York's constitution in 1821–1822, expanding the suffrage and curbing aristocratic influence, reforms that helped break De Witt Clinton's hold on the state Republican party. In 1821, Van Buren won election to the United States Senate, leaving behind a formidable political organization, popularly known as the "Albany Regency," that would manage the New York Republican party—and through it, the state—while he was away. The Regency maintained rigid discipline, rewarding loyalty with patronage appointments and disciplining errant members. Although centered in Albany, the organization's control also extended to local political organizations and clubs. Powerful as Van Buren's apparatus became, "It was not," one scholar of the period emphasizes, "so much the rewarding of partisans and the mass lopping off of rebellious heads that explained the Regency success as it was the skilful, highly judicious manner in which the power was exercised." Regency leaders took "the prejudices and feelings of local communities" into account in making their appointments and exercised equal care in making removals.[9]

Senator Van Buren: The "Little Magician"

Once in Washington, Van Buren set about organizing the New York congressional delegation, a difficult undertaking in light of the fact that John Taylor, the unofficial dean of the delegation and Speaker of the House of Representatives, was firmly in the Clinton camp. In an effort to curb Taylor's influence, Van Buren helped orchestrate the election of Virginia Representative Philip Barbour as House Speaker during the Seventeenth Congress, a narrow victory that increased his own influence while cementing his ties to Virginia Republicans. He tried but failed to block the appointment of a Federalist as postmaster of Albany, but his effort to derail the nomination, chronicled at length by the press, enhanced his reputation.[10]

In the 1824 presidential election, Van Buren backed the Republican caucus nominee, Treasury Secretary William H. Crawford. The two had a great deal in common: Crawford was a states' rights advocate, a strict constructionist, and—a consideration of overriding importance to Van Buren—a dedicated party man. But the Republican coalition was rapidly splintering, and many Republicans, calling for reform of the nominating process, refused to heed the will of the caucus. Four other candidates ultimately entered the race, all claiming membership in the party of Jefferson: Secretary of State John Quincy Adams, Secretary of War John C. Calhoun, Henry Clay, and Tennessee Senator Andrew Jackson. Consumed by his single-minded effort to secure Crawford's election, even after his candidate became so seriously ill that he could neither see,

hear, nor walk, Van Buren was bitterly disappointed when the House of Representatives elected Adams president.[11]

After the election, Van Buren, as the new acknowledged leader of the "Crawford" Republicans, also known as "Radicals," kept his peace while others denounced the "corrupt bargain" with Henry Clay that many suspected had elevated Adams to the White House. He voted to confirm Clay as secretary of state, but he broke his silence after Adams outlined an ambitious domestic and foreign policy agenda in his first annual address. Van Buren particularly objected to the president's plan to send representatives to a conference of South and Central American delegates in Panama and enlisted the aid of Vice President John C. Calhoun and his allies in an effort to prevent the confirmation of delegates to the conference. The Senate ultimately confirmed the nominees, but the debate over the Panama mission had helped forge a tentative coalition of "Radicals" and Calhoun supporters under Van Buren's leadership.[12]

In December 1826, the Little Magician formalized his alliance with Calhoun, who had already pledged his support for Andrew Jackson in the forthcoming presidential race. Each man had his own agenda: Calhoun intended to succeed Jackson, after serving a second term as vice president; Van Buren, alarmed by Adams' grandiose agenda and convinced that Republicans had strayed from the Jeffersonian creed, intended to restore the party to its "first principles." Jackson, he was convinced, should carry the reinvigorated party's standard in 1828. "If Gen Jackson . . . will put his election on old party grounds, preserve the old systems, avoid if not condemn the practices of the last campaign," he predicted, "we can by adding his personal popularity to the yet remaining force of old party feeling, not only succeed in electing him but our success when achieved will be worth something."[13]

By December 1827, Van Buren had assumed control of the Jackson campaign. The candidate remained in the background while the Little Magician orchestrated a battle plan of unprecedented energy and vigor. His campaigning was, in the words of one scholar, "little short of brilliant." Van Buren plunged wholeheartedly into the contest, serving as fund raiser, strategist, publicist, and counselor. Several states had, prior to the election, revised their election laws to expand the franchise. With parades, rallies, speeches, and calls for "reform," Van Buren and his lieutenants mesmerized these first-time voters, as well as others who had become disenchanted with the administration. "[T]he American people," a Jackson scholar concluded, "loved the performance put on for them." [14]

Keeping his fragile coalition together represented Van Buren's most difficult challenge, apart from persuading the candidate to suffer in dignified silence as the Adams camp levelled increasingly virulent attacks on his character. The growing protectionist sentiment in the West and in the Northeast posed particular problems for Van Buren, who could not afford to alienate southern free-trade advocates. Courting both camps, he studiously avoided making a definitive pronouncement on the tariff, even as he deftly guided a protectionist bill through the Senate. The 1828 tariff, known in the South as the "Tariff of Abominations," reassured westerners, who might otherwise have remained in the "Adams-Clay" fold, that a Jackson administration would take their interests into account. Van Buren realized that protectionism was anathema to southern agriculturalists, but he also realized that most southerners regarded Jackson as the lesser of two evils. As one scholar has conceded, during the tariff debate Van Buren "said some very equivocal things to Southerners," helping them convince themselves that, once elected, Old Hickory would support tariff reform. [15]

Secretary of State Van Buren

Jackson won an impressive victory in 1828, widely heralded as a triumph of the "common man." Writing his *Autobiography* many years after the fact, Van Buren attributed the outcome of this historic election to the "zealous union between that portion of the republican party who . . . had shown themselves willing to sacrifice personal preferences to its harmony, the numerous supporters of Gen. Jackson . . . and the friends of Mr. Calhoun . . . strengthened by the mismanagement of the administration." Van Buren achieved a personal victory as well, win-

ning election as governor of New York. But he served less than two months in this position, resigning to accept an appointment as secretary of state in the new administration. [16]

Van Buren was easily the most capable individual in Jackson's cabinet, an assortment of second-rank appointees chosen to achieve sectional and ideological balance. [17] During his two years as secretary of state from 1829 to 1831, he became one of the president's most trusted advisers. He arrived in the capital shortly after Jackson's inauguration to find the cabinet—and Washington society—at odds over Mrs. John C. Calhoun's adamant refusal to socialize with the wife of Secretary of War John Eaton, a woman with a spirited disposition and a notorious reputation. Several cabinet wives had followed suit, avoiding official functions for fear of encountering the tainted couple. The "Petticoat War" was, as Van Buren realized, much more than a dispute over protocol or public morals; it was a symptom of the deep divisions in an administration that included both free-trade advocates and protectionists. The tension became even more pronounced after Jackson delivered his first annual message. His speech, prepared with Van Buren's assistance, convinced Vice President Calhoun and his allies that they would obtain no relief from the Tariff of Abominations. As for Van Buren, he suspected—correctly, as it turned out—that Calhoun was somehow behind the talk of "nullification" emanating from South Carolina.

Van Buren at first tried to cure what he called "the Eaton malaria," the malaise that threatened to paralyze the administration, by entertaining the Eatons. As a widower with no wife to object if he showed courtesy to a woman of questionable repute, he had nothing to lose by entertaining Mrs. Eaton and everything to gain, given the high regard that Jackson felt for Peggy and her husband. He was no match for the formidable Floride Calhoun, however, and he soon became *persona non grata* among the Calhoun set, but his gallantry endeared him to the president. [18] Accompanying Jackson on horseback for their customary rides throughout the countryside surrounding Washington, Van Buren became the president's sounding board and friend, offering well-timed and perceptive counsel to the care-burdened and lonely old hero. He helped craft the president's memorable toast: "The Union: It must be preserved" that electrified the April 13, 1830, banquet commemorating Jefferson's birthday, and he helped persuade Jackson to run for a second term.

Calhoun simmered with resentment as the man he considered a "weasel" gained the upper hand in a rivalry that was becoming increasingly bitter. Van Buren, although every bit as ambitious as Calhoun, became increasingly discomfited at the widespread speculation that he, and not Calhoun, would succeed Jackson as president. Recoiling at the thought that his opponents might interpret his labors on Jackson's behalf as a crude form of electioneering, he informed the president in late March of 1831 that "there is but one thing" that would bring peace to Jackson's troubled administration: "my resignation." Old Hickory was at first reluctant to accept Van Buren's resignation, but eventually realized that the gesture offered him the opportunity to purge his cabinet of Calhoun partisans. Van Buren's departure precipitated the mass resignation of the entire cabinet, except for Postmaster General William Barry. The new cabinet was distinctly more sympathetic to Jackson—and to Van Buren. As a reward for his "highly patriotic" sacrifice, the Little Magician received an appointment as minister to England.[19]

Van Buren sailed for England before the Senate confirmed his nomination. His easy, elegant manners made him an instant hit in London. Almost immediately, he received the British foreign minister's pledge to respect the rulings of the panel arbitrating the longstanding boundary dispute between Maine and New Brunswick. Jackson had predicted that Van Buren's enemies would not dare oppose this appointment, for fear that "the people in mass would take you up and elect you vice Pres.," but, in late February 1832, Van Buren learned that the Senate had in fact rejected his nomination, with Vice President Calhoun casting the deciding vote. Jackson was furious when he heard the news but, after sober reflection, realized that he now had ample justification for removing Calhoun from the ticket in the coming election. He had already settled on Van Buren as his next vice president, but Calhoun's

effrontery strengthened his resolve. "The people will properly resent the insult offered to the Executive, and the injury intended to our foreign relations, in your rejection," he consoled Van Buren in mid-February, "by placing you in the chair of the very man whose casting vote rejected you." [20] Calhoun, his presidential prospects rapidly dimming as a consequence of his role in the nullification controversy, resigned before the end of his term—the first vice president to do so—to take a seat in the Senate. Once Van Buren's most formidable rival for the soul of the organization soon to be known as the Democratic party, he had become a sectional leader and would remain a sectional leader for the rest of his life.

The Election of 1832

Van Buren found every reason imaginable to remain abroad after learning of his rejection by the Senate. He could not break his lease or abruptly discharge his servants, he protested, nor could he pack up his household on such short notice. But his biographer suggests that he delayed his departure because he believed that the "opposition would splinter . . . if left alone; it stood a good chance of coalescing if he returned with undue haste for vindication." [21] Touring the Continent with his son John, Van Buren was still abroad when Democratic delegates assembled at Baltimore on May 21, 1832, to choose a vice-presidential candidate. Although antitariff southern Democrats had serious reservations about Van Buren, Jackson's sentiments prevailed. By an overwhelming margin, the convention chose Van Buren on the first ballot.[22]

Finally returning home in July 1832, the Little Magician was immediately summoned to Washington. Jackson needed his help in drafting a message to Congress explaining his impending veto of a bill to recharter the Second Bank of the United States. Van Buren approved of the veto message, a ringing denunciation of the bank as an instrument of privilege. At Jackson's request, he attended the Senate and the House of Representatives on July 10, in order to lobby against the inevitable attempt to override the veto. Also at Jackson's request, he lobbied for a compromise tariff designed to keep would-be nullifiers in the

Jacksonian camp. Successful in both efforts, he departed for New York after Congress adjourned. He remained in New York until shortly before the inauguration, attempting to reconcile die-hard New York protectionists to the compromise tariff.[23]

The 1832 election was, as one scholar of the period has observed, a referendum on the Second Bank of the United States, the first presidential election in which the candidates submitted a single, specific question to the electorate. Jackson was a "hard-money" man, deeply suspicious of banks, credit, and paper money after suffering near ruin in an early land speculation venture. Regarding the Second Bank of the United States, a government-chartered but privately owned institution, as an instrument of aristocratic, monied interests, he would have announced his intention to destroy the bank in his first annual message had his advisers not counseled restraint. Fully confident that the voters would signal their assent by electing him to a second term, Jackson had vetoed the bank recharter bill before the election. National Republican candidate Henry Clay, who considered the bank essential to the nation's fiscal stability, was quick to make an issue of the veto. Clay's partisans took aim at the Little Magician, as well, charging that his feats of legerdemain had secured the throne for a president who had abused his office. Political cartoons showed Jackson, Van Buren, and their cronies assaulting the bank with a battering ram, Van Buren crowning Jackson, and "King Andrew the First" brandishing the "veto." These and similar images helped make the contest one of the liveliest, if not the best illustrated, in the nation's history.

But the National Republicans were no match for the well-organized party that Van Buren had helped create. One scholar has suggested that the majority of American voters still regarded Jackson as their champion, even though they may well have approved of the bank, which provided the nation with the stable currency so essential to its prosperity. The Democrats, now a full-fledged political party, won a solid victory, although by a somewhat smaller margin than in 1828. Jackson was easily reelected, and Van Buren won a substantial victory over Clay's running mate, John Sergeant.[24]

Vice President Van Buren

Jackson had every reason to rejoice at the outcome of the election. The voters had, he believed, given him a mandate to destroy the bank, and he was rid of Calhoun. In Van Buren, Jackson had a vice president more to his liking. Old Hickory respected his second vice president and seems to have felt sincere affection for him, as well. Some longtime Jackson cronies were deeply jealous of the New Yorker, who, as one critic put it, stuck "close to the President as a blistering plaster."[25] But Van Buren was not, as critics of both men so frequently alleged, the "power-behind-the-throne." Jackson was a formidable tactician in his own right and a man of resolute convictions, fully capable of determining his own course of action. Van Buren was not his only confidant; throughout his two terms as president, Jackson also relied on his "Kitchen Cabinet," an informal group of trusted friends, supporters, kinsmen, and hangers-on, for advice and moral support.

In orchestrating the transfer of government deposits from the Bank of the United States to state depositories, for example, Jackson rejected the cautious course that Van Buren proposed in favor of the more precipitate approach advocated by Amos Kendall, the fourth auditor of the treasury. After Jackson informed his advisers early in his first term that he intended to remove the deposits, Kendall urged immediate action. Van Buren, sensitive to the political and financial repercussions of a hasty withdrawal but reluctant to challenge the president, advised Jackson to wait at least until the Twenty-third Congress convened in December 1833. Apprehensive—with good reason, as it turned out—that he would be regarded both as the author of this controversial move and as the pawn of Wall Street bankers who expected to benefit from the Philadelphia-based bank's demise, Van Buren was conspicuously absent from Washington that fall. The opposition would inevitably "relieve the question . . . from the influence of your well deserved popularity with the people," he wrote Jackson from New York in September, "by attributing the removal of the deposits to the solicitat[i]ons of myself and the monied junto in N. York, and as it is not your habit to play into the enemies hands you will not I know request me to come down unless there is some adequate inducement for my so doing." [26]

Van Buren did, however, enjoy a greater measure of influence in the administration than any previous vice president. He helped Treasury Secretary Roger B. Taney coax the president into a less belligerent posture when Jackson, outraged at France's failure to comply with the 1832 treaty for the payment of U.S. claims against France, threatened to seek congressional authorization to issue letters of marque, a move that Taney feared might lead to war. Upset that Jackson failed to follow his advice about France, Secretary of State Louis McLane resigned in protest. Van Buren then helped Jackson draft a reply to McLane's letter of resignation and suggested his longtime ally Senator John Forsyth of Georgia to fill the position. Van Buren shouldered a workload that, in the words of a biographer, "would have crushed lesser men." In addition to his labors in the Senate, he spent a considerable amount of time "advising members of the cabinet, ghosting significant parts of Jackson's messages, acting as the president's chief advisor on patronage and foreign affairs, feeling his way around the Kitchen Cabinet, while always keeping his eye on New York." [27]

Senate Committee Elections

Presiding over the Senate was easily Van Buren's most challenging and frustrating task, one that demanded all of his legendary tact and good humor. Jackson faced sustained opposition during his second term from an opposition coalition of National Republicans, nullifiers, states' rights advocates, and eventually from disaffected Democrats who came to regard him as an overreaching despot. By 1834, these disparate elements would unite to form a new party, calling themselves "Whigs" to signal their opposition to a chief executive they called King Andrew. The rhetoric was particularly heated in the Senate, where the opposition commanded a slim majority after the 1832 election. The coalition's ranks included such luminaries as Henry Clay,

the bank's most avid defender; Massachusetts Senator Daniel Webster, like Jackson a staunch unionist but also a defender of the bank; and Calhoun, the author of nullification. [28]

Van Buren began his duties in the Senate on December 16, 1833, two weeks after the Twenty-third Congress convened. Having served there from 1821 to 1828, he was familiar with the body's customs and procedures. He knew that the vice president was not expected to attend the Senate for several days at the beginning of each Congress, a practice that allowed the Senate to attend to organizational matters and appoint committees without interference from the executive branch. But in 1833 a unique combination of events prevented the Senate from attending to this important task before Van Buren arrived.

Under normal circumstances, President pro tempore Hugh Lawson White would have appointed the committee members and chairmen at the start of the Twenty-third Congress. The rule adopted in December 1828 governing the appointment of committees directed that "[t]he President pro tempore . . . shall appoint the committees of the Senate; but if there be no President pro tempore, the Senate . . . will proceed, by ballot," with a majority required to elect a committee chairman and a plurality required to elect the remaining members. [29] But White found himself in a "delicate" position. Although he was a long-standing friend and supporter of the president, he was becoming disillusioned with the administration, and he particularly resented Jackson's designation of Van Buren as his political heir. A firm defender of the Senate's prerogatives, he had refused to let Jackson dictate the composition of a select committee appointed to consider Clay's compromise tariff during the previous Congress, a stand that had deeply offended the president. White would eventually become a Whig, but at the start of the Twenty-third Congress, Clay and the rest of the opposition still regarded him as a Jackson man. [30]

On December 9, White stated that "he should have announced the standing committees this morning . . . had it not been that a resolution was offered by a Senator [Peleg Sprague] from Maine . . . which proposed to take away from the presiding officer the power of appointing any committees whatsoever.'' The Senate adopted the resolution the following day, returning to its earlier practice of choosing committees by ballot, with nearly all of the Jacksonians opposing the change.[31]

Van Buren finally arrived in Washington on the evening of December 14 and met with the president and Tennessee Senator Felix Grundy the following morning. He learned that Grundy, painfully aware that his party could no longer count on a majority in the Senate and reluctant to proceed with the selection of committees until Van Buren could provide advice, had offered a motion to postpone the elections until December 16. Webster had voted in favor of that motion, along with five other New England senators—a gesture that Grundy, rightly or wrongly, interpreted as an overture toward the administration. Webster's biographer discounts this possibility but admits that the Massachusetts senator's support for the administration during the nullification battle, and his differences with Clay over the tariff issue, had led to widespread speculation that he intended to form an alliance with the Jacksonians.

During his December 15 meeting with Van Buren, therefore, Grundy raised the possibility of an alliance with Webster, at least for the purposes of electing the Senate's committees. The vice president, however, refused to consider collaboration with Webster, the one individual he genuinely disliked and took pains to avoid. Such an arrangement would blur the very real differences between the administration and the New England opposition, he lectured, and would leave Jackson open to charges that he had placed politics above principle. Persuaded by the force of Van Buren's argument, Grundy deferred to the vice president. The Senate began the balloting to elect chairmen and members of its standing committees on December 16, Van Buren's first day in the chair. With only a slight majority, the Anti-Jackson forces did not win complete control of the committees. Jackson's ally, Thomas Hart Benton of Missouri, was reelected chairman of the Military Affairs Committee, and William Wilkins of Pennsylvania was elected chairman of the Foreign Relations Committee. But other coveted chairmanships went to opposition senators: the Finance Committee to Webster, the Judiciary Committee to John Clayton of Delaware, and the Committee on Public Lands to one of Jackson's most outspoken critics, George Poindexter of Mississippi.[32]

The Senate Censures Jackson: Van Buren Versus Clay

During the four years that Van Buren served as vice president, the president's war on the Bank of the United States was one of the most important and controversial subjects on the Senate's agenda. Anticipating Jackson's order to withdraw the government deposits, bank president Nicholas Biddle had persuaded the bank's directors to order sharp reductions in credit. The directors subsequently decreed that the bank would accept only hard currency from state banks with loans outstanding, a move that forced state banks to adopt similar measures and wreaked havoc in the credit-dependent West and in the nation's financial markets.[33]

When Van Buren assumed the chair on December 16, 1833, he found the Senate in a state of turmoil. The Senate's December 11 request that Jackson provide a copy of his withdrawal directive had been met with a curt response that infuriated opposition senators. "I have yet to learn," Jackson had notified the Senate on December 12, "under what constitutional authority that branch of the Legislature has a right to require of me an account of any communication." On December 27, Clay retaliated with two resolutions to censure Jackson, which the Senate adopted after three months of intense and heated debate. Van Buren's legendary poise served him well as Clay and his lieutenants began their attack, dropping not-so-thinly-veiled hints that the vice president was also to blame for the wave of bank and business failures sweeping the nation. Smiling and genial, he took care to maintain order in the chamber, ordering the galleries cleared when necessary. To all outward appearances, he seemed oddly unperturbed at the opprobrium that Clay and his allies heaped on the administration.[34]

Early in the debate, however, Van Buren had orchestrated a spirited rejoinder to Clay's attacks. Unable to join in the debate himself, he had persuaded Silas Wright, the New York senator widely regarded as his spokesman in the Senate, to deliver the administration's response. Unmoved by Wright's plea that "[t]he administration had several friends in the Senate more competent for the task than myself," Van Buren offered to "reduce all we want to have said to writing." On January 30, Wright presented an impassioned defense of Jackson's conduct and a ringing condemnation of the bank. His lengthy address—the product of Van Buren's pen—emphasized that the question before the public was "Bank or no Bank, . . . not the disposition of the Government deposits." The president, he argued, had been "instrumental in restoring the constitution of the country to what it was intended to be by those who formed it . . . relieving that sacred instrument from those constructive and implied additions under which Congress have claimed the right to place beyond the reach of the people, and without responsibility, a moneyed power." Wright concluded his remarks with an argument that Jackson partisans would use to good advantage in the months that followed. "The country . . . has approved the course of the Executive, in his attempts to relieve us from the corrupt and corrupting power and influence of a national bank," the New York senator stressed, "and it will sustain him in the experiment now making to substitute State institutions for such a fiscal agent."

Notwithstanding Wright's disclaimer that "he had given his opinion as an individual," everyone present realized the truth of Daniel Webster's observation that, knowing the senator's "political connexions, his station, and his relations," it was obvious that he had not "spoken one word which has not been deliberately weighed and considered by others." Van Buren's words, ably articulated by a senator generally regarded as the "clearest logician" of his day, provided a forceful rebuttal to Clay's charges. One senator pronounced the speech "a hit," while Webster fretted about the "effect which the recent debate in the Senate . . . may produce at the north." [35]

But even this triumph of sorts could not alleviate Van Buren's mounting discomfort as the lengthy debate dragged on. During one particularly heated March session, Clay addressed him directly, pleading with him to tell Jackson "in the language of truth and sincerity, the actual condition of his bleeding country." Van Buren listened politely as Clay, obviously playing to the galleries, reminded him of his "well-known influence" in the administration. At the conclusion of Clay's remarks, Van Buren handed the gavel to Hugh Lawson White and stepped down from the dais. Clay rose to his feet as the vice president deliberately approached his desk, and the crowds in the galleries fell silent. Then, with a deep bow, and a voice dripping with sarcasm, Van Buren returned fire: "Mr. Senator, allow me to be indebted to you for another pinch of your aromatic Maccoboy." The galleries erupted in a wave of laughter as Clay, speechless and humiliated, gestured helplessly at the snuff on his desk. Van Buren helped himself and returned to the chair, all the while maintaining his studied composure. [36]

When the Senate finally voted to censure the president on March 28, 1834, Van Buren was not unduly alarmed, convinced that the American people would not take kindly to this dramatic assault on their hero and champion. But he was deeply disturbed by the response that Jackson sent to the Senate in mid-April. The president's critics, and even some of his allies, were shocked to learn that Jackson, as he explained in his infamous "Protest," considered himself the direct representative of the American people—responsible, along with his appointees, for "every species of property belonging to the United States." Worried about the constitutional ramifications of this novel interpretation of presidential power and about the effect that the controversial pronouncement might have on his own prospects in the coming election, Van Buren persuaded Jackson to soften his rhetoric. He was greatly relieved when the 1834 midterm elections affirmed that the American people approved of the war that Jackson waged against the bank on their behalf. Jackson ultimately killed the bank, as he had predicted he would, but the struggle took its toll on Van Buren, who eventually came to regard his duties as president of the opposition-controlled Senate as "so distasteful and so wearing" that, according to a modern biographer, he suffered "more than his share of colds and debilitating upsets." [37]

The "Weasel"

Other issues before the Senate were equally troublesome for Van Buren, who was well aware that opposition senators, as well as some Jacksonians resentful of his influence, would exploit any apparent failing on his part in the coming election. The abolition movement, which sent scores of antislavery petitions to Congress during the 1830s, posed particular difficulties for a northern politician who had supported emancipation in his own state but was anxious to remain on good terms with southern voters and regarded slavery as a matter best left to the states. Like many northern voters at the time, Van Buren had little use for the abolitionists, dismissing their 1835–1836 crusade for emancipation in the District of Columbia as an attempt to "distract Congress and the country . . . in the midst of a Presidential canvas."

Van Buren's disclaimers failed to satisfy many southerners who considered him an abolitionist at heart, but some were heartened by his June 2, 1836, tie-breaking vote to proceed to the third and final reading of Calhoun's bill authorizing local postal officials to confiscate mailings prohibited by state law. The bill was similar to one that Jackson had proposed after a mass mailing of abolitionist literature to Charleston, South Carolina, caused a near-riot there the previous summer. But the administration proposal would have authorized the federal government to determine which materials should be embargoed, while Calhoun's would have delegated this function to the states. Calhoun engineered a tied vote on the motion to proceed to the third reading of his bill. If he did so to embarrass Van Buren, as one scholar of the period has suggested, he miscalculated. "The Vice President promptly voted yea, thus preventing Southerners from blaming him when the bill was finally defeated." [38] In fact, when the measure came up for the final vote less that a week later, [39] the Senate rejected it, a development that Van Buren, a shrewd judge of men and events, may well have anticipated. The "weasel," as Calhoun now disparagingly referred to Van Buren, [40] had once again outmaneuvered his rival.

A "Third-Rate Man"

On May 20, 1835, the Democratic nominating convention chose Van Buren as the party's 1836 presidential candidate. The unanimous vote of the delegates present belied serious divisions in a party that was, in the words of a contemporary journalist, comprised of "the Jackson party, proper; the Jackson-Van Buren party; the Jackson-anti-Van Buren party." More than a few disaffected Democrats, alarmed at the growth of presidential power during Jackson's two terms and reluctant to countenance more of the same under Van Buren, had grave reservations about the Little Magician. But Jackson had made his preference known. The president was equally adamant that Richard Mentor Johnson, a Kentucky Democrat and military hero who had served in both houses of Congress, should be Van Buren's running mate, a legacy that cost the ticket support among southern voters who regarded Johnson as an "amalgamator" because of his relationship with his slave mistress.

Van Buren was opposed by a field of regional opposition candidates endorsed by state and local Whig organizations. The Whigs, still more a coalition than a party, with no candidate capable of defeating Van Buren outright, hoped that each regional candidate would so weaken the Democratic ticket in his own section that the election would be thrown into the House of Representatives. During the campaign, opposition strategists reviled Van Buren as an abolitionist, a manipulator, and a trimmer—a "third-rate man," in the words of one detractor. David Crockett, formerly a member of the anti-Jackson coalition in the House and one of "Aunt Matty's" sharpest critics, ridiculed the vice president's appearance as he presided over the Senate, "laced up in corsets, such as women in a town wear, and, if possible, tighter than the best of them." Cartoonists portrayed Van Buren clutching the president's coattails, or donning Jackson's too-large greatcoat. More serious detractors warned that Van Buren would continue the aggrandizement of executive power that Jackson had begun. Democrats countered with pointed allusions to the Federalists, who had supported the First Bank of the United States, they reminded voters, as well as such equally repugnant measures as the Alien and Sedition Acts. They coupled these attacks with paeans of praise for the president who had slain the "monster bank."

Van Buren won the election, a triumph that owed more to the fragmented and poorly coordinated campaigns mounted by the opposition and to Jackson's continued popularity than to his own prestige. He assumed office under a cloud, overshadowed at his presidential inauguration by the crowds that flocked to catch a final glimpse of Old Hickory. He would never be as beloved or as respected as his predecessor. Richard Mentor Johnson had failed to receive an electoral majority after Virginia's electors withheld their votes in protest, forcing the vice-presidential election into the Senate for the first and only time in the nation's history. With his controversial personal history and complete disdain for prevailing norms of social discourse and personal hygiene, Johnson would remain a source of continuing embarrassment for Van Buren.[41]

"Martin Van Ruin"

The nation's worsening relations with Mexico posed a serious problem for the new president. American settlers in Texas had declared their independence in 1836, precipitating a war with Mexico, and a request for annexation by the United States was pending at the time of Van Buren's inauguration. Reluctant to involve the nation in a war that northern antislavery interests would inevitably characterize as a war to extend slavery, but equally reluctant to offend southern expansionists, he pursued a dilatory and evasive course until Texas ultimately withdrew its petition.[42]

Van Buren could not, however, afford to remain equally indecisive with respect to the economic maladies besetting the nation. On the day that he assumed office, one of the nation's most prominent trading houses suspended payments, the first in a wave of brokerage house failures that swept the nation during the panic of 1837. Jackson's "hard money" fiscal policies were only partly to blame for the panic. A trade imbalance

and a sharp decline in the price of American cotton had also contributed to the crisis, which was international in scope. But Whigs were quick to blame the nation's economic woes on Jackson and, by extension, on Van Buren, sometimes dubbed "Martin Van Ruin" during this period. He had inherited a situation that one scholar has characterized as a "potentially devastating emergency, probably the worst facing any new President on taking office until James Buchanan had to cope with slavery and the Dred Scott decision in 1837." Van Buren's solution was to "divorce" the government from the banking sector by establishing a treasury independent of the state bank-based system that, contrary to Jackson's expectations, had fuelled the speculative frenzy of the mid 1830s. Whigs succeeded in blocking this initiative until 1840, when Congress finally passed an independent treasury bill. In the meantime, the panic gave way to a depression of unprecedented severity. Up to one third of the factory workers in some northeastern towns were thrown out of work; in the South, vast expanses of once productive farmland went untilled. Prices of food and other necessities skyrocketed, with soup kitchens the only source of sustenance for many destitute residents of Washington, D.C., and other cities.[43]

Van Buren lost his 1840 bid for reelection to William Henry Harrison, a military hero touted as a "common man" by the Whig strategists who ran an extraordinarily effective campaign on his behalf. After one Democrat made the mistake of dismissing "Old Tippecanoe" as a cider-swilling rustic content to live in a log cabin, Whigs appropriated these symbols to their advantage. The log cabin and the cider barrel were powerful images during the depression, images that contrasted sharply with the picture that Whigs painted of Van Buren as a nattily attired, high-living schemer, a "used-up man" hopelessly out of touch with the American electorate. Out-maneuvered and out-campaigned, Van Buren's party lost not only the White House, but control of both houses of Congress, as well.[44]

A "Used-Up Man"

Van Buren was staggered by his humiliating defeat. He had received a mere 60 electoral votes, a dismal showing compared with Harrison's 234 electoral votes, and a defeat made even more galling by his failure to carry New York. He gave little outward sign of his disappointment and extended more than the customary courtesies to Harrison when "Old Tip" arrived in Washington shortly before the inauguration. Van Buren was anxious to return to private life, he cheerfully informed friends, and seemed to enjoy the rousing welcome that awaited him in New York City. (He had, of course, conveniently informed friends that he would arrive in the city on March 23, allowing them plenty of time to prepare a "surprise" in his honor.) But he was deeply shaken at the outcome of the election, and would have announced his retirement from politics had Silas Wright not intervened with a timely lecture about his responsibilities to the Democratic party.[45]

Van Buren retired to Lindenwald, his Kinderhook estate, cautiously pondering his prospects for 1844 while maintaining that "his ambition had been fully satisfied." But he made an extensive tour of the southern and western states in the spring and summer of 1842, drawing large crowds wherever he went. The voters who had turned him out of office were amazed to discover that the man demonized by Whigs as an insensitive dandy and a shrewd, cunning schemer was merely a plain-spoken, unassuming, and quite ordinary man. "Instead of a dwarf Dutchman, a little dandy who you might lift in a bandbox," Jackson observed, "the people found him a plain man of middle size, plain and affable." Cautiously and discreetly, Van Buren began laying the groundwork for another attempt at the presidency. The leading contender after the first ballot at the 1844 Democratic convention, he ultimately lost the nomination to James K. Polk, a darkhorse candidate who supported the immediate annexation of Texas. Resolved never again to seek elective office, he focused his energies on securing New York for Polk.[46]

After Polk's inauguration, Van Buren watched with mounting alarm as disagreement over the extension of slavery into the territory acquired from Mexico began to split his increasingly fragile party. He was deeply troubled by southern Democrats' claims that Congress could not bar slavery from the new territories; he had always believed that the institution, where it already existed, was a matter best left to the individual states. But when events in Texas offered southern slaveholders the opportunity to extend their reach toward the Southwest, Van Buren decided that he could not support the expansion of a practice that he regarded as evil. In 1848, the Free Soil party—a coalition of antislavery Democrats, antislavery Whigs and disaffected Whigs—nominated Van Buren as their presidential candidate. In this last attempt at elective office, he lost to Whig candidate Zachary Taylor, having received a mere 10 percent of the popular vote and no electoral votes.[47]

Van Buren died at Lindenwald on July 24, 1862. He had lived long enough to see the southern states secede from the Union, a bitter disappointment for the man who had forged a once-formidable coalition that had transcended sectional lines. His last public statement, made the year before his death, was a declaration of his "earnest and vigorous support to the Lincoln Administration for . . . the maintenance of the Union and the Constitution" in response to President Lincoln's call for troops to suppress the rebellion. Lincoln reciprocated with a stilted posthumous tribute: "The grief of his patriotic friends, will measurably be assuaged by the consciousness that while . . . seeing his end approaching, his prayers were for the restoration of the authority of the government of which he had been head, and for peace and good will among his fellow citizens."[48]

NOTES

[1] Donald B. Cole, *Martin Van Buren and the American Political System* (Princeton, NJ, 1984), p. 188.

[2] John Niven, *Martin Van Buren: The Romantic Age of American Politics* (New York, 1983), p. 298.

[3] James A. Hamilton, *Reminiscences of James A. Hamilton; or, Men and Events, at Home and Abroad, During Three Quarters of a Century* (New York, 1869), pp. 42, 97; Arthur M. Schlesinger, Jr., *The Age of Jackson* (Boston, 1945), pp. 47–50; Robert V. Remini, *Martin Van Buren and the Making of the Democratic Party* (New York, 1959; reprint of 1951 edition), pp. 2–3; Niven, pp. 7–8.

[4] Schlesinger, p. 49; Carl Sifakis, *The Dictionary of Historic Nicknames* (New York, 1984), p. 508.

[5] Also spelled Hoes.

[6] Niven, pp. 1–22; John C. Fitzpatrick, ed., *The Autobiography of Martin Van Buren* (New York, 1973; reprint of 1920 edition), 1:9–10.

[7] Niven, pp. 23–25, 60, 72, 162–63. Four of the five sons born to Martin and Hannah Van Buren survived infancy.

[8] Ibid., pp. 26–52.

[9] Remini, *Martin Van Buren*, pp. 5–11; Niven, p. 88.

[10] Niven, pp. 102–17.

[11] Remini, *Martin Van Buren*, pp. 36–92. For more on the 1824 election, see also Chapter 7, "John C. Calhoun," pp. 86–87.

[12] Remini, *Martin Van Buren*, pp. 91–113. For more about the Panama mission, see Chapter 7 of this volume, "John C. Calhoun," pp. 88–89.

[13] Ibid., pp. 120–32; Robert V. Remini, *Andrew Jackson and the Course of American Freedom, 1822–1832* (New York, 1981), pp. 113–15.

[14] Remini, *Martin Van Buren*, pp. 192–93; Remini, *Jackson and the Course of American Freedom*, pp. 116–42.

[15] Remini, *Martin Van Buren*, pp. 170–85. See also Chapter 7, "John C. Calhoun," p. 93.

[16] Fitzpatrick, ed., 1:220–24.

[17] Remini, *Jackson and the Course of American Freedom*, pp. 159–66.

[18] This incident is also discussed in Chapter 7, "John C. Calhoun," p. 95.

[19] Niven, pp. 232–71; Remini, *Jackson and the Course of American Freedom*, pp. 291–320.

[20] Niven, pp. 272–95; Remini, *Jackson and the Course of American Freedom*, pp. 345–55.

[21] Niven, pp. 295–98.

[22] Remini, *Jackson and the Course of American Freedom*, pp. 355–58; Niven, pp. 298–301.

[23] Niven, pp. 301–29. For a more detailed account of the nullification crisis, see Chapter 7 of this volume, "John C. Calhoun," pp. 94–96.

[24] Robert V. Remini, *Andrew Jackson and the Course of American Democracy, 1833–1845* (New York, 1984), pp. 374–92; Robert V. Remini, *Andrew Jackson and the Bank War: A Study in the Growth of Presidential Power* (New York, 1967), pp. 1–108.

[25] Remini, *Jackson and the Course of American Democracy*, p. 46.

[26] Remini, *Jackson and the Bank War*, passim; Niven, pp. 304, 330–47.

[27] Niven, pp. 368–72, 402; Remini, *Jackson and the Course of American Democracy*, pp. 201–18.

[28] At the beginning of the Twenty-second Congress, 20 of the Senate's 48 members belonged to the Jackson coalition; of the remainder, 26 belonged to the Anti-Jackson party and 2 were Nullifiers. U.S., Congress, Senate, *The Senate, 1789–1989*, by Robert C. Byrd, S. Doc., 100–20, 100th Cong., 1st sess., vol. 4, *Historical Statistics, 1789–1992*, 1993, p. 416.

[29] U.S., Congress, Senate, *Journal*, 20th Cong., 2d sess., p. 51.

[30] Nancy N. Scott, ed., *A Memoir of Hugh Lawson White, Judge of the Supreme Court of Tennessee, Member of the Senate of the United States . . . With Selections from His Speeches and Correspondence* (Philadelphia, 1856), pp. 265–300; Remini, *Jackson and the Course of American Democracy*, p. 39; Niven, p. 356.

[31] U.S., Congress, Senate, *Register of Debates in Congress*, 23d Cong., 1st sess., pp. 19–29; *Senate Journal*, 23d Cong., 1st sess., p. 39.

[32] Niven, pp. 356–58; Remini, *Jackson and the Course of American Democracy*, pp. 116–18; *Register of Debates in Congress*, 23d Cong., 1st sess., pp. 39–44; *Senate Journal*, 23d Cong., 1st sess., pp. 39–43; Maurice G. Baxter, *One and Inseparable: Daniel Webster and the Union* (Cambridge, 1984), pp. 224–28.

[33] Niven, pp. 333–54; Remini, *Jackson and the Bank War*, pp. 109–53.

[34] U.S., Congress, Senate, *The Senate, 1789–1989: Addresses on the History of the United States Senate*, by Robert C. Byrd, S. Doc. 100–20, 100th Cong., 1st sess., vol. 1, 1989, pp. 127–32; Niven, p. 354.

[35] John A. Garraty, *Silas Wright* (New York, 1970; reprint of 1949 edition), pp. 114–18; *Register of Debates in Congress*, 23d Cong., 1st sess., pp. 397–405.

[36] Robert V. Remini, *Henry Clay: Statesman for the Union* (New York, 1991), pp. 452–53; Niven, pp. 354–55.

[37] Byrd, *The Senate*, 1:127–41, 145–47; Niven, pp. 365–66; Remini, *Jackson and the Course of American Democracy*, pp. 150–60; Remini, *Jackson and the Bank War*, pp. 152–53.

[38] Niven, pp. 384–85, 390; Glyndon G. Van Deusen, *The Jacksonian Era* (New York, 1959), p. 107–9; Cole, pp. 269–72; *Senate Journal*, 24th Cong., 1st sess., pp. 396–400.

[39] *Senate Journal*, 24th Cong., 1st sess., pp. 414–16.

[40] Cole, p. 264.

[41] Ibid., pp. 256–90; Niven, pp. 386–402. For a more detailed account of the 1836 election, see Chapter 9 of this volume, "Richard Mentor Johnson," pp. 126–27.

[42] Cole, pp. 317–21.

[43] Ibid., pp. 285–360; Sifakis, p. 508; Niven, pp. 412–61.

[44] Cole, pp. 368–73.

[45] Ibid., pp. 372–75; Niven, pp. 471–83.

[46] Niven, pp. 484–548.

[47] Ibid., pp. 542–90; Cole, pp. 407–18.

[48] Niven, pp. 611–12.

Chapter 9

RICHARD MENTOR JOHNSON
1837–1841

RICHARD MENTOR JOHNSON

Chapter 9

RICHARD MENTOR JOHNSON

9th Vice President: 1837–1841

. . . I pray you to assure our friends that the humblest of us do not believe that a lucky random shot, even if it did hit Tecumseh, qualifies a man for the Vice Presidency.
—TENNESSEE SUPREME COURT CHIEF JUSTICE JOHN CATRON TO ANDREW JACKSON,
MARCH 21, 1835.[1]

The United States Senate elected Richard Mentor Johnson of Kentucky the nation's ninth vice president on February 8, 1837. His selection marked the first and only time the Senate has exercised its prerogative under the U.S. Constitution's Twelfth Amendment, which provides, "if no person have a majority, then from the two highest numbers on the list, the Senate shall choose the Vice-President." Johnson became Martin Van Buren's running mate after three decades in the House and Senate, a congressional career spanning the administrations of five presidents from Thomas Jefferson through Andrew Jackson. Detractors alleged, however, that he owed his nomination solely to the dubious claim that he killed the Shawnee chieftain Tecumseh in 1813 at the Battle of the Thames.

Johnson wielded substantial power in the House of Representatives during Jackson's two administrations, and his successful decade-long campaign to end imprisonment for debt won him a national following. For most of his career, the voters of his district held him in great esteem. They forgave him when he sponsored the 1816 Compensation Act, one of the most unpopular laws ever enacted by Congress, as well as on more than one occasion when he lined his own pockets with government funds.

During the 1836 presidential campaign and Johnson's single term as vice president, however, his popularity dissipated. The plain manners and

habits that had once endeared him to his constituents and supporters, combined with his controversial personal life and unfortunate penchant for lending his influence in support of questionable undertakings, proved serious liabilities. A campaign to remove him from the Democratic ticket in 1840 failed only because Van Buren, while no Johnson enthusiast, was unwilling to alienate the eastern labor vote and because party leaders were reluctant to force a potentially divisive confrontation. The 1840 election, resulting in a decisive victory for the Whig ticket headed by Johnson's former comrade-in-arms, William Henry Harrison, signalled the end of the Kentuckian's long and often controversial career.

A Frontier Youth

Little is known of Richard Mentor Johnson's early years. Nineteenth-century campaign biographies and a modern study based on these earlier accounts are heavily colored by the heroic rhetoric that Johnson and his supporters employed throughout his career.[2] Although he was, as he later claimed, "born in a cane-brake and cradled in a sap trough,"[3] the Johnsons were a powerful family of substantial means. The future vice president was born on October 17, 1780, at Beargrass, a Virginia frontier outpost near the site of present-day Louisville, Kentucky.[4] His father, Robert Johnson, had migrated from Orange County, Virginia, with his wife, Jemima Suggett

Johnson, in 1779. By 1812 Robert Johnson was one of the largest landholders in Kentucky. He served in the Virginia house of burgesses, attended both the 1785 convention that petitioned the Virginia legislature for Kentucky statehood and the 1792 Kentucky constitutional convention, and represented his district in the state legislature for several years after Kentucky's admission to the Union. After three of Richard Mentor Johnson's brothers achieved national office—James and John Telemachus served in the House of Representatives and Benjamin was a federal district judge—critics charged that the family sought "power in every hole and corner of the state." The Johnsons proved remarkably effective in obtaining government contracts and other favors for family members and allies, and their financial interests in local newspapers such as Amos Kendall's Georgetown *Minerva* and the Georgetown *Patriot* added to their considerable influence.[5]

Richard Mentor Johnson received enough of an early education to qualify him for apprenticeships reading law under Kentucky jurists George Nicholas and James Brown,[6] both former students of Thomas Jefferson's legendary teacher George Wythe.[7] The allusions that flavor his letters and speeches suggest at least a passing familiarity with the classics.[8] After his admission to the bar in 1802, he returned to the family's home near Great Crossings, Kentucky, to practice law.[9] He later operated a retail store at Great Crossings and engaged in other business and speculative ventures with brothers James, Benjamin, and Joel. These efforts, together with a sizeable bequest of land and slaves from his father, eventually made Johnson a wealthy man, although he never identified with the privileged classes. He routinely waived legal fees for the indigent land claimants he represented in suits against wealthy speculators,[10] and his home was a mecca for disabled veterans, widows, and orphans seeking his assistance. No one was refused hospitality at Blue Spring Farm, his estate near Great Crossings. An acquaintance "heard men say they were treated so well by Col. Johnson when they went out there, they loved to go."[11]

Early accounts describe the future vice president as a gentle and personable man, with a pleasant, if nondescript, appearance. Washington socialite Margaret Bayard Smith found him "[t]he most tender hearted, mild, affectionate and benevolent of men . . . whose countenance beams with good will to all, whose soul seems to feed on the milk of human kindness." He "might have been a fashionable man," she speculated, if not for his retiring nature and "plain . . . dress and manners."[12] He possessed, in the words of John C. Calhoun's biographer Charles M. Wiltse, "the rare quality of being personally liked by everyone."[13]

Soldier and Legislator

From 1804 to 1806, Johnson served as a delegate from Scott County in the Kentucky house of representatives, where he supported legislation to protect settlers from land speculators.[14] Elected to the United States House of Representatives from the district encompassing Shelby, Scott, and Franklin counties in 1806, he served six consecutive terms, retiring from the House in 1819 to seek election to the Senate.[15] Throughout his career, Johnson professed allegiance to the principles of "Thomas Jefferson, the patriarch of republicanism," and correspondence from his early years in Congress suggests that he enjoyed a cordial acquaintance with Jefferson.[16] In a rambling letter of February 1808, Johnson recommended a candidate for federal office and assured the president that "I feel in you a confidence, & attachment which is indescribable & can never be excelled." "Having procured the Books mentioned in the memorandum from you," the young congressman suggested, "a course of Historical reading would be gratefully received."[17] The acquaintance continued after Jefferson's retirement. In 1813, Johnson wrote that he "constantly recollected how much mankind are indebted to you," adding somewhat self-consciously that "I make no apologies for indulging feelings which I really feel."[18] During the War of 1812, he apprised the retired president of military developments and solicited his counsel "as to the manner of reading, & the Books to read, particularly as it respects Military history."[19]

As the representative of a frontier, predominantly agrarian district, Johnson shared his constituents' concern for the security of the interior settlements, as well as their inherent distrust of bankers, speculators, and other monied interests. An "administration man" with respect to defense and foreign policy matters, he voted against Secretary of the Treasury Albert Gallatin's proposal to recharter the Bank of the United States during the Madison administration.[20] "Great monied monopolies," he explained much later, "controlled by persons, irresponsible to the people, are liable to exercise a dangerous influence, and corporate bodies generally, especially when they have the power to effect the circulating medium of the country, do not well comport with genius of a republic."[21] He was a hardworking representative, popular among the voters of his district but otherwise undistinguished, until his heroism in the War of 1812 brought him national acclaim.[22]

Johnson was one of the vociferous young congressmen, led by his fellow Kentuckian House Speaker Henry Clay, known collectively as the "warhawks." During the Twelfth Congress, this group urged military redress for British violations of American frontiers and shipping rights,[23] and in June 1812 they voted to declare war against Great Britain.[24] Not wishing "to be idle during the recess of Congress,"[25] Johnson raised and led two mounted regiments that joined the northwestern army under the command of his future rival, General William Henry Harrison, in the fall of 1813. Johnson's Kentucky volunteers crossed the Canadian border in pursuit of a combined British and Shawnee force led by General Henry Proctor and overran the enemy position at the Thames River on October 5, 1813. A heroic cavalry charge led by Johnson and his brother James ensured a decisive American victory, in which Tecumseh, the Shawnee leader who had preyed upon American settlements in the Northwest since 1806, was among the presumed casualties. Although his remains were never identified, some witnesses claimed after the fact that Johnson had killed Tecumseh.[26]

Johnson returned to Congress a hero on March 7, 1814, still suffering from the extensive wounds that plagued him for the rest of his life. He turned his attention to war-related matters: the relief of veterans, widows and orphans; the compensation of veterans for service-related property losses; and the improvement of the young nation's military establishment.[27] Johnson's newfound popularity and his characteristic willingness to accede to his constituents' demands ensured his political survival through the furor over the 1816 Compensation Act, which for the first time granted members of Congress an annual salary, rather than paying them only for the days Congress was in session. The measure became controversial when a newspaper estimated that the new system would cost the government an additional $400,000 annually, and Congress repealed the law the next year. Although Johnson sponsored the bill, he quickly repudiated the measure after the public outcry cost many of his colleagues their seats.[28]

His nationalist perspective heightened by the war, Johnson joined with Henry Clay in advocating protection for frontier products and federal funding for internal improvements to give western producers readier access to eastern markets.[29] In 1817, he voted to override Madison's veto of the bonus bill, a proposal to fund internal improvements from the bonus and dividends from the Bank of the United States.[30] Widely regarded as an expert in military affairs as a consequence of his valor under fire, Johnson was one of several westerners whom President James Monroe considered to head the War Department after Henry Clay declined the post in 1817.[31] The nomination ultimately went to John C. Calhoun of South Carolina, but Johnson enjoyed considerable leverage over the department as chairman from 1817 to 1819 of the House Committee on Expenditures in the Department of War.[32] In 1818, Calhoun authorized an expedition to plant a military outpost at the mouth of the Yellowstone River, near the current site of Bismarck, North Dakota, and awarded the transportation and supply contract to the chairman's brother and partner, James Johnson.

The Yellowstone expedition departed from St. Louis just as the panic of 1819 brought postwar economic expansion to a halt and shortly before Treasury Secretary William H. Crawford issued a December 1819 report projecting a $5 million budget deficit. The venture grossly exceeded anticipated costs (in large part because of James

Johnson's malfeasance and Richard Mentor Johnson's repeated pleas for further advances). As a result, the expedition provided Calhoun's enemies in Congress with potent ammunition for an attack that ultimately led to drastic reductions in the War Department budget.[33] After Johnson requested yet another contract for James in the summer of 1820, Calhoun finally advised the president that, "to avoid all censure, the contracts ought to be made on public proposals."[34]

Johnson retired from the House long before the Yellowstone expedition stalled at Council Bluffs, Iowa, but the eventual outcry over the venture failed to diminish his stature in Kentucky.[35] As Monroe had earlier acknowledged, "the people of the whole western country" considered the expedition "a measure . . . to preserve the peace of the frontier."[36] The local press celebrated "the Herculean undertakings of the Johnsons," while accusing their critics of "political animosity."[37] On December 10, 1819, the Kentucky legislature elected Johnson to fill the unexpired portion of John J. Crittenden's Senate term.[38]

Relief for Debtors

Johnson began his Senate career heavily in debt. He mortgaged several properties to the Bank of the United States to settle accounts outstanding from the Yellowstone expedition and other speculative ventures. In 1822 Bank counsel Henry Clay won a substantial judgment against the Johnson brothers.[39] Still, Johnson weathered the depression better than many of his constituents and others who were left destitute after the panic of 1819 severely depressed credit and agricultural prices. Thousands of overextended farmers and laborers found themselves pressed by increasingly frantic creditors during the depression that followed the panic. Imprisonment for debt was a common punishment in state and local courts during the early nineteenth century, although few debtors were incarcerated for outstanding federal obligations.[40]

Both Johnson's own experience and the suffering in his district and elsewhere convinced him that "the principle is deemed too dangerous to be tolerated in a free government, to permit a man for any pecuniary consideration, to dispose of the liberty of his equal."[41] The movement to

end debt imprisonment began long before Johnson, on December 10, 1822, introduced a Senate bill to abolish use of the punishment by federal courts. He did, however, become one of the acknowledged leaders of the effort, first through his success in persuading the Kentucky legislature to abolish the practice in 1821 and then with his decade-long campaign in Congress that in 1832 achieved enactment of a federal statute.[42] Senator Thomas Hart Benton of Missouri later explained that the impact of the 1832 law extended far beyond the federal courts "in the force of example and influence." The statute "led to the cessation of the practice of imprisoning debtors, in all, or nearly all, of the States and Territories of the Union."[43]

A second legislative accomplishment that brought Johnson national distinction was a report that he prepared during his final Senate term, as chairman of the Committee on Post Offices and Post Roads, in response to a flood of petitions from religious congregations in the East demanding the suspension of Sunday mail deliveries. The January 19, 1829, report, widely reprinted in the press, argued that, as "a civil, and not a religious institution," the government could take no action sanctioning the religious convictions or practices of any denomination. After leaving the Senate, Johnson continued his crusade as a member of the House of Representatives. In 1830, as chairman of the House Committee on Post Offices and Post Roads, he submitted a second report. This, like the earlier Senate report, brought him widespread acclaim in the labor press as a champion of religious liberty. Some contemporaries doubted Johnson's authorship of the second report, however; and his biographer has conceded that Johnson's friends in the Post Office Department, including his landlord O.B. Brown, may have influenced his stance.[44]

During his ten years in the Senate from 1819 to 1829, Johnson gravitated toward the coalition, then emerging under the skilled leadership of Martin Van Buren, that eventually became the Democratic party, as well as toward the party's future standard bearer, Andrew Jackson.[45] The acquaintance dated at least from 1814, when Johnson wrote to Jackson at New Orleans to recommend a supply contractor.[46] He was Jackson's impassioned, if ineffective, defender in 1819 when Clay urged the House of Representatives to censure the general for his execution of two British subjects during the Seminole War.[47] Senator Johnson declared for Jackson after the 1824 presidential election was thrown into the House of Representatives[48]—and, by some accounts, after the candidate hinted that, if elected, he intended to name Johnson secretary of war.[49] When the House elected John Quincy Adams president, Johnson broke the news to Jackson that the new president had named as secretary of state Henry Clay, who had voted for Adams in spite of the Kentucky voters' clear preference for Jackson.[50] Johnson was absent when the Senate approved Clay's nomination on March 7, 1825.[51] A Washington journalist later reported that, after the election, Johnson "determined to enter the ranks of the opposition."[52] He had become, and would remain for the rest of his life, a steadfast "Jacksonian."

Johnson was reelected to a full Senate term in 1822 but in 1828 lost his reelection bid because Kentucky Democrats feared that controversy over his domestic life would jeopardize Jackson's chances in the national election. Johnson never married. Family tradition recounts that he ended an early romance, vowing revenge for his mother's interference, after Jemima Johnson pronounced his intended bride unworthy of the family.[53] He later lived openly with Julia Chinn, a mulatto slave raised by his mother and inherited from his father, until her death from cholera in 1833. Johnson freely acknowledged the relationship, as well as the two daughters born to the union, and entrusted Julia with full authority over his business affairs during his absences from Blue Spring Farm.[54]

The relationship provoked little comment in Johnson's congressional district, but as a member of the Senate, with an expanded constituency, he was vulnerable to criticism by large slaveholders and others who disapproved of open miscegenation. Threatened press exposure of the senator's personal life during the 1828 campaign unnerved Jackson supporters in the Kentucky legislature. They therefore attempted to dissociate the national candidate from the now-controversial Johnson, joining forces with the Adams faction

to oppose Johnson's reelection and ultimately forcing state legislator John Telemachus Johnson to withdraw his brother's name from the contest.[55] The defeat ended Johnson's Senate career. In his three later attempts to return to the Senate, he lost to Henry Clay in 1831 and 1848 and to John J. Crittenden in 1842.[56]

In the House Again

In 1829 the voters in Johnson's old district returned him to the House of Representatives,[57] where he remained during Jackson's two administrations. After chairing the Committee on Post Offices and Post Roads from 1829 to 1833, he served as chairman of the Committee on Military Affairs from 1833 to 1837.[58] An acknowledged power in the House, Johnson offered his services and advice to the administration on several occasions, albeit with noticeably less success than the more politically astute Martin Van Buren.[59]

Johnson was, by nature, a conciliator, whose vehement rhetoric belied a tendency to avoid politically risky confrontations. In 1830 he urged Jackson to sign a bill to fund an extension of the national road from Lexington to Maysville, Kentucky, warning in emphatic terms that "you will crush your friends in Kentucky if you veto that Bill." When the president proved intransigent, he conceded that a tax to fund the Maysville Road "would be worse than a veto." He failed to vote when the House sustained the veto on May 18, 1830.[60]

An early aspirant for the 1832 Democratic presidential nomination, Johnson refocused his sights on the vice-presidency after Jackson announced that he would seek a second term.[61] New York labor leader Ely Moore and members of the Workingmen's party supported Johnson for vice president,[62] but Democratic strategists questioned the wisdom of adding him to the ticket. A correspondent of Navy Secretary John McLean noted that "Gen. Jackson . . . is in feeble health; and may not live to the end of his second term" and questioned whether "Colo. Johnson's calibre will answer for so high a station."[63] Despite clear indications that Van Buren would replace Calhoun as the vice-presidential candidate, however, Johnson abandoned his campaign only after Jackson's adviser William B. Lewis convinced him to do so.[64] When, on May 22, 1832, the Democratic convention tapped Van Buren as Jackson's running mate on the first ballot, Johnson received only 26 votes from the Kentucky, Indiana, and Illinois delegations—a poor showing compared to Van Buren's 208 votes and the 49 votes of former House Speaker and Calhoun ally Philip P. Barbour. Jackson and Van Buren then went on to win an easy victory in the general election.[65]

As early as April 1833, shortly after Jackson's new term began, Duff Green's *Political Register* reported that "the western States are flooded with handbills nominating Col. Richard M. Johnson, of Kentucky, as a candidate for the Presidency in 1836." Johnson's friend William Emmons published *The Authentic Biography of Colonel Richard M. Johnson* in 1833, and Richard Emmons' play, *Tecumseh, of the Battle of the Thames,* soon followed. A poem by Richard Emmons supplied the slogan that Johnson enthusiasts trumpeted in the 1836 and 1840 campaigns: "Rumpsey, Dumpsey, Colonel Johnson killed Tecumseh!"

The candidate delighted in these overblown celebrations of his military prowess, boasting after a well-attended and well-received performance of *Tecumseh* that he had "more friends than ever."[66] But Johnson's following was based upon more than his military accomplishments, exaggerated though they were by his eager promoters. His efforts to abolish imprisonment for debt and to continue Sunday mail deliveries ensured him the support of the workingmen's movement in the urban centers, and his "hard-money," antibank fiscal policy appealed to the party's "radical" faction. He also enjoyed a strong following in the West, where Jackson's "Kitchen Cabinet" advisers Amos Kendall and Francis P. Blair considered him the only candidate who could neutralize Clay's overwhelming appeal.[67] Party regulars understood, however, that in selecting Van Buren as his running mate in 1832, Jackson had named the diminutive New Yorker his successor. Johnson eventually acceded to the president's wishes with his usual equanimity, refusing to run as an opposition candidate when approached in 1834 by a coalition of disaffected Tennesseans led by David Crockett

and John Bell.[68] Blair and Kendall quietly changed their tactics in hopes of securing the vice-presidential nomination for "Old Dick."[69] Perhaps they hoped that Johnson would thus become the "heir apparent" to succeed Van Buren, or perhaps they merely recognized the futility of opposing Old Hickory's will. Van Buren served as Jackson's "right hand" during his term as vice president, but this arrangement resulted more from his longstanding relationship with the president than from any commonly held assumptions regarding the role of the vice president.

1836 Election

When the Democratic convention met at Baltimore on May 22, 1835, to ratify Van Buren's nomination and select his running mate, Johnson's only serious opponent for the vice-presidential nomination was former senator William Cabell Rives of Virginia, who had served as minister to France during Jackson's first administration. Southern Democrats, and Van Buren himself, strongly preferred Rives. Although he counted "the gallant Colonel . . . among the bravest of the brave," Van Buren also feared that Johnson could not "be relied upon to check the cupidity of his friends." Jackson, however, concerned about the threat that opposition candidate Hugh Lawson White posed among western voters, strongly preferred his Kentucky lieutenant. His anger over Rives' diplomatic failures and his gratitude for Johnson's longstanding loyalty and support also weighed heavily in his decision. In spite of the president's considerable influence, however, Johnson received the required two-thirds vote only after New York Senator Silas Wright prevailed upon nondelegate Edward Rucker to cast the fifteen votes of the absent Tennessee delegation in his favor.[70]

The choice provoked bitter dissention in Democratic ranks. Virginia delegate Dr. R.C. Mason questioned Johnson's fidelity to the party's "great republican principles" and announced that his delegation would not support the nomination.[71] Johnson's letter of acceptance, explaining that "I consider the views of president Jackson, on the tariff and internal improvements, as founded in true wisdom," failed to mollify the Virginians.[72] Van Buren's ally Albert Balch had previously warned Jackson that "I do not think from what I hear daily that the nomination of Johnson for the Vice Presidency will be popular in any of the slave holding states except Ky. on account of his former domestic relations,"[73] and a Van Buren correspondent later predicted that "Col. Johnson's . . . weight would absolutely sink the whole party in Virginia."[74] Tennessee Supreme Court Chief Justice John Catron warned Jackson that Johnson was "not only positively unpopular in Tennessee . . . but affirmatively odious" and begged the president "to assure our friends that the humblest of us do not believe that a lucky random shot, even if it did hit Tecumseh, qualifies a man for the Vice Presidency." He predicted that "the very moment Col. J. is announced, the newspapers will open upon him with facts, that he had endeavored often to force his daughters into society, that the mother in her life time, and they now, rode in carriages, and claimed equality."[75]

The Whigs still formed a loose coalition bound by mutual opposition to Jackson's antibank policies but lacked the party unity or organizational strength to field a single ticket or define a coherent platform. Instead of a single nominee, they offered a series of sectional candidates nominated by local caucuses in hopes of defeating Van Buren in each region and throwing the election into the House of Representatives. The Whig presidential candidates were Daniel Webster, Tennessee Senator and former Jacksonian Hugh Lawson White, and Johnson's former commander, General William Henry Harrison. For vice president, opposition caucuses nominated New York Anti-Mason Francis Granger and former Democrat John Tyler of Virginia.[76]

In the bitter campaign that followed, Whigs attempted to attract disaffected Democrats by focusing on personalities rather than issues. In the South, opposition strategists raised the specter of abolition against Van Buren,[77] while attacking Johnson as a "great amalgamator," who had "habitually and practically illustrated" abolitionist principles in his own home.[78] Johnson not only cost his party southern votes, but he also failed to attract western votes as anticipated. His own state went for Harrison and Granger. In

spite of these disappointments, however, Van Buren still managed a narrow victory with just over fifty percent of the popular vote.[79]

On February 8, 1837, President pro tempore of the Senate William R. King of Alabama proclaimed to the members of Congress assembled in the House chamber to tally the electoral returns that Martin Van Buren, with 170 electoral votes, was the "duly elected President of the United States." Johnson, however, received only 147 electoral votes, 70 more than his closest contender, Francis Granger, but one less than the number required to elect. The Virginia electors had remained loyal to Van Buren, who carried the state by a close margin, but cast their votes in the vice-presidential contest for William Smith of Alabama. After King announced that "it devolved on the Senate of the United States . . . to choose . . . a Vice President of the United States," the Senate retired to its own chamber.[80]

After reassembling to elect the vice president, the Senate approved Tennessee Senator Felix Grundy's resolution to establish the voting procedure:

> [T]he Secretary of the Senate shall call the names of Senators in alphabetical order; and each Senator will, when his name is called, name the person for whom he votes; and if a majority of the whole number of Senators shall vote for either the said Richard M. Johnson or Francis Granger, he shall be declared by the presiding officer of the Senate constitutionally elected Vice President of the United States.

Secretary of the Senate Asbury Dickins called the roll, with 49 of the 52 senators present voting along strict party lines: 33 for Johnson, 16 for Granger. President pro tempore King then announced that Johnson had been "constitutionally elected Vice President of the United States for four years, commencing on the fourth day of March, 1837."[81]

Vice President

Notified of his election,[82] Johnson responded that his "gratification was heightened from the conviction that the Senate, in the exercise of their constitutional prerogative, concurred with and confirmed the wishes of both the States and the people." He explained that he had never paid "special regard to the minuteness of rules and orders, so necessary to the progress of business, and so important to the observance of the presiding officer" during his three decades in Congress. He was nonetheless confident—in words reminiscent of Jefferson's forty years earlier—that "the intelligence of the Senate will guard the country from any injury that might result from the imperfections of the presiding officer." While he hoped "that there may be always sufficient unanimity" to prevent equal divisions in the Senate, he would perform his duty "without embarrassment" in the event that he was called upon to cast a tie-breaking vote.[83]

President pro tempore King administered the oath of office to Johnson in the Senate chamber at 10:00 a.m. on March 4, 1837. In a brief address to the Senate, the new vice president observed that "there is not, perhaps, a deliberative assembly existing, where the presiding officer has less difficulty in preserving order." He attributed this characteristic to "the intelligence and patriotism of the members who compose the body, and that personal respect and courtesy which have always been extended from one member to another in its deliberations." At the conclusion of his remarks, the ceremony of newly elected senators presenting their credentials to the Senate and taking the oath of office was temporarily interrupted by the arrival of President-elect Van Buren and his party. The senators therefore joined the procession to the east portico of the Capitol for the presidential inauguration.[84]

Contemporary witnesses and scholarly accounts of the day's festivities mention Richard Mentor Johnson only in passing, if at all. The outgoing president, worn and emaciated from two terms in office and a recent debilitating illness but still towering over his immaculately attired successor, was clearly the focus of attention. Thomas Hart Benton, a dedicated Jackson supporter, later recounted the "acclamations and cheers bursting from the heart and filling the air" that erupted from the crowd as Jackson took his leave of the ceremony. From Benton's perspective, "the rising was eclipsed by the setting sun."[85]

Johnson's friendship with Jackson and his stature in the House had assured him access to the president and some measure of influence during Jackson's administrations. The controversy surrounding his nomination, however, together with his disappointing showing in the 1836 election, his longstanding rivalry with Van Buren, and the constitutional limitations of his new office severely curtailed his role in the Van Buren administration. Histories of Van Buren's presidency do not indicate that he ever sought his vice president's counsel.[86] Johnson's duties were confined to the Senate chamber, where he watched from the presiding officer's chair as Senate Finance Committee Chairman Silas Wright of New York introduced Van Buren's economic program.[87]

Johnson was, however, willing to use on behalf of his friends and cronies the limited influence he still commanded. When Lewis Tappan asked the vice president to present an abolition petition to the Senate, Johnson, who owned several slaves, averred that "considerations of a moral and political, as well as of a constitutional nature" prevented him from presenting "petitions of a character evidently hostile to the union, and destructive of the principles on which it is founded."[88] "Constitutional considerations" did not, however, prevent him from lobbying Congress on behalf of Indian subagent Samuel Milroy when Milroy, an Indiana Democrat who performed "special favors" for the vice president, sought the more lucrative position of Indian agent.[89]

Johnson was a competent presiding officer,[90] although not an accomplished parliamentarian. In keeping with Senate practice during the 1830s, he appointed senators to standing and select committees, a duty that President pro tempore William R. King performed when he was absent.[91]

Although he had hoped for "equanimity" in the Senate, Johnson was called upon to cast his tie-breaking vote fourteen times during his single term in office, more frequently than any previous vice president except John Adams and John C. Calhoun.[92] Three of his predecessors—Adams, George Clinton, and Daniel D. Tompkins—had addressed the Senate on occasion to explain their tie-breaking votes, but Johnson declined to do so.[93] In at least one instance, however, he did explain a vote to readers of the *Kentucky Gazette.* Justifying his support for a bill granting relief to the daughter of a veteran, Johnson reminded his former constituents that he had always "used my humble abilities in favor of those laws which have extended compensation to the officers and soldiers who have bravely fought, and freely bled, in their country's cause, and to widows and orphans of those who perished." [94] In other instances, however, Johnson voted with Democratic senators in support of administration policy. [95]

Notwithstanding his steady, if lackluster, service in the Senate, Johnson from the outset represented a liability to Van Buren. Still heavily in debt when he assumed office, he hoped to recoup his fortunes through the Choctaw Academy, a school he established at Blue Spring Farm during the 1820s that became the focus of the Jackson administration's efforts to "socialize" and "civilize" the Native American population. He received federal funds for each student from tribal annuities and the "Civilization Fund" established by Congress during the Monroe administration, [96] but revenues from the school failed to satisfy his mounting obligations. By the spring of 1839, Amos Kendall reported to Van Buren on the vice president's latest venture: a hotel and tavern at White Sulphur Spring, Kentucky. He enclosed a letter from a friend who had visited "Col. Johnson's Watering establishment" and found the vice president "happy in the inglorious pursuit of tavern keeping—even giving his personal superintendence to the chicken and egg purchasing and water-melon selling department." [97] Kendall wrote with consternation that Johnson's companion, "a young Delilah of about the complexion of Shakespears swarthy Othello," was "said to be his third wife; his second, which he sold for her infidelity, having been the sister of the present lady." [98] Although one of the most fashionable in Kentucky, [99] Johnson's resort also formed a source of considerable embarrassment for the administration.

As debts, disappointments, and the chronic pain he had suffered since 1813 took their toll, Johnson's once-pleasing appearance became dishevelled, and the plain republican manners that had in earlier days so charmed Margaret Bayard

Smith now struck observers as vulgar and crude, [100] especially compared to the impeccably clad and consummately tactful Van Buren. Henry Stanton observed Johnson presiding over the Senate in 1838 and pronounced him "shabbily dressed, and to the last degree clumsy," a striking contrast with his "urbane, elegant predecessor." [101] English author Harriett Martineau sat opposite the vice president at a dinner party, and predicted that "if he should become President, he will be as strange-looking a potentate as ever ruled. His countenance is wild, though with much cleverness in it; his hair wanders all abroad, and he wears no cravat. But there is no telling how he might look if he dressed like other people." [102] The trademark scarlet vest that Johnson affected while vice president (after he and stagecoach line operator James Reeside agreed to don vests to match Reeside's red coaches) [103] only accentuated his unkempt appearance and eccentric habits.

Van Buren and Johnson took office just as weakened demand for American products abroad and credit restrictions imposed by British banks and trading houses combined to produce a massive contraction in the economy. Critics focused their wrath on Jackson's fiscal policies, which were in part responsible for the panic of 1837, but Van Buren would not abandon his predecessor's "hard money" stance. He refused mounting demands to rescind the 1836 Specie Circular, Jackson's directive to end speculation and inflation by requiring purchasers of public land to pay in specie. During the September 1837 special session of Congress that Van Buren called to address the crisis, Senate Finance Committee Chairman Silas Wright of New York introduced the new administration's remedy, a proposal to end government reliance on the banking system. Congress finally approved Van Buren's independent treasury plan in the summer of 1840, but not before bitter debate and the worsening economy galvanized the Whig opposition. [104] Adding to Van Buren's considerable difficulties, and contributing to Democratic losses in the 1837 and 1838 local elections, were a border dispute with Canada, armed resistance to removal by the Seminole tribe in Florida, heightened sectional antagonism over slavery in Congress, and flagrant misconduct on the part of several administration appointees.[105]

1840 Campaign

Although Van Buren's renomination was never in doubt, Democratic strategists began to question the wisdom of keeping Johnson on the ticket in 1840. They feared, as Harriett Martineau had predicted, that "the slavery question . . . may again be to the disadvantage of the Colonel."[106] Even Jackson finally conceded that Johnson was a liability and insisted on former House Speaker James K. Polk of Tennessee as Van Buren's new running mate.[107] "I like Col. Johnson but I like my country more," he wrote Francis P. Blair shortly before the Democratic convention, "and I allway go for my Country first, and then for my friend."[108]

In spite of the entreaties of several southern Democrats, anonymous hints in the Democratic press that Johnson would not stand for reelection, and his own half-hearted offer to withdraw from the contest if asked to do so, he remained a candidate.[109] With William Henry Harrison, Johnson's former commander and comrade-in-arms and the "Hero of Tippecanoe," emerging as a likely Whig presidential contender, Van Buren was reluctant to drop the Democrats' own hero from the ticket. He was also well aware of "Old Dick's" following among "hard-money" Democrats in the Northeast.[110] Party leaders, unwilling to risk an open confrontation, approved Van Buren's compromise proposal that the 1840 convention would leave the selection of the vice-presidential candidate to the state party organizations, but they ultimately backed Johnson after two crucial states—New York and Pennsylvania—rallied behind him and other prospective candidates declined to run.[111]

Eastern Whigs' fear that Clay could not win the presidency, as well as Harrison's surprising showing in the 1836 contest, assured Harrison the 1840 Whig nomination. To balance his strength in the North and West, Whigs chose former Virginia Senator John Tyler as their vice-presidential candidate. Whigs portrayed Harrison as a champion of the people and a welcome corrective to the New York dandy whose economic policies had failed to relieve widespread suffering among ordinary folk.[112]

Van Buren remained aloof from the popular hoopla that distinguished the 1840 campaign from earlier contests, despite Johnson's warning that the campaign "would be hard run, and that he ought to go out among the voters as I intended doing."[113] The vice president plunged headlong into the fray, opening his shirt to display battle scars before an Ohio audience, revisiting the Battle of the Thames in progressively more lurid detail with each retelling, and delivering "rambling" diatribes on several occasions. He always also took care to remind western audiences that Van Buren had "raised himself from a poor Dutch orphan boy to the highest station in the world." During an Ohio campaign tour with Governor Wilson Shannon and Senator William Allen, the trio's inflammatory charges against Harrison touched off a riot in Cleveland.[114] Still, as Robert Gray Gunderson concluded in his study of the "log-cabin campaign," "Old Rumpsey Dumpsey conducted a more effective campaign than any other Democrat in 1840."[115]

Unprecedented public interest aroused by the campaign, coupled with broadened suffrage requirements in several states, ensured a record voter turnout. Harrison defeated Van Buren with 52.9 percent of the popular vote and 234 electoral votes to Van Buren's 60, and Whigs won majorities for the first time in both the House and the Senate.[116] Johnson's showing was particularly embarrassing: Kentucky voters again backed the opposing ticket, but this time the Whigs carried the vice president's own district as well.[117] One of the 23 Virginia electors, and all of South Carolina's 11 electors, voted for Van Buren but defected to James K. Polk and Littleton W. Tazewell of Virginia, respectively, in the vice-presidential contest.[118]

Johnson had the painful duty of presiding over the joint session of Congress that met in the House chamber on February 10, 1841, to count the electoral votes. After proclaiming Harrison's election, he announced that John Tyler "was duly elected Vice President of the United States for four years, commencing with the 4th day of March, 1841." He then appointed Whig Senator

William C. Preston of South Carolina to a joint committee to notify Tyler of his election,[119] and nine days later, he reported Tyler's acknowledgement of the message.[120]

Farewell

Johnson took his leave of the Senate on March 2, 1841, the day before the Twenty-sixth Congress adjourned, to allow the Senate "an opportunity of selecting a presiding officer, for the convenience of organization" when the next Congress convened two days later. Recalling his association with "a very great majority of the members of the Senate . . . for many years, in the councils of our common country," he reflected that his "personal relations" with them had "ever been kind and tender," notwithstanding "diversity of opinion . . . on minor points, or . . . points of greater magnitude." The "generous, the magnanimous course" of individual senators, and particularly "their indulgence" of a presiding officer "who never studied the rules of order technically," had rendered his service in the Senate "pleasant and agreeable" despite "momentary agitation and excitement in debate." As the Senate's presiding officer, he had tried to "act with perfect impartiality" and to treat "each Senator as the representative of a sovereign and independent State, and as entitled to equal consideration of me."

Johnson claimed that he retired "without the least dissatisfaction," obedient to "the great radical and fundamental principle of submission to the voice of the people, when constitutionally expressed." But his parting comments betrayed a sense of regret:

[A]nd when I am far distant from you—as time must separate us all even here, not to speak of hereafter—as long as I shall have my recollection to remember the associations which I have had with this body, I shall always be animated by the sentiment of kindness and friendship with which I take my final leave of the Senate.[121]

Later Years

Johnson's 1840 defeat effectively ended his political career. He was a candidate for the Senate in 1842 but lost to John J. Crittenden. Early efforts by Kentucky Democrats to secure the 1844 Democratic presidential nomination for "Colonel Dick," and his own tours of the northern states and the Mississippi Valley toward that end, met with polite but condescending resistance from Democrats who shared William L. Marcy's view that "he is not now even what he formally was. It may be there was never so much of him as many of us were led to suppose."[122] Jackson was characteristically blunt. Johnson, he warned Van Buren, would be "dead weight" in the forthcoming election.[123] An observer noted the old hero's mounting frustration: "Colonel Dick Johnson . . . seems to understand very well Mr. V Buren is stacking the cards . . . Dick . . . will be bamboozled as sure as a gun. . . . You never saw a more restless dissatisfied man in your life, than Dick is."[124] By 1843, Johnson partisans conceded that he had no chance of winning the presidential nomination, and a Kentucky Democrat assured Van Buren that "the friends of Col. Johnson do not ask anything more than a vote on the first ballot in his favor."[125] Several Democrats speculated that Johnson's real objective was the vice-presidential nomination, although he never formally declared himself a candidate.[126] But by early 1844 he realized that "his party doesn't even intend to place him upon the Vice Presidents ticket."[127]

Johnson made a final attempt to return to the Senate in 1848, but the Kentucky legislature sent his old colleague and adversary, Henry Clay, to Washington. Scott County voters elected Johnson to the state legislature two years later, but he was gravely ill when he took his seat on November 8, 1850. Shortly after the *Louisville Daily Journal* reported that "it is painful to see him on the floor attempting to discharge the duties of a member," Johnson suffered a stroke. He died on November 19, 1850, and, by resolution of the Kentucky legislature, was buried at the Frankfort cemetery. State Senator Beriah Magoffin eulogized the frontier hero as Johnson would have wished to be remembered: "He was the poor man's friend. . . . Void of ostentation, simple in his taste, his manners, and his dress—brave, magnanimous, patriotic and generous to a fault, in his earliest years he was the beau ideal of the soul and the chivalry of Kentucky."[128]

NOTES

[1] John Spencer Bassett, ed., *Correspondence of Andrew Jackson* (Washington, DC, 1931), 5:331.

[2] The first full-length account of Richard Mentor Johnson's career was William Emmons' highly laudatory campaign biography, *Authentic Biography of Colonel Richard M. Johnson* (New York, 1833). Ignatius Loyola Robertson's Sketches of Public Characters—Drawn from the Living and the Dead (New York, 1830), includes a brief and highly complimentary sketch of Johnson's career. Leland Winfield Meyer, *Life and Times of Colonel Richard M. Johnson* (New York, 1967, reprint of 1932 edition), pp. 176, 298, 342, 401, 405, 489. Meyer's biography, the only modern account of Johnson's life and career, accepts at face value many of the assumptions and assessments that color the earlier works.

[3] *Louisville Journal*, October 14, 1840, quoted in Meyer, p. 290.

[4] U.S., Congress, *Biographical Directory of the United States Congress, 1774–1989*, S. Doc. 100–34, 100th Cong., 2d sess., 1989, p. 1270.

[5] Meyer, pp. 13–48, 325–27.

[6] Ibid., pp. 290–91.

[7] Robert V. Remini, *Henry Clay: Statesman for the Union* (New York, 1991), p. 18.

[8] See, for example, Johnson's December 4, 1816, speech on the Compensation Law, U.S., Congress, House, *Annals of Congress*, 14th Cong., 2d sess., pp. 235–43.

[9] Meyer, p. 292.

[10] Ibid., pp. 290–342 and passim.

[11] Ibid., pp. 312–14 and Appendix, "Mr. James Y. Kelly's Reminiscences about 'Dick Johnson' Taken Down as He Spoke, April 2, 1929, to Leland W. Meyer," pp. 477–78.

[12] Mrs. Samuel Harrison Smith (Margaret Bayard Smith), *The First Forty Years of Washington Society* (New York, 1906), quoted in Meyer, pp. 293, 304–5.

[13] Charles M. Wiltse, *John C. Calhoun*, vol. 2, *Nullifier, 1829–1839* (New York, 1968; reprint of 1948 ed.), p. 37.

[14] Meyer, pp. 49–58.

[15] Ibid., p. 58; *Biographical Directory of the United States Congress*, p. 1270.

[16] R. M. Johnson to Andrew Stevenson et al., June 9, 1835, in James A. Padgett, ed., "The Letters of Colonel Richard M. Johnson of Kentucky," *Register of the Kentucky State Historical Society* 40 (January 1942): 83–86.

[17] Richard M. Johnson to Thomas Jefferson, February 27, 1808, in James A. Padgett, ed., "The Letters of Colonel Richard M. Johnson of Kentucky," *Register of the Kentucky State Historical Society* 38 (July 1940): 190–91.

[18] Richard M. Johnson to Thomas Jefferson, January 30, 1813, in ibid., p. 197.

[19] Richard M. Johnson to Thomas Jefferson, February 9, 1813 [1814?], in ibid., p. 198.

[20] Meyer, pp. 49–84.

[21] Richard Mentor Johnson to Dawson et al., February 6, 1836, printed in *Kentucky Gazette*, April 2, 1836, and reprinted in Meyer, p. 142.

[22] Meyer, pp. 49–84.

[23] Marshall Smelser, *The Democratic Republic, 1801–1815* (New York, 1968), pp. 208–9; John Niven, *John C. Calhoun and the Price of Union* (Baton Rouge, LA, 1988), p. 36; Harry W. Fritz, "The War Hawks of 1812," *Capitol Studies* 5 (Spring 1977): 28.

[24] Smelser, p. 216.

[25] Richard Mentor Johnson to John Armstrong, received February 23, 1813, quoted in Meyer, pp. 100–101.

[26] Smelser, pp. 210, 255–56; Meyer, pp. 101–35.

[27] Meyer, pp. 136–88.

[28] U.S., Congress, House, *Annals of Congress*, 14th Cong., 1st sess., pp. 1127–34, Appendix, p. 1801; 14th Cong., 2d sess., pp. 235–43, Appendix, p. 1278; Charles M. Wiltse, *John C. Calhoun*, vol. 1, *Nationalist, 1782–1828* (New York, 1968; reprint of 1944 edition), pp. 125–31; U.S., Congress, Senate, *The Senate, 1789–1989: Addresses on the History of the United States Senate*, by Robert C. Byrd, S. Doc. 100–20, vol. 2, 1991, pp. 350–51; Meyer, pp. 168, 172, 326–27.

[29] Meyer, pp. 162–67.

[30] *Annals of Congress*, 14th Cong., 2d sess., p. 1062.

[31] Harry Ammon, *James Monroe: The Quest for National Identity* (Charlottesville, VA, 1990), pp. 358–59.

[32] *Biographical Directory of the United States Congress*, p. 1270.

[33] John Niven, *John C. Calhoun and the Price of Union* (Baton Rouge, LA, 1988), pp. 59–80; Ammon, pp. 468–71; Meyer, pp. 189–206; Merrill D. Peterson, *The Great Triumvirate: Webster, Clay, and Calhoun* (New York, 1987), pp. 88–95; Chase C. Mooney, *William H. Crawford, 1772–1834* (Lexington, KY, 1974), pp. 151–57.

[34] John C. Calhoun to James Monroe, July 14, 1820, quoted in Meyer, p. 195.

[35] Meyer, pp. 202–5.

[36] James Monroe to John C. Calhoun, July 5, 1819, quoted in ibid., p. 202.

[37] *Kentucky Gazette*, October 8, 1819, quoted in ibid., p. 203.

[38] Meyer, pp. 183–88.

[39] Ibid., pp. 205–6; Remini, *Henry Clay*, pp. 207–8.

[40] Arthur M. Schlesinger, Jr., *The Age of Jackson* (Boston, 1945), pp. 134–36.

[41] Speech of Col. Richard M. Johnson to the Senate, January 14, 1823, quoted in Meyer, pp. 283–84.

[42] Schlesinger, pp. 134–36; Meyer, pp. 235, 282–89; *Annals of Congress*, 17th Cong., 2d sess., pp. 23–27.

[43] Thomas Hart Benton, *Thirty Years' View; or, A History of the Working of the American Government for Thirty Years, From 1820 to 1851* (New York, 1871; reprint of 1854 ed.), 1:291–92.

[44] Meyer, pp. 256–63, 293–94.

[45] Ibid., *passim*; Donald R. Cole, *Martin Van Buren and the American Political System* (Princeton, NJ, 1984), p. 125.

[46] Richard M. Johnson to Major General Andrew Jackson, November 21, 1814, in Padgett, ed., *Register of the Kentucky State Historical Society* 38: 326–27.

[47] Remini, *Henry Clay*, pp. 161–66.

[48] Meyer, p. 220.

[49] Ibid., pp. 221–22.

[50] Remini, *Henry Clay*, p. 268.

[51] Robert V. Remini, *Andrew Jackson and the Course of American Freedom, 1822–1832* (New York, 1981), p. 103; U.S., Congress, Senate, *Journal*, Appendix, 19th Cong., special session of March 4, 1825; U.S., Congress, Senate, *Executive Journal*, 19th Cong., special session, p. 441.

[52] *Niles' Weekly Register*, April 28, 1827, quoted in Meyer, pp. 220–21.

[53] Meyer, pp. 318–19.

[54] Ibid., pp. 317–22.

[55] Ibid., pp. 251–55.

[56] Remini, *Henry Clay*, pp. 373, 716; Meyer, p. 457.

[57] Meyer, p. 256.

[58] *Biographical Directory of the United States Congress*, p. 1270.

[59] Meyer, pp. 266–71; Robert V. Remini, *Andrew Jackson and the Course of American Democracy, 1833–1845* (New York, 1984), pp. 203–16, 305–6, 423; Richard M. Johnson to Andrew Jackson, February 13, 1831, in Padgett, ed., *Register of the Kentucky State Historical Society* 40: 69.

[60] Meyer, pp. 273–76; U.S., Congress, House, *Journal*, 21st Cong., 1st sess., pp. 763–64; Remini, *Jackson and the Course of American Freedom*, pp. 252–56.

[61] Remini, *Jackson and the Course of American Freedom*, p. 304; Meyer, pp. 393–400.

[62] Walter Hugins, *Jacksonian Democracy and the Working Class: A Study of the New York Workingmen's Movement* (Stanford, CA, 1960), pp. 63–64, 97.

[63] John Norvell to John McLean, January 23, 1832, and Worden Pope to John McLean, quoted in Meyer, p. 398.

[64] Schlesinger, p. 142.

[65] Robert V. Remini, "Election of 1832," in *History of American Presidential Elections, 1789–1968*, ed. Arthur M. Schlesinger and Fred L. Israel, (New York, 1971), 1:507–8; John Niven, *Martin Van Buren and the Romantic Era of American Politics* (New York, 1983), p. 300.

[66] Meyer, pp. 315–16, 398–402, 411.

[67] Major L. Wilson, *The Presidency of Martin Van Buren* (Lawrence, KS, 1984), pp. 15–16; Niven, *Martin Van Buren*, pp. 374–76; John Arthur Garraty, *Silas Wright* (New York, 1970; reprint of 1949 edition), p. 130; Remini, *Jackson and the Course of American Democracy*, p. 256; Meyer, pp. 393–429.

[68] Remini, *Jackson and the Course of American Democracy*, pp. 252–53.

[69] Ibid., pp. 182–83, 252–55, Niven, *Martin Van Buren*, p. 351, 372–76; Cole, p. 262; Wilson, p. 16.

[70] Remini, *Jackson and the Course of American Democracy*, pp. 256; Niven, *Martin Van Buren*, pp. 374–96; Wilson, p. 16; John C. Fitzpatrick, ed., *The Autobiography of Martin Van Buren* (Washington, DC, 1920), 2:754, quoted in Meyer, pp. 337–38.

[71] Niven, *Martin Van Buren*, p. 396; Meyer, p. 419.

[72] Richard M. Johnson to Andrew Stevenson, et al., June 9, 1835, in Padgett, ed., *Register of the Kentucky State Historical Society* 40: 83–86.

[73] Albert Balch to Andrew Jackson, April 4, 1835, quoted in Meyer, p. 413.

[74] C.S. Morgan to Martin Van Buren, January 9, 1936, quoted in Robert Bolt, "Vice President Richard M. Johnson of Kentucky: Hero of the Thames—Or the Great Amalgamator?" *Register of the Kentucky Historical Society* 75 (July 1977): 201.

[75] John Catron to Andrew Jackson, March 21, 1835, in Bassett, *Correspondence of Jackson*, 5:330–32.

[76] Joel Silbey, "Election of 1836," in Schlesinger and Israel, eds., 1:584–86.

[77] Silbey, pp. 586–91; Harry L. Watson, *Liberty and Power: The Politics of Jacksonian America* (New York, 1990), p. 204.

[78] *United States Telegraph*, June 3, 1835, quoted in Bolt, pp. 198–99.

[79] Niven, *Martin Van Buren*, pp. 401–2; Silbey, pp. 591–96; *Senate Journal*, 24th Cong., 2d sess., pp. 227–28.

[80] *Senate Journal*, 24th Cong., 2d sess., pp. 227–28; Niven, *Martin Van Buren*, pp. 401–2.

[81] *Senate Journal*, 24th Cong., 2d sess., pp. 229–31. South Carolina Senators John C. Calhoun and William C. Preston and Tennessee Senator Hugh Lawson White attended but did not vote. Wiltse, 2:303.

[82] *Senate Journal*, 24th Cong., 2d sess., p. 231.

[83] Ibid., pp. 238–39.

[84] Ibid., Appendix, special session of March 4, 1837, pp. 355–65.

[85] Benton, 1:735; Cole, pp. 289–90; Remini, *Jackson and the Course of American Democracy*, pp. 420–23; Stephen W. Stathis and Ronald C. Moe, "America's Other Inauguration," *Presidential Studies Quarterly* 10 (Fall 1980): 561; Watson, p. 205.

[86] See, for example, James C. Curtis, *The Fox at Bay: Martin Van Buren and the Presidency, 1837–1841* (Lexington, KY, 1970); Cole; Niven, *Martin Van Buren*; Wilson.

[87] Niven, *Martin Van Buren*, pp. 423–24; Cole, pp. 307–11, 318.

[88] Meyer, p. 431.

[89] Ronald M. Satz, *American Indian Policy in the Jacksonian Era* (Lincoln, NE, 1975), p. 183.

[90] Meyer, p. 431.

[91] Byrd, 2:219; *Senate Journal*, 25th Cong., 1st sess., pp. 27–28; 2d sess., pp. 25, 32–33; 3d sess., p. 5; 26th Cong., 1st sess., pp. 5, 10–11, 46.

[92] Henry Barrett Learned, "Casting Votes of the Vice-Presidents, 1789–1915," *American Historical Review* 20 (April

1915): 571; Byrd, *The Senate, 1789–1989*, vol. 4, *Historical Statistics, 1789–1992*, p. 642.

93 Ibid., p. 574.

94 *Kentucky Gazette*, March 14, 1839, quoted in Meyer, pp. 431–32.

95 *Senate Journal*, 25th Cong., 2d sess., pp. 181–82; 26th Cong., 2d sess., pp. 274–76; Francis Jennings, ed., *The History and Culture of Iroquois Diplomacy: An Interdisciplinary Guide to the Treaties of the Six Nations and Their Leagues* (New York, 1985), p. 206.

96 Satz, pp. 246–51; Meyer, pp. 337–39.

97 Letter to Amos Kendall, August 12, 1839, enclosed in Kendall's letter of August 22, 1839, to Van Buren, quoted in Meyer, p. 341.

98 Kendall to Van Buren, August 22, 1839, quoted in Meyer, p. 341.

99 Meyer, pp. 339–40.

100 Robert Gray Gunderson, *The Log-Cabin Campaign* (Lexington, KY, 1957), p. 80.

101 Henry B. Stanton, *Random Recollections* (New York, 1887), p. 61.

102 Harriett Martineau, "Life at the Capital," in *America Through British Eyes*, ed. Allan Nevins (New York, 1948; revised from 1923 edition), p. 150.

103 Joseph E. Morse and R. Duff Green, eds., *Thomas B. Searight's The Old Pike: An Illustrated Narrative of the National Road* (Orange, VA, 1971), pp. 105–6.

104 Glyndon Van Deusen, *The Jacksonian Era, 1828–1848* (New York, 1959), pp. 116–28; Watson, pp. 206–209; Cole, pp. 307–41, 347–60.

105 Niven, *Martin Van Buren*, pp. 425–52; Watson, p. 410; Van Deusen, pp. 132–40; Cole, pp. 318–42.

106 Harriett Martineau, "Life at the Capital," p. 150.

107 Remini, *Jackson and the Course of American Democracy*, pp. 463–64.

108 Andrew Jackson to Francis P. Blair, February 15, 1840, quoted in Remini, *Jackson and the Course of American Democracy*, p. 463.

109 Gunderson, p. 82; Meyer, pp. 435–36; Niven, *Martin Van Buren*, p. 463.

110 Niven, *Martin Van Buren*, p. 463; Gunderson, pp. 81–82; Cole, p. 358.

111 Niven, *Martin Van Buren*, p. 463; Gunderson, p. 83.

112 Gunderson, pp. 41–75; Peterson, pp. 248, 281–96; Remini, *Henry Clay*, pp. 545–67.

113 Washington *National Intelligencer*, September 24, 1840, quoting Wheeling *Gazette*, n.d., cited in Gunderson, p. 163; Wilson, p. 206.

114 Meyer, p. 433; Gunderson, pp. 241–46.

115 Gunderson, p. 246.

116 Remini, *Henry Clay*, pp. 566–67; Gunderson, pp. 253–54.

117 Gunderson, p. 255.

118 *Senate Journal*, 26th Cong., 2d sess., pp. 171–72.

119 Ibid., pp. 172–73.

120 Ibid., pp. 191–92.

121 Ibid., pp. 231–32.

122 Meyer, pp. 452–59.

123 Andrew Jackson to Martin Van Buren, September 22, 1843, quoted in Meyer, p. 460.

124 R.P. Letcher to John J. Crittenden, June 2, 1842, quoted in Meyer, p. 454.

125 General McCalla to Martin Van Buren, January 11, 1843, quoted in Meyer, p. 457.

126 Meyer, pp. 461–62.

127 R.P. Letcher to John J. Crittenden, January 6, 1844, quoted in ibid., p. 461.

128 Meyer, pp. 473–74.

Chapter 10

JOHN TYLER

1841

JOHN TYLER

Chapter 10

JOHN TYLER

10th Vice President: 1841

To this body [the Senate] is committed in an eminent degree, the trust of guarding and protecting the institutions handed down to us from our fathers, as well against the waves of popular and rash impulses on the one hand, as against attempts at executive encroachment on the other.

—VICE PRESIDENT JOHN TYLER

Go you now then, Mr. Clay, to your end of the avenue, where stands the Capitol, and there perform your duty to the country as you shall think proper. So help me God, I shall do mine at this end of it as I shall think proper.

—PRESIDENT JOHN TYLER

He held the office of vice president for only thirty-three days; he presided over the Senate for less than two hours. Despite this brief experience, John Tyler significantly strengthened the office by enforcing an interpretation of the Constitution that many of his contemporaries disputed. Tyler believed that, in the event of a vacancy in the office of president, the vice president would become more than just the acting president. He would assume the chief executive's full powers, salary, and residence as if he himself had been elected to that position. Taken for granted today, that interpretation is owed entirely to this courtly and uncompromising Virginian who brought to the vice-presidency a greater diversity of governmental experience than any of his predecessors.

Early Years

John Tyler was born on March 29, 1790, at Greenway, his family's twelve-hundred-acre James River estate in Charles City County, Virginia. He was the second son among the eight children of John and Mary Armistead Tyler. The elder John Tyler had been a prominent figure in the American Revolution and a vigorous opponent of the Constitution at the Virginia ratifying convention. Young John Tyler's mother died when he was only seven, leaving the boy's upbringing to his father. During John's late teens and early twenties, his father served as governor of Virginia and then as a federal judge. A modern biographer concluded: "The most important single fact that can be derived from John Tyler's formative years is that he absorbed in toto the political, social, and economic views of his distinguished father." [1]

Tyler received his early formal education at private schools; at the age of twelve he enrolled in the college preparatory division of the College of William and Mary. Three years later he began his college studies, chiefly in English literature and classical languages, and graduated in 1807, just seventeen years old. He studied law for two years, first under his father's direction, then with a cousin, and finally with Edmund Randolph, the nation's first attorney general. Randolph's advocacy of a strong central government ran counter to Tyler's interpretation of the limited extent to which the Constitution granted powers to the national government and his belief in the supremacy of states' rights. Tyler feared the Constitution would be used to subordinate the interests of the southern white planter class to those of northern merchants and propertyless working men, putting the South at an economic and political disadvantage.[2]

The young Virginian established his own legal practice in 1811 and soon developed a reputation as an eloquent and effective advocate in handling difficult criminal defense cases. That year also brought his election, at age twenty-one, to the Virginia house of delegates. He earned early acclaim through his work in persuading the house to pass a resolution censuring Virginia's two U.S. senators for their refusal to follow the legislature's "instructions" to vote against the recharter of the Bank of the United States.[3]

In March 1813, weeks after he inherited the Greenway plantation on his father's death, Tyler married the beautiful and introverted Letitia Christian. The death of both her parents soon after the marriage conveyed to the bride holdings of land and slaves that greatly expanded the wealth that John brought to their union. Reclusive and preferring domestic pursuits, Letitia took no active interest in her husband's public life. During the time of his service in Congress and as vice president, she visited Washington only once, preferring the tranquility of the family's plantation to the mud and grime of the nation's capital. Together they had seven children in a tranquil and happy union disrupted only when she suffered a paralytic stroke in 1839. She died in 1842.[4]

Tyler served five one-year terms in the Virginia house of delegates and was chosen to sit on the state executive council. In 1817, at the age of twenty-seven, he won election to the U.S. House of Representatives, serving there until 1821 without apparent distinction. He actively opposed legislation designed to implement Henry Clay's "American System," linking a federally sponsored network of canals, railroads, and turnpikes with a strong central bank and protective tariffs in an alliance that seemed designed to unite the North and West at the South's expense.

Tyler's views on slavery appeared ambivalent. In attacking the 1820 Missouri Compromise governing the future admission of "slave" and "free" states, Tyler sought without success to deny the federal government the right to regulate slavery. From his earliest days in the public arena, the Virginian appeared uncomfortable with the institution of slavery, although he owned many slaves throughout his lifetime and argued that slavery should be allowed to extend to regions where it would prove to be economically viable. He expected, however, that the "peculiar institution" would eventually die out and, on various occasions over the years, he advocated ending both the importation of slaves and their sale in the District of Columbia.[5]

At the end of 1820, suffering from financial difficulties, chronically poor health, and a string of legislative defeats, Tyler decided to give up his career in the House of Representatives. He wrote a friend, "the truth is, that I can no longer do any good here. I stand in a decided minority, and to waste words on an obstinate majority is utterly useless and vain."[6] In 1823, however, his health and political ambitions restored, Tyler returned to the Virginia house of delegates. Two years later, he won election as Virginia's governor and served two one-year terms until 1827, when he was elected to the U.S. Senate. Reelected in 1833, Tyler served until his resignation on February 29, 1836. While in the Senate he served briefly as president pro tempore in March 1835 and as chairman of the Committee on the District of Columbia and the Committee on Manufactures.

Philosophy

In the 1830s John Tyler identified himself with the Democratic party but differed often with President Andrew Jackson. The two men diverged both in temperament—a Tidewater aristocrat opposing a Tennessee democrat—and in political philosophy. Tyler supported the president's veto of legislation rechartering the Bank of the United States, but he opposed Jackson's removal of government funds from that institution. Although Tyler reluctantly advocated Jackson's election in both 1828 and 1832, he opposed many of the president's nominees to key administration posts. The final break between the two came in 1833 when Tyler, alone among Senate Democrats, chose to oppose the Force Act, which allowed Jackson to override South Carolina's ordinance nullifying the tariff of 1832. He feared the Force Act would undermine the doctrine of states' rights, to which he was deeply committed.

By 1834 Tyler joined Henry Clay in actively opposing Jackson's policies, and he voted with a Senate majority to "censure" the president for refusing to provide information concerning his removal of government funds from the Bank of the United States. In 1836, when the Virginia legislature "instructed" Tyler to reverse his censure vote, Tyler refused. Unlike some senators who by that time had come to ignore such legislative instruction, Tyler remembered his own vote years earlier against noncomplying senators and concluded that he had no honorable choice but to resign from the Senate.

In 1836 the emerging Whig party was united only in its opposition to Jackson. To avoid demonstrating their lack of unity, the Whigs chose not to hold a presidential nominating convention that year.[7] Party strategy called for fielding several regional candidates, nominated at the state and local level, in the hope that they would deny Jackson's heir Martin Van Buren a majority in the electoral college. Such an impasse would throw the contest into the House of Representatives where the outcome might be more easily influenced to produce a Whig president. Although there was little general interest expressed in the vice-presidential position, Tyler's name appeared for that post on the ballots in several states. He was listed as the running mate of William Henry Harrison in Maryland; of Hugh Lawson White in Tennessee, North Carolina, and Georgia; and of Willie Mangum in South Carolina. In Virginia, Tyler's name appeared on the ballot with both Harrison and White.

Van Buren won the presidency, but when the vice-presidential ballots were tallied, Tyler came in third, after Richard Mentor Johnson and Francis Granger, with 47 electoral votes from the states of Georgia, Maryland, South Carolina and Tennessee.[8] Under the provisions of the Constitution's Twelfth Amendment, as no candidate for the vice-presidency had secured a majority of the electoral votes, the Senate would make the selection from the top two candidates. On February 8, 1837, the Senate exercised this constitu-tional prerogative for the only time in its history and selected Johnson on the first ballot.

Senate Election Deadlock

In April 1838, Tyler won election to the Virginia house of delegates for the third time—this time as a Whig. On taking his seat early in 1839, he was unanimously chosen speaker. In that capacity, he presided over a debate in which he held an intense personal interest: the selection of a United States senator. William C. Rives, the Jacksonian Democrat who had succeeded Tyler in 1836, hoped to retain his Senate seat for another term. Tyler, however, decided that he would like to return to the Senate. The Democrats held a slight majority in the legislature, but among their members were a dozen so-called Conservatives, renegade Democrats who had supported Jackson but disagreed with the financial policies of his successor, Martin Van Buren. The legislature's regular Democrats tried to win the support of this maverick group to ensure that Virginia would marshal its sizeable number of electoral votes in favor of Van Buren in the 1840 presidential election. To this end, they offered to support Rives, one of Virginia's most prominent Conservatives. But Rives proved unwilling to lead Virginia's Conservatives back to the Democratic fold. Consequently, the Democrats turned to John Mason as their Senate candidate. Whig leaders might have been expected to support Tyler, who had resigned the seat in 1836 out of support for that party's doctrine. In fact, however, these party leaders were more willing to "sacrifice Tyler on the altar of party expediency" and promote Rives in return for cooperation from his fellow Conservatives in voting for a Whig presidential candidate in 1840.[9]

On February 15, 1839, each house first met separately to hear extended debate in support of Rives, Tyler, and Mason then convened in joint session to vote. With heavy support from the Whig rank-and-file, Tyler received a plurality on each of the first five ballots. On the sixth ballot, Whigs began to shift in favor of Rives, who moved into the lead but fell short of a majority in this and succeeding tallies. On February 25, after twenty-eight ballots and eight legislative days during which no other business was transacted, both houses agreed to suspend the voting indefinitely. The seat remained vacant for nearly two years until Tyler's election as vice president broke the deadlock and opened the way for the legislature to select Rives, who had recently changed his political allegiance to the Whig party.[10]

Contrary to his opponents' later charges, Tyler made no effort to obtain the vice-presidential nomination as a consolation prize for the Senate seat denied to him. "I do declare, in the presence of my Heavenly Judge, that the nomination given to me was neither solicited nor expected."[11]

Whig Nominating Convention

Going into their December 1839 presidential nominating convention, Whig leaders believed that Democratic President Martin Van Buren was easily beatable as long as they selected a challenger of moderate views who had not alienated large numbers of voters. Taking its name from the English political party of the seventeenth and eighteenth centuries that had formed in opposition to monarchial tyranny, the American Whig party was held together primarily by its opposition to the perceived executive tyranny of "King Andrew" and his successor, Van Buren.

Desiring a presidential candidate who would acknowledge the preeminent role of Congress as maker of national policy, the party could not ignore Henry Clay. As a leader of the Senate's Whigs and orchestrator of the 1834 Senate censure of Jackson, Clay personified the notion of congressional dominance. He was the best known of his party's potential candidates; he was the most competent; and, as a slaveholder and low-tariff advocate, he enjoyed considerable support in the South. Party leaders from other regions, however, argued that Clay's public record would work to his disadvantage and that, in any event, he could not be expected to carry the electorally essential states of New York and Pennsylvania.

Turning from a battle-scarred legislative veteran to military heroes of uncertain political leanings, the Whig convention, meeting in Harrisburg, Pennsylvania, considered War of 1812 generals Winfield Scott and William Henry Harrison. Harrison's heroism at the Battle of Tippecanoe was well known. He served as territorial governor of Indiana after the war and later represented Ohio in the House of Representatives and in the Senate, but he was hardly a national figure before the 1836 election.[12] That year he ran well in the presidential contest and in 1840 won the endorsement of Senator Daniel Webster, who sought to block his old rival, Clay. At the convention, Harrison gained the crucial support of New York political boss Thurlow Weed, who also wanted to prevent Clay from becoming the party's nominee. Weed manipulated the convention's voting rules to require a unit-rule system that had each state cast its entire vote for the candidate preferred by a simple majority of its delegates. Weed then led his state's influential delegation to secure a first-ballot victory for Harrison, a candidate unencumbered by a political record or strong opinions.[13]

The Whigs turned to the selection of a vice-presidential candidate as somewhat of an afterthought. In finding a running mate for Harrison, they sought an equally malleable candidate who would bring suitable geographical and ideological balance to the ticket. If Clay of Kentucky had been selected for the presidency, party leaders intended to find a vice-presidential candidate from a state closed to slavery. With Harrison the party's choice, they looked instead to the slave states for a suitable contender; they found John Tyler.

The courtly Virginian had run well in southern states during the 1836 contest and enjoyed a solid identification with the South and states' rights doctrine.[14] With Harrison rumored to be an abolitionist sympathizer, a slaveholder would nicely balance the ticket. The Whigs particularly hoped to pick up Virginia's twenty-three electoral votes, which had gone to the Democrats in 1836. (Both Tyler and Harrison had been born in the same Virginia county and their fathers had served terms as that state's governor.) The selection of Tyler, who had energetically campaigned for Clay through the final convention ballot— and was believed by some even to have shed tears at his defeat—was also intended to mollify Clay's disappointed supporters in the South. The convention's general committee quickly agreed on Tyler and recommended him to the assembled delegates, who voted their unanimous approval. In selecting Tyler, party leaders made no effort to determine whether his views were compatible with their candidate's, for their privately acknowledged campaign strategy was to "fool the voters and avoid the issues." [15]

The 1840 Campaign

At Harrison's request, Tyler remained inactive during most of the 1840 election campaign. His major contribution was his surname, which formed the rhyming conclusion of the party slogan "Tippecanoe and Tyler Too." Few Americans took much interest in his candidacy, for the sixty-seven-year-old Harrison appeared to be in good health and had vowed to serve only a single four-year term.

In the campaign's final weeks, word reached Tyler that President Van Buren's running mate, Vice President Richard Mentor Johnson, had been conducting a vigorous reelection campaign before enthusiastic crowds in Ohio and adjacent states. Tyler responded with a speaking tour of his own in portions of Virginia, Ohio, and Pennsylvania.[16] One Democratic editor concluded that he might as well have stayed home. "Mr. Tyler is a graceful, easy speaker, with all that blandness of manner which belongs to the Virginia character. But there is nothing forcible or striking in his speech; no bright thoughts, no well-turned expressions; nothing that left an impression on the mind from its strength and beauty—nothing that marked the great man." [17]

Saddled with responsibility for the economic crises that characterized his administration, Martin Van Buren had but a slim chance to win a second term. Harrison, for his part, avoided taking unpopular stands by repeating at every opportunity that he would take his direction from Congress—the best instrument for expressing the needs and wishes of the American people. Although the popular-vote margin was relatively slim, the Harrison-Tyler ticket won a resounding electoral vote victory (234 to 60) in an election that stimulated the participation of 80.2 percent of the eligible voters, the greatest percentage ever.

Although Tyler failed to carry his own state of Virginia, he took some satisfaction in believing that his Pennsylvania tour may have been responsible for winning that state's important electoral votes. The election also placed both houses of Congress under Whig control for the first time. A Whig newspaper summarized the consequences of the Harrison-Tyler victory: "It has pleased the Almighty to give the oppressed people of this misgoverned and suffering country a victory over their weak and wicked rulers. . . . The reign of incompetency, imposture and corruption, is at length arrested, and the country redeemed." [18]

A Brief Vice-Presidency

At 11 a.m. on March 4, 1841, the Senate convened in special session to play its constitutional role in inaugurating the Harrison presidency. After the secretary of the Senate called members to order, Henry Clay administered the oath of office to President pro tempore William R. King. Then, as a wave of excitement swept chamber galleries that had been packed to capacity since early morning, Tyler entered the room accompanied by former Vice President Richard M. Johnson, the Supreme Court, and the diplomatic corps. The court, somber "in their black robes with their grave, intellectual, reflecting countenances," sat in front-row seats to the presiding officer's right. To his left, in colorful contrast, sat the ambassadors decorated, "not only with the insignia of their various orders, but half covered with the richest embroidery in silver and in gold." [19]

John Tyler arose and proceeded with Vice President Richard Johnson to the presiding officer's chair to take his oath from President pro tempore King. The new vice president then assumed the chair and launched a three-minute inaugural address with a ringing tribute to his predecessors, calling it an honor "to occupy a seat which has been filled and adorned . . . by an Adams, a Jefferson, a Gerry, a Clinton, and a Tompkins." He then continued with a verbal bouquet to the Senate and "the high order of the moral and intellectual power which has distinguished it in all past time, and which still distinguishes it." In the next sentence, Tyler moved into his main theme—the centrality of the states' rights doctrine:

> Here [in the Senate] are to be found the immediate representatives of the States, by whose sovereign will the Government has been spoken into existence. Here exists the perfect equality among the members of this confederacy, which gives to the smallest State in the Union a voice as potential as that of the largest. To this body is committed in an eminent degree, the trust of guarding and protecting the institutions handed down to us from our fathers, as well against the waves of popular and rash impulses on the one hand, as against attempts at executive encroachment on the other.

Concluding in the spirit of Vice President Jefferson, Tyler confessed to his shortcomings as a presiding officer and asked of the Senate "your indulgence for my defects, and your charity for my errors. I am but little skilled in parliamentary law, and have been unused to preside over deliberative assemblies. All that I can urge in excuse of my defects is, that I bring with me to this chair an earnest wish to discharge properly its duties, and a fixed determination to preside over your deliberations with entire impartiality." [20]

When Tyler finished, senators beginning new terms took their oaths. At twenty minutes past noon, President-elect Harrison and the inaugural arrangements committee entered the chamber and took seats in front of the secretary's desk. After several minutes, the entire official party rose and proceeded to the Capitol's east portico where a crowd of fifty thousand awaited to witness the president's oath-taking. On that blustery spring day, Harrison spoke without hat or overcoat for more than ninety minutes. Following the ceremony, Tyler and the Senate returned to the chamber to receive the president's cabinet nominations, which were confirmed unanimously on the following day. Without caring to attend the series of inaugural parties or to preside over the Senate for the remainder of the special session that ended on March 15, Tyler promptly returned to Williamsburg. He traveled there, as one biographer noted, "with the expectation of spending the next four years in peace and quiet." [21]

Early in April, Secretary of State Daniel Webster sent word to Tyler that Harrison, worn out from the press of jobseekers, had fallen seriously ill. The vice president saw no compelling need, however, to return to Washington on account of the president's condition. As Senator Thomas Hart Benton observed, "Mr. Tyler would feel it indelicate to repair to the seat of government, of his own will, on hearing the report of the President's illness." [22] Then, at sunrise on April 5, 1841, two horsemen arrived at Tyler's plantation. They were State Department chief clerk Fletcher Webster, son of Secretary of State Daniel Webster, and Senate assistant doorkeeper Robert Beale, whose mission was to deliver a letter from the cabinet addressed to "John Tyler, Vice President of the United States." The letter reported that President Harrison had died of pneumonia the previous day. [23] After a quick breakfast, Tyler embarked on a hurried journey by horseback and boat that placed him back in the nation's capital at 4 a.m. the following day.

As word of Harrison's demise spread across a startled nation, John Quincy Adams despaired for the country's well-being:

> Tyler is a political sectarian, of the slave-driving, Virginian, Jeffersonian school, principled against all improvement, with all the interests and passions and vices of slavery rooted in his moral and political constitution—with talents not above mediocrity, and a spirit incapable of expansion to the dimensions of the station upon which he has been cast by the hand of Providence, unseen through the apparent agency of chance. No one ever thought of his being placed in the executive chair. [24]

Although Tyler at age fifty-one was younger than any previous president, he was also the most experienced in the ways of government. He had served as a member of both houses of his state legislature, both houses of the U.S. Congress, governor of his state, and vice president of the United States. [25] By appearance, he was cast for a leadership role. Standing slightly over six feet, he possessed all the "features of the best Grecian model" including a sharply defined aquiline nose. When a bust of Cicero was discovered during an excavation in Naples, two visiting Americans reportedly exclaimed "President Tyler!" 26

The Accidental President

Harrison's demise after only a month in office presented the nation with a potential constitutional crisis. The Constitution of that time contained no Twenty-fifth Amendment to lay out procedures governing the vice president's actions when the chief executive became disabled or when there was a vacancy before the end of the incumbent's term. The document provided only that the "Powers and Duties of the said Office . . . shall devolve on the Vice President . . . [who] shall act accordingly, until the Disability be removed, or a President shall be elected." In another section, the Constitution referred to the vice president "when he shall exercise [emphasis added] the Office of President of the United States." 27

These provisions had occasioned a theoretical discussion between those who believed a person does not have to become president to exercise presidential powers and others who held that the vice president becomes president for the balance of the term.28 As the first vice president to succeed to the presidency upon the death of his predecessor, Tyler was determined to transform theory into practice on behalf of the latter view, becoming president in his own right and not "Vice President, acting as President" as Harrison's cabinet was inclined to label him. Secretary of State Webster raised his concern about the constitutional implications of the succession with William Carroll, clerk of the Supreme Court. Carroll conveyed Webster's misgivings to Chief Justice Roger Taney, reporting that the "Cabinet would be pleased to see and confer with you at this most interesting moment." Taney responded with extreme caution, saying that he wished to avoid raising "the suspicion of desiring to intrude into the affairs which belong to another branch of government." 29

Tyler argued that his vice-presidential oath covered the possibility of having to take over as chief executive and consequently there was no need for him to take the separate presidential oath. The cabinet, major newspapers, and some Tyler advisers disagreed. To remove any doubt,

despite his own strong reservations, Tyler agreed to the oath, which was administered on April 6 at Brown's Indian Queen Hotel by Chief Judge William Cranch of the U.S. Circuit Court for the District of Columbia. Taking this step produced a significant reward, for it boosted Tyler's annual salary five-fold from $5,000 to $25,000.30

In his first official move, Tyler convened Harrison's cabinet and listened patiently as Secretary of State Daniel Webster advised that it had been Harrison's custom to bring all administrative issues "before the Cabinet, and their settlement was decided by the majority, each member of the Cabinet and the President having but one vote." Choosing his words with care, Tyler responded, "I am the President, and I shall be held responsible for my administration. I shall be pleased to avail myself of your counsel and advice. But I can never consent to being dictated to as to what I shall do or not do. When you think otherwise, your resignations will be accepted." 31

Outside of his cabinet, Tyler's assumption of the presidency's full powers evoked little general concern that he was overstepping proper constitutional boundaries, or that a special election should be called. Major newspapers argued that he was fully justified in his action, although for several months after he took office some journals continued to refer to him as "acting president." One suggested a compromise view; a special election would be required only if the presidency were to fall, in the absence of a vice president, to the Senate president pro tempore or the House Speaker, as designated by the presidential succession statute of 1792.32

As the epithet "His Accidency" grew in popularity, Congress convened on May 31, 1841, for its previously called special session and immediately took up the issue of Tyler's claim to be president in his own right. The question was raised as the House prepared a resolution authorizing a committee to follow the custom of informing the president that "Congress is now ready to receive any communication he may be pleased to make." 33 One member moved to amend the resolution by striking out the word "President" and substituting "Vice President now exercising the office of President." Members more sympathetic to Tyler's reading of the Constitution—and the need to get on with the business of the nation—offered a firm rebuttal, which the House then agreed to.

In the Senate, on the following day, a member posed a hypothetical question as to what would happen if the president were only temporarily disabled and the vice president assumed the office. He envisioned a major struggle at the time the disabled president sought to resume his powers, particularly if he and the vice president were of different parties. Senator John C. Calhoun reminded the Senate that this was not the situation that faced them, rendering further discussion pointless. And what about the Senate's president pro tempore? Should he assume the vice-presidency as the vice president had assumed the presidency? Former President pro tempore George Poindexter urged the incumbent president pro tempore, Samuel Southard, to claim the title. Southard ignored the advice, and the Senate then joined the House in adopting a resolution recognizing Tyler's legitimate claim to the presidency.[34]

Acting Vice President (President Pro Tempore)

In this early period of the Senate's history, when a vice president planned to be away from the Capitol, the Senate customarily elected a president pro tempore to serve for the limited time of that absence. This official would preside, sign legislation, and perform routine administrative tasks. Whenever the vice-presidency was vacant, as it was with the deaths of George Clinton and Elbridge Gerry in James Madison's administration, the post of president pro tempore, next in line of presidential succession, assumed heightened importance. Two individuals held this crucial post during Tyler's presidency: Samuel Southard, from 1841 to 1842, and Willie P. Mangum from 1842 to 1845.

Soon after Vice President Tyler left Washington on the day of Harrison's inauguration, the Senate followed Clay's recommendation and elected Senator Samuel Southard of New Jersey as president pro tempore. Southard had first entered the Senate in 1821 but resigned in 1823 to become secretary of the navy. In 1833, after moving through a series of state and national offices, Southard returned to the Senate, where he

helped to establish the Whig party. At a time when Clay was attempting to consolidate his control of the Senate, Southard proved to be a useful ally. When the Senate convened in May 1841, a month after Harrison's death, Southard's significance expanded. In this period of the Senate's history, the vice president or, in his absence, the president pro tempore made all committee assignments. Southard willingly accommodated Clay in the distribution of important chairmanships.

The next year, however, on May 3, 1842, the New Jersey Whig resigned from the Senate due to ill health and died soon thereafter. Several weeks later, on May 31, the Senate selected a new president pro tempore, Willie P. Mangum (W-NC), a leader of the Senate's Whig caucus. Mangum had served a Senate term in the 1830s and, as a Clay delegate to the 1839 Whig convention, had been considered briefly as a vice-presidential nominee. He returned to the Senate in 1840, where he remained as a Whig leader until 1853. His 1842 selection as president pro tempore occurred in recognition of his leadership in opposing Tyler. He held the post through the remainder of Tyler's administration.

Tyler's Presidency

Deep divisions over the issue of establishing a new banking system overshadowed Tyler's early presidency. In the Senate, Henry Clay led his party in a direction quite different from Tyler's. The two men had been good friends, despite their philosophical differences. Tyler had joined the Whigs because of his strong opposition to the policies of Andrew Jackson and Martin Van Buren. Ideologically, however, he had little sympathy for the Whig program of a national bank, internal improvements, and protective tariffs embodied in Clay's "American System." As a former states' rights Democrat, Tyler emphasized the importance of state sovereignty over national economic integration. Both Tyler and Clay held a typical nineteenth-century, anti-Jacksonian view of the presidency as a limited, relatively passive office responsible for providing Congress the necessary information to pass appropriate legislation. They saw the president's policy role as essentially limited to vetoing legislation that he believed to be either unconstitutional or not in the nation's best interests. Tyler, however, would have given the president sufficient power to keep Congress from actions that might erode states' rights. Clay made a sharper distinction, advocating an assertive Congress and a chief executive stripped of the powers acquired during Jackson's years in office. Admirers and foes alike began referring to Clay as "the Andrew Jackson of the Senate."

Although Clay had briefly opposed Tyler's move to take on full presidential powers after Harrison's death, he changed his mind and began to provide the new chief executive with valuable moral and political support. Yet Clay also realized that Tyler now blocked his own road to the presidency. Clay had appeared to be the obvious successor in 1845, based on Harrison's announcement that he intended to serve only one term.

Clay intended to lead the nation from the Senate and he expected Tyler to help him to that objective by supporting his policies. That expectation quickly proved to be misplaced. Despite Tyler's mild-mannered demeanor, he began to display a rock-like tenacity in pushing for his own objectives. Clay sought to reestablish a strong, private, central bank of the United States. Tyler, consistent in his concern for preservation of states' rights—and state banks—advocated a weaker bank, chartered in the District of Columbia, that would operate only in those states that chose to have it. When Clay urged Tyler to push for a new Bank of the United States during the May 1841 special session, Tyler said he wanted more time and intended to put the matter off until the regular session in December. Clay arrogantly responded that this would not be acceptable. Tyler is said to have countered, "Then, sir, I wish you to understand this—that you and I were born in the same district; that we have fed upon the same food, and have breathed the same natal air. Go you now then, Mr. Clay, to your end of the avenue, where stands the Capitol, and there perform your duty to the country as you shall think proper. So help me God, I shall do mine at this end of it as I shall think proper." [35]

In the interest of party harmony, Clay eventually agreed to a compromise bank measure, which the increasingly resentful Tyler promptly vetoed. Congress subsequently passed a modified "Fiscal Corporation" bill to meet the president's specific objections. Tyler also vetoed this act as an unconstitutional infringement on states' rights. On Saturday, September 11, 1841, in the final days of the special session, Tyler's entire cabinet—with the exception of Secretary of State Webster—resigned in a protest designed by Clay to force Tyler's own resignation. With the vice-presidency vacant, this would place Clay's protégé, Senate President pro tempore Southard, in the White House.

Refusing to be intimidated, Tyler responded the following Monday by sending the Senate a new slate of cabinet officers. Despite the president's break with the Senate's leaders, the body on September 13 quickly confirmed each of the nominees and then adjourned until December. Later that day, in a starkly dramatic move, sixty prominent Whigs assembled in the plaza adjacent to the Capitol. In a festive mood, they adopted a manifesto that asserted the supremacy of Congress in policy-making, condemned the president's conduct, and proclaimed that the Whig party could no longer be held responsible for the chief executive's actions. Tyler had become a president without a party. [36]

The chaos that ensued gave Tyler the unwanted distinction of having "the most disrupted Cabinet in presidential history." [37] During his nearly four years in office, he appointed twenty-two individuals to the administration's six cabinet seats. Many of these nominees were manifestly unqualified for their assignments, and the Senate refused to confirm four of them. Among those rejected was Caleb Cushing, whom Tyler chose to be secretary of the treasury. On the day of Cushing's initial rejection, Tyler immediately resubmitted his name. The Senate, irritated at this disregard of its expressed will, again said "no" but by a larger margin. For a third time, Tyler nominated Cushing and again the Senate decisively rejected him. The Senate's Whig majority, stalling for time in the expectation that Henry Clay would be elected president in 1844, also turned down, or failed to act on, four of Tyler's Supreme Court nominees—a record not before or since equalled.

Positioning himself to run in 1844 as the Whig candidate for the presidency, Clay resigned from the Senate in March 1842. Tyler continued the struggle with his party's congressional majority by vetoing two tariff bills. As government revenues fell to a dangerously low level, he finally agreed to a measure that became the Tariff Act of 1842. Although this action probably aided the nation's economy, it destroyed any remaining hope that Tyler might govern effectively. Northern Whigs condemned him for failing to push for a sufficiently protective tariff, and his former states' rights allies in the South abandoned him for supporting a measure that they considered excessively protective.

John Tyler sought to be a strong president, but his accomplishments proved to be modest. Stubborn, proud, and unpredictable, he decisively established the right of the vice president to assume the full powers of the presidency in the event of a vacancy to an unexpired term. He boldly exercised the veto ten times, a record exceeded only by Andrew Jackson among presidents who served in the nation's first seventy-five years. His chief contributions lay in the field of foreign policy. The annexation of Texas opened a new chapter in the nation's history. The Webster-Ashburton treaty prevented a costly war with Great Britain, and the Treaty of Wanghia obtained economically promising most-favored-nation status for the United States in China. [38]

Despite his earlier ambitions, Tyler became the first president not to seek a second term. (No party would have him as its candidate.) After leaving the White House on March 3, 1845, Tyler practiced law and was appointed to the board of visitors for the College of William and Mary. A year earlier, at the first presidential wedding to be conducted in the White House, he had married Julia Gardiner, a vivacious partner who, like his first wife Letitia, produced seven children. [39] In February 1861 the ex-president chaired a conference in Washington in a last-ditch effort to avert civil war. When that war began, he was elected to Virginia's secessionist convention and then to the provisional Congress of the Confederacy. He had won a seat in the Confederate Congress' house of representatives, but his death on January 18, 1862, came before he could begin his service.

Tyler biographer Robert Seager notes that he "lived in a time in which many brilliant and forceful men strode the American stage . . . and he was overshadowed by all of them, as was the office of the Presidency itself. . . . Had he surrendered his states' rights and anti-Bank principles he might have salvaged it. He chose not to surrender and the powerful Henry Clay crushed him." [40]

NOTES

[1] Robert Seager II, *And Tyler Too: A Biography of John & Julia Gardiner Tyler* (Norwalk, CT, 1963), p. 50.

[2] Ibid., pp. 52–53.

[3] Ibid., pp. 55–56.

[4] Ibid., pp. 56–58.

[5] Ibid., p. 53–54.

[6] Quoted in ibid., p. 72.

[7] Oliver Perry Chitwood, *John Tyler: Champion of the Old South* (New York, 1939), pp. 148–49.

[8] Ibid., p. 151–52.

[9] Ibid., pp. 157–61.

[10] Ibid., pp. 162–63.

[11] *National Intelligencer*, August 27, 1844; Seager, p. 135.

[12] Robert Gray Gunderson, *The Log-Cabin Campaign* (Lexington, KY, 1957), pp. 41–75; Merrill D. Peterson, *The Great Triumvirate: Webster, Clay, and Calhoun* (New York, 1987), pp. 248, 281–96; Robert V. Remini, *Henry Clay: Statesman for the Union* (New York, 1991), pp. 545–67.

[13] Norma Lois Peterson, *The Presidencies of William Henry Harrison & John Tyler* (Lawrence, KS, 1989), p. 21; Chitwood, pp. 164–67.

[14] Seager, pp. 134–35. There is some scholarly controversy over the reasons for Tyler's selection. The view that he was carelessly selected may not have been widely held until after Tyler broke with Whig party leaders after becoming president. For a discussion of this question, see Norma Peterson, *The Presidencies of William Henry Harrison & John Tyler*, p. 26; Chitwood, pp. 167–73.

[15] William O. Stoddard, *Lives of the Presidents*, 10 vols. (New York, 1888), 5:44; Chitwood, pp. 166–67; Norma Peterson, pp. 26–27.

[16] Chitwood, pp. 184–85.

[17] *Daily Pittsburgher*, October 8, 1840, quoted in ibid., p. 187.

[18] *Niles' National Register*, 59:163.

[19] *Niles National Register*, March 13, 1841, p. 19. This excellent source provides colorful descriptions of the events of March 4, 1841.

[20] Chitwood, pp. 200–201; U.S., Congress, Senate, *Congressional Globe*, 26th Cong., 2d sess., March 4, 1841, pp. 231–32.

[21] Chitwood, p. 202.

[22] Thomas Hart Benton, *Thirty Years' View*, 2 vols. (New York, 1871), 2:211.

[23] Ruth C. Silva, *Presidential Succession* (Ann Arbor, MI, 1951), p. 16.

[24] Charles Francis Adams, ed., *Memoirs of John Quincy Adams*, 12 vols. (Philadelphia, 1876), 10:456–57.

[25] Seager, p. 147.

[26] Quoted in Remini, p. 582.

[27] *U.S. Constitution*, Article II, section 1, clause 6; Article I, section 2, clause 10.

[28] Stephen W. Stathis, "John Tyler's Presidential Succession: A Reappraisal," *Prologue* 8 (Winter 1976): 223–24, especially footnote 1; Silva, pp. 2–3. See also Stephen W. Stathis, "The Making of a Precedent 1841 (The Presidential Succession of John Tyler)," (Master's Thesis, Utah State University, 1971).

[29] Samuel Tyler, *Memoir of Roger Brooke Taney* (Baltimore, 1872), pp. 295–96; Silva, pp. 16–17.

[30] Sharon Stiver Gressle, "Salaries, Executive," *Encyclopedia of the American Presidency* (New York, 1994), pp. 1344–46.

[31] Quoted in Seager, p. 149.

[32] Silva, pp. 18–20.

[33] *Congressional Globe*, 27th Cong., 1st sess., pp. 3–4.

[34] Stathis, p. 234; Chitwood, p. 206; Silva, pp. 21–22. Even after he left the presidency, Tyler continued to confront the issue of his proper title. On October 16, 1848, he wrote to Secretary of State James Buchanan to complain that the State Department, the government's official arbiter of protocol, had on three occasions addressed him in formal correspondence as "ex-vice president." "I desire only to say, that if I am addressed, and especially from the State department, by title, it must be that which the Constitution confers . . ." [quoted in Silva, p. 21]

[35] Chitwood, pp. 210–11; Seager, p. 147; Remini, p. 583.

[36] Norma Peterson, pp. 89–91; Seager, p. 160.

[37] Paul Finkelman, "John Tyler," *Encyclopedia of the American Presidency*, 4:1521.

[38] For a balanced assessment of Tyler's presidency, see Norma Peterson, chapter 15.

[39] Seager, pp. 1–16.

[40] Ibid., p. xvi.

Chapter 11

GEORGE MIFFLIN DALLAS
1845–1849

GEORGE M. DALLAS

Chapter 11

GEORGE MIFFLIN DALLAS

11th Vice President: 1845–1849

[Except that he is President of the Senate, the vice president] forms no part of the government:—he enters into no administrative sphere:—he has practically no legislative, executive, or judicial functions:—while the Senate sits, he presides, that's all:—he doesn't debate or vote, (except to end a tie) he merely preserves the order and courtesy of business . . . [When Congress is in recess] where is he to go? what has he to do?—no where, nothing! He might, to be sure, meddle with affairs of state, rummage through the departments, devote his leisure to the study of public questions and interests, holding himself in readiness to counsel and to help at every emergency in the great onward movement of the vast machine:—But, then, recollect, that this course would sometimes be esteemed intrusive, sometimes factious, sometimes vain and arrogant, and, as it is prescribed by no law, it could not fail to be treated lightly because guaranteed by no responsibility.

—GEORGE M. DALLAS, CA. 1845 [1]

George Mifflin Dallas admitted in his later years that his driving force in life was for historical fame. From the 1840s on through the latter part of the nineteenth century, Americans associated his name with the acquisition of Texas and the settlement of the Oregon boundary dispute. Texas memorialized his contributions to the state's history by renaming the town of Peter's Corner in his honor. In the 1850s, when officials in Oregon sought a name for the principal town in Polk County, they settled on the logical choice: Polk's vice president. Thus, while largely forgotten today as the nation's eleventh vice president, George Mifflin Dallas has won his measure of immortality in a large Texas city and a small Oregon town.[2]

For four years at the heart of the Senate's "Golden Age," Vice President George Dallas occupied a center stage seat in the nation's premier political theater. This courtly Philadelphia aristocrat—whose political ambition greatly exceeded his political energy—entered that arena in 1845 filled with optimism for the nation, the Democratic party, and his own presidential future. He departed in 1849 embittered and de-

pressed, his political chances obliterated. During his term, the nation fought and won a war with Mexico, acquired vast new territories, settled a chronic northwestern boundary dispute, discovered gold, and launched a communications revolution with the invention of the telegraph. In the Senate, where political party caucuses assumed new powers to appoint committee members and distribute patronage, the central debates occurred over the status of slavery in the territories and the very nature of the constitutional union. With increasing frequency, senators faced conflicting choices between the desires of their parties and of their constituencies. When such an unavoidable decision confronted Vice President Dallas in July 1846 on the then searing issue of tariff policy, he chose party over constituency—thereby forfeiting his political future.

Early Years

George Mifflin Dallas was born in Philadelphia on July 10, 1792, the second of Alexander and Arabella Smith Dallas' six children. Alexander Dallas, a politically well-connected Philadelphia lawyer, served as secretary for the Commonwealth of Pennsylvania and reporter for the opinions of the U.S. Supreme Court and other courts then meeting in that city, which was at the time the nation's capital and leading commercial center. In 1801, as a reward for the elder Dallas' assistance in his presidential election campaign, Thomas Jefferson appointed him U.S. district attorney for the eastern district of Pennsylvania. He remained in that post until 1814, when President James Madison selected him as his treasury secretary. In 1815, Alexander Dallas also served concurrently for a brief period as acting secretary of war. He then resigned the treasury position in 1816 to return to his law practice with the intention of expanding the family's financial resources. However, early the following year, a chronic illness led to his death at the age of fifty-nine, leaving his family without the wealth necessary to support its accustomed style of living.

George Dallas graduated with highest honors from the College of New Jersey at Princeton in 1810. He then studied law and in 1813, at age twenty, was admitted to the Pennsylvania bar. With little taste for legal practice, he sought military service in the War of 1812 but abandoned those plans on the objection of his ever-influential father. He then readily accepted an appointment to serve as private secretary to former treasury secretary and Pennsylvania political figure Albert Gallatin, who was about to embark on a wartime mission to secure the aid of Russia in U.S. peace negotiations with Great Britain. Dallas enjoyed the opportunities that travel to this distant land offered, but after six months orders took him from St. Petersburg to London to probe for diplomatic openings that might bring the war to an end.

In August 1814, as British troops were setting fire to the U.S. Capitol, young Dallas carried a preliminary draft of Britain's peace terms home to Washington and accepted President Madison's appointment as remitter of the treasury, a convenient arrangement at a time when his father was serving as that department's secretary. The light duties of his new post left Dallas plenty of time to pursue his major vocational interest—politics.[3]

In 1816, lonely and lovesick, Dallas left Washington for Philadelphia, where he married Sophia Chew Nicklin, daughter of an old-line Federalist family. (They would eventually have eight children.) His marriage extended his social and political reach but, as his modern biographer reports, "Prestige came without money, a circumstance that was doubly unfortunate because he had developed extravagant tastes as a youth. For this reason he continually lived beyond his means and was constantly in debt, a situation that caused him on more than one occasion to reject otherwise acceptable political posts."[4] At the start of his married life, Dallas achieved a measure of financial stability by accepting a position as counsel to the Second Bank of the United States, an institution his father had helped create while treasury secretary. The 1817 death of Alexander Dallas abruptly ended George's plans for a family law practice. He left the Bank of the United States to become deputy attorney general of Philadelphia, a post he held until 1820.

George Mifflin Dallas cultivated a bearing appropriate to his aristocratic origins. Tall, with soft hazel eyes, an aquiline nose, and sandy hair, he dressed impeccably in the finest clothes his fashionable city could offer, wrote poetry, and, when the occasion warranted, spoke perfectly nuanced French. He developed an oratorical style that capitalized on his sonorous voice and protected him from the barbs of quicker-witted legal adversaries. His biographer explains that, whether "by chance or design, his habit of talking slowly and emphasizing each word created the feeling that he was reasoning his way to a conclusion on the spot. Since he also prepared cases carefully in advance, his apparent groping for the right word—and finding it—reinforced the initial impression that a great mind was at work."[5]

Dallas, however, lacked both the intense drive necessary to achieve his high ambitions and a natural politican's gift for warm social interaction with those outside his immediate circle. "A silk-stocking Jeffersonian in an age of egalitarianism," he preferred to remain aloof from the rough-and-tumble world of political deal making. Only once in his public life, when he ran for the vice-presidency, did he submit himself to the decision of the voting public. The Pennsylvania state legislature awarded him his Senate term, and the rest of his offices were given by appointment. At crucial moments, Dallas pulled back from the wrenching political compromises and exhausting coalition building necessary to achieve his lifelong quest for the presidency.[6]

Buchanan Rivalry

Pennsylvania's chaotic political climate in the forty years that followed the War of 1812 promoted, shaped, and ultimately sidetracked Dallas' public career. Two factions within the state's Democratic party contended for power during that time. Led by Dallas, the Philadelphia-based "Family party" shared his belief in the supremacy of the Constitution and in an active national government that would impose protective tariffs, operate a strong central banking system, and promote so-called internal improvements to facilitate national commerce. In factional opposition to Dallas stood the equally patrician James Buchanan of Harrisburg, head of the rival "Amalgamators," whose strength lay among the farmers of western Pennsylvania.[7]

When the Family party gained control of the Philadelphia city councils, its members in 1828 elected Dallas as mayor. Boredom with that post quickly led Dallas—in his father's path—to the position of district attorney for the eastern district of Pennsylvania, where he stayed from 1829 to 1831. In December 1831 he won a five-man, eleven-ballot contest in the state legislature for election to the U.S. Senate to complete an unexpired term. In the Senate for only fourteen months, he chaired the Naval Affairs Committee and supported President Jackson's views on protective tariffs and the use of force to implement federal tariff laws in South Carolina.

A longtime supporter and financial beneficiary of the Second Bank of the United States, whose original charter his father had drafted, Dallas reluctantly parted company with the president on the volcanic issue of the bank's rechartering. As one Dallas biographer has written: "There was no question about how the people of Pennsylvania viewed the Second Bank of the United States. The Philadelphia-based institution was Pennsylvanian by interest, location, and legislative initiative."[8] Dallas complied with a directive from his state legislature that he support a new

charter, despite Jackson's unremitting opposition and his own view that the divisive recharter issue should be put off until after the 1832 presidential election. When Jackson vetoed the recharter act in July 1831 and Congress failed to override the veto, Dallas—always the pragmatist—dropped his support for the bank. Observing that "we ought to have it, but we can do without it," he mollified the president and angered his state's influential commercial interests.[9] Dallas realized that his chances for reelection to the Senate by the state legislature were uncertain. His wife Sophia, who refused to leave Philadelphia's comforts for muddy and cholera-ridden Washington, was growing increasingly bitter over the legislative and social demands of his life in the capital. Consequently, Dallas chose not to run for a full term and left the Senate in March 1833.[10]

Although off the national stage, Dallas remained active in state Democratic politics. The tension with Buchanan intensified when the latter returned from his diplomatic post in Russia and secured Pennsylvania's other seat in the U.S. Senate. Dallas turned down opportunities to return to the Senate and to become the nation's attorney general. Instead, he accepted an appointment as state attorney general, holding that post until 1835, when control of the state's party machinery shifted from the declining Family party to Buchanan's Amalgamators. In 1837, it was Dallas' turn for political exile, as newly elected President Martin Van Buren named him U.S. minister to Russia. Although Dallas enjoyed the social responsibilities of that post, he soon grew frustrated at its lack of substantive duties and returned to the United States in 1839. He found that during his absence in St. Petersburg Buchanan had achieved a commanding position in the home state political contest that had long engaged the two men.[11]

In December 1839, Van Buren offered the U.S. attorney-generalship to Dallas after Buchanan had rejected the post. Dallas again declined the offer and spent the following years building his Philadelphia law practice. His relations with Buchanan remained troubled throughout this period.

The 1844 Campaign and Election

Favoring Van Buren for the 1844 Democratic presidential nomination, Dallas worked successfully to blunt Buchanan's drive for that prize. Van Buren sought unsuccessfully to have the Democratic convention held in November 1843 rather than late May 1844. He had hoped to capture the nomination before his opposition to the annexation of Texas became public when Congress convened in early December. By April 1844, with Democratic support for annexation intensifying, Van Buren watched helplessly as his chances for regaining the White House slipped away.

Under the influence of Van Buren's opponents, the Democratic party's Baltimore convention in May adopted the Jackson-era rule that required a two-thirds vote to select its nominee. After eight deadlocked ballots at the superheated and violence-prone convention, supporters of Van Buren and his chief rival, Michigan's Lewis Cass, united on the unheralded former House Speaker James K. Polk of Tennessee—who thus became the first successful "darkhorse" candidate in American presidential history. To cement an alliance with the disgruntled Van Buren faction, Polk offered to support a Van Buren loyalist for the vice-presidential nomination, New York Senator Silas Wright. Although Wright was absent from the convention, those delegates who had not already left town willingly added him to the ticket.[12]

Four days earlier, Professor Samuel F. B. Morse had successfully demonstrated that his newly invented "Magnetic Electric Telegraph" could transmit messages over the forty-mile distance between the U.S. Capitol and Baltimore. Silas Wright was in the Capitol Rotunda reading other telegraphic reports from the Baltimore convention when news of his nomination arrived. Bitter at the convention's rejection of Van Buren, Wright dictated a response to Morse, who typed out the following message to the convention's waiting delegates: "WASHINGTON. IMPORTANT! MR. WRIGHT IS HERE, AND SAYS, SAY TO THE NEW YORK DELEGATION, THAT HE CANNOT ACCEPT THE NOMINATION." His party's remaining delegates in Baltimore did not fully trust this new invention and repeated their message. Morse replied: "AGAIN: MR. WRIGHT IS HERE, AND WILL SUPPORT MR. POLK CHEERFULLY, BUT CAN NOT ACCEPT THE NOMINATION FOR VICE-PRESIDENT." The unbelieving convention continued its request until Wright dispatched two members of Congress in a wagon—the evening train to Baltimore had already departed—bearing handwritten letters of rejection.[13]

With Wright out of the picture, and with no New York ally of Van Buren willing to accept the nomination, the convention turned to James Buchanan, but he immediately instructed his allies to withdraw his name. The searchlight then swept across several candidates from New England and came to rest on Maine's Senator John Fairfield, who received an impressive, but inconclusive, 106 votes on the first ballot. At the suggestion of party leader and Mississippi Senator Robert J. Walker (who was married to Dallas' niece), Pennsylvania delegates then sparked a move for Dallas, who was at home in Philadelphia. Dallas' views were generally compatible with Polk's, especially on the key issue of annexing Texas. His stand in favor of protective tariffs would appeal to northeastern commercial interests and offset Polk's ambiguous position on this sensitive issue. Party strategists realized that Pennsylvania, with its prize of nearly 10 percent of the total electoral votes, which were by no means safely in the Democratic camp, could prove decisive in the election. On the second ballot, the convention gave Dallas the nomination with 220 votes to just 30 for Fairfield.

On May 30, sixty high-spirited delegates left Baltimore for Philadelphia, arriving at the Dallas residence at 3 a.m. As a bewildered Dallas stood by his open door, the nocturnal visitors marched by double column silently into his parlor. Forming a semicircle, the men burst into applause as Senator Fairfield conveyed the surprising news and Dallas, uneasy at the prospect of returning to public life, accepted with less than abundant enthusiasm.[14]

The selection also came as news to presidential nominee Polk, whose advisers quickly assured him that Dallas would be an excellent complement to the ticket. Within Pennsylvania, opinion was sharply divided, as resentful Buchanan allies feared that the less-than-dynamic Dallas would cost their party the presidency in a contest against the aggressive and better-known Whig candidates, Kentucky's Henry Clay and New Jersey's Theodore Frelinghuysen.[15] One Pennsylvania Whig dismissively described Dallas as "a gentleman by birth and education, amiable in private life, very bland and courteous in manner . . . a reckless partisan totally devoid of principle and capable of upholding or relinquishing . . . opinions whenever his own or his party's interests require it."[16]

As was customary prior to 1845, the various states scheduled the presidential election on different days during November's first two weeks.[17] When the votes were finally tallied, the Polk-Dallas ticket won fifteen out of the twenty-six states by a comfortable margin of 170 to 105 electoral votes. They were far less convincing, however, in the popular vote, with a margin of only 6,000 out of the 2.7 million ballots cast. Polk narrowly lost his native Tennessee, while Dallas barely carried Pennsylvania. While analysts agreed that victories in New York and Pennsylvania made the difference for the Democratic ticket, no such consensus existed about Dallas' impact on this result.[18]

Preparing for Office

Like many of his contemporaries on the national political stage in 1845, George Dallas wanted to be president. In accepting the Democratic nomination, Polk committed himself to serving only one term, hoping this promise would encourage his party's warring factions to suspend their combat at least until the 1848 campaign.[19] Instead, his pledge instantly prompted maneuvering from many quarters for the 1848 nomination. Four of the nation's ten previous vice presidents had moved up to the presidency and Dallas saw no reason why he should not become the fifth. For his first two years in the second office, Dallas framed his behavior with that goal in mind.

Dallas met Polk for the first time on February 13, 1845, joining the president-elect for the final leg of his railroad journey to Washington. Dallas used the opportunity to follow up on his earlier suggestions for cabinet nominees he believed

would strengthen the party—and his own presidential chances.[20] He particularly sought to sabotage archrival James Buchanan's hopes of becoming secretary of state, the other traditional launching pad to the White House. Buchanan had arrogantly instructed Pennsylvania's presidential electors to recommend him for that post at the time they cast their ballots for the Democratic ticket. This infuriated Dallas, who promised a friend that, while he had become vice president "willy-nilly" and expected to endure "heavy and painful and protracted sacrifices, . . . I am resolved that no one shall be taken from Pennsylvania in a cabinet office who is notoriously hostile to the Vice President. If such a choice be made, my relations with the administration are at once at an end."[21]

Several weeks later, learning that Polk had indeed chosen Buchanan, Dallas failed to follow up on his dark oath. Instead, he began quietly to lobby for the appointment of Senator Robert J. Walker—his earlier choice against Buchanan for the state department—for the influential post of treasury secretary. Polk, realizing that he had offended Dallas and Walker's southern Democratic allies, awarded the treasury post to Walker. Dallas continued to be sensitive about the administration's distribution of major appointments, as he sought to strengthen his Pennsylvania political base in order to weaken the Buchanan faction and enhance his own presidential prospects. In his subsequent appointments, however, Polk continued to antagonize Dallas, as well as others in the Democratic party. Again, the president tried to appease the vice president. "I would have been pleased to explain to you some of the circumstances attending the appointments at Philadelphia which were made some time ago, but no opportunity for that purpose has occurred." Dallas responded that it was pointless to discuss these matters "in as much as you have not been able to gratify the few requests I have previously made." Despite his frustration and subsequent patronage losses to Secretary of State Buchanan, who was a far tougher and more persistent operator, the vice president endeavored to remain loyal to his president and party.[22]

President of the Senate

From 1789 to 1845, the Senate followed the practice of selecting its committees by ballot, with the exception of several years in the 1820s and 1830s when the power was specifically given to the presiding officer (1823–1826) or, more pointedly, to the president pro tempore (1828–1833), an officer selected by and responsible to the Senate.[23] When the Senate convened in March 1845 for its brief special session to receive the new president's executive nominations, Democratic party leaders engineered a resolution that revived the practice of having the vice president appoint the members of standing committees. Acknowledging that the vice president was not directly responsible to the Senate, administration allies asserted that his was a greater responsibility, as guaranteed in the Constitution, "to the Senate's masters, the people of these United States."[24] The goal was to pack the Committee on Foreign Relations with members sympathetic to the administration's position on the Oregon boundary question. Vice President Dallas made the desired appointments.

In December 1845, at the opening of the Senate's regular legislative session, party leaders again sought to give the appointment power to Dallas. On this occasion, however, four rebellious Democrats joined minority party Whigs to defeat the resolution by a one-vote margin. This action presented the Polk administration with the unappealing likelihood that, in balloting by the full Senate, Democrats hostile to its specific objectives would take control of key Senate committees. Dallas reported that the return to the usual procedure required him to work "unusually hard . . . to superintend some sixteen or twenty ballotings for officers and chairmen of Committees." He was "much encouraged by the kind manner in which I am complimented on my mode of presiding. But I assure you," he continued, "contrary to my expectations, it is not done without a great deal of preparatory labor. Now that [the anti-administration] hostility has shewn itself, I am bound to be ready at all points and against surprizes."[25]

To end this time-consuming process, Senate party leaders took a step of major importance for the future development of legislative political parties. The Democrats and Whigs each organized a party caucus to prepare lists of committee assignments, an arrangement that marked the beginning of the Senate seniority system. As long as committee members had been selected by secret ballot or appointed by presiding officers, a member's experience did not guarantee his selection. After 1845, seniority became a major determinant, particularly in the selection of committee chairmen. Legislative parties, charged with preparing slates of committee assignments, tended to become more cohesive. In this period the tradition also began of seating in the chamber by party—with the Democrats to the presiding officer's right and the Whigs (later the Republicans) to the left.

From his canopied dais, the vice president had the best seat in the nation's best theater. On one memorable occasion, he reported to his wife that "the speech of [Senator Daniel] Webster to-day would have overwhelmed and perhaps disgusted you. He attacked [Pennsylvania's Representative] Mr. C. J. Ingersoll with the savage and mangling ferocity of a tiger. For at least a half an hour, he grit his teeth, scowled, stamped, and roared forth the very worst & most abusive language I have ever heard uttered in the Senate." Dallas later observed that "[v]ast intellect, like Webster's, almost naturally glides into arrogance."[26]

In his brief inaugural address to the Senate, Dallas had acknowledged that he entered into his "tranquil and unimposing" new duties "[w]ithout any of the cares of real power [and] none of the responsibilities of legislation" except in rare instances when he might be called on to break tied votes. If anything, he would stand as "an organ of Freedom's fundamental principle of order."[27] Despite this noble disclaimer of partisanship, Dallas involved himself deeply in the struggle to help the president achieve his legislative agenda. He worked against strong contrary pressures from the party's western faction, led by Senator Thomas Hart Benton, and its southern bloc under the inspiration of Senator John C. Calhoun. In assessing these senators' motives, Dallas reported that Benton intended to oppose Calhoun wherever possible. "If Mr. Calhoun should support the [Polk] administration, Col. Benton will not be able to resist the impulse to oppose it:—on the contrary, if Mr. Calhoun opposes, Col. Benton will be our champion. Such are, in the highest spheres of action, the uncertainties and extravagancies of human passions!"[28]

At the start of his term as Senate president, Dallas was called on to make an administrative decision that had larger constitutional consequences. Since 1815, senators had received a compensation of eight dollars for each day they were present in Washington. Public opposition routinely frustrated persistent congressional efforts to move instead to an annual salary. In March 1845 several senators hit upon a novel way to supplement their compensation—to collect travel expenses to and from Washington for the special session that the Senate held at the start of each new administration to confirm presidential appointments. The problem was that senators had already been paid for their travel to the final regular session of the Congress that had adjourned the day before the special session began. When veteran Secretary of the Senate Asbury Dickins informed Dallas that "no distinct and controlling decision" had ever been made on this issue, Dallas ruled in a lengthy written opinion that each senator should be paid for travel at the beginning and end of each session "without any enquiry or regard as to where he actually was or how he was actually engaged . . . and without any enquiry or regard as to, where he intends to travel or remain when the Senate adjourns." This decision unleashed a flood of applications from current and former senators for compensation for travel to earlier special sessions, until Dallas advised that the ruling would not be applied retroactively. Several years later, in response to a Treasury Department challenge of the Dallas ruling, the attorney general concluded that the "president of the Senate is the sole judge of the amounts of compensation due and his certificate is conclusive" and that "mileage is part of a Senator's compensation, and not mere defrayment of travelling expenses, and hence actual travel is not necessary."[29]

Dallas followed the custom of members of Congress who rented rooms, for the duration of a congressional session, either on Capitol Hill or closer to the White House. During the regular session of the Twenty-ninth Congress, from December 1845 through August 1846, he resided at Henry Riell's boardinghouse within a short walk of the Capitol at Third Street and Maryland Avenue, NE. For the first session of the Thirtieth Congress, from December 1847 to August 1848, he lived at Mrs. Gadsby's on President's Square across from the White House. For his final session, from December 1848 to March 1849, he moved several blocks to Mr. Levi Williams' boardinghouse on the north side of Pennsylvania Avenue, between 17th and 18th Streets, Northwest.[30]

At the beginning of his first regular session in December 1845, Dallas set a daily routine in which he arrived at the vice president's office in the Capitol at 9 a.m., remained busily engaged there receiving visitors and presiding until 4 p.m., adjourned to his lodgings for lunch, and then returned to the Capitol until 9 or 10 p.m. For a diversion, he would stroll around the Capitol grounds or walk down Pennsylvania Avenue.[31] The newly refurbished Senate chamber he pronounced "redeemed from a thousand barbarisms." But he confided to his son that he expected the coming session to "be one of the most important, disturbed, and protracted" in the nation's history and feared that the weakness of administration supporters in the Senate "may exact more exertion from me than would otherwise fall my share."[32]

Dallas regularly complained about the inconveniences and demands of his daily life as vice president. His wife disliked Washington and remained in Philadelphia except for rare visits. He dined frequently with Treasury Secretary Robert Walker and his nephew U.S. Coast Survey Superintendent Alexander Dallas Bache (a great-grandson of Benjamin Franklin). His biographer reports that during these years, the vice president allowed himself one luxury—a stylish African American coachman who wore a distinctive black hat with broad band and steel buckle. Dallas was ill a great deal and complained of digestive disorders and sore feet, which he routinely bathed in hot water augmented with mustard or cayenne pepper.

Always concerned about earning enough money to support his desired social position and his wife's easy spending habits, Dallas supplemented his $5,000 government salary by maintaining an active law practice during his vice-presidency. He handled several high-profile cases against the federal government, including a claim against the Treasury Department for $15 million. The decision would be made by his close friend and relative by marriage, Treasury Secretary Robert Walker. Dallas, whose cocounsel in the case was Senator Daniel Webster, considered that "unless Walker has lost his intelligence and fairness, [the case] will be a lucrative one." To Dallas' dismay and veiled anger, Walker decided against his client.[33]

At the mid-point in his vice-presidency, Dallas accepted a $1,000 fee for a secondary role in representing wealthy Philadelphian Pierce Butler in his celebrated divorce from the Shakespearean actress Fanny Kemble. Fearing that the nation's top legal talent would be attracted to Kemble's side, Butler preemptively purchased much of that talent, including Dallas and Daniel Webster. Despite intense criticism by political opponents for cashing in on his national prominence, the vice president tossed off these attacks as the "hissing and gobbling" of "snakes and geese" and spent his final months in office arranging an expanded legal partnership with his son Philip.[34]

Tariffs and Westward Expansion

Dallas determined that he would use his vice-presidential position to advance two of the administration's major objectives: tariff reduction and territorial expansion. As a Pennsylvanian, Dallas had traditionally supported the protectionist tariff policy that his state's coal and iron interests demanded. But as vice president, elected on a platform dedicated to tariff reduction, he agreed to do anything necessary to realize that goal. Dallas equated the vice president's constitutional power to break tied votes in the Senate with the president's constitutional power to veto acts of Congress. At the end of his vice-presidential term, Dallas claimed that he cast thirty tie-breaking votes during his four years in office (although only nineteen of these have been identified in Senate records). Taking obvious per-

sonal satisfaction in this record, Dallas singled out this achievement and the fairness with which he believed he accomplished it in his farewell address to the Senate.[35] Not interested in political suicide, however, Dallas sought to avoid having to exercise his singular constitutional prerogative on the tariff issue, actively lobbying senators during the debate over Treasury Secretary Walker's tariff bill in the summer of 1846. He complained to his wife (whom he sometimes addressed as "Mrs. Vice") that the Senate speeches on the subject were "as vapid as inexhaustible. . . . All sorts of ridiculous efforts are making, by letters, newspaper-paragraphs, and personal visits, to affect the Vice's casting vote, by persuasion or threat."[36]

Despite Dallas' efforts to avoid taking a stand, the Senate completed its voting on the Walker Tariff with a 27-to-27 tie. (A twenty-eighth vote in favor was held in reserve by a senator who opposed the measure but agreed to follow the instructions of his state legislature to support it.) When he cast the tie-breaking vote in favor of the tariff on July 28, 1846, Dallas rationalized that he had studied the distribution of Senate support and concluded that backing for the measure came from all regions of the country. Additionally, the measure had overwhelmingly passed the House of Representatives, a body closer to public sentiment. He apprehensively explained to the citizens of Pennsylvania that "an officer, elected by the suffrages of all twenty-eight states, and bound by his oath and every constitutional obligation, faithfully and fairly to represent, in the execution of his high trust, all the citizens of the Union" could not "narrow his great sphere and act with reference only to [Pennsylvania's] interests." While his action, based on a mixture of party loyalty and political opportunism, earned Dallas the respect of the president and certain party leaders—and possible votes in 1848 from the southern and western states that supported low tariffs—it effectively demolished his home state political base, ending any serious prospects for future elective office. (He even advised his wife in a message hand-delivered by the Senate sergeant at arms, "If there be the slightest indication of a disposition to riot in the city of Philadelphia, owing to the passage of the Tariff Bill, pack up and bring the whole brood to Washington.") [37]

While Dallas' tariff vote destroyed him in Pennsylvania, his aggressive views on Oregon and the Mexican War crippled his campaign efforts elsewhere in the nation. [38] In his last hope of building the necessary national support to gain the White House, the vice president shifted his attention to the aggressive, expansionist foreign policy program embodied in the concept of "Manifest Destiny." He actively supported efforts to gain control of Texas, the Southwest, Cuba, and disputed portions of the Oregon territory.

The joint United States-British occupation of the vast western territory in the region north of the forty-second parallel and south of the boundary at fifty-four degrees, forty minutes, was scheduled for renewal in 1847. Dallas seized the opportunity in 1846 to call for a "settlement" at the 54° 40' line, even at the risk of war with Great Britain. For several months early in 1846, the vice president pursued this position—seeking to broaden his national political base—until President Polk and British leaders agreed to compromise on a northern boundary at the forty-ninth parallel. This outcome satisfied Dallas, as it removed his earlier fear that the United States would be caught in a two-front war, with Great Britain over the Oregon boundary and with Mexico over control of Texas. Now the nation would be free to concentrate on war with Mexico, a conflict that Dallas hoped would serve to unify the Democratic party and propel him to the White House. As the Mexican War continued into 1847, Dallas expanded his own objective to the taking of all Mexico. Again, a moderate course advanced by more realistic leaders prevailed and forced Dallas to applaud publicly the result that gained for the United States the Mexican states of California and New Mexico.

The events of 1846 extinguished Dallas' presidential fire. Although he remained strong in Philadelphia and its immediate precincts, Buchanan sapped his strength throughout the rest of their state. The vice president, incapable of the intense and sustained personal drive necessary to secure the nomination, nonetheless sought to bolster his political standing by advocating popular sovereignty as a solution to the crippling issue of allowing slavery in the territories. This stance only hardened the opposition against him and he soon abandoned his presidential quest. [39] Democratic party leaders originally looked to Mexican War hero Zachary Taylor as their 1848 standard-bearer. When the general cast his lot with the Whigs, Democrats turned to Michigan's Lewis Cass, who took the nomination at the Baltimore convention on the fourth ballot. They chose General William O. Butler as the vice-presidential candidate. With Martin Van Buren's third-party candidacy eroding the Democratic vote, Taylor and his running mate Millard Fillmore easily won the election.

By the end of the Mexican War in 1848, relations between Polk and Dallas had deteriorated to the point that the two men rarely spoke to one another. From the first days of his vice-presidency, Dallas complained to his wife Sophia and others that the president cared little for his advice on either small matters or major affairs of state. At the outbreak of the war with Mexico, Dallas confided, "In making the officers of the new Regiment of mounted riflemen, the tenant of the White House has maintained his consistency of action by excluding every one for whom I felt an interest." When Polk summoned the vice president to the White House for "a most important communication," Dallas told Sophia that Polk had a habit of "making mountains out of molehills." and that the meeting was "another illustration of the mountain and the mouse. I am heartily sick of factitious importance." Dallas considered Polk to be "cold, devious, and two-faced." When he received Thomas Macauley's newly published *History of England*, he noted that the author's description of Charles I's "defects of character"—faithlessness and cunning—"are so directly applicable to President Polk as almost to be curious." [40]

Last Session

Dallas entered the sunset of his vice-presidency at the three-month final session of the Thirtieth Congress, beginning on December 4, 1848. On the following day at noon, the Senate convened for the reading by its clerk of President

Polk's State of the Union message. Dallas listened for a while, until boredom compelled him to turn the chair over to Senator William King. "It was insufferably long, and some of its topics, a dissertation on the American system and one on the Veto Power especially, were almost ludicrous from their being misplaced and prolix."[41] This "lame duck" session, with its contentiousness and inaction, proved particularly frustrating as the Democrats sought to defer action on the volatile issues. "The great party project of the Session is to try hard to do nothing:—leaving all unsettled questions, and especially the free soil one, to harass Genl. Taylor next winter."[42]

Dallas was constantly aware of his responsibilities for maintaining order on the Senate floor. During the contentious final session, Mississippi's Henry Foote constantly baited Missouri's Thomas Hart Benton. While Benton never hesitated to bully other adversaries, he inexplicably refrained from challenging the diminutive Mississippian. As the Senate adjourned for the day on February 10, 1849, Benton approached Dallas and, in a whisper, asked whether he intended to act on his earlier request that alcoholic beverages be banned in the Senate. Dallas responded by asking whether any drinking had been taking place in the chamber. "Yes, in quantities, in every part, and at all times," responded the agitated Missourian. Dallas, believing that Benton's concern stemmed from an effort to curb Foote's behavior and "to excuse his own silent disregard of it in that way," instructed the sergeant at arms to ban liquor on the Senate side of the Capitol, except for members claiming to require it for medicinal purposes.[43]

Dallas told his wife that he was tempted to return home, leaving his Senate duties to a president pro tempore, but he felt obligated to remain at the Capitol for the important business of receiving the presidential electoral ballots, addressed to his attention, that were then arriving from the individual states. He explained that his duty was to "mark on each [envelope containing a state's ballots] the day and manner of receiving it, and file them with the Secretary [of the Senate], of course without breaking the seals. If a messenger hand me the list, I give him a certificate to that effect, on which he is entitled to be paid his expenses, at the Treasury Department."[44]

The president expressed to the vice president his ambivalence about his plans for the forthcoming inauguration of Zachary Taylor. If the planners reserved a place for him, he would attend, otherwise he would follow Van Buren's 1841 precedent and simply go home. Dallas said he would try to "follow the proper courtesies of public life," unless he too was intentionally slighted. He examined the practice of his predecessors and found Richard M. Johnson to be the only vice president to have attended the swearing in of his successor.

On March 2, 1849, Dallas followed the vice-presidential custom of delivering a farewell address to the Senate and then stepping aside so that the Senate could elect a president pro tempore to bridge the transition between administrations. In remarks more exalted in phrasing than the observations of his personal diary and correspondence, Dallas praised the Senate for the "elevated principle and dignified tone which mark [its] proceedings; the frank and yet forbearing temper of its discussions; the mutual manifestations of conciliatory deference, so just and appropriate among the delegates of independent States; and the consequent calmness and precision of its legislative action," which he believed had "attracted to it a very large share of veneration and confidence." He noted that, on occasion, tempers flared into "sudden impulses of feeling," but these "transient disturbances" were rare and passed "over the scene like flashes which do but startle, and then cease, [serving] only to exhibit in stronger relief the grave decorum of its general conduct."[45]

To a standing ovation, Dallas left the chamber in what he believed would be "the last scene of my public life." He recorded in his diary that "Mr. Filmore [sic] called at my chamber in the Capitol today, shortly I had left the Senate, and remained for an hour, making enquiries as to the forms of proceeding and the general duties annexed to the office he was about assuming. He was good enough to say that every body had told him I eclipsed as a presiding officer, all of my predecessors, and that he felt extreme diffidence in undertaking to follow me. Of course, after this, I took pleasure in answering all his questions." [46]

Dallas left Washington largely embittered about the price of success in public life, which he believed led "almost invariably to poverty and ignorance. Truth, Courage, Candour, Wisdom, Firmness, Honor and Religion may by accident now and then be serviceable:— but a steady perseverance in them leads inevitably to private life." [47] His only regret about leaving the Senate was that he would miss the "strange political tableau [that] would present itself on the floor of the Senate Chamber . . . on the 6. of March next [if] Mr. Clay, Genl. Cass, Mr. Van Buren, Mr, Calhoun, Mr. Webster, and Col. Benton were grouped together! Such a convocation of self-imagined gods could not fail to be followed by much thunder and lightening." But, he consoled himself, "All this galaxy, in the order of nature, may disappear in the course or two or three years. When then? Why, the Sun will still shine, the earth still roll upon its axis, and the worms of the Capitol be as numerous and phosphorescent as ever." [48]

Later Years

Dallas returned to private life until 1856, when James Buchanan resigned as minister to Great Britain to launch his presidential campaign challenging President Franklin Pierce for the Democratic nomination. Pierce, seeking to remove another potential rival for reelection, named Dallas to that prize diplomatic post. Philadelphia journalist John Forney, a longtime Buchanan ally who had once described Dallas as "below mediocre as a public man," thought the sixty-four-year-old Dallas fit the part. "I do not know anything more charming, always excepting a lovely woman, than a handsome old man—one who, like a winter apple, is ruddy and ripe with time, and yet sound to the heart. Such a man was George M. Dallas." [49] After Buchanan won the presidency, he retained Dallas at the Court of St. James but conducted sensitive diplomatic relations with Great Britain from the White House. Tired and longing for the comforts of home and family, Dallas resigned his post in May 1861. As a states' rights Unionist, he was deeply saddened by the eclipse of his Democratic party and its failure to prevent civil war. He died at the age of seventy-two on December 31, 1864.

NOTES

[1] George M. Dallas to unknown addressee, 1845 [?], in Roy M. Nichols, "The Library: The Mystery of the Dallas Papers (Part I)," *The Pennsylvania Magazine of History and Biography* 73 (July 1949): 373 [hereafter cited as Nichols-I].

[2] Lewis A. McArthur, *Oregon Geographic Names*, 5th ed. (Portland, OR, 1982), p. 205.

[3] John M. Belohlavek, *George Mifflin Dallas: Jacksonian Patrician* (University Park, PA, 1977), pp. 13–14.

[4] Ibid. pp. 4–5.

[5] Ibid., p. 15.

[6] Ibid., p. 5.

[7] Ibid., p. 27.

[8] Ibid., p. 37.

[9] Quoted in ibid., p. 43.

[10] Bruce Ambacher, "George M. Dallas and the Bank War," *Pennsylvania History* 42 (April 1975): 135.

[11] Belohlavek, p. 77.

[12] Charles Sellers, "Election of 1844," in *History of American Presidential Elections*, edited by Arthur M. Schlesinger, Jr., and Fred L. Israel (New York, 1971), 1:759–72.

[13] John Arthur Garraty, *Silas Wright* (New York, 1949), pp. 280–82.

[14] Belohlavek, pp. 86–88; Sellers, pp. 772–73.

[15] Belohlavek, p. 88.

[16] Sidney George Fisher quoted in ibid., p. 89.

[17] By the time of the presidential elections of 1840 and 1844, states were increasingly selecting presidential electors by popular vote, rather than by vote of their legislatures. With presidential elections scheduled on a variety of days throughout the states, conditions were ripe for election fraud. Both political parties organized gangs of voters who moved from state to state in an attempt to boost tallies in close elections. Finally, in 1845 Congress established a uniform date for presidential elections—the first Tuesday after the first Monday in November. Congressional elections were not similarly standardized until 1872. Peter H. Argersinger, "Electoral Processes," *Encyclopedia of American Political History* (New York, 1984), 2:496.

[18] Sellers, p. 795; Belohlavek, p. 97.

[19] Paul H. Beregeron, *The Presidency of James K. Polk* (Lawrence, KS, 1987), pp. 16–17.

[20] Dallas to Polk, December 15, 1845; Dallas to Sophia, February 14, 1845 in Nichols-I, pp. 355–60.

[21] Dallas to Robert J. Walker, November 6, 1844, quoted in Belohlavek, p. 100.

[22] Belohlavek, pp. 105–10.

[23] See Chapter 7 of this book, "John C. Calhoun," pp. 10–12.

[24] U.S., Congress, Congressional Globe, 29th Cong., 1st sess., p. 20.

[25] Ibid., pp. 19–22; Belohlavek, pp. 107–9; Dallas to Sophia, December 9, 1845, Nichols-I, p. 370.

[26] Ingersoll had accused Webster of corruption and embezzlement while serving as secretary of state. Dallas to Sophia, April 7, 1846, Nichols-I, pp. 375–76; Roy F. Nichols, "The Library: The Mystery of the Dallas Papers (Part II)," *The Pennsylvania Magazine of History and Biography* 73 (October 1949): 480 [hereafter cited as Nichols-II].

[27] U.S., Congress, Senate, Journal, 29th Cong., Extra Session, Appendix, p. 274.

[28] Dallas to Sophia, November 27, 1845, Nichols-I, p. 366.

[29] Ruth Ketring Nuermberger, "Asbury Dickins (1780–1861): A Career in Government Service," *The North Carolina Historical Review* 24 (July 1947): 311–12; Dallas to Sophia, March 17, 1845, Nichols-I, p. 365. On March 3, 1851, the president approved a statute (Chapter 42) ending the practice of paying members of the previous Congress for mileage to attend the Senate special session beginning on March 4, 1853, and every four years thereafter.

[30] Nichols-I, p. 391; Nichols-II, p. 475.

[31] Dallas to Sophia, December 2, 1845, Nichols-I, p. 369.

[32] Dallas to Sophia, November 27, 1845, ibid., p. 367.

[33] Belohlavek, pp. 134–35.

[34] Ibid., pp. 135–36; Dallas to Sophia, December 10, 1848, Nichols-II, p. 483.

[35] Senate *Journal*, 30th Cong., 2d sess., March 2, 1849, p. 294. Nineteen of the thirty votes that Dallas claimed to have cast have been identified in records of Senate floor proceedings. If Dallas' figure is accepted, he would hold the record among vice presidents for exercising this constitutional prerogative (although some scholars have credited John Adams with casting as many as thirty tie-breaking votes—see Chapter 1, note 1). If the lower figure is accurate, it still places him just behind John Adams—and just ahead of John C. Calhoun—for the number of ties broken in a four-year period. For a list of vice-presidential tie-breaking votes, see U.S., Congress, Senate, *The Senate, 1789–1989*, by Robert C. Byrd, S. Doc., 100–20, 100th Cong., 1st sess., vol. 4, *Historical Statistics, 1789–1992*, 1993, pp. 640–46.

[36] Dallas to Sophia, July 17, 1846, Nichols-I, pp. 384–85.

[37] Dallas' public letter quoted in Charles John Biddle, *Eulogy upon the Hon. George Mifflin Dallas Delivered before the Bar of Philadelphia, February 11, 1865* (Philadelphia, 1865), p. 36; Belohlavek, pp. 113–14; Dallas to Sophia, July 30, 1846, Nichols-I, p. 386.

[38] Belohlavek, p. 118.

[39] Charles McCool Snyder, *The Jacksonian Heritage: Pennsylvania Politics, 1833–1848* (Harrisburg, PA, 1958), pp. 205–7; Frederick Moore Binder, *James Buchanan and the American Empire* (Cranbury, NJ, 1994), p. 91.

[40] Dallas to Sophia, June 7, 1846, Nichols-I, pp. 381–82; Dallas diary, January 14, 1849, Nichols-II, pp. 492–93; Belohlavek, pp. 132–33.

[41] Dallas diary, December 5, 1848, Nichols-II, p. 475.

[42] Dallas to Sophia, December 7, 1848, ibid., p. 477.

[43] Dallas diary, February 10, 1849, ibid., pp. 512–13.

[44] Dallas to Sophia, December 7, 1848; Dallas diary, December 8, 1848, ibid., pp. 477–78.

[45] *Senate Journal*, 30th Cong., 2d sess., March 2, 1849, pp. 293–94.

[46] Dallas diary, March 2, 1849, Nichols-II, pp. 515–16.

[47] Dallas diary, January 28, 1849, ibid., p. 501; Dallas diary, March 2, 1849, ibid., pp. 516–17.

[48] Dallas diary, January 28, 1849, ibid., p. 502.

[49] Belohlavek, p. 107; John W. Forney, *Anecdotes of Public Men* (New York, 1881), 2:102.

Chapter 12

MILLARD FILLMORE
1849–1850

MILLARD FILLMORE

Chapter 12

MILLARD FILLMORE

12th Vice President: 1849–1850

I know how difficult it is to determine what is and what is not in order, to restrain improper language, and yet not abridge the freedom of debate. But all must see how important it is that the first departure from the strict rule of parliamentary decorum be checked, as a slight attack, or even insinuation of a personal character, often provokes a more severe retort, which brings out a more disorderly reply, each Senator feeling a justification in the previous aggression. There is, therefore, no point so proper to interpose for the preservation of order as to check the first violation of it.

—MILLARD FILLMORE, APRIL 3, 1850

The new vice president needed a clerk. Millard Fillmore suffered from an eye disorder that limited his ability to read by candlelight, yet his official duties kept him so busy during the daytime that he had to put off reading and preparing his correspondence until evening. A clerk would be most useful. When Fillmore's immediate predecessor, George Dallas, took office in 1845, no funding was provided for a vice-presidential clerk because there had been no vice president since 1841, when John Tyler had succeeded to the presidency after the death of William Henry Harrison. Senator Willie Mangum (W-NC), who had fulfilled the office's major constitutional function as Senate president pro tempore from 1842 to 1845, had considered his duties too light to justify continuing the perquisite that Vice President Richard M. Johnson had enjoyed during his 1837–1841 term. Aware of these precedents, Fillmore asked Mangum, one of the Whig party's senior senators, to introduce the necessary authorizing resolution. When Mangum did so, a Democratic senator immediately objected, noting that former Vice President Dallas had gotten along just fine without a clerk. Mangum responded by citing the example of Vice President Johnson, also a Democrat. The Democratic senator withdrew his objection and

Fillmore got his clerk. From this experience, Fillmore may have learned both how much the Senate valued precedent and how little some of its members regarded the office of vice president.[1]

Millard Fillmore rose to the vice-presidency, in part, because he was from New York. In presidential elections from 1812 to 1968, that state had the nation's largest congressional delegation and therefore was entitled to cast more votes in the electoral college than any other state. New York's electoral riches account for the fact that, during the century from 1801 to 1901, eight of the twenty-two vice presidents called that state home. In designing a presidential ticket that would attract large blocks of electoral votes, the national parties always paid very careful attention to New York political leaders.

Millard Fillmore would occupy the nation's second highest office for fewer than seventeen months. During his brief tenure, he suffered the fate of other vice presidents: his president ignored him, his state's party leaders undercut him, and the Senate over which he presided barely tolerated him. Yet the office benefitted him, just as he improved it. The experience ratified and extended his stature as a significant national figure. When Zachary Taylor's death thrust Fillmore into the presidency, few seriously doubted that he was up to the job. His close relations with senators at a time when the Senate served as the final arbiter of crucial national policy issues eased passage of the vital compromise legislation that staved off national political disintegration for another decade. To his role as the Senate's president, Fillmore brought a deep knowledge and understanding of the institution's rules, precedents, and culture. Aware that the incendiary climate in the Senate chamber during 1850 could foster an explosion of devastating national consequence, he insisted on order, decorum, and fair play. For his successors, he provided a valuable example, couched in the spirit of Thomas Jefferson a half century earlier.

Early Years

Millard Fillmore was born on January 7, 1800, into an impoverished farm family in the central New York frontier town of Locke. The second of Nathaniel and Phoebe Fillmore's nine children, Millard found little time for formal schooling and had barely learned to read by the age of seventeen. As a youth he worked on his father's farm—developing a muscular chest and broad shoulders that would remain a distinguishing physical characteristic for years to come—and he served apprenticeships to a cloth dresser and a textile mill operator. Aware of his educational deficiencies, young Millard struggled to improve his reading skills, carrying a dictionary on his daily rounds.[2] At age nineteen, he enrolled in a small academy in the town of New Hope, where he engaged in his first formal education, as well as a budding relationship with Abigail Powers, a local minister's daughter. When Millard returned to the central New York tenant farm, the judge who owned the property recognized his potential and provided him with essential financial and educational support to pursue a legal career. Young Fillmore taught in a local school and saved enough money to buy out the time remaining in his textile mill apprenticeship. When, before long, personal differences caused Millard and the judge to part ways, the young man once more returned to work on his father's farm. In 1820, the elder Fillmore moved his family west to the town of Aurora, eighteen miles from Buffalo. There Millard resumed his work as a teach-

er and as a law clerk, until he was admitted to the New York bar in 1824. He then opened a small law practice in East Aurora and in 1826 married Abigail Powers.[3]

In 1830 Millard and Abigail settled in Buffalo, the thriving western terminus of the Erie Canal. His practice flourished, as the local business community came to recognize him as an energetic, careful, and talented lawyer. An impressive figure, Fillmore stood six feet tall and handsome, with sparkling blue eyes, a pinkish complexion, a jovial and kindly demeanor, and polished manners. He enjoyed dressing in the latest fashions, displaying impeccable good taste that masked his humble origins. The Fillmore family, which now included a son and daughter, rose rapidly in Buffalo society. Millard and Abigail regularly entertained the city's elite and others with whom he associated in founding and promoting local educational, cultural, and civic institutions.

Buffalo's proximity to major water transportation routes predisposed Fillmore to be a strong supporter of John Quincy Adams' National Republicans and Henry Clay's "American System" of internal improvements, tariffs, and national bank. In 1828, Fillmore met Albany editor and political boss Thurlow Weed. Weed saw in Fillmore a natural politician and assisted his campaign, as a National Republican, for a seat in the state assembly. Despite the strong contrary tide that swept Democrat Andrew Jackson into the White House, Fillmore won his race. Over the next few years, he rose to leadership in western New York's newly emerging Whig party, sponsoring legislation beneficial to transportation, as well as financial and educational enterprises. Fillmore and Weed would remain close allies for many years.[4]

In the House of Representatives

In 1832, Anti-Mason and National Republican party voters in the congressional district that encompassed Buffalo elected Fillmore to the U.S. House of Representatives. There he served a single term and dedicated himself to merging those two parties into a strong Whig party in opposition to President Jackson's policies. Maneuvering to repair ill feelings between his supporting party factions, Fillmore removed himself from a reelection bid in 1834, but reentered the contest in 1836. He resumed his seat in the House the following year and served there until 1843.[5] When the Whigs took control of the White House and both houses of Congress for the first time in 1841, Fillmore's allies in the House nominated him for the post of Speaker. Although he came in second to a candidate supported by Henry Clay, he was subsequently elected chairman of the Committee on Ways and Means, a powerful position at this time of national financial crisis. His major accomplishment as chairman was to steer through his chamber's rough waters, and against the force of President John Tyler's opposition, the protective Tariff of 1842, a key revenue-raising component of his party's plan for economic recovery. The heads of executive branch agencies came to fear the chairman's quietly efficient scrutiny of their budget requests, as he routinely returned their spending estimates heavily marked in red pencil with notes asking for thorough justification of matters great and small.[6] At the end of the Twenty-seventh Congress, in March 1843, Fillmore again abandoned the political and social life of Washington, which he heartily disliked, for the quiet pleasures of Buffalo.

Neither Vice President nor Governor

Whig party elder statesman John Quincy Adams visited Buffalo in the summer of 1843 to praise publicly his former house colleague's achievements and to urge him to return to government service. Still enjoying the high regard of his party allies as a result of his successful management of the 1842 tariff, Fillmore had decided to launch a behind-the-scenes campaign for the Whig party's 1844 vice-presidential nomination. He learned, however, that state party strategist Thurlow Weed coveted that spot for his close ally, former New York governor William Seward, against whom Fillmore "harbored a jealousy that had in it something of the petulance of a child."[7] To derail this scheme, Fillmore made a bargain with John Collier of Binghamton, a New York City-supported antagonist of the party's Weed-Seward Albany faction. Fillmore would support Collier for governor and Collier would

put his influence behind Fillmore's vice-presidential quest. The plan fell apart when Seward declared he had no interest in the number two position. To protect against the election of his enemy Collier, Weed urged Fillmore to shift his focus and seek the governorship. Fillmore initially refused. Weed then quietly went to work to sabotage any chances that his faction-ridden party would award Fillmore its vice-presidential nomination. He hinted to delegates at the Whigs' Baltimore convention that Seward would accept a draft, while loudly proclaiming that no Whig but Fillmore could win the governorship. Seeing through Weed's machinations, Fillmore wrote an ally: "I need not tell you that I have no desire to run for governor. . . . I am not willing to be treacherously killed by this pretended kindness. . . . Do not suppose for a moment that I think they desire my nomination for governor."[8] Weed's tactics succeeded in denying Fillmore the vice-presidential nomination, as Theodore Frelinghuysen won a third-ballot nomination to join Henry Clay on the party's ticket.

Henry Clay made northern antislavery Whigs nervous. Soon after receiving the party's presidential nomination with a vow of opposition to the annexation of Texas, which seemed certain to become a slave state, he shifted to a more ambivalent stance. As abolitionists among New York's Whigs began to explore alliances with other parties, Weed redoubled his efforts to solidify the state party by putting Fillmore at the top of its ticket in the race for governor. Under Weed's pressure, John Collier withdrew in favor of Fillmore, who then received the unanimous nomination of the New York state Whig convention. Aware that the governorship could be a way station on the road to greater national ambitions, Fillmore set aside his earlier reluctance. He ran a strong campaign based on his opposition to Texas annexation, which he believed would benefit slaveholders at the expense of the rest of the country. Fillmore's views, however, proved unpopular with many voters, particularly recent immigrants who resented his party's nativist, anti-Catholic stance. In vain did Fillmore try to appeal to foreign-born voters by working to create a German-language newspaper in Buffalo.

He lost by ten thousand votes to Democrat Silas Wright, who earlier in the year had turned down his party's nomination as vice president in favor of this race.

The disaffection of New York's antislavery Whigs accounted for Fillmore's defeat, and the loss of that pivotal state also cost Henry Clay the presidency. Despite his setback, Fillmore emerged as his party's state leader, much to the irritation of Seward and Weed, who feared the New York Whig party's center of influence would thereby shift westward from their Albany power base to Fillmore's in Buffalo. Thus began a politically destructive geographical and ideological polarization between Fillmore in the state's western districts and the Seward-Weed forces in the east.[9]

Ambition for National Office

In his earlier life, Fillmore had shown no compelling ambition for public office, despite the evidence of his 1844 vice-presidential and gubernatorial campaigns. Twice he had given up his seat in the U.S. House of Representatives for other goals, and the center of his personal and political universe seemed to be the city of Buffalo, where his law practice was flourishing. By 1847, however, as in 1844, Fillmore had grown restless away from the larger state and national arenas. He had become deeply hostile toward President James K. Polk, whose administration was reversing Whig economic gains. In addition, the president was leading the nation in a war with Mexico aimed at acquiring western territories, presumably to feed slavery's insatiable appetite. In this frame of mind, Fillmore readily accepted his party's nomination for the influential post of state comptroller. (He would have preferred a U.S. Senate seat, but none was available.) By a wide margin over his Democratic opponent, Fillmore won the election, and his political star again began to rise. In Albany, he built a record of accomplishment that enlarged his already considerable popularity. While comptroller, Fillmore retained a national presence, regularly denouncing President Polk's war with Mexico, so that by 1848, northern Whigs had come to view the New York comptroller as a logical vice-presidential choice to balance the likely presidential candidacy of war hero General Zachary Taylor.[10]

The June 1848 Whig Convention

When the Whigs gathered at Philadelphia in June 1848, party leaders expected that General Taylor would win their presidential nomination. A Louisiana slaveholder, Taylor lacked partisan political experience and commitment. He had never voted in a presidential election, but he was an obviously electable military hero and had the important support of the southern or "Cotton Whig" branch of the party. Despite unhappiness among the party's antislavery elements in the North and West, and a sputtering effort to revive Henry Clay's candidacy (Clay lamented, "I wish I could slay a Mexican."[11]), Taylor gained the Whig nomination on the fourth ballot.

Following the selection of Taylor, convention chairman John Collier, a New Yorker and skillful parliamentary tactician, took the rostrum and gained control of Henry Clay's disappointed and angry forces, who threatened to disrupt the convention. Assuring the agitated delegates that New York would actively support Taylor, Collier presented a peace offering—a "surprise" candidate for vice president. On hearing the name of Millard Fillmore, many opponents of Taylor set aside their reservations and joined to support the new ticket. By the second ballot, the prize was Fillmore's.[12] Although Collier had skillfully associated Fillmore with Clay, playing on his well-established advocacy of Whig legislative programs, the nominee was by no means broadly sympathetic to the Kentucky statesman. However, the nervous delegates were in no mood for an extended examination of Fillmore's beliefs. Collier saw that Fillmore would balance the ticket and block fellow New Yorkers Seward and Weed, whose wishes for a return to a larger role in Whig affairs threatened to further polarize that party's factions. Weed reluctantly acquiesced to the nomination, while Seward remained deeply concerned.[13]

The same contentiousness reflected in the 1848 convention's proceedings made it inadvisable for party leaders to develop a specific platform. Instead, the Whig candidates devised their positions to fit the prejudices of specific regions. Candidate Fillmore told southern audiences that he "regarded slavery as an evil, but one with which the National Government had nothing to do." Under the Constitution, he contended, "the whole power over that question was vested in the several states where the institution was tolerated. If they regarded it as a blessing, they had a constitutional right to enjoy it; and if they regarded it as an evil, they had the power and knew best how to apply the remedy." As for Congress, Fillmore concluded that it had no power to interfere with slavery in the states where it existed. He dodged entirely the more ominous issue of slavery in the territories.[14]

In the weeks after the national convention, Thurlow Weed and other northern Whig leaders who suspected Taylor of Democratic sympathies considered moves to undercut his candidacy by influencing state party conventions to select panels of unpledged presidential electors. Fillmore defused this subversive strategy by persuading Taylor to write and publish a letter in which he distanced himself from his vocal Democratic supporters. In the so-called Allison Letter, Taylor asserted that Congress, not the president, should control the nation's policy agenda. "The personal opinions of the individual who may happen to occupy the executive chair ought not to control the action of Congress upon questions of domestic policy; nor ought his objections to be interposed where questions of constitutional power have been settled by the various departments of government, and acquiesced in by the people."[15]

Thanks in great measure to the influence of the Allison Letter and Fillmore's hard work, as well as to the Free Soil party candidacy of Martin Van Buren that divided traditional northern Democratic ranks, the Taylor-Fillmore ticket won New York state by a narrow margin, providing barely enough electoral votes to swing the election to the Whigs.[16] Expressing a common belief that the Whigs had sold out their principles with the selection of Taylor, journalist Horace Greeley, a Seward-Weed ally, concluded that the party was "at once triumphant and undone."[17]

A New Administration

Millard Fillmore shared Zachary Taylor's belief in a strong legislature and a compliant executive. In a letter written immediately after his election, he explained that in all areas not directly covered by the Constitution, "as to all other questions of mere policy, where Congress has the constitutional right to legislate, the will of the people, as expressed through their representatives in Congress, is to control, and that will is not to be defeated by the arbitrary interposition of the [executive] veto power." By adhering to this classic Whig doctrine, Taylor and Fillmore hoped to avoid the roiling sectional controversies that could easily wreck their administration, leaving them to the people's representatives in Congress. With guarded optimism, Fillmore saw the 1848 election "as putting an end to all ideas of disunion. It raises up a national party, occupying a middle ground, and leaves the fanatics and disunionists, north and south, without the hope of destroying the fair fabric of our constitution."[18] Yet, even as he wrote this, secessionist conventions were gathering in the South and antislavery societies in the North were stating their legislative demands. As word of the revolutions sweeping Europe reached the United States, it became clear that the political climate in the months ahead would hardly be free of grave challenges to the nation's constitutional order.

In the months before taking his oath of office, Fillmore had reason to believe his would be an active vice-presidency. Thurlow Weed heard that President-elect Taylor, fearing the unaccustomed administrative burdens that awaited him, had said "I wish Mr. Fillmore would take all of the business into his own hands." The ill-informed Taylor believed that the vice president would be an official member of his cabinet. Weed worried that Fillmore would use his new position to take control of New York state's lucrative federal patronage appointments, which would surely accelerate the political decline of that state's once-potent Weed-Seward political faction.[19]

In a typically crafty move to rescue their fortunes, Weed lobbied Fillmore to support Seward's candidacy for the Senate over that of John Collier, who had engineered Fillmore's vice-presidential nomination. In return, Weed promised full consultation in all state patronage matters. Anxious to secure his own political base in New York before moving onto the national stage, Fillmore abandoned Collier and yielded to Weed's entreaties, despite his misgivings based on twenty years of experience with the duplicitous political boss. As a result of Fillmore's shift, Seward obtained the necessary votes in the state legislature to win the Senate seat. He headed to Washington with the vice president-elect after both men, at a dinner with Weed in Albany, had agreed to consult with one another from time to time on the state's rich federal patronage. Outwardly cordial to Fillmore, Seward harbored a dark plot, conceived by Weed, to sabotage Fillmore's control over New York's federal appointments. Fillmore would pay dearly for his abandonment of Collier.[20]

In 1849, March 4 fell on a Sunday. In observance of the Christian sabbath, President-elect Taylor chose to defer his public oath-taking to the following day.[21] Thus, on a cloudy and brisk Monday morning, Fillmore met Vice President George Dallas at Willard's Hotel on Pennsylvania Avenue, the preferred lodging place of both men. At 11 a.m., the two men set out for Capitol Hill in an open carriage. Onlookers on Pennsylvania Avenue had difficulty telling the present and future vice presidents apart. Both were large, clean-shaven men, dressed in somber black with full heads of white hair. Only Fillmore's muscular torso, pink face, and sparkling blue eyes distinguished him. At this point in the transition process, as the president-elect was making key appointments to his cabinet and thereby setting the tone of his administration, Taylor and Fillmore had met only for social occasions. Yet, Fillmore seemed unconcerned that Taylor had not bothered to take advantage of his broad knowledge of party leaders and issues.[22]

An honor guard of senators escorted Fillmore into the mobbed Senate chamber where Vice President Dallas led him to the presiding officer's chair. Chief Justice Roger Taney administered the oath of office, and the new vice president delivered a brief inaugural address. Fillmore confessed his inexperience in the customs and procedures of legislative bodies and asked senators for their "indulgent forbearance." In cheerful words that he would soon have cause

to reconsider, Fillmore observed that "the senate is composed of eminent statesmen, equally distinguished for their high intellectual endowments and their amenity of manners, whose persuasive eloquence is so happily tempered with habitual courtesy, as to relieve your presiding officer from all that would be painful in the discharge of his duty, and render his position as agreeable as it must be instructive."[23] When he concluded his remarks, President Polk and General Taylor, after an awkward delay, entered the chamber and took their assigned seats. Pausing only briefly, the presidential party then formed ranks and proceeded with the senators to the inaugural platform on the Capitol's eastern portico.

In the weeks following the inauguration, Fillmore began to realize that on patronage matters Weed and Seward had already succeeded in weakening his limited influence with the new president. When the important post of marshal for New York's northern district opened, Seward and Weed, without consulting the vice president, sent word to Secretary of State John Clayton that they and Fillmore had agreed on P.V. Kellogg. Clayton forwarded Kellogg's name to the president, who made the selection. Learning of their duplicity, Fillmore asked Taylor to rescind the appointment, but the president refused to do so without consulting Clayton. Weed rushed to Washington and advised the president that Fillmore's anger reflected a parochial dispute between state factions that could best be avoided by placing New York's patronage recommendations in other hands. He suggested Governor Hamilton Fish, a "neutral" figure who was actually firmly within the Weed-Seward camp. Taylor naively agreed.[24] The extent of Weed's victory became clear when Fillmore recommended John Collier for the post of New York naval officer. Taylor ignored the request and appointed a Weed ally to that coveted position. The ultimate Fillmore defeat occurred in the vice president's own political back yard with the appointment of a Weed-Seward crony as collector for the port of Buffalo. A Buffalo newspaper under Weed's control gloated, "We could put up a cow against a Fillmore nominee and defeat him." Reflecting on his lowly status, Fillmore wrote Harvard President Edward Everett that since he had "no favors to bestow, either legislative or official," he expected a restful tenure.[25]

By November 1849, as Congress was about to convene for the first regular session of the Taylor administration, Fillmore complained to the president that the administration's appointments, influenced by Weed and Seward, were destroying his influence in New York. He asked the president whether in the future he would be "treated as a friend or foe?" Taylor promised to do better—and soon forgot his promise.

The "Memorable Senate of that fearful epoch"

Departing Vice President George M. Dallas had regretted that he would not be present in the presiding officer's chair in December 1849 to witness the constellation of illustrious figures among the sixty-member Senate of the Thirty-first Congress. Together again for what would prove to be their last legislative session were the members of the already legendary "Great Triumvirate." Returning from a seven-year absence, Henry Clay, whose initial Senate service dated back forty-three years to 1806, had been the Whig party's preeminent legislative leader. Daniel Webster, an eighteen-year Senate veteran, had taken a sabbatical to be secretary of state in the first Whig administration under Harrison and Tyler. And John C. Calhoun, gaunt, ill, and unlikely to survive the session, had been vice president in the John Quincy Adams and Andrew Jackson administrations, as well as Webster's successor as secretary of state in the Tyler presidency. Each of these men was by then identified as the congressional personification of his region. Also present among this eminent assembly were Stephen A. Douglas, the "Little Giant" of Illinois; Michigan's Lewis Cass, the recently defeated Democratic presidential candidate; Henry Foote and Jefferson Davis of Mississippi; Missouri's Thomas Hart Benton, approaching a thirty-year record of Senate service; Seward of New York; Salmon P. Chase of Ohio, an eventual U.S. chief justice; the fiery Sam Houston of Texas; and—at a lesser level of eminence—the Dodges, Henry of Wisconsin and Augustus Caesar of Iowa, the Senate's only father-son team.[26]

The 1848 treaty concluding the war with Mexico added to the nation's land mass 500,000 square miles of new western territories, including present-day California, Nevada, Utah, and much of New Mexico, Arizona, Wyoming, and Colorado. Confronting Congress and the new Taylor administration in 1849 was the explosive issue of how these territories would be organized with respect to slavery. Northern "free soil" advocates insisted that slavery be contained in the states where it already existed. Southern planters and their allies believed that their region's economic system should be allowed to operate without such crippling restrictions. In the 1848 presidential campaign, Democratic candidate Lewis Cass had supported the doctrine of "popular sovereignty," under which the residents of the territories would decide the issue for themselves. Former President Martin Van Buren, running as the Free Soil party candidate, demanded support for the 1846 Wilmot Proviso. This amendment to an appropriations bill had failed to pass the Senate, but it provided a rallying cry for antislavery forces by proposing the prohibition of slavery in the territory acquired from Mexico. The Whigs, standing on no platform, had simply ducked the issue during the election campaign. Southerners who at first had believed a Louisiana slaveholder would be a sympathetic president, soon had cause for concern when Taylor began to take advice from Senator Seward and other antislavery Whigs.

In his December 24, 1849, annual message to the newly convened Congress, Taylor sought to defuse this portentous issue by proposing that California and New Mexico apply immediately for statehood, bypassing the territorial stage and the Wilmot Proviso controversy. As Mexico had prohibited slavery in these regions, there would be few slaveholders to vote in favor of that institution. In fact, California had already approved a constitution that prohibited slavery. Southern members of Congress realized that the admission of an additional free state would destroy the balance between slave and free states that had made the Senate the principal forum for debate on the slavery issue since the 1820 Missouri Compromise. Taylor's message only further inflamed the festering controversy among southerners, who argued that if the territories had been taken with the blood of all Americans, they should not be closed to those citizens choosing to move with their property to those regions. Southern members introduced legislation designed to preserve the balance of new states and to toughen fugitive slave laws.

Conflicting northern proposals prompted Henry Clay in January 1850, with the assistance of Democrat Stephen A. Douglas, to fashion an "Omnibus Bill," a series of eight measures to address the slavery and territorial issues that collectively became known as the "Compromise of 1850." In the weeks that followed, the compelling oratory of Clay, Webster, Calhoun, and others drew capacity crowds to the Senate chamber. On March 7, Daniel Webster opened his classic address with these memorable lines of national reconciliation—and political suicide—addressed to Senate President Fillmore: "Mr. President, I wish to speak to-day, not as a Massachusetts man, nor as a northern man, but as an American." Four days later, Seward rose to denounce the proposed compromise. Acknowledging that the Constitution protected slavery, he asserted, "But, there is a higher law than the Constitution, which regulates our authority over the domain, and devotes it to the same noble purposes." These speeches drew new battle lines, with Seward and the mortally ill Calhoun representing their sections' hard-liners, while Webster and Clay sought a middle way. Suddenly secession seemed a real possibility.[27]

Obligation to Preserve Order

The death of John C. Calhoun on March 31 removed a tenacious opponent of the compromise. Fillmore presided at the statesman's funeral in the Senate chamber on April 2. On the following day, responding to the deeply unsettled atmosphere, the vice president took an extraordinary step for a presiding officer—he addressed the Senate. His topic: the vice president's "powers and duties to preserve order."[28] Speaking in a solemn manner, Fillmore stated that when he had first entered the office, he had assumed he would not be called on to maintain order in a body with such a strong reputation for courtesy

and deference. He soon realized that he had been naive. To arm himself against the challenge of recurring disorderly behavior, he had consulted old Senate records and manuals of parliamentary practice for guidance. He discovered, to no one's surprise, that the Constitution conferred on the vice president the general, if not express, power to maintain order. Rules 16 and 17, adopted during the First Congress in 1789, had defined the vice president's constitutional prerogatives. He alone possessed the authority to call a member to order, and his decision was to be considered final, not subject to appeal to the full Senate. In 1828 the Senate had adopted a rule that broadened the chamber's responsibility for taking notice of unruly senators, while weakening the vice president's role. Rule 6 provided that either the vice president or a senator could take action to silence a disorderly senator. When a senator called another senator to order, the offending words were to be written down so that the vice president could review them. Then the vice president would rule on the merits of the question, subject to an appeal to the Senate to confirm or override that ruling. The Senate adopted this rule after Vice President John C. Calhoun, in 1826, declared that he lacked authority to call a senator to order. He also objected to the arbitrary practice of not permitting an appeal to the full Senate.[29]

Fillmore acknowledged that senators were generally unwilling "to appear as volunteers in the discharge of such an invidious duty" as calling other senators to order. This reluctance placed a greater obligation on the vice president to exercise that power. The House of Representatives had recognized the unequal nature of the responsibility in the wording of its comparable rule, which provided that "the Speaker shall, or a member may, call to order." Fillmore concluded that, although some might charge him with impeding freedom of debate, he would do his duty to contain the first spark of disorder before it ignited a conflagration that would be more difficult to bring under control. "[A] slight attack, or even insinuation, of a personal character, often provokes a more severe retort, which brings out a more disorderly reply, each Senator feeling a justification in the previous aggression." [30] Exactly two weeks after Fillmore spoke these words, an altercation of historic proportions on the Senate floor dramatically validated his concern.

On Saturday, April 17, 1850, the Senate resumed its consideration of the volatile legislation related to the slavery issue and California statehood. Mississippi's senior senator, Henry S. Foote, made a motion to refer the various proposals to a special thirteen-member committee, which would reshape them into a new legislative plan. Since Missouri's Thomas Hart Benton favored compromise but disliked Henry Clay's specific plan, he offered an amendment to undercut Foote's motion. Seated in his accustomed place at the dais, Vice President Fillmore ruled that Benton's motion was in order, citing as his authority Thomas Jefferson's *Manual of Parliamentary Practice* (Section 35.2). Henry Clay rose in anger, charging that Fillmore's ruling was an attack on the Senate's "power," "consistency," and "dignity." He demanded that the Senate vote to reverse the decision.

Clay's complaint triggered an extended debate and a fiery exchange in which Benton charged Foote and his southern allies with alarming the country "without reason, and against reason." [31] Foote, who had been goading Benton for weeks, responded by asserting that Benton had unfairly maligned the "action of a band of patriots, worthy of the highest laudation, and who will be held in veneration when their calumniators, no matter who they may be, will be objects of general loathing and contempt." [32] As Foote sharpened his reference to Benton, "a gentleman long denominated the oldest member of the Senate—the father of the Senate," the burly sixty-eight-year-old Missourian rose from his seat separated from Foote by four desks on the rear row of the Democratic side, shoved back his chair, and advanced on the diminutive forty-six-year-old senator. Foote stepped away from Benton and into the chamber's nearby center aisle. He removed a "five-barrelled" pistol from his pocket, cocked the weapon, and pointed it at the floor. The Senate exploded in pandemonium. As alarmed senators called for order and blocked Benton's advance, the "father of the Senate" shrieked "I have no pistols! Let him fire! Stand out of the way, and let the assassin fire!" Foote handed over his pistol to a fellow senator, while Benton demanded to be searched to prove that he had no weapon. Fillmore called for order, but the chamber would not be quieted. As several senators shouted "Be cool!" Benton and Foote angrily hurled justifications of their actions. Accepting that no further business would be transacted that day, Fillmore recognized a senator who moved to adjourn. Despite his earnest preparations, the vice president now understood the near impossibility of maintaining order in such a deeply fractured Senate. [33]

On the following day, agreeing to Foote's interrupted proposal, the Senate appointed the Select Committee of Thirteen to prepare a suitable compromise measure. The committee reported on May 8, but for the remainder of the spring and into the summer the Senate heatedly debated the slavery-related issues that underlay the Benton-Foote controversy. Vice President Fillmore's estrangement from the Taylor administration deepened during this period and he turned his creative energies to service on the newly established Smithsonian Institution's board of regents.

On the Fourth of July, President Taylor celebrated the holiday by laying a ceremonial stone at the partially constructed Washington Monument and listening to a lengthy speech of reconciliation by Senator Henry Foote. Suffering from extended exposure to the sun, the president returned to the White House, ate some raw fruit and vegetables, which he washed down with large amounts of iced milk. He soon fell ill with the symptoms of acute gastroenteritis, which his doctors diagnosed as "cholera morbus." Under their treatment, his condition worsened. On July 7, 1850, Fillmore was called from the dais in the Senate chamber to the White House to keep vigil outside the president's bedroom. Late in the evening of July 9, a cabinet messenger went to Fillmore's quarters in the Willard Hotel to inform the sleepless vice president that Taylor was dead. [34]

MILLARD FILLMORE

President Fillmore

On the morning of July 10 a presidential messenger carried into the Senate chamber a letter in which Millard Fillmore announced the "most afflicting bereavement" of President Taylor's death and his own intention to take the presidential oath at noon in the House chamber. This time, unlike the first unplanned presidential transition less than a decade earlier, no one seriously questioned Fillmore's right to take on the full powers of the presidency. At the appointed hour, before a joint session of Congress, Fillmore took his presidential oath. Later in the day, the entire Taylor cabinet resigned to give the new chief executive the opportunity to set his own course.

As president, Fillmore moved to end the stalemate over the western lands issue. By the end of July, Clay's omnibus compromise bill was dead, replaced by a series of individual bills that Senator Stephen Douglas had proposed as a means to achieve Clay's objectives. Working closely and tactfully with legislative leaders, Fillmore succeeded in shaping these measures to be acceptable to all regions and sentiments. Within a few weeks, the individual bills became law. Passage of this Compromise of 1850 resulted in a major political realignment, which placed fatal pressures on the Whig party. Northern Whigs were furious about the Fugitive Slave Act, one of the laws enacted as part of the compromise, which Fillmore had only reluctantly signed. Thus, while Whigs in the South urged moderation, their northern counterparts embraced antislavery politics. A modern observer of the Whig party in 1850 characterized its many divisions, including the Seward-Fillmore animosity, as manifesting "the inescapable tension within Whiggery between progress and stability, between moral urgency and social order." [35]

Against this dark political landscape, Fillmore decided once again that he preferred the charms of life in Buffalo to the contentiousness of the nation's capital. Throughout 1851, the president let it be known that he would not seek a full term in 1852, hoping to advance Daniel Webster's candidacy. Webster, however, was too frail to attract the serious support of Whig national convention delegates. At the last minute, Fillmore half-heartedly decided to run, in order to prevent the nomination of Mexican War hero General Winfield Scott, the candidate of Fillmore's archenemy, William Seward. At the convention, delegates deadlocked between Seward, Scott, and Webster. After forty-six ballots, Fillmore tried to strike a bargain with Webster. The aging statesman, the weakest of the three, refused to transfer his delegates. They and others ultimately shifted to Scott, giving him the nomination on the fifty-third ballot. In the general election, southern Whigs abandoned their party to give the election to the Democratic candidate, New Hampshire's Franklin Pierce. The Whig party would never again be a significant national political force.

Anticipating his return to a happy life in Buffalo, Fillmore left a chilled White House on a bitterly cold March 4, 1853, to attend Pierce's inauguration. His wife, Abigail, who had suffered poor health for many months, stood through the extended proceedings with other dignitaries in the slush and lightly falling snow. The next day, she complained of cold symptoms, which developed into pneumonia. Her condition worsened and she died on March 30. Fillmore returned to Buffalo, where in July 1854 his favorite daughter, Mary Abigail, died at the age of twenty-two. Grief-stricken and seeking a diversion, he reentered the national political arena by accepting the 1856 presidential nomination of the anti-Catholic, anti-immigrant Know-Nothing party, composed of former Whig moderates and conservative southern unionists. In that ill-starred venture, the former president carried only Maryland.

In 1858 Fillmore married Caroline McIntosh, a wealthy Albany widow, and resumed his role as Buffalo's leading educator and philanthropist.[36] He served as the first chancellor of the University of Buffalo and the first president of the Buffalo Historical Society. Millard Fillmore died at the age of seventy-four on March 8, 1874.

NOTES

[1] U.S., Congress, Senate, *Congressional Globe*, 33d Cong., 1st sess., pp. 4–5.

[2] Robert J. Rayback, *Millard Fillmore: Biography of a President* (Norwalk, CT, 1959), pp. 4–7.

[3] Ibid., pp. 8–15.

[4] Elbert B. Smith, *The Presidencies of Zachary Taylor and Millard Fillmore* (Lawrence, KS, 1988), pp. 44–45.

[5] Rayback, pp. 81–85.

[6] U.S., Congress, House, *The Committee on Ways and Means: A Bicentennial History, 1789–1989*, by Donald R. Kennon and Rebecca M. Rogers, H. Doc. 100–244, 100th Cong., 2d sess., pp. 105, 125–29.

[7] Glyndon G. Van Deusen, *Thurlow Weed: Wizard of the Lobby* (Boston, 1947), p. 127.

[8] Rayback, pp. 148–51.

[9] Ibid., pp. 155–59; Glyndon Van Deusen, *William Henry Seward* (New York, 1967), pp. 100–103.

[10] Rayback, pp. 177–78.

[11] Quoted in Gil Troy, "Election of 1848," in *Running for President: The Candidates and Their Images*, ed. Arthur M. Schlesinger, Jr., vol. 1, (New York, 1994), p. 188.

[12] Rayback, pp. 183–86; Van Deusen, *Thurlow Weed*, p. 161.

[13] Thurlow Weed, *Autobiography* (1883), p. 585; Van Deusen, *William Henry Seward*, pp. 107–9.

[14] Rayback, pp. 186–87.

[15] W.L. Barre, *The Life and Public Services of Millard Fillmore* (New York, 1971; reprint of 1856 edition), p. 308.

[16] Smith, *The Presidencies of Zachary Taylor and Millard Fillmore*, p. 46.

[17] Troy, 1:193.

[18] Barre, p. 311.

[19] Rayback, p. 192; Van Deusen, *William Henry Seward*, pp. 114–15.

[20] Smith, *The Presidencies of Zachary Taylor and Millard Fillmore*, p. 165; Rayback, pp. 192–96; Van Deusen, *Thurlow Weed*, pp. 165–67; Van Deusen, *William Henry Seward*, pp. 111–12.

[21] Twenty-eight years had passed since an inauguration day had fallen on a Sunday. On that occasion, in 1821, President Monroe had taken Chief Justice John Marshall's advice to postpone "the oath until Monday unless some official duty should require its being taken on Sunday." (Stephen W. Stathis and Ronald C. Moe, "America's Other Inauguration," *Presidential Studies Quarterly*, 10 (Fall 1980): 553.) The story that Senate President Pro Tempore David Atchison served as "president for a day" on March 4, 1849, is without foundation. Since Atchison's Senate term expired on March 3, the Senate was without a president pro tempore, who under the presidential succession plan then in effect might have taken over. When the Senate convened on March 5 for the new Congress, it passed a resolution renewing Atchison's appointment as the temporary presiding officer. Based on the 1821 Monroe precedent, it was assumed that the new president began his term on March 4, but could not exercise the duties of the office until he had taken the formal oath. (George H. Haynes, "President of the United States for a Single Day," *American Historical Review* 30 (January 1925): 308–10.

[22] Rayback, pp. 196–97.

[23] Barre, pp. 212–13.

[24] Rayback, pp. 200–202; Van Deusen, *William Henry Seward*, pp. 114–15.

[25] Smith, *Zachary Taylor and Millard Fillmore*, p. 163, Rayback, pp. 203–4.

[26] Barre, p. 316.

[27] This familiar story is recounted in two modern-era studies: William W. Freehling, *The Road to Disunion: Secessionists at Bay, 1776–1854* (New York, 1990), Chapter 28, and Merrill D. Peterson, *The Great Triumvirate: Webster, Clay, and Calhoun* (New York, 1987), pp. 449–76.

[28] *Congressional Globe*, 31st Cong., 1st sess., pp. 631–32. Out of his concern for proper decorum, Fillmore reportedly ordered the removal of the large urn of snuff that had traditionally been placed on the vice president's desk. He acted because its availability caused members to congregate there, talking loudly and obscuring his view of the chamber. (This story is drawn from the recollections of Senate Assistant Doorkeeper Isaac Bassett as reported in the *New York Times*, June 7, 1894.)

[29] See Chapter 7, "John C. Calhoun," pp. 89–92.

[30] *Congressional Globe*, 31st Cong., 1st sess., p. 632.

[31] Ibid., p. 762.

[32] Ibid.

[33] Elbert B. Smith, *Magnificent Missourian: The Life of Thomas Hart Benton* (New York, 1958), pp. 271–72; Smith, *The Presidencies of Zachary Taylor and Millard Fillmore*, pp. 138–39; *Congressional Globe*, 31st Cong., 1st sess., pp. 762–64.

[34] Smith, *The Presidencies of Zachary Taylor and Millard Fillmore*, pp. 156–57; Rayback, pp. 238–39.

[35] Daniel Walker Howe, *The Political Culture of the American Whigs* (Chicago, 1979), p. 207; Mark J. Stegmaier, *Texas, New Mexico, and the Compromise of 1850: Boundary Dispute and Sectional Crisis* (Kent, OH, 1996), p. 319.

[36] Rayback, p. 416.

Chapter 13

WILLIAM RUFUS DEVANE KING

1853

WILLIAM R. KING

Chapter 13

WILLIAM RUFUS DEVANE KING

13th Vice President: 1853

The ceremony, although simple, was very sad and impressive, and will never be forgotten by any who were present. To see an old man, on the very verge of the grave, clothed with honors which he cared not for, and invested with authority which he could never exercise, was truly touching. It was only by persuasion that Mr. King would go through with the ceremony, as he looked on it as an idle form, for he said he was conscious he would not live many weeks.

—*National Intelligencer*, APRIL 8, 1853

Since the adjournment of Congress, the Vice President of the United States has passed from the scenes of earth, without having entered upon the duties of the station to which he had been called by the voice of his countrymen. Having occupied, almost continuously, for more than thirty years, a seat in one or the other of the two Houses of Congress, and having by his singular purity and wisdom, se- cured unbounded confidence and universal respect, his failing health was watched by the nation with painful solicitude. His loss to the country, under all circumstances, has been justly regarded as irreparable.

—FRANKLIN PIERCE, DECEMBER 5, 1853 [1]

On April 18, 1853, death cheated William King of his life's calling. Experience and temperament had uniquely prepared him to be the Senate's constitutional presiding officer, but tuberculosis denied him that role as vice president.[2] Between 1836 and 1850, King had won a record-breaking eleven elections to the post of Senate president pro tempore. At the time of his 1852 election to the vice-presidency, only one other member in the body's entire history had exceeded King's twenty-eight years and ten months of Senate service.[3] Warm-hearted and even-tempered, King personified balance and fairness in deeply disputatious times. Elected to the vice-presi- dential term that ran from March 4, 1853, to March 3, 1857, King was positioned to occupy center stage during such tumultuous future per- formances as the party rending 1854 struggle

over the Kansas-Nebraska Act and—the single most dramatic act in the Senate's history—the 1856 caning of Massachusetts Senator Charles Sumner by a South Carolina representative. One can now only speculate about the calming role that this natural mediator might have played in such events, although, ultimately, personalities and minds much stronger than his would direct the fateful course to national disunion and civil war.

William King was far from a genius and he had little talent as an orator. These qualities were so well noted during his lifetime that a fellow southerner, Senator Robert M. T. Hunter of Vir- ginia, felt free to remark on them even in the speak-no-evil context of a funeral oration. Hun- ter was quick to acknowledge, however, that this guileless and self-effacing man was an individual of integrity, sound judgment, and rich experience, who could be stern "when the public interests or his personal honor required it." Hunter and others lamented the demise of such a moderate and conciliatory statesman at "a period like this [April 1853], pregnant with change, and teeming, perhaps, with great and strange events."[4] Symbolic of the sectional balance that King tried to achieve, the Virginia senator's eulogy was followed by one from a longtime friend from Massachusetts, the renowned orator Edward Everett. Everett reminded all that when the Senate over the past several decades had needed a presiding officer in the absence of the vice president, its members "turned spontaneously" to Senator King. "He possessed, in an eminent degree, that quickness of perception, that promptness of decision, that familiarity with the now complicated rules of congressional proceedings, and that urbanity of manner, which are required in a presiding officer."[5]

Early Career

William Rufus Devane King was born in Sampson County, North Carolina, on April 7, 1786, the second son of William King and Margaret Devane. His father, a wealthy planter and justice of the peace, had fought in the Revolutionary War, served as a delegate in the state convention called to ratify the U.S. Constitution, and was an occasional member of the North Carolina state assembly. At the time of his son's birth, he owned more than two dozen slaves. Young William studied at local academies and at the University of North Carolina Preparatory School, a facility established in 1795 to cater to the educational needs of "raw, mostly untaught youths of diverse ages and acquirements."[6] He entered the University of North Carolina in the summer of 1801 and proved to be a capable student, but he left that institution at the end of his junior year.[7] Following a period of legal training with Fayetteville's William Duffy—one of the state's leading lawyers—he gained admission to the North Carolina bar in 1805. A Jeffersonian Republican, King served in the North Carolina legislature's house of commons from 1808 to 1809, and then as solicitor of the fifth circuit of the state superior court at Wilmington. In 1810, several

months short of the constitutionally prescribed age of twenty-five, he won the Wilmington district's seat in the U.S. House of Representatives.[8] There he joined with House Speaker Henry Clay, also a freshman member, John C. Calhoun, and other young, expansionist "warhawks" of the Twelfth Congress in a determined and successful campaign to initiate hostilities with Great Britain. In November 1816, King traded lawmaking for diplomacy by resigning from the House to serve as legation secretary under William Pinkney, recently appointed U.S. minister to Russia. Pinkney and King traveled first to the Kingdom of Naples in an unsuccessful attempt to obtain compensation for seized American ships. In January 1817, they reached St. Petersburg, where they served for a year. In February 1818, without waiting to be formally recalled, Pinkney and King returned to the United States.[9]

King then moved from North Carolina to the rich economic and political opportunities of the newly organized Alabama Territory. In October 1818, he purchased 750 acres of land and created an Alabama River estate, "King's Bend," six miles from the town of Cahaba, the new state capital. In March 1819, King and several others organized a land company and founded the nearby town of Selma, which he named for a site in classical legend that occupied high bluffs above a river.[10] The town prospered because of its proximity to Cahaba, which remained the state's capital until 1826. The former congressman and diplomat rose quickly to local prominence and was selected as a delegate to the territory's July 1819 constitutional convention and then, in December 1819, as one of Alabama's first United States senators.

Senator from Alabama

Despite his lengthy Senate service and his important role as conciliator in a fractious era, William King is not today counted among the great statesmen of the Senate's "Golden Age."[11] One scholar of the period, mindful of King's practice of wearing a wig long after such coverings had gone out of fashion, dismissed him as a "tall, prim, wigtopped mediocrity." Novelist John Updike, after his own extended research, took a more positive view of the slender and courtly statesman. Describing King's face as "darkly handsome and smolderingly receptive," he characterized the senator as "one of those eminences whose strong impression on their own times has suffered a gradual erasure upon the tablets of history." [12] A fellow senator offered the following assessment:

> He was distinguished by the scrupulous correctness of his conduct. He was remarkable for his quiet and unobtrusive, but active, practical usefulness as a legislator. He was emphatically a *business member* of the Senate, and, without ostentation, originated and perfected more useful measures than many who filled the public eye by greater display and daily commanded the applause of a listening Senate. . . . [T]o his honor be it spoken, he never vexed the ear of the Senate with ill-timed, tedious, or unnecessary debate. [13]

A moderate Democrat, King became an active supporter of Andrew Jackson soon after the 1825 decision of the House of Representatives to select John Quincy Adams over Jackson for president. In the 1828 presidential election, Alabama cast its electoral votes for Jackson, due in large measure to King's efforts. King generally supported the Jackson administration during its stormy eight-year life, although as a southerner he was also associated with the "little Senate" group considered loyal to Jackson's nemesis, South Carolina's John C. Calhoun. [14] The Alabama senator shared Jackson's hostility to Kentuckian Henry Clay's "accursed American System" of centralized governmental action against foreign competition through protective tariffs, a central banking system, and a public works program of canal and road-building.

In 1831 and 1832, King used his chairmanship of the Senate Committee on Public Lands to advance Jackson administration land policies. Consistent with his long-held views on the subject, he attacked the notion that public lands should be priced primarily to produce large amounts of federal revenue (that would go "to the East to pay the pensioners and support the fortifications"); he believed public lands should be sold only to those who actually planned to settle them. A reduction in land prices would simultaneously stimulate territorial settlement and national economic growth. [15] King also subscribed

to his region's hostility to high protective tariffs, arguing that high rates tax "the many for the benefit of the few," but he opposed John C. Calhoun's theory that the South had the right to "nullify" odious laws, such as the 1828 "Tariff of Abominations." "I view [nullification] as neither peaceful nor constitutional, but clearly revolutionary in its character, and if persevered in, must, in the nature of things, result in the severance of the Union. From such a calamity may God in His mercy deliver us." When Clay early in 1833 presented a compromise tariff bill that defused the building confrontation between federal force and state resistance, King, ever the moderate, quickly rose to support the measure. His moderation irritated both President Jackson and southern hard-liners, who charged that he had not worked hard enough to defend his region's interests. [16]

King contested Henry Clay's 1832 move to recharter the Bank of the United States, not because he opposed the bank, but because he objected to Clay's political opportunism, tied to that year's presidential election. When, as part of that controversy, Jackson ordered the removal of federal funds from the bank and then refused to respond to a Clay-inspired Senate demand for a copy of a related document, the Senate took the unprecedented action on March 28, 1834, of censuring the president. Administration partisans, led by Missouri Senator Thomas Hart Benton and King, launched a vigorous and ultimately successful campaign to expunge the censure from the Senate's journal. King, who had become widely respected for his knowledge of the Senate's rules and precedents, argued that Jackson's refusal to produce the document was in no way an assault on senatorial prerogatives. "The Senate was in no danger," he asserted, "it had never been so strong or so saucy as it was at the present moment; why, then, was it like the Italian beggar, continually wounding itself, for the purpose of exciting the commiseration and benevolence of the public." [17]

King's conflict with Clay and the dangerous tenor of the times are symbolized in the clash between the two men that took place in March 1841, as the Senate, under Clay's leadership, for the first time passed to the control of a new Whig majority. A great battle developed over Senate printing patronage as Clay sought to dismiss Democrat Francis P. Blair, editor of the *Washington Globe*, as official Senate printer. Clay "believed the Globe to be an infamous paper, and its chief editor an infamous man." King responded that Blair's character would "compare gloriously" to that of Clay. The Kentucky senator jumped to his feet and shouted, "That is false, it is a slanderous base and cowardly declaration and the senator knows it to be so." King answered ominously, "Mr. President, I have no reply to make—none whatever. But Mr. Clay deserves a response." King then wrote out a challenge to a duel and had another senator deliver it to Clay, who belatedly realized what trouble his hasty words had unleashed. As Clay and King selected seconds and prepared for the imminent encounter, the Senate sergeant at arms arrested both men and turned them over to a civil authority. Clay posted a five-thousand-dollar bond as assurance that he would keep the peace, "and particularly towards William R. King." Each wanted the matter behind him, but King insisted on "an unequivocal apology." On March 14, 1841, Clay apologized and noted that he would have been wiser to have kept quiet despite the intensity of his feelings against Blair. King then gave his own apology, after which Clay walked to King's desk and said sweetly, "King, give us a pinch of your snuff." King rose and both men shook hands as applause engulfed the chamber.[18]

Vice-Presidential Ambitions

In the late 1830s, as a leading southern moderate among long-serving, middle-aged senators, William King attracted attention within the Democratic party as a prospective vice-presidential candidate for the 1840 election. As early as 1838, dissatisfaction with Vice President Richard M. Johnson for his negative impact on the 1836 race and his scandalous personal life[19] caused party leaders to begin the search for a strong second-term running mate for President Martin Van Buren. King was a natural contender, having been on the national political stage for a quarter century and having routinely substituted for Johnson during the vice president's frequent absences from the Senate chamber. He enjoyed significant support in the electorally important state of Pennsylvania, thanks to his roommate and close ally Senator James Buchanan. Buchanan wished to thwart the 1844 presidential ambitions of both Senator Thomas Hart Benton and Secretary of State John Forsyth by blocking their paths to the vice-presidency in 1840. (In the closeness of their relationship in the years after 1834, King and Buchanan—both lifelong bachelors—became known as the "Siamese twins."[20]) King assured Buchanan that in return for the Pennsylvanian's help in obtaining the vice-presidency in 1840, he would refuse to run for the presidency in 1844, thus clearing the way for Buchanan. The Pennsylvania senator agreed to King's plan and circulated his name among leading Democratic newspaper editors. The anticipated renomination of President Van Buren, a New Yorker, required balancing by a southerner such as King. By the start of 1840, however, King's vice-presidential chances had evaporated because he was unable to generate support from Democratic leaders in the influential states of North Carolina and Pennsylvania. At the party's national convention in Baltimore, a motion to give the second spot to King failed to draw serious interest and party leaders decided to leave the vice-presidential selection to the individual state party organizations.[21]

In 1842, King's name again surfaced as a vice-presidential contender for the 1844 Democratic ticket. Supporters of a presidential bid by South Carolina's John C. Calhoun tried without success to dissuade King, as there would be room for no more than one southerner on a national slate. But by late 1843, the stronger candidacy of former President Van Buren smothered Calhoun's aspirations. For Van Buren's running mate, the names most frequently mentioned were James K. Polk and William King. King's supporters argued that, as a Jacksonian and resident of a southern state loyal to the Democratic party (a slap at Polk's Whig-inclined Tennessee), he deserved the vice-presidency.[22] However, in a repeat of his troubles four years earlier, King was unable to attract serious support in the electorally rich eastern states, so that his candidacy had lost its vitality by the eve of the 1844 Baltimore convention. Meanwhile, Van Buren had destroyed his own chances of becoming the presidential nominee with his announcement of opposition to the annexation of Texas. King hoped that party leaders would fill that void by selecting Buchanan, in which case he would again offer himself for the second spot on the grounds that his presence would help secure essential electoral votes from the wavering state of North Carolina.

On April 9, 1844, President Tyler ended King's preconvention maneuvering by appointing him minister to France. Throughout 1843 and into early 1844, angry with Tyler's policies, the Senate had rejected many of his nominations to major judicial, cabinet, and diplomatic posts. Among these was the appointment as minister to France of Virginia Representative Henry A. Wise, described by a modern historian as a "high-strung, tobacco-chewing extrovert." [23] As a result, this sensitive post had remained vacant for eighteen months until Tyler selected King, one of the Senate's most popular members. Easily confirmed, King left for Paris and soon succeeded in his central mission: to keep France from interfering with U.S. plans to annex Texas. [24]

From Paris, King kept actively in touch with national and Alabama political developments. In April 1846 he wrote his friend James Buchanan, now his boss as secretary of state, "Most sincerely do I wish that we had both remained in the Senate." [25] King therefore decided to run for his old Senate seat, then occupied by political rival and fellow Democrat Dixon H. Lewis. Desiring to return in time to influence the Alabama legislature's election, he left for the United States in November 1846. In a three-way race that included Whig leader Arthur Hopkins, the legislature took seventeen ballots during December 1847 but failed to make a selection. Throughout this hotly contested battle between unionist and states' rights forces—a battle that one modern historian of Alabama labeled "probably the most significant senatorial election in the antebellum period"—states rights' candidate Lewis led, followed by Hopkins and then unionist King. On the eighteenth ballot, in the only election defeat of his public career, King withdrew and the seat

went to Lewis. [26] King, however, did not have to wait long to fulfill his senatorial ambitions. Within seven months, Alabama's other Senate seat became vacant when President Polk named Arthur Bagby minister to Russia. On July 1, 1848, the governor appointed King to fill the eight months remaining in Bagby's term. Later that year, in a close race with his nemesis Arthur Hopkins, King won a full term. [27]

Compromiser in 1850

The national mood had darkened during King's four-year absence from the Senate. He told James Buchanan that he had doubts about the wisdom of returning in those troubled days. "A seat in the Senate is, I assure you, far from being desirable to me; bringing with it as it does at this particular time especially, great responsibility, great labor, and no little anxiety." [28] Characteristically, King tried to calm the brewing storm. He urged northern senators to resist intensifying pressures to introduce antislavery petitions. "I speak as a senator who has been here many years, and as one always anxious to see the members of this body preserve that decorum and kindness toward each other which secures to the body the respect in which it is held throughout the country and the world." [29] He supported the spirit, if not always the specifics, of Henry Clay's compromise measures. He opposed admitting California without the seasoning period of territorial status and he believed that Congress had "about as much constitutional power to prohibit slavery from going into the Territories of the United States as we have power to pass an act carrying slavery there." He believed that abolishing slavery in the District of Columbia would be unfair to the slaveholders in adjacent states, but he supported abolition of the slave trade there.

As the regional positions hardened in the tumultuous early months of 1850, King lamented the "banefull spirit of party" that in dividing the South encouraged northern extremists. In April, King's seniority and moderate views earned him a place as one of two southern Democratic representatives on the Senate's Select Committee of Thirteen, appointed to review Henry Clay's compromise resolutions regarding territories and slavery. With a majority of the committee's members, he agreed that slavery was a "rightful" subject for legislative attention, but only in the legislatures of states and not of territories. Thus, King took the view of southern conservatives that the Constitution protected owners in their control of slave property until a territory became a state.[30] At home, he met bitter opposition from a faction of "Southern Rights" secessionists who argued that his voting record better reflected the interests of Massachusetts, but an equally large group of supporters praised his support for compromise, union, and peace. He counseled patience, optimistically expecting the North to respect southern rights, but warning that if that section's actions jeopardized those rights—both constitutional and material—all southern men should "hurl defiance at the fanatical crew, and unitedly determine to defend their rights at every hazard and every sacrifice."[31]

Arbiter of Decorum

The Senate chamber in 1850 was frequently jammed to capacity as the major debates on slavery in the territories drew large crowds of House members, reporters, and the general public eager to get a glimpse of the likes of Henry Clay, Daniel Webster, Thomas Hart Benton, Stephen A. Douglas of Illinois, Sam Houston of Texas, and others of the nation's most notable public figures. As a frequent presiding officer, King regularly acted to restore decorum. In this electrically charged environment, he took every opportunity to remind other senators of his need for their support "to put down the least movement toward disorder, or the slightest indulgence in personal remarks."[32]

In May, while Vice President Millard Fillmore was presiding, a senator won adoption of a routine resolution to admit a local newspaper reporter to the Senate floor. Dissatisfied with such flagrant circumvention of the Senate's floor access rules, another member suggested referring the matter to a committee. Several senators proposed that the presiding officer be allowed to issue each member one admission permit to award as he saw fit. According to the proposal, with a guest waiting at the chamber's entrance, the host senator would go to the dais and request

his ticket from the vice president. New Jersey Senator William Dayton predicted there would be few takers. "All the multitudinous persons who hang around the Capitol will not have the face to ask Senators to go to the Vice President and formally get the permit to allow them to come on the floor every day." Others laughed at the dilemma of a senator having to decide between male and female guests and the idea of such a system that would have sixty senatorial guests contending with sixty senators and several hundred House members for floor space in such cramped quarters. Senator Jefferson Davis of Mississippi sounded the most realistic note: "It is utterly impossible to attempt to admit all who desire to come on the floor. . . . The evil can only be remedied by an enlarged chamber." As the member most identified with Senate decorum and tradition, King brought the debate to a close by moving to refer the matter to a special committee, knowing that another committee would soon propose the construction of new Senate and House chambers, each with ample public galleries.[33]

Finally Vice President

On July 10, 1850, Zachary Taylor's death placed Millard Fillmore in the White House and left the vice-presidency vacant. On July 11, the solemn Senate set aside the practice of having each party offer a nomination for the president pro tempore's post and unanimously selected King for the vacancy. This otherwise routine act took on special significance, for King would be in effect the acting vice president of the United States. King addressed the Senate in the tone of a vice president offering an inaugural oration. Noting the unusual bipartisan support for his election, King vowed to enforce the Senate's rules "mildly, but firmly, and I trust impartially. . . . Should I err, I look to my brother Senators, in a spirit of kindness, to correct my errors."[34] Continuing in the fashion of former Vice President Fillmore, King worked hard to calm the angry seas that swelled with increasing violence on the Senate floor.

King's long quest for the vice-presidency had resumed immediately after he returned from France in 1846. However, his failure that year to regain his Senate seat, coupled with deep ideological divisions within the Alabama Democratic party, denied him the support necessary to launch a vigorous national campaign. At the 1848 national convention in Baltimore, following the nomination of Michigan's Lewis Cass for the presidency, King's was among a half-dozen names placed before the delegates. On the first ballot, he came in third. On the second ballot, the convention selected Kentucky's General William O. Butler, a veteran of the War of 1812 and the Mexican War.[35]

In January 1852, the Alabama state Democratic convention endorsed the Compromise of 1850 and directed the state's national convention delegates to support King for either the presidency or vice-presidency. At the jam-packed, tumultuous Baltimore convention, delegates selected Franklin Pierce on the forty-ninth ballot. In a peace gesture to the Buchanan wing of the party, Pierce's supporters allowed Buchanan's allies to fill the second position, knowing that they would select King. On the second ballot, with only minor opposition, King finally captured his prize.[36] During the ensuing campaign, King's tuberculosis, which he believed he had contracted while in Paris, denied him the active behind-the-scenes role that he might otherwise have played, although he worked hard to assure his region's voters that New Hampshire's Pierce was a "northern man with southern principles." King's deteriorating physical condition clouded the victory that came in November; Pierce's unwillingness to consult the vice-president-elect on cabinet appointments deepened his malaise.

In November, King began to suffer from a worsening cough. A month later, he described himself as looking like a skeleton and told friends he doubted that he would ever recover. On December 20, two weeks into the short December-March congressional session, King resigned his Senate seat and made plans to regain his health away from wintertime Washington.[37] On January 17, 1853, King left for the more salutary climate of Cuba, by way of Key West, Florida; he reached Havana in early February. Soon realizing that he would be unable to return to Washington in time for the March 4, 1853, inauguration, King requested that Congress permit him to take his oath in Cuba.[38] Consequently, for the only time in this nation's history, Congress passed legislation allowing the vice-president-elect to be sworn in outside the country. On March 24, 1853, near Matanzas, a seaport town sixty miles east of Havana, the gravely ill statesman, too feeble to stand unaided, became the nation's thirteenth vice president. Deciding that he would make every effort to return to the United States, King set sail for Mobile on April 6. He reached his Alabama plantation on April 17, but his struggle was at an end. The sixty-seven-year-old King died there the following day. An opposition newspaper praised his "purity and patriotism" and concluded, "[t]hough not, perhaps, brilliant, he was better—sensible, honest, never running into ultraism, but in the contests between the State and the federal government, maintaining the true conservative medium, so necessary to the preservation of the constitution, the rights of the States and the Republic."[39]

NOTES

[1] U.S., Congress, Senate, *Journal*, 33d Cong., 1st sess., p. 25.

[2] On taking office as president pro tempore in January 1837, King offered the following observations about the Senate and the role of its presiding officer. They are similar in tone and formulation to those that Vice President Aaron Burr uttered on March 2, 1805.

The Senate of the United States, gentlemen, is, from its very organization, the great conservative body in this republic. Here is the strong citadel of liberty. To this body the intelligent and the virtuous, throughout our wide-spread country, look with confidence for an unwavering and unflinching resistance to the encroachments of power on the one hand, and the effervescence of popular excitement on the other. Unawed and unseduced, it should firmly maintain the constitution in its purity, and present an impregnable barrier against every attack on that sacred instrument, come it from what quarter it may. The demon of faction should find no abiding place in this chamber, but every heart and every head should be wholly occupied in advancing the general welfare, and preserving, unimpaired, the national honor. To insure success, gentlemen, in the discharge of our high duties, we must command the confidence and receive the support of the people. Calm deliberation, courtesy toward each other, order and decorum in debate, will go far, very far, to inspire that confidence and command that support. It becomes my duty, gentlemen, to banish (if practicable) from this hall all personal altercation; to check, at once, every remark of a character personally offensive; to preserve order, and promote harmony. . . . I earnestly solicit your co-operation, gentlemen, in aiding my efforts promptly to put down every species of disorder. (U.S., Congress, Senate, *Register of Debates in Congress*, 24th Cong., 2d sess., pp. 618–19.)

[3] As early as 1824, King regularly served as the chairman of the Committee of the Whole, a long-since-abandoned parliamentary form by which the full Senate could expedite its proceedings. (John Milton Martin, "William Rufus King: Southern Moderate," Ph.D. dissertation, University of North Carolina, 1955, p. 81.) Prior to 1890, the Senate elected its president pro tempore only when the vice president was away from the chamber. Election to that post during the Senate's first century was generally considered an acknowledgment of the Senate's respect for the individual's judicious temperament. In later years, the Senate designated a permanent president pro tempore for each Congress, usually the senior member of the majority party. (U.S., Congress, Senate, *The Senate, 1789–1989: Addresses on the History of the United States Senate*, by Robert C. Byrd, S. Doc. 100–

20, 100th Cong., 1st sess., vol. 2, 1991, Chapter 6; vol. 4, *Historical Statistics*, 1993, pp. 647–53.)

[4] U.S., Congress, Senate, *Congressional Globe*, 33d Cong., 1st sess, pp. 19–21. See also U.S., Congress, *Obituary Addresses on the Occasion of the Death of the Hon. William R. King, of Alabama, Vice President of the United States, Delivered in the Senate and House of Representatives of the United States, Eighth of December, 1853* (Washington, 1854), pp. 8–13, 37. Representative Sampson Harris (D-AL) also commented that King lacked "many of those great attributes of mind, which dazzle and lead captive the admiring throng . . ." (p. 37) and the *National Intelligencer* began its obituary, "Not endowed with shining talents, though of excellent sense . . ." (April 20, 1853).

[5] *Congressional Globe*, 33d Cong., 1st sess, p. 20.

[6] Martin, "William Rufus King: Southern Moderate," pp. 3–5, 11–12.

[7] No book-length biography of King exists. John Milton Martin, the only modern-era scholar to have given King's career serious consideration, prepared a 1955 doctoral dissertation ("William Rufus King: Southern Moderate," University of North Carolina) and articles in the early 1960s on King's role as a "Jacksonian Senator" and his multiple quests for the vice-presidency. Biographies of King's leading contemporaries and histories of nineteenth-century Alabama political life give him only passing reference. A small unorganized collection of his personal papers survives at the Alabama Department of Archives and History in Montgomery. Incomplete records at the University of North Carolina have led to conflicting accounts of his stay there. An error-ridden biographical article by E.S.W. Dameron in that institution's *University Magazine* (March 1905, p. 317–22) credits him with graduating in 1803, but notes that the "ravages of a century have despoiled his Alma Mater of all account of his college life." Others have accepted that information, including Thomas M. Owen in *History of Alabama and Dictionary of Alabama Biography*, vol. 3 (Chicago, 1921), p. 983, and Roy F. Nichols in "William Rufus Devane King," *Dictionary of American Biography* (vol. 10, p. 406). John M. Martin, King's only reliable modern biographer, disagrees, indicating that he withdrew in 1804, "William R. King and the Compromise of 1850," *The North Carolina Historical Review* 39 (October 1962): 500. In his University of North Carolina doctoral dissertation (pp. 20–22), Martin explores the matter in greater detail and concludes that King felt he was sufficiently prepared to begin his legal studies.

[8] By the time the Twelfth Congress convened on November 4, 1811, King had reached the required age of twenty-five. In those early years both houses of Congress occasionally ignored the minimum age requirement, which was generally applied at the time the oath of office was administered rather than on the date of election.

9 Martin, "William R. King and the Compromise of 1850," p. 500; Martin, "William Rufus King: Southern Moderate," Chapter 2.

10 Martin, "William Rufus King: Southern Moderate," pp. 61–65. King took the name "Selma" from the poem by James Macpherson, "the Song of Selma." Virginia O. Foscue, *Place Names in Alabama* (Tuscaloosa, AL, 1989), pp. 26–27, 125; Writers' Program, Alabama, *Alabama: A Guide to the Deep South* (WPA American Guide Series) (New York, 1941), pp. 47–50, 237–38.

11 The major documentary record of his Senate service is found in the quasi-official proceedings of Congress, the *Annals of Congress* (1811–1816; 1819–1824), the *Register of Debates in Congress* (1824–1838), and the *Congressional Globe* (1833–1853). Yet even this record is spare, as King made few substantive speeches, preferring to preside rather than to debate. He never married or had children, thus there were no direct heirs with a vested interest in preserving a useful record of his service.

12 Roy Nichols and Jeannette Nichols, "Election of 1852," in *History of American Presidential Elections, 1789–1968*, ed. Arthur M. Schlesinger, Jr., vol. 2 (New York, 1971), p. 942; John Updike, *Memories of the Ford Administration* (New York, 1992), pp. 227, 233.

13 *Congressional Globe*, 31st Cong., 1st sess., p. 21.

14 John M. Martin, "William R. King: Jacksonian Senator," *The Alabama Review* 18 (October 1965): 243–45.

15 Martin, "William R. King: Jacksonian Senator," pp. 247–51; Martin, "William Rufus King: Southern Moderate," p. 77.

16 Martin, "William R. King: Jacksonian Senator," pp. 253, 256.

17 Ibid., p. 262.

18 This story is derived from the account presented in Robert V. Remini, *Henry Clay: Statesman for the Union* (New York, 1991), p. 574. Remini consulted many sources beyond the quasi-official *Congressional Globe* (26th Cong., 2d sess., pp. 245, 247–249, 256–257), which was reported in the third person and without the detail that Remini located in contemporary newspapers, letters, and diary accounts. See also Martin, "William Rufus King: Southern Moderate," pp. 183–86.

19 See Chapter 9 of this volume, "Richard Mentor Johnson," p. 129.

20 Philip Shriver Klein, *President James Buchanan* (University Park, PA, 1962), p. 111; Novelist John Updike, in *Memories of the Ford Administration* (pp. 227–41), speculates at length on the nature of the intimacy between King and Buchanan.

21 John M. Martin, "William R. King and the Vice Presidency," *The Alabama Review* 16 (January 1963): 35–40; Klein, pp. 131–32.

22 Martin, "William R. King and the Vice Presidency," pp. 43–44.

23 John Niven, *John C. Calhoun and the Price of Union* (Baton Rouge, LA, 1988), p. 260.

24 St. George Leakin Sioussat, "John Caldwell Calhoun," in *American Secretaries of State and Their Diplomacy*, ed. Samuel Flagg Bemis, vol. 5 (New York, 1928), pp. 164–65, 169, 208, 300; Martin, "William Rufus King: Southern Moderate," Chapter 7.

25 Letter of April 30, 1846, quoted in Martin, "William Rufus King: Southern Moderate," p. 268.

26 William Warren Rogers, et al., *Alabama: The History of a Deep South State* (Tuscaloosa, AL, 1994), p. 155.

27 Martin, "William Rufus King: Southern Moderate," pp. 274–81, 290–91, 300–303.

28 Martin, "William R. King and the Compromise of 1850," p. 501.

29 *Congressional Globe*, 31st Cong., 1st sess., p. 342.

30 Remini, *Henry Clay: Statesman for the Union*, pp. 746–47.

31 Ibid.

32 *Congressional Globe*, 31st Cong., 1st sess., p. 915.

33 Ibid., pp. 1054–55.

34 Ibid., p. 1370.

35 Martin, "William R. King and the Vice Presidency," pp. 46–49.

36 *Congressional Quarterly's Guide to U.S. Elections*, 3d ed. (Washington, DC, 1994), p. 43.

37 *Congressional Globe*, 32d Cong., 2d sess., p. 89.

38 In King's absence, Senator Lewis Cass, as the Senate's oldest member, administered the oath of office to newly elected senators. President Franklin Pierce made no reference to his absent running mate during his inaugural address. Congress approved the necessary legislation on March 2, 1853. (*Congressional Globe*, 32d Cong., 2d sess., *Appendix*, p. 341.)

39 *Daily [Montgomery] Alabama Journal*, April 20, 1853.

Chapter 14

JOHN CABELL BRECKINRIDGE
1857–1861

JOHN C. BRECKINRIDGE

Chapter 14

JOHN CABELL BRECKINRIDGE

14th Vice President: 1857–1861

I trust that I have the courage to lead a forlorn hope.

—JOHN C. BRECKINRIDGE, 1860

The only vice president ever to take up arms against the government of the United States, John Cabell Breckinridge completed four years as vice president under James Buchanan, ran for president as the Southern Democratic candidate in 1860, and then returned to the Senate to lead the remnants of the Democratic party for the first congressional session during the Civil War. Although his cousin Mary Todd Lincoln resided in the White House and his home state of Kentucky remained in the Union, Breckinridge chose to volunteer his services to the Confederate army. The United States Senate formally expelled him as a traitor. When the Confederates were defeated, Breckinridge's personal secession forced him into exile abroad, bringing his promising political career to a bitter end.

An Illustrious Political Family

Born at "Cabell's Dale," the Breckinridge family estate near Lexington, Kentucky, on January 16, 1821, John Cabell Breckinridge was named for his father and grandfather. The father, Joseph Cabell Breckinridge, a rising young politician, died at the state capital at the age of thirty-five. Left without resources, his wife took her children back to Cabell's Dale to live with their grandmother, known affectionately as "Grandma Black Cap." She often regaled the children with stories of their grandfather, the first John Breckinridge, who, in addition to introducing the Kentucky Resolutions that denounced the Alien and Sedition Acts, had helped secure the Louisiana

Purchase and had served during the administration of Thomas Jefferson first as a Senate leader and then as attorney general. The grandfather might well have become president one day but, like his son, he died prematurely. The sense of family mission that his grandmother imparted shaped young John C. Breckinridge's self-image and directed him towards a life in public office. The family also believed strongly in education, since Breckinridge's maternal grandfather, Samuel Stanhope Smith, had served as president of the College of New Jersey at Princeton, and his uncle Robert J. Breckinridge started Kentucky's public school system. The boy attended the Presbyterian Centre College in Danville, Kentucky, where he received his bachelor's degree at seventeen. He then attended Princeton before returning to Lexington to study law at Transylvania University.[1]

A tall, strikingly handsome young man with a genial air and a powerful voice, considered by many "a perfect gentleman," Breckinridge set out to make his fortune on the frontier. In 1841 he and his law partner Thomas W. Bullock settled in the Mississippi River town of Burlingame, in the Iowa Territory. There he might have entered politics and pursued a career relatively free from the divisive issue of slavery, but Iowa's fierce winter gave him influenza and made him homesick for Kentucky. When he returned home on a visit in 1843, he met and soon married Mary Cyrene Burch of Georgetown. The newlyweds settled in Georgetown, and Breckinridge opened a law office in Lexington.[2]

A Rapid Political Rise

When the Mexican War began, Breckinridge volunteered to serve as an officer in a Kentucky infantry regiment. In Mexico, Major Breckinridge won the support of his troops for his acts of kindness, being known to give up his horse to sick and footsore soldiers. After six months in Mexico City, he returned to Kentucky and to an almost inevitable political career. In 1849, while still only twenty-eight years old, he won a seat in the state house of representatives. In that election, as in all his campaigns, he demonstrated both an exceptional ability as a stump speaker and a politician's memory for names and faces. Shortly after the election, he met for the first time the Illinois legislator who had married his cousin Mary Todd. Abraham Lincoln, while visiting his wife's family in Lexington, paid courtesy calls on the city's lawyers. Lincoln and Breckinridge became friends, despite their differences in party and ideology. Breckinridge was a Jacksonian Democrat in a state that Senator Henry Clay had made a Whig bastion. In 1851, Breckinridge shocked the Whig party by winning the congressional race in Clay's home district, a victory that also brought him to the attention of national Democratic leaders. He arrived in Congress shortly after the passage of Clay's Compromise of 1850, which had sought to settle the issue of slavery in the territories. Breckinridge became a spokesman for the proslavery Democrats, arguing that the federal government had no right to interfere with slavery anywhere, either in the District of Columbia or in any of the territories.[3]

Since Breckinridge defended both the Union and slavery, people viewed him as a moderate. The Pennsylvania newspaper publisher and political adventurer John W. Forney insisted that when Breckinridge came to Congress "he was in no sense an extremist." Forney recalled how the young Breckinridge spoke with great respect about Texas Senator Sam Houston, who denounced the dangers and evils of slavery. But Forney thought that Breckinridge "was too interesting a character to be neglected by the able ultras of the South. They saw in his winning manners, attractive appearance, and rare talent for public affairs, exactly the elements they needed in their concealed designs against the country." People noted that his uncle, Robert Breckinridge, was a prominent antislavery man, and that as a state legislator Breckinridge had aided the Kentucky Colonization Society (a branch of the American Colonization Society), dedicated to gradual emancipation and the resettlement of free blacks outside the United States. They suspected that he held private concerns about the morality of slavery and that he supported gradual emancipation. Yet, while Breckinridge was no planter or large slaveholder, he owned a few household slaves and idealized the southern way of life. He willingly defended slavery and white supremacy against all critics.[4]

The Kansas-Nebraska Controversy

In Congress, Breckinridge became an ally of Illinois Senator Stephen A. Douglas. When Douglas introduced the Kansas-Nebraska Act of 1854, which repealed the Missouri Compromise and left the issue of slavery in the territories to the settlers themselves—a policy known as "popular sovereignty"—Breckinridge worked hard to enact the legislation. Going to the White House, he served as a broker between Douglas and President Franklin Pierce, persuading the president to support the bill. He also spoke out in the House in favor of leaving the settlers "free to form their own institutions, and enter the Union with or without slavery, as their constitutions should prescribe."[5]

During those debates in March 1854, the normally even-tempered Breckinridge exchanged angry words on the House floor with Democratic Representative Francis B. Cutting of New York, almost provoking a duel. "They were a high-strung pair," commented Breckinridge's friend Forney. Cutting accused Breckinridge of ingratitude toward the North, where he had raised campaign funds for his tough reelection campaign in 1853. Breckinridge, "his eyes flashing fire," interrupted Cutting's speech, denied his charges, denounced his language, and demanded an apology. When Cutting refused, Breckinridge interpreted this as a challenge to a duel. He proposed that they meet near Silver

Spring, the nearby Maryland home of his friend Francis P. Blair, and that they duel with western rifles. The New Yorker objected that he had never handled a western rifle and that as the challenged party he should pick the weapons. Once it became clear that neither party considered himself the challenger, they gained a face-saving means of withdrawing from the "code of honor" without fighting the duel. When the two next encountered each other in the House, Breckinridge looked his adversary in the eye and said: "Cutting, give me a chew of tobacco!" The New Yorker drew a plug of tobacco from his pocket, cut off a wad for Breckinridge and another for himself, and both returned to their desks chewing and looking happier. Those who observed the exchange compared it to the American Indians' practice of smoking a peace pipe.[6]

Breckinridge supported the Kansas-Nebraska Act in the hope that it would take slavery in the territories out of national politics, but the act had entirely the opposite effect. Public outrage throughout the North caused the Whig party to collapse and new antislavery parties, the Republican and the American (Know-Nothing) parties, to rise in its wake. When the spread of Know-Nothing lodges in his district jeopardized his chances of reelection in 1855, Breckinridge declined to run for a third term. He also rejected President Pierce's nomination to serve as minister to Spain and negotiate American annexation of Cuba, despite the Senate's confirmation of his appointment. Citing his wife's poor health and his own precarious finances, Breckinridge returned to Kentucky. Land speculation in the West helped him accumulate a considerable amount of money during his absence from politics.[7]

The Youngest Vice President

As the Democratic convention approached in 1856, the three leading contenders—President Pierce, Senator Douglas, and former Minister to Great Britain James Buchanan—all courted Breckinridge. He attended the convention as a delegate, voting first for Pierce and then switching to Douglas. When Douglas withdrew as a gesture toward party unity, the nomination went to Buchanan. The Kentucky delegation nominated former House Speaker Linn Boyd for vice president. Then a Louisiana delegate nominated Breckinridge. Gaining the floor, Breckinridge declined to run against his delegation's nominee, but his speech deeply impressed the convention. One Arkansas delegate admired "his manner, his severely simple style of delivery with scarcely an ornament [or] gesture and deriving its force and eloquence solely from the remarkably choice ready flow of words, the rich voice and intonation." The delegate noted that "every member seemed riveted to his seat and each face seemed by magnetic influence to be directed to him." When Boyd ran poorly on the first ballot, the convention switched to Breckinridge and nominated him on the second ballot. Although Tennessee's Governor Andrew Johnson grumbled that Breckinridge's lack of national reputation would hurt the ticket, Buchanan's managers were pleased with the choice. They thought Breckinridge would appease Douglas, since the two men had been closely identified through their work on the Kansas-Nebraska Act. Being present at the convention, Breckinridge was prevailed upon to make a short acceptance speech, thanking the delegates for the nomination, endorsing Buchanan and the platform, and reaffirming his position as a "state's rights man." The nominee was thirty-six years old—just a year over the constitutional minimum age for holding the office—and his election would make him the youngest vice president in American history.[8]

Breckinridge spent most of the campaign in Kentucky, but he gave speeches in Ohio, Indiana, and Michigan, defending the Kansas-Nebraska Act. The election was a three-way race among the Democrats under Buchanan, the Republicans under John Charles Frémont, and the Know-Nothings under former President Millard Fillmore. Denouncing the antislavery policies of the Republicans and Know-Nothings, Breckinridge described himself not as proslavery but as a defender of the people's constitutional right to make their own territorial laws, a position that caused some Deep South extremists to accuse him of harboring abolitionist views. In November, Democrats carried all the slaveholding states except Maryland (which went Know-Nothing) and enough northern states to win the election. Breckinridge was proud that Kentucky voted for a Democratic presidential ticket for the first time since 1828.[9]

Strained Relations with Buchanan

Buchanan won the nomination and election primarily because nobody knew where he stood on the issues, since he had been out of the country for the past three years as minister to England. Although his supporters promoted him as "the man for the crisis," Buchanan was in fact the worst man for the crisis. Narrow, secretive, petty, vindictive, and blind to corruption within his administration, he proved unable to bind together either the factions of his party or the regions of his nation. A poor winner, Buchanan distrusted his rivals for the nomination and refused to invite Stephen Douglas to join his cabinet or to take seriously Douglas' patronage requests. Similarly snubbed, Breckinridge quickly discovered that he held less influence with Buchanan as vice president than he had as a member of the House with Pierce.[10]

Viewing Breckinridge as part of the Pierce-Douglas faction, Buchanan almost never consulted him, and rarely invited him to the White House for either political or social gatherings. Early in the new administration, when the vice president asked for a private interview with the president, he was told instead to call at the White House some evening and ask to see Buchanan's niece and hostess, Harriet Lane. Taking this as a rebuff, the proud Kentuckian left town without calling on either Miss Lane or the president. His friends reported his resentment to Buchanan, and in short order three of the president's confidants wrote to tell Breckinridge that it had been a mistake. A request to see Miss Lane was really a password to admit a caller to see her uncle. How Breckinridge could have known this, they did not explain. In fact, the vice president had no private meetings with the president for over three years.[11]

The new vice president bought property in the District of Columbia and planned to construct, along with his good friends Senator Douglas and Senator Henry Rice of Minnesota, three large, expensive, connected houses at New Jersey Avenue and I Street that would become known as "Minnesota Row." Before the construction was completed, however, the friendship had become deeply strained when Douglas fell out with President Buchanan over slavery in Kansas. A proslavery minority there had sent to Washington a new territorial constitution—known as the Lecompton Constitution. Buchanan threw his weight behind the Lecompton Constitution as a device for admitting Kansas as a state and defusing the explosive issue of slavery in the territory. But Douglas objected that the Lecompton Constitution made a mockery out of popular sovereignty and warned that he would fight it as a fraud. Recalling the way Andrew Jackson had dealt with his opponents, Buchanan said, "Mr. Douglas, I desire you to remember that no Democrat ever yet differed from an Administration of his choice without being crushed." To which Douglas replied, "Mr. President, I wish you to remember that General Jackson is dead." Between these two poles, the vice president vainly sought to steer a neutral course. He sided with Buchanan on the Lecompton Constitution but endorsed Douglas for reelection to the Senate.[12]

An Impartial Presiding Officer

As vice president in such a turbulent era, Breckinridge won respect for presiding gracefully and impartially over the Senate. On January 4, 1859, when the Senate met for the last time in its old chamber, he used the occasion to deliver an eloquent appeal for national unity. During its half century in the chamber, the Senate had grown from thirty-two to sixty-four members. The expansion of the nation forced them to move to a new, more spacious chamber. During those years, he observed, the Constitution had "survived peace and war, prosperity and adversity" to protect "the larger personal freedom compatible with public order." He recalled the legislative labors of Henry Clay, Daniel Webster, and John C. Calhoun, whose performance in that chamber challenged their successors "to give the Union a destiny not unworthy of the past." He trusted that in the future "another Senate, in another age, shall bear to a new and larger Chamber, this Constitution vigorous and inviolate, and that the last generation of posterity shall witness the deliberations of the Representatives of American States, still united, prosperous, and free." The vice president then led a procession to the new chamber. Walking two-by-two behind him were the political and military leaders of what would soon become the Union and the Confederacy.[13]

Breckinridge counseled against secession. A famous incident, recounted in many memoirs of the era, took place at a dinner party that the vice president attended. South Carolina Representative Lawrence Keitt repeatedly denigrated Kentucky's compromising tendencies. Breckinridge responded by recalling a trip he had made through South Carolina, where he met a militia officer in full military regalia. "I tell you, sah, we can not stand it any longer; we intend to fight," said the officer. "And from what are you suffering?" asked Breckinridge. "Why, sah, we are suffering from the oppression of the Federal Government. We have suffered under it for thirty years, and will stand it no more." Turning to Keitt, Breckinridge advised him "to invite some of his constituents, before undertaking the war, upon a tour through the North, if only for the purpose of teaching them what an almighty big country they will have to whip before they get through!"[14]

A Four-Way Race for President

Early in 1859 a *New York Times* correspondent in Washington wrote that "Vice President Breckinridge stands deservedly high in public estimation, and has the character of a man slow to form resolves, but unceasing and inexorable in their fulfillment." At a time when the Buchanan administration was falling "in prestige and political consequence, the star of the Vice President rises higher above the clouds." Later that year, Linn Boyd died while campaigning for the Senate, and Kentucky Democrats nominated Breckinridge for the seat, which would become vacant at the time Breckinridge's term as vice president ended. Breckinridge may also have been harboring even greater ambitions. Although he remained silent about the upcoming presidential campaign, many Democrats considered him a strong contender. In 1860, the Democratic con-

vention met in Charleston, South Carolina. Stephen Douglas was the frontrunner, but when his supporters defeated efforts to write into the platform a plank protecting the right of slavery anywhere in the territories, the southern delegates walked out. They held their own convention in Baltimore and nominated Breckinridge as their presidential candidate.[15]

For national balance, the breakaway Democrats selected Senator Joseph Lane, a Democrat from Oregon, for vice president. Lane had spent his youth in Kentucky and Indiana and served in the Mexican War. President James K. Polk had appointed him territorial governor of Oregon, an office he held from 1849 to 1850 before becoming Oregon's territorial delegate to Congress in 1851. When Oregon entered the Union in 1859, he was chosen one of its first senators. Lane's embrace of the secessionist spirit attracted him to the Southern Democrats. Had the four-way election of 1860 not been decided by the electoral college but been thrown into Congress, the Democratic majority in the outgoing Senate might well have elected him vice president. Instead, the race ended Lane's political career entirely, and Oregon became a Republican state.[16]

Breckinridge faced a campaign against three old friends: Stephen Douglas, the Democratic candidate; Abraham Lincoln, the Republican; and John Bell of Tennessee, the Constitutional Union party candidate. He was not optimistic about his chances. Privately, he told Mrs. Jefferson Davis, "I trust that I have the courage to lead a forlorn hope." At a dinner just before the nomination, Breckinridge talked of not accepting it, but Jefferson Davis persuaded him to run. Worried that a split in the anti-Republican vote would ensure Lincoln's victory, Davis proposed a scheme by which Breckinridge, Douglas, and Bell would agree to withdraw their candidacies in favor of a compromise candidate. Breckinridge and Bell agreed, but Douglas refused, arguing that northern Democrats would take Lincoln before they voted for any candidate that the southern firebrands had endorsed. The Illinois senator pointed out that, while not all of Breckinridge's followers were secessionists, every secessionist was supporting him. But Breckinridge also counted on the support of the last three

JOHN C. BRECKINRIDGE

Democratic presidential candidates, Lewis Cass, Franklin Pierce, and James Buchanan, as well as most of the northern Democratic senators and representatives. Despite these endorsements and the financial levies that the Buchanan administration made on all Democratic officeholders for him, Breckinridge failed to carry any northern states. In the four-way race, he placed third in the popular vote and second in electoral votes. Most disappointingly, he lost Kentucky to Bell.[17]

A Personal Secession

Following the election, Breckinridge returned to Washington to preside over the Senate, hoping to persuade southerners to abandon secession. But in December, South Carolina, Alabama, Mississippi, and Florida left the Union. In January, Mississippi Senator Jefferson Davis and other southerners bid a formal farewell to the Senate. In February, Vice President Breckinridge led a procession of senators to the House chamber to count the electoral votes, and to announce the election of Abraham Lincoln of Illinois. On March 4, Breckinridge administered the oath of office to his successor, Hannibal Hamlin, who in turn swore him into the Senate. When President Lincoln called Congress into special session on July 4, 1861, to raise the arms and men necessary to fight the Civil War, Breckinridge returned to Washington as the leader of what was left of the Senate Democrats. Many in Washington doubted that he planned to offer much support to the Union or the war effort. Breckinridge seemed out of place in the wartime capital, after so many of his southern friends had left. On several occasions, however, he visited his cousin Mary Todd Lincoln at the White House.[18]

During the special session, which lasted until August 6, 1861, Breckinridge remained firm in his belief that the Constitution strictly limited the powers of the federal government, regardless of secession and war. Although he wanted the Union restored, he preferred a peaceful separation rather than "endless, aimless, devastating war, at the end of which I see the grave of public liberty and of personal freedom." The most dramatic moment of the session occurred on August 1, when Senator Breckinridge took the floor to oppose the Lincoln administration's expansion of martial law. As he spoke, Oregon Republican Senator Edward D. Baker entered the chamber, dressed in the blue coat of a Union army colonel. Baker had raised and was training a militia unit known as the California Regiment. When Breckinridge finished, Baker challenged him: "These speeches of his, sown broadcast over the land, what meaning have they? Are they not intended for disorganization in our very midst?" Baker demanded. "Sir, are they not words of brilliant, polished treason, even in the very Capitol?" Within months of this exchange, Senator Baker was killed while leading his militia at the Battle of Ball's Bluff along the Potomac River, and Senator Breckinridge was wearing the gray uniform of a Confederate officer.[19]

After the special session, Breckinridge returned to Kentucky to try to keep his state neutral. He spoke at a number of peace rallies, proclaiming that, if Kentucky took up arms against the Confederacy, then someone else must represent the state in the Senate. Despite his efforts, pro-Union forces won the state legislative elections. When another large peace rally was scheduled for September 21, the legislature sent a regiment to break up the meeting and arrest Breckinridge. Forewarned, he packed his bag and fled to Virginia. He could no longer find any neutral ground to stand upon, no way to endorse both the Union and the southern way of life. Forced to choose sides, Breckinridge joined his friends in the Confederacy. In Richmond he volunteered for military service, exchanging, as he said, his "term of six years in the Senate of the United States for the musket of a soldier." On December 4, 1861, the Senate by a 36 to 0 vote expelled the Kentucky senator, declaring that Breckinridge, "the traitor," had "joined the enemies of his country."[20]

General Breckinridge

Commissioned a brigadier general, and later a major general, Breckinridge went west to fight at Shiloh, Stone's River, Chickamauga, and Chattanooga. He returned east to the battle of Cold Harbor, and in July 1864 he and General Jubal T. Early led a dramatic raid on Washington, D.C. Breckinridge's troops advanced as far as Silver Spring, Maryland, where they sacked Francis

Blair's home but did not destroy it, supposedly at the urging of Breckinridge, who had often been a guest there. Breckinridge got so close to Washington that he could see the newly completed Capitol dome, and General Early joked that he would allow him to lead the advance into the city so that he could sit in the vice-presidential chair again. But federal troops halted the Confederates, who retreated back to the Shenandoah Valley. There, at Winchester, Virginia, they confronted Union troops commanded by Philip H. Sheridan. The Confederate general John B. Gordon later recalled that Breckinridge was "desperately reckless" during that campaign, and "literally seemed to court death." When Gordon urged him to be careful, Breckinridge replied, "Well, general, there is little left for me if our cause is to fail." As they rode from their defeat on the battlefield, Jubal T. Early turned to ask, "General Breckinridge, what do you think of the 'rights of the South in the territories' now?" He received no answer.[21]

During the closing months of the war in 1865, Jefferson Davis made Breckinridge his secretary of war. He performed well in this final government position, firing the Confederacy's bumbling commissary general and trying to bring order out of the chaos, but these efforts came too late. When General Robert E. Lee surrendered his army, President Davis was determined to keep on fighting, but Breckinridge opposed continuing the war as a guerrilla campaign. "This has been a magnificent epic," he said; "in God's name let it not terminate in farce." Fleeing Richmond, Breckinridge commanded the troops that accompanied Davis and his cabinet. Davis was captured, but Breckinridge evaded arrest and imprisonment by fleeing through Florida to Cuba. From there he sailed for England. Subsequently, the Breckinridge family settled in Toronto, Canada. His daughter Mary later remarked that, while exile was a quiet relief for her mother, it was hard on her father, "separated from the activities of life, and unable to do anything towards making a support for his family." In Canada he met other Confederate exiles, including the freed Jefferson Davis. Once, Breckinridge and Davis rode to Niagara. Across the river they could see the red stripes of the American flag, which Breckinridge viewed nostalgically but the more embittered Davis described as "the gridiron we have been fried on."[22]

On Christmas Day, 1868, departing President Andrew Johnson issued a blanket pardon for all Confederates. John C. Breckinridge returned to the United States in February 1869. Stopping in many cities to visit old friends, he reached Lexington, Kentucky, a month later. He had not been back in Kentucky since he fled eight years before. In welcome, a band played "Home Sweet Home," "Dixie," and "Hail to the Chief." Breckinridge declared himself through with politics: "I no more feel the political excitements that marked the scenes of my former years than if I were an extinct volcano." Other than publicly denouncing the lawless violence of the Ku Klux Klan, he devoted himself entirely to private matters. The former vice president practiced law and became active in building railroads. Although he was only fifty-four, his health declined severely and he died on May 17, 1875. Despite his weakened condition at the end, Breckinridge surprised his doctor with his clear and strong voice. "Why, Doctor," the famous stump speaker smiled from his deathbed, "I can throw my voice a mile."[23]

NOTES

[1] Frank H. Heck, *Proud Kentuckian: John C. Breckinridge, 1821–1875* (Lexington, KY, 1976), pp. 1–11; James C. Klotter, *The Breckinridges of Kentucky, 1760–1981* (Lexington, KY, 1986), pp. 95–98.

[2] Heck, pp. 11–18; Klotter, p. 101.

[3] Heck, pp. 22, 30–31; William C. Davis, *Breckinridge: Statesman, Soldier, Symbol* (Baton Rouge, LA, 1974), p. 45.

[4] John W. Forney, *Anecdotes of Public Men* (New York, 1873), 2:41–42; Heck, pp. 30–31, 163–64; Klotter, p. 113.

[5] Heck, pp. 41–43.

[6] Forney, 2:301; Heck, pp. 44–46; Benjamin Perley Poore, *Perley's Reminiscences of Sixty Years in the National Metropolis* (Philadelphia, 1886), 1:439–42; L.A. Gobright, *Recollections of Men and Things at Washington During The Third of a Century* (Philadelphia, 1869), p. 138.

[7] Heck, pp. 47, 53–54; Mark W. Summers, *The Plundering Generation: Corruption and the Crisis of the Union, 1849–1861* (New York, 1987), p. 203.

[8] Davis, *Breckinridge*, p. 145; Heck, pp. 59–60; Klotter, p. 111.

[9] Klotter, pp. 111, 113; Heck, pp. 55–66.

[10] Frederick Moore Binder, *James Buchanan and the American Empire* (Cranbury, NJ, 1994), pp. 219–22.

[11] Ibid., p. 223; Heck, pp. 67–68; Davis, *Breckinridge*, p. 172.

[12] Heck, pp. 69–74; Davis, *Breckinridge*, pp. 171–72; Elbert B. Smith, *The Presidency of James Buchanan* (Lawrence, KS, 1975), p. 41; Forney, 1:41–42; Robert W. Johannsen, *Stephen A. Douglas* (New York, 1973), p. 652.

[13] U.S., Congress, Senate, *The Old Senate Chamber: Proceedings in the Senate of the United States upon Vacating their old Chamber on January 4, 1859*, S. Doc. 67, 74th Cong., 1st sess., pp. 4–15; Heck, pp. 75–76; Davis, *Breckinridge*, p. 194.

[14] Forney, 1:283–84; Poore, 2:47; Davis, *Breckinridge*, p. 175.

[15] Davis, *Breckinridge*, p. 197; Smith, p. 113.

[16] David M. Potter, *The Impending Crisis, 1848–1861* (New York, 1976), p. 438; see also Margaret Jean Kelly, *The Career of Joseph Lane* (Washington, 1942).

[17] William C. Davis, *Jefferson Davis: The Man and His Hour* (New York, 1991), pp. 282–83; Heck, p. 85; Smith, pp. 124–26; Summers, p. 274; Lowell H. Harrison, "John C. Breckinridge: Nationalist, Confederate, Kentuckian," *The Filson Club History Quarterly* 47 (April 1973): 128.

[18] Margaret Leech, *Reveille in Washington, 1860–1865* (New York, 1941), pp. 32, 87. As a sign of the public confusion over Breckinridge's loyalties, Mathew Brady's studio produced a photograph of Breckinridge retouched to make him appear to be wearing a Union army uniform. See Susan Kismaric, *American Politicians: Photographs from 1843 to 1993* (New York, 1994), p. 66.

[19] Heck, pp. 101–2; U.S., Congress, Senate, *The Senate, 1789–1989: Addresses on the History of the United States Senate*, by Robert C. Byrd, S. Doc. 100–20, 100th Cong., 1st sess., vol. 1, 1989, p. 250.

[20] Heck, pp. 101–2, 106; U.S., Congress, Senate, *United States Senate Election, Expulsion, and Censure Cases, 1793–1990*, S. Doc. 103–33, 103d Cong., 1st sess., 1995, p. 103.

[21] Klotter, p. 127; Leech, p. 345; Heck, pp. 111, 127–28; Harrison, p. 136.

[22] Heck, pp. 133–34; Davis, *Jefferson Davis*, pp. 600–601, 616–33, 658; Lucille Stilwell Williams, "John Cabell Breckinridge," *Register of the Kentucky State Historical Society* 33 (January 1935): 29.

[23] Heck, pp. 149, 157; Davis, *Breckinridge*, pp. 593, 623.

Chapter 15

HANNIBAL HAMLIN

1861–1865

HANNIBAL HAMLIN

Chapter 15

HANNIBAL HAMLIN

15th Vice President: 1861–1865

What can I do? The slow and unsatisfactory movements of the Government do not meet with my approbation, and that is known, and of course I am not consulted at all, nor do I think there is much disposition in any quarter to regard any counsel I may give much if at all.

—HANNIBAL HAMLIN, 1862

The emotional issue of slavery demolished the American political system during the 1850s: the Whig party disintegrated; the Democrats divided; and the Free Soil and American (or Know-Nothing) parties flourished briefly and died. Emerging from the wreckage of the old system, the Republican party, which ran its first presidential campaign in 1856, drew converts from all of these parties. Within the new party stood men who had spent years fighting each other under different political banners. In constructing a presidential ticket in 1860, therefore, Republicans needed candidates who would reflect their complex construction and reinforce their new unity. They picked a presidential candidate, Abraham Lincoln, who was not only a westerner but a Whig who claimed Henry Clay as his political role model. To balance Lincoln, Republicans chose as their vice-presidential candidate Hannibal Hamlin, an easterner who had spent the bulk of his political career as a Democrat and who had battled Henry Clay when they served together in the United States Senate. Despite their differences, Lincoln and Hamlin shared an opposition to the expansion of slavery into the western territories, without being abolitionists.[1]

Youth

Hannibal Hamlin owed his classical name to his grandfather Eleazer Hamlin, a man well read in history, who named his first son after the Roman general Scipio Africanus (everyone called the boy Africa) and called his twin sons Cyrus, after the great Persian conqueror, and Hannibal, after the Carthaginian general who crossed the Alps on elephants in his campaigns against Rome. Cyrus became a Harvard-trained medical doctor and moved to the village of Paris Hill, Maine, where on August 27, 1809, was born his son, whom he named after his brother Hannibal. The boy grew up in a prosperous family, living in an imposing, three-story white house. A natural leader among his peers, physically fit and athletic, Hannibal was also an avid reader. He was sent to local public schools and then to Hebron Academy.

Hannibal's ambition to become a lawyer was nearly sidetracked, first when his elder brother took ill, forcing him to leave school to run the family farm, and then when his father died, requiring him, under the terms of his father's will, to stay home and take care of his mother until he turned twenty-one. When he came of age, however, Hannibal left home to read law at the offices of Fessenden and Deblois, under Samuel C. Fessenden, an outspoken abolitionist and father of Hamlin's future political rival, William Pitt Fessenden. The association made Hamlin an antislavery man and launched him into his new profession. He set up his own law practice and became the town attorney in Hampden, Maine.[2]

HANNIBAL HAMLIN

Democratic Politics in Maine and Washington

Politically, from the 1830s to the 1850s, Maine was an entrenched Democratic state, and the politically ambitious Hamlin joined the Democratic party. In 1835 he was elected to the state house of representatives. Described as "tall, and gracious in figure, with black, piercing eyes, a skin almost olive-colored, hair smooth, thick and jetty, a manner always courteous and affable," he fit easily into legislative politics, became a popular member of the house, and was soon elected its speaker. His most notable legislative achievement was to lead the movement to abolish capital punishment in Maine. In 1840 he lost a race for the U.S. House of Representatives, but in 1843 (after the next election was delayed until the districts could be reapportioned) he won a seat in Congress. There he denounced Henry Clay's economic programs and voted very much as a Jacksonian Democrat. He became chairman of the Committee on Elections and won a coveted seat on the House Rules Committee. Hamlin enjoyed considerable luck in his career, particularly in February 1844, when he missed sailing on the U.S. Navy frigate *Princeton*, which was going to demonstrate its new guns. One of the guns exploded, killing Secretary of State Abel Upshur and several others.[3]

The extension of slavery into the territories was the most perplexing issue to face Congress during Hamlin's long career in the House and Senate. His state of Maine had entered the Union as a result of the Missouri Compromise, which admitted one free state for every slave state. But in 1846, when the United States entered a war with Mexico, the prospects of vast new conquered territories south of the Missouri Compromise line raised the question of the parameters of slavery. Hamlin joined with other radical antislavery men in the House to devise an amendment that would prohibit the introduction of slavery into any territory taken from Mexico as a result of the war. Pennsylvania Representative David Wilmot was selected to introduce the measure, which became known as the Wilmot Proviso. Hamlin introduced his own version of the proviso on an army appropriations bill, much to the anger of Democratic President James K. Polk. "Mr. Hamlin professes to be a democrat," the president wrote in his diary, "but has given indications during the present session that he is dissatisfied, and is pursuing a mischievous course . . . on the slavery question." The president attributed Hamlin's stand to a patronage quarrel with the administration, but Hamlin stood squarely on principle. "I have no doubt that the whole North will come to the position I have taken," he said. "Some damned rascals who may be desirous of disposing of myself, will mutter & growl about abolitionism but I do not care the snap of my fingers for them all."[4]

The Free Soil Challenge

In the House, Hamlin encountered many of the men with whom he would serve and against whom he would contend for the rest of his long career. Among others, he met Representatives Abraham Lincoln of Illinois, Andrew Johnson of Tennessee, and Jefferson Davis of Mississippi. He and Davis sparred frequently in the House and Senate over slavery. Tempers between the two men rose to such a level that for the only time in his life Hamlin thought it prudent to carry a pistol for self-protection. The unexpected death of Senator John Fairfield from malpractice by an incompetent physician opened a Senate seat from Maine, which Hamlin was elected to fill in 1848. That same year, antislavery Whigs and Democrats united to form a Free Soil party that nominated Martin Van Buren for president. Although Hamlin approved of their antislavery platform and had supported Van Buren in the past, he could not bring himself to abandon his party—to which he owed his Senate seat. As a Democratic senator, Hamlin strongly opposed Henry Clay's proposed Compromise of 1850. If the bill spread slavery into the West, he declared, "it will not be with my vote."[5]

As a temperance man, Senator Hamlin was distressed by the drinking habits of his colleagues. He observed that New York Senator Silas Wright was never sober and even sipped whiskey while he addressed the Senate. Hamlin estimated that as many as a third of the senators were drunk by the end of a daily session and that after a long executive session (held behind closed doors) two-thirds of the members left inebriated.

Nor did he approve of the ruffianly tendencies and tempers of some senators. After a dispute between Senator Thomas Hart Benton and Henry S. Foote, in which Foote pulled a pistol on the Senate floor, Hamlin wrote in disgust to a friend, "Don't you think the American Senate is a dignified body!!!!!!!!" [6]

Woolheads Versus Wildcats

The slavery issue split the Maine Democratic party into two factions. Hamlin's antislavery faction won the name "Woolheads" from its opponents. The Woolheads in turn labeled their adversaries, who opposed the Wilmot Proviso, "Wildcats." In addition to the slavery issue, temperance also divided the two factions, with Hamlin's "Woolheads" supporting prohibition laws and the "Wildcats" opposing them. In 1854, Hamlin denounced Senator Stephen Douglas' efforts to enact the Kansas-Nebraska bill and repeal the Missouri Compromise. "Shall we repeal freedom and make slavery?" he asked. "It comes to that." When the bill passed the Senate by a vote of 37 to 14, Hamlin was among only four Democrats to vote against it. [7]

As political turmoil reigned, Hamlin's attention was distracted by the illness of his wife, Sarah Jane Hamlin. Both Hannibal and Sarah Hamlin loved Washington's social life of dances, receptions, card playing, and theater-going. The senator, she wrote home to their son, "has had about ten invitations a week to dine, and he enjoys them very much, you know how much he enjoys a good dinner." But Sarah's health declined so severely in 1855 that for a while he considered resigning his Senate seat. Sarah Jane Hamlin died from tuberculosis in April 1856. That September, Hamlin married his wife's younger half-sister, Ellen, who was the same age as one of his sons. Characterized as plain but witty and warm-hearted, she bore two more of his children and offered him companionship through the rest of his long life. [8]

Becoming a Republican

To some degree, Sarah's illness provided political cover for Hannibal Hamlin at a time when he was under intense pressure to abandon the Democrats in favor of the newly formed Republican party. Republican leaders were anxious for the popular Hamlin to join their party to balance the radicals who threatened to gain control. "We have a great many men in our party who go off half cocked," wrote the young editor and politico, James G. Blaine. "They must be made to ride in the rear of the car instead of in the engine or else we are in constant danger of being thrown from the track." In 1856, Republicans wanted Hamlin to head their ticket as the Republican candidate for governor of Maine. Hamlin clung to his old party as long as he could, and also had no desire to leave the Senate. However, Republicans warned him that refusal to run for governor would end any chance of his being returned to the Senate. Hamlin agreed to run for governor, but only if the legislature would send him back to the Senate as soon as possible. An effective campaigner, Hamlin canvassed the state. Republicans won a smashing victory over both Whigs and Democrats, sweeping all six congressional districts and carrying the legislature. Since Maine's elections were held in September (because of the state's harsh winter weather), the early victory gave a psychological boost to the national Republican campaign that year. Hamlin won widespread credit for helping Republicans broaden their electoral base. [9]

Inaugurated governor on January 8, 1857, Hamlin resigned on February 25 to begin his third term as senator. In Washington he provided the Republicans with a strong voice against the "doughface" policies of James Buchanan's administration. (It was a decidedly Maine "Down East" voice, with Hamlin pronouncing "now" as "ne-a-ow," for instance.) While boarding at the St. Charles Hotel in Washington, Hamlin became reacquainted and favorably impressed with Andrew Johnson of Tennessee, with whom he had served in the House and who had just been elected to the Senate. As the 1860 elections approached, some Maine Republicans viewed Hamlin as a possible favorite-son candidate, in case the frontrunner, New York Senator William Seward, should falter. But James G. Blaine worked the Maine delegation to the Republican National Convention in favor of Abraham Lincoln's nomination. On the train ride to Chicago, Blaine convinced Governor Lot Morrill and other delegates to throw their support to Lincoln. When Lincoln upset Seward, the vice-presidential nomination was offered first to the Seward camp. The disappointed Seward men put no one forward for the second spot. There was strong support among the delegates for Cassius M. Clay, the Kentucky abolitionist, but Republican party leaders thought him too radical. By contrast, Hamlin seemed a more "natural" choice, more moderate, but with a spotless record against slavery, and a friend of Seward's in the Senate. Hamlin won the nomination on the second ballot.[10]

The nomination came as a shock to Hannibal Hamlin. While playing cards in his Washington hotel room, Hamlin heard a racket in the corridor. The door burst open and the room filled with excited men, led by Indiana Congressman Schuyler Colfax, who read a telegram from the convention and addressed him as "Mr. Vice-President." Stunned, Hamlin said he did not want the office, but Ohio Senator Ben Wade warned him that to decline would only give ammunition to the Democrats, suggesting that he was afraid to run on a losing ticket. Hamlin agreed, whispering to Wade and Colfax: "You people have spoiled a good lone hand I held." Afterwards, writing to his wife, Hamlin explained: "I neither expected or desired it. But it has been made and as a faithful man to the cause, it leaves me no alternative but to accept it." At least, he conceded, the duties of the office would "not be hard or unpleasant." Whether in cards or in politics, Hamlin had a lucky streak. As Blaine observed: "He always turns up on the winning side."[11]

Abra/Hamlin/coln

During the campaign, both Lincoln and Hamlin considered it prudent to make no speeches. However, Hamlin assured Lincoln, "While I have been silent, I have never been so busy thro' the Press and by personal effort endeavoring to strengthen the weak points all along the line." After Maine Republicans swept the September elections, Hamlin traveled to Boston in October to march in a torchlight parade, accompanied by Maine lumberjacks, Penobscot Indians, and party stalwarts. One of the favorite signs com-

bined the ticket into a single name: "Abra/Hamlin/coln." On a less friendly note, southerners denounced Lincoln and Hamlin as a radical abolitionists. Going even further, Robert Barnwell Rhett, editor of the *Charleston [S.C.] Mercury*, wrote that "Hamlin is what we call a mulatto. He has black blood in him." An amused New Yorker, George Templeton Strong, observed that Hamlin seemed "a vigorous specimen of the pure Yankee type. His complexion is so swarthy that I cannot wonder at the demented South for believing him a mulatto."[12]

Once the election had been won, Lincoln summoned Hamlin to meet him in Chicago on November 22. After some casual initial conversation—Hamlin noted that Lincoln had started to grow a beard, and both men reminisced about hearing each other's speeches during their term together in the House of Representatives—they got down to work. Lincoln wanted to discuss the composition of his cabinet and knew that Hamlin, as a senator, had worked with and taken the measure of many of the men he was considering for appointment. Lincoln was especially concerned about attracting his former rival, William Seward, into the cabinet as secretary of state. When the Senate convened in December, Senator Hamlin carried notes from Lincoln to Seward and pressed his colleague to accept the offer, which he did. Hamlin also successfully promoted Gideon Welles of Connecticut as a New England candidate for the cabinet as secretary of the navy. These early dealings hinted that Hamlin might play a more active role in the administration than had previous vice presidents. It soon turned out, however, that Hamlin's usefulness to Lincoln was tied mostly to his role as a senior senator and subsided almost as soon as he vacated his Senate seat for the vice-presidency.[13]

The Lincoln-Hamlin victory triggered the secession of the southern states. When asked by a friend from Maine what the future would hold, the new vice president replied, "there's going to be a war, and a terrible one, just as surely as the sun will rise to-morrow." Congress was out of session and Hamlin was in Maine when word came that Confederates had fired on Fort Sumter. The vice president devoted himself to raising a Maine regiment to fight for the Union. On his way back to Washington, Hamlin stopped in New York City, where he complied with President Lincoln's request to keep him advised daily on what troops were leaving New York to protect the capital.[14]

"A Contingent Somebody"

When the Senate convened on the Fourth of July in 1861 to take the legislative actions necessary for raising and funding an army for the Union, Vice President Hamlin discovered that he had far less power and patronage as vice president than he had as a senator. The loss of patronage particularly galled Hamlin, who was "noted for his fidelity to political friends." He also felt unhappy over being relegated to serving as an inactive observer of events. Hamlin considered himself the most unimportant man in Washington, ignored equally by the administration and the senators. He called his job "a fifth wheel on a coach" and identified the vice president as "a contingent somebody." When Jessie Benton Frémont asked Hamlin to intervene in favor of a new military command for her husband, the vice president replied: "What can I do? The slow and unsatisfactory movements of the Government do not meet with my approbation, and that is known, and of course I am not consulted at all, nor do I think there is much disposition in any quarter to regard any counsel I may give much if at all."[15]

Reflecting later on his office, Hamlin told an interviewer:

> There is a popular impression that the Vice President is in reality the second officer of the government not only in rank but in power and influence. This is a mistake. In the early days of the republic he was in some sort an heir apparent to the Presidency. But that is changed. He presides over the Senate—he has a casting vote in case of a tie—and he appoints his own private secretary. But this gives him no power to wield and no influence to exert. Every member who has a constituency, and every Senator who represents a state, counts for more in his own locality, and with the Executive who must needs, in wielding the functions of his office, gather around him, and retain by his favors, those who can vote in Congress and operate directly upon public sentiment in their houses.

Hamlin explained that he soon saw that his office was a "nullity" in Washington. He tried not to intrude upon the president, but always gave Lincoln his views, and when asked, his advice.[16]

Moreover, Hamlin found presiding over the Senate so boring that he was frequently absent. In contrast to his service as a senator, when he rarely missed a day of a session, as vice president he would leave for Maine well before the end of a session, turning his duties over to the president pro tempore. Hamlin's inattentiveness to Senate proceedings became an embarrassment when the Delaware Democrat Willard Saulsbury launched into a savage attack on President Lincoln as "a weak and imbecile man." Republican senators objected that the remarks were not in order, but Vice President Hamlin had to admit that "[t]he Chair was not listening to what the Senator from Delaware was saying, and did not hear the words." To this Saulsbury replied, "That is the fault of the Chair, and not of the Senator who was addressing the Chair." Hamlin finally ordered Saulsbury to be seated for questioning the motives of the senators who had raised the objection, and when Saulsbury refused to comply, the vice president ordered the sergeant at arms to place the senator in custody. After a brief conversation, Saulsbury accompanied the assistant sergeant at arms out of the chamber.[16]

Hamlin attributed Saulsbury's belligerence to his drinking. "He was very drunk—beastly so on the night of the transaction," the vice president wrote. "It was a most disgraceful scene." As a temperance man, Hamlin determined to banish liquor from the Senate chamber and committee rooms. The combination of his rule outlawing the sale of liquor in the Senate restaurant and the departure of the hard-drinking southern senators after secession sobered the institution. One visitor to the Capitol noted, "A few Senators were seen walking with unsteady gait from the cloak room to their desks, but thanks to the firmness of Hannibal Hamlin, the Senate became a pleasant place to the sober people who had to live there."[17]

Throughout the war, Hamlin identified more with the frustrated congressional radicals than with the more cautious President Lincoln. Those around Lincoln concluded that the vice president was not in close sympathy with the president but "was known as one who passively rather than actively strengthened a powerful cabal of Republican leaders in their aggressive hostility to Lincoln and his general policy." Lincoln did not appear to hold this against Hamlin. As one newspaper correspondent of the era observed: "Lincoln measured the men about him at their value. He knew their worth, their fidelity, and in no sense distrusted them." He did not require absolute loyalty in order to use a person. Hamlin, for instance, was among those who pressed Lincoln hard to issue an emancipation proclamation. Fearing at first that such a measure would divide the North, Lincoln resisted until he believed he could use the issue as a military advantage, to give a nobler purpose to the war. When Lincoln first drafted a proclamation, he invited Hamlin to dinner and let him be the first to see the document, asking for his suggestions. Hamlin later described Lincoln as "much moved at the step he was taking." [18]

Dumped from the Ticket

Despite Hamlin's grumbling about the powerlessness of the vice-presidency, he was willing to stand for reelection in 1864. Hamlin assumed that Lincoln supported his nomination, but the president—an entirely pragmatic politician—doubted that Hamlin would add much strength to the ticket in what was sure to be a difficult reelection campaign, with the survival of the nation at stake. Maine would vote Republican whether or not Hamlin was on the ticket, and he carried little weight in any other state. Lincoln sent emissaries to sound out several prominent War Democrats, among them Tennessee's war governor, Andrew Johnson. As the thinking went, to nominate a southerner like Johnson would be a way to "nationalize the Republican party." At the convention, to the surprise of Hamlin's supporters, the Tennessee governor outpolled the vice president on the first ballot and went on to win the nomination on the second. "To be Vice President is clearly not to be anything more than a reflected greatness," Secretary of the Senate John W. Forney wrote to console Hamlin. "You know how it is with the

Prince of Wales or the Heir Apparent. He is waiting for somebody to die, and that is all of it." Hamlin maintained a dignified silence but was vexed by his defeat. Years later he wrote: "I was dragged out of the Senate, against my wishes—tried to do my whole duty, and was then unceremoniously 'whistled down the wind.' While I have never complained to any one, I did not fail to feel and know how I was treated." [19]

During the summer of 1864, the lame-duck vice president briefly served in the Union army. When the war began in 1861, Hamlin had enlisted as a private in the Maine Coast Guard. His unit was called to active duty in 1864 and ordered to report to Fort McClary, at Kittery, Maine. Although Hamlin could have accepted a purely honorary place on the roll, he insisted upon active service. "I am the Vice-President of the United States, but I am also a private citizen, and as an enlisted member of your company, I am bound to do my duty." He added, "I aspire only to be a high private in the rear ranks, and keep step with the boys in blue." Promoted to corporal, Hamlin reported on July 7, drilled, and did guard duty and kitchen patrol along with the rest of the enlisted men. As vice president, however, he was assigned to officers' quarters. When his tour of duty ended in September, he left the company to campaign for the Republican ticket, first in Maine, and then down through New England to New York and Pennsylvania, doing what he could to aid Lincoln's reelection. [20]

In the Vice President's Room in the Capitol on inauguration day, Hamlin's successor, Andrew Johnson, approached him with a request. "Mr. Hamlin, I am not well, and need a stimulant," he said. "Have you any whiskey?" Hamlin explained that he had prohibited the sale of liquor in the Capitol, but when Johnson pressed his request, a messenger was sent to procure a bottle. Johnson poured a tumbler and downed it straight, then had two more drinks before going onto the Senate floor to give an embarrassingly drunken inaugural address. Recounting the scene later, Hamlin privately commented that if Johnson ordinarily drank that way, "he must be able to stand a great deal."

A few weeks after Hamlin returned to Maine, on the morning of April 15, 1865, he encountered a group of sorrowful men on the street in Bangor, who informed him that Lincoln had been assassinated. Hamlin boarded a steamer for Washington to attend the president's funeral. At the White House, he stood side by side with Andrew Johnson at Lincoln's casket, causing those who saw them to note the irony that Hamlin had within a matter of weeks missed the presidency. None could have realized how differently the nation's history might have developed if Lincoln had been succeeded by Hamlin, who favored a Radical Reconstruction of the South, rather than by Johnson, who opposed it.[21]

A Post-Vice-Presidential Political Career

After Hamlin's defeat for renomination as vice president, Lincoln had considered appointing him secretary of the treasury but concluded that "Hamlin has the Senate on the brain and nothing more or less will cure him." However, Hamlin was outmaneuvered for the Senate seat by his Maine Republican rival, William Pitt Fessenden. Massachusetts Senator Charles Sumner instead recommended that Hamlin be appointed collector of the port of Boston, and President Johnson made the nomination. In time, Hamlin became dismayed over Johnson's policies on Reconstruction and his abandonment of the rights of the freedmen. As other Republican officeholders resigned in protest, many looked to Hamlin to join them, but he held onto his collectorship. Finally, the governor of Maine wrote to Hamlin that his resignation would "strike a lofty note" and set a "high example" of sacrifice for principles. Realizing that his political future depended upon distancing himself from Johnson, Hamlin abandoned the office with a blast at the president.[22]

In 1868, against his wishes, Hamlin's name was put forward as a vice-presidential candidate on the ticket headed by U.S. Grant, but the nomination went to House Speaker Schuyler Colfax. At last in 1869 Hamlin was elected to another term in the Senate. He returned as a respected elder statesman and served two terms. One journalist who met Senator Hamlin in 1871 described him as attired in an antique blue swallow-tailed coat with big brass buttons, the type worn by antebellum statesmen. Hamlin mistook the journalist for a resident of Maine "and with the amiable humbug habit of many years wrung my hand warmly and affectionately inquired for the folks at the farm." The journalist took no offense, recognizing that "this trick of pretending remembrance is a venial sin with politicians and head waiters, great and small." Still, the incident gave an indication of how Hamlin had survived in politics for so long.[23]

In 1877, Hamlin fainted in the Senate Republican cloakroom, the first signs of his heart disease. He chose not to stand for reelection in 1880. The election that year of James Garfield as president made Maine's James G. Blaine secretary of state. Garfield and Blaine appointed Hamlin minister to Spain, a post that carried few duties and allowed him to make an extended tour of the European continent. The most amusing part of his brief diplomatic tenure was that the various foreign ministers he met "seemed to regard as of great importance" the fact that he had served as vice president. Hamlin retired from public service in 1882. He made his last public appearance at a Republican Club dinner at Delmonico's in honor of Lincoln's birthday in February 1891. There he was toasted as "The Surviving Standard-Bearer of 1860," to thunderous applause. A few months later, on the Fourth of July in 1891, thirty years to the day after he convened the Senate at the start of the Civil War, Hannibal Hamlin walked from his home to the Tarratine Club of Bangor, Maine. He had founded the social club, served as its president, and went there every afternoon (except Sunday) to play cards. While seated at the card table, Hamlin collapsed and fell unconscious, dying that night at the age of eighty-one.[24]

NOTES

[1] See William E. Gienapp, *The Origins of the Republican Party, 1852–1856* (New York, 1987).

[2] Charles Eugene Hamlin, *The Life and Times of Hannibal Hamlin* (Cambridge, MA, 1899), pp. 7–8; H. Draper Hunt, *Hannibal Hamlin of Maine: Lincoln's First Vice-President* (Syracuse, NY, 1969), pp. 1–11; Mark Scroggins, *Hannibal: The Life of Abraham Lincoln's First Vice President* (Lanham, MD, 1994), pp. 4–19.

[3] Hunt, pp. 23–26.

[4] Ibid., pp. 40–41; Scroggins, pp. 34–58.

[5] Hunt, pp. 44–47, 63; Hamlin, pp. 72–181; Frederick J. Blue, *The Free Soilers: Third Party Politics, 1848–54* (Urbana, IL, 1973), pp. 97–100.

[6] Hunt, pp. 48, 62. See description of the incident in Chapter 12 of this volume, "Millard Fillmore," p. 175.

[7] Hunt, pp. 68, 81; Gienapp, pp. 47, 77.

[8] Hunt, pp. 84–85; Scroggins, pp. 102–5, 117–18.

[9] Gienapp, pp. 208, 390–94.

[10] Hunt, pp. 114–18, 152; John Russell Young, *Men and Memories, Personal Reminiscences* (New York, 1901), pp. 48–50; Hans L. Trefousse, *Andrew Johnson: A Biography* (New York, 1989), p. 115.

[11] Hunt, pp. 118–19; Hamlin, p. 580.

[12] Hunt, pp. 121, 125–26, 152; Hamlin, pp. 354–55, 359.

[13] Hunt, pp. 127, 133; Hamlin, pp. 366–75.

[14] Hunt, pp. 148, 153.

[15] Ibid, p. 155; Benjamin Perley Poore, *Perley's Reminiscences of Sixty Years in the National Metropolis* (Philadelphia, 1886), 2:97–98.

[16] "Conversation with Hon. H. Hamlin," April 8, 1879, in Michael Burlingame, ed., *An Oral History of Abraham Lincoln: John G. Nicolay's Interviews and Essays* (Carbondale, IL, 1996), pp. 67–68.

[16] Hunt, pp. 157–58.

[17] Ibid, pp. 158, 188; Hamlin, p. 497.

[18] Hunt, pp. 160, 189; Young, p. 54.

[19] David Donald, *Lincoln* (New York, 1995), pp. 503–6; Hunt, pp. 177–89; Hamlin, pp. 461–89; James G. Blaine, *Twenty Years of Congress: From Lincoln to Garfield* (Norwich, CT, 1884), p. 522; David Donald, *Charles Sumner and the Rights of Man* (New York, 1970), pp. 169–73.

[20] Scroggins, pp. 210–12.

[21] Hamlin, p. 497; Hunt, p. 200; Poore, pp. 159–60.

[22] Scroggins, pp. 213–15; Hunt, pp. 194, 200; Beverly Wilson Palmer, ed., *The Selected Letters of Charles Sumner* (Boston, 1990), 2:326–27.

[23] Edward P. Mitchell, *Memoirs of an Editor* (New York, 1924), p. 314.

[24] Hunt, pp. 221, 250; Eric Foner, *Reconstruction: America's Unfinished Revolution, 1863–1877* (New York, 1988), p. 266.

Chapter 16

ANDREW JOHNSON
1865

ANDREW JOHNSON

Chapter 16

ANDREW JOHNSON

16th Vice President: 1865

The inauguration went off very well except that the Vice President Elect was too drunk to perform his duties & disgraced himself & the Senate by making a drunken foolish speech.
—SENATOR ZACHARIAH CHANDLER

Vice President-elect Andrew Johnson arrived in Washington ill from typhoid fever. The night before his March 4, 1865, inauguration, he fortified himself with whiskey at a party hosted by his old friend, Secretary of the Senate John W. Forney. The next morning, hung over and confronting cold, wet, and windy weather, Johnson proceeded to the Capitol office of Vice President Hannibal Hamlin, where he complained of feeling weak and asked for a tumbler of whiskey. Drinking it straight, he quickly consumed two more. Then, growing red in the face, Johnson entered the overcrowded and overheated Senate chamber. After Hamlin delivered a brief and stately valedictory, Johnson rose unsteadily to harangue the distinguished crowd about his humble origins and his triumph over the rebel aristocracy. In the shocked and silent audience, President Abraham Lincoln showed an expression of "unutterable sorrow," while Senator Charles Sumner covered his face with his hands. Former Vice President Hamlin tugged vainly at Johnson's coattails, trying to cut short his remarks. After Johnson finally quieted, took the oath of office, and kissed the Bible, he tried to swear in the new senators, but became so confused that he had to turn the job over to a Senate clerk.[1]

Without a doubt it had been the most inauspicious beginning to any vice-presidency. "The inauguration went off very well except that the Vice President Elect was too drunk to perform his duties & disgraced himself & the Senate by making a drunken foolish speech," Michigan Republican Senator Zachariah Chandler wrote home to his wife. "I was never so mortified in my life, had I been able to find a hole I would have dropped through it out of sight." Johnson presided over the Senate on March 6 but, still feeling unwell, he then went into seclusion at the home of an old friend in Silver Spring, Maryland. He returned to the Senate only on the last day of the special session, March 11. Rumors that had him on a drunken spree led some Radical Republicans to draft a resolution calling for Johnson's resignation. Others talked of impeachment. President Lincoln, however, assured callers that he still had confidence in Johnson, whom he had known for years, observing, "It has been a severe lesson for Andy, but I do not think he will do it again." [2]

Plebian Roots

Lost in his muddled inaugural was Johnson's celebration of his dramatic rise from "plebeian" roots. He had been born in a log cabin in Raleigh, North Carolina, on December 29, 1808, to Jacob Johnson, an illiterate bank porter and city constable, and his wife, Mary, known as "Polly the Weaver" for her work as a seamstress and laundress. When Andrew was three his father died. His mother remarried and later apprenticed her sons William and Andrew at James Selby's tailor shop. Young Andy Johnson was something of a hell-raiser and at fifteen he and his brother got into trouble by pelting a neighbor's house with pieces of wood. When the woman threatened to sue, the boys fled from Raleigh, causing their employer Selby to post a ten-dollar reward for their return.[3]

Johnson went to Laurens, South Carolina, where he worked in a tailor shop. He fell in love with a local girl, but her mother objected to her marriage with a penniless tailor. Disappointed, he abandoned South Carolina and walked to Tennessee. There he worked in a tailor shop and in 1827 married Eliza McCardle, daughter of a Greenville shoemaker. Eliza did not teach her husband to read, as some stories later had it, but she aided his further efforts at self-education. Short, stocky, and swarthy, but always impeccably dressed, as befitted his trade, Johnson built a solid business as a tailor, invested in real estate, raised a growing family, joined a debating society, and won the title "Colonel Johnson" for his rank in the state militia. With his steadily increasing wealth and status, he also bought a few slaves. A staunch supporter of the Democrat Andrew Jackson, Johnson became active in local politics. In 1829, he won his first race as alderman. He was chosen mayor of Greenville in 1834 and elected to the Tennessee state legislature the following year. In the legislature he introduced a homesteading bill that would give poor men 160 acres of public land if they would live on it— a measure he persisted in pushing when he moved to the U.S. Congress, until it became federal law in 1862.[4]

A Rising Political Star

Tennessee Democrats, spotting Andrew Johnson as a rising star and a pugnacious debater, sent him around the state to campaign for their ticket in the 1840 election. Governor James K. Polk received reports that Johnson was "a strongminded man who cuts when he does cut not with a razor but with a case knife." In 1843, Johnson won election to the U.S. House of Representatives, where he attracted attention as an outspoken and unbending defender of Jeffersonian-Jacksonian principles. He opposed Whig programs for protective tariffs and internal improvements as unnecessary public expenditures.

He proposed cutting the number of government clerks, voted against raising soldiers' pay, assailed military academies as aristocratic, opposed purchasing paintings of past presidents for the White House, and opposed accepting the funds bequeathed to the United States by James Smithson to create a Smithsonian Institution, on the grounds that if the funds were unwisely invested the taxpayers would have to support the enterprise. Among those with whom he served in Congress who had the opportunity to take his full measure were the Whig representative from Illinois, Abraham Lincoln, and the Democratic representative from Mississippi, Jefferson Davis. Johnson particularly sparred with Davis, whom he portrayed as part of the South's "illegitimate, swaggering, bastard, scrub aristocracy."[5]

In 1852, Tennessee elected Johnson governor. During his term he succeeded in enacting tax-supported public education for his state. He won reelection over intense opposition and served until 1856, when the legislature elected him to the U.S. Senate. Once more, Johnson pressed for passage of a Homestead bill, which he succeeded in moving through Congress in 1860, only to have it vetoed by President James Buchanan. While Johnson was preoccupied with his Homestead bill, his party was breaking up over the issue of slavery in the territories. In 1860, Johnson supported the Southern Democratic candidate, John C. Breckinridge, but he strenuously opposed the secessionists within his party. After Lincoln's election, Johnson fought to keep Tennessee in the Union. To Andrew Johnson, secession appeared simply a continuation of John C. Calhoun's discredited policy of nullification, against which his hero Andrew Jackson had stood his ground. Johnson threw his support behind Lincoln as the new embodiment of Jackson.[6]

War Democrat

In the spring of 1861, Johnson took the train from Washington back to Tennessee and was mobbed at several stops in Virginia. The senator had to pull a pistol to defend himself. Although Union sympathies were strong in the eastern mountains of Tennessee, where Johnson's hometown of Greenville was located, he found Confederate flags flying around the town. There were enough Union sympathizers in Tennessee to defeat an effort to call a state convention to secede, but after the firing on Fort Sumter, sentiment in the state swung more heavily to the Confederates. To avoid arrest, Johnson left Tennessee and returned to the Senate. As the only southern senator to remain loyal to the Union after his state seceded, Johnson became a hero in the North. As a leader of the "War Democrats," he denounced "Peace Democrats" and defended President Lincoln's use of wartime executive power. "I say, Let the battle go on—it is Freedom's cause. . . . Do not talk about Republicans now; do not talk about Democrats now; do not talk about Whigs or Americans now; talk about your Country and the Constitution and the Union."[7]

When federal troops conquered Nashville and its immediate vicinity, President Lincoln sent Andrew Johnson back to Tennessee in 1862 as war governor. Johnson still identified himself as a Democrat, but as one who put the Union before party. He denounced the state's aristocratic planting class who had supported the war, and said that if freeing their slaves would help to end the war, then he was in favor of emancipation. "Treason," he said, in a much-publicized quote, "must be made odious and traitors punished." In 1863, Tennessee held elections for a civilian government. Much to Johnson's chagrin, a conservative, proslavery candidate won the race for governor. President Lincoln wired Johnson to ignore the results and not recognize the new governor. "Let the reconstruction be the work of such men only as can be trusted for the Union," Lincoln instructed. "Exclude all others. . . . Get emancipation into your new state constitution." Following Lincoln's advice, Johnson made anyone who wished to vote take an oath of loyalty, which was then followed by a six-month waiting period. Since this meant that only those who had opposed the Confederacy could vote, Johnson's Radical forces swept the next state elections.[8]

Lincoln faced a difficult campaign for reelection in 1864, and he doubted that his vice president, Maine Republican Hannibal Hamlin, would add much to his ticket. Officially, the president maintained a hands-off attitude to-

ward the choice of a vice president, but privately he sent emissaries to several War Democrats as potential candidates on a fusion ticket. General Benjamin F. Butler let the president know he had no interest in the second spot, but Johnson of Tennessee and Daniel S. Dickinson of New York both expressed eagerness to be considered. Secretary of State William Seward, who counted New York as his own political base, wanted no part of Dickinson in the cabinet and threw his weight behind Johnson. The fearless, tough-minded war governor of Tennessee captured the imagination of the delegates. As John W. Forney judged Johnson's wartime record: "His speeches were sound, his measures bold, his administration a fair success." Johnson won the nomination on the first ballot.[9]

Becoming a Household Word

During the campaign, the great Republican orator Robert G. Ingersoll wrote to Johnson saying:

The people want to see and hear you. The name of Andrew Johnson has become a household word all over the great West, and you are regarded by the people of Illinois as the grandest example of loyalty in the whole South.

Traveling to Logansport, Indiana, in October, Johnson told the crowd that a Democratic newspaper had accused the Republicans of nominating "a rail-splitter" at the head of their ticket and "a boorish tailor" at its tail. Rather than see this as a rebuke, Johnson took pride in having risen up "from the mass of the people." The aristocrats were offended that he was a tailor, he said, but he had learned "that if a man does not disgrace his profession, it never disgraces him." Johnson acquitted himself well during the campaign but at times had trouble restraining himself in the excitement of facing a crowd, whether hostile or supportive. Late in October 1864 he addressed a large rally of African Americans in Nashville. Johnson noted that, since Lincoln's emancipation proclamation had not covered territories like Tennessee that were already under Union control, he had issued his own proclamation freeing the slaves in Tennessee. He also asserted that society would be improved if the great plantations were divided into many small farms and sold to honest farmers. Looking out over the crowd and commenting on the storm of persecution through which his listeners had passed, he wished that a Moses might arise to "lead them safely to their promised land of freedom and happiness." "You are our Moses," shouted people in the crowd. "We want no Moses but you!" "Well, then," replied Johnson, "humble and unworthy as I am, if no other better shall be found, I will indeed by your Moses, and lead you through the Red Sea of war and bondage, to a fairer future of liberty and peace." [10]

Vice President

Success on the battlefield brought Lincoln and Johnson victory in the election of 1864. As the Civil War approached its end, the equally monumental challenge of reconstructing the Union lay ahead. In Congress, the Radical Republicans wanted a victor's peace, enforced by federal troops, that would allow the former Confederate states to return to the Union only on terms that protected the rights of the freedmen. They offered their plan as the Wade-Davis bill of 1864, which Lincoln killed by a pocket veto. Lincoln wanted to be free to pursue a more lenient, flexible approach to Reconstruction. Having gotten the United States into the Civil War during a congressional recess in 1861, Lincoln anticipated ending the war and reconstructing the South during the long recess between March and December 1865. He presumed that his new vice president would be in sympathy with these plans, since in July 1864 Johnson had congratulated Lincoln on his veto of the Wade-Davis bill, saying that "the real union men" were satisfied with the president's approach. [11]

The vice president-elect hesitated in leaving Tennessee. In January 1865, Johnson wrote to Lincoln pointing out that the final abolition of slavery in Tennessee could not be taken up until the new civilian legislature met that April. He wanted to remain as war governor until that time, before handing power over to the elected representatives of the people. Johnson suggested that his inaugural as vice president be delayed until April. His friend, John W. Forney, secretary of the Senate, had checked the records and found that several vice presidents (John Adams, George Clinton, Elbridge Gerry, Daniel Tompkins, Mar-

tin Van Buren, and William R. King) were sworn in on dates after March 4. With the war still underway, however, Lincoln replied that he and his cabinet unanimously believed that Johnson must be in Washington by March 4. Had Johnson not complied, he might not have taken the oath of office before Lincoln's death on April 14, adding more constitutional confusion to the aftermath of the assassination. [12]

An Assassination Plot

During Johnson's six weeks as vice president, he faced greater danger than he knew. The assassination plot that would make Johnson president included him as a target. The circle of conspirators that John Wilkes Booth had gathered at Mrs. Mary Surratt's boardinghouse had at first planned to capture President Lincoln and whisk him off to the Confederacy. But the war was ending sooner than they anticipated, and when the attempted capture went awry, Booth decided to kill Lincoln, Vice President Johnson, and Secretary of State William H. Seward, thereby throwing the North into confusion and anarchy. Booth intended to kill Lincoln himself, and assigned Lewis Payne to assassinate Seward. For the vice president, whom he considered the least important victim, Booth assigned his weakest partner, George Atzerodt. A German carriage maker from Port Tobacco, Maryland, Atzerodt had spent the war years ferrying Confederates across the Potomac River to circumvent the Union blockades.

On the morning of April 14, 1865, Atzerodt registered at Kirkwood House, a hotel at the corner of Twelfth Street and Pennsylvania Avenue, between the White House and the Capitol. He took a room almost directly above the ground-floor suite occupied by the vice president. So incompetent at conspiracy was Atzerodt that he signed his right name to the hotel register. His notion of surveillance was to spend the afternoon in the hotel bar asking suspicious questions about the vice president and his guard. Sufficiently fortified with liquor, Atzerodt armed himself and asked the desk clerk to point out the vice president's suite. When informed that Johnson had just come back to his rooms, Atzerodt reacted in shocked surprise, and left the hotel.

Shortly afterwards, Johnson also left for an appointment with Lincoln.

When Booth arrived at the Kirkwood House and learned that Atzerodt was gone, he lost hope that this weak man would have the nerve to carry out his assignment. If he could not have Johnson killed, Booth improvised a way of discrediting him. He asked for a blank card, which he filled out: "Don't wish to disturb you. Are you at home? J. Wilkes Booth." Booth assumed that Johnson would have a hard time explaining the card, since it suggested that the vice president was himself part of the conspiracy. Fortunately for Johnson, his secretary, William A. Browning, picked up the mail at the desk and assumed that the card was for him, since he had once met Booth after a performance.

A pounding at the door later that evening awakened Andrew Johnson. Rather than George Atzerodt with a pistol, the excited man at the door was former Wisconsin Governor Leonard Farwell, who had just come from Ford's Theater and who exclaimed, "Someone has shot and murdered the President." Johnson ordered Farwell to go back to the theater to find out what he could about the president's condition. Farwell returned with the District of Columbia's provost marshal, who assured Johnson and the crowd that had gathered in his room that President Lincoln was dying and that Secretary of State William Seward was dead, as part of a gigantic plot (in fact, Seward had been badly wounded but not killed). Johnson wished to leave immediately to be with the president, but the provost marshal urged him to wait until order had been restored in the streets. At dawn, Johnson, receiving word from Secretary of War Edwin Stanton that Lincoln was dying, insisted on going to the president's side. Flanked by Governor Farwell and the provost marshal, the vice president walked the few blocks to the Petersen house, just across from Ford's Theater, where Lincoln had been carried. Admitted to the bedroom where the cabinet and military leaders were gathered around the president's deathbed, Johnson stood with his hat in his hand looking down saying nothing. He then took Robert Lincoln's hand, whispered a few words to him, conversed with Stanton, and went to another parlor to pay his respects to Mary Todd Lincoln. Somberly, he walked back to Kirkwood House. There, in his parlor, at ten o'clock that morning after Lincoln's death, Johnson took the oath of office from Chief Justice Salmon P. Chase.[13]

A Stormy Presidency

Lincoln's death stunned the nation and elevated the often harshly criticized wartime president to a sanctified martyr. In Washington, some Radical Republicans viewed Lincoln's death as a godsend. They held, as Johnson's friend Forney wrote in the Philadelphia *Press*, that "a sterner and less gentle hand may at this juncture have been required to take hold of the reins of Government." Johnson's fiery rhetoric in the Senate and as war governor, his early embrace of the "state suicide" theory that secession had reduced the southern states to the status of territories, to be readmitted under terms set by Congress, his call for expropriation of plantation lands, his authorship of the Homestead Act, all suggested that the new president would act more sympathetically toward Radical Reconstruction than would Lincoln. "Johnson, we have faith in you," the Radical Republican Senator Ben Wade told the new president. "By the Gods, there will be no trouble now in running this government."[14]

Johnson also won admiration for his gallant treatment of Mrs. Lincoln, who was too distraught to leave the White House for more than a month after her husband's death. Rather than move into the White House, which served as the president's office as well as his residence, President Johnson worked out of a suite of rooms in the Treasury Department (marked today by a plaque on the door). However, the spirit of good will evaporated almost a soon as Johnson began making decisions regarding Reconstruction.

Showing a strange amalgam of political courage and "pigheaded" stubbornness, Andrew Johnson confounded both his supporters and his adversaries. By the end of May 1865, it became clear that, like Lincoln, he intended to pursue a more lenient course toward Reconstruction than the Radicals in Congress wanted. Members of Congress grumbled when Johnson handed pardons to former Confederate leaders, suspected that the plebeian president took pride in having former aristocrats petition him. Congress was further shocked when the new governments formed under Johnson's plan enacted "Black Codes" that sought to regulate and restrict the activities of the freedmen. There was fear also that the former Confederate states would send Confederate officers and officeholders to reclaim their seats in Congress and undo the legislative accomplishments of the wartime Republican majorities. When the president opposed granting political rights to the freedmen, white southerners looked to him as a defender of white supremacy and as their protector against Radical retribution. The Democratic party considered Johnson as one of their own, who might be induced to return to their fold.[15]

The predominantly Republican Washington press corps had at first embraced President Johnson, assuring their readers that he supported black suffrage and other Radical measures. Forney celebrated his old friend as a "practical statesman" whose policies offered a common ground for "all earnest loyalists." Whatever honeymoon the new president enjoyed with Congress and the press ended in February 1866 when Johnson vetoed the Freedmen's Bureau bill. The veto shocked Republican conservatives and drove them into alliance with the Radicals against the president. The press and even Forney deserted Johnson. That fall, Johnson conducted a disastrous "swing around the circle," campaigning by train in favor of congressional candidates who supported his policies. Egged on by hecklers, he made intemperate remarks that further alienated the voters and resulted in the election of an even more hostile Congress. The new Congress seized the initiative on Reconstruction from the president—most notably with a constitutional amendment giving the freedmen the right to vote—and passed legislation to limit his responses. Among these laws, the Tenure of Office Act prohibited the president from firing cabinet officers and other appointees without Senate approval. Johnson considered the act unconstitutional—as indeed the Supreme Court would later declare it—and in February 1868 he fired his secretary of war, Edwin Stanton, for insubordination.[16]

The Impeachment of Andrew Johnson

Although Johnson's term was coming to a close and he had little chance of nomination by any party, the House of Representatives voted to impeach the president. The New York *Tribune*'s editor Horace Greeley thought this a foolhardy tactic. "Why hang a man who is bent on hanging himself?" Greeley asked. But the Republican members of Congress and their allies in the press wanted to take no chance of the president's sabotaging congressional Reconstruction during his last months in office. Said Thaddeus Stevens, leader of the House impeachers: "I don't want to hurt the man's feelings by telling him he is a rascal. I'd rather put it mildly, and say he hasn't got off that inaugural drunk yet, and just let him retire to get sobered." The House voted for impeachment, and on March 5, 1868, the United States Senate convened as a court to consider removing Johnson from the presidency. As the trial opened, the majority of the northern press favored conviction, but as the proceedings wound on, a profound sense of disillusionment set in among the correspondents, who communicated their dismay to their readers.[17]

Correspondent George Alfred Townsend described Johnson's Senate trial as "a more terrible scene than the trial of Judas Iscariot might be before the College of Cardinals." Not a single Democrat countenanced the impeachment, he pointed out, "It was purely within the political organization which had nominated the offender." Although Townsend was a Republican who considered Johnson a barrier against any settlement of "the Southern question," when he arrived at the Capitol he found none except Charles Sumner and Thaddeus Stevens who seemed excited over Johnson's policies. "It was his abuse of the party patronage which was an unforgiven sin." Johnson took patronage away from his critics and purged over 1,600 postmasters. In addition, Townsend noted: "He had disobeyed an act of Congress, of doubtful validity, taking away from him the power to make ad-interim appointments, or those made between sessions of Congress. This was a challenge to every member of Congress in the regular caucus ranks that off straight come the heads of HIS post-master, HIS revenue officials, HIS clerks, and HIS brothers-in-law." [18]

Rather than appear in the Senate chamber personally, President Johnson wisely left his defense to his attorneys. Although Republicans enjoyed a more than two-thirds majority in the Senate at the time, seven Republicans—fearing impeachment's negative impact on the office of the presidency—broke with their party. As a result, the impeachers failed by a single vote to achieve the two-thirds majority necessary to convict the president. In the 1868 elections, Johnson endorsed the Democratic candidate, Horatio Seymour, and was deeply disappointed over the victory of the Republican, U.S. Grant. Refusing to attend Grant's inauguration, Johnson left the White House in March 1869, discredited but not disgraced. Out of office for the first time in thirty years, he could not stay retired. That fall he campaigned for a Senate seat from Tennessee and lost. Never giving up, Johnson tried again in January 1875 and won back a seat in the Senate that had once tormented him. [19]

The only former U.S. president ever to return to serve in the Senate, Johnson saw his election as a vindication and came back to Washington in triumph. He took his oath of office on March 5, along with Lincoln's other vice president, Hannibal Hamlin, reelected a senator from Maine. (Both men had begun their congressional service in the House of Representatives on the same day, thirty-two years earlier.) Hamlin in 1866 had resigned as collector of the port of Boston as a public protest against Johnson's policies on Reconstruction. The oath was administered by Vice President Henry Wilson, who as a senator had voted for Johnson's conviction and for his disqualification from holding future office. When Johnson stepped forward to shake hands first with Hamlin and then Wilson, the chamber erupted into cheers. A reporter asked if he would use his new position to settle some old scores, to which Johnson replied, "I have no enemies to punish nor friends to reward." The special session ended on March 24, and Johnson returned to Tennessee. At the home of a granddaughter, he suffered a stroke and died on July 31, 1875. A marble bust of Johnson, sculpted with a typically pugnacious and defiant expression, looks down from the gallery at the Senate chamber, where he served on three occasions as a senator, briefly presided as vice president, and was tried and acquitted in a court of impeachment. [20]

NOTES

[1] H. Draper Hunt, *Hannibal Hamlin of Maine: Lincoln's First Vice-President* (Syracuse, NY, 1969), pp. 196–98; Lloyd Paul Stryker, *Andrew Johnson: A Study in Courage* (New York, 1929), p. 167.

[2] Hans L. Trefousse, *Andrew Johnson: A Biography* (New York, 1989), pp. 188–91; John W. Forney, *Anecdotes of Public Men* (New York, 1873), 1:177.

[3] Trefousse, Andrew Johnson, pp. 20–23.

[4] Ibid., pp. 35–50.

[5] Ibid, pp. 43, 51–83; Donald W. Riddle, *Congressman Abraham Lincoln* (Urbana, IL, 1957), pp. 144, 147, 159.

[6] Trefousse, *Andrew Johnson*, pp. 84–127; Eric Foner, *Reconstruction: America's Unfinished Revolution, 1863–1877* (New York, 1988), p. 176; LeRoy P. Graf, ed., *The Papers of Andrew Johnson*, vol. 7, *1864–1865* (Knoxville, TN, 1986), p. 9.

[7] Christopher Dell, *Lincoln and the War Democrats: The Grand Erosion of Conservative Tradition* (Rutherford, NJ, 1975), pp. 36–37, 80.

[8] Ibid., pp. 202, 238–39, 289; Foner, pp. 43–44.

[9] Hunt, pp. 178–89; Trefousse, *Andrew Johnson*, pp. 176–79; Stryker, pp. 121–23; Forney, 1:166–67, 2:48.

[10] Graf, ed., 7:110, 222, 251–53.

[11] Ibid., 7:30.

[12] Ibid., 7:420–21, 427.

[13] See Jim Bishop, *The Day Lincoln Was Shot* (New York, 1955).

[14] Dell, p. 323; Foner, p. 177.

[15] Graf, ed., 7:639; Foner, pp. 176–216; Joel H. Silbey, *A Respectable Minority: The Democratic Party in the Civil War Era, 1860–1868* (New York, 1877), pp. 178–79.

[16] Donald A. Ritchie, *Press Gallery: Congress and the Washington Correspondents* (Cambridge, MA, 1991), pp. 79–90; Foner, pp. 261–71.

[17] Ritchie, pp. 83–84; Hans L. Trefousse, *Impeachment of a President: Andrew Johnson, the Blacks, and Reconstruction* (Knoxville, TN, 1975), pp. 146–64; Benjamin Perley Poore, *Perley's Reminiscences of Sixty Years in the Nation's Metropolis* (Philadelphia, 1886), 2:229.

[18] George Alfred Townsend, *Washington, Outside and Inside* (Hartford, CT, 1873), pp. 506–7; Foner, p. 266.

[19] Michael Les Benedict, *The Impeachment and Trial of Andrew Johnson* (New York, 1973), pp. 126–80.

[20] Trefousse, *Andrew Johnson*, pp. 353–79; Stryker, pp. 805–11, Hunt, pp. 202–5.

Chapter 17

SCHUYLER COLFAX

1869–1873

SCHUYLER COLFAX

Chapter 17

SCHUYLER COLFAX

17th Vice President: 1869–1873

The Vice Presidency is an elegant office whose occupant must find it his principal business to try to discover what is the use of there being such an office at all.

—*Indianapolis Journal,* MARCH 7, 1871

As amiable a man who ever served in Congress, good-natured, kindly, cordial, and always diplomatic, Indiana's Schuyler Colfax won the nickname "Smiler" Colfax. Through two of the most tumultuous decades in American public life, Colfax glided smoothly from the Whig to Know-Nothing to Republican parties, mingling easily with both conservatives and radicals. He rose to become Speaker of the House and vice president and seemed poised to achieve his goal of the presidency. Along the way, there were those who doubted the sincerity behind the smile and suspected that for all his political dexterity, Colfax stood for nothing save his own advancement. Those close to President Abraham Lincoln later revealed that he considered Speaker Colfax an untrustworthy intriguer, and President Ulysses S. Grant seemed relieved when the Republican convention dumped Vice President Colfax from the ticket in 1872. Even the press, which counted the Indiana editor as a colleague and pumped him up to national prominence, eventually turned on Colfax and shredded his once admirable reputation until he disappeared into the forgotten recesses of American history.[1]

Early Years

Schuyler Colfax was born into a family of distinguished heritage but depleted circumstances. His grandfather, who had fought in the American Revolution and served closely with George Washington, married Hester Schuyler, a cousin of General Philip Schuyler, and named one of his sons for Washington and another for Schuyler. Schuyler Colfax, Sr., became a teller in a bank on New York City's Wall Street. In 1820 he married Hannah Stryker, the daughter of a widowed boardinghouse keeper. He died of tuberculosis two years later, as his wife was expecting her first child. Four months after his father's death, Schuyler, Jr. was born in New York City on March 23, 1823.

As a boy, Colfax attended public schools until he was ten, when he was obliged to work as a clerk in a retail store to help support himself, his mother, and his grandmother. Three years later, his mother married George W. Matthews, and the family moved to New Carlisle, Indiana. Young Colfax worked in his stepfather's store, which served also as the village post office. Townspeople later recalled that Colfax would sit on barrels reading newspapers as they arrived by post. He borrowed whatever books he could get to provide himself with an education. In 1841, the family moved to South Bend, where Matthews was elected as the Whig candidate for county auditor and hired Schuyler as his deputy. Enjoying politics, the boy became active in a "moot legislature," where he gained his first experience in debate and parliamentary procedure.[2]

SCHUYLER COLFAX

Politics and the Press

At sixteen, Colfax wrote to Horace Greeley, editor of the influential Whig newspaper, the *New-York Tribune*, offering to send occasional articles. Always open to new talent, Greeley agreed and published the boy's writings on Indiana politics, beginning a correspondence and friendship that lasted for the rest of their lives. Colfax also reported on the Indiana legislature for the *Indiana State Journal*, and when he was nineteen local Whigs engaged him to edit the South Bend *Free Press*. The young editor described himself as an "uncompromising Whig." He idolized Henry Clay and embraced all of the Whig reforms, taking a pledge of abstinence from alcoholic spirits (but not from the cigars he loved). In 1844 he married a childhood sweetheart, Evelyn Clark, and by the next year was able to purchase the *Free Press*, renaming it the *St. Joseph Valley Register*. The writer Harriet Beecher Stowe later proclaimed it "a morally pure paper."[3]

Advancing from the editorial page into politics, Colfax served as a delegate to the Whig convention of 1848 and to the convention that drafted a new constitution for Indiana in 1849. He led the opposition to a provision in the constitution that barred African Americans from settling in Indiana or those already in the state from purchasing land. Despite his efforts, this racial barrier stood until ruled unconstitutional as a consequence of the Thirteenth Amendment to the Constitution in 1865. In 1851, the Whigs chose Colfax to run for Congress. At that time, Indiana was a Democratic state and Colfax narrowly lost to the incumbent Democrat. He declined to run again in 1852. Dismayed over the disintegration of the Whig party and offended by Senator Stephen A. Douglas' Kansas-Nebraska Act that repealed the Missouri Compromise, Colfax again ran for Congress in 1854 as an Anti-Nebraska candidate. His friend and fellow editor Horace Greeley, who had served a brief term in 1849, encouraged him: "I thought it would be a nuisance and a sacrifice for me to go to Congress," he advised Colfax, "but I was mistaken; it did me lasting good. I never was brought so palpably and tryingly into collision with the embodied scoundrelism of the nation as while in Congress."[4]

Building a New Party

Antislavery Whigs like Colfax sought to build a new party that combined the antislavery elements among the Whigs, Democrats, and Free Soilers, a coalition that eventually emerged as the Republican party. For a brief time, however, it seemed likely that a nativist organization, the Know-Nothings, might become the new majority party. The first Know-Nothing lodge in Indiana opened in early 1854 and by election time the party had grown, in the words of one Methodist minister, "as thick as the Locusts in Egypt." The Know-Nothings opposed slavery and alcohol but turned their greatest passions against Catholics and immigrants. Although Colfax shared these nativist prejudices (arguing that "Protestant foreigners, who are thoroughly Americanized" should be admitted into the party), he made it clear that he would remain only if the Know-Nothings kept a firm antislavery plank in their platform. When the new congressman arrived in the House of Representatives in 1855, it was unclear which members belonged to what party. The *New-York Tribune Almanac* estimated that there were 118 Anti-Nebraska representatives, a number that included Republicans, anti-Nebraska Democrats, and antislavery Know-Nothings, comprising a slight majority of the House. By the following year, the Know-Nothings had already peaked and declined, and Colfax announced that he would run for reelection as a Republican.[5]

The House of Representatives proved an ideal arena for Colfax's talents. Short and stocky, fair-haired, with a ready smile, he got along well with his colleagues in private but never hesitated to do battle with the opposition on the House floor. When Republicans held the majority, he served energetically as chairman of the Committee on Post Offices and Post Roads, handling the kind of patronage that built political organizations. Never having been a lawyer, he could put complex issues of the day into layman's terms. In 1856, his speech attacking laws passed by the proslavery legislature in Kansas became the most widely requested Republican campaign document. His speech raised warnings that it was a short step between enslaving blacks and suppressing the civil liberties of whites. Watching Colfax battle southern representatives over the slavery issue, James Dabney McCabe recorded that "Mr. Colfax took an active part in the debate, giving and receiving hard blows with all the skill of an old gladiator."[6]

Colfax traveled widely, spoke frequently, and helped fuse the various Republican and antislavery groups into a unified party for the 1860 election. When the southern Democrats seceded and put House Republicans in the majority, he considered running for Speaker, but after testing the waters declined to be a candidate. He resumed his chairmanship of the Post Office Committee. Colfax took a moderate position on emancipation and other issues of the day, maintaining close ties with both wings of his party. He enjoyed direct access to President Lincoln and often served as a conduit of information and opinion from Horace Greeley and other Republican editors. He worked tirelessly on behalf of the Union, recruiting regiments and raising public spirits. Yet antiwar sentiments ran strong in Indiana and many other northern states, and in 1862 Colfax faced a tough campaign for reelection against David A. Turpie. Winning a narrow victory further elevated Colfax within the party at a time when many other Republicans, including House Speaker Galusha Grow, were defeated. When the Thirty-eighth Congress convened in December 1863, House Republicans—with their numbers considerably thinned—elected Schuyler Colfax Speaker, despite President Lincoln's preference for a Speaker less tied to the Radical faction of his party.[7]

Speaker of the House

As Speaker of the House, Schuyler Colfax presided, in the words of the journalist Ben: Perley Poore, "in rather a slap-dash-knock-'em-down-auctioneer style, greatly in variance with the decorous dignity of his predecessors." He had studied and mastered the rules of the House, and both sides considered his rulings fair. Credited as being the most popular Speaker since Henry Clay, Colfax aspired to be as powerful as Clay. Certainly, he shared Clay's sense of the dramatic,

once stepping down from the presiding officer's chair to urge the House to expel an Ohio Democrat who had advocated recognizing the independence of the Confederacy. Another time the Speaker broke precedent by requesting that his vote be recorded in favor of the Thirteenth Amendment. Yet with the exception of the power to appoint members to committees, the Speaker of the House was still mostly a figurehead. Observers declared the real power in the House to be the tough-minded Pennsylvanian Thaddeus Stevens, chairman of the Appropriations Committee and de facto Republican floor leader.[8]

Washington newspaper correspondents celebrated the election of one of their own as Speaker and threw a dinner in his honor. "We journalists and men of the newspaper press do love you, and claim you as bone of our bone and flesh of our flesh," said correspondent Sam Wilkeson. "Fill your glasses, all, in an invocation to the gods for long life, greater success, and ever-increasing happiness to our editorial brother in the Speaker's Chair." In reply Colfax thanked the press for sustaining him through all his elections. Trained in journalism, Speaker Colfax applied the lessons of his craft to his political career, making himself available for interviews, planting stories, sending flattering notes to editors, suggesting editorials, and spreading patronage. A widower (his wife died in 1863) with no children, Colfax was free to socialize nightly with his friends on Washington's "Newspaper Row." He hoped to parlay his popularity with the press into a national following that would make him the first journalist to occupy the White House.[9]

The press lavished more attention on Speaker Colfax than they had on Galusha Grow or any of his immediate predecessors. They praised the regular Friday night receptions that the Speaker and his mother held and commended him for the "courtesy, dignity, and equitability which he exhibited in the discharge of the important duties of the chair." It was harder for the press to detect whether Speaker Colfax actually had any influence on specific legislation. He gave the radical firebrands wide latitude, while speaking with moderation himself. At one point, when Radical Republicans were prepared to introduce a resolution in the party conference that defended the Republican record and called for the use of black soldiers in the Union army, Colfax outflanked them with a motion that substituted patriotic flag waving for partisanship, calling instead for all loyal men to stand by the Union. His action was taken as an effort to give the Republican party a less vindictive image that would build a broader base for congressional elections.[10]

On April 14, 1865, Colfax called at the White House to talk over Reconstruction and other matters with President Lincoln before Colfax left on a long tour of the western states and territories. With the war won, Lincoln was in an ebullient mood and held a long and pleasant conversation with the Speaker (whom Lincoln privately regarded as "a little intriguer—plausible, aspiring beyond his capacity, and not trustworthy"). The president invited the Speaker to join his party at Ford's Theater that night, but Colfax declined. Later that evening, he was awakened with news that the president had been shot and rushed to spend the night in the room where Lincoln died.[11]

Reconstructing the South

During the summer of 1865, Colfax toured the mining regions between the Rocky Mountains and the Pacific. Newspaper correspondent Albert Richardson, who accompanied him, recorded that the trip proved to be "one continuous ovation" for Colfax, with brass bands, banquets, and public receptions, during which the Speaker made seventy speeches. He returned to a capital still uncertain over how the new President Andrew Johnson would handle the reconstruction of the southern states. Radicals in Congress trusted that Johnson would use federal troops to support tough policies toward the former Confederacy, but there were signs that Johnson favored a speedier, more lenient readmission of the states. That November, at a serenade to mark his return to Washington, Speaker Colfax made some remarks that seemed impromptu but that may have been prearranged. He endorsed Johnson's attempts to begin Reconstruction prior to congressional legislation and set as a minimum for the return of the southern states a guarantee that freedmen would be treat-

ed equally under the law. He made no mention of the radical demand that the freedmen also have the right to vote. The speech won widespread praise in the North, where it was perceived as the firm foundation of Republican policy on which both the president and Congress could stand.[12]

Colfax's efforts at party harmony and a moderate course of Reconstruction were short lived. Johnson resented Colfax's preempting his own statement of policy on the subject. The president's plans to reconstruct the South showed little regard for the rights of the freedmen, and he vetoed such relatively moderate congressional efforts as the Freedmen's Bureau bill. His action drove moderate and radical Republicans into an alliance that brought about congressional Reconstruction of the South. Finally, Johnson's dismissal of Secretary of War Edwin Stanton in violation of the Tenure of Office Act convinced even moderates like Colfax that the president must be impeached. Through all of these dramatic events, Colfax's most astonishing success was his ability to retain the support of all sides in his party and to hold House Republicans together. The party defections that saved Johnson took place in the Senate rather than the House.[13]

From Speaker to Vice President

As the 1868 presidential election approached, Speaker Colfax believed the nomination of Ulysses S. Grant to be "resistless." As for himself, he declined to run either for the Senate or for governor of Indiana, leaving the door open for the vice-presidential nomination. Colfax insisted that presiding over the House as Speaker was "the more important office" than presiding over the Senate as vice president. But the vice-presidency was the more direct avenue to the presidency. At the convention, his chief rivals for the second spot were Senate President pro tempore Ben Wade and Massachusetts Senator Henry Wilson. Colfax polled fourth on the first ballot and gained steadily with each subsequent ballot. The temperance forces were delighted that Colfax's headquarters distributed no liquor, in contrast to Senator Wade, who handed out spirits freely among the delegates. Among Republicans there was a collective sense that the abstinent Colfax would balance a ticket with Grant, who had been known to drink heavily.[14]

Colfax stayed in Washington while the Republican convention met in Chicago. His good friend, William Orton, head of the Western Union Telegraph Company, arranged for Colfax to receive dispatches from the convention every ten minutes. On May 21 Colfax was in the Speaker's Lobby when he received Orton's telegram announcing his nomination. Cheers broke out, and the room quickly filled with congressmen wishing to offer congratulations. As he left the lobby, Colfax was greeted by House staff members, who "gathered around him in the most affectionate manner and tendered him their regards." Citizens hailed him as he walked across the Capitol grounds. On the Senate side, Bluff Ben Wade received the news that he had been beaten and said, "Well, I guess it will be all right; he deserves it, and he will be a good presiding officer." The news was received with seemingly universal applause. "His friends love him devotedly," wrote one admirer, "and his political adversaries . . . respect him thoroughly."[15]

For years, Colfax had addressed Sunday schools and temperance revival meetings, quoting from the Bible and urging his listeners to a life of virtue. He won support from the religious magazines as a "Christian Statesman." One campaign biography praised his "spotless integrity" and declared, "So pure is his personal character, that the venom of political enmity has never attempted to fix a stain upon it." Democrats, however, lambasted Colfax as a bigot for the anti-Catholicism of his Know-Nothing past. Republicans dismissed these charges as mudslinging and organized Irish and German Grant and Colfax Clubs to court the Catholic and foreign-born vote. (Although it was not known at the time, U.S. Grant had also once joined the Know-Nothings and apparently shared their anti-Catholic prejudices.)[16]

In November 1868, Grant and Colfax were narrowly elected over the Democratic ticket headed by New York Governor Horatio Seymour. Days after the election, the vice president-elect married Ellen Wade, niece of the Ohio senator he had defeated for the vice-presidential nomination. The groom was forty-five and the bride "about thirty," an attractive and charming woman. By April 1870 their son Schuyler III was born. This domestic bliss would in fact contribute to Colfax's political undoing. As a married man, he found less time to socialize with his old friends in the press, and invitations to the lavish receptions at his new home became harder for reporters to receive, causing considerable resentment among his old friends on Newspaper Row, who thought he was putting on airs. Not a wealthy man, the new vice president could never say no to a gift. He grew indiscreet in his acceptance of everything from sterling silver to free railroad passes. In 1868 Colfax also accepted some railroad stocks from his friend Representative Oakes Ames, who promised handsome dividends. Neither suspected the political price that the stock would ultimately exact.[17]

Plans to Retire

The first Speaker of the House ever elected vice president (a previous former Speaker, James K. Polk, had won the presidency in 1844), Colfax moved easily to the Senate chamber as a man long familiar with the ways of Capitol Hill. The Senate proved an easier body to preside over, leaving him with time on his hands to travel, lecture, and write for the press. The Indianapolis *Journal* observed that "the Vice Presidency is an elegant office whose occupant must find it his principal business to try to discover what is the use of there being such an office at all." Colfax consulted periodically with President Grant, but, as one Democratic paper sneered, the vice president carried "more wind than weight." His distance from the president proved not to be a disadvantage when various scandals began to tarnish Grant and his administration. Speculation soon arose that Colfax would replace Grant in the next election. There was much surprise, therefore, when in September 1870, at age forty-seven, Colfax announced that he intended to retire at the end of his term. "I will then have had eighteen years of continuous service at Washington, mostly on a stormy sea—long enough for any one; and my ambition is all gratified and satisfied." This was an old tactic for Colfax, who periodically before had announced his retirement and then changed his mind. Some believed he intended the announcement to further separate himself from the Grant administration and open the way for the presidential nomination in 1872. But the national press and Senator Henry Wilson took the announcement at face value, and before long the movement to replace him went further than Colfax had anticipated.[18]

Colfax predictably changed his mind early in 1872 and acceded to the wishes of his friends that he stand for reelection on "the old ticket." President Grant may have questioned Colfax's intentions. In 1871 the president had sent his vice president an extraordinary letter, informing him that Secretary of State Hamilton Fish wished to retire and asking him "in plain English" to give up the vice-presidency for the State Department. Grant appeared to be removing Colfax as a potential rival. "In all my heart I hope you will say yes," he wrote, "though I confess the sacrifice you will be making." Colfax declined, and a year later when Senator Wilson challenged Colfax for renomination, the president chose to remain neutral in the contest.[19]

For a man who had assiduously courted the press for so long, Colfax found himself abandoned by the Washington correspondents, who overwhelmingly supported Henry Wilson. Colfax's slide in the opinion of the Washington press corps had its roots in a dinner at the beginning of his term as vice president, when he had lectured them on the need to exercise their responsibilities prudently, since in their hands lay the making and unmaking of great men. The reporters had noted archly that Colfax, like other politicians, had never complained about the "making" of their reputations, just the "unmaking." Mary Clemmer Ames, a popular newspaper writer in Washington, attributed Colfax's downfall to envy within the press corps. He did not invite them to his dinners and receptions, so they decided to "write him down." The naturally cynical and skeptical reporters, apparently considering the vice president's sanctimoniousness contradictory to his newfound riches and opulent lifestyle, sought to take him down a few pegs. One correspondent likened Colfax to "a penny dip burning high on the altar among the legitimate tapers of State." By contrast, the reporters liked Senator Wilson, who leaked so freely that they dubbed him "the official reporter of the [secret] executive sessions of the Senate." Colfax bitterly charged that Wilson had invited newspapermen in "nearly every evening, asking them to telegraph that he was gaining steadily, that I did not care for it." When he lost the nomination, the vice president magnanimously shook Senator Wilson's hand, but one observer noticed that his famous smile had become "a whitened skeleton of its former self." At least Colfax's defeat spared him having to run against his old mentor, Horace Greeley, presidential candidate that year on a fusion ticket of Democrats and Liberal Republicans.[20]

The Crédit Mobilier Scandal

As a man still in his forties, Colfax might well have continued his political career after the vice-presidency, except for his connection to the worst scandal in nineteenth-century U.S. political history. In September 1872, as the presidential campaign was getting underway, the *New York Sun* broke the four-year-old story about the Crédit Mobilier, a finance company created to underwrite construction of the transcontinental Union Pacific Railroad. Since the railroad depended on federal subsidies, the company had recruited Massachusetts Representative Oakes Ames to distribute stock among the key members of Congress who could help them the most. Some members had paid for the stock at a low value, others had put no money down at all but simply let the generous dividends pay for the stock. On Oakes Ames' list were the names of both Schuyler Colfax and Henry Wilson, along with such other Washington luminaries as Representatives James Garfield and James G. Blaine. In South Bend, Indiana, Vice President Colfax made a public statement that completely dissociated himself from Crédit Mobilier, assuring his listeners that he never owned a dollar of stock that he had not paid for.[21]

On January 7, 1873, the House committee investigating the Crédit Mobilier scandal called the vice president to testify. Ames claimed that, since Colfax had lacked the money to buy the stock, the stock had been paid for by its own inflated dividends. Ames' notes indicated that Colfax had received an additional $1,200 in dividends.

On the stand, Colfax swore flatly that he had never received a dividend check from Ames, but his testimony was contradicted by evidence from the files of the House sergeant at arms. Without missing a beat, Colfax insisted that Ames himself must have signed and cashed the check. Then the committee produced evidence from Colfax's Washington bank that two days after the payment had been made, he had deposited $1,200 in cash—and the deposit slip was in Colfax's own handwriting. Taking two weeks to explain, Colfax claimed that he had received $200 from his stepfather (who worked as a clerk in the House of Representatives) and another $1,000 from George Nesbitt, a campaign contributor by then deceased. This story seemed so patently self-serving and far-fetched that even his strongest supporters dismissed it. Making matters worse, the committee disclosed evidence suggesting that Nesbitt, who manufactured stationery, had bribed Colfax as chairman of the House Post Office Committee in order to receive government contracts for envelopes. A resolution to impeach Colfax failed to pass by a mostly party-line vote, in part because just a few weeks remained in his term. The pious statesman had been exposed, and the public was unforgiving. Colfax left the vice-presidency in disgrace, becoming a symbol of the sordidness of Gilded Age politics. Later in 1873, when the failure of the transcontinental railroads to make their bond payments triggered a disastrous financial collapse on Wall Street, plunging the nation into a depression that lasted for the rest of the decade, one ruined investor muttered that it was "all Schuyler Colfax's fault, damn him." [22]

Later Years

Others implicated in Crédit Mobilier survived politically. Henry Wilson was elected vice president. James Garfield became president in 1880, and James G. Blaine won the Republican presidential nomination, but not the election, in 1884. Colfax, however, returned to private life in South Bend, Indiana. Briefly, there was talk that his friend William Orton would put up the funds to enable him to purchase the prestigious *New-York Tribune* after Horace Greeley's death in 1872, but the deal fell through. Then a new opportunity developed. Called upon to deliver a short speech at the unveiling of a statue of Abraham Lincoln in Springfield, Illinois, Colfax discovered that the public had an insatiable appetite for information about their martyred president. He commenced a lucrative career as a public lecturer (up to $2,500 per speech) on his wartime relationship with Lincoln. From time to time, Colfax's name surfaced as a candidate for the House or the Senate, or for the presidential nomination, but he declined to become a candidate. "You can't imagine the repugnance with which I now view the service of the many headed public," he wrote, "with all its toils, its innumerable exactions of all kinds, the never ending work and worry, the explanations about everything which the public think they have a right to, the lack of independence as to your goings and comings, the misunderstandings, the envyings, backbitings, etc., etc., etc." On January 13, 1885, on his way to a speaking engagement in Iowa, Colfax was stricken by a heart attack and died while waiting at a railroad station in Mankato, Minnesota, where the temperature dipped to thirty below zero. Unrecognized by those around him, the former Speaker and vice president was identified only by papers in his pocket. [23]

Doggerel from a critical newspaper perhaps served as the epitaph for Schuyler Colfax's rise to national prominence and precipitous fall from grace:

> A beautiful smiler came in our midst,
> Too lively and fair to remain;
> They stretched him on racks till the soul of
>   Colfax
> Flapped up into Heaven again,
> May the fate of poor Schuyler warn men of a
>   smiler,
> Who dividends gets on the brain! [24]

NOTES

[1] James G. Blaine, *Twenty Years of Congress: From Lincoln to Garfield* (Norwich, CT, 1884), 1:497–98; Neil MacNeil, *Forge of Democracy: The House of Representatives* (New York, 1963), p. 69; Allan G. Bogue, *The Congressman's Civil War* (New York, 1989), p. 117.

[2] Willard H. Smith, *Schuyler Colfax: The Changing Fortunes of a Political Idol* (Indianapolis, 1952), pp. 1–7; Albert D. Richardson, *A Personal History of Ulysses S. Grant with a Portrait and Sketch of Schuyler Colfax* (Hartford, CT, 1868), p. 553.

[3] Smith, pp. 13–16; Edward Winslow Martin [James Dabney McCabe], *The Life and Public Service of Schuyler Colfax* (New York, 1868), p. 15.

[4] Richardson, pp. 554–55; Donald A. Ritchie, *Press Gallery: Congress and the Washington Correspondents* (Cambridge, MA, 1991), p. 43.

[5] William E. Gienapp, *The Origins of the Republican Party, 1852–1856* (New York, 1987), pp. 109, 180–81, 240–41, 245.

[6] Ibid, p. 359; Martin [James Dabney McCabe], p. 109.

[7] Charles Edward Russell, *Blaine of Maine: His Life and Times* (New York, 1931), p. 237; Bogue, p. 116; David Herbert Donald, *Lincoln* (New York, 1995), pp. 468–69.

[8] Benjamin Perley Poore, *Perley's Reminiscences of Sixty Years in the National Metropolis* (Philadelphia, 1887) 2:211; McNeil, pp. 69, 171; James G. Blaine, *Twenty Years of Congress: From Lincoln to Garfield* (Norwich, CT, 1884), 1:325–26, 497–98; Albert G. Riddle, *Recollections of War Times: Reminiscences of Men and Events in Washington, 1860–1865* (New York, 1895), p. 222.

[9] Ritchie, pp. 63–64, 67.

[10] Bogue, pp. 116, 125.

[11] Smith, pp. 202–9.

[12] Richardson, p. 559; Michael Les Benedict, *A Compromise of Principle: Congressional Republicans and Reconstruction 1863–1869* (New York, 1974), p. 130; Eric Foner, *Reconstruction: America's Unfinished Revolution, 1863–1877* (New York, 1988), pp. 181, 226.

[13] Benedict, pp. 168, 255; Smith, pp. 222–26.

[14] Foner, p. 338; Smith, p. 284, Russell, p. 237.

[15] Martin [James Dabney McCabe], pp. 246–47, 253.

[16] Russell, p. 237; Richardson, p. 560; Tyler Anbinder, *Nativism and Slavery: The Northern Know Nothings and the Politics of the 1850s* (New York, 1992), pp. 271–74.

[17] Smith, pp. 308–9, 312; Mark Wahlgren Summers, *The Era of Good Stealings* (New York, 1993), p. 66; McNeil, p. 198.

[18] Smith, pp. 316–17, 324, 326, 333; Ernest A. McKay, *Henry Wilson: Practical Radical: A Portrait of a Politician* (Port Washington, NY, 1971), p. 225.

[19] George S. Sirgiovanni, ''Dumping the Vice President: An Historical Overview and Analysis,'' *Presidential Studies Quarterly* 24 (Fall 1994): 769–71.

[20] Poore, 2:243; Ritchie, pp. 96, 106; Richard H. Abbott, *Cobbler in Congress: The Life of Henry Wilson, 1812–1875* (Lexington, KY, 1972), p. 243; Smith, pp. 358–59; Summers, *Era of Good Stealings*, p. 66; Mark Wahlgren Summers, *The Press Gang: Newspapers and Politics, 1865–1878* (Chapel Hill, NC, 1994), pp. 152–53.

[21] Smith, pp. 369–74; Ritchie, pp. 102–3.

[22] Smith, pp. 374–416; Russell, pp. 243–45; Sean Dennis Cashman, *America in the Gilded Age: From the Death of Lincoln to the Rise of Theodore Roosevelt* (New York, 1984), p. 197; Summers, *The Era of Good Stealings*, pp. 52–53, 66, 242; see also W. Allan Wilbur, ''The Credit Mobilier Scandal, 1873,'' in *Congress Investigates: A Documented History, 1792–1974*, ed. Arthur M. Schlesinger, Jr. and Roger Bruns (New York, 1975), pp. 1849–63.

[23] Merrill D. Peterson, *Lincoln in American Memory* (New York, 1994), p. 138; Smith, pp. 422, 430, 438–39; O.J. Hollister, *Life of Schuyler Colfax* (New York, 1886), pp. 385–91.

[24] Summers, *The Press Gang*, p. 154.

Chapter 18

HENRY WILSON
1873–1875

HENRY WILSON

Chapter 18

HENRY WILSON

18th Vice President: 1873–1875

He was not learned, he was not eloquent, he was not logical in a high sense, he was not always consistent in his political actions, and yet he gained the confidence of the people, and he retained it to the end of his life.

—SENATOR GEORGE BOUTWELL

Long before public opinion polling, Vice President Henry Wilson earned recognition as a master at reading the public's mind. During his eighteen years in the United States Senate, Wilson traveled relentlessly through his home state of Massachusetts. A typical day would find him visiting shops and factories around Boston. Then he would board the night train to Springfield, where he would rouse some political friend at 2 a.m. and spend the rest of the night talking over current issues, departing at dawn to catch the early train to Northampton or Greenfield. "After a week or two spent in that way," his friend George F. Hoar observed,

> never giving his own opinion, talking as if he were all things to all men, seeming to hesitate and falter and be frightened, so if you had met him and talked with him you would have said . . . that there was no more thought, nor more steadiness of purpose, or backbone in him than in an easterly cloud; but at length when the time came, and he had got ready, the easterly cloud seemed suddenly to have been charged with an electric fire and a swift and resistless bolt flashed out, and the righteous judgment of Massachusetts came from his lips.[1]

Such systematic sampling of public opinion enabled Wilson to represent the prevailing sentiments of his constituents and to make remarkably accurate political prognoses. This skill helped him build political alliances and parties and win elections. It also added an element of opportunism to Wilson's political maneuvering that brought him distrust, even from his political allies. Yet he did not simply follow the winds of public opinion whichever way they blew. Throughout his long political career, Wilson remained remarkably consistent in his support for human freedom and equality of rights for all men and women regardless of their color or class.

The Rise of Jeremiah Jones Colbath

Henry Wilson's life resembled a Dickens novel. Like Pip, David Copperfield, and Nicholas Nickleby, he overcame a childhood of hardship and privation through the strength of his character, his ambition, and occasional assistance from others. He was born Jeremiah Jones Colbath on February 16, 1812, in Farmington, New Hampshire. His shiftless and intemperate father named the child after a wealthy bachelor neighbor in vain hope of inheritance. The boy grew to hate the name, and when he came of age had it legally changed to Henry Wilson, inspired either by a biography of the Philadelphia school teacher Henry Wilson or by a portrait of the Rev. Henry Wilson in a volume on English clergymen. The Colbaths lived from hand to mouth; "Want sat by my cradle," he later recalled. "I know what it is to ask a mother for bread when she has none to give."[2]

When the boy was ten years old, his father apprenticed him to a nearby farmer, binding him to work until his twenty-first birthday. The apprenticeship supposedly allowed one month of school every year, so long as there was no work to be done, but he rarely had more than a few days of school at any time. Lacking formal education, he compensated by reading every book in the farmhouse and borrowing other books from neighbors. He read copiously from history, biography and philosophy. Also as part of his self-improvement efforts, at age nineteen he took a pledge of total abstinence from alcohol, which he maintained thereafter. In 1833 he reached twenty-one and was freed from his apprenticeship. Long estranged from his parents, the newly renamed Henry Wilson set out for new horizons. He hunted for employment in the mills of New Hampshire and then walked one hundred miles from Farmington to Boston. Just outside of Boston he settled in the town of Natick, where he learned shoemaking from a friend.[3]

The ambitious young cobbler worked so hard that by 1836 his health required he get some rest. Gathering his savings, Wilson traveled to Washington, D.C., to see the federal government. His attention was caught instead by the sight of slaves laboring in the fields of Maryland and Virginia and of slave pens and auctions within view of the Capitol Building. He left Washington determined "to give all that I had . . . to the cause of emancipation in America," he said. Wilson committed himself to the antislavery movement and years later took pride in introducing the legislation in Congress that ended slavery in the District of Columbia. Home from his journey, he enrolled briefly in three academies and then taught school for a year, falling in love with one of his students, Harriet Malvina Howe. They were married three years later, in 1840, when she turned sixteen.[4]

From Shoemaker to Politician

Although he harbored political aspirations, Wilson returned to the shoemaking business. Even during the economic recession that swept the country in the late 1830s, he prospered. Abandoning the cobbler's bench himself, he hired contract laborers and supervised their work, vastly increasing his production. As a factory owner, Wilson was able to build a handsome house for his family and to devote his attention more fully to civic affairs.[5]

An active member of the Natick Debating Society, Wilson became swept up in the leading reform issues of his day, temperance, educational reform, and antislavery, and these in turn shaped his politics. Although the Democratic party in Massachusetts appealed to workers and small businessmen like Wilson, he was drawn instead to the more upper-crust Whig party because it embraced the social reforms that he supported. At a time when the Whigs were seeking to expand their political base, Wilson's working-class background and image as the "Natick Cobbler" appealed to the party. During the 1830s and 1840s, the Whigs ran him repeatedly for the state legislature, and he won seats in its upper and lower houses. Unlike many other Whigs, Wilson mingled easily in the state's factories and saloons. He gathered political lieutenants around the state and invested some of his shoemaking earnings in the Boston *Republican*, which he edited from 1848 to 1851. He also joined the Natick militia, rising to brigadier general and proudly claiming the title "General Wilson" through the rest of his long political career.[6]

As a self-made man, Henry Wilson felt contempt for aristocrats, whether Boston Brahmins or southern planters. "I for one don't want the endorsement of the 'best society' in Boston until I am dead," he once declared, "—for it endorses everything that is dead." He reserved even greater contempt for aristocratic southerners who lived off the labor of their slaves, swearing that slavery must be ended. "Freedom and slavery are now arrayed against each other," he declared; "we must destroy slavery, or it will destroy liberty." Although the Whigs promoted numerous reforms, as a national party they included many southerners who supported slavery. In Massachusetts, the party split between "Cotton Whigs," with political and economic ties between the New England cotton mills and the southern cotton plantations, and the "Conscience Whigs," who placed freedom ahead of patronage and profits. Sensing the changing tides of public opinion, Wilson predicted that, if antislavery supporters in all the old parties could bind together to form a new party, they could sweep the northern elections and displace southerners from power in Washington. In 1848 he abandoned the Whigs for the new Free Soil party, which nominated Martin Van Buren for president on an antislavery platform.[7]

A Residue of Distrust

The Free Soil party proved to be premature. Wary voters defeated Wilson in his campaigns as the Free Soil candidate for the U.S. House of Representatives in 1852 and governor in 1853. Sadly disappointed in 1853 at the defeat of a new state constitution for which he had labored long and hard, Wilson responded by secretly joining the Order of the Star Spangled Banner, also known as the American or Know-Nothing party—an anti-Catholic and anti-immigrant, nativist movement. Given the collapse of the established parties, the Know-Nothings flourished briefly, offering Wilson an unsavory opportunity to promote his personal ambitions—despite the party's conflict with his political ideals of racial and religious equality. At the same time, Wilson called for the creation of "one great Republican party" in opposition to the Kansas-Nebraska Act, which threatened to open the western territories to slavery. In 1854, he ran as the Republican candidate for governor, but his strange maneuvering during and after the campaign convinced many Republicans that Wilson had sold them out by throwing the gubernatorial election to the Know-Nothings in return for being elected a U.S. senator by the Know-Nothings in the Massachusetts legislature, with the aid of Free Soilers and Democrats. Although Wilson identified himself as a Republican, his first Senate election left a residue of distrust that he would spend the rest of his life trying to live down.[8]

In the Senate, Henry Wilson was inevitably compared with his handsome, dignified, scholarly senior colleague from Massachusetts, Charles Sumner. An idealist and fierce foe of slavery, Sumner laced his speeches with classical allusions and gave every indication that he would appear quite natural in the toga of a Roman senator. Henry Wilson would have seemed ludicrous in Roman garb or in attempting to match Sumner's grandiloquent addresses. Listeners described Wilson instead as "an earnest man" who presented "the cold facts of a case" without relying on flamboyant oratory. George Boutwell, who served with him in Massachusetts and national politics, judged Wilson an especially effective speaker during elections and estimated that during the course of Wilson's career he spoke to more people than anyone else alive. Boutwell concluded of Wilson:

> He was not learned, he was not eloquent, he was not logical in a high sense, he was not always consistent in his political actions, and yet he gained the confidence of the people, and he retained it to the end of his life. His success may have been due in part to the circumstance that he was not far removed from the mass of the people in the particulars named, and that he acted in a period when fidelity to the cause of freedom and activity in its promotion satisfied the public demand.[9]

Despite their different backgrounds and personalities, Wilson and Sumner agreed strongly on their opposition to slavery and pooled their efforts to destroy the "peculiar institution." Even when people distrusted Wilson's wily political maneuvering or disdained his plebeian roots, they gave him credit for showing backbone in his fight against slavery. Massachusetts returned him to the Senate for three more terms, until his election as vice president.

Chairman of the Military Affairs Committee

During the 1850s, Wilson fought from the minority. When the southern states seceded in 1860 and 1861 and the Republicans moved into the majority, Henry Wilson assumed the chairmanship of the Senate Committee on Military Affairs, a key legislative post during the Civil War. In the months that Congress stood in recess, impatient Radical Republicans demanded quick military action against the South. In July 1861, at the war's first battle, along Bull Run creek in Manassas, Virginia, Wilson rode out with other senators, representatives, newspaper reporters, and members of Washington society to witness what they anticipated would be a Union victory. In his carriage, Senator Wilson carried a large hamper of sandwiches to distribute among the troops.

Unexpectedly, however, the Confederates routed the Union army. Wilson's carriage was crushed and he was forced to beat an inglorious retreat back to Washington.[10]

Defeat at the "picnic battle," sobered many in the North who had talked of a short, easy war. In seeking to assign blame for the debacle, rumors spread that Wilson himself might have tipped off the enemy through his friendly relationship with a Washington woman, Mrs. Rose O'Neal Greenhow. When she was arrested as a Confederate spy, "the Wild Rose" held a packet of love letters signed "H." But the letters were not in Wilson's handwriting, and Mrs. Greenhow knew many other senators, members of Lincoln's cabinet, and other highly placed sources of information.[11]

Wilson went back to Massachusetts to raise a volunteer infantry, in which he wore the uniform of colonel. However, once the regiment reached Washington, he resigned his commission and returned to his Senate seat. Wilson also served as a volunteer aide-de-camp to General George McClellan, who commanded the Union armies. When he reported to the general's camp, he was ordered to accompany other officers on a horseback inspection of the capital's fortifications. As the Boston newspaper correspondent Benjamin Perley Poore observed, "Unaccustomed to horsemanship, the ride of thirty miles was too much for the Senator, who kept his bed for a week, and then resigned his staff position." Still, this brief association made Wilson more sympathetic to McClellan than were other Radical Republicans in Congress. The Radicals established a Joint Committee on the Conduct of the War, in part to bypass Wilson's Military Affairs Committee in scrutinizing and attacking the various officers of the Union army. Wilson at first defended the army, arguing that Democratic generals were opposed to the Republican administration but not to the war. Over time, he grew disheartened by the protracted war and impatient with McClellan's overly cautious military tactics. However, he made it a point, as committee chair, to avoid public criticism of the military operations of any general.[12]

Wilson and the Radicals

Henry Wilson soon stood among the inner circle of Radical Republicans in Congress beside Charles Sumner, Benjamin Wade, Thaddeus Stevens, and Henry Winter Davis. He introduced bills that freed slaves in the District of Columbia, permitted African Americans to join the Union army, and provided equal pay to black and white soldiers. Wilson pressed President Lincoln to issue an emancipation proclamation and worried that the final product left many people still enslaved in the border states. Known as one of the most persistent newshunters in Washington, Wilson brought knowledgeable newspaper reporters straight from the battlefield to the White House to brief the president. Despite his intimacy with Lincoln, Wilson considered him too moderate and underestimated his abilities. The senator was once overheard denouncing Lincoln while sitting in the White House waiting room. He hoped that Lincoln would withdraw from the Republican ticket in 1864 in favor of a more radical presidential candidate.[13]

Following Lincoln's assassination, Wilson initially hoped that the new president, his former Senate colleague Andrew Johnson, would pursue the Radical Republican agenda for reconstruction of the South. He was deeply disappointed in Johnson's endorsement of a speedy return of the Confederate states to the Union without any protection for the newly freed slaves. When the Thirty-ninth Congress convened in December 1865, Wilson introduced the first civil rights initiative of the postwar Congress. His bill aimed at outlawing the Black Codes and other forms of racial discrimination in the former Confederacy but, deemed too extreme by the non-Radical Republicans, it was defeated. Wilson also proposed that the Constitution be amended to prohibit any effort to limit the right to vote by race.[14]

Johnson's more lenient policies for Reconstruction and his veto of the Freedmen's Bureau bill and other congressional efforts to protect black southerners eventually drove moderate Republicans into an alliance with the Radicals. Over time, Wilson saw his objectives added to the Constitution as the Thirteenth, Fourteenth, and

Fifteenth amendments. He supported the use of federal troops to enforce congressional Reconstruction, to permit freedmen to vote, and to establish Republican governments in the southern states. When Johnson stubbornly resisted the Radical programs, Wilson endorsed efforts to impeach the president. He accused the president of "unworthy, if not criminal" motives in resisting the will of the people on Reconstruction and cast his vote to remove Johnson from office. However, seven moderate Republican senators broke ranks with their party, and the Radicals failed by a single vote to achieve the two-thirds necessary to remove the president.[15]

National Ambitions

Prior to the presidential election of 1868, Henry Wilson made an extended speaking tour throughout the southern states. Many journalists interpreted this effort as a means of promoting himself as a presidential candidate. In fact, Wilson supported U.S. Grant, the hero of Appomattox, for president and sought the vice-presidential nomination for himself. Always a political mechanic bent on building coalitions, Wilson felt certain that the southern Republican party could survive only if it became biracial. "I do not want to see a white man's party nor a black man's party," he told a black audience in New Orleans. "I warn you to-night, as I do the black men of this country everywhere, to remember this: that while a black man is as good as a white man, a white man is as good as a black man. See to it while you are striving to lift yourselves up, that you do not strive to pull anybody else down." By urging southern blacks to take a conciliatory, nonviolent approach toward those who had so recently enslaved and oppressed them, Wilson stunned his Radical Republican colleagues in Congress. "Wilson is a —————— fool!" wrote Ohio Senator Ben Wade. Nevertheless, southern delegates to the Republican convention generally supported Wilson's candidacy.[16]

On the first ballot for vice president at the Chicago convention, Ben Wade led with Wilson not far behind. That ballot marked Wilson's peak, and he lost support steadily on subsequent ballots. When House Speaker Schuyler Colfax

gained strength, Wilson's delegates switched to Colfax, giving him the nomination. Grant's election brought expectations that Wilson might be named to the cabinet, but the senator asked that his name be removed from consideration, citing his wife's critically ill health—she died in 1870. Still, Wilson remained an influential and frequently consulted senator throughout Grant's first term.

Grant's Second Vice President

By Grant's inauguration in 1869, Massachusetts boasted the most powerful delegation in Congress. Wilson chaired the Senate Military Affairs Committee, while Sumner chaired Foreign Relations. In the House, four Massachusetts representatives chaired committees, including Appropriations and Foreign Affairs. Commenting on the state's two senators, Massachusetts Representative George F. Hoar noted that, while Sumner was a man of great learning, great principle, and great ego, "Wilson supplied almost everything that Sumner lacked." Wilson was the more practical politician, with his finger on the public pulse. He recognized the value of party organization and "did not disdain the art and diplomacies of a partisan." Wilson also combined practical politics with a strong inclination for reform. He spoke out for civil rights for the freedmen, voting rights for women, federal aid to education, federal regulation of business, protection of women, and prohibition of liquor. Hoar judged that no other man in the Senate, "not even Sumner, had more influence over his colleagues" than did Henry Wilson.[17]

During Grant's first term, the imperious Sumner challenged the new president and defeated his plans for incorporating Santo Domingo into the United States. President Grant retaliated by goading the Senate Republican caucus to remove Sumner as chair of the Foreign Relations Committee (Wilson spoke in defense of retaining Sumner's chairmanship). A wounded Sumner opposed Grant's renomination in 1872, raising concerns that he and his allies might bolt to the Liberal Republican-Democratic fusion ticket headed by the eccentric newspaper editor Horace Greeley. After Vice President Schuyler Colfax released word that he did not intend to stand for a second term, many Republican leaders calculated that selecting Wilson for vice president would outflank Sumner and strengthen Grant with workers and with the "old anti-slavery guard." Saluting the working-class origins of their ticket, Republican posters showed idealized versions of Grant, "the Galena Tanner," and Wilson, "the Natick Shoemaker," attired in workers' aprons.[18]

Just as the presidential campaign got underway in September 1872, the *New York Sun* published news of the Crédit Mobilier scandal, offering evidence that key members of Congress had accepted railroad stock at little or no cost, presumably to guarantee their support for legislation that would finance construction of a transcontinental line. On the list were the names of Grant's retiring vice president, Colfax, and his new running mate, Henry Wilson. Newspaper correspondent Henry Van Ness Boynton sent the *New York Times* a dispatch reporting that Senator Wilson had made a "full and absolute denial" that he had ever owned Crédit Mobilier stock. In truth, Wilson had purchased the stock in his wife's name but had later returned it. Called to testify before a House investigating committee, Boynton recounted how he had gone to see Wilson to ask if he would deny the charges against him and that Wilson had given him an absolute denial, knowing that he would file the story that night. Wilson did not contradict the reporter. "General Boynton is a man of character and truth," he told the committee, "and I should take his word." Although the committee cleared Wilson of any wrongdoing in taking the stock, it concluded that the information Wilson had given the *Times* had been "calculated to convey to the public an erroneous impression."[19]

The Ravages of Ill Health

The Crédit Mobilier scandal did not dissuade voters from reelecting Grant and making Henry Wilson vice president. Wilson helped the ticket by embarking on an ambitious speaking tour that took him some ten thousand miles to deliver ninety-six addresses, ruining his health in the process. In May 1873, the sixty-one-year-old Wilson suffered a stroke that caused him to lose control of his facial muscles and to speak thickly whenever fatigued. Although doctors ordered him to rest, the advice went against his nature. A friend wrote, "You know he was never still for five minutes, and it is more difficult for him than for most persons to sit quietly and dream away the time." After spending the summer recuperating in Massachusetts, Wilson traveled to Washington in December for the opening of the new Congress, but by January his poor health forced him to return home once again. Instead of presiding over the Senate, he spent his time writing a multi-volume history of the rise and fall of the slave power, memorializing his own role in the great events of the Civil War and Reconstruction.[20]

Wilson's ill health kept him from playing any role of consequence as vice president but did not suppress his political concerns and ambitions. He lamented that a "Counter-Revolution" was overtaking Reconstruction and urged his old antislavery veterans to speak out against efforts to limit the rights of the freedmen. Wilson blamed the decay of Reconstruction on the Grant administration. According to Representative James Garfield, the vice president had asserted that "Grant is now more unpopular than Andrew Johnson was in his darkest days; that Grant's appointments had been getting worse and worse; that he is still struggling for a third term; in short that he is the millstone around the neck of our party that would sink it out of sight." Yet Wilson could not bring himself to admit that his own involvement in the Crédit Mobilier scandal, as well as the involvement of other members of Congress in the many other scandals of the era, had dimmed the moral fervor of the antislavery movement and congressional Reconstruction, thus undermining public confidence in an active federal government. For the rest of the nineteenth century, political trends moved away from Wilson's cherished reforms. A new generation of genteel reformers advocated limited government, civil service reform, and other administrative solutions and abandoned support for the voting and civil rights of the freedmen, women's rights, and other social reforms that Wilson esteemed.[21]

In the spring of 1875, Vice President Wilson made a six-week tour of the South, raising suspicions that he intended to "advertise himself" for the presidential nomination the next year. He returned home optimistic about the chances that the Republicans could build political and economic ties to conservative southerners by appointing a southern ex-Whig to the cabinet and by offering economic aid to southern business (policies later adopted by the next president, Rutherford B. Hayes). Although Grant desired a third term, Wilson's friends felt sure that the vice president could win the presidential nomination and election.[22]

Wilson's great ambition went unfulfilled. That fall, he consulted Dr. William Hammond, complaining of pain in the back of his head and an inability to sleep. "I enjoined rest from mental labor," the doctor noted, but the vice president replied that he could not comply with those wishes "as fully as desirable." Dr. Hammond saw Wilson again in early November and noted "vertigo, thickness of speech, twitching of the facial muscles, irregularity of respiration, and the action of the heart, slight difficulty of swallowing, and intense pain in the back of the head and nape of the neck." He observed that the vice president's "hands were in almost constant motion and he could not sit longer than a few seconds without rising and pacing the floor, or changing to another chair." Wilson insisted that he must travel to Washington for the new Congress but promised his doctor not to work too hard. He told a friend that "he would at least be able to preside at the opening of the Senate, and perhaps through most of the session."[23]

During the nineteenth century, many members of Congress lived in boardinghouses and hotels where the plumbing left much to be desired. To accommodate them, the Capitol provided luxurious bathing rooms in its basement for the House and Senate. There members could soak in large marble tubs, enjoy a massage, and have their hair cut and beards trimmed. On November 10, 1875, Wilson went down to soak in the tubs. Soon after leaving the bath, he was struck by paralysis and carried to a bed in his vice-presidential office, just off the Senate floor. Within a few days, he felt strong enough to receive visitors and seemed to be gaining strength. When he awoke in his Capitol office on November 22, he was informed that Senator Orris Ferry of Connecticut had died. Wilson lamented the passing of his generation, commenting "that makes eighty-three dead with whom I have sat in the Senate." Shortly thereafter, he rolled over and quietly died, at age sixty-three. His body lay in state in the Rotunda, and his funeral was conducted in the Senate chamber, the vice-presidential chair arrayed in black crepe.

In his memory, the Senate in 1885 placed a marble bust of Wilson by the sculptor Daniel Chester French in the room where the vice president died.[24] There the Senate also installed a bronze plaque, with an inscription written by his old friend and colleague, George F. Hoar:

IN THIS ROOM
HENRY WILSON
VICE PRESIDENT OF THE UNITED STATES
AND A SENATOR FOR EIGHTEEN YEARS,
DIED NOVEMBER 22, 1875

The son of a farm laborer, never at school more than twelve months, in youth a journeyman shoemaker, he raised himself to the high places of fame, honor and power, and by unwearied study made himself an authority in the history of his country and of liberty and an eloquent public speaker to whom Senate and people eagerly listened. He dealt with and controlled vast public expenditure during a great civil war, yet lived and died poor, and left to his grateful countrymen the memory of an honorable public service, and a good name far better than riches.[25]

NOTES

[1] George F. Hoar, *Autobiography of Seventy Years* (New York, 1903), 1:218.

[2] Richard H. Abbott, *Cobbler in Congress: The Life of Henry Wilson, 1812–1875* (Lexington, KY, 1972), pp. 1–6; Elias Nason and Thomas Russell, *The Life and Public Services of Henry Wilson, Late Vice-President of the United States* (New York, 1969; reprint of 1876 ed.), p. 17.

[3] Nason and Russell, pp. 18–21; Ernest A. McKay, *Henry Wilson: Practical Radical: A Portrait of a Politician* (Port Washington, NY, 1971), pp. 6–12.

[4] Nason and Russell, pp. 29–34; Abbott, p. 11.

[5] McKay, *Henry Wilson: Practical Radical*, p. 16; Abbott, pp. 14–15.

[6] Abbott, pp. 30, 36.

[7] Ibid, pp. 27, 53.

[8] Ibid., pp. 46–63; Ernest A. McKay, "Henry Wilson: Unprincipled Know Nothing," *Mid-America* 46 (January 1964): 29–37; David Herbert Donald, *Charles Sumner and the Coming of the Civil War* (Chicago, 1960), p. 268; William E. Gianapp, *The Origins of the Republican Party, 1852–1856* (New York, 1987), pp. 135–36.

[9] Allan G. Bogue, *The Earnest Men: Republicans of the Civil War Senate* (Ithaca, NY, 1981), pp. 33–34; Abbott, p. 18; George S. Boutwell, *Reminiscences of Sixty Years in Public Affairs* (New York, 1968; reprint of 1902 ed.), 1:228–29.

[10] Abbott, p. 116; McKay, *Henry Wilson: Practical Radical*, pp. 146–47.

[11] Abbott, p. 117; Margaret Leech, *Reveille in Washington, 1860–1865* (New York, 1941), pp. 134–38.

[12] Abbott, pp. 125–26; McKay, *Henry Wilson: Practical Radical*, p. 161; Benjamin Perley Poore, *Perley's Reminiscences of Sixty Years in the National Metropolis* (Philadelphia, 1887), 2:99.

[13] Wilson also introduced a bill to permit women to vote and hold office in the District. Bogue, pp. 109–10, 152, 167, 169; T. Harry Williams, *Lincoln and the Radicals* (Madison, WI, 1941), pp. 161, 309, 316; J. Cutler Andrews, *The North Reports the Civil War* (Pittsburgh, 1955), p. 332.

[14] Earl M. Maltz, *Civil Rights, The Constitution, and Congress, 1863–1869* (Lawrence, KS, 1990), pp. 43, 148; Michael Les Benedict, *A Compromise of Principle: Congressional Republicans and Reconstruction, 1863–1869* (New York, 1974), p. 24.

[15] Abbott, pp. 200–202.

[16] Ibid., pp. 196–99; Benedict, pp. 259–60.

[17] Hoar, pp. 213, 215, 217–18; Abbott, p. 225. Henry Wilson, *History of Antislavery Measures of the Thirty-Seventh and Thirty-Eighth Congresses* (Boston, 1865); *History of the Reconstruction Measures of the Thirty-Ninth and Fortieth Congress* (Chicago, 1868); *History of the Rise and Fall of the Slave Power in America*, 3 vols. (Boston, 1872–1877).

[18] William B. Hesseltine, *Ulysses S. Grant, Politician* (New York, 1935), pp. 276–77; McKay, *Henry Wilson: Practical Radical*, pp. 222–23.

[19] Donald A. Ritchie, *Press Gallery: Congress and the Washington Correspondents* (Cambridge, MA, 1991), pp. 105–6.

[20] Abbott, p. 249.

[21] Eric Foner, *Reconstruction: America's Unfinished Revolution, 1863–1877* (New York, 1988), p. 527; William S. McFeely, *Grant: A Biography* (New York, 1981), p. 406; see also Mark Wahlgren Summers, *The Era of Good Stealings* (New York, 1993).

[22] Abbott, p. 255.

[23] William A. Hammond, *On The Cause of Vice-President Wilson's Death* (Cambridge, MA, 1875), pp. 7–8.

[24] In 1886 the Senate began the practice of acquiring marble busts of all former vice presidents.

[25] Hoar, p. 219.

Chapter 19

WILLIAM ALMON WHEELER
1877–1881

WILLIAM A. WHEELER

Chapter 19

WILLIAM ALMON WHEELER

19th Vice President: 1877–1881

Who is Wheeler?

—RUTHERFORD B. HAYES

In the wake of the Grant-era scandals, both the Republican and Democratic parties searched for untarnished candidates as they approached the presidential election of 1876. Democrats chose one of their most prominent leaders, New York Governor Samuel J. Tilden, who had won national attention by taking on the Tweed Ring in New York City. Republicans passed over their party's bigger names, men who had been stained by various exposés in the press, and settled instead on a ticket of Ohio Governor Rutherford B. Hayes and New York Representative William A. Wheeler. Although neither man was very well known to the nation, both had reputations for scrupulous honesty and independence. If history remembers William Wheeler at all, it is for his character. In his introduction to John F. Kennedy's *Profiles in Courage*, the historian Allan Nevins reproduced a colloquy between Wheeler and Senator Roscoe Conkling, the Republican political boss of New York. "Wheeler, if you will act with us, there is nothing in the gift of the State of New York to which you may not reasonably aspire," Conkling tempted; to which Wheeler replied, "Mr. Conkling, there is nothing in the gift of the State of New York which will compensate me for the forfeiture of my self-respect." [1]

A Cautious Politician

Among the stranger individuals to occupy the vice-presidency, William Almon Wheeler seems to have been scarred by his father's ill health, which left him neurotically obsessed with his own well-being. An excessively cautious politician—to the point of timidity—he straddled the various factions in his party, avoided all commitments, and advanced himself politically while covering himself with obscurity. William Wheeler was born on June 30, 1819, in the upstate New York town of Malone, near the Canadian border. His father, Almon Wheeler, had attended the University of Vermont and was a promising young attorney and local postmaster who died at the age of thirty-seven, when William was just eight years old. Left in debt, his mother, Eliza, took in boarders from the nearby Franklin Academy to support her two children. William attended the academy, farmed, and did whatever he could to save money for college. At nineteen, with the help of a loan from a friend, he entered the University of Vermont in Burlington. There he studied for two years, at times living on bread and water, until "an affection of the eyes" caused him to drop out. [2]

He returned to Malone, taught school and studied law. In 1845, shortly after he was admitted to the bar, he married one of his former students, Mary King. A Whig, Wheeler was soon running for office. He became town clerk, school commissioner, and school inspector. In later years he recalled that the thirty dollars a year he earned as town clerk, recording deeds and laying out roads, "were of more value to me than the thousands I have since attained." He served as district attorney for Franklin County from 1846 to 1849 and, from 1850 to 1851, served in the state assembly, where he chaired the ways and means committee. Joining the new Republican party, he moved to the state senate in 1858 and was elected its president pro tempore. Wheeler also conducted a private law practice until "throat trouble" interfered with his courtroom advocacy and convinced him to abandon the law in favor of running a local bank and serving as a railroad trustee, positions that he held until "driven from business in 1865, by broken health."[3]

A Silent Member of the House

Wheeler was elected to serve in the U.S. House of Representatives from 1861 to 1863. He then returned to New York, where he chaired the state constitutional convention, a prestigious body whose members included two future presidential candidates, Horace Greeley and Samuel J. Tilden. Although Wheeler spoke infrequently, his words carried weight, and he gained high marks for fairness as presiding officer. In 1868 he again won election to the House, where he chaired the Committee on Pacific Railroads. It was at this time that Iowa Representative Oakes Ames, acting as an agent for the Crédit Mobilier, the construction company for the Union Pacific Railroad, began spreading railroad stock among high-ranking members of Congress, "where it would do the most good." Wheeler not only refused all stocks offered to him, but resigned his chairmanship to avoid further temptation. In 1872, when the Crédit Mobilier scandal broke in the newspapers, Wheeler remained clean as some of the most prominent members of Congress were caught with the stock. His rectitude even inspired him to oppose an appropriation to construct a post office in his home town of Malone.

Wheeler stayed aloof from the New York state political machine run by Senator Roscoe Conkling. In 1872, Conkling maneuvered to make Wheeler Speaker of the House in place of his hated rival, James G. Blaine. Wheeler declined to have anything to do with the scheme and supported Blaine, who apparently had promised, but never delivered on the promise, to make Wheeler chairman of the House Appropriations Committee. Wheeler also cited his poor health as a reason for not putting himself for-

ward, and only the persuasiveness of his wife and friends kept him from retiring from Congress.[4]

In the House, Wheeler generally kept silent unless he was managing a bill, but then he always proved to be well prepared and highly effective. He remained in the political shadows until 1874, when as a member of the House Committee on Southern Affairs he investigated a disputed election in Louisiana. The election of 1872 had torn apart the Republican party in the state, with half of the party machinery supporting William Pitt Kellogg for governor, and the other half joining the Democrats on a fusion ticket. The election board declared the Democratic candidates the victors, but Republicans refused to concede. They created their own election board, which gave the governorship to Kellogg and a number of disputed elections to their candidates for the state legislature. After President Grant recognized Kellogg as governor, a battle erupted on the streets of New Orleans that left fifty-six people dead. A mob ousted Kellogg, but federal troops restored him to office.[5]

The Wheeler Compromise

Traveling to Louisiana, Wheeler and other committee members heard highly emotional and contradictory testimony from both sides. It was Wheeler who forged the compromise that let Kellogg remain as governor and allowed the committee to arbitrate the disputed seats in the legislature, most of which went to the Democrats. In March 1875, the House endorsed the "Wheeler compromise," a plan which essentially undid federal Reconstruction of the state and held out hope for peace between the North and South a decade after the Civil War had ended. When Louisiana Democrats violated the spirit of the compromise by unseating even more Republican state legislators, in order to elect a Democrat to the U.S. Senate, most northern politicians and newspapers ignored the violations. The North seemed relieved to escape the responsibilities of Reconstruction. Representative Wheeler observed that northerners had expected too much from the South and declared that it was time to admit the failure of efforts to promote peace with the sword. His compromise taught northern Republicans how to cut their losses. Thereafter the party concentrated on preserving its power in the North while scaling down its military efforts in the South, even if that meant abandoning the political rights of the freedmen.[6]

Wheeler was content in his life as a member of the House of Representatives and dreamed of becoming Speaker. However, in early 1876 some Republicans began talking of him as a candidate for president or vice president. The politically astute manager of the Western Associated Press, William Henry Smith, predicted that the GOP ticket would be Hayes and Wheeler. Upon hearing this forecast, Ohio Governor Rutherford B. Hayes wrote to his wife, "I am ashamed to say, Who is Wheeler?" Because Wheeler had served in the House from 1861 to 1863 and again from 1869 to 1877, while Hayes had been a representative during the intervening years from 1865 to 1867, there had been no overlap in their service.[7]

A Quiet Candidate

At the Republican convention in Cincinnati, Wheeler received a handful of votes for president, but the major contest was between Senator Conkling, House Speaker Blaine, and Governor Hayes. When Conkling's nomination seemed impossible, his party machine, the "stalwarts," threw their support to Hayes as the best way of stopping Blaine, leader of the "half-breed" faction. Having helped Hayes win the presidential nomination, the stalwarts considered the vice-presidency theirs to name and they put forward New York Representative Stewart Woodford. The half-breeds, however, wanted the stalwarts off the ticket. Massachusetts half-breed Senator George F. Hoar promoted his friend Wheeler as a man of high moral character. Hoar approached the distinguished author James Russell Lowell, a member of the Massachusetts delegation, on Wheeler's behalf. When Lowell replied that he was unwilling to vote for anyone about whom he knew so little, Hoar responded, "Mr. Lowell, Mr. Wheeler is a very sensible man. He knows The Bigelow Papers by heart." Lowell, the author of *The Bigelow Papers*, said nothing but later was overheard telling other delegates, "I understand that Mr. Wheeler is a very sensible man."[8]

Former Vermont Senator and Representative Luke Poland placed Wheeler's name in nomination, while Conkling's lieutenant Tom Platt nominated Woodford. The publicity Wheeler had received for his compromise, coupled with his independence from the Conkling machine, appealed to the delegates, who voted for him overwhelmingly. When the roll call of the states reached New York, the stalwarts realized they were about to lose and withdrew Woodford's name. The New York delegation voted unanimously for Wheeler—a bitter pill for Conkling's supporters to swallow.[9]

During the campaign, Democrats vainly sought scandals in the pasts of the Republican candidates but could find nothing that would tar Wheeler's reputation. One campaign biography boasted that, at the time when it was fashionable for congressmen "to dabble in railroad stocks and bonds," Wheeler had neither bought nor sold a share of stock or a single bond in any Pacific railroad. He had served his country in Congress for ten years without adding to the personal wealth that he brought to Washington. "With simple tastes," his biographer extolled, "he has never been greedy of gain either for its own sake or for the luxury it would buy. As a legislator, the thought never occurred to him that his influence could bring riches, and not the shadow of a stain rests on his name." Wheeler had also voted against the "salary grab"—an unpopular attempt by members of Congress to raise their pay retroactively—and refused the increase in his own salary.[10]

Wheeler also appealed to the professional songwriters, who in 1876 were just taking over the business of writing campaign songs from the amateurs who had long prevailed. The Tin Pan Alley men leaned towards puns, alliteration and other word-plays in their songs. Thus the sheet music for "We'll Go for Hayes! We'll Wheel'er in on Time" showed Wheeler pushing Hayes in a wheelbarrow toward the White House.[11]

While Wheeler did not detract from the ticket, he added little to it and even refused to campaign. The Democratic vice-presidential nominee Thomas Hendricks spoke in the swing state of Indiana, but Wheeler declined all invitations from the Republicans. In a remarkable reply to

James G. Blaine's invitation to speak to a series of mass meetings in Maine, Wheeler cited his frailty and insomnia as excuses:

I greatly regret my physical inability to do little in the way of speaking in his canvass. But I have no reserve of strength to draw upon. I was driven from business in 1865, by broken health and have never been strong since. . . . My trouble for years has been wakefulness at night. No resident of the grave or a lunatic asylum has suffered more from this cause than I have. Speaking, and the presence of crowds, excite me and intensify my wakefulness. . . . Gov. Hayes wrote me, asking me to go to Indiana and Ohio, to which I answered as I write you. . . . I regret that I was nominated. You know I did not want the place. I should have gone back to the House, and into a Republican majority. I should have almost to a certainty, been its Speaker, which I would greatly prefer to being *laid away*.[12]

All that Wheeler would do was to issue the traditional letter of acceptance of his nomination. The conciliatory tone of that letter toward the South was seen as part of the Republicans' strategy of trying to detach the old southern Whigs from the southern Democrats. Candidate Hayes issued a similarly ambiguous endorsement of reconciliation with the South. At the Republican convention, the civil rights leader Frederick Douglass had challenged the delegates to decide whether they meant to uphold for blacks the rights they had written into the Constitution or whether they could "get along without the vote of the black man in the South." The Hayes and Wheeler ticket suggested that the party had chosen the latter course.[13]

The Contested Election

On election night, it looked as if Tilden and Hendricks had defeated Hayes and Wheeler, especially after Democrats captured Wheeler's home state of New York. Republican newspapers conceded the election, but Zachariah Chandler, chairman of the Republican National Committee, saw hope in the southern electors and dispatched telegrams to party leaders in those southern states still under Reconstruction rule, alerting them that the election was still undecided. Three southern states each sent two sets of electoral ballots, one set for Tilden and one set for Hayes. One of the disputed states was Louisiana, where only a year earlier Wheeler had found evidence that the state board of election had produced fraudulent returns. Now his election as vice president depended upon that same board.[14]

After a specially created electoral commission awarded all of the disputed ballots to Hayes, a joint session of Congress still had to count the ballots, and there was talk of angry Democrats marching on Washington by the thousands to prevent this "steal" of the election. To avoid bloodshed, friends of both candidates met at the Wormley Hotel in Washington in late February 1877. There they agreed to a compromise that settled the election and ended Reconstruction. In return for Hayes' election, Republicans offered federal funds to build railroads through the ravaged South and otherwise restore the southern economy, promised to appoint a southerner to the cabinet, and—most important—pledged to remove all federal troops from the southern states. When members of the Democratic majority in the House of Representatives still tried to block the counting of the electoral ballots, a Louisiana representative assured them that an acceptable arrangement had been negotiated at the Wormley Hotel. The revolt fizzled, and at 4 a.m. on March 2, senators marched to the House chamber to declare Hayes president. Hayes upheld the bargain and removed the federal troops, abandoning black voters to disfranchisement and segregation.[15]

Hymn Singing and Square Talk

Although they had not known each other before their nomination, Hayes and Wheeler developed an unusually friendly relationship while in office. The Hayes family—scorned by many Washington politicos for their old-fashioned manner and strict adherence to temperance—became a surrogate family to the lonely vice president, a sixty-year old widower with no children. The vice president was fond of hymn singing, and each Sunday evening the Hayes family invited Wheeler and a few other friends to the White House library, where Secretary of the Interior Carl Schurz played the piano and the vice president distributed copies of *The Presbyterian Hymn and Tune Book* for "a revelry of sweet sounds and mingling of souls."[16]

Wheeler also provided Hayes with advice about appointments, recommending that selections be made according to "personal character, recognized capacity and experience." He especially warned Hayes about the hostility that the Conkling machine exhibited toward the new administration. At one point, Hayes noted in his diary that Wheeler was critical of cabinet members who, when approached by jobseekers, responded equivocally. "When there is no hope tell the man so," Wheeler asserted. "He will be disappointed at the time, but it is the best way." Hayes observed that Wheeler was right. "Prompt and square talk is in the long run safest and is just to the parties concerned. I must also bear this in mind."[17]

Despite their friendship, Hayes rarely consulted Wheeler and did not include him within his circle of advisers. Wheeler spent his vice-presidency presiding over Senate debates, a job he found dull and monotonous, comparing his role of repeating set phrases to that of a parrot. During his term, he cast six tie-breaking votes, including one that helped his old friend William Pitt Kellogg to be seated as senator from Louisiana. Wheeler grew particularly frustrated at being left out of both cabinet meetings and party caucuses and feeling that he was generally ignored. The greatest trial of being vice president, he once commented, was attending church. "I hear the minister praying for the President, his Cabinet, both Houses of Congress, the Supreme Court, the governors and legislatures of all the states and every individual heathen . . . and find myself wholly left out."[18]

A Forgotten Man

Wheeler made it easy for his nation to forget that he existed. A more assertive man might have risen to lead the opposition to the Conkling machine, but Wheeler contented himself with sneering at Conkling rather than challenging him. The vice president urged President Hayes not to appear weak and yielding to Conkling. But when Hayes took on Conkling by removing his lieutenants Chester A. Arthur and Alonzo Cornell from

their lucrative posts at the New York custom-house, Wheeler disapproved the action because he feared it might split the party. Wheeler even endorsed Cornell's candidacy for governor of New York.[19]

In December 1879, the Republican National Committee met in Washington, as a first step toward nominating the presidential ticket for 1880. Hayes had let it be known that he would not stand for a second term, and sentiments within the party seemed to be roughly divided between Grant and Blaine. In his diary Hayes commented, "If New York could with a fair degree of unity, present a man like say the Vice President . . . he would probably be nominated." But there was no hope of the factions in New York uniting, especially over someone who opposed Roscoe Conkling.[20] At the convention, James A. Garfield defeated Grant, Blaine, and other candidates on the thirty-sixth ballot to become the Republican nominee. He and his running mate Chester A. Arthur went on to win the election.

In March 1881, Wheeler turned over the vice-presidency to his successor, Conkling's confederate Chet Arthur. Within months, Conkling launched his last great political battle against the new president. In May, both New York senators, Conkling and Tom Platt, dramatically resigned and returned to Albany, where they expected the state legislature to reelect them as a sign of solidarity in their patronage struggles with Garfield. Instead, the legislature rebelled. A number of candidates entered the Senate race, including former Vice President Wheeler. On several ballots, Wheeler ran ahead of Conkling. Although neither won the election, Conkling's biographer concluded that "the ambition of former Vice-President Wheeler was a major contributing cause" to Conkling's defeat. Crushed by his defeat and by Garfield's assassination, Conkling retired from politics to a lucrative Wall Street law practice. William A. Wheeler also retired from public life, turning down an appointment from President Chester Arthur to serve on a commission to study the tariff because, he said, his health was not up to it. He died on June 4, 1887, in Malone, a forgotten man.[21]

NOTES

[1] John F. Kennedy, *Profiles in Courage* (New York, 1956), p. xiv.

[2] William Dean Howells, *Sketch of the Life and Character of Rutherford B. Hayes, Also a Biographical Sketch of William A. Wheeler* (New York, 1876), pp. 5–7; see also James T. Otten, ''Grand Old Partyman: William A. Wheeler and the Republican Party, 1850–1880,'' (Ph.D. dissertation, University of South Carolina, 1976), pp. 1–11, 285–86.

[3] Howells, p. 10; Keith Ian Polakoff, *The Politics of Inertia: The Election of 1876 and the End of Reconstruction* (Baton Rouge, LA, 1973), p. 123.

[4] Otten, pp. 63–79, 288–89.

[5] Polakoff, p. 181.

[6] Ibid; William Gillette, *Retreat from Reconstruction, 1869–1879* (Baton Rouge, LA, 1979), pp. 133, 294.

[7] Howells, p. 12; Polakoff, p. 37.

[8] Herbert Eaton, *Presidential Timber: A History of Nominating Conventions, 1868–1960* (New York, 1964), pp. 55–59; Richard E. Welch, Jr., *George Frisbie Hoar and the Half-Breed Republicans* (Cambridge, MA, 1971), p. 55.

[9] Polakoff, pp. 67–68; David M. Jordan, *Roscoe Conkling of New York: Voice in the Senate* (Ithaca, NY, 1971), p. 241.

[10] Howells, pp. 16–17, 20.

[11] Irwin Silber, *Songs America Voted By* (Harrisburg, PA, 1971), p. 115.

[12] Mark Wahlgren Summers, *The Era of Good Stealings* (New York, 1993), p. 281; Polakoff, p. 123.

[13] Gillette, pp. 304, 419.

[14] Ibid., p. 332; Otten, p. 218.

[15] For details of the compromise, see C. Vann Woodward, *Reunion and Reaction; The Compromise of 1877 and the End of Reconstruction* (New York, 1991; reprint of 1951 edition); Eric Foner, *Reconstruction: America's Unfinished Revolution, 1863–1877* (New York, 1988); and Polakoff. See also Chapter 21 of this volume, ''Thomas Andrews Hendricks,'' p. 263.

[16] Kenneth E. Davison, *The Presidency of Rutherford B. Hayes* (Westport, CT, 1972), pp. 84–85.

[17] Otten, p. 171; T. Harry Williams, ed., *Hayes: The Diary of a President, 1875–1881* (New York, 1964), pp. 69, 129.

[18] Howells, p. 26; Otten, pp. 176, 181, 292; U.S., Congress, Senate, *The Senate, 1789–1989*, by Robert C. Byrd, S. Doc. 100–20, 100th Cong., 1st sess., vol. 4, *Historical Statistics, 1789–1992*, 1993, p. 644.

[19] Williams, ed., p. 302; Otten, pp. 209, 256, 263.

[20] Williams, ed., pp. 256–57.

[21] Jordan, pp. 407–8; Otten, pp. 277–79.

Chapter 20

CHESTER ALAN ARTHUR
1881

CHESTER A. ARTHUR

Chapter 20

CHESTER ALAN ARTHUR

20th Vice President: 1881

Such an honor and opportunity comes to very few of the millions of Americans, and to that man but once. No man can refuse it, and I will not.

—CHESTER A. ARTHUR

Following the Civil War and Reconstruction, "boss rule" and "machine politics" flourished in the United States, and nowhere more intensely than in New York, the most populated state in the Union. The Tweed Ring ran the Democratic party's Tammany Hall apparatus in New York, and an equally powerful machine operated within the state's Republican party. Throughout the 1870s, that party's "stalwart" faction, led by Senator Roscoe Conkling, dominated New York politics until it reached both its apex and nadir within the space of a few months in 1881. Although responsible for some of the most tawdry politics in American history, Conkling's machine also produced two vice presidents, Chester Alan Arthur and Levi P. Morton, one of whom—Arthur—became president of the United States under tragic circumstances and turned against the machine and its spoilsmen.

A spellbinding orator with a commanding presence, Senator Roscoe Conkling was the uncrowned leader of the Senate in an era before majority and minority leaders were formally designated. One woman newspaper correspondent described him as the most alluring politician of his time and "the Apollo of the Senate." New York's other senator, Thomas C. Platt, similarly considered Conkling one of the handsomest men he had ever met.

He was over six feet tall, of slender build, and stood straight as an arrow. . . . A curl, described as Hyperion, rolled over his forehead. An impe-

rial [air] added much to the beauty of his Apollo-like appearance. His noble figure, flashing eye and majestic voice made one forget that he was somewhat foppish in his dress. A physical fitness fanatic, Conkling boxed to keep in shape for his political battles, and a journalist noted that Conkling also "loved to use words as a prize-fighter loves to use his fists." No one admired Conkling's talents and abilities more than he himself. A vain and haughty man with a monumental ego, he believed himself unfettered by the rules that governed lesser mortals. These impulses led him to carry on a scandalous affair with Kate Chase Sprague, the wife of his Senate colleague William Sprague, and to challenge openly two presidents—Rutherford B. Hayes and James A. Garfield—for power and patronage.[1]

Conkling built his political machine on a rich source of patronage, the New York customhouse, headed by the collector of the port of New York. Before income taxes, the chief sources of federal revenue were the duties charged on imported goods. The busy port of New York served as the point of deposit for many imports, and its customhouse became the largest federal office in the government, taking in more revenue and handing out more jobs than any other. Since the days of Andrew Jackson, the "spoils system" had prevailed in the hiring and retention of federal employees. Each new administration cleaned house, regardless of the ability of individual civil servants, making room for its own appointees. As was the case at the city and state level, these federal jobs provided the glue that united political party organizations. Yet increasingly in the post-Civil War era, federal offices like the New York customhouse became symbols of waste, fraud, and incompetence that cost the government millions of dollars.[2]

Political Lieutenant in the Conkling Machine

From 1871 to 1877, the head of the New York customhouse was Roscoe Conkling's close ally, Chester Alan Arthur. Born in North Fairfield, Vermont, on October 5, 1829, Arthur was the son of a Baptist minister who held a succession of pastorates throughout Vermont and upstate New York. When his father finally settled at a church in Schenectady, young Arthur was able to attend Union College, from which he graduated Phi Beta Kappa in 1848. For a few years he taught school and was a principal. He then studied law and gained admission to the bar in New York City in 1854. During the Civil War, he became a judge advocate general and later the quartermaster general of the New York militia. Although he never saw combat, these posts enabled him to campaign as "General Arthur" in his later political career.

Arthur married Virginia-born Ellen Lewis Herndon in 1859 and established his family in a handsome brownstone on Lexington Avenue near Gramercy Park. His law practice enabled him to live in a conspicuously stylish fashion. At first, Arthur was identified with the conservative wing of his party, led by former Governor William H. Seward and Albany boss Thurlow Weed. But at the state convention in 1867, he entered the orbit of the rising political star Roscoe Conkling. An upstate Republican, Conkling needed alliances with New York City men and recruited Arthur into his organization. Conkling's biographer David Jordan assessed Arthur as "a shrewd, imaginative, and meticulous political manager; he was a master organizer, a necessity for Conkling's new organization." The popular "Chet" Arthur rose quickly within the ranks of the machine. In 1871, President Ulysses S. Grant rewarded Conkling's loyalty to his administration by appointing Arthur to the highly lucrative post of collector of the port of New York.[3]

Numerous scandals within the administration of President Ulysses S. Grant led Republicans to seek a less-tarnished candidate for the 1876 contest. Chet Arthur supported Conkling's bid for the Republican presidential nomination, but when the nomination went instead to the reform-conscious governor of Ohio, Rutherford B. Hayes, Arthur threw the support of his office behind Hayes, raising funds and getting out voters to help Hayes carry New York and win the election. Rather than showing his gratitude, however, President Hayes appointed a commission to investigate the New York customhouse. When the group's report exposed inefficiency, graft, and a bloated payroll, Hayes issued an order forbidding federal officeholders to take part in political activities, so that the customhouse could be run under a merit system. Conkling's lieutenants, Arthur as collector and Alonzo Cornell as naval officer of the port—both members of the Republican State Committee—should have resigned under this order, but they refused. Hayes then fired both men and nominated Theodore Roosevelt, Sr. (father of the future president) and L. Bradford Prince to replace them. An outraged Conkling persuaded the Senate to reject both nominations.[4]

The Stalwarts and the Half-Breeds

As the election of 1880 approached, Hayes chose not to seek a second term. Rather than become a candidate himself, Conkling threw his support behind former president U.S. Grant. Conkling particularly wanted to block the nomination of his longtime rival, Senator and former House Speaker James G. Blaine of Maine. Back in 1866, when they were both members of the House, Blaine had delivered a sarcastic speech that mocked Conkling's "turkey-gobbler strut" and "Hyperion curl." Delighted political cartoonists had seized on these characteristics to mock Conkling. Although Blaine and Conkling served together in the House and Senate for another fourteen years, they never spoke to one another again. Each dedicated himself to blocking the other from becoming president.[5]

At the national convention in June, Conkling proposed a unit rule to force the entire New York delegation to support Grant, but William H. Robertson, a Blaine supporter, led a minority of the delegation to rebel against the stalwarts. Robertson's faction, known dismissively as "half-breeds," joined with other independent delegates to defeat the unit rule. The result was an extended deadlock that was broken only when the Blaine forces swung their support to a darkhorse candidate, Ohio Representative James A. Garfield. Garfield's supporters realized that they needed a New Yorker on the ticket, not only for the state's large potential harvest of electoral votes but also to mollify Conkling. Garfield at first wanted Levi P. Morton, his friend from the House of Representatives, but Morton felt he could not accept without Conkling's approval. When Conkling made it clear that no friend of his should join the ticket, Morton declined. The Garfield forces next turned to Chet Arthur, who showed no such reluctance. "Such an honor and opportunity comes to very few of the millions of Americans, and to that man but once," Arthur told Conkling. "No man can refuse it, and I will not."[6]

The selection of Chet Arthur for vice president did not pacify Conkling, whom Garfield knew was a man "inspired more by his hates than his loves." In August 1880, Garfield went to New York to make peace with Conkling's machine. In the Fifth Avenue Hotel rooms of Levi Morton, Garfield met with Arthur, Platt, and other machine leaders—but not with Conkling, who stayed away. The Conkling men sought an understanding about patronage in a Garfield administration. In return for assurances that he would take their wishes into consideration for New York appointments, they agreed to raise funds for his campaign. According to Platt, Garfield also disavowed any close relations with Hayes' civil service proposals. With these guarantees, the Conkling machine threw its weight behind Garfield, enabling him to win a very narrow victory in November. It was said that, while Garfield owed his nomination to Blaine, he owed his election to Conkling.[7]

Party reformers were chagrined at the choice of Chet Arthur, the recently deposed collector of the port of New York and a symbol of corrupt machine politics, as Garfield's running mate. Most Republican newspapers held the vice-pres-

idential candidate in low esteem. One campaign biography devoted 533 pages to Garfield and only 21 pages—almost as an embarrassed aside—to Arthur. Enumerating his "good" qualities, the campaign tract observed that his face was "full, fat and fair," that he did not talk with "offensive accents," that he dressed "in perfect good taste," and that he was "fairly corpulent as his pictures very well suggest."[8] Arthur probably gained some public sympathy for his wife's death in 1880, which left him to raise a son and young daughter.

An Evenly Balanced Senate

Once elected, Vice President Arthur proved crucial to his party's fortunes in the Senate. At the beginning of the Forty-seventh Congress, the party balance in the Senate was exactly equal, a situation in which the vice president's vote might be needed to give the Republicans a majority to organize the body and chair its committees. When the Senate met on March 4, 1881, there were 37 Republicans, 37 Democrats, and 2 Independents. One of the Independents, former Supreme Court Justice David Davis, announced that he planned to vote with the Democrats to organize the chamber. If the other Independent, William Mahone of Virginia, could also be persuaded to join them, the Democrats would take the majority. Rumors spread that the White House was plying Mahone with "champagne and satisfaction," or promises of patronage, to win him for the Republicans. With a noisy mob watching from the galleries, Vice President Arthur directed the clerk to call the roll. When Mahone's name was reached, the Virginia senator, sitting on the Democratic side of the aisle, voted with the Republicans, giving Arthur the deciding vote. For his vote, Mahone received a basket of flowers from the White House, the chairmanship of the Agriculture Committee, and control of federal patronage in Virginia. Democrats, however, intended to fight the administration at every turn, making every vote—especially the vice president's—critical.[9]

At this juncture, a fissure disrupted Republican ranks. Much to Roscoe Conkling's chagrin, President Garfield had named James G. Blaine as secretary of state, and from that post Blaine plotted against his longtime rival. While a number of offices went to Conkling men, they were excluded from the cabinet seats they desired—especially the secretary of the treasury, which had jurisdiction over the collector of the Port of New York. On the day before their inauguration, Arthur had visited Garfield, along with Senators Conkling and Platt, to plead for their candidate for treasury secretary. As Garfield noted in his diary, Conkling seemed "full of apprehension that he had been or was to be cheated." [10]

"A Square Blow at Conkling"

Conkling had good reason for apprehension. On March 23, Vice President Arthur, while presiding over the Senate, received a list of presidential nominations. His eye fell on the name of New York state senator William H. Robertson for collector of the port of New York, which, as one reporter described it, represented "a square blow at Conkling." Arthur folded the document so that Robertson's name appeared uppermost and had a page deliver it to Senator Conkling. From the press gallery, reporters watched Conkling walk rapidly to his colleague Platt and hold a "whispered conference." Conkling made it known that he considered the nomination personally offensive, and Vice President Arthur joined with Senators Conkling and Platt in a letter asking the president to withdraw Robertson's name. At the Republican caucus, Conkling delivered a long, eloquent, and bitter attack on the president for his breach of senatorial courtesy. He persuaded Senate Republicans to postpone the customs collectors' nominations and take up less controversial posts. President Garfield retaliated by withdrawing the nominations of five of Conkling's men. When it began to look as if Senate Democrats would contribute enough votes to confirm Robertson, Conkling and his colleague Tom Platt decided to resign from the Senate and return to New York, where they expected the state legislature to reelect them as a sign of endorsement in their power struggle with the president. [11]

Vice President Arthur had no trouble deciding which side to take in this epic struggle between his president and his party boss. After the Senate adjourned, Arthur also journeyed to Albany, where he lobbied for Conkling's reelection. J. L. Connery, the editor of the New York *Herald*, which the Conkling machine courted, recalled Arthur telling him in confidence that Garfield had been neither honorable nor truthful. "It is a hard thing to say of a President of the United States, but it is, unfortunately, only the truth," said Arthur. "Garfield—spurred by Blaine, by whom he is easily led—has broken every pledge made to us; not only that, but he seems to have wished to do it in a most offensive way." Garfield's supporters, however, never forgave Arthur for his betrayal of the president. [12]

A Presidential Assassination

The strategy of the Conkling forces unraveled when the New York legislature reacted negatively to the "childish" resignations of its two senators. Led by state senate president pro tempore William Robertson (the customs collector nominee), the half-breeds called on legislators to "stand by the administration," and the legislature entered a month-long deadlock over the senatorial elections. On July 2, Platt withdrew from the race in a last-ditch attempt to improve Conkling's chances of reelection. That same day, on the brink of victory, President Garfield walked arm in arm with Secretary of State Blaine through Washington's Baltimore and Ohio railroad station. A crazed assassin shot the president in the back and then identified himself with Conkling's stalwarts. After lingering throughout the summer, the mortally wounded Garfield died on September 19. By then the New York legislature had rejected Conkling's bid for reelection. "How can I speak into a grave?" Conkling complained. "How can I battle with a shroud. Silence is a duty and a doom." [13]

Garfield's death elevated to the presidency a man who had shared an apartment in Washington with Conkling and who had sided with Conkling against Garfield. Political observers naturally assumed that Conkling would dominate Chet Arthur's administration. Newspaper correspondent Theron Crawford later noted that Conkling "had been in the habit of patronizing Mr. Arthur, and had given him political orders for so many years that he could not imagine this pleasure-loving, easy-going man capable of rebellion." Arthur was in New York when Garfield died, and it was Roscoe Conkling who carried the new president's bag to the station when he left for Washington.

Less than a month later, Conkling arrived in Washington and held a private meeting with Arthur. Reporters speculated that the two had chosen a new cabinet, yet no announcement was made to the press. Neither man would publicly acknowledge what had transpired, but their associates described a stormy session. Conkling presented his patronage demands: he wanted William Robertson dismissed as collector and he himself was willing to accept a cabinet portfolio. But Conkling underestimated how deeply the assassination had shocked and sobered Chester Arthur. Senator Platt described Arthur as "overcome with grief," particularly after newspapers quoted the assassin saying "I am a Stalwart, and I want Arthur for President." Feeling the weight of his new office and calculating that public opinion would never tolerate Robertson's removal, the president rejected Conkling's advice. A New York Republican leader told a friend in the press that President Arthur felt very bitter over the demands Conkling had made on him. "You can put it down for a fact that 'Conk' wanted 'Chet' to remove Robertson and appoint one of our fellows collector." When Arthur refused, Conkling stormed out, swearing that all of his friends had turned traitor to him.[14]

Conkling's mistress, Kate Chase Sprague, tried to intercede with the president, reminding him of "the vital importance of placing a robust, courageous, clear-headed man at the head of the Treasury," and arguing that Conkling would be a "tower of strength" in the cabinet. But Arthur offered neither a cabinet appointment nor the removal of Robertson as collector. Instead, Conkling went into permanent political exile. Although Arthur later named Conkling to the Supreme Court, his former leader declined. At the same time, Arthur accepted Blaine's resignation as secretary of state, feeling that by doing so he had neutralized the heads of both warring factions and could steer a course between them. Senator Chauncey Depew later judged that, while Arthur tried to govern fairly, "he was not

big enough, nor strong enough, to contend with the powerful men who were antagonized."[15]

Support for Civil Service Reform

Since the martyred President Garfield was regarded as a "victim of that accursed greed for spoils of office," his death rallied public support behind civil service reform legislation. In Arthur's first annual message to Congress in December 1881, he pledged his willingness to enforce any reform legislation that Congress might enact modeled on the British civil service system. Democratic Senator George H. Pendleton of Ohio sponsored a measure that became known as the Pendleton Act, which President Arthur signed in January 1883. The Pendleton Act established a bipartisan Civil Service Commission to set rules by which federal jobs would be filled. The act placed about 14,000 jobs, about one-tenth of the total federal employment at the time, under civil service. Although by no means a complete reversal of the spoils system, it took a large step in that direction. As the journalist Henry Stoddard mused, it was a strange turn of events that a spoilsman like Chester Arthur should sign the first effective civil service law and also be the first president to veto a river and harbor appropriations bill as excessive "—the bill that had come to be known as the 'pork barrel' bill into which both parties dug deep."[16]

The initial reaction to Vice President Arthur's elevation to the presidency had been one of universal dismay: "Chet Arthur in the White House!" But, as chief executive, Chester Alan Arthur replaced Chet Arthur. The new president acted in a dignified manner, made strong appointments, and won approval for the "elevated tone" of his administration. He redecorated the White House and entertained regally. He became famous for his fourteen-course dinners that often kept his guests at the table until after midnight, consuming fine wines and rich foods. Overeating and underexercising did not help Arthur's health, and during his presidency he suffered from kidney disease that slowly sapped his strength. In 1884, he made himself available for renomination. "Arthur has given us a good administration, but it has been negatively rather than positively good," wrote one dubious journalist. "He has done well, in other words, by not doing anything bad. This kind of goodness does not count for much in presidential campaigns."[17]

Arthur's attempt to steer a course between the stalwarts and half-breeds succeeded only in alienating both sides. At the Republican convention, the remnants of the stalwart wing (led by Tom Platt) supported James G. Blaine, on the grounds that Arthur had deserted them. When they tried to persuade Conkling, now a highly successful New York attorney, to emerge from his political retirement and endorse Blaine's presidential candidacy, Conkling acidly replied, "No thank you, I don't engage in criminal practice." Blaine lost New York by a whisker—and with it the election. Grover Cleveland, who had owed his election as governor of New York to the split between the stalwarts and the half-breeds, now became the first Democratic president since the Civil War. Chester Arthur returned to his New York law office. Rapidly declining in health, he died on November 17, 1886, less than two years after leaving the White House. He had been chosen as vice president without much expectation but, when thrust into the presidency, he rose to the occasion and conducted the office with style.[18]

NOTES

[1] David J. Rothman, *Politics and Power: The United States Senate, 1869–1901* (Cambridge, MA, 1966), pp. 27–30; Donald A. Ritchie, *Press Gallery: Congress and the Washington Correspondents* (Cambridge, MA, 1991), p. 156; Louis J. Lang, ed., *The Autobiography of Thomas Collier Platt* (New York, 1910), p. 55; Henry L. Stoddard, *As I Knew Them: Presidents and Politics from Grant to Coolidge* (New York, 1927), p. 115.

[2] Ari Hoogenboom, *Outlawing the Spoils: A History of the Civil Service Reform Movement, 1865–1883* (Urbana, IL, 1961), pp. 1–32.

[3] David M. Jordan, *Roscoe Conkling of New York: Voice in the Senate* (Ithaca, NY, 1971), pp. 146–48.

[4] Ibid., pp. 155–78; Chester L. Barrows, *William M. Evarts: Lawyer, Diplomat, Statesman* (Chapel Hill, NC, 1941), p. 326.

[5] Ritchie, pp. 136–37.

[6] Jordan, p. 341; Stoddard, pp. 118–19; Chauncey M. Depew, *My Memories of Eighty Years* (New York, 1924), pp. 122–23.

[7] Justus D. Doenecke, *The Presidencies of James A. Garfield & Chester A. Arthur* (Lawrence, KS, 1981), pp. 26–27; Jordan, p. 439; Lang, ed., pp. 128–32; Alfred R. Conkling, *The Life and Letters of Roscoe Conkling, Orator, Statesman, Advocate* (New York, 1889), p. 614. See also Chapter 22 of this volume, "Levi P. Morton," p. 271.

[8] James S. Brisbin, *From The Tow-Path to the White House: The Early Life and Public Career of James A. Garfield* (Philadelphia, 1880), pp. 546–47.

[9] "The Great Senate Deadlock: 1881," *Senate History* 9 (July 1984): 1, 9–10.

[10] Harry James Brown and Frederic D. Williams, eds., *The Diary of James A. Garfield* (East Lansing, MI, 1981), 4:552.

[11] Ben: Perley Poore, *Perley's Reminiscences of Sixty Years in the National Metropolis* (Philadelphia, 1886), pp. 400–402; Conkling, p. 640; Doenecke, p. 45.

[12] Theodore Clarke Smith, *The Life and Letters of James Abram Garfield* (New Haven, CT, 1925), 2:1128–29; T.B. Connery, "Secret History of the Garfield-Conkling Tragedy," *Cosmopolitan* 23 (June 1897): 145–62.

[13] Jordan, pp. 379–409; Henry L. Stoddard, p. 114.

[14] Theron C. Crawford, *James G. Blaine: A Study of His Life and Career, from the Standpoint of a Personal Witness of the Principal Events in his History* (Philadelphia, 1893), p. 525; Thomas C. Reeves, *Gentleman Boss: The Life of Chester A. Arthur* (New York, 1975), p. 256; William C. Hudson, *Random Recollections of an Old Political Reporter* (New York, 1911), p. 127; Lang, ed., pp. 162–63.

[15] Katherine Chase Sprague to Chester A. Arthur, October 21, 1881, Chester A. Arthur Papers, Library of Congress; Crawford, pp. 508, 546; Depew, p. 118.

[16] Hoogenboom, pp. 213–53; Stoddard, p. 122.

[17] Poore, p. 431; Stoddard, pp. 117, 285; Francis Carpenter, ed., *Carp's Washington* (New York, 1960), p. 30; Doenecke, pp. 76–77, 80, 183–84.

[18] Lang, ed., p. 181; Ritchie, p. 137.

Chapter 21

THOMAS ANDREWS HENDRICKS
1885

THOMAS A. HENDRICKS

Chapter 21

THOMAS ANDREWS HENDRICKS

21st Vice President: 1885

There were no neutral tints in his own political colors.

—SENATOR DANIEL VOORHEES

American political parties have traditionally been coalitions of contradictory and contentious forces. The electoral college is largely responsible for the loose-knit nature of these political parties. Victory requires a majority of electors from throughout the nation, a feat nearly impossible for any party rooted in a single region or clustered about one ideology or interest group. To build such national coalitions, politicians must reach out to those with whom they may disagree. The Democratic party emerged from Thomas Jefferson's defense of the yeoman farmer against Alexander Hamilton's efforts to use the government to promote American industry and finance. Yet to build a national party, Jefferson needed to embrace New York's Tammany Hall, which represented urban interests. Nearly a century later, Indiana's Thomas A. Hendricks confronted that same split. He was a "soft-money" agrarian reformer, who ran twice for vice president on Democratic tickets headed by two different "hard-money" New York governors.

Early Years

A son of the Mississippi Valley, Thomas A. Hendricks was born on a farm near Zanesville, Ohio, on September 7, 1819, to John and Jane Thomson Hendricks. When just six months old, he moved with his parents to Indiana, where his father's older brother, William, was a U.S. rep-

resentative and a soon-to-be governor of that new state. Hendricks was raised as a staunch Presbyterian and a Jacksonian Democrat, the two pillars of his thinking throughout his life. He attended the Presbyterian-run Hanover College in Indiana, where he proved an average student but a skillful debater. After graduating, he went east to Pennsylvania to study at a law school run by one of his uncles. In 1843 he was admitted to the bar and practiced in Shelbyville, Indiana. That same year, he met Eliza Morgan, a vivacious teenager from Ohio who was visiting in Indiana. After two years of correspondence, he felt financially secure enough to propose, and they were married in 1845. Their only child died at age three. In later years, an old neighbor said that he doubted whether Hendricks could have achieved his political success without Eliza. "She is generous, wise and discreet. The man born to get on in the world always marries that kind of woman, it appears." [1]

Slavery and Politics

Always ambitious, Hendricks plunged into politics. He was elected to the Indiana house of representatives in 1848, served as a delegate to the state constitutional convention in 1849, and won a seat in the U.S. House of Representatives in 1850. A popular member of the House, he became a follower of Illinois Democratic Senator

THOMAS A. HENDRICKS

Stephen A. Douglas and supported Douglas' controversial Kansas-Nebraska Act. That statute repealed the Missouri Compromise and permitted residents of the territories to determine whether or not to permit slavery, a concept known as "popular sovereignty." Public outrage in the North caused the dissolution of the old Whig party and a period of political instability that eventually resulted in the emergence of the new Republican party. Hendricks believed his vote for the Kansas-Nebraska Act reflected the sentiments of his constituents, although it was later cited as the cause of his defeat for reelection in 1854. He was opposed by a former Democrat representing a coalition of Free Soilers, abolitionists, temperance advocates, Know-Nothings, and Whigs. Hendricks denounced the nativism of the Know-Nothing movement and defended the rights of immigrants and religious minorities. Despite these admirable stands for minority rights, he had a blind eye on racial issues. As a delegate to the Indiana constitutional convention in 1849, he had led the move to enact "Black Laws" that promoted segregation and restricted the migration of free blacks into the state.[2]

After losing his seat in Congress, Hendricks in 1855 accepted an appointment from President Franklin Pierce to become commissioner of the General Land Office in the Interior Department, a post he held through 1859. As a Douglas Democrat, he felt increasingly out of step with the anti-Douglas administration of James Buchanan and resigned his office to return to Indiana, where in 1860 he ran unsuccessfully for governor. He then moved to Indianapolis to practice law.[3]

A Pro-Union Democrat

When the Civil War erupted in 1861, the Democratic party in Indiana divided between peace and pro-Union factions. Jesse D. Bright, the president pro tempore of the U.S. Senate, led the party's peace wing, while Hendricks became a leading "War Democrat." Bright, an imperious man who had tolerated no opposition in his twenty-year domination of the state Democratic party, was expelled from the Senate in February 1862, when it was discovered that he had written a letter addressed to Jefferson Davis as "President of the Confederate States," recommending that the Confederacy purchase rifles from an Indiana manufacturer. Bright expected that the Indiana legislature would reelect him, but instead Judge David Turpie was chosen to fill the few months remaining in his term. The legislature elected Thomas Hendricks to take the seat during the next full term. Bright thereafter blamed Hendricks for his defeat.[4]

When peace Democrats in the state legislature attempted to pass antiwar resolutions, pro-Union members bolted. Hendricks recognized that the peace movement would discredit the party, and he was sufficiently familiar with the legislature to be certain that there were enough pro-Union Democrats to defeat the resolutions. Accepting both his reasoning and his head counting, the bolters resumed their seats and defeated the peace resolutions.[5]

Hendricks took his oath as a U.S. senator in 1863, becoming one of only ten Democrats facing thirty-three Republicans. He soon assumed the role of his party's recognized leader in the Senate. Hendricks was a thorough partisan. "There were no neutral tints in his own political colors," future Indiana Democratic Senator Daniel Voorhees later commented. But even Republican senators acknowledged that his speeches were well prepared and that his arguments were plausible—if one accepted all of his premises. Assessing Hendricks' Senate career, the journalist A.K. McClure later said, "He was a Democratic Senator in the most trying times of the war, when many less faithful or less discreet men made hopeless shipwreck of their political future, but the record of Mr. Hendricks has stood the severest test and is conspicuous for its freedom from the partisan blunders which then and since have ranked as crimes."[6]

President Abraham Lincoln cultivated the support of War Democrats like Hendricks. As Congress prepared to adjourn in March 1865, Hendricks paid a last visit to the president, who told him, "We have differed in politics, Senator Hendricks, but you have uniformly treated my administration with fairness." During the period of congressional Reconstruction of the South that followed the war, Hendricks never missed an opportunity to remind Republican senators that

President Lincoln had opposed such radical Reconstruction measures as the Wade-Davis bill and had wanted a speedy return of the southern states to the Union. Hendricks consistently opposed repealing the fugitive slave laws until slavery was constitutionally abolished, and he tried to prevent African Americans from gaining the right to vote. "I say we are not of the same race," Hendricks declared; "we are so different that we ought not to compose one political community."[7]

Hendricks emerged as one of the few prominent Democrats not to be stigmatized as a Copperhead (or southern sympathizer) during the war. As a result, his name arose for the 1868 Democratic presidential nomination. He lost the nomination to New York Governor Horatio Seymour but went back to Indiana, where he was nominated to run for governor. In the fall, both Seymour and Hendricks were defeated. Hendricks returned to his law practice and bided his time for a revival of Democratic fortunes. Looking toward the 1872 presidential election, former Iowa Senator A.C. Dodge recommended Hendricks as a "worthy, able and excellent man." He believed that there was strong support throughout the Midwest for the Indianan, although he doubted that Hendricks would run well in the East. The Democrats instead nominated the eccentric newspaper editor Horace Greeley for president on a fusion ticket with liberal Republicans who opposed the corruption of the Ulysses Grant administration. That same year, Indiana Democrats nominated Hendricks to run again for governor and, while Greeley went down to a crashing defeat, Hendricks won the Indiana state house.[8]

Tilden-Hendricks

His victory in that important swing state made Hendricks a frontrunner for the Democratic presidential nomination in 1876. However, after the panic of 1873 and the widespread economic crisis that followed, Hendricks became publicly identified with agrarian reform and "soft money." Currency reformers believed that postwar contractions of the currency had caused the economic depression and that inflation of the currency through issuance of greenbacks or increased minting of silver currency would lower farmers' costs of repaying their debts. Such arguments struck fear into eastern financial circles, whose members supported sound currency based on gold and believed that any debasing of the currency would rob creditors of just returns on their investments. The hard-money element within the Democratic party rallied behind the nomination of Samuel J. Tilden, known in some circles as the "Great Forecloser." To balance Tilden, the party nominated the soft-money Hendricks for vice president.

The Republican candidate, Ohio governor Rutherford B. Hayes, carried every midwestern state except Hendricks' Indiana. On election night, it appeared that the Tilden-Hendricks ticket had won both the popular and the electoral vote, but the outcome in three southern states still controlled by Reconstruction governments remained in dispute. Both Republicans and Democrats claimed these electoral votes. The Democrats needed just one more state to win, the Republicans needed all of the disputed votes. When a deadlock developed between the Republican Senate and the Democratic House over counting the electoral votes, both sides reluctantly agreed to set up a special electoral commission. Republicans gained an 8-to-7 majority on the commission, and by that straight party vote the commission assigned all of the disputed electoral votes to Hayes, who was sworn in as president. To prevent a new civil war, Tilden and Hendricks accepted the outcome, but thereafter Democrats charged that the election had been stolen from them.[9]

Hobbled by Illness

After the electoral disappointment, Hendricks and his wife consoled themselves with a long journey through Europe. He returned to his law practice and continued to speak out on the issues of the day. Hoosiers were "a speech-loving people," as one of Hendricks' biographers noted, and large crowds always showed up for his orations. In 1880, Indiana once again boosted Hendricks for president, but while he was vacationing at Hot Springs, Arkansas, Hendricks suffered a stroke. Two years later, he developed a lameness in one foot—a result, claimed the journalist

Ben: Perley Poore, of Hendricks' frequent public speaking engagements:

> While speaking he was in the habit of bending forward on the tip of his right foot, resting the entire weight upon it. From the pressure of his right shoe a swelling arose on one of his toes. . . . In twenty-four hours erysipelas [an acute skin inflammation] developed, and it was only after an illness of six months that he recovered. But he always afterwards was somewhat lame, especially when he was fatigued.[10]

As the 1884 election approached, Samuel Tilden, who had also suffered a paralytic stroke, mentioned to a newspaper reporter that his old running mate Thomas Hendricks wanted a reprise of the 1876 ticket of Tilden and Hendricks, "and I do not wonder, considering my weakness!" Tilden announced his withdrawal from the race, which left the Democratic nomination wide open. No one doubted that Hendricks was available for the nomination in 1884, but his constant availability in every presidential election since 1868 had devalued his candidacy. The party looked for a new face to unite them and lead them to victory after so many years in the minority. Hendricks was dismissed as a man of "inordinate ambition."[11]

Cleveland-Hendricks

Hendricks attended the Democratic National Convention in 1884 not as a candidate but rather as a delegate who would nominate former Indiana Senator Joseph E. McDonald. His appearance at the convention drew much enthusiastic applause, since he represented the "old ticket" of 1876 that had been robbed of victory. As the convention moved toward nominating the reform governor of New York, Grover Cleveland, Cleveland's opponents—especially New York City's Tammany Hall—concluded that Hendricks was the only man around whom the opposition could be united. They planned a strategy to stampede the convention to Hendricks the next day. Just as Indiana swung its vote to him, Hendricks entered the convention hall through a door facing the delegates. The band struck up a tune as Tammany Hall boss John Kelly and his henchmen leaped from their seats and began shouting for Hendricks. As the delegates paraded, Hendricks sat calmly. "To those near him," Indiana Senator Daniel Voorhees asserted, "he simply appeared to enjoy in a quiet silent way the popular approval of his long and faithful services."[12]

These tactics might have worked, except that Cleveland's managers got wind of the conspiracy and sent messages to all the delegates warning them not to get caught up in any spurious demonstrations. Cleveland's supporters argued that New York was essential for a Democratic victory and that Cleveland, a hard-money reform governor, could attract liberal Republican voters, a group known as the mugwumps. These arguments prevailed, and the Hendricks boom fizzled when Illinois increased its vote for Cleveland, followed by enough other states to give Cleveland the nomination at the end of the second ballot. Hendricks was rewarded with the vice-presidential nomination, once again to balance a hard-money presidential candidate and to offer the promise of carrying the swing state of Indiana.[13]

The prospect of victory invigorated Hendricks, and he campaigned valiantly, proving "a tower of strength for the ticket" in what has often been described as the "dirtiest" campaign in American political history. He attacked the incumbent Republican administration, helped stop a party bolt by Tammany Hall, drew large crowds to his speeches, and dramatically survived a late-night train wreck while campaigning in Illinois. Hendricks won praise as an "urbane leader." He stood five feet nine inches tall and was described as "well proportioned and stoutly built, though not corpulent." His once light hair had turned silver, and he wore "the least of side whiskers, which are light gray, and his complexion is fair." As a speaker he was clear and forceful, while in conversation he was "easy, courteous, cautious, and deferential.[14]

Vice President of the Spoilsmen

In 1884, Democrats won their first presidential election since 1856, and Thomas Hendricks returned as presiding officer to the Senate where he had once served in a pitifully small minority. From the start, however, Hendricks found himself at odds with President Cleveland, a scrupulously honest man with good intentions but limited vision. Unlike Hendricks, who had long called for more government intervention in the economy to promote agrarian reform, Cleveland advocated laissez-faire economics and was a Social Darwinist who thought the slightest hint of government paternalism would undermine the national character.[15]

Mugwump reformers waited to see if Cleveland would expand the Civil Service System recently established by the Pendleton Act, but Democrats, long out of power, demanded patronage. Vice President Hendricks and many Democratic senators, furious when Cleveland ignored the patronage requests of their state party organizations, considered the president's conduct "treacherous." Cleveland dismissed these complaints as the howls of old Jacksonian spoilsmen and wild-eyed currency reformers, among whom he counted his vice president. But by midsummer 1885, Cleveland buckled at the threat of revolt within his party. He replaced his civil-service-reform-minded assistant postmaster general with former Illinois Congressman Adlai Stevenson, "who understood practical politics." Given free rein, Stevenson replaced Republican postmasters with deserving Democrats at a fast clip, until more than 40,000 federal jobs changed hands.[16]

The Indiana Democratic organization was particularly outspoken about its dissatisfaction with Cleveland's skimpy patronage, and Vice President Hendricks became known as "Vice President of the spoilsmen." The label "spoilsman" distressed Hendricks. As one senator who knew him explained, Hendricks felt the charge came from those who "had been wont to linger in the shade and slumber while he and the 'boys,' as he loved sometimes to call the party workers, had borne the heat and dust and burden of the battle."[17]

In September, Hendricks left Washington to attend the thirty-fifth anniversary reunion of the surviving members of the constitutional convention of Indiana and to rest in anticipation of the coming session of Congress in December. While

at home in Indianapolis, he died in his sleep on November 25, 1885.

Death of the Vice President

Hendricks' death eliminated the leader of the possible rival camp to Cleveland's presidency, but also for the second time in a decade deprived the nation of a vice president for more than three years, raising concerns about the problem of presidential succession. If Cleveland should die, who would become president? The Presidential Succession Act of 1792 provided that the Senate's president pro tempore and the Speaker of the House, in that order, should succeed. There was concern that one of these offices might soon be filled with members of the opposition rather than members of Cleveland's party, since both posts were vacant at the time of Hendricks' sudden death and, while Democrats controlled the House, Republicans controlled the Senate. On the recommendation of Massachusetts Republican Senator George F. Hoar, Congress in 1886 adopted a law that eliminated congressional officers from the line of succession in favor of cabinet officers, in order of their rank. This system prevailed until 1947, when the death of a president had again left the vice-presidency open for almost an entire term, stimulating another reevaluation and a different solution to the problem.[18]

When President Cleveland ran for reelection in 1888, Democrats had to choose a replacement for Thomas Hendricks. The honor went to former Ohio Senator Allen G. Thurman. This time, Cleveland faced a Hoosier Republican, Senator Benjamin Harrison. Without Hendricks on the ticket, the Democrats failed to carry Indiana. Although Cleveland won a plurality of the popular vote, he lost the electoral college and with it the presidency.

Hendricks' death, as the veteran journalist Ben: Perley Poore judged, "removed an official around whom the disaffected Democrats could have crystallized into a formidable opposition," for Hendricks had not been disposed to accept being what Hannibal Hamlin had described as the fifth wheel on a coach.[19]

NOTES

[1] W.U. Hensel, "A Biographical Sketch of Thomas A. Hendricks," in William Dorsheimer, *Life and Public Services of Hon. Grover Cleveland* (New York, 1884), pp. 184–95; John W. Holcombe and Hubert M. Skinner, *Life and Public Services of Thomas A. Hendricks with Selected Speeches and Writings* (Indianapolis, 1886), p. 93.

[2] Hensel, pp. 210–12; Holcombe and Skinner, pp. 117–18; Ralph D. Gray, "Thomas A. Hendricks: Spokesman for the Democracy," in *Gentlemen from Indiana: National Party Candidates, 1836–1940*, ed. Ralph D. Gray (Indianapolis, 1977), p. 126.

[3] Gray, p. 128.

[4] Holcombe and Skinner, pp. 195, 245.

[5] Christopher Dell, *Lincoln and the War Democrats: The Grand Erosion of Conservative Tradition* (Rutherford, NJ, 1975), p. 201.

[6] U.S., Congress, *Memorial Addresses on the Life and Character of Thomas A. Hendricks* (Washington: Government Printing Office, 1886), pp. 26, 38–39; Hensel, p. 225.

[7] Holcombe and Skinner, p. 267; Hensel, p. 226; Eric Foner, *Reconstruction: America's Unfinished Revolution, 1863–1877* (New York, 1988), pp. 278–79.

[8] Horace Samuel Merrill, *Bourbon Democracy of the Middle West, 1865–1896* (Seattle, 1967; reprint of 1953 edition), p. 71.

[9] The best account of the disputed election is Keith Ian Polakoff, *The Politics of Inertia: The Election of 1876 and the End of Reconstruction* (Baton Rouge, LA, 1976). See also Chapter 19 of this volume, "William Almon Wheeler," p. 246.

[10] Hensel, pp. 279, 284; Ben: Perley Poore, *Perley's Reminiscences of Sixty Years in the National Metropolis* (Philadelphia, 1887), 2:503–4.

[11] Herbert Eaton, *Presidential Timber: A History of Nominating Conventions, 1868–1960* (New York, 1964), pp. 102–7; Allan Nevins, *Grover Cleveland, A Study in Courage* (New York, 1932), pp. 146–47; *Memorial Addresses*, p. 25.

[12] Nevins, p. 154; *Memorial Addresses*, p. 29.

[13] Eaton, p. 111; Nevins, p. 154; Poore, p. 284; Richard E. Welch, Jr., *The Presidencies of Grover Cleveland* (Lawrence, KS, 1988), pp. 28–29.

[14] Nevins, p. 177; Hensel, p. 255; Holcombe and Skinner, pp. 7, 363–64.

[15] Vincent P. De Santis, "Grover Cleveland: Revitalization of the Presidency," in *Six Presidents from the Empire State*, ed. Harry J. Sievers (Tarrytown, NY, 1974), pp. 90–91.

[16] John A. Garraty, *The New Commonwealth, 1877–1890* (New York, 1968), pp. 288–90; Horace Samuel Merrill, *Bourbon Leader: Grover Cleveland and the Democratic Party* (Boston, 1957), p. 99. See also Chapter 23 of this volume, "Adlai Ewing Stevenson," pp. 280–81.

[17] Nevins, pp. 237, 247; *Memorial Addresses*, p. 63.

[18] Chester L. Barrows, *William M. Evarts: Lawyer, Diplomat, Statesman* (Chapel Hill, NC, 1941), p. 446; Richard E. Welch, Jr., *George Frisbie Hoar and the Half-Breed Republicans* (Cambridge, MA, 1971), p. 137; John D. Feerick, *From Failing Hands: The Story of Presidential Succession* (New York, 1965), pp. 140–46.

[19] Poore, 2:503–4.

Chapter 22

LEVI PARSONS MORTON
1889–1893

LEVI P. MORTON

Chapter 22

LEVI PARSONS MORTON

22nd Vice President: 1889–1893

Business experience had taught him conservatism. He never was influenced by crazy theorists.
—SENATOR THOMAS C. PLATT

Like a hero from the pages of a Horatio Alger novel, Levi P. Morton worked his way up by pluck and luck to fame and fortune. From a boy toiling in a country store, he rose to become one of the nation's wealthiest and most influential bankers and vice president of the United States. Morton might have become president as well, had his political acumen matched his financial ability.

Youth

Born on May 16, 1824, in the little village of Shoreham, Vermont, Levi Parsons Morton was named for his uncle, the first American missionary to Palestine. He was the son of a Congregational preacher, who moved his family from church to church in New England, never accruing much wealth. Although young Morton wanted to attend college, his father was too poor to send him. An older brother advised him not to worry about further schooling since "a self-taught man is worth two of your college boys." Instead, Morton took a job in a country store. After getting his fill of heavy manual labor, he sought respite as a teacher in a country school. Then he took another clerkship in the general store of W.W. Estabrook, in Concord, New Hampshire, where he learned the bookkeeper's art of calculating profit and loss.[1]

Estabrook dispatched Morton to run his store in Hanover, New Hampshire. There the young Morton lived with the family of a Dartmouth College professor and met Lucy Young Kimball, whom he would eventually marry thirteen years later. But first he had a fortune to earn. Morton later recalled that he was happiest "when I was learning how to accomplish things; when I was building up my business." When his employer went bankrupt, the chief creditor, James M. Beebe, came to New Hampshire to inspect the situation and was impressed enough with Morton's industriousness to invite him to join James M. Beebe & Co. in Boston—"the business Mecca for every Yankee boy." Beebe & Co., Boston's largest importing firm, soon took Junius Spencer Morgan as a partner, thus introducing Levi Morton to Morgan's son, J.P. Morgan, who would one day become his principal rival as a banker. In 1854, Beebe sent Morton to New York City to take charge of the company's operations there. A year later, Morton formed his own dry goods company in New York. Finally wealthy and secure enough to settle down, he married Lucy Kimball in 1856. The new Mrs. Morton disliked his Old Testament name of Levi and began calling her husband "L.P.," as he became known among family and friends thereafter.[2]

Banking and Politics

Morton's chief business was importing cotton from the South for New England's textile industry and exporting manufactured goods from the North to the agricultural South. When the Civil War broke out in the spring of 1861, his loss of southern clients forced him to suspend business. For the next decade, Morton worked to pay back his own creditors, dollar for dollar. Although the war soon stimulated the northern economy and rebuilt Morton's financial base, he saw a safer and more profitable future in banking. In 1863, he founded a Wall Street banking house, later named Morton, Bliss & Co., with a London firm called Morton, Rose. By the end of the war, Morton's bank could challenge the powerful Jay Cooke & Co. for the right to handle government transactions. In 1873 Cooke's bank failed, leaving Morton as one of the preeminent bankers in the nation.[3]

Morton's gracious manners and generous campaign contributions made him many friends in Washington, among them President Ulysses S. Grant and Grant's strongest supporter in Congress, Senator Roscoe Conkling of New York. Morton and his British partner, Sir John Rose, expanded their financial and political fortunes by facilitating U.S. negotiations with Great Britain to settle the "Alabama Claims." During the war, Britain had violated its neutrality by allowing the construction of Confederate shipping on its soil. Senator Charles Sumner, chairman of the Foreign Relations Committee, pressed the administration to demand large-scale compensation from Britain, including the annexation of Canada, even if those claims led the two nations to war. Morton and Rose persuaded the British and Americans to accept international arbitration of their war claims; the U.S. to reduce its demands; and the British to pay $15 million in damages, for which the house of Morton, Rose acted as disbursing office. When advised that the government's position would be strengthened by using Morton, Rose as its agent, President Grant questioned whether Morton's firm was strong because of the government's patronage rather than the other way around.[4]

After his wife Lucy died in 1871, L.P. Morton married Anna Livingston Reade Street in 1873. Anna's connections as a member of New York's old Knickerbocker society helped propel Morton into New York's political scene. From all accounts, Anna Morton combined great charm, wisdom and prudence, making her admirably suited to be the wife of a political man. In 1876, Morton became financial chairman of the Republican National Committee. Aware that success in this position might reward him with an attractive diplomatic post, he was also considering a race for Congress. Morton asked his friend Whitelaw Reid, editor of the New-York Tribune, "If elected, and I wanted a foreign mission, could I well resign and accept that, or if defeated, what then?" adding "I have never made a speech in my life." Reid encouraged him not to worry about speechmaking but advised that a resignation from a newly won office would create some bitterness. When Morton declared his candidacy for a House seat from New York's Eleventh District, a fashionable residential area around upper Fifth Avenue, he ran on a platform of sound currency based on the gold standard. That plank would remain consistent through his next quarter century in politics. His opponents pictured him as a plutocrat and "a tool of Wall Street," charges that would similarly follow him in every election. Morton lost by a narrow margin but won when he ran again for the seat in 1878.[5]

The Conkling Machine

In politics, Morton identified himself with the New York political faction, the "stalwarts," headed by Republican Senator Roscoe Conkling. Opposing the stalwarts were the "half-breed" Republicans who rallied behind Senator James G. Blaine of Maine. Conkling and Blaine were bitter personal and political rivals, yet few substantive differences existed between their rival factions on the issues of the day. Conkling's machine was more identified with New York's financial interests and made sound currency its chief legislative aim, while the half-breeds placed more emphasis on railroads, industry, and the protective tariff. Both organizations, however, thrived on government patronage and opposed civil service reform. Morton's presence in the Conkling machine attested to its connections with Wall Street financiers.

Entering Congress in 1879, Morton acted as much as a representative of Morton, Bliss & Co. as he did as a representative of the Eleventh District, since he saw no difference between his own interests and those of his constituents. The newspaper reporter George Alfred Townsend described Morton as "not a loquacious man, and yet an interesting talker, and one of the pleasantest expressions of his face is that of the respectful, intelligent listener." He stood six feet tall, straight-limbed and erect, and walked with "flexible and quiet movements." With close-cropped hair and a square jaw, his face had a cosmopolitan appearance, "though the New England lines are decided." The "whole tone of his talk and character are toward tranquillity," Townsend observed. In the House, Morton was "a close listener, a silent critic, a genial answerer; neither intrusive nor obtrusive." Since Morton was wealthier than his colleagues, he was able to establish his family in a handsome house on Lafayette Square that became a popular meeting place for politicos and high society. Morton won a reputation for his urbanity and generous hospitality. Among the friends he made was Representative James Garfield of Ohio.[6]

Declining the Vice-Presidency

In 1880, Morton went to the Republican convention as a Conkling lieutenant, dedicated to winning a third-term nomination for Ulysses S. Grant. Conkling's stalwarts were equally determined to stop the nomination of Blaine. When a deadlock developed, Blaine's half-breeds threw their support to Garfield, a darkhorse candidate. Once Garfield won the nomination, he realized that he would need a New Yorker on the ticket and immediately thought of his wealthy and well-positioned friend, L.P. Morton. Morton scurried to find Conkling, who objected. When Morton declined the offer, the vice-presidential nomination went instead to another Conkling man, Chester A. Arthur, who had fewer scruples about breaking with the boss.

Still trying to make peace with the Conkling faction, Garfield came to New York in August 1880 for a meeting in Morton's suite at the Fifth Avenue Hotel. There, Garfield promised to support the Conkling machine's patronage demands, which included the post of secretary of the treasury. The Treasury Department oversaw the New York customhouse, upon whose patronage the New York machine had been built. Morton agreed to chair Garfield's campaign finance committee, assuming that the treasury portfolio would be his. After winning the election, however, Garfield insisted that he had made no spe-

cific pledges. In December 1880, Garfield recorded in his diary that Morton was "under misapprehension" that he had been promised the Treasury Department. "This was not my understanding and seems wholly inadmissable. It would be a congestion of financial power at the money centre and would create jealousy at the West."[7]

Blaine, who had been named secretary of state, pronounced Morton "unfit" for the treasury, while Senator Conkling traveled to Garfield's home in Mentor, Ohio, to lobby for Morton. Conkling wanted to balance Blaine in the cabinet, to protect his organization's control over the New York customhouse, and to remove Morton from a hotly contested race for the other Senate seat from New York, which Conkling wanted for Tom Platt. Haughtily, Conkling told the president-elect that New York would rather be passed over completely in the cabinet if it could not obtain the Treasury Department. Even Garfield's wife Lucretia joined the fray when she wrote from a New York shopping trip:

> Mr. [Whitelaw] Reid told me this morning that Morton had been very ugly in his talk about you, using the expression that seems to be so gratifying to the Conkling clique, "That Ohio man cannot be relied upon to stand by his pledges."[8]

Shortly before the inauguration, Garfield offered Morton the secretaryship of the navy, which he accepted. But Conkling and Arthur roused Morton from his bed in the middle of the night and persuaded him to decline the post. The next day Garfield recorded: "Morton broke down on my hands under the pressure of his N.Y. friends, who called him out of bed at 4 this morning to prevent his taking the Navy Dep't. . . . The N.Y. delegation are in a great row because I do not give the Treasury to that state." Despite his exasperation, Garfield still owed Morton something for his work as campaign finance chairman and settled on making him minister to France.[9]

Collapse of the Conkling Machine

As president, Garfield confronted the Conkling machine by appointing the half-breed Republican William Robertson to be collector of the port of New York and head of the customhouse. His action triggered a series of events that culminated in the resignations of Senators Conkling and Platt, who expected to be reelected by the New York legislature as a show of support. Instead, both were defeated. In the midst of this monumental struggle, on July 2, 1881, President Garfield was shot by a deranged follower of Conkling's stalwarts. On July 20, when Morton sailed for France, Garfield was still lingering and recovery seemed possible. But on September 19, the president died, making Chester Arthur—and not L.P. Morton—president of the United States. Morton spent the next four years in the diplomatic service, attending largely to the ceremonies connected with France's gift of the Statue of Liberty to the United States. But he still harbored ambitions for a seat in the Senate.[10]

By the time Morton returned to the United States, Roscoe Conkling had quit politics for a lucrative law practice and Tom Platt had picked up Conkling's leadership of the New York party. In 1884 Platt decided to support Blaine for president, on the grounds that Chet Arthur had deserted his former friends. Morton followed the Platt machine into the Blaine camp. He was one of the two hundred businessmen who attended the infamous "millionaires' dinner" given in Blaine's honor at Delmonico's restaurant on October 29, 1884. At that dinner, a Protestant minister rose to denounce the Democrats as the party of "rum, Romanism, and rebellion." Blaine ignored the remark, but Democrats seized upon it and publicized it widely among Irish voters. Blaine lost New York by a narrow margin and with it the presidency.[11]

Platt put Morton forward unsuccessfully for senator in 1885 and 1887. In the former instance, Morton was perceived as the frontrunner, having greater resources and the full backing of Platt's machine. But Platt's men had made the mistake of taking all the key committee posts in the state assembly, causing the "soreheads" who had been left out to unite behind another candidate, who snatched away the coveted Senate seat. The 1887 election was a three-man race, in which another candidate appeared to have a better chance of winning for the stalwarts. Morton's withdrawal from the race, seen as an expression of his selfless sense of duty to his party (or faction of the party), raised his chances for the vice-presidential nomination in 1888.[12]

A Strange Victory

When James G. Blaine, declining in health, made it clear he would not run again for president in 1888, Tom Platt threw New York's support to Indiana Senator Benjamin Harrison—the grandson of former President William Henry Harrison. Blaine recommended Harrison as the best candidate and suggested for vice president former Representative William Walter Phelps of New Jersey. However, Platt's support of Morton helped the banker defeat Phelps by a margin of five to one. The ticket of Harrison and Morton put together a strange victory in the presidential election. They lost the popular vote by 90,000 but still managed to beat the incumbent President Grover Cleveland in the electoral college, 233 to 168. The journalist Arthur Wallace Dunn attributed the Republican success in 1888 to the combined political shrewdness of Republican National Committee chairman and Pennsylvania Senator Matt Quay and New York party boss Tom Platt.[13]

As president, however, Benjamin Harrison would not allow Platt and Quay to dictate his cabinet and other federal appointments. Although principled, his stand against the spoilsmen alienated him from those most responsible for his election. A thoughtful man, Harrison was cold in person but articulate and compelling as a public speaker. By contrast, Vice President Morton was no public speaker, but "a loveable personality," who "filled every position with grace, dignity, and ability." In an era of greed, corruption, and excess, Harrison and Morton both epitomized family life and puritanical religious values. Harrison's cabinet was conservative and business oriented, with the department store magnate John Wanamaker serving as postmaster general. The political officeseekers ridiculed the publicity received by Harrison's family, particularly his granddaughter, known as Baby Ruth (namesake of the candy bar); they scoffed that the supposedly puritanical Morton owned Washington's Shoreham Hotel (which he named after his Vermont birthplace), where liquor was sold; and they belittled the attention given to Wanamaker's Sunday school teaching. As a spoilsmen's verse put it:

The baby rules the White House,
    Levi runs the bar,
Wanny runs the Sunday school,
    And dammit here we are! [14]

Due to Mrs. Harrison's illnesses and death in 1892, Anna Morton often entertained on behalf of the administration at the vice president's mansion on Scott Circle. "Mrs. Morton became the leader of society in Washington, and there was never a more brilliant and popular leader than she," according to one account. "It was her innate graciousness, her innate tact, and her kindness of heart . . . which won her admiration and respect of all." Morton, whose only child by his first marriage had died in infancy, had five daughters by his second wife and boasted a lively home. [15]

The Businessman's Cabinet and the Millionaires' Club

Just as Harrison's cabinet was called the "businessman's cabinet" for its inclusion of Wanamaker and the Vermont marble baron Redfield Proctor, the Senate over which Vice President Morton presided was dubbed a "millionaires' club." In the late nineteenth century, businessmen had steadily gained control over both the Republican and Democratic parties and used their political positions to advance their economic interests. Senators became identified as spokesmen for railroads, timber, mining, and other industries. As California Senator George Hearst, who had made his millions in mining, proclaimed: "the members of the Senate are the survivors of the fittest." It seemed appropriate, therefore, that the Senate's presiding officer should be one of the nation's most prominent bankers. [16]

President Harrison considered the greatest failure of his administration to be its inability to pass the federal elections bill sponsored by Henry Cabot Lodge. Known as the "Force bill," it was intended to force the South to permit black men to vote and thereby protect their civil rights. After Republican losses in the congressional elections of 1890, the Senate had taken up the Lodge bill again, only to encounter a Democratic filibuster by those who believed it would restore a

Reconstruction-like Republican rule in the South. Harrison summoned Republican senators to the White House and urged them to do everything possible to pass the bill. But western silver Republicans believed that the nation's most pressing need was an inflated currency to cure economic ills. These Republicans joined Democrats in passing a resolution to take up a new currency measure in place of the elections bill.

The elections bill reached the Senate floor only because of Vice President Morton's tie-breaking vote. But the bill immediately encountered another filibuster, and Morton did nothing to help Republican efforts to break it. Republican senators hoped to persuade Morton to vacate his chair, in order to allow a more sympathetic member to preside, but Morton insisted on being present throughout the debate. Because the vice president had announced that he planned to preside as a neutral figure and not follow the dictates of the Republican caucus, he was accused of doing little to maintain party discipline and compared unfavorably to Speaker of the House Thomas Brackett Reed, who presided with an iron fist. Massachusetts Senator George F. Hoar sneered at Morton as one of those vice presidents who "asserted their authority with as little show of force as if they were presiding over a company of guests at their own table." Finally on January 22, 1891, a resolution to replace the elections bill with another was passed 35 to 34, and the elections bill died. [17]

Unceremoniously Dumped

As the Republican convention approached in 1892, Morton's supporters floated his name for the presidency, but he lacked the necessary delegate votes. Then Secretary of State Blaine resigned from Harrison's cabinet to become a candidate himself. The "Old Guard" bosses, notably Pennsylvania's Quay and New York's Platt, supported Blaine, but President Harrison held the majority of the delegates. Morton was unceremoniously dumped from the ticket in favor of another New Yorker, his supposed friend Whitelaw Reid. President Harrison apparently had never cared much for his vice president—or forgiven him for his neutrality over the Force bill—and did not demand his renomination. At the same time, the "Platt Contingent" at the convention determined that a Harrison ticket was doomed to defeat, and they had better plans for Morton.[18]

In 1894, Platt ran Morton for governor of New York, a race that he won handily. Platt later memorialized Morton as "the safest Governor New York ever had. Business experience had taught him conservatism. He never was influenced by crazy theorists, but conducted his administration as he did his great private financial institutions." Senator Chauncey Depew similarly credited Morton as bringing to the governorship "business ability which had made him one of the great merchants and foremost bankers." In 1896, Platt put the seventy-two-year-old Governor Morton forward as New York's favorite son for the Republican presidential nomination, to stop the nomination of Ohio Governor William McKinley, whose past flirtation with free silver worried the gold standard men of the East. Platt organized banquets and planted newspaper editorials that encouraged Morton to envision himself in the White House. But these efforts were routed by the campaign strategies of the brilliant businessman-tactician Mark Hanna, who engineered McKinley's nomination.[19]

Morton retired from politics and returned to his banking career, organizing the Morton Trust Company. In 1909, when Morton was in his eighties, an offer came from J.P. Morgan to merge the Morton bank into the Morgan Guaranty Trust Company. Morton deeply regretted that, as a result of the merger, the company bearing his name was retired from the business world. L.P. Morton died on his ninety-sixth birthday in 1920, already a long-forgotten name in both banking and politics.[20]

NOTES

[1] Robert McNutt McElroy, *Levi Parsons Morton: Banker, Diplomat and Statesman* (New York, 1975; reprint of 1930 edition), pp. 25–26.

[2] Ibid., pp. 20–37, 39; George Alfred Townsend, "Levi P. Morton: A Biography," in Lew Wallace, *Life of Gen. Ben Harrison* (Philadelphia, 1888), p. 361.

[3] McElroy, pp. 42, 51.

[4] David M. Jordan, *Roscoe Conkling of New York: Voice in the Senate* (Ithaca, NY, 1971), pp. 151–52; William S. McFeely, *Grant, A Biography* (New York, 1981), pp. 333, 336, 355.

[5] Royal Cortissoz, *The Life of Whitelaw Reid* (New York, 1921), 1:351; McElroy, pp. 71–74.

[6] McElroy, pp. 84–88, 97; Townsend, pp. 354–55, 372.

[7] Theodore Clarke Smith, *The Life and Letters of James Abram Garfield* (New Haven, CT, 1925), 2:1047, 1055; Louis J. Lang, ed., *The Autobiography of Thomas Collier Platt* (New York, 1910), pp. 128, 131–32. See also Chapter 20 of this volume, "Chester Alan Arthur," p. 253.

[8] Smith, pp. 1074, 1078, 1083–84.

[9] Ibid., pp. 1090–91: Harry James Brown and Frederick D. Williams, *The Diary of James A. Garfield* (East Lansing, MI, 1981), 4:552; Jordan, p. 376.

[10] Smith, p. 1072; Justus D. Doenecke, *The Presidencies of James A. Garfield & Chester A. Arthur* (Lawrence, KS, 1981), pp. 20–21, 30, 95.

[11] Lang, ed., p. 181; Jordan, pp. 416–17.

[12] Chester L. Barrows, *William M. Evarts: Lawyer, Diplomat, Statesman* (Chapel Hill, NC, 1941), pp. 436–37; Lang, ed., pp. 187–92; Paul Lancaster, *Gentleman of the Press: The Life and Times of an Early Reporter, Julian Ralph of the Sun* (Syracuse, NY, 1992), p. 141.

[13] Robert F. Wesser, "Election of 1888," in *History of American Presidential Elections, 1789–1968*, ed. Arthur M. Schlesinger, Jr., and Fred L. Israel (New York, 1969), 2:1635; Arthur Wallace Dunn, *From Harrison to Harding: A Personal Narrative, Covering a Third of a Century, 1888–1921* (Port Washington, NY, 1972; reprint of 1922 edition), 1:8.

[14] Homer Socolofsky and Allan B. Spetter, *The Presidency of Benjamin Harrison* (Lawrence, KS, 1987), pp. 19–45; Frank Carpenter, *Carp's Washington* (New York, 1960), p. 305; Chauncey M. Depew, *My Memories of Eighty Years* (New York, 1924), p. 220; Herbert Adams Gibbons, *John Wanamaker* (New York, 1926), 1:328.

[15] *Great Leaders and National Issues of 1896* (New York, 1896), p. 287.

[16] Thomas C. Corchran and William Miller, *The Age of Enterprise: A Social History of Industrial America* (New York, 1942), pp. 162–64.

[17] McElroy, pp. 188–91; Socolofsky and Spetter, pp. 64–65; Charles W. Calhoun, "Civil Religion and the Gilded Age Presidency: The Case of Benjamin Harrison," *Presidential Studies Quarterly* 23 (Fall 1993): 658; George F. Hoar, *Autobiography of Seventy Years* (New York, 1903), 2:68.

[18] McElroy, pp. 194–205; H. Wayne Morgan, *From Hayes to McKinley: National Party Politics, 1877–1896* (Syracuse, NY, 1969), p. 415.

[19] Lang, ed., pp. 332–33; Depew, pp. 147, 218, 220; James A. Kehl, *Boss Rule in the Gilded Age: Matt Quay of Pennsylvania* (Pittsburgh, 1981), pp. 199–203; Morgan, p. 491.

[20] McElroy, p. 320.

Chapter 23

ADLAI EWING STEVENSON
1893–1897

ADLAI E. STEVENSON

Chapter 23

ADLAI EWING STEVENSON

23rd Vice President: 1893–1897

"Has Mr. Cleveland yet consulted you to that extent?" Vice President Stevenson was once asked. "Not yet," he replied. "But, there are still a few weeks of my term remaining."

In February 1900, the *Chicago American* ran a photograph of former Vice President Adlai Stevenson holding his new grandson, Adlai Ewing Stevenson II. That year the grandfather was again nominated to run for vice president on the Democratic ticket. A half century later, the grandson would run twice as the Democratic nominee for president and gain even greater national and international prominence. Yet it was the grandfather who came closest to becoming president of the United States—when President Grover Cleveland underwent critical surgery.[1]

Youth

The Stevenson family were Presbyterians from Northern Ireland who migrated first to Pennsylvania and then to North Carolina and Kentucky. Adlai E. Stevenson, son of John Turner Stevenson and Eliza Ewing Stevenson, was born on the family farm in Christian County, Kentucky, on October 23, 1835. He attended the common school in Blue Water, Kentucky, presided over by a "dreaded schoolmaster," Mr. Caskie. Years later, when as vice-presidential candidate Stevenson was about to speak at a barbecue in Kentucky, the elderly schoolmaster approached the platform and inquired, "Adlai, I came twenty miles to hear you speak; don't you remember me?" Stevenson instantly replied, "Yes, Mr. Caskie, I still have a few marks left to remember you by!"[2]

In 1852, when Adlai was sixteen, frost killed the family's tobacco crop. His father set free their few slaves and moved to Bloomington, Illinois, where he operated a sawmill. Adlai worked in the mill and taught school, earning money for college. He attended the Presbyterian-run Centre College in Danville, Kentucky, headed by the Reverend Lewis Warner Green. Adlai fell in love with Green's daughter Letitia, but family problems delayed their marriage for nine years. His father's death prompted Adlai to return to Bloomington to run the sawmill; then, when the Reverend Green died, Letitia and her mother moved near Bloomington. Mrs. Green considered the Stevensons socially inferior and did not favor a marriage between the young people, even though Adlai had studied law and had been admitted to the bar in 1858. Not until 1866 did Adlai and Letitia finally marry. They had three daughters and a son, Lewis, who became father to the later presidential candidate.[3]

A Democrat in Republican Territory

As a young lawyer, Stevenson encountered such celebrated Illinois attorneys as Stephen A. Douglas and Abraham Lincoln, campaigning for Douglas in his 1858 Senate race against Lincoln. Stevenson also made speeches against the "Know-Nothing" movement, a nativist group opposed to immigrants and Catholics. That stand helped cement his support in Illinois' large German and Irish communities. In a predominantly Republican area, the Democratic Stevenson won friends through his storytelling and his warm and engaging personality. In 1860 at the age of twenty-five, he was appointed master in chancery (an aide in a court of equity), his first public office, which he held during the Civil War. In 1864 Stevenson was elected district attorney, and at the end of his term in 1868 he entered law practice with his cousin, James S. Ewing. Stevenson & Ewing became one of the state's most prominent law firms.[4]

In 1874, when Stevenson ran for the House of Representatives as a Democrat, local Republican newspapers painted him as a "vile secessionist," but the continuing hardships from the economic panic of 1873 caused voters to sweep him into office with the first Democratic congressional majority since the Civil War. In the presidential election year of 1876, however, the Republican ticket headed by Rutherford B. Hayes carried his district, and Stevenson was narrowly defeated for reelection, taking 49.6 percent of the vote. Then, in 1878, he ran on both the Democratic and Greenback tickets and won. Returning to a House from which one-third of his earlier colleagues had either voluntarily retired or been retired by the voters gave Stevenson a sense of the swiftly changing tides of politics. In 1880, again a presidential election year, he once more lost narrowly, and he was defeated in his final race for Congress in 1882.[5]

The Headsman of the Post Office

Stevenson served as a delegate to the Democratic convention of 1884 that nominated Grover Cleveland for president. Cleveland's reform record as governor of New York helped win over Republican reformers, the mugwumps, who enabled him to defeat the popular but scandal-ridden Republican candidate James G. Blaine. When Cleveland took office as president, the mugwumps expected him to carry out the goals of civil service reform rather than return to the spoilsmanship of Jacksonian Democracy. They felt reassured at first when Cleveland appointed an able Republican as postmaster of New York City. But job-hungry Democrats besieged the administration for patronage, and the president had to respond to the angry rumblings from his party on Capitol Hill.

Particularly at stake were the 55,000 fourth-class postmasters. Although paying just a thousand dollars a year, these offices were critically important to local political operations. In small towns, the postmaster knew everyone, as well as the mail they received and the newspapers and magazines they read. This knowledge placed the postmasters in an excellent position to keep the national party organization informed on public opinion. The local postmasters would also distribute party literature in bulk more cheaply than if it were individually addressed. Former Democratic nominee Samuel J. Tilden, a master political organizer, reminded the Cleveland administration that these rural post offices essentially served as their party's local headquarters. To leave them in the hands of Republicans would be "infidelity to the principles and causes of the Administration."[6]

When First Assistant Postmaster General Malcolm Hay, a civil service reformer, resigned due to ill health after only three months in office, Cleveland appointed the more partisan Adlai Stevenson to succeed him. Given free rein to remove Republican officeholders, Stevenson thoroughly enjoyed swinging the axe. One Republican journalist described Stevenson as "an official axman who beheaded Republican officeholders with the precision and dispatch of the French guillotine in the days of the Revolution." Dubbed "the Headsman" for replacing some 40,000 Republicans with deserving Democrats, he once "decapitated sixty-five Republican postmasters in two minutes." Republicans protested but recognized that they had swung the same axe, and even the mugwumps realized that true civil service reform probably could not be achieved until greater balance was achieved between Democratic and Republican officeholders.[7]

Cleveland rewarded Stevenson with a judicial nomination to the supreme court of the District of Columbia, but Senate Republicans refused to confirm the man who had discharged so many of their postmasters. When Cleveland was defeated for reelection in 1888, President Benjamin Harrison appointed James S. Clarkson as first assistant postmaster general, and Clarkson promptly undid Stevenson's handiwork by replacing 32,335 of the fourth-class postmasters. When the Democrats chose Cleveland once again as their standard bearer in 1892, they appeased party regulars by the nomination of the "headsman of the post-office," Adlai Stevenson, for vice president. As a supporter of using greenbacks and free silver to inflate the currency and alleviate economic distress in the rural districts, Stevenson balanced the ticket headed by Cleveland, the hard-money, gold-standard supporter. Just before the election, Cleveland learned that Republicans were planning a lurid exposé of Stevenson's soft-money record. Cleveland's campaign manager caught Stevenson at a speaking engagement in West Virginia and handed him a letter endorsing sound money. Stevenson signed the letter and released it to the press, thus defusing the issue. The winning Cleveland-Stevenson ticket carried Illinois, although not Stevenson's home district.[8]

Civil service reformers held out hope for the second Cleveland administration but saw Vice President Stevenson as a symbol of the spoils system. He never hesitated to feed names of Democrats to the Post Office Department. Once he called at the Treasury Department to protest against an appointment and was shown a letter he had written endorsing the candidate. Stevenson told the treasury officials not to pay attention to any of his written endorsements; if he really favored someone he would tell them personally.[9]

Silver and Gold

While such stories about "Uncle Adlai" brought smiles around Washington, Stevenson's presence as next in line to the presidency frightened Cleveland's more conservative supporters. Just before Cleveland took office, a financial panic on Wall Street had plunged the nation into depression. As a staunch advocate of limited government, Cleveland disapproved of any government program to reduce economic suffering. By contrast, Vice President Stevenson represented the "populist doctrines" of currency reform that were creeping into the Democratic party. In June 1893, after Cleveland proposed repeal of the Sherman Silver Purchase Act and a return to the gold standard, one of his hard-money supporters wrote Cleveland saying: "I wish you had Congress in session now. You may not be alive in September. It would make a vast

difference to the United States if you were not." The writer did not know that Cleveland faced a potentially fatal operation. A habitual cigar-smoker, Cleveland had developed cancer of the mouth that required immediate surgery. The president insisted that the surgery be kept secret to avoid another panic on Wall Street over the thought of a silverite like Stevenson in the White House. While on a yacht in New York harbor that summer, Cleveland had his entire upper jaw removed and replaced with an artificial device, an operation that left no outward scar. The cancer surgery remained secret for another quarter century. Cleveland's aides explained that he had merely had dental work. His vice president little realized how close he came to the presidency that summer.[10]

Meanwhile, a major battle loomed in the Senate over currency reform. In 1890, the Republican President Harrison had supported the Sherman Silver Purchase Act in return for silver Republicans' support of the protective tariff named after Ohio Representative—and future President—William McKinley. But in the 1890 elections the unpopular McKinley tariff defeated many Republicans, including McKinley, restored Democratic majorities in Congress, and bolstered the populist movement that was demanding more government intervention in railroad regulation, currency reform, and farm relief. Disdainful of the populists, Cleveland interpreted the Republican defeat as vindication of his policies. Upon reentering the White House in 1893, he was determined to repeal the Sherman Act to restore business confidence and therefore called Congress into extraordinary session in August to consider the issue.[11]

In October 1893, efforts to repeal the Sherman Silver Purchase Act met with a filibuster in the Senate. Indiana Senator Daniel Voorhees, leader of the Cleveland Democrats, announced that the Senate would remain in continuous session until a vote was taken. Opponents made repeated calls for quorums, feigned illness, and refused to appear even when summoned by the Senate sergeant at arms. Those conducting the filibuster benefitted from the cooperation of the presiding officer. Vice President Stevenson refused to turn his back on the silverites, who had helped to nominate him, and gave no aid to the administration in whipping the dissenters into line. The prominent Washington correspondent Julian Ralph knew that the Senate had no formal cloture procedure but heard that it might be possible for the vice president to cut off debate by simply ordering a vote. Ralph asked the opinion of former House Speaker Thomas B. Reed, who had broken similar dilatory actions in the House by counting the minority as present even if they failed to answer the roll. Reed asserted that the vice president "could do whatever he pleased if he had a majority behind him." But Democrat Isham G. Harris of Tennessee, the president pro tempore, strongly disagreed. "Why, sir, I don't believe he would live to accomplish it," said Harris (who later repudiated the threatening quote when it appeared in the Ralph story).[12]

New York Democratic Senator David Hill followed Ralph's suggestion by circulating a petition to force the vice president to overrule all dilatory motions, but it failed to attract many signers. Nor were Democrats able to agree on adoption of a cloture rule. Finally, the Senate accepted a compromise arranged by Maryland Democratic Senator Arthur Pue Gorman that established a gradual reduction of silver purchases over a three-year period. Although this agreement made possible passage of the repeal, President Cleveland never forgave Gorman for his compromise and thereafter rarely consulted this important Democratic leader. Repeal of the Sherman Silver Purchase Act only contracted the currency and further weakened the economy. Silverites called it the "Crime of 1893." The Democrats became tagged as the party of the "empty dinnerpail" and suffered sweeping congressional defeats in 1894.[13]

A Notable Sense of Humor

Adlai Stevenson enjoyed his role as vice president, presiding over "the most august legislative assembly known to men." He won praise for ruling in a dignified, nonpartisan manner. In personal appearance he stood six feet tall and was "of fine personal bearing and uniformly courteous to all." Although he was often a guest at the White House, Stevenson admitted that he was less an adviser to the president than "the

neighbor to his counsels." He credited the president with being "courteous at all times" but noted that "no guards were necessary to the preservation of his dignity. No one would have thought of undue familiarity." For his part, President Cleveland snorted that his vice president had surrounded himself with a coterie of free-silver men dubbed the "Stevenson cabinet." The president even mused that the economy had gotten so bad and the Democratic party so divided that "the logical thing for me to do . . . was to resign and hand the Executive branch to Mr. Stevenson," joking that he would try to get his friends jobs in Stevenson's new cabinet.[14]

Toward the end of his term, "Uncle Adlai" was a dinner guest at the home of Senator Gorman. The vice president had a strong sense of humor, which he suppressed while presiding over the Senate but let loose in private. At dinner, Stevenson said he resented the familiar charge that vice presidents were never consulted by the president and told a story about Vice President John Breckinridge once being consulted by President James Buchanan—about the wording of his Thanksgiving message. "Has Mr. Cleveland yet consulted you to that extent?" Senator Gorman asked. "Not yet," Stevenson replied. "But, there are still a few weeks of my term remaining."[15]

Stevenson was mentioned as a candidate to succeed Cleveland in 1896. Although he chaired the Illinois delegation to the Democratic National Convention, he gained little support. As one Democrat noted, "the young men of the country are determined to have something to say during the next election, and are tired of these old hacks." Stevenson received a smattering of votes, but the convention was taken by storm by a thirty-six-year-old former representative from Nebraska, William Jennings Bryan, who delivered his fiery "Cross of Gold" speech in favor of a free-silver plank in the platform. Not only did the Democrats repudiate Cleveland by embracing free silver, but they also nominated Bryan for president. Many Cleveland Democrats, including most Democratic newspapers, refused to support Bryan, but Vice President Stevenson loyally endorsed the ticket. In the fall, Bryan conducted the nation's first whistle-stop campaign, traveling extensively around the country and capturing people's imaginations. Although he did far better than expected, he lost the election to Ohio's Republican governor, William McKinley.[16]

A bimetallist himself, McKinley ran on a gold-standard platform. But McKinley wanted to enact a protective tariff, and, to win support from silver Republicans, he promised to appoint a bipartisan commission to negotiate an international agreement on bimetallism. Silverites hoped that a prominent Democrat might be appointed, but when their leading candidates declined they settled for "a man of no particular weight," the former vice president. The work of the commission came to naught. Stevenson found more satisfaction as a political speaker, addressing all things "purely and absolutely Democratic."[17]

After the 1896 election, Bryan became the titular leader of the Democrats and frontrunner for the nomination in 1900. Much of the newspaper speculation about who would run as the party's vice-presidential candidate centered on Indiana Senator Benjamin Shively. But when reporter Arthur Wallace Dunn interviewed Shively at the convention, the senator said he "did not want the glory of a defeat as a vice presidential candidate." A disappointed Dunn said that he still had to file a story on the vice-presidential nomination, and then added: "I believe I'll write a piece about old Uncle Adlai." "That's a good idea," said Shively. "Stevenson is just the man. There you have it. Uniting the old Cleveland element with the new Bryan Democracy. You've got enough for one story. But say, this is more than a joke. Stevenson is just the man." For the rest of the day, Dunn heard other favorable remarks about Stevenson, and by that night the former vice president was the leading contender, since no one else was "very anxious to be the tail of what they considered was a forlorn hope ticket."[18]

The Populists had already nominated the ticket of Bryan and Charles A. Towne, a silver Republican from Minnesota, with the tacit understanding that Towne would step aside if the Democrats nominated someone else. Bryan preferred his good friend Towne, but Democrats wanted one of their own, and the regular element of the party felt comfortable with Stevenson. Towne withdrew and campaigned for Bryan and Stevenson. As a result, Stevenson, who had run with Cleveland in 1892, now ran with his nemesis Bryan in 1900. Twenty-five years senior to Bryan, Stevenson added age and experience to the ticket. Nevertheless, their effort never stood a chance against the Republican ticket of McKinley and Theodore Roosevelt. Stevenson returned again to private practice in Illinois, making one last attempt at office in an unsuccessful race for governor in 1908. After that, he retired to Bloomington, where his Republican neighbors described him as "windy but amusing."[19]

Grandfather and Grandson

Through Stevenson's long career, his wife Letitia was a "keen observer and judge of people, and a charming hostess." Although suffering from migraine headaches and severe rheumatism that forced her to wear leg braces when standing at receptions, she dutifully supported his many political campaigns. Letitia also helped establish the Daughters of the American Revolution as a way of healing the divisions between the North and South after the Civil War. She succeeded Mrs. Benjamin Harrison as the DAR's second president-general. Adlai Stevenson II remembered his grandparents' home as "a very formal household." The vice president addressed his wife as "Mrs. Stevenson" and she called him "Mr. Stevenson." Young Adlai considered his grandfather "one of the great raconteurs of his day" and learned much about American history and politics from him. At his grandfather's house in Bloomington he met many "distinguished Democrats" from around the land, including William Jennings Bryan. He recalled that hanging on the wall was a lithograph, "The Lost Bet," depicting a gentleman in top hat and frock coat paying off an election bet by pulling a wagon down a street beneath a banner that read: "Grover Cleveland and Adlai E. Stevenson."[20]

Adlai Stevenson died in Bloomington on June 14, 1914. Thirty-eight years later, his grandson and namesake, then serving as governor of Illinois, agonized over whether to make himself available for the Democratic nomination for president. When Adlai E. Stevenson II appeared on the television news show *Meet the Press*, a reporter from the *Chicago Daily News* pressed him for a commitment by saying: "Wouldn't your grandfather, Vice President Stevenson, twirl in his grave if he saw you running away from a chance to be the Democratic nominee in 1952?" Stevenson, who loathed giving up his governorship for what most likely would be a futile campaign against the war hero Dwight Eisenhower, blanched at the comparison and replied, "I think we have to leave Grandfather lie." [21]

NOTES

[1] Jeff Broadwater, *Adlai Stevenson and American Politics: The Odyssey of a Cold War Liberal* (New York, 1994), p. 1.

[2] Adlai E. Stevenson, *Something Of Men I Have Known* (Chicago, 1909), p. 47.

[3] Porter McKeever, *Adlai Stevenson: His Life and Legacy* (New York, 1989), pp. 15–18; Jean H. Baker, *The Stevensons: A Biography of an American Family* (New York, 1996), pp. 82–95.

[4] George Spiel, *The Battle of 1900* (Chicago, 1900), p. 475; Broadwater, p. 1.

[5] McKeever, p. 17; Stevenson, p. 47; Baker, pp. 112–22.

[6] Horace Samuel Merrill, *William Freeman Vilas, Doctrinaire Democrat* (Madison, WI, 1954), pp. 100, 102–3.

[7] David S. Barry, *Forty Years in Washington* (Boston, 1924), p. 191; Solomon X. Griffin, *People and Politics: Observations by a Massachusetts Editor* (Boston, 1923), p. 307; Wayne Morgan, *From Hayes to McKinley: National Party Politics, 1877–1896* (Syracuse, NY, 1969), p. 446; Merrill, *William Freeman Vilas*, p. 105.

[8] Griffin, pp. 307, 327; McKeever, p. 17; Herbert Eaton, *Presidential Timber: A History of Nominating Conventions, 1868–1960* (New York, 1964), pp. 145–47; Allan Nevins, *Grover Cleveland, A Study in Courage* (New York, 1932), pp. 504–5.

[9] Nevins, p. 518.

[10] Horace Samuel Merrill, *Bourbon Democracy of the Middle West, 1865–1896* (Seattle, 1967; reprint of 1953 edition), pp. 216, 237; Morgan, p. 450; Richard E. Welch, Jr., *The Presidencies of Grover Cleveland* (Lawrence, KS, 1988), pp. 60, 106, 119; Robert H. Ferrell, *Ill-Advised: Presidential Health and Public Trust* (Columbia, MO, 1992), pp. 3–11.

[11] Paolo E. Coletta, ''The Democratic Party, 1884–1910,'' in *History of U.S. Political Parties*, ed. Arthur M. Schlesinger, Jr. (New York, 1980), 2:996.

[12] Paul Lancaster, *Gentleman of the Press: The Life and Times of an Early Reporter, Julian Ralph of the Sun* (Syracuse, NY, 1992), p. 221.

[13] John R. Lambert, *Arthur Pue Gorman* (Baton Rouge, LA, 1953), pp. 193, 195, 199; Baker, pp. 163–71.

[14] Stevenson, pp. 63, 243–44; Spiel, p. 477; Allan Nevins, ed., *Letters of Grover Cleveland, 1850–1908* (Boston, 1933), p. 380.

[15] David S. Barry, *Forty Years in Washington* (Boston, 1924), pp. 191–92.

[16] Merrill, *William Freeman Vilas*, p. 198.

[17] Leon Burr Richardson, *William E. Chandler, Republican* (New York, 1940), p. 551; Spiel, p. 477.

[18] Arthur Wallace Dunn, *From Harrison to Harding: A Personal Narrative, Covering a Third of a Century, 1888–1921* (Port Washington, NY, 1972; reprint of 1922 edition), 1:344; Baker, pp. 174–77.

[19] Louis W. Koenig, *Bryan: A Political Biography of William Jennings Bryan* (New York, 1971), p. 324; Broadwater, p. 2.

[20] McKeever, p. 18; John Bartlow Martin, *Adlai Stevenson* (New York, 1952)., p. 41; Baker, pp. 154–63.

[21] McKeever, p. 185.

Chapter 24

GARRET AUGUSTUS HOBART
1897–1899

GARRET AUGUSTUS HOBART

Chapter 24

GARRET AUGUSTUS HOBART

24th Vice President: 1897–1899

For the first time in my recollection, and the last for that matter, the Vice President was recognized as somebody, as a part of the Administration, as a part of the body over which he presided.
—Veteran Newspaper Correspondent

It seems startling that someone who never held prior office outside of a state legislature could be nominated and elected Vice President of the United States, as was Garret Augustus Hobart in 1896. By the time convention delegates chose the last nineteenth-century vice president, they had come to regard that office as little more than a "fifth wheel to the executive coach." The nomination was in their view simply a device for balancing the ticket, either by ideology or by region. "Gus" Hobart, an easterner chosen to run with a middle westerner, William McKinley of Ohio, completely shared McKinley's conservative political philosophy. With warm feelings for Hobart, President McKinley decided to rescue the vice-presidency from its low estate. McKinley so embraced the vice president as his friend, associate, and confidant that Hobart's home on Lafayette Square became known as the "Little Cream White House," and Hobart as the "Assistant President." [1]

Youth

Hobart was the descendant of a long line of clergymen, with a family tree that dated back to the Massachusetts Bay Colony of the early seventeenth century. In 1841 his father had left New England to open a primary school in Long Branch, New Jersey. There, on June 3, 1844, Garret Augustus Hobart was born. Young Hobart attended his father's school and then went to boarding school. As a member of the Reformed Church, he attended Rutgers College, which was then under that church's control. He graduated at the top of his class in 1863. Although the nation was deeply engaged in the Civil War, Hobart did not join the Union army. Instead, he studied law in Paterson, New Jersey, under the tutelage of Socrates Tuttle, a childhood friend of his father's. He became a lawyer in 1866, and on July 21, 1869, married Tuttle's daughter, Jennie. Hobart's family had long been Democrats, but marriage into the Republican Tuttle household converted the young man to the Grand Old Party. [2]

Not a Conventional Politician

After service as clerk of a grand jury, Hobart was elected a judge in Paterson in 1868. In 1871, after his father-in-law became mayor, Hobart was appointed to the post of city counsel. The following year he went to the state assembly, rising speedily to become speaker in 1874. In 1876 he won election to the state senate, which chose him as senate president in 1881, according him the distinction of being the first person to head both houses of the New Jersey legislature. Despite these achievements, Hobart was no politician in the conventional sense. "He was not fond of standing in the public eye," a friend later assessed. "He did not seek popularity by those methods which usually evoke the applause and admiration of the multitude. He was not spectacular." [3]

GARRET A. HOBART

A rotund, jovial, hospitable man, Hobart displayed much tact, charm, and ability to work with other people. These qualities, which made him an outstanding state legislator, should have helped him move up to the national legislature, if it had not been for his increasingly lucrative law practice in New Jersey. The many banks and railroads among his clients made him wealthy, and he was loath to abandon his comfortable family life in New Jersey for the demands of a political career in Washington. (The Hobart home, "Carroll Hall," was reputedly the "largest and most sumptuous in Paterson.") Several times Hobart stood for the United States Senate but never fought hard enough to win election from a state legislature in which he was immensely popular. He served instead as chairman of the State Republican Committee from 1880 to 1891 and as a member of the party's national committee.[4]

A Homesick Candidate

Since the Civil War, New Jersey had leaned toward Democratic presidential candidates. President Grover Cleveland had carried the state in 1892, but, during the economic depression that followed, both houses of the legislature and the governorship of New Jersey went Republican, suggesting that the state could be taken by the national ticket in 1896. Looking over the scene, the Democratic *New York Graphic* noted that there was no other Republican in New Jersey as strong as this "sturdy, bright faced, genial gentleman."[5]

In 1896, the New Jersey delegation went to the Republican convention in St. Louis determined to nominate Hobart for vice president, as a way of consolidating the party's recent gains within their state. When Ohio Governor McKinley defeated House Speaker Thomas Reed and several other prominent candidates for the presidential nomination, newspapers identified some twenty potential candidates for the vice-presidency. All of them were governors, cabinet members, senators, and representatives, with the exception of Hobart, who remained unknown outside of his state. Yet when the vote was taken, Hobart, who had attended the convention as a delegate, emerged the nominee.

Hobart insisted that he had not sought the nomination but that it was handed to him as "a tribute from my friends." It came equally as a tribute from Marcus A. Hanna, the Cleveland industrialist and political strategist who masterminded McKinley's nomination. Hanna wanted a ticket to satisfy the business interests of America, and Hobart, a corporate lawyer, fit that requirement perfectly. Hanna's biographer noted that, even if Hobart did little to strengthen the ticket, "he did nothing to weaken it."[6]

Hobart himself felt ambivalent about the honor. Ambitious for national office, he was realistic enough to know what it would ultimately cost him. From the convention, he wrote to his wife:

> I have been too busy to be homesick, but, to tell the honest truth, I am heart-sick over my own prospects. It looks to me I will be nominated for Vice-President whether I want it or not, and as I get nearer to the point where I may, I am dismayed at the thought. . . . If I want a nomination, everything is going my way. But when I realize all that it means in work, worry, and loss of home and bliss, I am overcome, so overcome I am simply miserable.[7]

Unlike the Democratic presidential candidate William Jennings Bryan, who barnstormed the country making speeches, William McKinley stayed at home in Canton, Ohio, running his campaign from his front porch. Hobart similarly limited his speaking to his portico in New Jersey. McKinley and Hobart stood firm for the gold standard and the protective tariff. Bryan, for his part, ran on a "Free Silver" platform and attracted many desperate farmers and debtors to his crusade. But economic conditions—and corporate interests—favored the Republicans. McKinley won by a half million votes, or 51 percent of the total cast. His Republican ticket carried 23 of the 45 states, including Hobart's New Jersey.

The Little Cream White House

For a running mate, McKinley had preferred Speaker Thomas B. Reed, with whom he had worked for many years in the House, but Reed would accept only the top spot on the ticket. Although McKinley and Hobart were strangers by comparison, the president had no difficulty warming up to Gus Hobart. The wealthy Hobarts leased a house at 21 Lafayette Square, which became known as the "Little Cream White House." Built in 1828 by Col. Ogle Tayloe, the house had hosted Washington's high society during the antebellum years. At the outset of the Civil War, General George McClellan had taken it as his headquarters. After the war, Pennsylvania Senator Don Cameron had remodeled and restored the old house. The Hobarts used it to entertain lavishly—particularly because President McKinley's wife was an invalid who could not shoulder the traditional social burdens of the White House. The president frequently attended Hobart's dinners and afternoon smokers, where he could meet informally with party leaders from Capitol Hill.[8]

No previous vice president had visited the White House as often as Gus Hobart, due in part to the warm friendship that developed between Ida McKinley and Jennie Hobart. Mrs. McKinley suffered from epilepsy, which left her a recluse in the White House. President McKinley doted on his wife and grew to depend on Jennie Hobart, who visited Ida daily. "The President constantly turned to me to help her wherever I could," Mrs. Hobart wrote in her memoirs, "—not because I was Second Lady, but because I was their good friend." Whenever McKinley had to be away from his wife in the evenings, he would entrust her to Jennie Hobart's care. He also invited Mrs. Hobart to White House social functions because her presence "gave him confidence." In addition to seeing each other in Washington, the McKinleys and Hobarts vacationed together at Bluff Point on Lake Champlain.[9]

McKinley looked on Hobart as a trusted adviser. Although the vice president was not invited to join meetings of the cabinet, the president and cabinet members consulted with him freely. The mutual regard between the two men made them, in the words of one acquaintance, "coadjustors in the fixing of the policies of the Administration to an extent never before known." Arthur Wallace Dunn, a newspaper correspondent who covered presidents from Benjamin Harrison to Warren Harding, mar-veled that "for the first time in my recollection, and the last for that matter, the Vice President was recognized as somebody, as a part of the Administration, and as a part of the body over which he presided." Dunn described Hobart as a "business politician," whose knowledge of the "relations between business and politics" made his judgments extremely useful. McKinley even turned to his vice president for personal financial advice. Having once suffered the embarrassment of declaring personal bankruptcy, McKinley turned over a portion of his monthly presidential salary, which Vice President Hobart invested for him.[10]

The Splendid Little War

Although Hobart socialized more frequently and worked more closely with the president than had most of his predecessors, his primary function remained that of presiding over the Senate. In his brief, self-deprecatory inaugural address, Hobart had told the senators that, while he was unfamiliar with their rules and procedures, he would work to the best of his abilities, feeling confident that they would indulge him as considerately as they had all of the previous occupants of the chair. Hobart's experiences presiding over the New Jersey assembly and state senate served him well, and he soon won favorable notices for impartial and informed rulings. Massachusetts Senator Henry Cabot Lodge applauded Hobart for abandoning his predecessors' habit of "submitting nearly every question of order to the Senate," and instead ruling promptly on these points himself, "as every presiding officer ought to do." One newspaper correspondent wrote that, initially, Hobart's "business-like advice and warning intimations rather nettled many of the Senators," but that over time he appeared to captivate the Senate with his genial good nature.[11]

Hobart settled comfortably into the job. Senate vouchers show that he purchased for the Vice President's Room in the Capitol silk mohair carpeting, Neapolitan silk curtains, Persian throw rugs, and "a silk velour slumber robe" made to match the velour cushions on his sofa. Hobart also ordered the grandfather clock and the imposing mahogany desk that his successors continue to use.[12] Presiding over the Senate was no easy task, however. In 1898, following the unexplained sinking of the U.S. battleship *Maine* in Havana harbor, sentiment in the Senate swung sharply toward war with Spain, which at that time still ruled Cuba as a colony. President McKinley's cautious attempts to avoid going to war made him seem indecisive. When McKinley's friend Senator William Mason of Illinois announced in favor of war, a demonstration broke out on the Senate floor that Hobart found impossible to quiet. As Mrs. Hobart recalled, the vice president was "worried to desperation" over the rising rebelliousness of the Senate, and took his concerns to McKinley. "Mr. President, I can no longer hold back the Senate," he warned. "They will act without you if you do not act at once." Accepting the inevitable, McKinley called on Congress to declare that a state of war existed with Spain. Hobart sent the president a pen to sign the declaration.[13]

The "splendid little war" with Spain was fought and won within a six-month period. At the conclusion of the Fifty-fifth Congress, Vice President Hobart congratulated the Senate on this remarkable achievement, noting that "unlike any other session in the history of our country, this Congress has witnessed the inception, prosecution, and conclusion of a war." More than just a war Congress, it had also been a peace Congress, having approved the ratification of the Treaty of Paris that ended the Spanish-American War.

The vice president played a significant part in one aspect of that peace treaty. Although the United States had pledged not to take Cuba as its own territory, it did decide to hold the Philippine Islands, unexpectedly acquired from Spain. After the Senate had approved the peace treaty by the necessary two-thirds vote, Georgia Democrat Augustus O. Bacon had sponsored an amendment promising independence to the Philippines if it established a stable government. Due to the absence of several administration supporters, the vote was tied at 29 to 29. Hobart assured the taking of the territory for the United States by casting the deciding vote against Bacon's amendment.[14]

The Vice President's Valedictory

The vice president's speech concluding the second session of the Fifty-fifth Congress was in fact his valedictory, for he would die before the next Congress convened. In addressing the senators for the last time, he noted that "the Senate of the United States is a peculiar body. . . . made up, as you know of many elements, and in its membership you will find not only straight and stalwart Republicans, to whose active efforts the country is now looking for relief, but Bimetallists, Populists, Silverites—both Republican and Democratic—and a few gold Democrats." Despite the senators' many differences, Hobart as presiding officer observed that each of them stood on the common ground of patriotism, pride in the nation's history, zealousness for its Constitution, and devotion to its flag. For a generation old enough to remember the Civil War, the Spanish-American War appeared to represent the end of the old divisions that had led to secession. Former Union and Confederate soldiers supported a common war effort, with some from both sides donning uniforms once again.[15]

Beginning in early 1899, Hobart suffered from fainting spells triggered by serious heart problems. He never fully recovered. Yet that summer he performed a last major service for the McKinley administration when he helped the gentle president to fire his secretary of war, General Russell A. Alger. A large, affable man with presidential ambitions, Alger had become tarred by scandals that emerged during the Spanish-American war—particularly charges that unscrupulous war suppliers had fed "embalmed beef" to American soldiers. McKinley saw the need to sacrifice his secretary of war to the demands of public opinion, but could not bring himself to fire a friend. When Secretary of State John Hay declined to deliver the bad news, the task fell to Hobart. That summer, Alger and his wife regularly spent weekends with the Hobarts at their summer house at Norwood Park, New Jersey. One evening, Hobart took Alger into the smoking room and suggested that he find some excuse for retiring from the cabinet. During the next week, newspapers published stories that Alger had been pressured to step down but that the president was standing loyally by him. The oblivious Alger returned to Hobart's seaside home the next weekend and insisted that in light of the president's loyal backing he had no reason to leave the cabinet. Now Hobart bluntly explained that the president would feel "very much relieved" if the secretary would resign. Alger could not believe what he was hearing until Hobart admitted that he was speaking with the president's authorization. The shaken secretary of war hurried back to Washington and at nine o'clock on Monday morning handed his resignation to President McKinley.[16]

As Hobart suffered increasingly debilitating attacks and his strength declined, rumors spread that his illness would keep him from running again for vice president. In the fall of 1899, as McKinley was preparing a grand reception to honor the return of Admiral George Dewey from the Philippines, he invited the Hobarts to stay at the White House. "I can imagine no place where you will be more comfortable than here." But Hobart declined. He conceded that he must remain in Paterson and could not return to Washington either for the Dewey reception or to preside again over the Senate when it reconvened that December. This public announcement was an admission that the vice president was "in virtual retirement," with no hope of recovery. Hobart died on November 21, 1899. Arriving at the Hobart home in Paterson for the funeral, President McKinley told the family, "No one outside of this home feels this loss more deeply than I do."[17]

History has remembered Garret Hobart less for his life than for his death. The void he left was quickly filled. The powerful Senator Mark Hanna moved into the "Little Cream White House," and the vacant vice-presidency was soon occupied by one of America's most dynamic political leaders, Theodore Roosevelt. McKinley's second running mate in 1900 bore little resemblance to the man he succeeded. In short order the young, energetic Roosevelt—and the progressive reform movement he embodied—eclipsed not only Hobart but McKinley as well, as the United States entered the twentieth century.

NOTES

[1] David S. Barry, *Forty Years in Washington* (Boston, 1924), p. 246; David Magie, *Life of Garret Augustus Hobart, Twenty-fourth Vice-President of the United States* (New York, 1910), p. 169.

[2] Magie, pp. 1–26, 42; Jennie Tuttle Hobart, *Memories* (Paterson, NJ., 1930), p. 3.

[3] *Address of Honorable John W. Griggs at the Unveiling of the Statue of Garret Augustus Hobart, Late Vice-President of the United States at Paterson, New Jersey, June 3, 1903* (Paterson, NJ, 1903), p. 4.

[4] Magie, pp. 27–57; Edward S. Ellis, et al., *Great Leaders and National Issues of 1896* (William Ellis Scull, 1896), p. 542.

[5] Magie, p. 50.

[6] Ibid., pp. 58, 74; Margaret Leech, *In The Days of McKinley* (New York, 1959), p. 83; Herbert D. Croly, *Marcus Alonzo Hanna* (New York, 1912), p. 191.

[7] Magie, p. 79.

[8] Barry, pp. 245–46; Magie, pp. 116–17; H. Wayne Morgan, *William McKinley and His America* (Syracuse, NY, 1963), pp. 220, 274.

[9] Leech, p. 435; Magie, p. 170; Hobart, pp. 13–14, 19, 29.

[10] *Address of Honorable John W. Griggs,* p. 9; Arthur Wallace Dunn, *From Harrison to Harding: A Personal Narrative, Covering a Third of a Century, 1888–1921* (Port Washington, NY, 1972; reprint of 1922 edition), 1:224–25; Morgan, p. 321.

[11] U.S., Congress, Senate, *Congressional Record,* 55th Cong., special session, p. 1; Magie, pp. 151–52, 156.

[12] Hobart's purchases are documented in the reports of the Secretary of the Senate and in a booklet published by the Office of the Senate Curator, *The Vice President's Room.*

[13] Horace Samuel Merrill and Marion Galbraith Merrill, *The Republican Command, 1897–1913* (Lexington, KY, 1971), p. 49; Leech, pp. 184–85, 193; Hobart, pp. 58–60.

[14] Harold U. Faulkner, *Politics, Reform and Expansion, 1890–1900* (New York, 1959), p. 258; Lewis L. Gould, *The Presidency of William McKinley* (Lawrence, KY, 1980), p. 150.

[15] Magie, pp. 162–63.

[16] Barry, pp. 256–59; Magie, pp. 209–11.

[17] Magie, pp. 176, 212–17, 231; Hobart, p. 68.

Chapter 25

THEODORE ROOSEVELT
1901

THEODORE ROOSEVELT

Chapter 25

THEODORE ROOSEVELT

25th Vice President: 1901

I would a great deal rather be anything, say professor of history, than Vice-President.
—THEODORE ROOSEVELT [1]

Senator Thomas C. Platt of New York declared that he went to the presidential inaugural of 1901 "to see Theodore Roosevelt take the veil." [2] Roosevelt, the governor of New York, had been elected vice president the previous autumn on William McKinley's Republican ticket, and Platt looked forward to having the maverick governor in seclusion for four years. The new vice president was not entirely certain of his own prospects, stating that "it [the vice-presidency] is not a steppingstone to anything except oblivion"—hardly a ringing endorsement of the nation's second highest office. [3] Yet this was the prevailing opinion about the vice-presidency at the beginning of the twentieth century. Most of Roosevelt's nearest predecessors were men of limited qualifications and interests whose functions were primarily social. Some observers hoped that this office would finally tame the firebrand Roosevelt, but if the Rough Rider's active and adventurous past was any indication, the vice-presidency was in for some changes.

Youth

The life of Theodore Roosevelt is one of the great American stories. He was born on October 27, 1858, in New York City to a prominent family of moderate wealth. Theodore Roosevelt, Sr., a partner in the importing firm of Roosevelt and Son, was a well-known philanthropist, teaching in mission schools and founding the Children's Aid Society. His wife, Martha Bulloch, was a woman of remarkable beauty and refined taste. The couple made a striking contrast: Theodore being a vigorous entrepreneur of somewhat mercurial temperament, while Martha, a Georgian, was the stereotypical "southern belle." Theodore, Jr., the second of four children, was a frail boy, frequently suffering from severe asthmatic attacks. As an adolescent, however, he had taken his father's advice to "make" his body, so that by the time he entered Harvard in 1876, he was an accomplished athlete and outstanding boxer. At Harvard, Roosevelt excelled in natural science and politics, graduating twenty-first in a class of 177.

Upon graduation, Roosevelt had a number of careers open to him. He had long considered science his greatest strength—his first published work, *The Summer Birds of the Adirondacks*, appeared in 1877 while he was still an undergraduate—but was gradually losing professional interest in the topic. He began studying law at Columbia and undertook his first work of history, *The Naval War of 1812* (published in 1882). It was politics, however, that most piqued his interest. This possible vocation horrified Roosevelt's family and social peers, most of whom considered politics a low and dirty activity dominated by corrupt bosses and ill-bred immigrants. Theodore, however, decided that he "intended to be one of the governing class," a determination that would dominate the rest of his life. [4]

THEODORE ROOSEVELT

Legislator, Cowboy, and Naturalist

In 1881, at the age of twenty-three, Roosevelt was elected to the New York state assembly as a Republican. He quickly established himself as the leader of a group of young independent-minded Republican legislators, known as the "Roosevelt Republicans," who fought to clean up New York politics by opposing the power of both the Republican state machine and the Tammany Hall Democrats of New York City. Roosevelt gained a widespread reputation for honesty, integrity, and vigor. In his second term, he was made minority leader of the assembly and in his third term collaborated often with Democratic Governor Grover Cleveland to pass reform legislation, especially civil service reform.[5]

This seemingly charmed career was sidetracked in February of 1884, when Roosevelt suffered the deaths of both his wife and his mother. He had met the beautiful Alice Lee while he was at Harvard and they had married on October 27, 1880, a handsome couple who delighted in the social life of New York. Alice became ill with Bright's Disease immediately after giving birth to their first child, also named Alice. At the same time, Martha Roosevelt lay ill with typhoid fever in an upstairs room. On Valentine's Day, 1884, Martha died, followed the next morning by Alice, who died in her husband's arms. The blow was tremendous, causing Theodore to lament in his diary, "The light has gone out of my life." He never spoke of Alice Lee Roosevelt again. He declined to run for reelection to the assembly, deciding instead to go west and forget his sorrows by becoming a cowboy. He purchased a ranch in the Dakota Territory and spent the next two years tending to a large herd of cattle, chasing outlaws, writing popular books about the West such as *Hunting Trips of a Ranchman* (1885), and creating an image as one of the nation's most enigmatic cowboys.[6]

These sojourns in the West helped to expand one of Roosevelt's greatest interests, his love of nature. As a young man Roosevelt had enjoyed studying the plant and animal life of his native New York. The Dakota Territory opened up new experiences and also fostered a concern for the vanishing wildlife of the nation. Throughout his subsequent political career, he would maintain an interest in preserving America's natural beauty, despite his penchant for shooting at much of it on western hunting trips. Whether it was the founding of Boone and Crockett Clubs throughout the country or setting up wildlife preserves as president, this interest would remain a constant throughout his life. Another constant interest was history. In all, Roosevelt wrote fourteen books on various topics, as well as numerous articles. While not recognized as great works of history, his *Naval War of 1812*, *Thomas Hart Benton* (1886), and *Winning of the West* (1889) were considered standard works for decades. All of this he accomplished while pursuing an active career in politics.[7]

Even in his attempts at seclusion, Roosevelt could not entirely escape from politics. Before leaving for the Dakotas in 1884, he led the New York delegation to the Republican National Convention in an attempt to block the presidential nomination of James G. Blaine. When this effort failed, Roosevelt declined to follow the example of other reformers, who switched their allegiance to the Democratic candidate, Grover Cleveland. As he boarded his train for the Dakotas, he indicated that he would support the Republican nominee. The reform press reacted with outrage, excoriating their former hero from afar. During his years as a cowboy, Roosevelt made frequent trips back east to attend to family business and regaled reporters with tales of his exotic adventures. This ensured that his name remained in the papers in New York, as well as spreading to more western locales. He remained enough in the public eye, in fact, that upon one of his return trips in 1886, the party nominated him for mayor of New York City.[8]

Politics and War

After losing the three-way mayoral race of 1886 and spending a few years on his literary pursuits, Roosevelt held a succession of appointed posts in which he performed well and continued to enhance his public reputation. In 1889 he became a civil service commissioner under President Benjamin Harrison. He left this position in 1895 to become a New York City police commissioner, and then, in 1897, President

William McKinley appointed him assistant secretary of the navy. Roosevelt found himself in this office when the United States declared war on Spain in 1898. Never one to miss the action, Roosevelt promptly resigned his post to form a volunteer regiment of western cowboys and eastern adventurers that the press dubbed "Roosevelt's Rough Riders." The Spanish-American War did not last long, but it was long enough for the Rough Riders to ride (or march, since only Colonel Roosevelt was actually mounted) into American folklore. After the well-chronicled Battle of San Juan Hill, Roosevelt returned to the United States as the most famous man in the nation.[9]

In the summer of 1898, the New York Republican party was searching for a gubernatorial candidate. As the current Republican administration was plagued with scandals and falling popularity, the prospects of a Democratic victory in the fall were rising daily. It quickly became obvious to party leaders that only a man of tremendous popularity and an impeccable reputation for honesty and "clean government" could rescue the party from defeat. That man was the vigorous colonel just returned from Cuba, Theodore Roosevelt. The man whose opinion mattered most, however, was not so sure. Senator Thomas Platt had risen to power in the party the old-fashioned way, by climbing up through the party machinery. By 1898, he had established himself as the unquestioned leader of the state GOP. Known as the "Easy Boss," Platt was in a position to decide who the state convention would nominate for governor. As a veteran New York politician, Platt had seen Roosevelt in action and was suspicious of the young man's reform attitude, his lack of sympathy for the machine, and his immense personal popularity. The last thing the Easy Boss wanted was a challenge to his power within the party. On the other hand, Roosevelt had shown his party regularity by not bolting the Blaine campaign in 1884, and his most virulent tirades were usually reserved for the Democratic Tammany Hall machine in New York City. Most of all, Platt saw in the famous colonel a way to keep the party in office, an out-

come far preferable to the election of a hostile Democratic administration.[10]

On September 17, Roosevelt went to see Platt at the senator's apartment in the Fifth Avenue Hotel in order to come to some sort of working agreement. The reformers once more cried out in protest that their leader was consorting with the enemy. Roosevelt's ambiguous relationship with many vocal reform advocates was a recurring theme during his career. Those who worked to overthrow the machines did not see how a politician could further the cause of reform while still working with men like Tom Platt. Roosevelt was, above all else, a man of action who measured success by results. He was willing to compromise in order to accomplish gradual changes. He was contemptuous of what he called "professional reformers," men who refused to bend their ideals to the realities of power. While others railed at the system from without, Roosevelt would try to reform it from within, but to do this required power.[11]

Governor of New York

Senator Platt agreed to Roosevelt's nomination after the candidate promised to consult him on appointments to office and important policy matters. Roosevelt's campaign was rather simple; he promised merely to run a "clean" administration and capitalized on his popularity with the voters. Although he may not have had a clear program in mind while running for office, once in, he quickly showed that he had no intention of being a mere caretaker for the machine. It became apparent that he and Senator Platt had different definitions of "consultation." One of the governor's first decisions was to appoint a new administrator for the state canal system. It was in this office that most of the worst scandals of the previous administration had taken place. Senator Platt had promised the position to Francis J. Hendricks of Syracuse. When Roosevelt refused to make the appointment (because Hendricks was from a "canal county"), Platt was incensed. Roosevelt managed to calm the situation by drawing up a list of names, all good party men, and allowing Platt to choose from it. By this method, most future appointments were made amicably, but the governor had shown his independence and given the Easy Boss an uneasy feeling about the future.[12]

Conflicts over policy would be a more difficult matter. Governor Roosevelt supported legislation authorizing the state supreme court to inspect the books of corporations, endorsed antimonopoly legislation, pushed for better civil service laws, supported an eight-hour-day law for public employees, and advocated a minimum wage for New York City's school teachers. These and other measures ran afoul of Senator Platt's wishes, but the issue which most disturbed him was Roosevelt's support for a tax on public franchises. Platt's political machine was financed primarily by large corporations in New York, many of which held public franchises. Nothing was more hateful to these interests than corporate taxes, especially on companies that were, in their eyes at least, providing a public service such as water or gas. By forcing the franchise tax through the legislature, Roosevelt made powerful enemies who informed Senator Platt of their disapproval. The boss worried that his hold on the party was fading because of his inability to control his governor. He began reconsidering his relationship with Theodore Roosevelt.[13]

Getting rid of Governor Roosevelt did not promise to be easy. While the impetuous governor may have made enemies in the business community, he was immensely popular with the public. In fact, it was this popularity that made him such an effective governor. One reason Senator Platt had acquiesced in Roosevelt's nomination was that the senator anticipated controlling the state assembly. As long as Platt's will was supreme in the legislature, the governor's most threatening schemes could be defeated. Roosevelt, however, had developed a weapon capable of changing the minds of wavering legislators. During his campaign for election, the governor had demonstrated the power of his personality; as one observer remarked, "Teddy . . . [was] a wonder . . . there were immense gatherings of enthusiastic people at every stopping place. . . . [Even when] the speech was nothing, . . . the man's presence was everything. It was electrical, magnetic." Roosevelt was aware of his hold on the public imagination. As the most vigorous governor most New Yorkers had ever

seen, Roosevelt used constant publicity to push for his programs. He regularly held two press conferences a day and consulted experts of all kinds on complex issues.[14] The growing media of the day feasted on this constant flow of information, and the public loved it. Under such intense public scrutiny, only the most intransigent of legislators cared to challenge Roosevelt. This method of public persuasion would serve Roosevelt well in the future, as it defined his political style and formed his most lasting contribution to the political process in the twentieth century.

Deciding Whether to Run for Vice President

During Roosevelt's term as governor, many of his friends and admirers began once more to consider his future. As governor of New York, he naturally became a potential candidate for president. Even Senator Platt realized this when he was considering Roosevelt's gubernatorial nomination, saying, "If he becomes Governor of New York, sooner or later, with his personality, he will have to be President of the United States. . . . I am afraid to start that thing going."[15] In 1900 however, the Republicans already had a candidate in incumbent President William McKinley. Few doubted that Roosevelt would be a candidate in 1904; the problem was what he should do until then. Even if Roosevelt were reelected governor, he could only serve until 1902, leaving two years before he could run for president. Roosevelt himself did not believe that his current popularity could last another four years.[16] His friends, however, found a solution to his problem: they would make him vice president.

The most conspicuous proponent of this idea was Massachusetts Senator Henry Cabot Lodge. Roosevelt and Lodge had been close friends for many years, and Lodge had no doubt about his friend's presidential destiny. Lodge was sure that the vice-presidency was the way to the Executive Mansion. This must have sounded odd to many since the vice-presidency was widely perceived as "a spot to gain four years of rest and a good income,"[17] hardly the sort of office to appeal to an active man like Roosevelt. Lodge, however, knew his friend well enough to realize that all Roosevelt needed to succeed was a place in the spotlight. As Lodge later put it,

> I do not pretend to say that the office [of vice president] in itself is suited to you and to your habits, but for the future it is, in my judgement, invaluable. It takes you out of the cut-throat politics of New York, where I am sure they would have destroyed your prospects, if you had remained two years longer, and it gives you a position in the eyes of the country second only to that of the President.[18]

Some of Roosevelt's other friends also speculated that the vice president's role as presiding officer of the Senate would keep him in the public eye much more effectively than his current position as governor of New York. Finally, many of his western supporters were eager for the opportunity to promote their man for a national office, especially after his appearance at the Rough Riders' reunion in Las Vegas in 1899. Newspapers all over the West championed him for the vice-presidency in 1900 and the presidency in 1904. Some even suggested replacing McKinley in 1900.[19] The movement was gathering momentum, and Vice President Garret A. Hobart's death in November 1899 only increased the pace—but what about the candidate?

While flattered by all the support for his candidacy, Roosevelt did not relish the idea of being vice president. He worried that as vice president he "could not do anything."[20] For a man who thrived on the "strenuous life," it was an unpleasant prospect indeed. He would have few responsibilities in the office, and it would restrict his ability to speak out on issues that greatly concerned him. He worried that "if I did anything [as vice president] I would attract suspicion and antagonism." He considered the potential for a vice president to be active in formulating policy to be "infinitesimal."[21] As governor of New York, at least, he was actively doing the work that so stimulated him; as vice president that would not be possible.

Presiding over the Senate did not appeal to him either. The job would undoubtedly be a "bore" and might, in fact, prove quite maddening. As he wrote to Lodge, "I should be in a cold shiver of rage at inability to answer hounds like

[Senator Richard] Pettigrew [D-SD] and the scarcely more admirable [Senator William] Mason [R-IL] and [Senator Eugene] Hale [R-ME]. . . . I would be seeing continually things that I would like to do, and very possibly would like to do differently from the way in which they are being done." The vice president had little, if any, real authority in the Senate, and Roosevelt was adamant that he would "not like to be a figurehead."[22]

There were also financial reasons for Roosevelt's reluctance to run. He was, by his own standards, a man of "very moderate means." The vice president was expected to carry on an active social life in Washington, which required "the expenditure of a good deal of money for entertaining and the like." Roosevelt could certainly not entertain on a scale comparable to that of Levi Morton and Garret Hobart, the two most recent Republican vice presidents. Still, if the office held opportunities to do valuable work, Roosevelt would have tolerated the financial problems.[23] Unfortunately, the vice-presidency offered few such possibilities and promised to be a financial strain as well.

The more Roosevelt thought about it, the less appealing the vice-presidency became. He continually expressed this opinion to anyone who asked, finally stating, "I would a great deal rather be anything, say professor of history, than Vice-President."[24] It was not, however, a teaching position that attracted his attention. The position that Roosevelt really wanted was secretary of war, but McKinley appointed Elihu Root to that recently vacated post. Roosevelt's second choice was governor general of the Philippines, but the president, not trusting Roosevelt's impetuous nature, was unlikely to grant him that office.[25] With these options unavailable, the governor's mansion seemed the best place for him. It was left for the Easy Boss to step in and supply the final piece to the nomination puzzle.

Senator Platt was looking for a way to get Governor Roosevelt out of New York. The corporations and large financial interests of the state were increasingly disturbed by the governor's performance, especially his support of the franchise tax, and were anxious to return to business as usual. They placed growing pressure on Senator Platt to do something about his governor. While reluctant to resort to a potentially disastrous fight against Roosevelt's renomination for governor, the boss saw an opportunity in all the talk about the vice-presidency. If he could push Roosevelt into that position devoid of power, he would get the young reformer out of the way, appease his financial supporters, and be free to select a more pliable governor as Roosevelt's replacement. It seemed the perfect solution.[26]

The boss proceeded to push Roosevelt's name to party leaders and hinted to the governor that he might not support him for a second gubernatorial term. This challenge from the machine, however, only raised the fighting spirit in Roosevelt, who was never one to a retreat from political battle. In February 1900 Roosevelt therefore attempted to remove himself from the vice-presidential race, telling the *New York Tribune* that "under no circumstances could I, or would I, accept the nomination for the vice presidency."[27] The boom for his nomination, however, continued, with friends and foes alike fanning the flames.

Meanwhile, in Washington, President McKinley remained silent on the issue. The president had never been greatly impressed by Governor Roosevelt for reasons of both personality and policy. Yet, after Hobart's death, he gave no indication of preference in the selection of his new running mate. Most Republican leaders believed Roosevelt would bring a new kind of glamor and excitement to their ticket. The governor was a recent war hero, whose record in office had been very popular and less radical than some had feared. There were also no other similarly attractive candidates available.[28] McKinley may have been opposed to Roosevelt, but he proposed no alternatives, and his silence seemed to indicate acceptance.

Election of 1900

By the time the Republican National Convention opened in June in Philadelphia, it had become obvious that Roosevelt was the favorite to receive the vice-presidential nomination. When he continued to protest that he would rather be governor of New York, Lodge warned him that, if he attended the convention, his nomination

was assured. But Roosevelt could not stay away, claiming that to do so would look like cowardice.[29] As a result, despite his protestations, his magnetic presence at the convention fired the enthusiasm of his partisans to a fever pitch. When he appeared for the opening session clad in a black hat reminiscent of the Rough Riders' Cuban campaign—what one delegate called "an acceptance hat"—his nomination was sealed. Scores of western delegates spent that night parading and chanting "We want Teddy." As Senator Platt put it, "Roosevelt might as well stand under Niagara Falls and try to spit water back as to stop his nomination by this convention."[30] Ohio Senator Mark Hanna, who opposed the Roosevelt nomination, tried to block the movement from his position as convention chairman, but without support from the president he could do little against the combined forces of Platt, Pennsylvania boss Matthew Quay (who had an old score to settle with Hanna), and genuine popular will. In desperation, Hanna could only protest, "Don't you realize that there's only one life between this madman and the White House?"[31]

Theodore Roosevelt really did not want to be vice president, but he was a confirmed political realist with presidential ambitions. He knew that regaining the nomination for governor of New York would be difficult, if not impossible, against the open opposition of Senator Platt, and even a successful gubernatorial campaign promised only two years of political struggle against growing corporate hostility. Although Roosevelt continued to fight his own nomination, his protests grew gradually weaker, until, by the time of the convention, they were no longer convincing. Everything pointed to the vice-presidency, and Theodore Roosevelt knew how to read the signs. He did not pursue the office, but when it was thrust upon him, he accepted it. For good or ill, he was now President McKinley's running mate and he was determined to make the best of it.

Republican strategy in 1900 was to let their youthful vice-presidential candidate take to the hustings while President McKinley conducted his "front porch campaign," just as he had in 1896, except this time he received guests at the

White House rather than his home in Canton, Ohio. This strategy suited the vigorous Roosevelt extremely well, as he proclaimed himself to be "strong as a bull moose." It allowed him to tour the West and Midwest, taking on Democratic presidential candidate William Jennings Bryan on issues of the tariff, the gold standard, and American empire. These two great orators set standards of stamina never before seen. Roosevelt covered 21,000 miles in twenty-four states, making over 600 speeches.[32] Roosevelt's tour helped the GOP compensate for Bryan's popularity in the West and it added life to an otherwise dull campaign. The vice-presidential candidate radiated energy, while McKinley sat on his porch in Washington, reminding the nation how prosperous it was.

For Roosevelt, the campaign also provided an opportunity to perform on a national stage. Everywhere he went, he drew huge crowds and constant public attention. As historian John Milton Cooper, Jr., has put it, "The sheer fascination of his presence among people who had already read or heard about him, together with the pungency of his personality, made him the sensation of the 1900 campaign."[33] Roosevelt's nationwide tour helped accelerate the growing trend toward direct, personal campaign techniques. Throughout the nation, "boy orators" such as Roosevelt, Bryan, and Robert M. LaFollette of Wisconsin were altering the system of party campaigning that had persisted for decades. Rather than relying solely on their parties to obtain office, they used whistle-stop campaigns and the burgeoning mass media to take their message directly to the voters. They pushed for direct primaries in order to bypass the party machines and relied on public indignation to insist on reforms. Theodore Roosevelt was helping to lead the way for changes in American political campaigns that would reverberate throughout the twentieth century.[34] Of course, the press played its part in promoting these changes. Roosevelt, as the most interesting candidate in 1900, received more press coverage than even the presidential candidates, and certainly more than the Democratic nominee for vice president, Adlai Stevenson. Reporters loved Roosevelt because he was always good

news copy. While other politicians relied on editors for favorable press coverage, Roosevelt had an ongoing rapport with reporters. They could go to any politician for opinions; they could go to Roosevelt for stories. His campaign dominated the news. As journalist Finley Peter Dunne's favorite character "Mr. Dooley" put it, "'Tis Teddy alone that's r-runnin', an' he ain't runnin', he's gallopin'."[35]

An Unenthusiastic Presiding Officer

McKinley's reelection was nearly a foregone conclusion. The nation was prosperous and the administration was popular. On election day, McKinley received 51.6 percent of the vote, up from 51 percent in 1896. He lost only one state (Kentucky) from the previous election while adding Washington, Wyoming, Utah, South Dakota, Kansas, and Nebraska. Roosevelt's popularity in the West may have influenced these states, but the prosperity of McKinley's first term had also reduced the impact of "free silver" as a decisive issue, depriving Bryan of his greatest western appeal.[36]

Roosevelt was not overjoyed at being vice president but was proud of helping the ticket achieve victory. He did, however, show early signs of frustration at the prospect of inactivity. He declined an invitation to speak in February 1901, "chiefly for the excellent reason that I have nothing whatever to say."[37] His penchant for speaking out would return soon enough, but this initial hesitation reflected the uncertainty of Roosevelt's new position. Accustomed to the aggressive pursuit of his own policies, he now had to be careful not to offend either his president or the party leadership, a goal he had failed to achieve in New York. It was a potentially trying situation for an active and outspoken young man.

The first task of the new vice president was to preside over the Senate, meeting in a special session for four days beginning March 4. This brief appearance did not give Roosevelt much time to make an impression, but in those four days he impressed no one. He had not been looking forward to this role, but as he characteristically put it, "Now all that there is for me to do is to perform with regularity and dignity the duty of presiding over the Senate, and to remember the fact that the duty not being very important is no excuse for shirking it."[38] He proved as ill-suited for the role as he was unenthusiastic. His mind wandered, and he had a limited grasp of Senate procedures. As Senator Joseph Foraker tactfully put it, "his peculiar qualifications for the public service fitted him better for wider, broader and more useful fields."[39] Roosevelt confessed to being "the poorest presiding officer the Senate ever had."[40] The first impressions made by the new vice president in the Senate were hardly encouraging.

Once the Senate adjourned, Roosevelt returned home to New York to spend the summer with his wife and seven children, his most enjoyable vacation in years. Two years after the death of his first wife, Theodore had married his childhood sweetheart, Edith Carow. Edith was a very private woman who never seemed entirely comfortable with the publicity that always surrounded her husband. Privately, however, her influence went even beyond the difficult task of raising the rambunctious Roosevelt children. She controlled the family's finances—Theodore having never been good at managing his money—and it was later suspected that she was influential in his presidential appointments because she was considered a better judge of character than he was. (From 1901 to 1909, as first lady, Edith would help transform the White House into a centerpiece for the social and cultural life of Washington and the nation.) The lack of pressing business as vice president allowed Theodore to spend time playing football with his sons and sparring with his tempestuous older daughter, Alice. Theodore's relationship with Alice would become increasingly strained during his presidency as she struggled for greater independence. As he later put it, "I can be President of the United States, or I can attend to Alice. I can't do both." During Roosevelt's presidency, "Princess Alice" would become a celebrity as a Washington socialite and a prominent model of the independent young woman of the new century. She would eventually marry Republican Congressman Nicholas Longworth of Ohio, a future Speaker of the House, in 1906, and become one of the most famous matrons of Washington society.[41]

Because of his lack of interest in the official duties of his new office, Roosevelt in the summer of 1901 began looking for other activities and focused on two. First, he resumed a regular speaking schedule. These speeches reveal that, without more immediate matters to deal with, his thoughts were increasingly turning to one of his favorite topics: foreign policy. He spoke to crowds in New York and New England about the need for an effective navy and the threat from a newly powerful Germany.[42] Perhaps Roosevelt saw this as an area in which he would have some freedom, because he and McKinley, while not always in complete accord, had similar views on foreign policy. Roosevelt's more virulent criticism was aimed at anti-imperialist Democrats, who were McKinley's enemies as well. By spending his time attacking the Democrats on foreign policy, he might avoid disturbing the Old Guard in his own party with his progressive views on domestic matters.

Vice President Roosevelt's second activity revealed his ambition. He spent considerable time lining up support for a presidential bid in 1904. Despite his concerns that opposition from the party in New York would deny him the nomination, he cautiously pursued a course designed to build a broad base of popular support. He concentrated his efforts especially in the West, where he was already popular and where the Bryanite Democrats represented a significant electoral challenge. Friends such as William Allen White in Kansas, Philip B. Stewart in Colorado, and Booker T. Washington in the South began acting as unofficial campaign managers, and he planned a national speaking tour for 1902. Roosevelt also undertook a potentially more risky strategy of supporting progressive-minded Republicans in state elections. He volunteered to assist Albert B. Cummins of Iowa in his campaign for governor. Cummins had defeated an Old Guard opponent for the nomination and in supporting him too heartily, Roosevelt ran the risk of offending the national party leadership. He may have been willing to take that chance in order to build a separate base of party support and appeal to the growing public interest in progressive candidates. Roosevelt was preparing once more for political battle, and, on the whole, the odds looked good.[43]

It appeared that Vice President Roosevelt's official responsibilities were to be limited, at least for the moment, since President McKinley did not consult him either on policy or appointments. Although McKinley had used Vice President Hobart as his liaison with the Senate, Roosevelt was poorly suited for this role, since he shone more as a public spokesman than as a parliamentary operator. In addition, the Senate was dominated by Old Guard Republicans, most of whom were wary of Roosevelt's insurgent impulses. In any event, McKinley was not likely to entrust his impetuous vice president with legislative responsibilities, because he distrusted the younger man's lack of caution. Roosevelt, for his part, chafed under the restraints of McKinley's slowness in dealing with contentious issues. As a result, while the relations between the two men were amicable and professional, they were not close.[44]

Early in September 1901, everything changed. On September 5 President McKinley, a longtime advocate of protective tariffs, delivered a major policy speech at the Pan American Exposition in Buffalo, New York. In his address, the president called for a new era of reciprocal trade with other nations, in which the old trade barriers must fall. "The period of exclusiveness is past . . . the expansion of our trade and commerce is the pressing problem," he declared. The next day, September 6, the president held a public reception in the Temple of Music. At slightly after 4 p.m., a young anarchist named Leon Czolgosz walked up to the president with a gun in his right hand, hidden in a bandage. He fired two shots at the president: one bounced off a button, but the other lodged in McKinley's stomach. For a week, the president struggled to survive, but on September 14 he expired, whispering the title of his favorite hymn, "Nearer, My God, To Thee."[45] McKinley's pathbreaking initiative for lower tariffs died with him.

Upon hearing of the shooting, Roosevelt had rushed to Buffalo, but when the doctors had been encouraged by the president's progress after three days, the vice president had departed for the Adirondacks. On September 13, he was recalled by a note from Secretary of War Elihu Root, "The President appears to be dying, and members of the Cabinet in Buffalo think you should lose no time in coming." Making a furious trip by buckboard and special train, Roosevelt arrived in Buffalo on the fourteenth to find the president already dead. After paying his respects to Mrs. McKinley, he met with the cabinet, telling them, "I wish to say that it shall be my aim to continue, absolutely unbroken, the policy of President McKinley for the peace, the prosperity, and the honor of our beloved country." He then took the oath of office, becoming, at forty-two, the youngest president in the nation's history.[46]

A Popular President

Roosevelt's pledge to continue McKinley's policies was not only meant to calm the nation, but was consistent with his conception of the role of the vice president. In an article for *Review of Reviews* in 1896, Roosevelt, then New York City's police commissioner, had described the vice president as a "functionless official" except for the possibility of becoming "the head of the whole nation." He therefore stressed:

> The Vice-President should so far as possible represent the same views and principles which have secured the nomination and election of the President, and he should be a man standing well in the councils of the party, trusted by his fellow party leaders, and able in the event of any accident to his chief to take up the work of the latter just where it was left.[47]

Of course, the man holding the office in September 1901 did not fit this model. Roosevelt had not been selected because of his similarities to McKinley and, now that he was president, would not take long to go his own way. He almost immediately began pursuing a nature conservation program and in a few months would instigate an antitrust suit against the Northern Securities Company. He would genuinely attempt to steer a middle course between the Old Guard and the insurgent Republicans, but pressure for change was rising and Roosevelt's heart had always been with the reformers.[48] His first annual message to Congress, calling for some regulation of corporations, served notice that life under Roosevelt would be different from life under McKinley.

President Roosevelt inherited a number of advantages from his predecessor. The first was a powerful and efficient party organization, built by Mark Hanna, which Roosevelt immediately began making his own. He used appointments and the connections he had already made to give power to his supporters and prepare for the convention of 1904. He also inherited a talented and able cabinet. He would rely a great deal on men like Secretary of State John Hay, Secretary of War Elihu Root, and McKinley's personal secretary George Courtelyou. Roosevelt had also learned some things about press relations from McKinley's White House. The McKinley administration, thanks primarily to the enterprising Cortelyou, had made innovative changes in handling the media. McKinley had used press releases, pre-released speech transcripts, and "trial balloons" to shape news reports as no other president had ever done. Roosevelt combined this efficiency with his own tremendous personality to dominate the news. His control of the information the papers reported gave him extraordinary power to shape his own publicity.[49]

Because Roosevelt was vice president for so short a time, he had little impact on the office, but thanks to his skill at publicity, the potential certainly existed for him to have played an influential role in that office. Roosevelt had defied conventional practice by waging an active national campaign for the vice-presidency,[50] demonstrating his ability to publicize the Republican cause and reach out to the voters in a way that McKinley could not. It seems likely that McKinley, a man well aware of the power of the press, might have continued to use Roosevelt in a similar fashion, as a sort of "public persuader" for the administration.[51] McKinley had indicated that he would pursue trade reciprocity agreements in his second term, had begun to prepare an antitrust agenda, and had hinted that he might take up the tariff issue.[52] If so, Roosevelt would have been the ideal man to sell these programs to the public.

Theodore Roosevelt became one of the nation's most active and popular presidents, easily winning reelection in 1904. He pursued important domestic legislation, such as the Hepburn Act (for greater regulation of railroads) and the Pure Food and Drug acts, and he led the nation into a more active role in international relations. In 1906, he became the first American to receive the Nobel Prize for Peace for his mediation of the Russo-Japanese War.

After leaving office in 1909, Roosevelt embarked on a hunting safari in Africa, returning home in 1910 to a hero's welcome. In 1912, disenchanted with the policies of his presidential successor William Howard Taft, Roosevelt decided to run for president once more. Denied the nomination by the Republicans, he formed his own party, the Progressive or Bull Moose party, chose Hiram Johnson of California as a running mate, and ran against Taft. The three contenders, Roosevelt, Taft, and Democrat Woodrow Wilson, the eventual winner, together produced one of the most memorable presidential campaigns in U.S. history. When the ballots were counted, Roosevelt's independent candidacy came in second, ahead of Taft's Republican ticket.[53]

After the campaign of 1912, Roosevelt retired once more into private life. He would not, however, remain in the background. Upon the outbreak of World War I in Europe in 1914, Roosevelt called for immediate entry by the United States on the side of the Allies. When President Wilson adopted a policy of neutrality, Roosevelt became the president's most vociferous critic. After the United States entered the war in 1917, Roosevelt proposed to lead a division of volunteers, a reincarnation of the Rough Riders, to fight in France and was outraged when President Wilson refused him a command. Roosevelt continued to criticize Wilson throughout the war, but late in 1918, as peace negotiations proceeded in Paris, Roosevelt fell ill. On January 6, 1919, at the age of sixty, Theodore Roosevelt died in his sleep.[54]

As Henry Cabot Lodge had predicted, the vice-presidency proved a stepping stone for Roosevelt to the White House, though not in the way he had foreseen. Theodore Roosevelt was elected vice president thanks to a combination of Senator Platt's desire to get him out of the way and a popular movement among friends and admirers within the GOP. Despite Platt's hope that he would fade from view, Roosevelt appeared to be on the path to the presidency, poised to use the vice-presidency in novel ways to build his own support for 1904. Lodge thus proved a better prophet than either Roosevelt or Platt. The vice-presidency led, not to oblivion, but to the White House.

NOTES

[1] Elting E. Morison, ed., *The Letters of Theodore Roosevelt*, vol. 2, *The Years of Preparation, 1898–1900* (Cambridge, 1951), p. 1174.

[2] Quoted in Irving G. Williams, *The Rise of the Vice Presidency* (Washington, D.C., 1956), p. 81.

[3] Morison, 2:1439.

[4] Edmund Morris, *The Rise of Theodore Roosevelt* (New York, 1979), pp. 32–36, 60–70, 128, 135–56. This is the most detailed and colorful account of Roosevelt's life and early career.

[5] Ibid., pp. 159–201, 227–67; William Henry Harbaugh, *Power and Responsibility: The Life and Times of Theodore Roosevelt* (New York, 1961), pp. 27–28. Harbaugh provides the most thorough scholarly account of Roosevelt's public career.

[6] Morris, pp. 240–45, 270–341. As chairman of the Stockman's Association, Roosevelt was automatically a deputy sheriff of Billings County, a responsibility he took very seriously.

[7] Ibid., pp. 382–85, 153–56, 386–93. Boone and Crockett Clubs were dedicated to preserving wildlife throughout the nation and to westward expansion.

[8] Ibid., pp. 261–68, 345–47.

[9] Ibid., Chapters 16–25.

[10] Ibid., pp. 665–66; Harbaugh, *Power and Responsibility*, pp. 108–11.

[11] Harbaugh, *Power and Responsibility*, pp. 109–11.

[12] Ibid., pp. 111–14.

[13] Ibid., pp. 114–21.

[14] Ibid., pp. 113–22; John Morton Blum, *The Republican Roosevelt*, 2d ed. (New York, 1964), pp. 15–16.

[15] Quoted in Morris, p. 666.

[16] Henry Cabot Lodge, ed., *Selections from the Correspondence of Theodore Roosevelt and Henry Cabot Lodge, 1884–1918* (New York, 1925), 1:426.

[17] David J. Rothman, *Politics and Power: The United States Senate, 1869–1901* (Cambridge, MA, 1966), p. 157.

[18] Lodge, 1:467.

[19] Morison, 2:1157; Harbaugh, *Power and Responsibility*, p. 123.

[20] Morris, p. 718.

[21] Lodge, 1:435, 442.

[22] Morison, 2:1157; Lodge, 1:448.

[23] Morison, 2:1140; Lodge, 1:442.

[24] Morison, 2:1174.

[25] G. Wallace Chessman, "Theodore Roosevelt's Campaign Against the Vice-Presidency," *Historian* 14 (Spring 1952): 174–75; Lodge, 1:442.

[26] Williams, p. 73; Morison, 2:449.

[27] Quoted in Chessman, "Theodore Roosevelt's Campaign Against the Vice-Presidency," p. 179.

[28] John Milton Cooper, Jr., *Pivotal Decades: The United States, 1900–1920* (New York, 1990), p. 29. This work offers an outstanding general synthesis of the politics of this era.

[29] Lodge, 1:460.

[30] Quoted in Harbaugh, *Power and Responsibility*, p. 135.

[31] Quoted in Blum, p. 22.

[32] Harbaugh, *Power and Responsibility*, pp. 137–38.

[33] Cooper, *Pivotal Decades*, pp. 29–30.

[34] Ibid., pp. 28–30.

[35] Chalmers M. Roberts, *The Washington Post: The First 100 Years* (Boston, 1977), p. 57; David S. Barry, *Forty Years in Washington* (Boston, 1924), p. 270; Morris, p. 731.

[36] William H. Harbaugh, "The Republican Party, 1893–1932," in *History of U.S. Political Parties*, ed. Arthur M. Schlesinger, Jr., vol. 3, *1910–1945, From Square Deal to New Deal* (New York, 1973), p. 2080; Cooper, *Pivotal Decades*, pp. 24–25.

[37] Morison, 2:1422; Lodge, 1:484.

[38] Morison, 2:1446.

[39] Quoted in Barry, p. 273.

[40] Quoted in Williams, p. 81.

[41] Harbaugh, *Power and Responsibility*, pp. 143–44; Morris, pp. 26, 313, 359, 372; Lewis Gould, *The Presidency of Theodore Roosevelt* (Lawrence, KS, 1991), pp. 102–4, 226.

[42] Lodge, 1:484–88, 492–94.

[43] Morison, 3:121, 129; G. Wallace Chessman, *Theodore Roosevelt and the Politics of Power* (Boston, 1969), pp. 79–83; Blum, p. 40; Williams, p. 81; Gould, *The Presidency of Theodore Roosevelt*, p. 128.

[44] Chessman, *Theodore Roosevelt and the Politics of Power*, p. 77; Lewis Gould, *The Presidency of William McKinley* (Lawrence, KS, 1980), p. 215; Morison, pp. 56–57.

[45] Gould, *The Presidency of William McKinley*, pp. 251–52; Harbaugh, *Power and Responsibility*, pp. 144–45.

[46] Harbaugh, *Power and Responsibility*, pp. 144–46.

[47] Theodore Roosevelt, "The Three Vice-Presidential Candidates and What They Represent," *American Monthly Review of Reviews* 14 (September 1896): 289–91.

[48] Harbaugh, "The Republican Party, 1893–1932," p. 2080; Chessman, *Theodore Roosevelt and the Politics of Power*, pp. 82–84.

[49] Chessman, *Theodore Roosevelt and the Politics of Power*, pp. 80–82; Blum, pp. 38–44; Gould, *The Presidency of Theodore Roosevelt*, pp. 16–21; Robert C. Hilderbrand, *Power and the People: Executive Management of Public Opinion in Foreign Affairs, 1897–1921* (Chapel Hill, NC, 1981), pp. 52–61; John Milton Cooper, *The Warrior and the Priest: Woodrow Wilson and Theodore Roosevelt* (Cambridge, 1983), pp. 65, 70.

[50] Although most scholars have credited Roosevelt with being the first vice-presidential candidate to wage a national campaign, Richard Mentor Johnson also did so in

1840. See Chapter 9 of this volume, "Richard Mentor Johnson," p. 130.

[51] This role is suggested in Horace Samuel Merrill and Marion Galbraith Merrill, *The Republican Command, 1897–1913* (Lexington, KY, 1971), p. 95.

[52] Gould, *The Presidency of William McKinley*, pp. 249–51; Cooper, *The Warrior and the Priest*, p. 77. McKinley's untimely death permits only speculation about his full intentions, but his public and private statements indicate preparations for a more active agenda of antitrust and tariff legislation.

[53] For the most penetrating discussions of Roosevelt's presidency see Blum's *Republican Roosevelt* and Gould's *Presidency of Theodore Roosevelt*. Chessman's *Theodore Roosevelt and the Politics of Power* is also helpful. For the election of 1912, see Cooper's *The Warrior and the Priest*.

[54] The fullest account of Roosevelt's post-presidential activities appears in Harbaugh's *Power and Responsibility*.

Chapter 26

CHARLES WARREN
FAIRBANKS
1905–1909

CHARLES W. FAIRBANKS

Chapter 26

CHARLES WARREN FAIRBANKS

26th Vice President: 1905–1909

My name must not be considered for Vice President and if it is presented, I wish it withdrawn. Please withdraw it.

—CHARLES WARREN FAIRBANKS [1]

In the summer of 1904 Senator Charles Warren Fairbanks wanted to be president of the United States. Many in 1900 had seen him as the natural successor to his good friend President William McKinley. Now, however, it was not the fallen McKinley who occupied the White House, but Theodore Roosevelt, and the president appeared on his way to easy renomination at the 1904 Republican convention. When members of the Republican Old Guard suggested Fairbanks for vice president, the senator saw an opportunity for advancement. After all, the second spot had led to the presidency for Roosevelt, it might do the same for him. The vice-presidency might prove a good place from which to maneuver for the 1908 convention, and anything could happen with the impetuous Roosevelt in the White House. As Finley Peter Dunne's fictional character Mr. Dooley speculated, "Th' way they got Sinitor Fairbanks to accipt was by showin' him a pitcher iv our gr-reat an' noble prisidint thryin to jump a horse over a six-foot fence." [2] Most of all, Roosevelt's prodigious shadow seemed a natural place for a man described by friends as "a safe and popular politician" to wait for his turn in the White House. [3] If ever a man seemed destined to remain in the political shadows, it was Charles Warren Fairbanks.

Youth

Charles Fairbanks was born on May 11, 1852, in a modest log house in Ohio. His father, Loriston Fairbanks, was a farmer and wagon maker who had moved from New York to go into business for himself. He became active in Union County as a member of the agricultural board, and his wife, Mary Adelaide Smith, was a local temperance advocate. As a moderately wealthy farmer, Fairbanks could afford to send his son Charles to college at Ohio Wesleyan. Charles excelled at his studies, graduating eighth out of forty-four in the class of 1874. He continued his education at Cleveland Law College, taking only six months to complete his courses and pass the bar. [4]

On October 6, 1874, Charles married Cornelia Cole and moved with her to Indianapolis, Indiana, where, with the help of an uncle, Charles took a position as attorney with the Chesapeake and Ohio railroad system. Over the next decade, young Fairbanks built a sterling reputation—as well as a personal fortune—as a lawyer for numerous railroad interests in the Midwest. He specialized in dealing with bankrupt railroads and he prosecuted strikers after the Indianapolis railroad strike in 1877. These activities brought the young lawyer to the attention of Indiana's Republican party.[5]

Leader of the Indiana Republicans

In 1884, Indiana's Republicans split in their support of presidential candidates, some favoring Walter Q. Gresham and others preferring Benjamin Harrison. The election of Harrison in 1888 seemingly jeopardized Fairbanks' prospects, since he had been active on behalf of the Gresham faction. Harrison's lackluster performance in the White House, however, followed by impressive Democratic victories in 1892, gave Fairbanks the opportunity to return to prominence in the state by helping to rebuild the party. The campaign of 1892 also brought him into contact with the governor of Ohio, William McKinley. The two men formed a friendship that lasted until McKinley's untimely death in 1901 and proved extremely beneficial to the careers of both men.[6]

Even though he held no office, Fairbanks managed to gain control of the Indiana Republican party, primarily because of his wealth. He spent freely on campaigns and consistently urged party unity behind candidates at all levels. Persistent letter writing and encouragement endeared him to GOP officeholders throughout the state, and he used his connections with the railroads to obtain passes for political allies. Perhaps most importantly, he secretly owned a majority interest in the state's largest newspaper, *The Indianapolis News*. By 1901, he had also purchased the major opposition daily, *The Indianapolis Journal*. Fairbanks' control of the press significantly promoted the Republican cause in Indiana.[7]

As leader of his state's Republican party, Fairbanks stood in an excellent position to command the attention of the national party. With the parties almost evenly balanced in the late nineteenth century, a small shift in the voting patterns of one of the more densely populated industrial states could win or lose a presidential election. Indiana was one of these vital states. In the thirteen presidential elections from 1868 to 1916, eleven of the national tickets boasted a Hoosier candidate, usually running for vice president. Charles Fairbanks thus became an important man in Republican electoral considerations.[8]

When William McKinley ran for president in 1896, he made his friend Fairbanks a key player in his campaign strategy. Fairbanks ran McKinley's campaign in Indiana and delivered a united Hoosier delegation for McKinley at the Republican National Convention in St. Louis. As temporary chairman of that convention, Fairbanks uncharacteristically delivered a stirring keynote address, in which he lambasted the Democrats and advocated the gold standard for currency.[9] McKinley won the Republican nomination handily, then defeated Democrat William Jennings Bryan in the general election. Indiana, which he won by only about 18,000 votes, proved instrumental to his victory.[10]

On the state level, the Republicans also did well enough to regain control of the Indiana legislature, guaranteeing that they would determine that body's choice of a United States senator. Speculation naturally turned to Charles Fairbanks. The wealthy lawyer had assisted many of the Republican legislators during their campaigns; now they could return the favor. With a little help from President McKinley, Fairbanks easily won election to his first political office.[11]

A Senator with Presidential Ambitions

Fairbanks' Senate career proved competent if unspectacular. He stuck to the party line and was well respected among his colleagues. As chairman of the Immigration Committee, he favored restricting immigration and requiring a literacy test before entry into the United States—both popular positions. When the Immigration Committee proved too contentious for his liking, Fairbanks moved to the chairmanship of the more agreeable Committee on Public Buildings and Grounds. Although he had originally opposed the pressure for war with Spain in 1898, he faithfully followed President McKinley's lead when war came. The president appointed him to the Joint-High Commission to decide the U.S.-Canadian boundary in Alaska. No settlement was reached, but Fairbanks helped his own popularity by declaring, "I am opposed to the yielding of an inch of United States territory." The people of Alaska showed their appreciation by naming the city of Fairbanks in his honor. Perhaps Fairbanks' only controversial stand in the Senate was his support for the demands of black soldiers fighting in Cuba that they be commanded by black officers. Thanks to the senator's intervention, Indiana became the first state to accept this position as general policy for its militia units.[12]

Fairbanks' calm demeanor and "safe" Republican views made him very popular in the Senate. As a senator from a pivotal state and a consistent defender of the McKinley administration, Fairbanks emerged as a natural successor to McKinley. He certainly looked like a president: tall (approximately six feet, four inches), dignified, always clad in a proper Prince Albert coat.[13] In 1900 some conservatives, most notably Ohio Senator Mark Hanna, tried to maneuver Fairbanks into a vice-presidential nomination.[14] The conservative attempt to block the nomination of New York Governor Theodore Roosevelt ended in failure, but the mention of Fairbanks for vice president fueled the senator's already growing ambition. The Indianan turned down Hanna's offer for practical reasons and because he had set his sights higher. As one journalist put it, "[Fairbanks] had dreams of the White House. He preferred to remain in the Senate until the real call came."[15]

Charles Fairbanks' political fortunes changed dramatically on September 6, 1901, when President McKinley was assassinated while visiting the Pan-American Exposition in Buffalo. He lost not only a friend, but also a political patron. Although McKinley's successor, Theodore Roosevelt, promised to continue the fallen president's policies, Fairbanks' close connection to the White House was severed. Beyond these personal considerations, the nation's political environment was about to change—partly in response to Roosevelt—in ways that would leave Fairbanks in the shadows. President Roosevelt brought a new glamour to the presidency. He dominated the news and shifted the national debate to new issues.[16] None of these changes proved helpful to Fairbanks' presidential ambitions.

Conditions were also changing in Indiana. In 1899 the state legislature had elected a young firebrand named Albert J. Beveridge to the Senate. The new junior senator from Indiana was a powerful orator who shot to prominence by advocating a policy of overseas expansion for the United States. His growing power in Indiana represented a challenge to Fairbanks. The threat became increasingly severe as Beveridge gradually broke away from the party's Old Guard and began siding with the insurgents in calling for greater regulation of railroads and business trusts. No longer merely over party power, the battle had come also to concern policies. To make matters worse for Fairbanks, President Roosevelt quite obviously preferred the counsel of Senator Beveridge.[17]

This smoldering conflict erupted in 1901 when a federal judgeship became available in Indiana. Beveridge recommended an old friend, Francis Baker, whom Fairbanks adamantly refused to endorse. The squabble became public and was widely seen as a test of prestige within the state. Because this type of patronage could crucially affect a politician's ability to accumulate and wield power, the dispute had serious repercussions for Fairbanks. When Roosevelt nominated Baker, apparently without much concern for the prerogatives of the senior senator, there was little question which of Indiana's senators had the favor of the White House.[18]

Vice-Presidential Candidate

Charles Fairbanks saw his presidential hopes gradually slipping away. President Roosevelt effectively maneuvered throughout 1902 and 1903 to gain control of the party and ensure his renomination in 1904. Some conservatives considered supporting Mark Hanna for the nomination, but Hanna's death in February 1904 ended any real opposition to Roosevelt within the GOP. With Hanna gone, Fairbanks became more closely identified as the heir to McKinley, but Roosevelt's presence—rather than McKinley's spirit—had come to dominate the party.

Still, the Old Guard could not simply be dismissed. If one of their own could not be the presidential nominee, they would choose the vice-presidential candidate. Fairbanks was the obvious choice, since conservatives thought highly of him yet he managed not to offend the party's more progressive elements. Roosevelt was far from pleased with the idea of Fairbanks for vice president. He would have preferred Representative Robert R. Hitt of Illinois, but he did not consider the vice-presidential nomination worth a fight. For his part, Fairbanks followed Roosevelt's example from 1900 by declaring that he was not a candidate. His friends, however, had little doubt of his interest in the position, and he privately informed Roosevelt that he would serve in any way the president indicated. With solid support from New York, Pennsylvania, and Indiana (thanks to the acquiescence of Senator Beveridge) Fairbanks was easily placed on the 1904 Republican ticket in order to appease the Old Guard.[19]

By avoiding controversy and contentious issues, Fairbanks made himself a useful running mate, conservative enough to alleviate business uneasiness about Roosevelt but not so outspoken as to be unacceptable to the insurgents. Still, the reaction was not entirely favorable. The *New York Journal* called Fairbanks "a mere blank wall upon which the influences that control the Republican party can paint what they will."[20]

If the goal of constructing a national presidential ticket is to achieve a complementary balance between its two members, the Republican ticket of 1904 came close to being ideal. Roosevelt and Fairbanks differed from one another in nearly every way. The ticket offered balance both geographically, between New York and Indiana, and ideologically, from progressive to conservative. Perhaps the greatest contrast was one of personality. The vigorous and ebullient Roosevelt differed markedly from the calm and cool Fairbanks. One wag called the 1904 ticket "The Hot Tamale and the Indiana Icicle." Fairbanks' cool demeanor often led cartoonists to portray him as a block of ice.[21] Although friends claimed he was a very genial fellow in private and only appeared austere,[22] the icy image remained the popular one, providing an interesting contrast to the "strenuous life" of President Roosevelt.

Mrs. Fairbanks partially offset this impression of coldness. Cornelia Fairbanks had become one of the most popular hostesses in Washington, renowned for her charm and tact. She also remained active as president-general of the Daughters of the American Revolution. The Fairbanks' Washington home, the Van Wyck House near

Dupont Circle, occupied a prominent place in the capital's social landscape.[23]

Charles Fairbanks assumed the principal Republican campaign duties for the ticket in 1904, as tradition dictated that incumbent presidents remain at work in the White House. He toured all the northern states and spent the final week ensuring a Republican victory in Indiana.[24] His task turned out to be relatively easy thanks to Theodore Roosevelt's enormous popularity and the Democratic nomination of the rather lifeless Judge Alton B. Parker of New York. The Republicans' landslide victory over Democrats Parker and Henry G. Davis unquestionably resulted from Roosevelt's popularity, but Fairbanks was now vice president and he hoped his star was on the rise once more. He began making plans to pursue an even higher calling in 1908.

President of the Senate

In an 1896 article for *Review of Reviews*, Roosevelt, while New York City police commissioner, had argued that the vice president should participate actively in a presidential administration, including attendance at cabinet meetings and consultation on all major decisions. He even posited that the vice president should be given a regular vote in the Senate.[25] Now that he was president, however, Roosevelt displayed no intention of following his own advice. He did not invite Fairbanks to participate in the cabinet and consulted the vice president about nothing of substance. Roosevelt certainly showed no inclination to support granting Fairbanks a vote in the Senate and, given Fairbanks' conservative tendencies, would probably have opposed any attempt to do so. Discussing the office abstractly turned out to be quite different from dealing with a flesh-and-blood occupant.

The new vice president spent much of his time presiding over the Senate. He undoubtedly felt comfortable dealing with his old friends on Capitol Hill, and President Roosevelt gave him nothing else to do. As Senate president, Fairbanks had little direct power to affect the course of legislation, but working in tandem with the Republican leadership he was able to play a role in passing the president's ambitious legislative program that included the Hepburn Act regulating railroad rates, the Pure Food and Drug Act, and an employer's liability law for the District of Columbia.

Fairbanks, Republican Senate leader Nelson Aldrich of Rhode Island, and Speaker of the House Joe Cannon of Illinois also worked together effectively to bury unwanted legislation in hostile committees and to rule opposition speakers "out of order" at every opportunity.[26] Fairbanks never had a chance to break a tied vote, but he seldom missed a session and opposition speakers remained sensitive to his vigilance in the chair.

In 1907, Fairbanks wielded the power of his office against his old foe Albert Beveridge. When the Senate considered legislation for government inspection of packaged meat, Beveridge advocated charging the inspection fees to the meat packers, but was unsuccessful in his attempts. Later in the session, he offered this plan as an amendment to the agriculture appropriations bill. In order to stop the amendment, Senator Francis Warren of Wyoming raised a point of order that the amendment contained "general legislation" and, therefore, under Senate rules, could not be added to an appropriations bill. The presiding officer, Vice President Fairbanks, could either rule on the point of order himself or present it to the Senate for a decision. Senator Jacob Gallinger of New Hampshire submitted a list of precedents in which previous officers had referred similar points of order to the Senate for determination. Fairbanks promptly ignored these precedents and ruled Beveridge's amendment out of order, observing, "During the present session the Chair has frequently been invited by Senators to submit to the Senate points of order on amendments which were not in order, and in every case of such invitation the Chair has felt obliged to decline to do so." Fairbanks took further pleasure in chastising Beveridge for offering an amendment that was very similar to a bill Beveridge had introduced the previous December. If the matter were of "such large consequence," he asserted, the Senate would have dealt with it then, in "an orderly and appropriate way."[27] The vice-presidency may not have had much power, but Fairbanks knew how to use what he had.

The most famous instance of Fairbanks' effectiveness as presiding officer came in May 1908 during debate over the conference report on the Aldrich-Vreeland Emergency Currency Act. This legislation authorized the issuance of emergency currency based on state bonds, municipal bonds, and railroad bonds. The inclusion of bonds from railroad companies enraged many midwestern and southern progressives, who saw it as an example of the railroads' control of Congress. As Senator Robert C. Byrd observed in discussing this incident in a 1989 address to the Senate, "Filibusters are inherently much more difficult to wage successfully on conference reports than on bills, because conference reports are not amendable."[28] Nevertheless, Republican Senator Robert La Follette of Wisconsin, leading the small but determined opposition to the legislation, decided to filibuster. By holding the floor, La Follette and Democratic Senators Thomas Gore of Oklahoma and William Stone of Missouri hoped to force the leadership to drop railroad bonds from the measure. La Follette began speaking at 12:20 p.m. on Friday, May 29. Either Gore or Stone was to take the floor when he finished and, by speaking in rotation, they could stifle Senate business indefinitely.

A filibuster in the early twentieth century could be particularly unpleasant. In the summer, an extremely hot Senate chamber customarily drove senators to the cloakrooms for relief. During a filibuster, however, if too many members left the chamber, the speaker, or an ally, could suggest the absence of a quorum without losing control of the floor. This procedure required the vice president to direct that the roll be called, and, if a quorum (forty-seven members at that time) were not present, the Senate would adjourn until a quorum could be obtained, further contributing to the filibuster's objective of delay. In any event, the quorum call allowed the speaker a few moments to seek water or food and some fresh air. When Robert La Follette took the floor on May 29, 1908, he brought a clerk with him to keep track of the number of senators present. Since the day turned out to be especially warm, senators had no desire to linger in the sweltering chamber. Whenever the count of members in the chamber fell below the required number, La Follette would stop his speech to suggest the absence of a quorum, forcing his colleagues to file back into the chamber to answer the roll. This cycle continued for hours. When Vice President Fairbanks ordered La Follette's clerk, who had been keeping count for his boss, to leave the chamber, other members friendly to the Wisconsin senator's cause took up the counting. Finally, at about 11:45 that night, after thirty-two quorum calls, Fairbanks, under the guidance of party leader Aldrich, managed to limit the tactic by making a resourceful parliamentary ruling that some business other than debate must take place between quorum calls. Not until 2:25 a.m. on Saturday, May 30, did La Follette finally establish the absence of a quorum, at which point the Senate adjourned until the sergeant at arms roused enough senators from bed to begin debate once more, at 3:40 a.m., allowing La Follette a short nap.

La Follette continued until 7:00 a.m. William Stone followed, holding the floor until 1:30 p.m., and then yielded to Senator Gore. Gore was to speak until 4:30 p.m., when Stone would return. At the appointed time, Gore, who was blind, heard that Stone had returned, but when Gore yielded the floor, Stone, either by mistake or through chicanery, had stepped outside the chamber for a moment. Vice President Fairbanks, alert to his opportunity, immediately recognized Nelson Aldrich, who moved that the vote be taken on his bill. Fairbanks, ignoring other speakers shouting for recognition, directed the clerk to call the yeas and nays, and Aldrich, first on the roll, answered in the affirmative. Under Senate rules, once a vote began, it could not be stopped for further debate. After more than twenty-eight hours, the filibuster was broken.[29]

The passage of the Aldrich-Vreeland Act pleased President Roosevelt, but his vice president's other Senate rulings would not always produce such agreeable results. Roosevelt spent most of 1907 and 1908 fighting with Congress. The Senate, especially, erected roadblocks to the president's legislative initiatives, particularly those seeking to expand the powers of the executive branch. Roosevelt believed that Congress was incapable of making the kind of informed,

disinterested decisions necessary to regulate the nation's powerful trusts. He preferred to rely on executive agencies, staffed by experts whom he considered capable of maintaining a careful watch over the nation's business community. He argued that efficient executive power, rather than clumsy intermittent legislation, would most effectively deal with the trusts. The Hepburn bill included provisions allowing the Interstate Commerce Commission to set railroad rates, and Roosevelt pursued legislation to allow executive agencies to set maximum prices for certain commodities. While the Senate eventually agreed to the Hepburn bill with some modifications, it jealously guarded its prerogatives against what it saw as presidential encroachment. Even a president as persuasive as Theodore Roosevelt had difficulty convincing Congress to expand the executive's power.[30]

Opposition from his own party in the Senate constantly frustrated Roosevelt, who attempted to rouse public opinion in support of greater executive power. For their part, many Republican senators bristled at the seemingly endless flow of presidential messages from the White House, as well as at Roosevelt's constant public criticism of their cherished institution.[31] Vice president Fairbanks' sympathies plainly lay with the Senate, and when his term ended in 1909, he used his farewell address to launch a vigorous defense of his Senate colleagues. He supported the record of the recent session against "erroneous" criticism that it was unresponsive to the popular will. "The Senate of the United States," he said, "was designed by our fathers to be a deliberative chamber in the fullest and best sense—a chamber where the passions of the hour might be arrested and where the better judgement of the people would find ultimate expression." Offering a Senate response to Roosevelt's "bully pulpit," he declared, "A servile Senate was not contemplated by its founders." [32]

Pursuit of the Presidency

During his vice-presidency, Fairbanks also spent considerable time trying to secure the Republican presidential nomination in 1908. In this endeavor, he faced serious obstacles. His own lackluster image offered cartoonists and writers a favorite target. When President Roosevelt told columnist Finley Peter Dunne that he was considering taking a ride in a submarine, Dunne advised, "You really shouldn't do it—-unless you take Fairbanks with you." [33] Fairbanks even earned a short mention in David Graham Phillips' 1906 exposé *The Treason of the Senate*, where he is referred to as the "presiding genius" of the Senate. [34]

Fairbanks' popularity increased somewhat after a supposed attempt on his life. While the vice president was laying the cornerstone for a new federal building in Flint, Michigan, police arrested a man in the crowd carrying a thirty-two-caliber revolver and pockets full of "socialistic literature." This incident surely evoked memories of the assassination of President McKinley. Fairbanks also tried to use favorable publicity to bolster his image. He spent the summer of 1905 on a farm he owned in Illinois trying to appeal to the farm vote. He had himself photographed chopping down a tree and cutting it up, perhaps trying to emulate Roosevelt's much-admired vigor. Still, no one outside the inner circle of the Republican party seemed to pay much attention. The *New York Daily News* committed his obscurity to verse, saying:

> Fairbanks was in town two days
>   Yet no one seemed the wiser;
> He yearned to meet the public gaze
>   His own press advertiser.
> He strolled about the town at will
>   Without much molestation,
> The only effect was a heavy chill
>   And his own great agitation.
> A stranger on a foreign shore
>   Would scare up more attention;
> And he is feeling extra sore
>   For lack of even mention. [35]

In his effort to attract support, Fairbanks' oratory proved less than appealing. *The Nation* declared, "No public speaker can more quickly drive an audience to dispair." [36] He seemed both uninspiring and out of step with the times. During an era of growing clamor for progressive reforms, Fairbanks' speeches were full of what one observer called "splendid verbosity," simply equating the Republican party with prosperity. During the congressional races of 1906, he spoke often for GOP candidates, stressing the theme

"Let Well Enough Alone." *Collier's Weekly* summed up his performance with another poem:

> Then Mr. Fairbanks waxed quite warm;
>   His voice ris to a roar.
> He yelled: "I say to you, my friends,
>   That two and two make four,"
> And thereupon all doubts dissolved,
>   All fears were put to rout;
> Pie-seekers said that Fairbanks knew
>   Just what he was about.
> He did not name unbusted trusts
>   Or mention Standard Oil;
> He did not talk of railroad graft
>   Nor speak of children's toil.
> He said the crops looked mighty well,
>   The cattle all seemed fat,
> The sky was blue, the grass still grew,
>   And the G.O.P. stood pat.
> And he let it go at that. [37]

The only substantive issue that really seemed to hold Fairbanks' attention was the gold standard. He had demanded a strong gold plank in the Indiana platform in 1896 and succeeded in helping McKinley make that a major part of the 1896 campaign. [38] After McKinley's victory in 1900, however, the gold standard had ceased to be a salient issue for the public. Fairbanks' continued reliance on it seemed safe and popular, but not likely to create a groundswell of support. It was merely one more instance of Fairbanks' failure to keep up with the rapid political changes of the new century.

An even more serious problem for Fairbanks loomed in the form of opposition from Theodore Roosevelt. The president had already announced he would not run in 1908, but he intended to choose his own successor. His list clearly did not include Fairbanks. Roosevelt preferred Secretary of State Elihu Root, but his age (over sixty) and background in corporate law made him an unlikely choice. The president, therefore, settled on his secretary of war and close friend, William Howard Taft, using the power of his office to secure convention delegations loyal to Taft. By the time the convention began, Taft's selection was nearly determined. [39] Against the power of a popular incumbent president, Fairbanks never had a chance.

Roosevelt could hardly conceal his scorn for Fairbanks. The president liked to tell amusing stories about his uninspiring vice president and would often discuss his preferred successors in

Fairbanks' presence without mentioning the gentleman from Indiana.[40] When Fairbanks and New York Governor Charles Evans Hughes both showed some strength as possible nominees in the summer of 1908, Roosevelt seemed stunned. As he exclaimed to a Hughes supporter before the convention, "Do you know whom we have most trouble in beating? Not Hughes—but Fairbanks! Think of it—Charley Fairbanks! I was never more surprised in my life. I never dreamt of such a thing. He's got a hold in Kentucky, Indiana, and some other states that is hard to break. How and why is beyond me."[41] This strength, though, was illusory compared to the influence wielded by Roosevelt on behalf of Taft. After gaining the nomination, Taft went on to win an easy victory over William Jennings Bryan in November.

Still Active in Politics

After the inauguration of Taft and new Vice President James Sherman in March 1909, Fairbanks returned to Indiana to live the life of a country gentleman. He remained marginally active in Indiana politics but tried to maintain a low profile during the disastrous party split in 1912. In 1914, the former vice president returned to prominence once more as the advocate of party unity. The Indiana delegation to the 1916 Republican National Convention supported him as a "favorite son" candidate for president, in hopes of a deadlocked convention. When Charles Evans Hughes obtained the nomination, there was talk of proposing Fairbanks for vice president. The prospect of reacquiring his old position did not appeal to Fairbanks. He wired his friends in the Indiana delegation, "My name must not be considered for Vice President and if it is presented, I wish it withdrawn. Please withdraw it." When, despite Fairbanks' wishes, he was nominated on the first ballot,[42] his loyalty to the party induced him to accept the nomination and fulfill his duty as a candidate. He toured the country calling for a return to the high tariff policies that Democratic President Woodrow Wilson had abandoned. Neither Fairbanks nor his opponent and fellow Hoosier, Democratic Vice President Thomas Marshall, aroused much enthusiasm. As the *New Republic* put it,

"Mr. Marshall is an argument for the election of Mr. Hughes. Mr. Fairbanks is an argument for the re-election of Mr. Wilson." Hughes and Fairbanks suffered a narrow defeat in 1916, but Fairbanks could take comfort that Indiana swung once more into the Republican column.[43]

After the election, Charles Fairbanks again retired to private life. He remained active in the Indiana Forestry Association, a conservation group of which he was founder and first president (perhaps his only similarity to Roosevelt). During the First World War, he visited several army camps to encourage the troops and spoke for the Liberty Loan campaigns. Fairbanks died on June 14, 1918, at the age of sixty-six.

Ironically, the message from the Republican National Convention in 1904 notifying Charles Fairbanks of his nomination for the vice-presidency spoke in glowing terms of the party's unity. It lamented previous selections that had been made to appease defeated factions and rejoiced that this selection was not such a case. It compared the hoped-for collaboration between Roosevelt and Fairbanks to that of McKinley and Garret Hobart (conspicuously passing over McKinley and Roosevelt).[44] The author of this message surely must have been aware of its inaccuracy. Roosevelt accepted Fairbanks because he did not consider the office worth a fight. Fairbanks took the position in hopes that it would lead to the presidency. The two men never cooperated well and spent the last two years of the administration actually working at cross purposes. Roosevelt thwarted Fairbanks' bid for the presidential nomination, while Fairbanks helped to bottle up Roosevelt's legislation in the Senate.

Charles Fairbanks was neither a great orator nor a brilliant political thinker. He succeeded by mastering the intricacies of the Senate and by avoiding controversy. Like so many other Indiana politicians, Fairbanks excelled as a political insider. He was skilled in the arts of political management and compromise.[45] Those skills made him a valued member of the Senate and an influential state politician but were far less useful in presidential politics. Perhaps an observer in 1897 had him pegged best when he said, "Fairbanks may not be a great Statesman, but he certainly is a great Politician."[46] By understanding party politics, Fairbanks advanced as far as the vice-presidency. Yet, in an era dominated by the likes of Roosevelt, Wilson, Bryan, and La Follette, Fairbanks' political skills were not sufficient to allow him to escape the shadows of those men.

NOTES

[1] Quoted in Herbert J. Rissler, "Charles Warren Fairbanks: Conservative Hoosier," (Ph.D. dissertation, Indiana University, 1961), p. 266.

[2] James H. Madison, "Charles Warren Fairbanks and Indiana Republicanism," in Ralph D. Gray, ed., *Gentlemen From Indiana: National Party Candidates, 1836–1940* (Indianapolis, 1977), p. 184.

[3] William Henry Smith, *The Life and Speeches of Hon. Charles Warren Fairbanks* (Indianapolis, 1904), p. 7.

[4] Rissler, pp. 5–27.

[5] Ibid., pp. 28–35.

[6] Ibid., pp. 40–62; Smith, p. 39.

[7] John Braeman, *Albert J. Beveridge: American Nationalist* (Chicago, 1971), pp. 73–77; Madison, p. 177; Donald A. Ritchie, *Press Gallery: Congress and the Washington Correspondents* (Cambridge, MA, 1991), p. 182.

[8] Rissler, preface; Ralph D. Gray, ed., *Gentlemen From Indiana: National Party Candidates, 1836–1940* (Indianapolis, 1977), Chapters VII–XI.

[9] Smith, pp. 44–55; Rissler, pp. 64–72; Madison, p. 179.

[10] *Congressional Quarterly's Guide to U.S. Elections*, 3d. ed. (Washington, 1994), p. 444.

[11] Rissler, pp. 76–77; Madison, p. 179.

[12] Rissler, pp. 80–97.

[13] Madison, pp. 181–82.

[14] Lewis L. Gould, "Charles Warren Fairbanks and the Republican National Convention of 1900: A Memoir," *Indiana Magazine of History* 77 (December 1981): 370.

[15] Henry L. Stoddard, *As I Knew Them: Presidents and Politics From Grant to Coolidge* (New York, 1927), p. 248.

[16] For the most thorough discussion of Roosevelt's presidency, see Lewis L. Gould, *The Presidency of Theodore Roosevelt* (Lawrence, KS, 1991). For a discussion of Roosevelt's vice-presidency, see Chapter 25 of this volume, "Theodore Roosevelt," pp. 303–5.

[17] For the life and career of Albert J. Beveridge, see Braeman, *Albert J. Beveridge: American Nationalist* and Claude G. Bowers, *Beveridge and the Progressive Era* (New York, 1932).

[18] Braeman, pp. 76–77; Bowers, 175–76.

[19] Gould, *The Presidency of Theodore Roosevelt*, p. 135; Rissler, pp. 135–50; Irving G. Williams, *The Rise of the Vice Presidency* (Washington, 1956), pp. 86–87.

[20] Rissler, p. 115.

[21] Ibid., p. 151; Gould, "Charles Warren Fairbanks," p. 361.

[22] George F. Sparks, ed., *A Many Colored Toga: The Diary of Henry Fountain Ashurst* (Tucson, 1962), p. 79.

[23] Thomas R. Shipp, "Charles Warren Fairbanks, Republican Candidate for Vice President," *American Monthly Review of Reviews* 30 (August 1904): 181.

[24] Rissler, pp. 157–58.

[25] Theodore Roosevelt, "The Three Vice-Presidential Candidates and What They Represent," *American Monthly Review of Reviews* 14 (September 1896): 289–97.

[26] Williams, p. 90.

[27] Braeman, p. 109; Asher C. Hinds, *Hind's Precedents of the House of Representatives of the United States*, vol. 2 (Washington, 1907), pp. 883–85.

[28] U.S., Congress, Senate, *The Senate, 1789–1989: Addresses on the History of the United States Senate*, by Robert C. Byrd, S. Doc., 100–20, 100th Cong., 1st sess., vol 2, 1991, p. 108.

[29] Belle Case La Follette and Fola La Follette, *Robert M. La Follette, June 14, 1855–June 18, 1925* (New York, 1953), pp. 238–56. This source gives the most detailed and interesting, if one sided, account of the filibuster.

[30] John M. Blum, *The Republican Roosevelt*, 2d ed. (New York, 1964), pp. 87, 95–96, 105, 107–8.

[31] Gould, *The Presidency of Theodore Roosevelt*, pp. 276–77, 291–94.

[32] U.S., Congress, Senate, *Congressional Record*, 60th Cong., 2d sess., 1909, p. 3825.

[33] Jules Witcover, *Crapshoot: Rolling the Dice on the Vice Presidency* (New York, 1992), p. 58.

[34] David Graham Phillips, *The Treason of the Senate* (Chicago, 1964; reprint of 1906 edition), p. 198.

[35] Rissler, pp. 169–72.

[36] Ibid., pp. 145–46.

[37] Ibid., pp. 178–79, 202.

[38] Ibid., pp. 69–70; Stoddard, p. 239.

[39] Gould, *The Presidency of Theodore Roosevelt*, pp. 271–73, 283–84.

[40] Williams, pp. 88–89.

[41] Stoddard, p. 335.

[42] Rissler, pp. 265–66.

[43] Ibid., pp. 266–71; *Congressional Quarterly's Guide to U.S. Elections*, p. 449.

[44] Smith, pp. 234–35.

[45] For an excellent overview of Indiana politics and the general skills of Hoosier politicians, see Philip R. VanderMeer, *The Hoosier Politician: Officeholding and Political Culture in Indiana 1896–1920* (Urbana, IL, 1985).

[46] Madison, p. 173.

Chapter 27

JAMES SCHOOLCRAFT SHERMAN
1909–1912

JAMES SCHOOLCRAFT SHERMAN

Chapter 27

JAMES SCHOOLCRAFT SHERMAN

27th Vice President: 1909–1912

You will have to act on your own account. I am to be Vice President and acting as a messenger boy is not part of the duties as Vice President.
—JAMES SCHOOLCRAFT SHERMAN TO PRESIDENT WILLIAM HOWARD TAFT

A marble bust of James Schoolcraft Sherman has the distinction of being the only vice-presidential bust in the United States Capitol with eyeglasses. Sherman apparently had thought that no one would recognize him without his glasses. However, over time he has grown so obscure that no one recognizes him even *with* his glasses.[1] Capitol visitors often confuse him with the more famous Senator John Sherman, author of the Sherman Antitrust Act. Yet while he never authored a famous bill, "Sunny Jim" Sherman was a powerful leader in the House of Representatives, a skilled parliamentarian, and a popular presiding officer of the Senate during his vice-presidency under William Howard Taft.

Youth

James S. Sherman was born on October 24, 1855, in Utica, New York, where his grandfather, Willett Sherman, ran a profitable glass factory and owned an impressive farm. In later years, Senator Elihu Root recalled spending summers at his own grandfather's farm and "the big, white house, with the great columns," of Sherman's grandfather's adjoining farm. Root believed that Sherman inherited his probusiness politics from his grandfather. Sherman's father, Richard U. Sherman, headed a food canning company and published a Democratic newspaper.

Young James Sherman graduated from Whitestown Seminary in 1874 and then attended Hamilton College, where he achieved recognition for his skills in oratory and debate. His genial temperament made him "the most popular man in his class." He graduated from Hamilton in 1878, received his law degree there the following year, and was admitted to the New York state bar in 1880, practicing in a firm with his brother-in-law. In 1881, he married Carrie Babcock of East Orange, New Jersey; they would have three sons.

Sherman was a joiner. In college he had joined the Sigma Phi fraternity. He was active in the Dutch Reformed Church. He was a member of the Royal Arcanum, the Order of Elks, and of all the local clubs in Utica. In politics, he broke with his Democratic father to become a Republican and at the age of twenty-nine won election as mayor of Utica. Two years later, in 1886, his district elected him to the U.S. House of Representatives. Except for the two years following his defeat for reelection in 1890, he remained in national public office for the rest of his life.[2]

A Jolly Coterie in the House

As a Republican committed to a high protective tariff, Sherman blamed his single defeat on an angry voter reaction to the McKinley Tariff of 1890, which had swept many members of his party out of Congress (including William McKinley). In 1892 Sherman narrowly defeated Democrat Henry Bentley, who had beaten him in 1890, and returned to Congress. There Sherman reestablished himself as the leader of a "jolly coterie" of New York Republicans. Speaker Thomas B. Reed, who enjoyed the company of these younger men, promoted Sherman in the House hierarchy. Democratic Leader Champ Clark identified him as among the "Big Five" in the House Republican leadership, but Sherman never held a party leadership post or chaired a major committee. He served on the committees on the Judiciary, Census, Industrial Arts and Expositions, Interstate and Foreign Commerce, and Rules; and for fourteen years he chaired the Indian Affairs Committee. Democratic Representative John Sharp Williams believed that Sherman could have had a seat on either of the most important House committees, Appropriations or Ways and Means, "for the asking." But the New Yorker always stood aside in favor of friends who wanted those appointments, "thereby making the task of the Speaker, who was in those days always the party leader, easier and the pathway of his friends pleasanter." [3]

The secret of Sherman's success in the House was his recognized parliamentary ability. Whenever House Speakers Tom Reed, David Henderson, and Joseph Cannon had to leave the chair, they knew that they could trust Sherman with the gavel, because he was a "decisive, self-possessed, and able parliamentarian." Unlike the smaller Senate, the House regularly used the device of a "committee of the whole" as a means of suspending its rules and moving ahead more speedily on legislation, since a smaller quorum was needed for the committee of the whole, and debate was limited. Amendments could be voted upon, but the final bill had to be reported back to the full House to be voted upon in regular session. Officially known as the Committee of the Whole House on the State of the Union, this committee comprised all House members and met in the House chamber. To indicate that the House was meeting in the committee of the whole rather than in regular session, the House sergeant at arms lowered the House mace from its pedestal,

and the Speaker stepped down as presiding officer in favor of another member. Henry Cabot Lodge declared that Sherman "gradually came to be recognized as the best Chairman of the Committee of the Whole whom that great body had known in many years." Presiding effectively over the committee of the whole, said Lodge, was "a severe test of a man's qualities, both moral and mental. He must have strength of character as well as ability, quickness in decision must go hand in hand with knowledge, and firmness must always be accompanied by good temper." [4]

While in the House, Sherman was a leader in the fight to preserve the gold standard against Populist proposals for "free silver"—by which farmers hoped to reduce their debts by fueling inflation through an expansion of the amount of money in circulation. Sherman also fought Democratic President Grover Cleveland's efforts to lower the tariff. When the Republicans returned to power with the election of William McKinley as president in 1896, Sherman played a key role in passage of the Dingley Tariff that reversed Democratic efforts and restored the high protective tariff. As usual, Speaker Reed turned the gavel over to Sherman to chair the committee of the whole throughout most of the debate on the Dingley Tariff. When Speaker Reed retired in 1900, Sherman sought the Speakership but lost to David Henderson. He became Henderson's right-hand man and continued to play that role under Henderson's successor, the powerful "Uncle Joe" Cannon. [5]

McKinley's assassination in 1901 transferred the presidency to the dynamic Theodore Roosevelt, whose strong personality stimulated a national reform movement that had grown out of a series of local responses to the human abuses of industrialism. Progressives demanded change, which conservative leaders in Congress resisted. Sherman stood with the Old Guard. "He was preeminently a stand-patter and proud of it," recalled Senator Chauncey Depew. Having inherited the presidency of the New Hartford Canning Company from his father, Sherman fought progressive efforts to require accurate labeling of the weights and measures of canned jelly, catsup, corn, and other foods. He proposed a substitute amendment that required only that if a canner did label the weight and measure of the product, that such labeling must be accurate. This caused Dr. Harvey Wiley, who led the crusade for pure food and drug laws, to rename "Sunny Jim" Sherman as "Short-weight Jim." [6]

The Republican Congressional Campaign Committee

Sherman chaired the Republican Congressional Campaign Committee during the congressional elections of 1906, raising large campaign contributions from business interests and gaining further recognition from his party's leaders. Sherman himself faced a hard fight for reelection that year. At one point, he turned desperately to an old fraternity brother, Elihu Root, then secretary of state in the Roosevelt administration. Sherman invited Root to speak for him and for the New York Republican gubernatorial candidate, Charles Evans Hughes, who was locked in battle with the Democratic candidate, newspaper publisher William Randolph Hearst. Other Republican leaders, fearing that Hearst might exploit Root's corporate connections to embarrass the Republican ticket, pleaded with Root to cancel his trip. But Sherman begged Root to reconsider. Root made the speech, in which he strongly and eloquently denounced Hearst, an attack that was credited with helping Hughes and Sherman win their elections.[7]

In 1908, Sherman chaired the Republican state convention for the third time (having previously done so in 1895 and 1900). His supporters then launched a vice-presidential boom for him. President Theodore Roosevelt had announced that he would not stand for a third term, and had anointed Secretary of War William Howard Taft as his successor. The New York delegation went to the convention pledged to their governor, Charles Evans Hughes, for president, but as one journalist observed, the state's delegation was actually anxious to nominate Sherman for the second place on the ticket. Fortunately for Sherman's ambitions, Governor Hughes did nothing to promote his candidacy. Hughes' cool aloofness inspired a Gridiron Club parody of an old spiritual:

Swing low, sweet chariot,

You'll have to if you're after me;
Swing low, sweet chariot,
For I'm lying low, you see.[8]

A Machiavellian Nomination

Taft won the nomination and would have preferred a progressive running mate, someone of the stature of Indiana Senator Albert Beveridge or Iowa Senator Jonathan Dolliver. But House members, led by Speaker Cannon, pressed for the nomination of James Sherman. On the surface, it seemed as though Sherman won the nomination by default, after the more progressive possibilities withdrew their names from consideration. But years later, in his memoirs, Senator Chauncey Depew revealed a more Machiavellian version of what had happened. The New York delegation had lobbied hard to convince Taft's managers that New York would be a critical state in the election, and that a New Yorker would most strengthen the ticket headed by a "westerner" like Taft of Ohio. Since Taft's managers had already discussed the nomination with several other potential candidates, they could not turn to Sherman without first dissuading these people—and doing so without offending their states. As Depew explained:

The method adopted by one of the leading managers was both adroit and hazardous. He would call up a candidate on the telephone and say to him: "The friends of Mr. Taft are very favorable to you for vice-president. Will you accept the nomination?" The candidate would hesitate and begin to explain his ambitions, his career and its possibilities, and the matter which he would have to consider. Before the prospective candidate had finished, the manager would say, "Very sorry, deeply regret," and put up the telephone.

When the nomination was made these gentlemen who might have succeeded would come around to the manager and say impatiently and indignantly: "I was all right. Why did you cut me off?" However, those gentlemen have had their compensation. Whenever you meet one of them he will say to you: "I was offered the vice-presidency with Taft but was so situated that I could not accept." [9]

Straddling Party Divisions

House Democratic minority leader Champ Clark agreed that Sherman stood prominently in the House, but no more so than a half dozen other Republicans. In Clark's estimation, Sherman was "an industrious, level-headed, capable member, and a capital presiding officer," but in truth he received the nomination as a means of placating the GOP's conservative wing, which viewed Taft suspiciously as a progressive. "The Stand-patters selected Sherman partly because he wanted it, partly because they could trust him, and partly because he was perhaps the most acceptable of all the Old Guard chieftains in the House to President Roosevelt," Clark assessed. The vice-presidential nomination was clinched when Speaker Cannon stepped onto the platform, hiked up his sleeves, and offered an impassioned endorsement of Sherman. With the Old Guard's stamp of approval, "the two wings flapped together."[10]

While well-known in Washington, Sherman had little popular identification across the nation, and it is doubtful that he brought many votes to the Taft ticket. The opposition Democratic candidate was William Jennings Bryan, who had twice before lost the presidency, in 1896 and 1900. Few Republicans would have voted for Bryan regardless of who ran with Taft, but Sherman campaigned with good grace. When the Democratic candidate for vice president, John Worth Kern, came to Utica he received a telegram from Sherman, who was campaigning elsewhere, welcoming Kern to his home city and urging him to call upon the Sherman family.[11]

For the third and last time, William Jennings Bryan went down to defeat as Taft and Sherman were elected. While Taft prepared to enter the White House, Theodore Roosevelt made arrangements to leave the country for an extended hunting trip in Africa and tour of Europe, to give his successor a chance to establish himself. Even Taft had trouble in accepting the departure of the dynamic Roosevelt from the presidency. "When I hear someone say Mr. President," said Taft, "I look around expecting to see Roosevelt." Facing Taft was the problem of keeping together the warring conservative and progressive factions of the Republican party. Roosevelt had finessed party unity by talking publicly of reform while working privately with conservative leaders in Congress, and by steering absolutely clear of such divisive issues as the tariff. Taft came into office with a reputation for progressivism but with the support of such powerful conservatives as Rhode Island Senator Nelson Aldrich, who had worked quietly behind the scenes for Taft's nomination. During the campaign, Taft had managed to straddle party divisions, but once he assumed the office, he would have to choose sides.[12]

No Messenger Boy

At first, Taft thought he had a perfect role for Sherman. The president-elect said that he had no intention of having anything to do with the reactionary House Speaker Cannon. "I am going to rely on you, Jim, to take care of Cannon for me," said Taft. "Whatever I have to do there will be done through you." "Not through me," Sherman declined. "You will have to act on your own account. I am to be Vice President and acting as a messenger boy is not part of the duties as Vice President." A month later, Taft invited Cannon to visit him, and thereafter Taft and Cannon met regularly at the White House. It was the beginning of a drift to the right that would eventually alienate Taft from Republican progressives.[13]

Whatever ill-will may have resulted from Sherman's refusal to cooperate over handling Speaker Cannon evaporated in the glow of the inaugural festivities. Taft's wife, Helen, later wrote that Vice President and Mrs. Sherman shared a box with them at the inaugural ball. "They also had with them a large family party and were both so jolly and so much in the festive spirit that formality disappeared."[14]

When Taft met with Speaker Cannon in December 1908, he learned that the House Ways and Means Committee was at work on major tariff revisions. Taft favored lowering tariff rates and negotiating reciprocal trade agreements with other nations to stimulate international trade, but congressional conservatives remained committed to high tariff duties to protect American industries. House Ways and Means Committee chairman Sereno Payne eventually produced the Payne bill, which pleased Taft by its moderate tariff reductions. In the Senate, however, Finance Committee chairman Nelson Aldrich amended the tariff with massive increases in rates. Insurgent Republicans led by Wisconsin Senator Robert La Follette fought the Payne-Aldrich Tariff, but Aldrich prevailed. Never in doubt was the stance of the Senate's new presiding officer, Vice President Sherman, a lifelong high-tariff man. In the end, President Taft sided with Sherman and the protectionists and signed the bill. As progressives began to reevaluate their assessment of Taft, the president compounded his problems by speaking out in defense of the Payne-Aldrich Tariff at Winona, Wisconsin, in Senator La Follette's home state, describing the tariff as "the best bill that the Republican party ever passed." At the same time, Vice President Sherman was telling people that the Republican party "had fulfilled every campaign pledge in passing the Aldrich bill." [15]

Growing Relationship Between Taft and Sherman

The more conservative the president became, the closer he grew to his vice president. Taft found that he liked Sherman, a man who "hated shams, believed in regular party organization, and was more anxious to hold the good things established by the past than to surrender them in search for less certain benefits to be derived from radical changes in the future." Like Taft, Sherman possessed a jovial spirit, and the president credited the vice president with accomplishing much on Capitol Hill by his "charm of speech and manner, and his spirit of conciliation and compromise." Sherman succeeded through a "sunny disposition and natural good will to all." Yet he also manifested what Taft called "a stubborn adherence" to his principles. "In other words," said Taft, "it would be unjust to Mr. Sherman to suggest that his sunny disposition and his anxiety to make everybody within the reach of his influence happy, was any indication of a lack of strength of character, of firmness of purpose, and of clearness of decision as to what he thought was right in politics." [16]

From all accounts, Sherman showed fairness, judicial temperament, and good humor in his ca-

pacity as presiding officer. "In the Senate we have no rules," observed New York Senator Chauncey Depew. Sherman had risen in the House because of his mastery at presiding over the House, whose rules were more rigid and its precedents voluminous. He thus found it quite a change to "preside over a body which is governed practically by no rules whatever, but is a rule unto itself." Depew noted that the older senators resented any effort on the part of the chair to curb their wanderings or their "very unregulated wills." He recalled how the vice president had ruled against Texas Democrat Joseph W. Bailey, one of the most quarrelsome senators, who

> instantly declared that the independence of the Senate had been invaded by the Vice President who was not a member of the Senate but only its Constitutional presiding officer; that he had no right to use a position which was largely one of courtesy to violate the traditions of the most august body in the world and deny, or attempt to deny, to a Senator the rights to which every Senator was entitled.

Throughout this attack, Sherman showed no trace of emotion.

> He was the presiding officer personified. With perfect calmness, good humor, and dignity, he stated the case to a breathless Senate. He did it so clearly and convincingly that the Senate sat down upon the tumultuous senator, and Sherman's decisions were never after questioned. [17]

Always showing his sunny disposition in public, Sherman played tough-minded, hard-ball politics in private. "Sherman's indictments," President Taft once complained, "are as abrupt and severe as a school master's." When progressives revolted against the Payne-Aldrich tariff, Sherman advised: "Mr. President, you can't cajole these people. You have to hit them with a club." Sherman recommended cutting off postmastership appointments to the progressives as punishment for their disloyalty, to which Taft replied: "I hate to use the patronage as a club unless I have to." "It is your only club," Sherman rebutted. "You have other weapons, but the appointing power is your only club." [18]

Roosevelt and Taft Split

In January 1910, Taft fired Theodore Roosevelt's good friend Gifford Pinchot as head of the U.S. Forest Service, after Pinchot had accused Taft's secretary of the interior, Richard Ballinger, of undermining the conservation program in favor of business interests. Sherman strongly backed Taft's decision, and when a joint congressional committee was established to investigate the Ballinger-Pinchot controversy, the vice president made sure to name only Taft supporters to the committee. Not surprisingly, the committee exonerated Ballinger, but the incident further divided the Republican party.[19]

As the 1910 congressional elections approached, Taft dispatched Vice President Sherman on a number of political missions. In Wisconsin, Taft tried to block the renomination of the Senate's leading insurgent, Robert La Follette. Although the state had abandoned party nominating conferences in favor of primary elections, conservatives had organized a "true Republican meeting." The president sent Sherman to bestow the administration's blessing. Despite their efforts, however, La Follette easily won renomination and reelection.[20]

Sherman then plunged into New York state politics, where Governor Charles Evans Hughes' resignation to become a Supreme Court justice had triggered open warfare between conservative and progressive Republicans. William Barnes of Albany, who led the party's Old Guard, selected Vice President Sherman as temporary chairman of the state convention to nominate the next governor. But Representative Herbert Parson, the Republican national committeeman for New York and leader of the party organization in New York City, appealed to former president Theodore Roosevelt for help. Roosevelt, who had just returned from his long overseas journey, was deeply angered over the Ballinger-Pinchot affair, and dismayed by the increasingly conservative tendencies of the Taft administration. Roosevelt agreed to run against Sherman for chairman to help insure the nomination of a progressive candidate for governor and a more progressive platform.[21]

Roosevelt maintained that his candidacy was directed against Sherman and not against the administration. He portrayed Sherman as having spread the erroneous impression of having Taft's support. Yet Sherman remained in close communication with Taft by telephone throughout the New York convention fight, and at one point the president laughed as he told aides, "They have defeated Theodore." But Sherman could not overcome Roosevelt's immense popularity, and convention delegates voted, 568 to 443, to reject Sherman in favor of Roosevelt. Although Taft maintained public neutrality, Sherman's defeat was widely perceived as a defeat for the president.[22]

The internal split proved a disaster for the Republican party in the 1910 congressional midterm elections. Republicans lost eight seats in the Senate—where insurgents now held the balance of power—and lost their majority in the House to the Democrats. In the hope of restoring harmony, Taft invited the leading insurgent senators to the White House to discuss patronage. All but the implacable La Follette attended. But these efforts alarmed the party's conservatives, who warned that, if Taft embraced the progressives, the Old Guard might throw their support to Vice President Sherman in 1912. Harmony was the last thing that the hapless Taft could achieve.[23]

Death and Defeat

At first, Senator La Follette emerged as the principal challenger to Taft's renomination, but when the overworked and exhausted La Follette suffered a breakdown in February 1912, Theodore Roosevelt jumped into the race for the Republican nomination. In a series of bitter confrontations, Roosevelt won the popular primaries but Taft retained control of the party machinery that chose a majority of the delegates. In New York, Sherman's forces managed to gain 78 delegates for Taft, with only 12 for Roosevelt.[24] Denied the nomination, the former president walked out of the Republican convention to form the Progressive ("Bull Moose") party. Democrats meanwhile had nominated the progressive governor of New Jersey, Woodrow Wilson, who became the frontrunner by virtue of the Republican split.

With Taft's defeat in the November elections an almost foregone conclusion, the Republican convention renominated Sherman with little fuss or attention. He became the first sitting vice president to be renominated since John C. Calhoun, eighty years earlier. New York Republicans continued to argue that Sherman would bring the most strength to the ticket. In fact, Sherman was too ill to campaign that year. Since 1904 he had suffered from Bright's disease, a serious kidney ailment. During the long session of the Senate in 1912, Sherman's discomfort had been increased by the Senate's inability to elect a Republican president pro tempore who might spell him as presiding officer. He returned to Utica, where his family doctor diagnosed his condition as dangerous and prescribed rest and relaxation. His doctor urged him not even to deliver his speech accepting the nomination, at ceremonies planned for late August. "You may know all about medicine," Sherman responded, "but you don't know about politics." Sherman went through with the ceremonies and spoke for half an hour. Two days later, his health collapsed, leaving him bedridden. By mid-September, Sherman felt well enough to travel to Connecticut, where he checked into an oceanside hotel to recuperate. When reporters caught up with him and asked why he had avoided campaigning, Sherman replied, "Don't you think I look like a sick man?" [25]

His longtime colleague and adversary, Robert La Follette, later noted that "the hand of death" had been upon Sherman throughout his vice-presidency. "From the first its shadow went with him in and out of this Chamber, stood over him at his desk, followed him down the corridors, pursued him to his home. Month after month, waking or sleeping, in social cheer or the still hours of the night, it was his constant companion. Before all others he was the first to know what threatened him." Yet Sherman never allowed his illness to hamper him. "He bore an outward geniality and spirit that dispelled fear from all his friends." [26]

On October 30, 1912, President Taft was at a dinner at the Brooklyn Navy Yard, after launching the battleship *New York*, when word came that Vice President Sherman had died. He was fifty-seven years old. Taft asked the diners to adjourn in Sherman's memory and later issued a statement that he felt "a sense of personal bereavement in the loss of a friend." Privately, Taft fretted that Sherman's death might dissuade people from voting for the ticket. Mrs. Taft considered Sherman's death "very unfortunate" coming just before the election. "You have the worst luck," she commiserated with her husband. [27]

A Deceased Running Mate

Taft considered naming the progressive governor of Missouri, Herbert S. Hadley, to replace Sherman, but members of the national committee persuaded the president that it would be poor politics to choose someone who was unlikely to carry his own state in the election. So Taft put off the decision and went into the election with a deceased running mate. It mattered little, since the Democratic candidate, Woodrow Wilson, won the presidency with 435 electoral votes; the Progressive candidate, Theodore Roosevelt, took second place with 88 electoral votes; and Taft came in a dismal third, with only the 8 electoral votes of Vermont and Utah. In January, the Republican National Committee named another New Yorker, Columbia University president Nicholas Butler, to fill out the Republican ticket for purposes of receiving electoral votes, which were counted on February 12, 1913. Taft's reelection campaign remains one of the worst defeats ever suffered by a Republican presidential candidate (in 1936, Alf Landon tied Taft by winning only 8 electoral votes). [28]

Various memorial services were held to honor the deceased vice president. Senator Elihu Root paid tribute to Sunny Jim, whose "smile was always bright; his fair, ruddy face was always glowing with kindly feeling; and the impression produced by his just and sweet and serene temperament was so strong that the world thought of him as a bright and cheerful man. It was all real; there was none of it put on." Senator Chauncey Depew commended Sherman's steadfast defense of the protective tariff, "the fundamental principle of all his political career."

Democratic Senator John Worth Kern, who had lost the vice-presidency to Sherman in 1908, recalled his arrival in the Senate in 1911. Vice President Sherman had been so anxious to show his good will that within minutes after Kern had taken the oath of office, Sherman invited him to take the gavel and preside over the Senate. "I protested that I was a stranger, not only to this body but its procedure," said Kern,

> but he insisted, saying, "It will be only for a few minutes and it is for my own pleasure and gratification that I ask you to do me this personal favor." And from that time on until the last he never lost an opportunity to make me feel that however wide our political differences—and they were irreconcilable—I had in him a friend on whose fidelity I might always rely.

Senator Charles Curtis of Kansas, who had served with Sherman in the House, and who would follow him as vice president during Herbert Hoover's administration, described Sherman as a fatherly man: "He was at once interested in the things in which you were interested, and immediately took upon himself the cloak of helper and adviser. He was thus particularly useful and congenial to new Members, and commanded for himself respect and support in everything he undertook." [29]

An Unexpected Reappearance

Despite these eulogies, James Schoolcraft Sherman quickly disappeared from public memory. He remained the least-remembered twentieth-century vice president until 1974, when he made an unexpected reappearance in E.L. Doctorow's best-selling novel *Ragtime*. At a climactic moment in the book, Sarah, a black domestic, tried to intercede on behalf of her husband, when Vice President Sherman attends a campaign rally in New Rochelle, New York:

> When the Vice-President's car, a Packard, rolled up to the curb and the man himself stepped out, a cheer went up. Sunny Jim Sherman was a New York State politician with many friends in Westchester. He was a round balding man and in such ill health that he would not survive the campaign. Sarah broke through the line and ran toward him calling, in her confusion, President! President! Her arm was extended and her black hand reached toward him. He shrank from the contact. Perhaps in the dark windy evening of impending storm it seemed to Sherman's guards that Sarah's black hand was a weapon. A militiaman stepped forward and, with the deadly officiousness of armed men who protect the famous, brought the butt of his Springfield against Sarah's chest as hard as he could. She fell. A Secret Service man jumped on top of her. The Vice-President disappeared into the hotel. [30]

That scene, which led to Sarah's death in the novel, was entirely fictitious. Sherman simply served as the novelist's metaphor of an unhealthy and unresponsive political system. Although perhaps better than total obscurity, it was not the way "Sunny Jim" would have wanted to be remembered.

NOTES

[1] Senate Curator James Ketchum provided the following information in response to the popular belief that Sherman's marble bust was damaged in the 1983 explosion that took place on the second floor of the Capitol's Senate wing, adjacent to the Sherman bust. "As Bessie Potter Vonnoh began working on the translation of her Sherman bust from plaster to marble, she discovered an imperfection near the surface of the stone. She raised her concern about its possible effect on the finished piece with the Senate Library Committee. In response, Chairman George Peabody Wetmore asked architect Thomas Hastings (of the firm of Carrere and Hastings) and sculptor James Earle Fraser to look into the matter. Both agreed that the discoloration on the right cheek was of little concern. Unfortunately, as the carving progressed, the dark spot became more apparent. There was little that could be done to minimize it and the work proceeded to completion. After the 1983 bombing of the Capitol, it was erroneously reported that the area in question, located just below Sherman's glasses, resulted from the explosion. The bust of J.S. Sherman, including his glasses, survived that bombing unscathed."

[2] *Memorial Services in Honor of the Memory of the Late James Schoolcraft Sherman, Vice-President of the United States* (New York, 1913), pp. 12, 34–35.

[3] Ibid., pp. 5–6; Samuel W. McCall, *The Life of Thomas Brackett Reed* (Boston, 1914), p. 164; *James Schoolcraft Sherman, Late Vice President of the United States, Memorial Addresses Delivered at a Joint Session of the Senate and the House of Representatives of the United States, February 15, 1913* (Washington, 1913), p. 50.

[4] *Memorial Addresses*, pp. 38–39, 50.

[5] Ibid., pp. 21–22.

[6] Ibid., p. 23; Mark Sullivan, *Our Times, 1900–1925* (New York, 1953), 2:521; James Harvey Young, *Pure Food: Securing the Federal Food and Drugs Act of 1906* (Princeton, NJ, 1989).

[7] Henry F. Pringle, *Theodore Roosevelt, A Biography* (New York, 1956), p. 318; Philip C. Jessup, *Elihu Root* (New York, 1938), 2:114–15, 122.

[8] Arthur Wallace Dunn, *From Harrison to Harding: A Personal Narrative, Covering a Third of a Century, 1888–1921* (Port Washington, NY, 1971; reprint of 1922 edition), 2:73, 201; Arthur Wallace Dunn, *Gridiron Nights* (New York, 1915), p. 201.

[9] Chauncey M. Depew, *My Memories of Eighty Years* (New York, 1924), pp. 176–77.

[10] Champ Clark, *My Quarter Century of American Politics* (New York, 1920), 2:284–87.

[11] *Memorial Addresses*, p. 43.

[12] Henry F. Pringle, *The Life and Times of William Howard Taft* (Norwalk, CT, 1967; reprint of 1939 edition), p. 399; Horace Samuel Merrill and Marion Galbraith Merrill, *The Republican Command, 1897–1913* (Lexington, KY, 1971), p. 274.

[13] Henry L. Stoddard, *As I Knew Them: Presidents and Politics from Grant to Coolidge* (New York, 1927), p. 347.

[14] Mrs. William Howard Taft, *Recollections of Full Years* (New York, 1914), p. 345.

[15] Merrill and Merrill, pp. 277–98; George E. Mowry, *Theodore Roosevelt and the Progressive Movement* (New York, 1946), p. 70.

[16] *Memorial Services*, pp. 9–10.

[17] Ibid., p. 28; Clark, 2:285.

[18] Judith Icke Anderson, *William Howard Taft, An Intimate History* (New York, 1981), pp. 132, 187.

[19] William Manners, *TR and Will: A Friendship That Split the Republican Party* (New York, 1969), pp. 104–23.

[20] George E. Mowry, *The Era of Theodore Roosevelt, 1900–1912* (New York, 1958), p. 267; Belle Case La Follette and Fola La Follette, *Robert M. La Follette, June 14, 1855–June 18, 1925* (New York, 1953), 1:298–99.

[21] Stoddard, p. 381.

[22] Elting E. Morison, et al., eds., *The Letters of Theodore Roosevelt* (Cambridge, MA, 1954), 7:116, 140, 147; Henry F. Holthusen, *James W. Wadsworth, Jr.: A Biographical Sketch* (New York, 1926), pp. 64–65.

[23] James Holt, *Congressional Insurgents and the Party System, 1910–1916* (Cambridge, MA, 1967), p. 44.

[24] Holthusen, p. 80.

[25] *New York Times*, September 17, October 31, 1912.

[26] *Memorial Services*, p. 48.

[27] *New York Times*, October 31, 1912; *Washington Post*, October 31, 1912; Manners, p. 289.

[28] *New York Times*, November 3, 1912, January 5, 1913.

[29] *Memorial Services*, pp. 14, 19; *Memorial Addresses*, pp. 44, 54.

[30] E.L. Doctorow, *Ragtime* (New York, 1974), p. 159.

Chapter 28

THOMAS R. MARSHALL
1913–1921

THOMAS R. MARSHALL

Chapter 28

THOMAS R. MARSHALL

28th Vice President: 1913–1921

[I]t has not been the practice for Presidents to throw any of the burdens of their office upon the Vice President. He rules the dignified and at times irascible Senate and reflects upon the inactive character of his job. . . . He has an automobile provided for him . . . but has to buy his own tires, gasoline and supplies.

—WASHINGTON EVENING STAR, MARCH 2, 1913 [1]

Vice President Thomas R. Marshall, who served two terms with President Woodrow Wilson from 1913 to 1921, claimed that most of the "nameless, unremembered" jobs assigned to him had been concocted essentially to keep vice presidents from doing any harm to their administrations. One of these chores, according to Marshall, was that of regent of the Smithsonian Institution. The vice president recalled that at his first board meeting the other regents, including the chief justice of the United States and the inventor Alexander Graham Bell, discussed funding an expedition to Guatemala to excavate for traces of prehistoric man. With the breezy manner of a self-described "light-hearted Hoosier," Marshall asked if the Smithsonian had ever considered excavating in Washington, D.C. Judging from the specimens walking about on the street, he said, they would not have to dig far below the capital to discover prehistoric man. "And then the utter uselessness and frivolity of the vice-presidency was disclosed," Marshall confessed, "for not a man smiled. It was a year before I had courage to open my mouth again." [2]

This typically self-deprecating story revealed much about Marshall's lamentable vice-presidency. His feelings of inadequacy in both himself and the position he held were reflected again in his reaction to an invitation from President Wilson to attend cabinet meetings. Vice President

Marshall stopped going after a single session. When asked why, he replied that he realized "he would not be listened to and hence would be unable to make any contribution." Marshall similarly attended only one meeting of the Senate Democratic Caucus. "I do not blame proud parents for wishing that their sons might be President of the United States," he later said. "But if I sought a blessing for a boy I would not pray that he become Vice-President." [3]

Woodrow Wilson, a supremely self-confident intellectual, regarded Marshall as a "small-caliber man" and had not wanted him on his ticket in 1912. [4] During their eight years together, Wilson undoubtedly made Marshall feel uncomfortable. The editor William Allen White once described presenting a proposal to Wilson at the White House. Wilson "parried and countered quickly, as one who had heard the argument I would present and was punctiliously impatient. He presented another aspect of the case and outtalked me, agreeing in nothing. I could not tell how much he assimilated." [5] For a more insecure man like Marshall, such a response must have been excruciating. Convinced that the president and other high-ranking officials did not take him seriously enough to listen to him, Marshall learned not to speak, not to attend meetings, and not to offer suggestions. He became the epitome of the vice president as nonentity. But this condition moved from comedy to tragedy when President Wilson suffered a paralytic stroke in 1919. Faced with the crisis of having to determine whether the president was able to fulfill the duties of his office, Marshall failed miserably.

A Man of Contradictions

Thomas Riley Marshall had been little known outside his home town of Columbia City, Indiana, before he was elected governor in 1908. Born in Indiana on March 14, 1854, he was the only child of a country doctor and his sickly wife. After moving to Illinois and Kansas for Mrs. Marshall's health, the family returned to Indiana where Thomas attended Wabash College. From his youth he intended to become a lawyer and spent many of his Saturdays in the courtroom listening to such prominent Indiana lawyer-politicians as Benjamin Harrison, Thomas Hendricks, and Daniel Voorhees—who became president, vice president, and senator, respectively. Marshall read law and went into practice in Columbia City. In his early years he was a hard-drinking man, who "wanted a barrel, not a drink." His intemperance persisted for years, and he often appeared hung over in court. A seemingly confirmed bachelor, he lived with his mother until her death. Shortly thereafter, however, at the age of forty-one, he married Lois Kimsey, a deputy in the office of her father, the county clerk in nearby Angola, Indiana. After several difficult years, his wife persuaded him to stop drinking, and after 1898 he never touched another alcoholic beverage.[6]

Marshall's biographer, Charles M. Thomas, summarized the contradictions of his subject's personality:

> He was prior to 1898, a most pronounced drinker and at the same time a leader in the church and a temperance lecturer. He was inconsistent, yet he was trusted. He was a fundamentalist in religion, yet not sectarian [that is, not intolerant]. He was enjoyed as the biggest wit in town, yet his judgment was respected by those who knew him, and his leadership was accepted. His later political career proves that, despite his conflicting traits, there was something in his character which made men like him.[7]

An Indiana Democrat

Marshall came from a traditionally Democratic family who traced their political roots back to the age of Andrew Jackson. Marshall himself was always a regular party man. In 1876 he became secretary of the Democratic County Convention and spoke for many Democratic candidates. In 1880 he lost an election for prosecuting attorney. For years that defeat dissuaded him from campaigning for office. Although he became a member of the Democratic State Central Committee, he did not run again until 1908, when he sought the Democratic nomination for governor. When the frontrunning candidates eliminated each other from the race, Marshall won the nomination. He campaigned against Republican Representative James "Sunny Jim" Watson, who would later become Senate majority leader. Marshall was elected governor that year, even though in the presidential election Republican William Howard Taft carried Indiana against William Jennings Bryan, whose vice-presidential candidate, John W. Kern, was a Hoosier. It was the first time that Indiana Democrats had won the governorship since 1896.[8]

The "boss" of the Indiana Democratic party at that time was the Irish-born Thomas Taggart, owner of a nationally famous hotel, health resort, and gambling casino at French Lick, Indiana.[9] After William Jennings Bryan's two unsuccessful campaigns for president in 1896 and 1900, Tom Taggart had helped the anti-Bryan Democrats and regular machine organizations to nominate the more conservative Judge Alton B. Parker for president in 1904. Taggart managed Parker's campaign as Democratic party national chairman.

Bryan recaptured the Democratic nomination in 1908, but Taggart, a national committeeman, had enough influence in the party to ensure the choice of Indiana's John Worth Kern for vice president. In 1912 Taggart went to the Democratic convention with similar plans to recognize Indiana Democrats by winning the second spot for the governor, who could not succeed himself in the statehouse. A conventional, middle-of-the-road politician, Marshall as governor had been neither in Taggart's pocket nor much identified with his party's more progressive wing. But Indiana was a pivotal state, carried by every winning presidential candidate since 1880. Moreover, having Marshall on the national ticket would help state Democrats elect the machine's new candidate for governor.

Tom Taggart disliked New Jersey Governor Woodrow Wilson, whom progressive Democrats were supporting. Instead Taggart hoped for the nomination of House Speaker Champ Clark. But the party boss was shrewd enough to keep Indiana's 29 votes united for Marshall as their "favorite son," until he could determine how to use them to the best advantage. The Democratic convention required a two-thirds vote to nominate a presidential candidate. On the first ballot, Clark had 440 delegates to Wilson's 324. Despite his majority of votes, Clark peaked on the tenth ballot. On the fourteenth ballot, William Jennings Bryan endorsed Wilson. Sensing the way the wind was blowing, Taggart on the twenty-eighth ballot gave all of Marshall's delegates to Wilson, who went on to win the nomination on the forty-sixth ballot. Wilson would have preferred Alabama Representative Oscar W. Underwood for vice president, but when Underwood declined, Taggart clinched the nomination for Governor Marshall. As for Marshall, he had hoped that the frontrunning Wilson and Clark would eliminate each other, giving him the presidential nomination as the darkhorse candidate. When awarded the vice-presidential nomination instead, Marshall's first inclination was to decline on the ground that the job did not pay enough. But Mrs. Marshall had always wanted to go to Washington, and her tears of disappointment convinced him to change his mind and accept. In a multi-candidate race, the Democratic ticket won with 435 electoral votes to 88 for Theodore Roosevelt's "Bull Moose" ticket and only a meager 8 for Republican William Howard Taft.[10]

Vice President

Thomas R. Marshall went to Washington "with the feeling that the American people might have made a mistake in setting me down in the company of all the wise men in the land." His job as vice president required him to preside over the Senate, but other than delivering his gu-

bernatorial messages to the Indiana legislature, Marshall had no legislative experience. He assumed that as presiding officer of the Senate he had some authority, but it did not take him long to discover "that the Senate was not only a self-governing body but that it was a quite willful set of men, who had not the slightest hesitancy in overruling a presiding officer." Marshall and his wife also found that they were invited everywhere to social functions in Washington. After a while, however, he decided that these invitations were less out of respect for him and his office, than Washington's efforts to "size up" a new man under the microscope. With whatever illusions he might have had about his office quickly dispelled, Marshall came to agree with the early senator who had suggested that Vice President John Adams be titled "His Superfluous Excellency."[11]

A slight, bespectacled man, with his hat pushed back on his head, a pipe or cigar always ready in his hand, Marshall knew that he "was too small to look dignified in a Prince Albert coat," and so he continued his ordinary manner of dress. "He is calm and serene and small; mild, quiet, simple and old-fashioned," as one Indiana writer described him. "His hair is gray and so is his mustache. His clothes are gray and so is his tie. He has a cigar tucked beneath the mustache and his gray fedora hat shades his gray eyes." Another observer characterized Marshall's voice as "musical, pleasant in tone, and . . . sufficient for stump-speaking out of doors, altho you wouldn't think it to hear its soft notes in conversation."[12]

In later years, President Franklin D. Roosevelt loved to tell the story of Vice President Marshall's arrival aboard the cruiser *San Diego*, anchored off the Panama-Pacific Industrial Exposition, that took place in 1915 in San Francisco. As assistant secretary of the navy, FDR had designed the first vice-presidential flag, which was flown when Marshall came on board. Apparently, the vice president had not been instructed about naval etiquette. He came up the gangplank in the formal attire that the occasion required: silk hat, frock coat, gloves, and cane, and his ever-present cigar. When the band struck up the "Star Spangled Banner," the vice president "realized his predicament," shifted the cane from right hand to left, took the cigar out of his mouth, got the hat off his head and saluted. But when the first gun went off: "the whole works went two feet into the air." After the hat, gloves, cane and cigar were retrieved, Marshall tried to shake hands with the first saluting sailor he approached. "By that time," Roosevelt recalled, "the Admiral and I had sprinted across the deck and rescued the Vice President." Later at the exposition, Roosevelt and Marshall watched a motion picture that included the scene aboard the cruiser. "My God," said Marshall, "if I looked like that I will never go on board another ship as long as I live!" [13]

Witty but Overshadowed

From these descriptions, it is not surprising that Vice President Marshall gained a reputation as a rustic provincial. He also won notice for his folksy stories and down-home wit. In those days the Capitol guides escorted visitors through the corridor behind the Senate chamber. Whenever the vice president left the door to his office open, he could hear the guides pointing him out as if he were a curiosity. One day he went to the door and said, "If you look on me as a wild animal, be kind enough to throw peanuts at me." Seeking more space and more privacy, Marshall requested and received an office in the recently opened Senate Office Building, where he could "put his feet on the desk and smoke." [14]

Compared with the president, or even the Speaker of the House, Vice President Marshall could boast few perquisites of office. He had to share his small quarters in the Capitol with a secretary and stenographer. His $12,000 annual salary compared poorly with the president's $75,000 stipend, and he lacked travel and housing allowances. Awarded an automobile and a $1,000-per-year chauffeur, Marshall had to finance auto repairs from his personal resources. Each of the recent vice presidents had accepted from the Senate a solid silver inkstand as a memento of their office, but Vice President James Sherman had declined the honor, leaving Marshall to wrestle with the inevitable questions of propriety. [15]

Serving under a vigorous and innovative president, Marshall had difficulty determining his own role. Woodrow Wilson broke tradition in April 1913 by personally coming to the Capitol to address a joint session one day and the next by visiting the President's Room outside the Senate chamber to lobby senators in support of his tariff proposals. It was clear that the president intended to be his own lobbyist on Capitol Hill and had no particular use for his vice president. Marshall quickly ascertained that he was "of no importance to the administration beyond the duty of being loyal to it and ready, at any time, to act as a sort of pinch hitter; that is, when everybody else on the team had failed, I was to be given a chance." Marshall was probably also aware of Wilson's belittling comments about the vice-presidency in his 1885 book *Congressional Government*. The position, Wilson the scholar of government declared, "is one of anomalous insignificance and curious uncertainty," whose chief importance "consists in the fact that he may cease to be Vice President." [16]

Although both men had served as Democratic governors and both were Calvinist Presbyterians, Wilson and Marshall in fact had little in common. Marshall had considered himself a progressive governor of his state, but the president and his closest advisers looked upon him as a conservative. The White House rarely consulted him, and many months often elapsed between meetings of the president and vice president. Marshall loyally supported Wilson's program but was by nature too iconoclastic to embrace wholeheartedly Wilson's idealism. For instance, the vice president never reconciled himself to child labor laws or woman suffrage. Certainly Marshall lacked Wilson's imagination and determination, two qualities that the vice president admired greatly in his chief executive. "Whether you may like Woodrow Wilson, or not, is beside the point," Marshall wrote, "this one thing you will be compelled to accord him: he had ideas and he had the courage to express them. He desired things done, and he had the nerve to insist on their being done." [17]

Even in the Senate, Marshall was overshadowed by his two fellow Indianans, both progressive Democrats. Indiana's senior senator was

Benjamin Shively, whom Marshall described as "one of the finest specimens of physical manhood in the Senate—tall, commanding, of striking appearance, and his brain was as large as his body." Shively was also "a great orator, and a great logician, and when he spoke his words commanded careful consideration." The junior senator from Indiana was John Worth Kern, chairman of the Democratic caucus and floor leader for Wilson's New Freedom program. Kern was "strong in debate, gentle as a woman in his relations with his fellow-men, full of good ways and good works." The majority leader had "a weakness for the telling of stories, and he told them in an inimitable way." [18]

Correspondent Louis Ludlow, who covered Washington for various Indiana newspapers, rated Marshall highly for his irrepressible wit. Marshall's funny remarks "at the expense of the Senate's dignity" had at first shocked the older and more staid senators, "but out in the cloakroom they would laugh over his sayings until their sides ached." Marshall described the Senate as "the Cave of Winds" and used humor to belittle "the idols of clay" that populated it. [19] President Wilson apparently enjoyed hearing Marshall's stories and often repeated them at cabinet meetings and dinner parties. But Wilson's close confidant, Colonel Edward House, believed that Marshall's wit diminished his standing as a serious statesman and made him appear just a jester. "An unfriendly fairy godmother presented him with a keen sense of humor," House commented. "Nothing is more fatal in politics." [20]

Ironically, Vice President Marshall did not deserve authorship of his most famous quip about "a good five-cent cigar." Although there are many versions of this story, the most often repeated alleges that Kansas Senator Joseph Bristow had been making a long-winded speech with the repeated refrain "What this country needs—" causing the vice president to lean over and whisper to one of the Senate clerks: "Bristow hasn't hit it yet. What this country needs is a good five-cent cigar." Newspapers repeated the quote and cigar makers gratefully showered the vice president with their products. Immortalized in every dictionary of quotations, the "five-cent cigar" quote remains just about the only thing

for which Thomas R. Marshall is remembered today. But historian John E. Brown has traced the quotation back to the Indiana newspaper cartoonist Kin Hubbard, who put the words in the mouth of his popular character "Abe Martin." As a fan of the cartoon strip, Marshall simply picked up the phrase, repeated it, and became its surrogate father. [21]

In 1916, the Democratic Convention renominated Wilson and Marshall. Wilson gave little indication whether he wanted to retain or replace Marshall. In late 1915, Arizona Senator Henry F. Ashurst had learned of a plan to "ditch" Marshall from the ticket and had called on the president to endorse Marshall for a second term, but Wilson simply replied: "I have a very high regard for Vice-President Marshall and I wish you would tell him so." When the senator pressed harder, asking if he could say that President Wilson was for Marshall's renomination, Wilson "gurgled out" a positive response. Nevertheless, Secretary of War Newton Baker had the strong impression that the president would have preferred him for a running mate. Meanwhile, Marshall had increased his income by giving numerous after-dinner talks on the lecture circuit whenever Congress was not in session and had made himself a nationally popular figure. With a difficult reelection campaign ahead, the Democrats hesitated to drop the well-liked (if not necessarily well-respected) vice president from the ticket. In November, Wilson and Marshall won a narrow victory over the Republican ticket of Charles Evans Hughes and Charles Fairbanks (also from Indiana—which went Republican in the election). Marshall became the first vice president since John C. Calhoun, almost a century earlier, to be reelected to a second term. [22]

A Stressful Second Term

Marshall's second term proved difficult and stressful. In April 1917, the United States entered the First World War, joining the allied forces against Germany. Marshall spent much of the war speaking at rallies to sell Liberty bonds. Victory on the battlefield then thrust the United States into the negotiations to end the war and determine the future of Europe and the world. On December 4, 1918, President Wilson sailed for

France to negotiate the peace treaty. Except for the few days between February 24 and March 5, 1919, Wilson remained out of the country until July, after the Treaty of Versailles had been signed. During Wilson's unprecedented long absences from the United States, he designated Vice President Marshall to preside over cabinet meetings in his place. The request startled Marshall, but he complied gamely. On December 10, 1918, he presided over the cabinet for the first time, and Navy Secretary Josephus Daniels recorded in his diary that Marshall "was bright & full of jest." However, a photograph taken of him presiding showed a man trying to look resolute but appearing decidedly uncomfortable. As Louis Ludlow noted: "This was the first instance in history when a President showed an inclination to make a real use of his spare tire." [23]

Marshall presided only briefly over the cabinet, withdrawing after a few sessions on the grounds that the vice president could not maintain a confidential relationship with both the executive and legislative branches. Still, he had established the precedent of presiding over the cabinet during the president's absence, making it particularly difficult to understand why he failed to carry out that same duty in October 1919, after Wilson suffered a paralytic stroke. Initially, Wilson's wife Edith, his personal physician Admiral Cary Grayson, and his secretary Joe Tumulty, kept the vice president, the cabinet, and the nation in the dark over the severity of Wilson's illness. Noting with understatement that the eighteen months of Wilson's illness were "not pleasant" for him, Marshall recalled that the standing joke of the country was that "the only business of the vice-president is to ring the White House bell every morning and ask what is the state of health of the president." In fact, Marshall was admittedly afraid to ask about Wilson's health, for fear that people would accuse him of "longing for his place." [24]

Secretary of Agriculture David Houston met Marshall while lunching at the Shoreham Hotel, and recorded in his memoirs:

The Vice President was evidently much disturbed and expressed regret that he was being kept in the dark about the President's condition. He asked me if I could give him the real facts, which I was unable to do. . . . The Vice President expressed the view that he ought immediately to be informed; that it would be a tragedy for him to assume the duties of President, at best; and that it would be equally a tragedy for the people; that he knew many men who knew more about the affairs of the government than he did; and that it would be especially trying for him if he had to assume the duty without warning. [25]

Tumulty eventually sent word to Marshall through a friendly intermediary, *Baltimore Sun* correspondent J. Fred Essary, that the president's condition was so grave that he might die at any time. A stunned Marshall sat absolutely speechless. "It was the first great shock of my life," he later told Essary. Still, he could not bring himself to act, or to do anything that might seem ambitious or disloyal to his president. It was Secretary of State Robert Lansing rather than Vice President Marshall who determined to call cabinet meetings in the president's absence. Without the participation of either the president or vice president, the cabinet met regularly between October 1919 and February 1920, presided over by Secretary of State Lansing, or in his absence, Secretary of the Treasury Carter Glass. When Wilson recovered sufficiently, he fired Lansing for attempting to "oust" him from office by calling these meetings. Wilson, who was never himself after his stroke, argued that these meetings held no purpose since no cabinet decisions could be made without the president. Yet Wilson himself had sanctioned the cabinet meetings over which Marshall had presided a year earlier. If nothing else, for the cabinet to hold regular meetings at least assured the American public that their government continued to function. [26]

The Constitution declares that the vice president could assume the duties of president in case of the president's "Inability to discharge the Powers and Duties of the said Office," but until the Twenty-fifth Amendment was adopted in 1967, the Constitution said absolutely nothing about how he should do it. [27] Marshall was clearly in a difficult situation. As editor Henry L. Stoddard observed, "Wilson's resentment of Lansing's activities is proof that Vice President Marshall would have had to lay siege to the

White House, had he assumed the Presidency."[28] The eminent historian of American diplomacy Thomas A. Bailey noted that President Wilson "clung to his office, without the power to lead actively and sure-footedly, but with unimpaired power to obstruct." In his classic study of Wilson's handling of the Treaty of Versailles, Bailey speculated that if Wilson had died rather than been incapacitated by his stroke, the results would have been far more positive, and that Wilson's historical reputation would have eclipsed even Abraham Lincoln as a martyr. Had Wilson died, the Senate might well have been shamed into action on the League of Nations. "Much of the partisanship would have faded, because Wilson as a third-term threat would be gone, and Vice President Marshall, a small-bored Hoosier, was not to be feared," wrote Bailey:

> Marshall of course would have been President for seventeen months. Having presided over the Senate for more than six years, and knowing the temper of that body, he probably would have recognized the need for compromise, and probably would have worked for some reconciliation of the Democratic and Republicans points of view. In these circumstances it seems altogether reasonable to suppose that the Senate would have approved the treaty with a few relatively minor reservations.[29]

Indeed, Marshall presided over the Senate during the "long and weary months" of debate on the Treaty of Versailles. Although he stood loyally with the president, he believed that some compromise would be necessary and tried unsuccessfully to make the White House understand. "I have sometimes thought that great men are the bane of civilization," Marshall later wrote in his memoirs, in a passage about the clash between Woodrow Wilson and Senator Henry Cabot Lodge: "[T]hey are the real cause of all the bitterness and contention which amounts to anything in the world. Pride of opinion and authorship, and jealousy of the opinion and authorship of others wreck many a fair hope."[30] Despite assurances from members of both parties in Congress that they would support him

should he assert his claim to the presidency, Thomas R. Marshall never sought to fill Woodrow Wilson's place. His years in Washington had convinced him that he desired the good will of others rather than the "pomp or power" of the presidency. Rather than act as president, or even preside over cabinet meetings, Marshall contented himself with replacing Wilson as "official host" for the many visiting European royalty and other dignitaries who came to Washington to offer thanks for American assistance during the First World War.[31] By shrinking from a distasteful duty, Marshall gave himself peace of mind but deprived the nation of whatever leadership he might have offered in trying times.

Marshall himself told the story of riding on a train behind a man and a woman who were discussing the news that President Wilson had removed Secretary of State Lansing for holding cabinet meetings. "Why what else could Mr. Lansing have done?" the woman asked. "Here the President was sick. A lot of big questions had to be talked over and there was the Vice President, who doesn't amount to anything. The only thing Mr. Lansing could do, I tell you, was to call these Cabinet meetings, and I think he did the right thing." Said Marshall, "There you have it in a nutshell. The woman was right. I don't amount to anything."[32]

Although Thomas Marshall publicly hinted that he would accept the Democratic nomination for president in 1920, few delegates outside of Indiana cast any votes for him. Instead, Democrats nominated James M. Cox and Franklin D. Roosevelt, who lost overwhelmingly to the Republican ticket of Warren G. Harding and Calvin Coolidge. Marshall left office as vice president in March 1921 and returned to Indiana. He died while visiting Washington on June 1, 1925, at age seventy-one. In 1922 President Harding had appointed him to serve on the Federal Coal Commission to settle labor troubles in the coal mines, but otherwise Marshall insisted he had retired. "I don't want to work," he said. "[But] I wouldn't mind being Vice President again."[33]

NOTES

1 "Vice President Marshall Has Fallen Into a Big Job With Little Work, Many Peculiar Customs and Much Social Strain," *Washington Evening Star*, March 2, 1913, part 4, p. 6.

2 Thomas R. Marshall, *Recollections of Thomas R. Marshall, Vice-President and Hoosier Philosopher: A Hoosier Salad* (Indianapolis, 1925), pp. 16–18.

3 Ray Stannard Baker, *Woodrow Wilson, Life and Letters* (Garden City, N.Y., 1931), 4:104–9; and Daniel C. Roper, *Fifty Years of Public Life* (Durham, NC, 1941); John E. Brown, "Woodrow Wilson's Vice President: Thomas R. Marshall and the Wilson Administration, 1913–1921" (Ph.D. dissertation, Ball State University, 1970), p. 216.

4 Charles M. Thomas, *Thomas Riley Marshall, Hoosier Statesman* (Oxford, OH, 1939), p. 129.

5 William Allen White, *The Autobiography of William Allen White* (New York, 1946), pp. 615–16.

6 Thomas, pp. 27–28; Marshall, p. 96.

7 Thomas, p. 35.

8 Ibid., pp. 40–55.

9 *Indianapolis News*, March 6, 1929.

10 Josephus Daniels, *The Wilson Era: Years of Peace, 1910–1917* (Chapel Hill, NC, 1944), p. 550; Thomas, pp. 112–39; Brown, p. 146; *Congressional Quarterly's Guide to U.S. Elections*, 3d ed. (Washington, DC, 1994), p. 390. The 1912 election is also discussed in Chapter 25 of this volume, "Theodore Roosevelt,", p. 306, and Chapter 27, "James Schoolcraft Sherman," pp. 330–31.

11 Marshall, pp. 221–25, 229.

12 Ibid., p. 233; Brown, pp. 50–51.

13 Brown, pp. 250–51.

14 Marshall, p. 230; Thomas, p. 141; *Washington Evening Star*, March 2, 1913, part 4, p. 6; March 4, 1913, p. 1; and March 6, 1913, "Senate takes day off."

15 *Washington Evening Star*, March 2, 1913, part 4, p. 6.

16 Marshall, p. 233; Woodrow Wilson, *Congressional Government: A Study in American Politics* (Baltimore, 1981; reprint of 1885 edition), p. 162.

17 Brown, pp. 157–59, 171; Daniels, pp. 552–53; Thomas, pp. 142–44; Marshall, p. 241.

18 Marshall, pp. 292–93.

19 Louis Ludlow, *From Cornfield to Press Gallery; Adventures and Reminiscences of a Veteran Washington Correspondent* (Washington, DC, 1924), pp. 311–15.

20 Thomas, p. 153.

21 Ludlow, pp. 313–14; Brown, pp. 188–93.

22 George F. Sparks, *A Many-Colored Toga: The Diary of Henry Fountain Ashurst* (Tucson, AZ, 1962), pp. 42–43; Thomas, pp. 234–36.

23 E. David Cronon, ed., *The Cabinet Diaries of Josephus Daniels, 1913–1921* (Lincoln, NE, 1963), p. 354; Ludlow, p. 301.

24 Daniels, p. 558; Marshall, p. 368.

25 David F. Houston, *Eight Years With Wilson's Cabinet, 1913 to 1920* (Garden City, NY, 1926), pp. 36–38.

26 Thomas, p. 207; see also Herbert Hoover, *The Ordeal of Woodrow Wilson* (Baltimore, 1992; reprint of 1958 edition), pp. 270–78; Robert H. Farrell, *Ill-Advised: Presidential Health and Public Trust* (Columbia, MO, 1992), p. 16.

27 See Birch Bayh, *One Heartbeat Away: Presidential Disability and Succession* (Indianapolis, 1968).

28 Henry L. Stoddard, *As I Knew Them: Presidents and Politics from Grant to Coolidge* (New York, 1927), pp. 539–47.

29 Thomas A. Bailey, *Woodrow Wilson and the Great Betrayal* (New York, 1945), pp. 137–38.

30 Marshall, pp. 363–64.

31 Ibid., p. 368.

32 Brown, pp. 418–19.

33 Ludlow, p. 312.

Chapter 29

CALVIN COOLIDGE
1921–1923

CALVIN COOLIDGE

Chapter 29

CALVIN COOLIDGE

29th Vice President: 1921–1923

If the Vice-President is a man of discretion and character so that he can be relied upon to act as a subordinate in that position, he should be invited to sit with the Cabinet, although some of the Senators, wishing to be the only advisers of the President, do not look on that proposal with favor.

—CALVIN COOLIDGE

Calvin Coolidge came to the vice-presidency from the governorship of Massachusetts, but he was at heart a Vermonter. Born in Vermont on the Fourth of July 1872, he died in Vermont sixty-one years later, on January 5, 1933. During the years between, he lived most of his adult life in Massachusetts and worked out of the statehouse in Boston but never identified with Back Bay society. "I come from Boston," a lady once identified herself to him when he was president. "Yes, and you'll never get over it," Coolidge replied dryly. One of Coolidge's first biographers, Claude Fuess, identified him as the archetypical Yankee, "with his wiry, nervous body, his laconic speech, his thrift, his industry, his conservative distrust of foreigners and innovations, and his native dignity." This dour, taciturn man served eight years as vice president and president during the "Roaring Twenties," an era remembered for its speakeasies, flappers, and anything-goes attitudes. Calvin Coolidge, as journalist William Allen White aptly recorded, was "A Puritan in Babylon." [1]

Youth

Calvin Coolidge grew up in the bucolic setting of rural Vermont in the late nineteenth century. He was a slight, red-headed, blue-eyed boy whose decided nasal twang was made worse by numerous childhood allergies until it gave his voice a quacking sound. His invalid mother died when he was just twelve years old, and he was raised by his father, Colonel John Coolidge, a talented jack-of-all-trades, who ran a general store and farmed, as well as serving as justice of the peace and a member of the state legislature. For all these accomplishments, Colonel Coolidge was not a man who could express his emotions openly, and one senses from reading Calvin Coolidge's *Autobiography* that he spent much of his life trying to earn his father's respect and approval. As Coolidge later noted, "A lot of people in Plymouth can't understand how I got to be President, least of all my father!" [2]

A Shy Politician

A painfully shy boy, Coolidge would go into a panic at the sound of a stranger's voice in the house. Writing in a letter to a friend years later, he recalled that when visitors would sit with his parents in the kitchen, he found it difficult to go in and greet them. "I was almost ten before I realized I couldn't go on that way. And by fighting hard I used to manage to get through that door. I'm all right with old friends, but every time I meet a stranger, I've got to get through the old kitchen door, back home, and it's not easy." [3]

Shortly after his mother died, Coolidge escaped from the drudgery of farm work to attend the Black River Academy in Ludlow, Vermont, his "first great adventure," which he described as "a complete break with the past." His parents and a grandmother had attended the school briefly, but Coolidge embraced schoolwork more thoroughly, going on to Amherst as the first member of his family to attend college. He did well enough to be chosen one of the three commencement speakers at his graduation, assigned to deliver the "grove oration," which was to describe the class members in a witty and humorous manner. Coolidge later related that he learned from the experience "that making fun of people in a public way was not a good method to secure friends, or likely to lead to much advancement." [4]

After college he read law with the firm of Hammond and Field in Northampton, Massachusetts, before joining the bar in 1897. Politically a conservative Republican, Coolidge had marched in a torchlight parade for Benjamin Harrison's unsuccessful reelection campaign in 1892 and wrote letters to the local papers in support of William McKinley's election in 1896. In December 1898 he won his first election to the Northampton city council, an unsalaried job that he saw primarily as a means of making useful contacts for his law practice. He was then elected city solicitor, a post that paid six hundred dollars annually, which he believed would make him a better lawyer. Next came election to the Massachusetts house of representatives, and appointment to its judiciary committee, which he again considered more in terms of promoting himself as a lawyer than as a politician. He ran for mayor of Northampton, "thinking the honor would be one that would please my father, advance me in my profession, and enable me to be of some public service." As a local office, it would not "interfere seriously with my work." [5]

Coolidge always insisted that he never planned his political career. He meant only "to be ready to take advantage of opportunities." [6] In 1911 he ran for the state senate and soon became its president, a role that took him from local to statewide office. Coolidge summed up his philosophy as a legislator in a letter to his father upon the elder Coolidge's election to the Vermont Senate:

It is much more important to kill bad bills than to pass good ones, and better to spend your time on your own committee work than to be bothering with any bills of your own. . . . See that the bills you recommend from your committee are so worded that they will do just what they intend and not a great deal more that is undesirable. Most bills can't stand that kind of test. [7]

A Return to Conservatism

Coolidge began his ascendancy in statewide politics at a time when the Massachusetts Republican party was still divided between conservatives and progressives. In 1912, Theodore Roosevelt had walked out of the Republican party and campaigned for president on the ticket of the Progressive ("Bull Moose") party. In that election, the Republican nominee, William Howard Taft, had come in a distant third behind the more progressive candidacies of Roosevelt and Woodrow Wilson. Coolidge was far from comfortable with the reform politicians and muckraking magazines of the era. "It appeared to me in January, 1914, that a spirit of radicalism prevailed which unless checked was likely to prove very destructive," he later wrote. "It consisted of the claim in general that in some way the government was to be blamed because everybody was not prosperous." He believed that progressive reforms and "unsound legislative proposals" would destroy business and that the country needed "a restoration of confidence in our institutions and in each other, on which economic progress might rest." Fittingly, Coolidge's first address as president of the state senate appealed "to the conservative spirit of the people." [8]

Coolidge correctly anticipated the shift in public opinion. Even before the First World War, a conservative reaction to the progressive era was apparent as voters grew tired of political crusades. In 1914, an economic recession that was especially severe on the East Coast also hurt progressive candidates. Conservative challengers argued that more laws and more regulations would only mean more taxes. In one sign of the changing atmosphere, when the first direct elections for U.S. senators were held in 1914, progressive candidates went down to defeat. Conservative Republicans swept the field in many states, reducing the Democratic majorities in both the Senate and House. Most symbolically, the staunchly conservative Senator Boies Penrose of Pennsylvania beat one of the nation's most prominent progressives, Gifford Pinchot. "The most curious part," Pinchot confessed, "is that no one seemed to know in advance that we were to be beaten and certainly no one thought the defeat would be so complete." [9]

Calvin Coolidge's fortunes rose as those of the progressives fell. In 1915 he was elected lieutenant governor, and on January 1, 1919, he was inaugurated as governor of Massachusetts. Before that year was out, unexpected events had made him one of the most famous and admired men in the country. "No doubt it was the police strike of Boston that brought me into national prominence. That furnished the occasion and I took advantage of the opportunity," Coolidge wrote with characteristic understatement in his *Autobiography*. [10]

Boston's police force was badly underpaid and overworked. As a legislator, Coolidge had achieved a reasonably favorable record toward labor, and as governor he tried unsuccessfully to persuade the legislature to improve the policemen's lot. The police then organized the Boston Social Club and sought to affiliate with the American Federation of Labor, but Boston Police Commissioner Edwin Curtis had no intention of dealing with a police union, and he suspended the police union organizers from the force. Angry police voted to go out on strike, throwing the city into a panic. There was an increase in looting and robberies, and volunteers turned out to police the streets. Governor Coolidge ignored all appeals to intervene, and his inactivity undoubtedly allowed the situation to worsen. Finally, after much confusion and delay, Coolidge sided with the hard-line Police Commissioner Curtis, who had announced that the striking police would not be reinstated. More than for his actions, "Silent Cal" became famous for his words. In a telegram to AFL President Samuel Gompers, who had sought his support for the police, Coolidge asserted, "There is no right to strike against the public safety by anybody, anywhere, any time." At a time when the nation was rocked by a series of often violent postwar labor disputes, many citizens welcomed this message. Coolidge became the "law and order" governor.

His photograph appeared on the front pages of newspapers nationwide, and thousands of telegrams and letters poured in to congratulate him. There was talk of running Calvin Coolidge for president in 1920. [11]

The Coolidge Phenomenon

New York Times correspondent Charles Willis Thompson was among the many journalists curious about this new phenomenon. Thompson noted that Coolidge began making political speeches outside of Massachusetts but not in such likely places as Chicago and New York. Instead, Coolidge went to Oregon and to the Rocky Mountain states, and his speeches were always on nonpolitical themes. "Each one of these nonpolitical speeches had in it that quality of arrest; there was something in it, unpretentious as it was as a whole, that made you stop and think," Thompson observed. "There was nothing spectacular about him yet, or ever." The 1920 Republican convention opened in Chicago with many candidates and no clear frontrunner. The real story was not in the primaries or in the main convention hall, but in the back rooms, which became immortalized as the "smoke-filled room" where decisions were made by a coterie of Republican senators. When the convention became deadlocked between General Leonard Wood and Illinois Governor Frank Lowden, the senators met privately to pick a candidate and prevent a rift in the party. They were determined to name someone who would reduce the powers of the presidency, which they believed had expanded disproportionately during the administrations of Theodore Roosevelt and Woodrow Wilson. To this end, they chose one of their most pliable colleagues, Ohio Senator Warren G. Harding, as the Republican presidential nominee. [12]

Harding had been far from a leading contender among the delegates, who nominated him without much enthusiasm. Seeking to balance the conservative Harding, and hoping to make it an all-senatorial ticket, the senators first offered the vice-presidential nomination to California Senator Hiram Johnson, who turned it down. They next went to progressive Senator Irvine Lenroot of Wisconsin. When Illinois Senator Medill McCormick stepped to the podium to nominate

Lenroot, a delegate from Portland, Oregon, former Judge Wallace McCamant, called out loudly, "Coolidge! Coolidge!" Other delegates took up the cry. When Senator McCormick finished his address, McCamant leaped on a chair among the Oregon delegation and nominated Governor Calvin Coolidge of Massachusetts for vice president. Showing enthusiasm for the first time, the delegates demonstrated spontaneously in Coolidge's behalf. Lenroot would be "just one too many Senators on the presidential ticket," a reporter observed. Delegates for other candidates who felt they had been denied their choice for the top spot were determined to have a voice in the second place. They voted 674 for Coolidge to 146 for Lenroot.[13]

Coolidge himself was back in Boston, in the hotel where he lived as governor, nursing his disappointment that all of his quiet campaigning had seemingly made no impact on the presidential race. That evening as he and Mrs. Coolidge were preparing to go down to dinner, he received news about McCamant's surprising speech and the demonstration that followed. The phone rang again, and Coolidge turned to his wife to utter a single word: "Nominated."

"You aren't going to take it are you?" asked Mrs. Coolidge.

"Well—I suppose I'll have to." said Coolidge.[14]

It had been perhaps the most unusual and independent vice-presidential nomination in American political history. Where parties normally balance, both Harding and Coolidge were unabashed conservatives and comprised the most conservative ticket since the party had gone down to disastrous defeat in 1912. But in 1920 that proved to be exactly what the nation wanted, and in November the Harding-Coolidge ticket overwhelmed the Democratic ticket of James M. Cox and Franklin D. Roosevelt. At his inauguration as vice president, Calvin Coolidge took satisfaction that "the same thing for which I had worked in Massachusetts had been accomplished in the nation. The radicalism which had tinged our whole political and economic life from soon after 1900 to the World War period was passed."[15]

An Impassive Senate President

"More hotel life, I suppose," Grace Coolidge commented on their move to Washington, D.C. The U.S. vice president still had no official place of residence, and Coolidge was not prepared to spend his $12,000 a year salary on purchasing a house commensurate with his position. "There is no dignity quite so impressive, and no independence quite so important, as living within your means," he observed. The Coolidges moved into the suite of rooms at the Willard Hotel being vacated by Vice President and Mrs. Thomas R. Marshall, for which they paid eight dollars a day. As vice president, he occupied an office in the Capitol and another in the Senate office building. His staff consisted of a secretary, a clerk, an assistant clerk, and a chauffeur. He inherited Vice President Marshall's Cadillac.[16]

"Presiding over the Senate was fascinating to me," Coolidge later wrote. Although the Senate's methods at first seemed peculiar, he soon became familiar with them and suggested that they were "the best method of conducting its business. It may seem that debate is endless, but there is scarcely a time when it is not informing, and, after all, the power to compel due consideration is the distinguishing mark of a deliberative body." However, as Coolidge tried to master the Senate rules, he soon discovered that there was but one fixed rule: "that the Senate would do anything it wanted to do whenever it wanted to do it. When I had learned that, I did not waste much time on the other rules, because they so seldom applied."[17]

Vice President Coolidge presided in a remarkably impassive manner. Once James A. Reed, a Missouri Democrat, and Porter J. McCumber, a North Dakota Republican, engaged in a shouting match on the Senate floor. Other senators and the galleries joined in the uproar, while Coolidge simply watched the commotion. When the parliamentarian begged him to use his gavel to restore order, the vice president replied, "Yes I shall if they get excited."[18]

Doomed to be an Outsider

Coolidge's most controversial moment as vice president came in July 1921. Midwestern progressive Republicans were seeking federal relief for farmers, whose sales and purchasing power had collapsed after the war. Senator George Norris of Nebraska introduced a bill that would make it easier to market American farm products overseas. The Harding administration countered with a bill sponsored by Minnesota Senator Frank Kellogg to make domestic marketing of farm goods easier. Norris had asked Coolidge, as presiding officer, to recognize Senator Joseph E. Ransdell, a Louisiana Democrat, first. Coolidge had agreed, but then he left the chair and asked Charles Curtis of Kansas, a tough-minded partisan senator, to preside in his place. When Ransdell stood and sought recognition, Curtis ignored him and instead called upon Kellogg, who in fact was still in his seat and had not even risen to seek recognition. After the ensuing hubbub, as Kellogg claimed the floor, Coolidge reentered the chamber and once again presided. Progressive Republicans and Democrats long remembered this maneuver and never fully trusted Coolidge again. His biographer, Donald McCoy, concluded, "The episode may have doomed Coolidge to be an outsider for the rest of his time as Vice President and even have contributed to his troubles with Congress while he was President. He was now distrusted by the progressives and perhaps even disliked by the regulars for violating one of the unwritten rules of the Senate." He had gone back on his word.[19]

Coolidge lacked either the jovial good humor of his predecessor Thomas Marshall or the type of personality that would attract senators to him. In the Senate restaurant, Coolidge ate alone, in a corner, facing the wall. "Is that how you treat your presiding officer?" someone asked Senator Edwin Ladd of North Dakota. "Nobody has anything to do with him," said the Senator. "After this, of course, he's through." Coolidge cast no tie-breaking votes and spoke only as required—and as briefly as possible. Biographer Donald McCoy noted that, while Coolidge had been a success as presiding officer in Massachusetts, in the U.S. Senate he was "almost a nonentity."[20]

Largely overlooked in the Senate, Coolidge won more notice for all of the "dining out" that he and his wife did. "As the President is not available for social dinners of course the next officer in rank is much sought after for such occa-

sions," he noted. On an average they ate out three times a week during the congressional season. At first the Coolidges enjoyed these social dinners, since as the ranking guests they were able to arrive last and leave first. He considered it an opportunity to become acquainted with official Washington. But Washington proved a cruel atmosphere for the Yankee Coolidge. Stories spread through the city that the new vice president was either very dumb or very shy. Coolidge's table manners were peculiar to say the least. He sat quietly, nibbling nuts and crackers and saying next to nothing to those around him. Soon it became a Washington parlor game to tease the vice president into talking. One famous story had a Washington socialite telling him that she had bet her friends she could get him to say three words. "You lose," Coolidge replied. "They provoked him to Yankee aphorisms and he knew what they were up to," wrote William Allen White. "So he clowned a little for his own delight, played the dumb man, impersonated the yokel and probably despised his tormentors in his heart." New Hampshire Senator George Moses told of a stag party where Coolidge was a guest, when several senators spiked the punch—this during Prohibition—to loosen up the vice president, but the more Coolidge drank, the quieter he became. The longer he stayed in Washington, the more suspicious he grew of everyone he met. When an old friend warned that this was an unhealthy state of mind, Coolidge replied: "I do not think you have any comprehension of what people do to me. Even small things bother me." Later, when he was president, Coolidge declined an invitation to a fashionable Washington home. "When I lived at the Willard and was vice president they didn't know I was in town," Coolidge exploded. "Now that I am President they want to drag me up to their house for one of their suppers and show me off to a lot of people, and I'm not going. . . . I'm not going, and I'm not going to let that wife of mine go."[21]

Coolidge was blessed with a wife, Grace Goodhue Coolidge, whose warmth and charm more than made up for his aloofness and eccentricities. However, Coolidge tightly restricted her activities, forbidding her to drive, ride horseback, or fly, from wearing slacks, bobbing her hair, or expressing her opinion on any political issue. In the age of the liberated woman of the 1920s, he wanted Grace to be the model of old-fashioned womanhood. As if this were not enough, he also made her the target for his pent-up anger and unhappiness. Always a quiet man in public, Coolidge would explode in private by throwing temper tantrums. Historian Donald McCoy has noted that "the reserved and unathletic New Englander could not release his frustrations in a healthy way. Whatever release he got came in the form of tantrums, the brunt of which his wife bore. Anything that was unexpected could lead him to prolonged moods of sulking and even to fits of yelling." Most likely, Coolidge's private outbursts resulted from his disappointment in the vice-presidency, which left him in the shadows, powerless.[22]

Sitting with the Cabinet

A major exception to Coolidge's isolation during this period was President Harding's invitation to him to sit with the cabinet. This was probably a response to the unhappy situation in the last years of the Wilson administration, when Vice President Marshall had declined to preside over the cabinet during the president's illness, and Secretary of State Robert Lansing had been fired by Wilson for holding cabinet meetings without his authorization. Harding had made the offer first to Irvine Lenroot, when he was considered for the vice-presidency, and then to Coolidge.[23] When they met after the convention, Harding told the press:

> I think the vice president should be more than a mere substitute in waiting. In reestablishing coordination between the Executive Office and the Senate, the vice president can and ought to play a big part, and I have been telling Governor Coolidge how much I wish him to be not only a participant in the campaign, but how much I wish him to be a helpful part of a Republican administration.[24]

Coolidge joined the cabinet meetings, becoming the first vice president to do so on a regular basis. He sat at the farthest end of the table from Harding, listening to what was said and saying almost nothing himself. In his *Autobiography*, Coolidge wrote, "If the Vice-President is a man of discretion and character so that he can be relied upon to act as a subordinate in that position, he should be invited to sit with the Cabinet, although some of the Senators, wishing to be the only advisers of the President, do not look on that proposal with favor." Coolidge believed that, although the vice president could probably offer little insight about the Senate, and virtually nothing about the House, a vice president needed to be fully informed of what was going on in case he should become president. "My experience in the Cabinet," he concluded, "was of supreme value to me when I became President." By contrast, Coolidge's own vice president, Charles Dawes, disagreed and let it be known publicly that he did not consider it wise for vice presidents to be invited to cabinet meetings because of the separation of powers between the branches.[25]

The Harding administration meanwhile had become mired in scandal. The Senate had launched an investigation of improper leasing of naval oil reserves at Teapot Dome in Wyoming. There were also indications of scandals brewing in the Veterans Administration and the Department of Justice. Whether Harding would be reelected, whether he would keep Coolidge on the ticket, and whether the ticket could be reelected in the face of these scandals were all unanswerable questions in the summer of 1923, when a dispirited Harding traveled to Alaska and the Pacific Coast. Vice President Coolidge was on vacation at his father's home in Plymouth, Vermont, when on the night of August 2, 1923, he was awakened by his father calling his name. "I noticed that his voice trembled. As the only times I had ever observed that before were when death had visited our family, I knew that something of the gravest nature had occurred," Coolidge recorded. Colonel John Coolidge informed his son that a telegram had arrived announcing that President Harding had died in San Francisco. As Calvin Coolidge noted, his father "was the first to address me as President of the United States. It was the culmination of the lifelong desire of a father for the success of his son." Coolidge quickly dressed, and in a downstairs parlor, lit by a flickering kerosene lantern, his father as a notary public administered to him the oath of office as president. Arizona Senator Henry Fountain Ashurst, a Democrat, observed that "the simplicity of this episode fired the public imagination." Harding's death and "the sportsmanship of the American people," Ashurst believed, built public support for Coolidge's presidency and revived Republican spirits.[26]

A Surprisingly Popular President

After his unsatisfying years as vice president, Coolidge became a surprisingly popular president, easily winning reelection in 1924. Correspondent Charles Willis Thompson, a keen observer of presidents during the first decades of this century, believed that the nation found psychological relief in Coolidge after the high-minded oratory of Wilson and the bombast of Harding. Recognizing that he did not have the voice of an orator, Coolidge "never wasted time trying to acquire it." His message was straightforward, with "no purple . . . no argument, no stock official phrases. He told Congress what he thought would be for the good of the country and told it as briefly as he could." Thompson concluded that Coolidge was as good as elected the day he sent his first message to Congress in 1923. "Congress, with its historic political wisdom, banged him around the Capitol walls by the hair of his head," but the people loved him, and decided to "Keep Cool With Coolidge."[27]

Coolidge had the advantage of being everything that Harding was not—which provided him some comfortable distance as the news of the Harding administration's scandals broke. Harding was tall and handsome. Coolidge was smaller, five feet nine inches tall, and weighed perhaps a hundred and fifty pounds. Harding had a famous smile. Coolidge's skin was smooth, one biographer noted, "because of lack of exercise in either frowning or smiling." Harding was gregarious. Coolidge was aloof. Harding tolerated his friends, even the most corrupt of them. Coolidge preached thrift and honesty. During the 1924 campaign, the Democratic and Progressive candidates tried to tar Coolidge with the

Teapot Dome scandal but not a trace stuck to him.[28]

The press, which had belittled Coolidge during his vice-presidency, now helped build up his public image. Coolidge said very little, but newspaper reporters must have news. "So we grasped at little incidents to build up human interest stories," explained correspondent Thomas L. Stokes. At first the press pictured Coolidge as a "strong, silent man," so much so that the *Baltimore Sun*'s veteran Washington correspondent Frank R. Kent accused his press corps colleagues of inflating Coolidge to make him look good. Kent compared Coolidge's "weak and watery utterances" at his press conferences with the "forceful and vigorous" dispatches that reporters produced. He charged reporters with turning a passive, indecisive chief executive into "a red-blooded, resolute, two-fisted, fighting executive, thoroughly aroused and determined." This mythical presidential image served reporters' interests by appealing to the illusions of their readers and their editors. But as time passed and it became clear that Coolidge was neither strong nor silent, newspapers shifted their emphasis to his dry wit and created a national character: "Cal." "Everyone spoke of him fondly as 'Cal.' He was one of us," observed correspondent Stokes. "He was the ordinary man incarnate." Another veteran correspondent, Delbert Clark, speculated that the press enjoyed writing, and even manufacturing, homey little stories about Coolidge because "the mounting evidence he gave of being a very small, very solemn man in a very big job, intrigued them by reason of the contradictions involved."[29]

The presidency was far more gratifying for Coolidge than the vice-presidential years had been. He claimed to maintain as much simplicity in life as possible, clearly disliking most formal ceremonies. Yet he also enjoyed the pomp and circumstance of office, and he could not hide the pleasure on his face when the band played "Hail to the Chief." But the presidency was not always a happy time for Calvin Coolidge. In July 1924, he was devastated by the death of his son, Calvin, Jr. In playing lawn tennis on the White House South Grounds, the boy had raised a blister on his toe which resulted in blood poisoning.

"In his suffering he was asking me to make him well. I could not," Coolidge remarked. "When he went the power and the glory of the Presidency went with him." [30]

Coolidge was never an innovative or active president. He was largely uninterested in foreign policy. Embracing a laissez-faire philosophy opposed to government intervention, he had no bold domestic programs but carried on the policies begun under Harding. As he had throughout his political life, he felt more comfortable blocking legislation that he opposed than he did in proposing new measures. Thus, he vetoed such legislation as the soldiers' bonus, the McNary-Haugen farm bills, and Senator Norris' efforts to develop water power in the Tennessee River Valley. He believed in reducing government regulation, cutting taxes, and allowing business to operate with as little restraint as possible. His presidency coincided with a period of tremendous economic prosperity, for which he reaped full credit. The stock market soared, although an investigation by the Senate Banking and Currency Committee a few years later concluded that fully half of the fifty billion dollars worth of stocks sold during the 1920s had been "undesirable or worthless." His secretary of commerce, Herbert Hoover, repeatedly urged Coolidge to increase federal controls on private banking and stock trading practices. (Coolidge could barely hide his distaste for his active, energetic commerce secretary, whom he mocked as "The Wonder Boy.") But the government continued its "hands-off policies" under Coolidge's dictum that "the business of America is business." Coolidge left the presidency in March of 1929. By November the stock market had crashed, taking the Coolidge prosperity with it. By the time he died in January 1933, the nation was paralyzed in the worst depression of its history. Although his successor Herbert Hoover bore the weight of blame for that depression, historians have found Calvin Coolidge culpable of contributory neglect. [31]

Calvin Coolidge never made any pretensions to greatness. "It is a great advantage to a President and a major source of safety to the country, for him to know that he is not a great man," he recorded in his *Autobiography*. That seems the most fitting epitaph for the man. [32]

NOTES

[1] Claude M. Fuess, *Calvin Coolidge: The Man from Vermont* (Boston, 1940), p. 5; William Allen White, *A Puritan in Babylon: The Story of Calvin Coolidge* (New York, 1938).

[2] Calvin Coolidge, *The Autobiography of Calvin Coolidge* (New York, 1929), pp. 99, 174; White, p. vii.

[3] Donald R. McCoy, *Calvin Coolidge, The Quiet President* (Lawrence, KS, 1988), p. 8.

[4] Coolidge, p. 71.

[5] Ibid., pp. 83–99.

[6] Ibid., p. 99.

[7] Fuess, pp. 107–8.

[8] Coolidge, p. 107.

[9] Gifford Pinchot to Lady Jonstone, November 9, 1914, Gifford Pinchot Papers, Library of Congress.

[10] Coolidge, p. 141.

[11] McCoy, pp. 83–94.

[12] Charles Willis Thompson, *Some Presidents I Have Known and Two Near Presidents* (Indianapolis, 1929), pp. 327–29, 361; Coolidge, p. 148; Andrew Sinclair, *The Available Man: The Life Behind the Masks of Warren Gamaliel Harding* (New York, 1965), pp. 142–49.

[13] Thompson, pp. 362–64; Fuess, pp. 234–67; Herbert F. Margulies, "Irvine L. Lenroot and the Republican Vice-Presidential Nomination of 1920," *Wisconsin Magazine of History* 61 (Autumn 1977): 21–31.

[14] White, p. 214.

[15] Coolidge, p. 158.

[16] Fuess, p. 287; McCoy, p. 134.

[17] Coolidge, pp. 161–62.

[18] Irving G. Williams, *The Rise of the Vice Presidency* (Washington, 1956), p. 124.

[19] McCoy, p. 136.

[20] Ibid., pp. 134–35, 145.

[21] Ibid., p. 162; Coolidge, pp. 160, 173; White, p. 222; Fuess, p. 303.

[22] McCoy, p. 145; White House Chief Usher Ike Hoover later wrote: "Those who saw Coolidge in a rage were simply startled. The older employees about the White House who had known [Theodore] Roosevelt used to think he raved at times, but in his worst temper he was calm compared with Coolidge." Relating the tempers of various other presidents, Hoover concluded, "It remained for Coolidge, the one who from his reputation would be least suspected, to startle the household with sparks from his anger. Many times, too, the cause was of but trifling importance. He would just work himself up to a real explosion." Irwin Hood (Ike) Hoover, *Forty-Two Years in the White House* (Boston, 1934), p. 233.

[23] Margulies, p. 25. See Chapter 28 of this volume, "Thomas R. Marshall," p. 342.

[24] McCoy, p. 123.

[25] Coolidge, pp. 163–64; George H. Haynes, *The Senate of the United States: Its History and Practice* (Boston, 1938), 1:225, 228–29.

[26] Coolidge, pp. 174–75; George F. Sparks, ed., *A Many-Colored Toga: The Diary of Henry Fountain Ashurst* (Tucson, AZ, 1962), pp. 211, 223.

[27] Thompson, pp. 354–55.

[28] McCoy, p. xv; John D. Hicks, *The Republican Ascendancy, 1921–1933* (New York, 1960), p. 81.

[29] Thomas L. Stokes, *Chip Off My Shoulder* (Princeton, NJ, 1940), pp. 135–41; Donald A. Ritchie, *Press Gallery: Congress and the Washington Correspondents* (Cambridge,, MA, 1991), p. 210; Delbert Clark, *Washington Dateline* (New York, 1941), pp. 62–66.

[30] White, p. 413; Coolidge, p. 190.

[31] Stokes, p. 138; Donald A. Ritchie, "The Pecora Wall Street Expose," in *Congress Investigates: A Documented History, 1792–1974*, ed. Arthur M. Schlesinger, Jr., and Roger Bruns, (New York, 1975), pp. 2555–56; David Burner, *Herbert Hoover: A Public Life* (New York, 1979), pp. 244–45; William E. Leuchtenburg, *The Perils of Prosperity, 1914–32* (Chicago, 1958), p. 246.

[32] Coolidge, p. 173.

Chapter 30

CHARLES G. DAWES
1925–1929

CHARLES G. DAWES

Chapter 30

CHARLES G. DAWES

30th Vice President: 1925–1929

I should hate to think that the Senate was as tired of me at the beginning of my service as I am of the Senate at the end.

—CHARLES G. DAWES

It is ironic that "Silent Cal" Coolidge should have a vice president as garrulous as Charles Gates Dawes. A man of action as well as of blunt words, "Hell'n Maria" Dawes (the favorite expression by which he was known) was in so many ways the opposite of President Coolidge that the two men were never able to establish a working relationship. The president probably never forgave his vice president for stealing attention from him at their inaugural ceremonies, nor did he ever forget that Dawes was responsible for one of his most embarrassing defeats in the Senate. As a result, although Dawes was one of the most notable and able men to occupy the vice-presidency, his tenure was not a satisfying or productive one, nor did it stand as a model for others to follow.

Charles Dawes was not Calvin Coolidge's choice for a running mate. It would have taken a far more self-confident president to want a vice president with a longer and more distinguished career than his own. Dawes had been a prominent official in the McKinley administration when Coolidge was still a city council member in Northampton, Massachusetts. Dawes became a highly decorated military officer during the First World War, was the president of a prestigious financial institution, was the first director of the Bureau of the Budget, and devised the "Dawes Plan" to salvage Europe's postwar economy, for which he received the Nobel Peace Prize. Dawes had a keen concern for foreign affairs, in which Coolidge showed little interest. As an activist in domestic policy, Dawes convinced the Senate to pass the McNary-Haugen farm relief bill; Coolidge vetoed the bill. Dawes was a problem solver, Coolidge a problem avoider. The 1920s might have been a very different decade if the Republican ticket in 1924 had been Dawes-Coolidge rather than Coolidge-Dawes.

Banking, Business and Politics

Born in Marietta, Ohio, on August 27, 1865, Charles Dawes was the great-great grandson of William Dawes, who had ridden with Paul Revere to warn the colonists that the Redcoats were coming. Dawes' father, Rufus Dawes, was a Civil War veteran and lumber merchant who served as a Republican for one term in the U.S. House of Representatives. Young Charlie, who even as a boy had a reputation for "flying off the handle" when something angered him, attended the Marietta Academy in Ohio and graduated from Marietta College in 1884. Two years later he received his law degree from the Cincinnati Law School. While in law school he worked during the summers as a civil engineer for the Marietta, Columbus & Northern Ohio Railway Company.[1]

In 1887, former Ohio Governor Rufus Walton hired Dawes to go to Lincoln, Nebraska, and look after his real estate holdings. Dawes was admitted to the bar in Nebraska and opened the law office of Dawes, Coffroth & Cunningham. He established a reputation for handling railroad rate cases under the Interstate Commerce Act of 1887 and as a "people's advocate against the railroad lobby." The same year that Dawes opened his law office, William Jennings Bryan started his law practice in the same building in Lincoln. Dawes, who was then twenty-two, and Bryan, who was twenty-seven, attended Sunday services and Wednesday night prayer meetings at the same Presbyterian church and even lived two houses apart on the same street. As a consequence, the two men, from different parties and with very different views on the issues, had many opportunities to meet and debate politics. (In 1924, Dawes would run for vice president against Bryan's brother Charles, the Democratic vice-presidential candidate.) Dawes became director of the American Exchange National Bank, a small bank in Lincoln, which he and other directors fought hard to save during the panic of 1893. As a bank director, he strongly disagreed with Bryan's advocacy of free silver to stimulate inflation and help the indebted farmers. Dawes became so engrossed in the currency issue that he published his first book, *The Banking System of the United States and Its Relation to the Money and Business of the Country*, in 1894.[2]

"I struck Lincoln right at the top of a boom," Dawes noted, "then it started sliding." The panic of 1893 had undermined his business and banking career in Lincoln, sending him in search of new business ventures elsewhere. Attracted by the utilities industry, he bought control of the La Crosse, Wisconsin, Gas Light & Coke Company, and became president of the People's Gas Light & Coke Company of Chicago. In January 1895, he moved his family to Chicago to make that city the center of his business interests. But within two weeks he met the Cleveland industrialist Marcus A. Hanna, who was promoting the presidential aspirations of Ohio Governor William McKinley. Writing in his diary that "McKinley seems to be the coming man," Dawes was bitten by the political bug. He managed McKinley's preconvention campaign in Illinois, winning that state's delegates away from the erstwhile "favorite son" candidate, Senator Shelby M. Cullom. Not only did McKinley win the Republican nomination, but Dawes' old friend William Jennings Bryan won the Democratic nomination. While Dawes disagreed profoundly with the logic of free silver, he listened to Bryan's "Cross of Gold" speech with a feeling of great pride "for the brilliant young man whose life for so many years lay parallel to mine, and with whom the future years may yet bring me into conflict as in the past."[3]

Comptroller of the Currency

Mark Hanna put Dawes in charge of the Chicago headquarters, which largely ran the McKinley campaign. Dawes also served on the Republican National Executive Committee as McKinley's "special representative." McKinley's victory led to Dawes' appointment as comptroller of the currency, a post in which he sought to reform banking practices that had led to the depression of the 1890s. McKinley treated Dawes "as a father would a son." Dawes frequently had lunch at the White House with McKinley and his invalid wife Ida and returned for an evening of cards or of playing the piano for the McKinleys' entertainment. (A self-taught pianist, Dawes later wrote a popular piano piece, "Melody in A Major," and when lyrics were added in 1951 it became the well-known song "It's All in the Name of the Game.") More than a companion to the president, Dawes was a trusted adviser. In 1900 when Mark Hanna tried to block the vice-presidential nomination of New York Governor Theodore Roosevelt, it was Dawes who intervened with McKinley on Roosevelt's behalf.[4]

In June 1901, Dawes decided to resign as comptroller of the currency to return to Illinois and run for the Senate. He was assured of McKinley's endorsement, but his resignation did not take place until October, a month after McKinley's assassination. Dawes' political ambitions were thwarted by new President Theodore Roosevelt, who endorsed another candidate, and by the "blond boss" of the Illinois Republican party, William Lorimer. Running for vice president in 1924 and reflecting on his only other run for elected office in 1901, Dawes remarked: "I don't know anything about politics. I thought I knew something about politics once. I was taken up on the top of a twenty story building and showed the promised land—and then I was kicked off."[5]

A day after losing the Senate nomination, the thirty-six-year-old Dawes began to organize the Central Trust Company of Illinois. He became its president and devoted his attentions to banking and to family life until the First World War. Dawes had married Caro Blymyer in 1889. They had two children and later adopted two more. In the late summer of 1912, Dawes suffered the greatest tragedy of his life when his only son drowned at Lake Geneva, Wisconsin, while on a brief vacation before returning to Princeton University. Deeply saddened, Dawes and his wife withdrew from most social life and turned to philanthropy. In memory of their son, they founded the Rufus Fearing Dawes Hotel for Destitute Men in Chicago and Boston, and later established the Mary Dawes Hotel for Women in honor of Dawes' mother.[6]

Supplying the War in Europe

When the United States entered the First World War in 1917, Dawes received a telegram from Herbert Hoover, who had organized American relief efforts in Europe and was now serving as Food Administrator. Searching for talented administrators, Hoover wanted Dawes to take charge of grain prices. But instead of a desk job in Washington, Dawes longed to be in uniform. Hoover considered that a mistake. "I can find a hundred men who will make better lieutenant colonels of engineers, and I want you right here," he argued. "No, Mr. Hoover, I don't want to consider it," Dawes replied. A few days later, Dawes at age fifty-two received his commission as a major in the 17th Railway Engineers, bound for France, and, just as Hoover predicted, he was soon a lieutenant colonel.[7]

The American Expeditionary Force (AEF) was commanded by General John J. Pershing, who had known Dawes since the 1890s when Pershing was a military instructor at the University of Nebraska in Lincoln. In August 1917, Pershing summoned Dawes to Paris and made him chief of supply procurement for the American forces in Europe, assigning him to head the board that collected supplies and to coordinate purchases to hold down inflation and duplication of orders.

Dawes rose to the rank of brigadier general. When the Allied command was unified, General Dawes became the U.S. member of the Military Board of Allied Supply. While representing the United States Army in conferences with other Allied armies and governments, Dawes particularly admired men of action rather than those who simply talked. "Action, then, is everything—words nothing except as they lead immediately to it," he commented, adding, "I came out of the war a postgraduate in emergency conferences."[8] After the Armistice in 1918, he remained in Europe to oversee the disposition of surplus military property. In 1919 he resigned his commission and returned to the United States. His wartime experiences in negotiating and coordinating efforts with his Allied counterparts left him an internationalist in outlook, advocating ratification of the Treaty of Versailles and United States membership in the League of Nations. After the war, everyone called him "General Dawes," despite his protests to the contrary.[9]

In 1920 Dawes supported his good friend, Illinois Governor Frank Lowden, for the Republican presidential nomination, but that prize went to Ohio's Warren G. Harding. In February 1921, however, an event occurred that brought Dawes to the attention not only of president-elect Harding but of the entire nation. A House of Representatives committee to investigate war expenditures called Dawes to testify. Republicans—who held the majority—were clearly eager to uncover any information about "extravagant purchases" in the AEF that might tarnish the outgoing administration of Woodrow Wilson. Journalist Bascom Timmons recorded that Dawes, a busy man, had resented being called by the committee. On the morning that he was due to testify, he walked around the Capitol waiting for the committee to assemble, getting angrier all the time. It took only a spark to set him off. In the course of the interrogation, Representative Oscar Bland, an Indiana Republican, pressed Dawes on how much the American army had paid for French horses.[10]

"Hell'n Maria!" Dawes exclaimed, jumping up from his seat and striding to the mahogany table where the committee sat. "I will tell you this, that we would have paid horse prices for sheep, if they could have hauled artillery!" Peppering his remarks with profanity, Dawes lectured the committee on the urgency of getting supplies to soldiers who were being shot at. He recounted how he had cut through the red tape and "had to connive with the smuggling of horses over there," but he got the horses to drag the cannon to the front. Turning the fire on "pinhead" politicians, Dawes roared: "Your committee can not put a fly speck on the American Army. . . . I am against that peanut politics. This was not a Republican war, nor was it a Democratic war. It was an American war."[11]

Afterwards, Dawes explained that he had "suddenly decided that so far as I could bring it about either the Committee or I would go out of business." His "Hell 'n Maria" testimony took up seven hours for three sessions of the committee, with the official stenographers complaining that he often spoke too rapidly. Dawes' defense of the AEF won great praise from both parties. The newspapers, and especially the editorial cartoonists, loved Dawes' indignant outburst and quaint expletive. His published testimony, even with the expletives deleted, became a Government Printing Office best seller. The incident made him a national figure, and in July 1921, when Congress created the Bureau of the Budget, Harding appointed Dawes as its first director. Adding to his colorful personality, Dawes at this time adopted his trademark pipe. For years he had smoked as many as twenty cigars a day, but during the war a British officer had given him a pipe. Soon after his appointment to the Bureau of the Budget, a newspaper photograph showed him smoking his pipe on the Treasury Department steps. A Chicago pipe manufacturer sent him a new, strangely shaped pipe with most of its bowl below rather than above the stem. Dawes tried it, liked it, and ordered a gross more. From then on, he was rarely seen without this distinctive pipe, which together with his wing-tip collars and hair parted down the middle, reinforced his individualistic, iconoclastic, and idiosyncratic public image.[12]

The Nobel Peace Prize

After spending a year setting up the first federal budget under the new act, Dawes returned to Illinois, concerned about graft and political corruption, especially in Chicago. He organized "The Minute Men of the Constitution," to watch elections and prevent vote fraud. The group opposed the political activities of the Ku Klux Klan, and it also assailed what it considered to be unfair labor union practices. Dawes insisted that his group was not anti-union, but that it opposed the closed union shop. At one point the "Minute Men" had a membership of 25,000, but after his election as vice president the group disbanded.

In 1923, the economy of Germany had deteriorated drastically. Since Germany was unable to repay its war debts, France sent troops to occupy the industrial Ruhr valley. President Harding appointed Dawes to head a commission to study and solve the German financial problem. The "Dawes Plan" offered ways to stabilize the German currency, balance its budget, and reorganize its Reichbank, but the plan postponed action on the most difficult issue of delaying and reducing the German war reparations. Nevertheless, the "Dawes Plan" was recognized as a significant enough contribution to world peace to win Dawes the 1925 Nobel Peace Prize, which he shared with his British counterpart, Sir Austen Chamberlain. Dawes donated his share of the prize money to the Walter Hines Page School of International Relations at Johns Hopkins University.

The Second Choice for the Second Spot

At the Republican convention in 1924, Calvin Coolidge was nominated without significant opposition, but the front-running candidate for vice president, Governor Lowden, had let it be known that he did not want the second spot on the ticket. Nor did the popular Idaho Senator William E. Borah want to be the number two man. A story at the time recorded that President Coolidge had offered Borah a place on the ticket. "For which position?" Borah had supposedly replied. On the second ballot, the delegates nominated Lowden, but he declined to run, as threatened. Republican National Chairman William

Butler promoted Commerce Secretary Herbert Hoover, but Hoover remained too unpopular with the farm states for his price fixing as food commissioner during the war, and the delegates on the third ballot chose Charles G. Dawes for vice president. President Coolidge, who had already sent a congratulatory note to Frank Lowden, accepted Dawes as someone who would add strength to the campaign and who he expected would remain personally loyal to him.[13]

When the unexpected news came over the radio, Dawes was back at his birthplace of Marietta, Ohio, delivering the commencement address to his alma mater. "There is one recollection I shall always treasure," he later wrote. "It is of the gathering of thousands of the people of the town, the next day, to hear me speak briefly from the front porch of the old family home; and the church bells of the town were rung in honor of the occasion. Some people may claim that the vice-presidency does not amount to much, but just then it seemed to me the greatest office in the world."[14]

During the campaign, Coolidge maintained his stance of speaking infrequently and keeping his remarks as bland and inoffensive as possible. He left it to Dawes to attack the Democratic candidate, John W. Davis, and the Progressive candidate, Wisconsin Senator Robert M. La Follette. Dawes entertained his audiences with the type of "Hell'n Maria" speeches they expected, shaking his fist and denouncing La Follette—whose platform among other things advocated allowing Congress to overturn Supreme Court decisions—as a demagogue and dangerous radical "animated by the vicious purpose of undermining the constitutional foundation of the Republic." Dawes went so far as to suggest that La Follette was a Bolshevik, although La Follette had publicly rejected Communist support and had been attacked by them.[15]

Coolidge and Dawes were overwhelmingly elected in 1924, winning more votes than the Democratic and Progressive candidates combined. "When Coolidge was elected President the world desired tranquility," Dawes noted in his journal, "—a reaction of its peoples from the excesses of war."[16] But tranquility was not Charles Dawes' style.

An Assault on the Rules of the Senate

At his swearing-in in the Senate chamber in March 1925, Dawes was called upon to deliver a brief inaugural address, a tradition that dated back to John Adams in 1789. What the audience heard, however, was far from traditional. As the Senate's new presiding officer, Dawes addressed himself to "methods of effective procedure," rather than any particular policies or programs. He then launched into an attack on the Senate rules, "which, in their present form, place power in the hands of individuals to an extent, at times, subversive of the fundamental principles of free representative government." The rules of the Senate, he declared, ran contrary to the principles of constitutional government, and under these rules "the rights of the Nation and of the American people have been overlooked."[17]

Dawes focused his attack on filibusters, which at that time were being carried out most frequently by the small band of progressive Republicans, such as Robert La Follette, Sr., and George Norris, who held the balance of power in the Senate. Dawes declared that Rule 22, which required a two-thirds majority of those present and voting to shut off debate, "at times enables Senators to consume in oratory those last precious minutes of a session needed for momentous decisions," thus placing great power in the hands of a minority of senators. "Who would dare oppose changes in the rules necessary to insure that the business of the United States should always be conducted in the interests of the Nation and never be in danger of encountering a situation where one man or a minority of men might demand unreasonable concessions under threat of blocking the business of the Government?" he asked. Unless the rules were reformed, they would "lessen the effectiveness, prestige, and dignity of the United States Senate." He insisted that "reform in the present rules of the Senate is demanded not only by American public opinion, but I venture to say in the individual consciences of a majority of the Members of the Senate itself." He concluded by appealing to senators' consciences and patriotism in correcting these defects in their rules.[18]

Since Dawes had not given advance copies of the speech to the press or anyone else, no one had anticipated his diatribe. In the audience, President Calvin Coolidge attempted indifference, but could not hide his discomfort. Dawes had managed to upstage the president's own inaugural address, which was to follow at ceremonies outside on the Capitol's east front. As the senators proceeded to the inaugural platform, they talked of nothing else but their anger over Dawes' effrontery, making Coolidge's address anticlimactic. After the ceremony, Dawes compounded the ill will when he joined the president to ride back to the White House, instead of returning to the chamber to adjourn the Senate. In the Senate chamber, there was considerable confusion. Senator James A. Reed of Missouri noted that the Senate did not adjourn, nor did it recess. "It simply broke up." [19]

Most senators were less than receptive to Dawes' advice. "Dawes showed as little knowledge of the Senate's rules as he did good taste," snapped Democratic minority leader Joseph T. Robinson. "It was exactly what should not have been said," added Robinson's colleague from Arkansas, Thaddeus Caraway. "I regret that such occasion was perverted into a farce," complained Senator Claude Swanson of Virginia. "I have an opinion of the spectacle but do not care to express it," was George Norris' response, and Republican majority leader Charles Curtis declined to make any public comment on the vice president's remarks. But while the senators disapproved, columnist Mark Sullivan observed that the public was delighted. Sullivan described Dawes as a hero who had finally made a dent "in that fine old encrusted Senatorial tradition, buttressed by antique rules and practices, and solemnly defended by conservative and radical Senators alike." [20]

An Irritated President

After upstaging the president on inaugural day, Dawes compounded his error by writing to inform Coolidge that he did not think the vice president should attend cabinet meetings. President Harding had invited Coolidge to cabinet meetings on a regular basis, but Dawes did not believe that Harding's action should necessarily set a precedent for future presidents. He took the initiative by declining even before Coolidge had offered him an invitation. "This was done to relieve him—if he shared my views—of any embarrassment, if he desired to carry them out," Dawes later explained, "notwithstanding the fact that he had accepted Harding's invitation." Dawes dismissed suggestions by the "busybodies and mischievemakers" in Washington, who imagined "unpleasant relations between Coolidge and myself." What Coolidge thought is less certain. In his *Autobiography*, Coolidge counted his experiences in the cabinet as being "of supreme value" to him when he became president and suggested that the vice president should be invited to sit with the cabinet, if he was "a man of discretion and character so that he can be relied upon to act as a subordinate in that position." The implication was that Dawes did not fit that description. In addition, Coolidge never mentioned Dawes by name in his memoirs.[21]

Coolidge also felt irritated over an incident that occurred on March 10, only days after Dawes started presiding over the Senate. Up for debate was the president's nomination of Charles Warren to be attorney general. In the wake of Teapot Dome and other business-related scandals, Democrats and Progressive Republicans objected to the nomination because of Warren's close association with the "Sugar Trust." At midday, six speakers were scheduled to address Warren's nomination. Desiring to return to his room at the Willard Hotel for a nap, Dawes consulted the majority and minority leaders, who assured him that no vote would be taken that afternoon. After Dawes left the Senate, however, all but one of the scheduled speakers decided against making formal remarks, and a vote was taken. When it became apparent that the vote would be tied, Republican leaders hastily called Dawes at the Willard. The roused vice president jumped in a taxi and sped toward the Capitol. But enough time intervened to persuade the only Democratic senator who had voted for Warren to switch his vote against him. By the time Dawes arrived there was no longer a tie to break, and the nomination had failed by a single vote—the first such rejection in nearly sixty years. President Coolidge angrily held Dawes responsible for his most embarrassing legislative defeat, and the rest of Washington could not resist teasing the vice president over the incident. The Gridiron Club presented him with a four-foot high alarm clock. And Senator Norris read a parody of "Sheridan's Ride" on the Senate floor:

> Hurrah, Hurrah for Dawes!
>   Hurrah! hurrah for this high-minded man!
> And when his statue is placed on high,
>   Under the dome of the Capitol sky,
> The great senatorial temple of fame—
>   There with the glorious General's name
> Be it said, in letters both bold and bright,
>   "Oh, Hell an' Maria, he has lost us the
>   fight." [22]

Stimulating a National Debate

Dawes bore the criticism surprisingly well. He was never a man to shy away from controversy, and he enjoyed being at the center of attention. He also enjoyed occupying the Vice President's Room behind the Senate chamber, which he found impressive, with its tall mahogany cabinet, Dolly Madison mirror, Rembrandt Peale portrait of Washington, and chandelier that once hung in the White House. When the Senate was not in session, large delegations of visitors would tour the corridor outside his office, and since the door was generally kept open for better ventilation they would always "stop and peek in." The senators, too, would stop and talk with the vice president who took such an active interest in their rules and proceedings. But Dawes found it curious that conversation always seemed to get around to whether "this or that Senator will be willing to concede the right-of-way to this or that piece of general legislation as a measure of surpassing public importance." He remained convinced that, by allowing unlimited debate, the Senate rules granted an intolerable power to the minority. [23]

Rather than cease his criticism, Dawes continued to seek public forums to denounce the Senate filibuster. During the summer recess in 1925, he toured the country addressing public meetings on the subject. He pointed out that filibus-

ters flourished during the short sessions of Congress, held between December and March following each congressional election, and that these protracted debates tied up critical appropriations bills until the majority would agree to fund some individual senator's pet project. He frequently cited a filibuster by Senator Benjamin Tillman that brought a $600,000 appropriation to South Carolina. Dawes praised the work of Senators Francis Warren, chairman of the Appropriations Committee, and Reed Smoot, chairman of Finance. "It is they and their like who perform most of the difficult, disagreeable and necessary work, speaking only when they have something to say and accomplish." By contrast to such "constructive" senators, he had no use for legislative showmen, radicals, and filibusterers. [24]

Dawes' campaign stimulated a national debate on the Senate rules. A significant rebuttal to his assertions came from the political scientist Lindsay Rogers, who argued that filibusters served a useful purpose. Too much legislation was hammered out in committees that met in secret, where powerful corporate interests held sway, and where progressive reformers had little influence. Rogers pointed out that "the powers of delay given individual Senators force into pending bills some amendments that the Senate leaders would not accept were they free to act as they desired." He also pointed out that despite the filibuster, the Senate got a "creditable amount of business" done each session. Changing the rules would be inadvisable, since it would silence the minority and allow the majority to act unimpeded. [25]

Although the Senate did not change its rules during his vice-presidency, Dawes noted with satisfaction that it invoked cloture more frequently than ever before. After 1917, when the cloture rule was first adopted, the Senate had voted to cut off debate on the Versailles Treaty in 1919 but failed to invoke cloture on tariff legislation in 1921 and 1922. During the Sixty-ninth Congress, which ran from 1925 to 1927, the Senate cast seven votes on cloture, and three times gained the two-thirds majority sufficient to cut off filibusters. Not until the Ninety-third Congress, from 1973 to 1975, after a rules change had reduced the majority needed to vote cloture from two-thirds to three-fifths of the members, did the Senate equal and surpass that number of successful cloture votes.

Farm Relief and Banking Reform

Dawes also personally intervened in other attempts to cut off debate, and his efforts led to the Senate's passage of bills that extended the Federal Reserve banks and would have provided farm relief. Agitation for farm relief became a pressing issue during the 1920s, when American farmers were shut out of the general prosperity of the era. After the First World War, farm prices had fallen and never recovered. Members of Congress from midwestern and plains states therefore formed the Farm Bloc, consisting of some twenty-five senators and one hundred representatives. Holding the balance of power in Congress, they promoted legislation to solve the problem of distributing surplus farm produce. Each year between 1924 and 1928, Senator Charles McNary of Oregon and Representative Gilbert Haugen of Iowa, both Republicans, sponsored the McNary-Haugen bill to permit the federal government to buy crop surpluses and sell them abroad while at the same time maintaining a high tariff on the importation of farm goods. The result would have raised prices in the United States.

Robert M. La Follette, Jr., who had succeeded his late father in the Senate, led a filibuster against the McFadden-Pepper bill to extend the charters of the Federal Reserve Banks. By holding up passage of the bank bill, La Follette sought to pressure the Senate to vote on the McNary-Haugen bill. The only way to break this logjam, as far as Dawes could see, was to form a coalition "between the conservatives favoring the bank bill and certain radicals favoring the farm bill." The vice president intervened, calling representatives of both groups to a meeting in his room. One of the participants, Pennsylvania Senator George Wharton Pepper, commented that "by sheer force of his personality, [Dawes] forced an agreement that both measures should be voted upon. This agreement was carried out. Both bills passed." Pepper gave Dawes the chief credit for enacting these bills, as did Senator James E. Watson, the Indiana Republican who would soon become majority leader. In the course of a speech on equalization fees, Watson noted, "This explanation of the equalization fee was prepared by the Vice President, who is a supporter of the McNary-Haugen bill." Although Watson deleted this indiscretion from the *Congressional Record*, alert reporters in the press gallery had already publicized the statement. Dawes' interest in this legislation did not further endear him to President Coolidge, who twice vetoed the McNary-Haugen bills that his vice president had helped the Senate pass. Coolidge complained that "the McNary-Haugen people have their headquarters in [Dawes'] chambers."[26]

An Irksome Job for a Man of Action

As a man of action, Charles Dawes found the job of presiding over Senate debates "at times rather irksome." He felt more comfortable in executive and administrative positions with "specific objectives and well-defined authority and responsibilities." He preferred clear statements of fact to speeches that appealed to prejudice or emotion. As presiding officer, he enjoyed making decisions about rulings from the chair and took some pride in the fact that the Senate had never overturned one of his decisions, but he attributed much of his success to the Senate's young journal clerk, Charles Watkins. Watkins had studied the rules and compiled the *Senate Precedents*, making himself "the actual parliamentarian" of the Senate. "Senate precedents are almost always conflicting, and when Charley Watkins gives me a choice of precedents to follow, I sometimes make my own decision. But it is chiefly upon his advice that I act." A decade later, Watkins became the Senate's first official parliamentarian, a post he held until his retirement in 1964.[27]

Dawes similarly bristled over the social requirements of the vice-presidency, and as one Washington hostess recorded, "his social tactics, no less than his insubordination to the Senate, brought down blame upon him in Washington." Although he frequently dined out and entertained generously, it was always on his own terms. He would arrive late, leave early, and smoke his pipe at the dinner table. Caro Dawes also disappointed Washington's social set. Lacking the stamina that Mrs. Thomas Marshall and

Mrs. Calvin Coolidge had shown for attending a continuous procession of luncheons and receptions, Mrs. Dawes declined many invitations. She never seemed to enjoy "presiding over the Ladies of the Senate," and looked visibly relieved when her guests departed. Yet even her critics conceded that her "manner was sweet and gentle, her conversation cultured, and her dignity unimpeachable," providing a gentle counterpart to her "Hell 'n Maria" husband. The vice president's estrangement from the president further shaded his social standing. As one Senate wife later confided, "I have always had a feeling which many share, that a slightly different attitude on the part of the Coolidges might have done much to relieve the strain so far as the Dawes were concerned."[28]

In 1927, President Coolidge stunned the nation with his announcement that he did not choose to run for reelection the following year. Although pundits debated whether Coolidge wanted to accept a draft, his announcement opened a spirited campaign for the Republican presidential nomination. Although Dawes was frequently mentioned for the presidency, he announced that he was not a candidate and instead favored his longtime friend, Illinois Governor Frank Lowden. The nomination went instead to Commerce Secretary Herbert Hoover, whose supporters considered putting Dawes on their ticket as vice president. But President Coolidge let it be known that he would consider Dawes' nomination as a personal affront. Instead, the nod went to Senate Majority Leader Charles Curtis of Kansas. For the third straight time, the Republican ticket swept the national election.[29]

A Travesty Upon Good Government

As Dawes' term of office approached its end, a senator told him how much the members of the Senate thought of him, adding "but the Senate got very tired of you at the beginning of your service." Dawes replied, "I should hate to think that the Senate was as tired of me at the beginning of my service as I am of the Senate at the end."[30]

At about this time, Dawes attended the annual Gridiron Dinner. He and his successor, Charles Curtis, were ordered to stand while the "Dawes Decalogue, or the Letter of a Self-made Has-Been to His Successor" was read, listing several commandments drawn from "the depths of my experience":

> Don't steal the first page on Inauguration Day, and you may be invited to sit in the Cabinet.
> Don't be afraid to criticize the Senate. You know how much it needs it. The public likes it and the Senate thrives on it. . . .
> Don't try to change the Senate Rules.
> Don't buck the President if you want to stay more than four years.
> Don't do your sleeping in the day time.[31]

Ironically, Dawes spent his last days in the Senate watching another filibuster, napping on the couch in his office and responding when the quorum bells rang. When the Senate dispatched its sergeant at arms to "arrest" absent senators, Dawes considered listening to the profanity of the arrested senators as they were brought in "one of the few pleasant incidents of such proceedings." He noted with some dismay that the galleries were filled to watch the filibuster and grumbled that "a travesty upon good government in the Senate is regarded as an amusement rivaling a picture show." In his farewell speech to the Senate on March 4, 1929, Dawes reiterated his objections to the Senate rules, saying, "I take back nothing."[32]

Dawes had resigned as chairman of the board of the Central Trust Company of Illinois when he was elected vice president. After his term in Washington, he returned as honorary chairman, when it merged to become the Central Republic Bank & Trust Co. He became chairman of a financial commission to the Dominican Republic, and chairman of a committee to finance the exposition "A Century of Progress, Chicago, 1933." In April 1929, President Hoover appointed Dawes U.S. ambassador to Great Britain, a post he held until 1932. He was scheduled to head the American delegation to the World Disarmament Conference in Geneva, Switzerland, when President Hoover persuaded him to take charge of the Reconstruction Finance Corporation, which Congress had just created to assist corporations and banks in need of relief from the Great Depression. Dawes' national standing rose so high that some Republicans talked of dumping Vice President Curtis from the ticket in favor of Dawes as a "rip-snorting, hell-raising" candidate to boost Hoover's chances of reelection. Then in June 1932, Dawes abruptly resigned as chairman of the RFC. His own financial base, the Central Republic Bank of Chicago was near collapse and required a ninety million dollar loan from the RFC to keep it alive and to keep the entire Chicago banking structure from collapsing. Dawes had to resign to avoid a conflict of interest.[33]

Dawes, whose early career was shaken by the panic of 1893, was now confronted by an even greater financial crisis, one that shook his natural self-confidence and ended whatever remaining political chances he might have had. Reporter Thomas L. Stokes met Dawes shortly after his resignation from the RFC and found him "a dejected, dispirited man." Dawes was distributing a typewritten statement to the press predicting business improvement. "That's all he had to say," wrote Stokes. "He was manifestly uneasy and nervous, not the hail fellow, the 'Hell and Maria' I had known about Washington for several years. I wondered at the time what was wrong." Several days later Stokes heard rumors about the shaky banking situation in Chicago and then about the RFC loan. Eventually the Central Republic Bank was placed in receivership and liquidated. Dawes reorganized it as the City National Bank & Trust Company of Chicago and paid back the RFC loans. He remained associated with the bank until he died at the age of eighty-five, on April 23, 1951.[34]

Historians have concluded that if Dawes was not really a leader, he acted like one. As vice president, he would not accept direction from the president, and whenever his views did coincide with Coolidge's his lobbying on behalf of administration measures was more likely to hurt rather than help. Dawes' forthrightness and tactlessness incurred the anger of many senators. Although his "bull-like integrity" won Dawes recognition as an outstanding vice president, that quality antagonized the Coolidge Administration more than aiding it. As for Dawes, he believed that the vice-presidency "is largely what the man in it makes it." And for his part, he made the most of it.[35]

NOTES

[1] Paul R. Leach, *That Man Dawes* (Chicago, 1930), p. 32.

[2] Ibid., pp. 40–48; Bascom N. Timmons, *Portrait of an American: Charles G. Dawes* (New York, 1953), p. 26; Charles G. Dawes, *A Journal of the McKinley Years* (Chicago, 1950), pp. vii–viii; Dawes was also the author of *Essays and Speeches* (1915), *A Journal of the Great War* (1921), *The First Year of the Budget of the United States* (1923), *Notes as Vice President* (1935), *How Long Prosperity?* (1937), *A Journal of Reparations* (1939), *A Journal as Ambassador to Great Britain* (1939), and *A Journal of the McKinley Years* (1950).

[3] Timmons, p. 18; Dawes, *A Journal of the McKinley Years*, pp. 51, 89.

[4] Charles G. Dawes, *Notes as Vice President, 1928–1929* (Boston, 1935), p. 49; *National Cyclopedia of American Biography* (New York, 1958), p. 7; Dawes, *A Journal of the McKinley Years*, pp. 232–33.

[5] Leach, p. 102.

[6] Dawes, *A Journal of the McKinley Years*, pp. 443–49.

[7] Leach, p. 149.

[8] Dawes, *Notes as Vice President*, p. 10.

[9] Leach, p. 167.

[10] Timmons, pp. 194–95.

[11] The "Hell 'n Maria" reference does not appear in the hearing transcripts. As the subcommittee chairman explained: "Objection has been made by members of the committee to the fact that at the request of the witness, Mr. Dawes, the many fluent expressions of profanity were omitted from the transcript." U.S. Congress, House of Representatives, Select Committee on Expenditures in the War Department, *War Expenditures*, 66th Cong., 2d sess (Washington, 1921), pp. 4427, 4492, 4515; Timmons, pp. 195–98; Leach, pp. 175–78.

[12] Dawes, *Notes as Vice President*, pp. 10–12; Leach, pp. 186–88.

[13] Claude M. Fuess, *Calvin Coolidge: The Man From Vermont* (Boston, 1940), pp. 345–46.

[14] Dawes, *Notes as Vice President*, p. 18.

[15] Donald R. McCoy, *Calvin Coolidge: The Quiet President* (Lawrence, KS, 1988), pp. 254–59; William Leuchtenburg, *The Perils of Prosperity, 1914–32* (Chicago, 1958), p. 134.

[16] Dawes, *Notes as Vice President*, p. 32.

[17] McCoy, pp. 264–65; U.S., Congress, Senate, *Congressional Record*, 69th Cong., special sess., p. 3.

[18] Ibid., pp. 3–4.

[19] Ibid., p. 8; Fuess, p. 361.

[20] Leach, pp. 249–50; Mark Sullivan, *Our Times: The United States, 1900–1925* (New York, 1935), 6:634–36.

[21] Dawes, *Notes as Vice President*, pp. 33–34; Calvin Coolidge, *The Autobiography of Calvin Coolidge* (New York, 1929), pp. 163–64.

[22] Richard Lowitt, *George W. Norris: The Persistence of a Progressive, 1913–1933* (Urbana, IL, 1971), pp. 279–80.

[23] Dawes, *Notes as Vice President*, pp. 154, 169.

[24] McCoy, pp. 268–69; Dawes, *Notes as Vice President*, pp. 110, 288.

[25] Lindsay Rogers, *The American Senate* (New York, 1926), pp. 188–90.

[26] Dawes, *Notes as a Vice President*, pp. 62–70; McCoy, p. 323; Leach, p. 273; see also George Wharton Pepper, *In The Senate* (Philadelphia, 1930).

[27] Dawes, *Notes as Vice President*, pp. 107, 179–80.

[28] Frances Parkinson Keyes, *Capital Kaleidoscope: The Story of a Washington Hostess* (New York, 1937), pp. 140–43.

[29] "Heap Big Chief," *American Mercury* 17 (August 1929): 404.

[30] Dawes, *Notes as Vice President*, p. 255.

[31] Ibid., pp. 183–84.

[32] Ibid., pp. 299, 304, 316.

[33] David Burner, *Herbert Hoover, A Public Life* (New York, 1979), p. 275.

[34] Thomas L. Stokes, *Chip Off My Shoulder* (Princeton, NJ, 1940), pp. 329–30.

[35] McCoy, p. 247; Dawes, *Notes as Vice President*, p. 4.

Chapter 31

CHARLES CURTIS
1929–1933

CHARLES CURTIS

Chapter 31

CHARLES CURTIS

31st Vice President: 1929–1933

His politics were always purely personal. Issues never bothered him.

—WILLIAM ALLEN WHITE

In the spring of 1932, George and Ira Gershwin's Broadway musical, "Of Thee I Sing," spoofed Washington politics, including a vice president named Alexander Throttlebottom, who could get inside the White House only on public tours. The tour guide, who failed to recognize Throttlebottom, at one point engaged him in a discussion of the vice-presidency:

> Guide: Well, how did he come to be Vice President?
>
> Throttlebottom: Well, they put a lot of names in a hat, and he lost.
>
> Guide: What does he do all the time?
>
> Throttlebottom: Well, he sits in the park and feeds the peanuts to the pigeons and the squirrels, and then he takes walks, and goes to the movies. Last week, he tried to join the library, but he needed two references, so he couldn't get in.[1]

Audiences laughed heartily at these lines, in part because they could easily identify the hapless Throttlebottom with the incumbent vice president, Charles Curtis. Curtis was never close to President Herbert Hoover and played no significant role in his administration. Despite Curtis' many years of experience as a member of the House and Senate and as Senate majority leader, his counsel was rarely sought on legislative matters. His chief notoriety as vice president came as a result of a messy social squabble over protocol, which only made him appear ridiculous. Many Republicans hoped to dump Curtis from the ticket when Hoover ran for reelection. Given Curtis' Horatio Alger-style rise in life, and his

long and successful career in Congress, how did he become such a Throttlebottom as vice president?

Formative Years on the Reservation

Although colorful in itself, Charles Curtis' actual life story often became obscured by its political mythology.[2] He began life in 1860 in North Topeka, Kansas, where he spent his earliest years partly in the white and partly in the Native American community. The son of Orren Curtis, a white man, and Ellen Pappan, who was one-quarter Kaw Indian, Charles Curtis on his mother's side was the great-great grandson of White Plume, a Kansa-Kaw chief who had offered assistance to the Lewis and Clark expedition in 1804. White Plume's daughter married Louis Gonville, a French-Canadian fur trader, and their daughter, Julie Gonville, married Louis Pappan. As a result of the Kansa-Kaw treaty of 1825, the tribe relinquished its claims to its traditional lands in Missouri and Kansas. A two-million-acre reservation was established west of Topeka for full-blooded Indians, while a series of fee-simple land grants along the Kansas river were set aside for "half-breeds"—those who had intermarried with whites. Curtis' grandmother Julie Gonville Pappan received "Half-Breed Reservation No. Four," directly across the river from the Kansas capital, where she and her husband ran a profitable ferry business.

Reflecting his mother's heritage, Charles Curtis spoke French and Kansa before he learned

English. His mother died in 1863, about the time that his father left to fight in the Civil War. Soon thereafter, Orren Curtis remarried, divorced, remarried again, and was dishonorably discharged from the Union army. At the end of the war, Curtis was court martialled for having hanged three prisoners in his custody—or as the charges read for "executing the bushwakers." Sentenced to a year's hard labor at the Missouri State Penitentiary, he was pardoned a month later and returned to Kansas. Given Orren's unstable circumstances and roving nature, young Charley remained in the custody of his paternal grandparents. In 1865, his maternal grandparents, Louis and Julie Pappan Gonville, left North Topeka to return to the Kaw reservation at Council Grove, concerned that otherwise they might be excluded from future land settlements and compensation. The next year, young Charley went to live with them on the reservation.[3]

Since Charley could speak the Kaw language, he fit comfortably into the tribe. "I had my bows and arrows," he later recalled, "and joined the other boys in shooting arrows at nickles, dimes, and quarters which visitors would place in split sticks." In those still-frontier days, the Kaw reservation was frequently raided by nomadic Cheyenne Indians, and during one attack Charley was sent on a mission to inform Topeka. "I volunteered to make the trip," he later told audiences. "When we heard the Cheyennes were coming, the horses and ponies were driven to pasture, some distance from my grandpa's home, so there was no horse or pony to ride. I therefore, started out on foot, traveling during the night." The next day, he arrived in Topeka, some sixty miles away. Curtis' "cross-country run" made him a celebrity in North Topeka, but the incident also convinced his paternal grandparents, William and Permelia Curtis, that their grandson should be raised in the more "civilized" atmosphere of Topeka rather than return to the reservation.[4]

Curtis had learned to ride Indian ponies bareback and won a reputation as a "good and fearless rider." Back in North Topeka, his grandfather William Curtis had built a race track, and in 1869 Charles Curtis rode in his first race. He soon became a full-fledged jockey and continued

to ride until 1876. A fellow jockey described Curtis as "rather short and wiry" and "just another brush boy jockey," explaining that eastern riders "called us brush boys because we rode in what would be called the sticks." As a winning jockey, Curtis was known throughout Kansas as "The Indian Boy." His mounts made a lot of money for the local gamblers and prostitutes who bet on him, and he recalled that after one race a madam bought him "a new suit of clothes, boots, hat and all," and had a new jockey suit made for him; others bought him candy and presents. "I had never been so petted in my life and I liked it," Curtis reminisced.[5]

His family, however, had greater ambitions for the boy than horse racing. In 1871, grandfather William Curtis brought suit on behalf of Charley and his sister Elizabeth to establish their claim, over that of their father, for title to their mother's share of the Half-Breed Lands in North Topeka. When Curtis' father lost this suit, he left Topeka for good. Grandfather Curtis wanted Charley to stop racing and go back to school, but after his grandfather's death in 1873, the boy set out to join his other grandparents Louis and Julie Pappan, who were traveling with the Kaw Tribe from Kansas to the Indian Territory of Oklahoma. Still on the tribal roll, and "longing for the old life," he wanted to live on the reservation. Grandmother Julie talked him out of it. She invited him to her wagon and asked why he wanted to go to the Indian Territory. While she would have liked nothing better than to have him live with her, she told him that on the reservation he would end up "like most of the men on it," without an education or future prospects. If Charley expected to make something of himself, he should return to Topeka and attend school. "I took her splendid advice and the next morning as the wagons pulled out for the south, bound for Indian Territory, I mounted my pony and with my belongings in a flour sack, returned to Topeka and school," Curtis recounted. "No man or boy ever received better advice, it was the turning point in my life."[6]

A Passion for Politics

In Topeka, Curtis lived with grandmother Permelia Hubbard Curtis, a decidedly strongminded woman. "She brooked no opposition," recalled Charley's half-sister, Dolly. "I think she regarded being both a Methodist and a Republican as essential for anyone who expected to go to heaven." When Charley was offered a contract to race at the Philadelphia Centennial in 1876, Permelia Curtis put her foot down. Instead, he retired as a jockey and went to high school. After graduating, he studied law, supporting himself by working as a custodian in a law firm and by driving a hack. When he had no customers, he would stop under street lamps to read his law books. In 1881, at the age of twenty-one, Charles Curtis was admitted to the Kansas bar. Although his life appeared to be a rags-to-riches story, Curtis had in fact a considerable inheritance in land in North Topeka. The young lawyer plunged into real estate, selling lots and building houses. He also opened his own firm and practiced criminal law. In 1884, Charles Curtis married Anna Baird. They had three children and also took in his half-sister Dolly when her mother died.[7]

As a young man, Curtis showed a passion for politics. In 1880, during James Garfield's campaign for president, Curtis donned an oilcloth cap and carried a torch in a Republican parade through Topeka. It was only a matter of time before the popular "Indian jockey" ran for office himself. In 1884, after shaking every hand in the district, Curtis won election as Shawnee county attorney. Since both his father and grandfather Curtis had operated saloons in North Topeka, he was supported by the liquor interests, which had also retained his law firm. But once elected, Curtis insisted on enforcing the state's prohibition laws and closed down all of the saloons in the county. He won attention not only as a "dry," but as a law-and-order prosecutor.[8]

By a single vote in 1889, Curtis lost the nomination to fill a vacancy in the U.S. House of Representatives. It was a time of agrarian depression, when voters in the West were turning away from conservatives like Curtis in favor of the more radical solutions put forward by the Farmers' Alliance and its political offspring, the Populist party. In 1891, William Allen White, editor of the *Emporia Gazette*, first met the "young prince,"

Charles Curtis, and later provided this description:

> He came down from Topeka to campaign the county, sent by the Republican state central committee. His job was to fight the Farmers' Alliance. He had a rabble-rousing speech with a good deal of Civil War in it, a lot of protective tariff, and a very carefully poised straddle on the currency question (which, I was satisfied then—and still think—that he knew little about, and cared nothing for). For his politics were always purely personal. Issues never bothered him. He was a handsome fellow, five feet ten, straight as his Kaw Indian grandfather must have been, with an olive skin that looked like old ivory, a silky, flowing, handlebar mustache, dark shoe-button eyes, beady, and in those days always gay, a mop of crow's wing hair, a gentle ingratiating voice, and what a smile![9]

For three days, White and Curtis toured the county together, with White making the introductions and Curtis making the speeches. Never had White met anyone who could charm a hostile audience as effectively as did Curtis, whose personality could overshadow whatever he was speaking about. This trait helped Curtis defeat the Populist and Democratic fusion candidate for a seat in the House in 1892—the same election that saw Kansas vote for the Populist presidential candidate and elect a Populist governor. Curtis' upset victory brought him to the attention of prominent easterners, such as House Republican leader Thomas B. Reed, who were delighted that someone who thought the way they did on tariff, railroad, and currency issues could win election in so Populist a state as Kansas. Reed took a particular liking to "the Indian," as he called Curtis, and made him one of his lieutenants.[10]

"Our Charley"

When Curtis first came to Washington, Democrats firmly controlled the federal government. Grover Cleveland had just been elected to his second term as president, and in the House Democrats held 218 seats, Republicans 124, and the Populists 14. Then in 1893 a severe economic depression dramatically reversed party fortunes. Campaigning against the Democrats as the party of the "empty dinner pail," Republicans won 254 seats in the next Congress, leaving the Democrats with 93 and the Populists with 10. Tom Reed, who had resumed the speakership with the return of a Republican majority, trusted Curtis' political judgment. According to an often-repeated story, Curtis once entered Speaker Reed's office and found a group of Republicans discussing the restoration of the gold standard. "Indian, what would you do about this?" Reed asked. Curtis suggested taking the matter out of the hands of the standing committees that had been dealing with it, since it was apparent they would never agree. Instead, he recommended appointing a special committee to write a new bill. Reed liked the idea so much that he appointed Curtis as a member of the special committee that drafted the Gold Standard Act of 1900.[11]

Curtis devoted most of his attention to his service on the Committee on Indian Affairs, where he drafted the "Curtis Act" in 1898. Entitled "An Act for the Protection of the People of the Indian Territory and for Other Purposes," the Curtis Act actually overturned many treaty rights by allocating federal lands, abolishing tribal courts, and giving the Interior Department control over mineral leases on Indian lands. Having reinstated his name on the Kaw tribal rolls in 1889, Curtis was able, through his position on the House Indian Affairs Committee, to calculate the benefits he might receive from government allotments to his tribe. In 1902, he drafted the Kaw Allotment Act under which he and his children received fee simple title to Kaw land in Oklahoma.[12]

Congressman Curtis, hailed throughout Kansas as "Our Charley," assiduously built his political base in the state. William Allen White recalled that Curtis carried with him little books containing the names of all the Republicans in each township and used to mumble these names "like a pious worshiper out of a prayer book" to commit them to memory. When Curtis greeted a voter, he could recall the man's name and ask about his wife, children, and business. He left voters convinced that they were intimates. In 1903, Curtis made a bid for a Senate seat, competing against fellow Republican Representative Chester Long. Both men had strong support

from the railroads, Long being allied with the J. P. Morgan interests and Curtis identified with the Jay Gould railroads. Editor William Allen White grumbled that the money and influence in the election came from the railroads and "the people had nothing to do with it."[13]

When the Republicans deadlocked, Long and Curtis reached an agreement that Long would gain the nomination in 1903 and would then support Curtis for the next Senate opening—which occurred sooner than anyone anticipated. In 1904, Kansas Senator Joseph R. Burton was indicted by a federal grand jury in St. Louis, Missouri, for representing clients for a fee before the Post Office in violation of federal statutes. Although the U.S. Supreme Court overturned this conviction on the grounds that Missouri lacked jurisdiction, Burton was tried and convicted again in 1905. In May 1906, the Supreme Court upheld Burton's second conviction, and as the Senate prepared to expel him, Burton resigned on June 4, 1906.

At that time, state legislatures still elected U.S. senators, but since the Kansas legislature was not in session, the governor appointed Alfred W. Benson to fill the vacancy. When the legislature reconvened, Curtis and several other Republicans challenged Benson for the seat. Kansas progressives promoted the candidacy of Joseph L. Bristow, arguing that he would more faithfully support the reform legislation of President Theodore Roosevelt. Curtis turned for help to Roosevelt's chief conservative opponent, Rhode Island Senator Nelson W. Aldrich. As chairman of the Senate Finance Committee, Aldrich handled all tariff legislation and was able to channel considerable amounts of money from business interests to pro-tariff politicians. Aldrich supplied Curtis with funds to purchase newspapers that would support his senatorial candidacy. William Allen White, who supported Bristow, warned President Roosevelt that attorneys for every railroad in the state were for Curtis. "Two railroad attorneys when I asked them why they were for Curtis, frankly told me in confidence of friendship that orders came from higher up to be for Curtis and they are obeying orders," White wrote to the president. But Roosevelt seemed less concerned, assuring White that "so far my experience with Curtis has been rather more pleasant than with the average of his colleagues." [14]

A High-Tariff Man

The state legislature elected Charles Curtis senator on January 23, 1907, and he took his seat a week later. Just as he had worked closely with Tom Reed in the House, Curtis became a chief lieutenant for Senator Aldrich. Then in his last years in the Senate, and having outlasted his most powerful allies, Aldrich came to rely on a group of younger, high-tariff colleagues, including Curtis, W. Murray Crane of Massachusetts, Eugene Hale of Maine, and Reed Smoot of Utah. In 1909, Curtis played an influential role in the passage of the Payne-Aldrich Tariff, which raised rates so high that it helped split the Republican party into warring conservative and progressive factions. Two years later, that split claimed Curtis as a victim, when he was defeated for renomination by a progressive Republican—who in turn was defeated by a Democrat. [15]

As a result of the ratification of the Seventeenth Amendment, the first direct popular elections of senators were held in 1914. Progressives were confident that the people would support their candidates, but with an economic recession at home and war in Europe, voters nationwide instead turned to conservative candidates. After defeating the progressive incumbent Joseph Bristow for the Republican Senate nomination, Charles Curtis went on to defeat both a Democratic and a Progressive party opponent that November. [16]

Curtis returned to the Senate in 1915 as a symbol of the rewards of party regularity and the defeat of insurgency. Following the pattern set by Senate Democrats, who had created the post of party whip in the previous Congress, Senate Republicans appointed New York Senator James Wadsworth as both conference secretary and whip. Then, within a week, the party decided to split these posts and elected Charles Curtis Republican whip. He served under the party leadership of New Hampshire Senator Jacob Gallinger from 1915 to 1918 and of Massachusetts Senator Henry Cabot Lodge from 1918 to 1924. In 1918, when Republicans won back the majority in the Senate, Curtis' role as whip expanded, as he led much of the Republican opposition to the Wilson administration. "No one ever accused him of being a Progressive," wrote one Washington correspondent, "but the feminists nevertheless called him friend, and it is one of the proudest of his claims that he led the floor fight for the Nineteenth Amendment," granting women the right to vote. [17]

Senator Curtis went to the 1920 Republican convention in Chicago as head of the Kansas delegation. When the convention reached a stalemate between the presidential candidacies of General Leonard Wood and Illinois Governor Frank Lowden, Curtis was one of the senators who gathered in the famous "smoke-filled room" and anointed their colleague, Ohio Senator Warren G. Harding, as the party's nominee. Curtis then returned to the Kansas delegation and told them frankly, as William Allen White recalled, "that it had been decided (the phrase was his) to give Harding a play." The hot and tired delegates were glad to take orders and break the deadlock. Kansas switched from Wood to Harding, whose bandwagon began its roll toward the White House. [18]

Harding's election took Curtis into the inner circle of Washington power, where he remained a poker-playing adviser to Harding throughout that ill-fated presidency. In 1923, as Harding considered running for a second term, Curtis inquired about his intentions of keeping Vice President Calvin Coolidge on the ticket, perhaps hoping for the job himself. "We are not worrying about that little fellow in Massachusetts," Harding supposedly told him. "Charlie Dawes is the man!" Harding's sudden death elevated Coolidge to the presidency, and the following year it was indeed Dawes, not Curtis, who won the nomination for vice president. [19]

Senate Majority Leader

In 1923, Curtis became chairman of the Senate Rules Committee, and two years later he succeeded Lodge as majority leader—becoming the first Republican to hold the official title of party floor leader. He did not occupy the front-row desk that was subsequently reserved for the party's leaders but instead led from the back-row seat on the center aisle. As floor leader, Curtis limited his role to that of a legislative tactician who tried to keep his party united. "You boys tell me what you want, and I'll get it through," Curtis promised. He was said to know "every senator's feelings on any pending legislation so thoroughly that he can tell in advance how that senator is going to vote." Remarkably, Curtis maintained good relations with both the conservative and progressive wings of his party. The conservative Pennsylvania Senator George Wharton Pepper recorded that Curtis as majority leader "displayed a remarkable talent for accomplishing good results for his party by what in international parlance are termed 'conversations' with the other side. He was unusually adept at making deals." The progressive Nebraska Senator George Norris noted that, while he often disagreed with Curtis on legislative matters, he never knew Curtis to violate his word or fail to carry out an agreement. Idaho Senator William Borah acclaimed Curtis "a great reconciler, a walking political encyclopedia and one of the best political poker players in America." [20]

Journalists described majority leader Curtis as one of the greatest "whisperers" in Congress. "Whenever he took his favorite pose, with a short fat arm coiled around another Senator's shoulders, the Press Gallery got busy," wrote one reporter. "It was a sure sign that something was doing. . . .'Talk, talk, talk,' he would complain to the reporters about the endless Senate deliberations." Curtis believed "that everything can be fixed by friendly and confidential getting together." The press depicted Curtis as taciturn, not given to long speeches, and unhappy with the Senate's penchant for filibustering (Curtis had supported creating a cloture rule as early as 1911). He had a "poker face" that masked his feelings, which some attributed to his Indian ancestry.[21]

As majority leader, Curtis loyally supported the Coolidge administration, but as a farm-state senator he strongly advocated the kind of federal farm relief that the president opposed. He consistently voted for the McNary-Haugen bills that Coolidge vetoed. In May 1928, however, he shifted his vote to sustain—by a one-vote margin—Coolidge's veto. He explained that, regardless of his belief in the issue, he felt it was his duty as leader to stand by the president. This was not an easy vote for Curtis, who at the time was an announced candidate to succeed Coolidge in that year's presidential election, and who was counting on strong support from the farm states. Significantly, another senatorial candidate for the presidency, Indiana's "Sunny Jim" Watson (who later followed Curtis as majority leader), voted to override the veto.[22]

Presidential Candidate

Curtis had harbored presidential ambitions for some time. In 1924 he had been widely mentioned as a vice-presidential candidate, but his wife, Anna, was seriously ill at the time. His sister Dolly volunteered to stay with her, so that Curtis could attend the convention and improve his chances for the vice-presidential nomination. "Dolly," he replied, "I would not leave Anna now to be President of the United States, and certainly not for the Vice Presidency." (Anna Curtis died on June 29, 1924.) In 1927 President Coolidge jolted the nation by announcing that he did not choose to run in 1928. Potential candidates and the press speculated endlessly about what Coolidge meant—whether he expected the convention to deadlock and then draft him or whether he would not run under any circumstances. Curtis assumed that Coolidge was out of the race and felt assured that Coolidge favored him for president. Even Commerce Secretary Herbert Hoover privately conceded that Curtis "was a natural selection for Mr. Coolidge's type of mind." [23]

Hoover was the frontrunner, but the farm states had remained strongly opposed to him ever since his service as "Food Czar" during the First World War, as well as because he opposed the McNary-Haugen bills. Curtis and Hoover had never been close. Recalling that Hoover had campaigned for Democratic candidates in 1918, Curtis had tried to prevent President Harding from appointing Hoover to the cabinet. Hoover saw Curtis as one of a half-dozen senators who were trying to stop his nomination by heaping attacks on him. "Their favorite name for me was 'Sir Herbert,' a reference to my periodic residence in England," Hoover recalled with some indignation.[24]

After announcing for president, Curtis made no speeches and continued to devote his attention to his functions as Senate majority leader. The *New York Times* called his campaign "quieter than gumshoes." This was how Curtis wanted it. Serving as his own campaign manager, he planned to work the back rooms as he always had, hoping that if the convention frontrunners deadlocked, he would emerge as the compromise candidate—in the way the delegates had turned to Warren Harding in 1920. About the only publicity his campaign received occurred when a Senate page stamped the words "Curtis for President" in the snow around the Capitol. Not until Curtis reached the convention in Kansas City did he speak out against Hoover. He warned that the Republicans could not afford to nominate a candidate who would place the party "on the defensive from the day he is named." Despite caravans of farmers who protested against Hoover, the commerce secretary easily won the Republican nomination on the first ballot.[25]

Eating Bitter Words

To balance the ticket, Republicans sought a farm-state man for vice president and chose Charles Curtis of Kansas. Insisting that he had never sought the vice-presidency, Curtis agreed to run because of his loyalty to the party. Reporters viewed the choice of Curtis as "the perfect touch of irony" for the convention, given his earlier opposition to Hoover. "I can see him yet as he stood before the convention gulping at his pride under the klieg lights," recalled reporter Thomas L. Stokes:

> He had eaten his bitter words, but he was suffering from indigestion, you could see. His bald head gleamed, as if still feverish under the indignity of second place on the ticket. His mustache twitched in pain, as he tried to smile. It was only a contorted grin that creased his swarthy face. In the press section we nudged each other and chuckled cruelly.[26]

During the campaign, Curtis visited the incumbent vice president, Charles Dawes. Sympa-thetically, Dawes noted that Curtis looked pretty worn out, his hand was in a sling because a car door had slammed on his fingers, and he had not much voice left. Later, however, listening to Curtis speak on the radio, Dawes bristled when Curtis referred to the vice-presidency as amounting to nothing. Although he recognized that the remark was intended to sound modest and was made in jest, Dawes recorded in his journal, "But when I find him tired, with a husky voice and bandaged arm, resting after a five thousand-mile trip and preparing to start on ten thousand miles more, I am inclined to think that he places quite a high value on the office." [27]

The Hoover-Curtis ticket rode to victory that November over the Democratic ticket of Alfred Smith and Joseph T. Robinson. Each of the vice-presidential candidates served as his party's floor leader in the Senate, and, despite their political differences, the two were known as "chums." Curtis was celebrated as a "stand patter," the most regular of Republicans, and yet a man who could always bargain with his party's progressives and with senators from across the center aisle. Newspapers claimed that Curtis knew the Senate rules better than any other senator and declared him "the most competent man in Congress to look after the legislative program of the administration." [28]

This was not to be. Hoover and Curtis remained alienated after the strains of campaigning against each other for the nomination. Since their ticket had been a marriage of convenience, there was little love to lose over the next four years. Neither man mentioned the other in his inaugural address, and except for formal occasions they seem to have had as little to do with each other as possible. A politico not identified with issues or ideas, Curtis could never measure up to Hoover's standards and never became an inside player. Although Curtis attended some cabinet meetings, his advice was neither sought nor followed. He spent his vice-presidency presiding over the Senate, and on a few occasions casting tie-breaking votes. Sixty-nine years old when he took office, Curtis was no longer the vigorous politician of his youth.[29]

A Subtle Transformation

Curtis enjoyed the status of the vice-presidency and made much of his rise "from Kaw tepee to Capitol." As the first American of Indian ancestry to reach high office, he decorated his office with Native American artifacts and posed for pictures wearing Indian headdresses. But the press who covered him noted that Charles Curtis had changed in many ways, both subtle and conspicuous. As a senator, he had always been a "placid, humble, unchanging, decent fellow," but when he began to harbor presidential ambitions "his humility turned inside out." Curtis grew pompous, demanding that past intimates address him as the vice president of the United States and giving the impression that he felt that he, rather than Herbert Hoover, should be occupying the White House. Perhaps sensing that resentment, the Hoover White House never trusted Curtis as a legislative lieutenant. Reporters who watched him believed that the frustrated Curtis, having been so busy and influential as majority leader, "just had to have something to do" as vice president. He found his outlet as "a stern and unbending disciplinarian in the Senate and a defiant defender of vice presidential rank and precedent there and elsewhere, particularly at dinner tables." Or, as one Washington hostess noted archly, "Mr. Curtis openly exulted in the ephemeral effulgence of the limelight which shone upon him." [30]

Curtis' search for status revived the issue of an official vice-presidential residence. The wealthy widow of Missouri Senator John B. Henderson lived in a brownstone castle on 16th Street, on a hillside several blocks north of the White House. For years Mrs. Henderson had lobbied to rechristen 16th Street as the Avenue of the Presidents and had persuaded many embassies to locate along the street—by selling them inexpensive parcels of land. Mrs. Henderson became convinced that the street would be the perfect location for a permanent vice-presidential dwelling, suitable for entertaining, and she offered to give the government a house overlooking Meridian Hill Park, whose land she had also contributed to the city. Earlier, Vice President Calvin Coolidge had declined a similar offer, but Curtis was much more receptive, and sent his sister Dolly Curtis Gann out to inspect the property. She pronounced the house "lovely" and appropriate for its purposes, arguing that a vice president "should not have the social duties now incumbent upon him unless he is to be in a position to fulfill them properly and comfortably." But a member of the Henderson family objected to the elderly Mrs. Henderson's penchant for giving away her property, and the deal fell through. Not for another half century would vice presidents have an official residence. [31]

A Tempest in a Teapot

When the stock market crashed in 1929, the nation began to slip into the worst economic depression in its history. At a moment when people wanted positive action from their political leaders, poor Curtis became embarrassingly embroiled in a "tempest in a teapot." His sister Dolly openly feuded with Alice Roosevelt Longworth, the daughter of Theodore Roosevelt and wife of House Speaker Nicholas Longworth, over their relative positions in protocol. "Princess Alice" admitted making a "little mischief" over the affair. After Curtis' wife died, Dolly had invited him to live at her Washington home and had acted as his official hostess. Dolly Gann asserted that as hostess for the vice president she should be seated ahead of the congressional and diplomatic wives at Washington dinners. "At that there was a cackle of excited discussion about the propriety of designating any one not a wife to hold the rank of one," observed Alice Longworth. Alice raised the issue with her husband Nick, who disapproved of Dolly Gann's pretensions and used the controversy as an excuse to avoid going to Prohibition-era "dry" dinner parties that he hated to attend. All this caused a "torrent of newspaper publicity," predominantly negative. William Allen White's *Emporia Gazette* proclaimed:

> If Washington does not do right by our Dolly, there will be a terrible ruckus in Kansas. We will be satisfied with nothing less than that she be borne into the dinner on the shoulders of Mrs. Nick Longworth, seated in the center of the table as an ornament with a candelabra in each hand

and fed her soup with a long-handled spoon by the wife of the Secretary of State.[32]

Bad press dogged Curtis and he assumed the public image of a Throttlebottom, especially as a result of his panicky response to the bonus marchers in 1932. World War I veterans had marched on Washington to demand that Congress pass legislation enabling them to receive early payment of their promised bonus for wartime service. As a senator, Curtis had sponsored an earlier bonus bill and, although he himself had never served in the military, he frequently cited his father's Civil War service in seeking veterans' support for his campaigns. But when the marchers camped around Washington and paraded to the Capitol, Curtis urged President Hoover to call out the troops. The president, however, tried to keep calm and maintain the peace.[33]

The Depression Sinks the Ticket

In July 1932, some four hundred men marched to the Capitol grounds. When the architect of the Capitol had the lawn sprinklers turned on, the marchers gave up their idea of camping on the grounds and instead began a single-file march around the Capitol Building. A nervous Vice President Curtis announced that "Neither Speaker [John Nance] Garner nor I issued any permits to parade inside Capitol Grounds, and for this reason I believe they should be kept off." The vice president had a "stormy session" with the District of Columbia's police chief, Pelham Glassford, who informed him that only the president could call out the army. Curtis then contacted the U.S. Marines to have them stand ready for an emergency. But the marines took the vice president too literally and sent two companies wearing trench helmets to the Capitol, riding on the city trollies. Curtis claimed to have been mis-understood, but his calling out the marines made him even more the subject of national jokes.[34]

As the depression worsened and the presidential election approached, many Republicans talked of dumping Curtis from the ticket in favor of a stronger candidate who might help Hoover's chance of reelection. Curtis himself recognized his vulnerability and talked of running for the Senate seat from Kansas instead. But with his sister Dolly rallying support among the delegates, Curtis was renominated on the Hoover ticket to face Franklin D. Roosevelt and John Nance Garner. In the depth of the depression, the Hoover-Curtis campaign never stood a chance. Hecklers challenged Curtis when he spoke. Why had he not fed the veterans in Washington? they yelled at one stop. "I've fed more than you have, you dirty cowards!" Curtis shouted back at the crowd. "I'm not afraid of you!" The crowd chanted "Hurrah for Roosevelt!"[35]

A landslide defeat in November 1932 retired Charles Curtis from a political career that had begun almost fifty years earlier when he ran for Shawnee County district attorney. Now, to the surprise of many Kansans, Curtis seemed to have "lost interest in Kansas." Having spent so much of his life in the nation's capital, he remained in Washington, where he practiced law and talked politics. In 1935 he became chairman of the Republican senatorial campaign committee, hoping the party could win back the Senate majority the next year, but he died in February 1936 at his sister Dolly's home. A party regular—"one-eighth Kaw Indian and a one-hundred per cent Republican" as he liked to tell audiences—he had been yoked to one of the most intellectual and least political of all American presidents, and the incompatibility of the team made his vice-presidency a dismal failure.[36]

NOTES

[1] Quoted in Chalmers Roberts, *First Rough Draft: A Journalist's Journal of Our Times* (New York, 1973), p. 268.

[2] For an especially egregious example, see Don C. Seitz, *From Kaw Teepee to Capitol: The Life Story of Charles Curtis, Indian, Who Has Risen to High Estate* (New York, 1928).

[3] William E. Unrau, "The Mixed-Blood Connection: Charles Curtis and Kaw Detribalization," in *Kansas and the West: Bicentennial Essays in Honor of Nyle H. Miller*, ed. Forrest R. Blackburn, et al. (Topeka, KS, 1976), pp. 151–61; William E. Unrau, *Mixed-Bloods and Tribal Dissolution: Charles Curtis and the Quest for Indian Identity* (Lawrence, KS, 1989), pp. 9–10, 58, 64–65; Marvin Ewy, "Charles Curtis of Kansas: Vice President of the United States, 1929–1933," *Emporia State Research Studies* 10 (December 1961): 6–9.

[4] Unrau, *Mixed-Bloods and Tribal Dissolution*, pp. 70–75.

[5] Ibid., pp. 61–62, 81–82; *New York Times*, June 17, 1928; Seitz, p. 128.

[6] Unrau, *Mixed Bloods and Tribal Dissolution*, pp. 92–93; Ewy, p. 11.

[7] Dolly Gann, *Dolly Gann's Book* (Garden City, NY, 1933), pp. 1, 4–5; Unrau, *Mixed Bloods and Tribal Dissolution*, pp. 97–98.

[8] Unrau, *Mixed Bloods and Tribal Dissolution*, pp. 99–101; Ewy, pp. 15–17.

[9] William Allen White, *The Autobiography of William Allen White* (New York, 1946), p. 196.

[10] Ibid., pp. 196–97.

[11] Seitz, pp. 161–62; Ewy, p. 23.

[12] Unrau, *Mixed-Bloods and Tribal Dissolution*, pp. 119–23; Unrau, "The Mixed-Blood Connection," p. 159.

[13] White, pp. 304, 352, 366.

[14] Horace Samuel Merrill and Marion Galbraith Merrill, *The Republican Command, 1897–1913* (Lexington, KY, 1971), pp. 26, 288.

[15] Ibid., pp. 27, 295.

[16] Ewy, pp. 27–29.

[17] Ibid., pp. 30–31; "Heap Big Chief," *American Mercury* 17 (August 1929): 401.

[18] Andrew Sinclair, *The Available Man: The Life Behind the Masks of Warren Gamaliel Harding* (New York, 1965), pp. 143–49; White, p. 546.

[19] Curtis served as an honorary pallbearer at Harding's funeral, and was later active in the effort to suppress news of Harding's illegitimate child by Nan Britton. Francis Russell, *The Shadow of Blooming Grove: Warren G. Harding in His Times* (New York, 1968), pp. 571, 597, 626.

[20] Irving G. Williams, *The Rise of the Vice Presidency* (Washington, D.C., 1956), p. 144; Seitz, pp. 172, 178; George Wharton Pepper, *In The Senate* (Philadelphia, 1930), p. 35: *New York Times*, June 19, 1928; Washington *Evening Star*, February 8, 1936.

[21] "Heap Big Chief," p. 410; Seitz, pp. 172–73.

[22] *New York Times*, May 26, 1928.

[23] Gann, p. 74; Herbert Hoover, *The Memoirs of Herbert Hoover: The Cabinet and the Presidency, 1920–1933* (New York, 1952), p. 194.

[24] John D. Hicks, *Republican Ascendancy, 1921–1933* (New York, 1960), p. 201; Sinclair, p. 184; Russell, p. 433; Hoover, p. 192.

[25] *New York Times*, February 3, April 26, June 11–15, 1928; Ewy, pp. 38–39.

[26] Thomas L. Stokes, *Chip Off My Shoulder* (Princeton, NJ, 1940), pp. 230–31.

[27] Charles G. Dawes, *Notes as Vice President, 1928–1929* (Boston, 1935), p. 123.

[28] *New York Times*, September 2, November 11, 1928.

[29] Williams, p. 146; Ewy, p. 43.

[30] "Heap Big Chief," pp. 401–6, 411; Gene Smith, *The Shattered Dream: Herbert Hoover and the Great Depression.* (New York, 1970), p. 185; Frances Parkinson Keyes, *Capital Kaleidoscope: The Story of a Washington Hostess* (New York, 1937), p. 245.

[31] Gann, pp. 191–92.

[32] Alice Roosevelt Longworth, *Crowded Hours* (New York, 1933) pp. 73, 330–33; David Burner, *Herbert Hoover: A Public Life* (New York, 1979), p. 291.

[33] Daniel J. Lisio, *The President and Protest: Hoover, Conspiracy, and The Bonus Riot* (Columbia, MO, 1974), p. 218.

[34] Fleta Campbell Springe, "Glassford and the Siege of Washington," *Harpers* 165 (November 1932): 649–51; Smith, p. 149.

[35] Williams, p. 147; Ewy, pp. 51–52; Lisio, p. 244.

[36] Unrau, *Mixed-Bloods and Tribal Dissolution*, p. 112.

Chapter 32

JOHN NANCE GARNER
1933–1941

JOHN NANCE GARNER

Chapter 32

JOHN NANCE GARNER

32nd Vice President: 1933–1941

My belief has always been in Executive leadership, not Executive rulership.

—JOHN NANCE GARNER

"There is hardly any limitation upon the ways in which the Vice President might be of service to the President," wrote Franklin Delano Roosevelt in a 1920 issue of the *Saturday Evening Post* when he was the Democratic vice-presidential candidate. The vice president, Roosevelt suggested, should be entrusted with "carrying the large burden of interpreting administration policies to Congress and to the public." Like the vice president in a modern corporation, he should be a "super handy man," handling various matters of detail and "leaving the president free to deal mainly with matters of policy." [1]

Upon becoming president a dozen years later, however, Roosevelt had adjusted his image of the vice-presidency to more closely match the predispositions of the man that the Democratic National Convention nominated to be his running mate, John Nance Garner. As vice president, Garner would indeed work extensively at "interpreting administration policies to Congress," as the White House's chief liaison to Capitol Hill, but he did little to communicate these policies to the public because he refused to be a spokesman or campaigner. He did provide the administration with expertise on "matters of detail" but limited this advice mostly to the intricacies of maneuvering legislation through Congress.

Garner's long career in the House of Representatives had prepared him for the vice-presidency. He had rarely originated innovative ideas to answer the problems of the country, yet once someone else conceived an idea for legislation, Garner was often called upon to serve as a parliamentary midwife. He would expertly guide the plan through the House, from negotiations in smoky back rooms to a debate and vote on the floor.

On the surface, there appears to be little mystery about John Nance Garner. Plainspoken and refreshingly unpretentious, "Cactus Jack" from the tiny back-country town of Uvalde, Texas, was by all accounts a man of common words, simple tastes, a frugal lifestyle, and an unswerving pragmatism that prompted Roosevelt to dub him "Mr. Common Sense." Yet, for all his uncomplicated personality, Garner remains an enigmatic presence in history. For thirty-eight years in Washington, from 1903 to 1941, Garner continued to be a secretive back-room operator. Because nearly all of his most important political activities took place out of the public eye and off the record, his personal motivations or convictions remain unclear. It is particularly difficult to gauge the degree to which, in his role as vice president, Garner should be credited for the legislative successes of the first Roosevelt administration or be blamed for the failures of the second. [2]

Youth

Garner was born on November 22, 1868, in Red River County, Texas. Although political promoters later romanticized his modest upbringing in a mud-chinked log cabin, his mother, Rebecca

Walpole Garner, was the daughter of the town banker and a descendent of English aristocracy. At age eighteen, young Garner set off to enroll at the University of Tennessee, the state in which both sides of his family had roots. Finding himself handicapped by an insufficient preparatory education and various respiratory problems, however, the young man soon returned home and found work in a law office. By studying in his spare time, Garner gained entrance to the bar in 1890. He then failed in his first bid for political office as a twenty-one-year-old candidate for city attorney.

A Back-Room Politician

Garner moved to Uvalde, Texas, for the health benefits of its dry climate. During his successful campaign for judge of Uvalde County, he met Ettie Rheiner, who soon became his cherished partner as both beloved wife and career-long personal secretary.[3] Garner served as county judge from 1893 to 1896, followed by a tenure in the Texas state legislature from 1898 to 1902. When Texas gained an additional congressional seat after the 1900 census, Garner managed to secure the chairmanship of a special redistricting committee. He used this position to carve out an advantageous congressional district, from which he ran successfully in 1902 for the U.S. House of Representatives.

During his first several years in the House, Garner was a silent backbencher who ingratiated himself with his colleagues by cultivating friendships and by his record of party loyalty. He was eventually rewarded with coveted committee appointments, and by the 1920s his seniority had made him the ranking Democrat on the Ways and Means Committee and chairman of the Democrats' Committee on Committees, which chose that party's members for all House committees. His vociferous attacks on Treasury Secretary Andrew Mellon's economic programs earned him a national reputation as "a Jefferson/Jackson Democrat—egalitarian, rural, states' rights oriented, and populist."[4]

In 1929, Garner was elected the floor leader of a House Democratic party whose morale and representation had suffered a crushing blow in the 1928 elections. As minority leader, Garner re-lied upon informal methods to strengthen the party's influence. He enjoyed a close rapport with Republican Speaker Nicholas Longworth, his debonair alter ego. Said Garner, "I was the heathen and Nick was the aristocrat." This congressional odd couple cohosted a daily bipartisan gathering of lawmakers in a small room, deep in the bowels of the Capitol, which became known as the "Bureau of Education." Like The Boar's Head Club, the site of Speaker Joe Cannon's drinking and gambling congregations that Garner had attended decades earlier, the bureau provided a place for politicians to relax and get to know one another over a cordial drink, ignoring the Eighteenth Amendment's ban on alcoholic beverages. The bureau also served as an informal forum for constructive, off-the-record communications and negotiations between the two parties. In this setting, Longworth said that Garner operated as "a one man cabal"[5]

Garner presented only four major bills to Congress under his own name in his entire three decades in the House, a fact a longtime House colleague, James F. Byrnes of South Carolina, attributed to Garner's collaborative parliamentary style: "It was his policy, whenever he had an idea . . . to induce a prospective opponent or a doubtful supporter to sponsor the legislation. When he achieved that, he knew his purpose was accomplished." As a result, Byrnes noted, "The *Congressional Record* will not show the remarkable influence he exercised upon the members of the House and Senate during his long service." Garner himself later asserted that he had "no more useful years than those in the ranks of or as the leader of the opposition to the majority."[6]

Between the 1930 congressional elections and the opening of the Seventy-second Congress on December 7, 1931, fourteen members-elect, including Longworth, died.[7] After special elections were held to replace the deceased, the Democrats emerged with a 219 to 214 advantage, enabling Garner to become Speaker and the titular head of his party as its highest national officeholder. Garner did not share the same close personal friendship with the new Republican minority leader, New York's Bertrand Small, that he had enjoyed with Longworth. The two parties were becoming increasingly polarized in their approaches to solving the crisis that gripped the national economy. In addition, a decade in the minority had permitted many House Democrats to lapse into habits of frequent absenteeism and maverick voting patterns, which the party with its slim majority could now ill afford.

The new Speaker enforced party discipline with a severity that inspired Sam Rayburn to call him, "a terrible, table-thumping Democrat." Under the slogan "You've got to bloody your knuckles!" Garner regularly summoned House Democrats to caucus or bureau meetings, where they wrangled out consensus policies to which he would then "bind" all of their votes. "And if they didn't stay bound," he recalled, "I'd put 'em down in my book and they'd never get through paying for it." Of his overriding concern for party solidarity, Garner once declared, "I have always done what I thought was best for my country, never varying unless I was advised that two-thirds of the Democrats were for a bill and then I voted for it." [8]

In his response to the Great Depression, this dedication to maintaining a governing consensus eventually outweighed Garner's normally conservative principles, and he grew increasingly supportive of federal intervention in economic affairs. At first, the Speaker attempted to forge bipartisan cooperation in support of Herbert Hoover's economic programs, such as the Reconstruction Finance Corporation and the Glass-Steagall banking bills. This conciliatory approach meant reversing his previous opposition to such measures as a manufacturers' sales tax designed to increase government revenue in the face of mounting deficits—favored by business groups for more than a decade—and establishment of a moratorium on foreign debts in order to relieve some of the financial burden on the nation's European trading partners. [9]

By 1932, however, the overwhelming consensus among congressional Democrats and the public against the sales tax and in favor of additional relief measures convinced Garner to repudiate Hoover's program. He proposed his own federal relief spending bill through a massive public works program. This action was highly uncharacteristic, given his reluctance to offer his own proposals and his long record of opposition to increased government spending. Hoover vetoed the bill, condemning it as "the most gigantic pork barrel raid ever proposed to an American Congress!" Relations between the two men never recovered. [10]

The Election of 1932

A "Garner for President" movement emerged in January 1932. Instigated by an editorial campaign in the newspapers of William Randolph Hearst, it was independent of any initiative or encouragement by Garner. Over such other prospective nominees as Franklin Roosevelt, Al Smith, and former Secretary of War Newton Baker, Hearst endorsed Garner as the candidate he considered most likely to adhere to his own agenda, which included instituting a national sales tax and keeping the United States out of the League of Nations. [11] The Garner bandwagon included many conservative southern and western politicians who felt ideologically and personally comfortable with Garner. A contemporary journalist attributed the attraction of the Garner candidacy to the desire of "the rank and file Democrats to get away from everything the East implies and to find a good, safe politician with an innocuous record, what they want is a Democratic Coolidge." Others supported Garner only as a stalking-horse for another candidate or as one of a variety of candidates whose delegates could collectively block Roosevelt. [12]

Garner himself was less interested in becoming president than in ensuring his tenure as Speaker by nominating a candidate who could capture the White House with long enough coattails to solidify the party's majority in Congress. Roosevelt's candidacy, he concluded, was the best bet to unite and strengthen the party enough to achieve this goal. Garner therefore ignored the efforts of his promoters and refused to proclaim himself a candidate, although he never actually ordered them to desist. As a consequence, Garner found himself holding a tiger by the tail at the Democratic National Convention in Chicago, where he placed third on the first ballot behind Roosevelt and Smith. After three ballots, during which Garner's numbers increased marginally, Roosevelt's strategists realized that without Garner's support they would never achieve the necessary two-thirds vote that the party's century-old rule mandated for nomination. They feared they were about to lose the Mississippi delegation, which operated under a rule that gave all twenty of its votes to the candidate favored by a simple majority of its members. To break the impasse, Roosevelt campaign manager James Farley called Garner's campaign manager, Representative Sam Rayburn, to a meeting in Mississippi Senator Pat Harrison's hotel room. They agreed to ask Garner to transfer his delegates to Roosevelt in return for the vice-presidential nomination. Garner reluctantly agreed in order to avoid the type of deadlocked convention that in 1924 had produced the unsatisfying compromise candidacy of John W. Davis and his losing campaign. Garner consoled himself with the thought that the apparently less demanding office "might be a nice way for me to taper off my career."[13]

Roosevelt wanted to use Garner's homespun appeal in extensive campaigning as a sort of "Texas Al Smith." But Garner refused, believing that such efforts would be irrelevant, since he regarded elections as merely a referendum on the incumbent's performance. He made only two speeches and was briefly employed as Roosevelt's peacemaking mediator to Smith before being dismissed to go home to Uvalde. There he was reelected to his House seat on the same day he was elected vice president of the United States.[14]

Between the November 1932 election and the March 1933 inauguration, Roosevelt frequently phoned Garner in Uvalde to solicit his opinions about proposals for legislation and organizing the new government. Although Garner offered relatively few legislative proposals, he did advocate government guarantees of banking deposits, an idea he promoted in Congress despite the objections of the president-elect. Eventually, the groundswell of congressional support for the plan won Roosevelt over, and he endorsed the Vandenberg Amendment to the Glass-Steagall Banking Act, creating the Federal Deposit Insurance Corporation. In this case, Garner appeared to be ahead of the "New Deal" curve, belying his later reputation as an inflexible reactionary.

Inauguration Day in 1933 marked a ceremonial demonstration of mutual affection and gratitude between the outgoing Speaker and his House colleagues as the procession of 400 House members and another 150 members-elect escorted Garner through the Capitol to the Senate chamber, where he thanked them with an emotional farewell speech in which he grieved, "my heart will always be in the House."[15]

First Term—Supporting the President's Program

In many respects, Garner's new job was a step down. He called the vice-presidency "the spare tire on the automobile of government," "a no man's land somewhere between the legislative and the executive branch," and "not worth a bucket of warm spit." He bemoaned the fact that the vice president had "no arsenal from which to draw power," believing that only when men "have friendship for him and faith in and respect for his judgement can he be influential."[16]

In the Senate, the new vice president renewed political alliances with over twenty of his former colleagues who had moved there from the House, including such influential Democratic senators as Arkansas' Joe Robinson, Mississippi's Pat Harrison, Kentucky's Alben Barkley, Virginia's Carter Glass, South Carolina's James Byrnes, Texas' Morris Sheppard, and Maryland's Millard Tydings. These men were products of the Wilsonian progressive New Freedom movement, but by the 1930s some of them had become the leaders of the party's conservative wing of southern and western Democrats, who held the key committee chairmanships. Garner's vice-presidency enhanced the influence of these men because he often sympathized with them in their efforts to limit the liberalism of the New Deal.[17]

Garner's familiarity with the mechanics and personalities of Congress initially proved invaluable to the new Roosevelt administration. Before committing himself to the innovative experiments of his "Brains Trust," Roosevelt asked for Garner's realistic assessment of congressional reaction. After observing Garner in cabinet meetings, Roosevelt's Postmaster General James Farley came "to look upon him as one of the truly great public men of this generation" because of

Garner's mastery of "such intricate problems as government financing, taxation, tariffs, and revenue bills." Once Roosevelt decided on a new proposal, Garner acted as his political general, personally leading the White House troops as they stormed Capitol Hill.[18]

Most of Garner's political generalship was of the guerrilla variety. He continued to host regular Bureau of Education meetings in a room near the Senate floor. Darrell St. Claire, assistant secretary of the Senate, remembered that "the whiskey vapor would come flowing into the chamber from the formal office, along with the laughter." Garner would lure guests there from both the legislative and the executive branches, ambushing them with bombardments of reason and liquor designed to "hypnotize, mesmerize and otherwise to get our friends to approve matters in a helpful way."[19]

Garner did not always agree with Roosevelt's policies during the "First One Hundred Days" of the new administration, but he encouraged other reluctant lawmakers to follow him in supporting the president because it was "good politics and good patriotism." "Sometimes conditions in a country justify temporary violations of deep principles of government," he reasoned to one congressman, "if ever there was such a time it is now." To another Democrat who was skeptical of Roosevelt, "It doesn't matter what kind of a fool you think he is; he's your fool just as long as he's President and the leader of your party." In a letter responding to criticism of the administration from a Texas lumberman friend named John Henry Kirby he admitted, "You can't do everything you want to and I can't do half of what I would like to do. You can't control everybody you would like to and I am in a similar fix."[20]

One historian of the vice-presidency rated Garner as "a combination presiding officer, Cabinet officer, personal counselor, legislative tactician, Cassandra and sounding board" for the administration and "undoubtedly one of the most powerful of the twentieth century Vice-Presidents."[21] However, there were some tasks that Garner stubbornly avoided, especially those that would involve publicity, which he felt was inappropriate for a vice president. He refused to act as a spokesman for the administration because, he told Roosevelt, "Any speech or statement I made would be searched to find a difference between you and me." Instead, when the press begged him for comments, he declared, "I'm a member of a firm—the junior member. Go to headquarters for the news." Just as he had in 1932, he begged out of campaigning publicly for his party in the national and statewide elections. He also declined a radio station's offer to give weekly fifteen-minute addresses at $1,500 each, which he thought would be exploitative of his office.[22]

Garner further absolved himself of the traditional vice-presidential obligations to represent the administration at a variety of ceremonial and gala affairs. He adamantly protected his privacy and his personal time with his wife, refusing even the accompaniment of the Secret Service. "I don't want those constables protecting me. There is not anybody crazy enough to shoot a Vice-President," he declared.[23]

Thanks to the large Democratic majorities, Garner needed to cast a tie-breaking vote in the Senate on only two minor matters, but he still made his presence felt as presiding officer. One of the cagey veteran's favorite parliamentary tricks was to "buggy-whip" bills through debate with an unexpected staccato call of "There-being-no-objections-the-bill-is-passed" and a sudden rap of the gavel. He also descended frequently from the dais to lobby the senators in attendance.[24]

The cantankerous Garner had little patience with the flamboyant senator from Louisiana, Huey Long. Long once asked Garner to require all of his colleagues to stay and listen to his filibuster on the National Recovery Act, to which Garner retorted: "In the first place the Senator from Louisiana should not ask that. In the second place, it would be cruel and unusual punishment." Another time he remarked to humorist Will Rogers before the convening of a session, "Will, sometimes I think the hearing in my right ear and the vision in my right eye isn't as good as it used to be. Long sits on my right. . . . I may not be able to hear or see Huey this morning."[25]

Long antagonized Garner on another occasion by drawling: "Mr. President, I rise to make a parliamentary inquiry. How should a Senator who is half in favor of this bill and half against it cast his vote?" Snapped an exasperated Garner: "Get a saw and saw yourself in two. That's what you ought to do anyway!" [26]

Roosevelt's first term was not without a few points of contention between the president and his vice president, foreshadowing their later problems. Garner had grave misgivings about the National Recovery Act, diplomatic recognition of Russia, and the embargo clause in the Neutrality Act. Roosevelt was somewhat dissatisfied with Garner's choices when the Senate authorized him to select one member to the London Economic Conference in 1933 and three to the Nye munitions industry investigation committee. The president also suspected that Garner had botched his plan to slip the soldier's bonus bill of 1935 through Congress by leaking the strategy to his congressional friends. [27]

At the 1936 Democratic National Convention in Pittsburgh, the cumbersome 1832 rule requiring that two-thirds of all delegates approve both the presidential and vice-presidential nominations was overturned in favor of a simple majority. The rules change enabled future Democratic presidential nominees to choose their own running mates, rather than accept the consensus of the convention. Initiated by Roosevelt, this reform was passed largely in deference to his personal prestige. Yet Garner's presence on the ticket also must have made the delegates feel comfortable in doing so. It is difficult to imagine the same rule passing in 1940, when Roosevelt offered as his running mate Henry Wallace, a less popular man within the party, who would not likely have been approved under the former rules.

Second Term—An Obstacle to Roosevelt

The second term of the Roosevelt-Garner administration saw the breakdown of the working relationship between the president and vice president. Garner objected to Roosevelt's determination to escalate the New Deal's centralizing of the federal government, expanding government regulation and spending programs, and "revolutionizing" the Democratic party.

The first issue over which the two men had a truly acrimonious dispute was Roosevelt's labor agenda. Garner objected to such New Deal pro-labor legislation as the Wagner-Connery Act of 1935 and the Black-Connery bill of 1937. He fiercely opposed organized labor's 1936 sit-down strikes, considering them a violation of business owners' property rights. When the president proved reluctant to repudiate these tactics, Garner secretly lobbied Congress in support of efforts by Texas Representative Martin Dies, Jr., and South Carolina Senator James Byrnes to pass congressional resolutions condemning the strikes. When Republican Senator Arthur Vandenberg of Michigan gave a ringing speech on the floor of the Senate in support of Byrnes' amendment, Garner jumped down from his presiding seat to offer his congratulations. [28]

On February 5, 1937, Roosevelt called Garner and a handful of Democratic congressional leaders to a meeting at the White House, where he stunned them with an audacious plan to reorganize the Supreme Court. Up to six new justices would be chosen by the president in an attempt to ensure many years of judicial approval for his liberal legislative agenda.

Garner himself was not among those critics who considered the proposal to be a threat to the judiciary's independence, believing that "no President can control that court." However, he was deeply concerned about the threat to party unity posed by Roosevelt's somewhat reckless method of handling such a controversial proposal. Garner complained that the president sent the plan to Congress, "without notice after saying he had no legislative program other than outlined . . . it was not in the party platform nor was it taken after consultation with Congressional leaders who would have to put it through. Party policy is not made by one man without consultation with elected officials from another branch of government." [29]

While never issuing a public statement against the bill, Garner demonstrated his disapproval with two symbolic gestures. First, he held his nose and gave an emphatic "thumbs-down" sign as the bill was introduced on the floor of the Senate. Then, during the subsequent congressional debate, Garner suddenly departed from the capital in June to return to Texas. It was the first time he had left Washington while Congress was in session. Roosevelt was furious. "Why in hell did Jack have to leave at this time for?" he fumed, "This is a fine time to jump ship." In response to widespread speculation in the press about a rift between the president and himself, Garner issued a public statement from Texas declaring that his departure was in no way meant as a protest. "I asked the Boss," he claimed, "and he told me it was all right for me to go fishing." Garner eventually returned to Washington, but the death of Senate Democratic Majority Leader Joseph Robinson in July 1937 mortally wounded Roosevelt's court proposal. The faithful Robinson had tenaciously led the fight for the bill on the president's behalf. After his passing, Roosevelt assigned that task to the unenthusiastic Garner. Meanwhile, Roosevelt's intervention to help loyal New Dealer Alben Barkley succeed Robinson as majority leader provoked resentment from many senators, as well as the vice president. When the Judiciary Committee reduced Roosevelt's Court packing plan to the point where it became unrecognizable, Roosevelt was convinced that Garner had collaborated with the opposition. For his part, Garner blamed Roosevelt for antagonizing the Senate by interfering in its internal affairs. Neither man completely trusted the other again. [30]

Roosevelt and Garner had fundamentally different styles and philosophies of governing. Garner was a strict traditionalist in his attitudes toward party affairs and a strict and unbending constructionist in his literal interpretations of the constitutional doctrine of separation of powers. He was a staunch defender of the sovereignty of the legislature from undue interference by the executive. Citing the low-key approach of Calvin Coolidge as a model, he once stated "My belief has always been in Executive leadership, not Executive rulership." [31]

Roosevelt, in contrast, used the powers of the presidency to set the agenda of his party and the tone of the legislative debate. Under Roosevelt, the White House increasingly issued preemptive public announcements to marshal public support to gain political leverage. Garner objected to Roosevelt that this threatened to "jeopardize the legislative program by giving out premature information." He complained privately that Roosevelt wanted too much power. "He has changed in office. He does not delegate. His nature is [to] want to do everything himself." [32]

Purging the Party

By 1938, the president was sufficiently frustrated by the conservative Democrats in Congress to attempt a "purge" of the party. He embarked on a campaign through southern and western states to endorse liberal candidates in primary challenges to such conservative incumbents as Senators Millard Tydings of Maryland, Walter George of Georgia, and Guy Gillette of Iowa. Garner argued to Roosevelt that his intervention in local elections was an unfair invasion of a local politician's "own constituency and his own orbit" and could only provoke resentment from voters who would regard it as "Presidential arrogance." He warned Roosevelt, "You can't defeat the Southern Democrats and if you defeat the Democrats in the North you will get Republicans instead." [33]

This prediction proved true, as the November elections resulted in the Republicans gaining eighty-one House and eight Senate seats. Although only one of Roosevelt's primary election targets (Representative John J. O'Connor of New York City) lost, several of Garner's close friends in the Senate, including Connecticut's Augustine Lonergan, New Hampshire's Fred Brown, and Wisconsin's Francis Duffey, were among the Democratic casualties in the general elections. Roosevelt then further insulted conservatives by appointing to key administrative posts several New Dealers who had been defeated in the elections. Garner lamented to Postmaster General James Farley that Roosevelt had "stirred up a hornet's nest" by entering into the primary fights. "There are now twenty men—Democrats—in the Senate who will vote against anything he wants." [34] In 1939, Congress denied virtually everything Roosevelt requested, including an undistributed profits tax, government reorganization, increased funding for the Works Progress Administration, and revision of the neutrality laws. Convinced that the crisis of the depression was essentially over and that continued relief programs threatened to create a complacently dependent lower class, Garner considered it time to roll back some of the regulatory legislation and "pump-priming" expenditures that had been passed for emergency relief during the first term.[35]

Privately, Garner confided his suspicions of several ardent New Dealers in the Roosevelt "Brains Trust." "I am not worried about the Boss. It's the people around him. I have no confidence in them." Another time Garner claimed, "I have more honest affection for him [Roosevelt] in my little finger that they have in their whole bodies." This hostility was mutual. The New Dealers were contemptuous of Garner's conservatism and his occasionally coarse behavior and disdained his somewhat shady style of old-fashioned, back-room horse trading. Identifying Garner as a convenient scapegoat for Roosevelt's frustrations in guiding his agenda through Congress, liberals within the administration launched assaults to discredit his character. Harold Ickes, writing in a June 1939 issue of *Look* magazine, accused Garner of "a traitorous knifing in the back of the commander in chief."[36]

The coming 1940 presidential election sparked the final break. Garner claimed that at the inauguration ceremony in 1937 he and the president had taken a mutual pledge to retire at the end of that term. As tumultuous events unfolded abroad, however, it became increasingly apparent that Roosevelt intended to run for an unprecedented third term, arguing that the volatility of the international situation made his presence indispensable.[37]

In December of 1939, Garner announced that, while he would not actively campaign, he would not reject the presidential nomination if he were offered it at the 1940 convention, regardless of whether Roosevelt chose to retire or run again. He thus became the first vice president of the modern era to challenge his own chief executive for the office. Garner admitted that his passive candidacy was hopeless if Roosevelt really wanted to be reelected and that he would be happy to retire to Uvalde. But his opposition to a third term motivated him to join the "Stop Roosevelt" movement. He considered himself the only candidate with a chance of attracting enough support to convince the president to retire.

During the last two years of Roosevelt's second term, Garner was the consistent frontrunner among the possible successors to Roosevelt in public opinion polls. Although the public rarely got to observe Jack Garner's actions directly, what they did know about him—or at least what they thought they knew—captured their imagination. His wheeler-dealer image, self-made wealth, and free-market convictions made him a symbol of the emerging business age. At the same time, as a rugged, individualistic frontiersman, he was a nostalgic throwback to a vanishing age, a reassuringly simple figure in an increasingly complex world. It was obvious to all that "Cactus Jack" had earned his nickname because he was a hardy survivor with a tough hide, stumpy stature, prickly disposition, and deep Texas roots.

Conservative congressmen praised Garner to their favorite reporters. The press, in turn, was usually eager to carry "good copy" about the legendary cowboy vice president who rode herd on Washington and plotted in the cloakrooms. Complained one contemporary critic, "the newspaper men have never lost an opportunity to apotheosize his mediocrity." Despite this build-up, Roosevelt correctly doubted that Garner possessed enough ambition or standing to mount a serious challenge in 1940. Yet Garner believed Roosevelt resented the press attention that was often lavished on his vice president. Postmaster General James Farley noted that Roosevelt sometimes seemed quick to blame Garner for the administration's legislative failures and that the president "did not like to see the trees grow too tall around him."[38]

Hitler's offensive across Western Europe in 1940 and the patriotic rallying around the president that the crisis inspired effectively precluded any challenge to Roosevelt's nomination. He was renominated on the first ballot at the Democratic National Convention in Chicago with the votes of 946 delegates. Farley and Garner were far behind with 72 and 61 votes, respectively. Not only did Garner not campaign for Roosevelt, he could not even bring himself to vote in the 1940 election. He went home to Uvalde, where he lived in retirement until his death at the age of ninety-eight twenty-seven years later.

Conclusion

Years after his retirement from politics, Garner mused that the country might have benefited more had he retained the speakership and used it to check the growth of Franklin Roosevelt's ambitions and powers in much the way Speaker Cannon had restrained Theodore Roosevelt. "I think I could have talked him out of a lot of things. That could have been my contribution. I would have had no desire to dictate his decisions," Garner told Bascom Timmons, his newspaper correspondent biographer, "but there would have been times when I would have told him what he could not do."[39] In a 1957 interview, Garner lamented, "If I hadn't been nominated for Vice President, I might still be speaker today." This claim does not seem farfetched, given Garner's relish for the position, his robust health, and the preservation of a Democratic majority in the House for all but two congresses during the rest of his long life.[40]

The memory of his sour second term with Garner encouraged Roosevelt to redefine drastically what he was looking for in a vice president in 1940. Henry Agard Wallace was in many ways the antithesis of Garner. As vice president, Wallace was without either the inclination or access to make his own clandestine alliances and deals that might undermine the president's authority. While Garner was a parochial thinker with isolationist convictions, Wallace was fascinated with foreign affairs and peoples and entertained ideas about how Americans could help solve their problems. An administrator rather than a politician like Garner, Wallace lacked legislative experience and extensive party ties. To some degree, Wallace resembled the corporate vice president that Roosevelt had advocated in 1920, who could handle "matters of detail."[41]

The vice-presidency of John Nance Garner stands as a watershed in the evolution of the office. His first term marked the apex of the parliamentarian as vice president; his second term represented its nadir. Perhaps no other vice president had as much impact, both positive and negative, on the legislative efforts of his administration. Garner was a specialist in an office that would soon require generalists. He was the last vice president whose duties were primarily legislative. Garner was also the last of the largely silent, Washington-based vice presidents before the coming age of modern telecommunications and travel enabled future vice presidents to assume higher profiles as representatives of their administrations, as wide-ranging campaigners, public spokesmen, and foreign emissaries.[42]

During his first term, Garner may have made a more valuable and positive contribution to his administration than any of his predecessors, but his actions in the second term did more to undermine the administration than those of any vice president since John C. Calhoun. Chosen to balance the ticket in 1932, Garner felt obligated to use all of the formal and informal powers of his office to protect the interests of the party's conservative wing that had, against his better judgment, moved him from Speaker to vice president.

NOTES

[1] Franklin D. Roosevelt, "Can the Vice President Be Useful?" *Saturday Evening Post* 193 (October 16, 1920): 8. Roosevelt also wrote that the very ambiguity of the office placed its occupant in a unique position to serve as an "additional set of eyes and ears" and as "a kind of roving commission" to study the fundamental structural problems in government, "especially where the jurisdiction or control does not rest in one department but partly in one and partly in others." By the time Roosevelt finally attempted to realize his longtime ambition to radically reorganize the federal government in 1937, however, he chose a commission of academicians rather than his vice president to study the matter and make recommendations. See Richard Polenberg, *Reorganizing Roosevelt's Government, 1936–1939* (Cambridge, MA, 1966).

[2] Attempts to solve the mysteries of Garner's career are not helped by the fact that he burned all of his personal papers soon after retiring from Washington. "I didn't want to go through the files myself," he explained. "I needed all my own energies for present activities." Bascom N. Timmons, *Garner of Texas: A Personal History* (New York, 1948), p. 286. An excellent bibliography of sources on Garner can be found in Donald R. Kennon, *The Speakers of the U.S. House of Representatives: A Bibliography, 1789–1984* (Baltimore, 1986), pp. 226–36.

[3] See Mrs. John N. [Marietta] Garner, "30 Years of Dictation," *Good Housekeeping* 94 (May 1932): 28.

[4] For an account of Garner's maneuvers for position and influence within his party, see Alex Arnett, "Garner versus Kitchin: A Study of Craft and Statecraft" in Vera Largent, ed., *The Walter Clinton Jackson Essays in the Social Sciences* (Chapel Hill, NC, 1942), pp. 133–45; Ronald M. Peters, Jr., *The American Speakership: The Office in Historical Perspective* (Baltimore, 1990), p. 111.

[5] D. B. Hardeman and Donald C. Bacon, *Rayburn: A Biography* (Austin, TX, 1987), pp. 114, 303; Timmons, p. 122.

[6] Timmons, pp. 110, 293.

[7] The 14 House members who died between the November 4, 1930, elections and the December 7, 1931, convening of the 72nd Congress were Ernest Ackerman (R-NJ), James Aswell (D-LA), Henry Cooper (R-WI), Charles Edwards (D-GA), Fletcher Hale (R-NH), George Graham (R-PA), Nicholas Longworth (R-OH), Samuel Major (D-MO), Charles Mooney (D-OH), David O'Connell (D-NY), Matthew O'Malley (D-NY), John Quayle (D-NY), Bird Vincent (R-MI), and Harry Wurzbach (R-TX).

[8] Hardeman and Bacon, pp. 116, 346; Allan Andrew Michie, *Dixie Demagogues* (New York, 1939), p. 25.

[9] For highly critical views of Garner's speakership see George Milburn, "The Statesmanship of Mr. Garner," *Harper's Magazine* (November 1932), pp. 669–82; Jordan A. Schwarz, "John Nance Garner and the Sales Tax Rebellion of 1932," *Journal of Southern History* 30 (May 1964): 162–80; and Jordan A. Schwarz, *The Interregnum of Despair: Hoover, Congress and the Depression* (Urbana, IL, 1970), chapter 5.

[10] Milburn, p. 679.

[11] Roosevelt waited until February 2, 1932, to announce his own repudiation of the League of Nations, after Hearst had endorsed Garner. Irving G. Williams, *The Rise of the Vice Presidency* (Washington, DC, 1956), p. 150.

[12] Schwarz, "John Nance Garner and the Sales Tax Rebellion of 1932," p. 165; Douglas Craig, *After Wilson: The Struggle for the Democratic Party, 1920–1934* (Chapel Hill, NC, 1992), p. 244.

[13] Hardeman and Bacon, pp. 137–38; David Robertson, *Sly and Able: A Political Biography of James F. Byrnes* (New York, 1994), pp. 138–40.

[14] Williams, p. 152.

[15] Timmons, p. 174.

[16] Jules Witcover, *Crapshoot: Rolling the Dice on the Vice Presidency* (New York, 1992), p. 400; Timmons, pp. 176, 178.

[17] See James Patterson, *Congressional Conservatism and the New Deal* (Lexington, KY, 1967).

[18] James A. Farley, *Jim Farley's Story: The Roosevelt Years* (New York, 1948) pp. 91, 163; James A. Farley, *Behind the Ballots: The Personal History of a Politician* (New York, 1973).

[19] *Darrell St. Claire, Assistant Secretary of the Senate,* Oral History Interviews, December 1976-April 1978 (U.S. Senate Historical Office, Washington, DC); John Michael Romano, "The Emergence of John Nance Garner as a Figure in American National Politics, 1924–1941," (Ph.D. dissertation, St. John's University, 1974), p. 231.

[20] Timmons, pp. 182, 183; Patterson, p. 40; Michie, p. 39.

[21] Williams, pp. 159, 175.

[22] Timmons, pp. 140, 202; *U.S. News and World Report*, November 21, 1958, p. 107.

[23] Timmons, p. 208.

[24] Besides presiding regularly over the Senate, he also frequented the Senate Democrats' party conferences. See Romano, pp. 185, 212.

[25] Timmons, p. 186. In fact, Garner admitted in an interview in *U.S. News and World Report*, November 21, 1958, pp. 101–2, that he had been diagnosed as permanently hard of hearing in his left ear sometime during the Taft administration but had managed to keep the fact a secret throughout his career.

[26] Paul Boller, *Congressional Anecdotes* (New York, 1991), p. 255.

[27] Romano, pp. 219, 268; Farley, *Jim Farley's Story,* p. 54.

[28] Patterson, p. 137.

[29] Timmons, pp. 219, 225.

[30] Farley, *Jim Farley's Story,* p. 84; Henry M. Hyde, "White House No-Man," *Saturday Evening Post* 25 (June 25, 1938): 23.

[31] Timmons, pp. 291–92.

[32] Ibid., pp. 228, 255.

[33] Ibid., pp. 234–35.

[34] Farley, p. 137.

[35] Romano, p. 291; Timmons, pp. 291–92.

[36] Farley, *Jim Farley's Story*, p. 206; Ickes quoted in Romano, p. 99.

[37] See Bernard Donahoe, *Private Plans and Public Dangers* (South Bend, IN, 1965).

[38] Milburn, p. 669; Farley, *Jim Farley's Story*, pp. 230, 168, 172, 70.

[39] Timmons, p. 279.

[40] *U.S. News and World Report*, March 8, 1957, p. 68. See also *U.S. News and World Report*, November, 21, 1958, pp. 98–105, and January 16, 1967, pp. 44–45. Garner's greatest contribution to the office of the Speaker may have occurred during his vice-presidency, when in 1936 he endorsed his longtime apprentice Sam Rayburn for House majority leader, the stepping stone to his speakership.

[41] Garner had a low opinion of his successor, whom he considered "a dangerous character . . . not because he's bad at heart, but because he doesn't know where he's going." Farley, *Jim Farley's Story*, p. 205.

[42] Ironically, the parochial Garner became the first vice president to be sent abroad. In 1935, he led a delegation to the Far East, although he merely silently attended ceremonies as an official representative while Secretary of War George H. Dern spoke for the president. Later that year, Garner went to Mexico as part of the "Good Neighbor" policy and gave a speech on the Laredo Bridge. Williams, p. 162.

Chapter 33

HENRY AGARD WALLACE
1941–1945

HENRY A. WALLACE

Chapter 33

HENRY AGARD WALLACE

33d Vice President: 1941–1945

No matter what he does, it is always going to seem faintly ridiculous, and no matter how he acts,
it is always going to seem faintly pathetic—at least to the cold-eyed judgments of the Hill.

—ALLEN DRURY

Prefaced by the stormy Democratic nominating convention of 1940, the vice-presidency of Henry A. Wallace concluded with the equally tempestuous 1944 convention. In 1940, when Vice President John Nance Garner broke with President Franklin D. Roosevelt and withdrew to Texas, Roosevelt designated Wallace as his running mate over the considerable objection of many convention delegates. Four years later, in 1944, Roosevelt jettisoned Wallace in favor of Harry S. Truman, who then succeeded to the presidency following Roosevelt's death. During his single term, Henry Wallace became more involved in administrative and foreign policy matters than any of his predecessors. Although widely judged a failure as vice president, Wallace was in many ways a forerunner of the modern vice presidents, who often serve as executive assistant and international emissary for the president.

As Roosevelt planned to run for a third term in 1940, he wanted to revolutionize the role of the vice president and make the office into an "additional set of eyes and ears." He sought someone who could handle administrative questions and large national policies without being a member of the cabinet. As an active secretary of agriculture and a committed New Dealer, Henry Wallace seemed the ideal person for the job. But Wallace's visionary social liberalism, his mysticism, his curiously shy and introspective personal demeanor, and his political insensitiv-

ity, all prevented him from gathering the support from congressional leaders that would have enabled him to sustain a successful political career in Washington. Because few senators came to know Wallace personally, they often judged his character on the basis of his poorly delivered speeches and unusual appearance. Journalist Allen Drury, who observed the vice president often from the Senate press gallery, described Wallace as follows: "A shock of silver-graying hair sweeps over to the right of his head in a great shaggy arc. He looks like a hayseed, talks like a prophet, and acts like an embarassed schoolboy." Drury recorded sympathetically in his diary that he found it difficult to "put into exact words the combination of feelings he arouses. The man's integrity and his idealism and his sainted other-worldliness are never in question; it's just the problem of translating them into everyday language and making them jibe with his shy, embarrassed, uncomfortable good-fellowship that is so difficult." Drury considered Henry Wallace doomed by fate. "No matter what he does, it is always going to seem faintly ridiculous, and no matter how he acts, it is always going to seem faintly pathetic—at least to the cold-eyed judgments of the Hill." [1]

Youth

Henry A. Wallace was born on October 7, 1888, near the town of Orient, Iowa, an oddly appropriate location for someone who would become

[399]

so fascinated with oriental philosophy. Wallace was also deeply influenced by Iowa's rural culture. The agrarian lifestyle and communal society of turn-of-the-century Iowa formed his values, especially the idealism for which he is remembered. As a student at Iowa State College he studied plant genetics and crossbreeding. He discovered and patented a successful strain of corn that produced a greater yield while resisting disease better than normal corn. This triumph allowed the young Wallace to found his own business to manufacture and distribute the plants, a venture that gave him valuable experience for his later career in public service.

The future vice president was actually the third Henry Wallace. The first, his grandfather, had been a Presbyterian preacher turned farmer, who became editor of the *Iowa Homestead* and publisher of *Wallace's Farmer*. These heavily read agricultural journals spread the Wallace name over the Iowa countryside and throughout the rural Midwest. The vice president's father, Henry Cantwell Wallace, served as secretary of agriculture in the administrations of presidents Warren G. Harding and Calvin Coolidge from 1921 until his death in 1924. Henry Agard Wallace took over as publisher of the family journal when his father went to Washington, continuing in that role until he himself moved to Washington as secretary of agriculture in 1933.[2]

The Wallaces had traditionally been a Republican family, but the shock of the Great Depression and its impact on rural America forced Henry A. Wallace to reevaluate his political affiliations. Disgruntled by the Coolidge and Hoover agricultural policies, Wallace threw his support to the Democrats. In 1932, Wallace supported Franklin Roosevelt, who in turn selected Wallace as his secretary of agriculture.

Secretary of Agriculture

An active secretary of agriculture, Wallace took to heart the needs and fears of his agricultural constituents. In addition to helping American farmers sustain themselves during the economic downturn, his Department of Agriculture oversaw the creation and development of the food stamp and school lunch programs that greatly aided urban America. In 1934, Wallace

published a book about the economic turbulence of the depression and its repercussions on farmers, which he titled *New Frontiers*. In it Wallace outlined the visionary politics that he employed in his subsequent writings and speeches. Later observers would compare both the title and the themes of this book with the ideas espoused by John F. Kennedy.[3]

Drastic times called for drastic measures. A firm supporter of government economic intervention, Wallace vigorously implemented the controversial measures of the Agricultural Adjustment Act of 1933. Never before in peacetime, had the federal government sought to regulate production in American farming, with government planning designed to battle overproduction and low prices. Additionally, Wallace offered hog and cotton farmers a single opportunity to improve their stagnating markets by ploughing under ten million acres of cotton and slaughtering six million pigs. For these losses, the government would issue relief checks totalling millions of dollars. Although it earned him the nickname "The Greatest Butcher in Christendom," the program essentially worked, and the market experienced a 50-percent rise in prices. Wallace scorned those who ridiculed his plans without considering the logic behind them, observing, "Perhaps they think that farmers should run a sort of old-folks home for hogs."[4]

Having proved himself an effective, energetic cabinet member, Wallace remained in office through Roosevelt's first two terms. By 1940, with Europe plunged into war, there was talk of an unprecedented third term, and Wallace was among those who endorsed the president's reelection. Because Vice President John Nance Garner, who aspired to the presidency himself, strongly opposed a third term, Roosevelt sought a new running mate for the 1940 election once he made the decision to run. FDR's choice of Wallace marked a turning point in the history of the vice-presidency. Never before had the president so openly made the selection. In the past, the main function of a vice president was usually to balance the ticket, to unite the party, and to pull in voters not normally drawn by the presidential candidate himself, with comparatively little attention paid to the compatibility of the two men. Presidential candidates generally acceded to the wishes of their party conventions in completing the ticket.

The 1940 Election

The Republicans in 1940 had chosen a dynamic darkhorse candidate for president, Wendell Willkie, and to balance the ticket the convention had selected the Republican Senate minority leader, Charles McNary of Oregon. During the 1920s, McNary had chaired the Senate Agriculture Committee and had won national attention, particularly in agricultural areas, for his sponsorship of the McNary-Haugen bills. Vetoed by presidents Coolidge and Hoover, these bills were forerunners of the New Deal's agricultural program. Seeking to neutralize McNary's popularity in the farm belt, FDR decided to make his secretary of agriculture his vice president. Roosevelt also felt confident that, if anything happened to him, Wallace would vigorously pursue the liberal objectives of the New Deal. Democratic convention delegates were furious, however, since they considered the former Republican Wallace as an outsider, lacking any of the qualities of a typical politician. When warned that the delegates might revolt, Roosevelt made it clear that "they will go for Wallace or I won't run, and you can jolly well tell them so." Party leaders reluctantly capitulated to the president's demand and nominated Wallace, but the convention's mood was so sour that Wallace decided not to make an acceptance speech.[5]

Shortly after Wallace became the vice-presidential candidate, stories circulated about his religious beliefs. Having abandoned the Calvinism of his youth, he had studied Catholicism, Judaism, Buddhism, Islam, Zoroastrianism, and Christian Science, finally settling into the Episcopal Church in Washington. But Wallace had also fallen under the influence of a Russian-born "guru" named Nicholas Roerich. During the 1930s, Wallace had written a series of letters to one of Roerich's associates, detailing his spiritual beliefs and his candid observations about contemporary political leaders. These so-called "guru letters" fell into the hands of Republicans, who considered releasing them to embarrass Wallace during the campaign. Democrats countered with evidence that presidential candidate Willkie had carried on an extramarital affair. Although the two parties eventually agreed to a quid pro quo that suppressed both the "guru letters" and the Willkie affair, the news shook some of Roosevelt's confidence in his running mate. Nonetheless, the Democratic team swept the election.[6]

Wartime Vice President

When he first took office, Wallace found the job of vice president untaxing. During the early months of his tenure, he had more time for tennis than ever before, but as the United States moved closer to war the vice president began to assume unprecedented duties, being assigned executive tasks to allow Roosevelt more freedom to deal with international affairs. One of Wallace's biographers, Richard Walton, has asserted that "never before, nor since, has a Vice President had so much direct executive authority." Others referred to him as the first "working" vice president. Named a member of FDR's secret "war cabinet," Wallace chaired the Economic Defense Board, the Supply Priorities and Allocations Board, and the Board of Economic Warfare. Journalists began to refer to him as "Mr. Assistant President." [7]

Divided into an Office of Imports, Office of Exports, and Office of War Analysis, the Board of Economic Warfare (BEW) supported the Allied war effort through procurement of strategic resources. As chairman, Wallace freed himself to deal with long-term policy matters by delegating the day-to-day management of the BEW to Milo Perkins, an associate from the Agriculture Department. Like many special boards created by President Roosevelt, the BEW came in for its share of interdepartmental bickering, rivalries, and conflicts of authority. Although Roosevelt expressly forbade federal government agencies to publicly criticize each other during the war, Wallace, after eight years of fighting within the cabinet, failed to recognize that the president was serious about this order.[8] Wallace's diary traces his fight to gain greater autonomy for the BEW and his many clashes with cabinet officers like Secretary of State Cordell Hull and Secretary of Commerce Jesse Jones. These established bureaucrats did not relish the thought of an activist vice president assuming responsibilities that their departments normally held. Wallace believed that the wartime emergency required drastic action to deal with problems like rubber shortages, while Jones and Hull believed that existing mechanisms could solve even wartime demands. Wallace's assertion of his authority to purchase materiel vital to the war effort spawned conspicuous political battles.[9]

When Roosevelt signed an executive order in April 1942 allowing the BEW to negotiate contracts with foreign governments, Secretary Hull saw it as an attempt to create a second Department of State. Wallace's goals for social justice ran against the grain of Hull's State Department policies. For instance, Wallace was firmly convinced that the Latin American rubber supply could be increased dramatically if the living standards of that region's rubber workers were raised to reduce the incidence of chronic malnutrition and malaria. He attempted to force negotiated contracts to provide for socially beneficial improvements to the Latin American infrastructure, with the United States funding half the cost of these programs. Wallace's acquisition of executive authority had been unpopular with the rank and file in Congress, and most members supported Hull, a former senator, in his attacks on the BEW and its chairman. A growing consensus that Wallace had pushed a too active program in Latin America caused Roosevelt to issue another executive order, which preserved the State Department's monopoly on negotiations with foreign governments, a blow aimed directly at Wallace's authority.[10]

The BEW controversy climaxed in February 1943, when Wallace tried to place the purchasing authority of the Reconstruction Finance Corporation (RFC) under the BEW's jurisdiction. An infuriated Commerce Secretary Jesse Jones roundly denounced what he considered Wallace's arrogant action. When Wallace retaliated by accusing Jones of delaying shipments of quinine to marines dying of malaria, the imbroglio became too hot for Roosevelt to ignore. The embattled vice president wrote to the president, asking for either complete vindication for his actions in the matter or relief of his duties as chairman of the

BEW. Roosevelt responded on July 15, 1943, by dissolving the BEW and reconstituting its function under a new Foreign Economic Administration, headed by Leo Crowley, a known supporter of Jones. By revealing the strained relations between the president and vice president, the order substantially weakened Wallace's position in Washington politics. Until then, Wallace had been "the ideal and inspiration of every little world-planner in Washington," wrote the commentator Raymond Moley. "After Roosevelt abolished the BEW . . . it was clear to them that they must forsake their high priest and follow the president."[11]

As Senate President

In spite of his earlier success as agriculture secretary, Wallace demonstrated acute political insensitivity in his failure at BEW. "I did not look on myself as very much of a politician," he said, revealingly. Wallace disliked the formalities and superficialities of the political world, particularly as practiced on Capitol Hill, and he lacked the small-talk abilities critical in a system so dependent on unofficial meetings and social politics. Senate staff member Richard Riedel judged Wallace "the least congressional of all the Vice Presidents" and recorded that he possessed "none of the political talents that enable public figures to mingle with and influence each other."[12]

Wallace never fit into the Senate's club-like atmosphere, in part because he refused to join the club. One of his first acts as president of the Senate was to close down the private bar that "Cactus Jack" Garner had maintained to entertain senators in his office—Wallace himself neither drank nor smoked. Later, when Wallace hit a home run during a congressional baseball game, a senator observed that it clearly "furnished more pleasure [for him] than any political contest." The Spartan, health-conscious Wallace chose to demonstrate his physical prowess over the men who held him at a political arm's length. During a friendly boxing match, he knocked out Louisiana Senator Allen Ellender, who had been less than supportive of Wallace's vice-presidency.[13]

As the Senate's presiding officer, Wallace found his duties monotonous and boring. He disdained the senators' right of unlimited debate and slumped down "unceremoniously" in the presiding officer's chair during the proceedings. When he tried to intervene in debate, the senators slapped him down. Wallace once suffered an embarrassing browbeating from Tennessee's crusty Kenneth McKellar, who had been arguing over the rules of the Senate for several hours. When Wallace, from the chair, declared this tirade a "parliamentary trick," McKellar launched into an attack on the presiding officer and ultimately forced Wallace to apologize for his impetuous insult. Left only with his constitutional role of breaking tie votes, Wallace was able to cast only four votes—the most satisfying being to prevent the Senate from terminating the Civilian Conservation Corps.[14]

A Roving Vice President

It soon became clear that Wallace's aspirations lay beyond the Senate chamber. More interested in the issues of the world, he became the first vice president to take an active role in foreign policy, serving as the president's personal ambassador. Wallace made his first trip in late 1940, when Roosevelt sent him to the inauguration of Mexican President Camacho, whose disputed election threatened Mexican political stability and U.S. access to Mexican trade. Having studied the language, Wallace eagerly delivered a speech in Spanish to the crowd gathered at the Mexican capital—an effort that won him thunderous applause. In 1943 Wallace made an official tour of Costa Rica, Panama, Chile, Bolivia, Peru, Ecuador, and Colombia. At every stop he took pains to meet the common people and converse with them in their native tongue. He traveled without a large entourage and refused to accept costly ceremonial gifts. The images of bitter suffering and poverty that he encountered in these underdeveloped countries convinced Wallace of the need for U.S. humanitarian aid and strengthened his resolve to struggle for a lasting postwar peace.[15]

In 1944 the president asked Wallace to make an even more ambitious and dangerous trip to China and the Soviet Union. Historians continue to speculate on whether Roosevelt expected Wallace to accomplish anything diplomatically or simply wanted the vice president out of the country while preparing to dump him from the Democratic ticket. Whatever was at stake, Wallace felt exuberant and optimistic about the possibilities of his venture. FDR asked him to foster greater cooperation between Chiang Kai-shek and the Communist forces in China and to prod the Nationalists into stepping up their campaign against the Japanese.[16]

Arriving in Siberia, Wallace tried again to meet the indigenous population as he had in Latin America. Even though he spoke little Russian and had to use an interpreter, he insisted on delivering an address in Russian at Irkutsk. He visited the collective farms in several Siberian villages and seemed most impressed with their productivity. These observations planted the seeds of Wallace's respectful impression of the Soviet Union. Later analysis revealed that his visit had been considerably more orchestrated by the Soviets than Wallace or the rest of his party had realized. Wallace saw the famous Soviet Academy of Science but not the advanced atomic experiments being conducted there. Similarly, he was never taken to visit the nearby forced-labor camps and consequently gained a distorted view of Soviet life.[17]

After touring Russia, Wallace's modest entourage of diplomats arrived in Chungking to begin their most difficult and least successful task—trying to solve China's major wartime problems. Unprepared for the sad state of Chiang Kai-shek's regime, Wallace concluded that cooperation between the Nationalists and Communists would be nearly impossible. Nevertheless, he managed to negotiate an agreement by which U.S. forces were to enter northern China to set up weather stations to aid in bombing raids against the Japanese. Although the publicity from Wallace's first two goodwill tours had been highly positive and had helped him to redefine the vice president's role in foreign relations, his final journey gravely damaged his political career.[18]

Wallace's favorable view of the Soviet Union became increasingly pronounced and more widely discussed. Shortly before his marathon tour of Russia and China, Wallace wrote an article for the *New York Times*, called "The Dangers of American Fascism," in which he condemned the rising tide of anti-Soviet propaganda. Seeking to break down the wall of ignorance between the Russian and American cultures, he anticipated that the two peoples would eventually find they shared the same hopes and fears and could live together in friendship. His visit to Russia, and the warm welcome he received there, further softened his views. Wallace compared the Soviet citizens he visited in Siberia with the farm families of the Midwest whom he had known as a boy. His warm regard for the Soviet Union earned him a liberal identity during the war and a heretical image during the cold war that followed.[19]

Wallace's Idealism

Wallace envisioned a postwar era governed by an international peacekeeping force and an international court, rather than through balance-of-power politics. His plan also called for an end to European imperialism in Asia and Africa. In an address to the Free World Association on May 8, 1942, Wallace outlined his "Century of the Common Man," in which he endorsed federal support for education and collective health care for workers. These proposals would have required continuing the initiatives of the New Deal era that Wallace so admired, but the administration lacked sufficient political capital to promote an expanded program of domestic social welfare, because of the enhanced executive war powers adopted by the president. More than the New Deal inspired Henry Wallace. Christian morality and the social gospel formed the fundamental inspiration behind his speeches. As a product of Protestant liberalism, he adhered to the principles of the Sermon on the Mount and saw himself as bound to accomplish the work of the Lord.[20]

President Roosevelt admired and sought to harness his vice president's idealistic liberalism, while at the same time trying to teach him how the political machinery of Washington really operated. Roosevelt thought that Wallace was a few years ahead of his time and expected that his ideas would eventually be realized. Yet Wallace's inability to grasp Washington politics led to a marked decline in the vice president's stat-

ure on Capitol Hill in the final year of his tenure. Growing hostility between the executive branch and the conservatively oriented Congress finally convinced FDR that Wallace had become an expensive political liability.

The 1944 Election

As the 1944 elections approached, four influential Democrats decided to ensure that Wallace was not nominated in the next Democratic convention. Terming themselves the "Conspiracy of the Pure in Heart," the four consisted of Democratic party chairman Robert Hannegan, Postmaster General Frank Walker, New York Democratic party chief Ed Flynn, and Democratic party treasurer Edwin Pauley. The Democratic leadership had unsuccessfully opposed Wallace in the 1940 nomination convention, but this time they had the advantage of Roosevelt's declining health and his increasing preoccupation with wartime diplomacy.[21]

Roosevelt himself appears to have grown dissatisfied with the vice president's record. Wallace had not proved himself to be the political partner Roosevelt had hoped he would become. The president's motivation in sending Wallace overseas at a critical political time at home may therefore have been devious. The Asian journey allowed Wallace no time to campaign and made him vulnerable to political attack. When Wallace returned to Washington's National Airport, he faced reporters who asked if he planned to withdraw from the race. The vice president replied, "I am seeing the president at 4:30. I have a report to make on a mission to China. I do not want to talk politics."

But Wallace did try to make a compelling case that he should continue as FDR's running mate, indicating that he had the support of labor leaders and rank and file Democrats.[22] In that conversation on July 11, Roosevelt appeared sympathetic to keeping Wallace on the team. Wallace asked the president to communicate his support in writing to the Democratic leadership, assuming that the endorsement of the terribly popular chief executive would resolve the matter as it had four years earlier. Roosevelt's letter, however, emphasized that he had no desire to dictate to the convention. This approach left the door open to the "Conspiracy of the Pure in Heart" to find a replacement for Wallace. These party leaders first considered the director of the Office of War Mobilization, James F. Byrnes of South Carolina, a former senator and Supreme Court justice, before finally settling on Senator Harry Truman of Missouri. In effect, FDR had astutely removed his hand from the process, knowing full well what would happen to Wallace without his active support.[23]

Nonetheless, at the 1944 Democratic convention in Chicago, Wallace showed surprising popularity among the delegates, threatening to ruin the Democratic leadership's carefully orchestrated plan to dump him. After his rousing speech, cheering delegates began to shout for "Wallace in '44." The convention chairman, Indiana Senator Samuel D. Jackson, noted the crowd's enthusiasm and feared that Wallace might win on the first ballot. He therefore called for an adjournment until the next day, blaming fire code infractions due to the more than capacity crowd at the convention center. Although the nays drowned out the ayes on the motion, the chairman declared the session adjourned. During the night, Roosevelt's ambiguous letter of support circulated among the delegates and undermined Wallace's position. The next day, the delegates selected Senator Truman for vice president. Jubilant Democratic leaders later boasted of their role in the affair. Party chairman Hannegan told friends that his epitaph should read, "Here lies the man who kept Henry Wallace from being President of the United States."[24]

Commerce Secretary

Although defeated for renomination, Wallace did not retire from politics. His active campaigning for FDR's fourth term led the president to reward his loyalty with appointment as secretary of commerce. Some have suggested that Roosevelt believed the Senate would never confirm Wallace. In his letter firing Jesse Jones as commerce secretary, FDR admitted that Wallace's appointment was a repayment for his "utmost devotion to our cause." This letter caused a storm of debate in Congress and the press. Members of Congress expressed serious doubt about Wallace's abilities and were particularly dis-

turbed at the prospect that he would take charge of the billions of dollars of loans made by the Reconstruction Finance Corporation (RFC). As a compromise, senators who wished to let the president have his appointment yet shuddered at giving their former presiding officer power, voted to transfer the money-lending responsibilities of the RFC out of the Commerce Department's jurisdiction. Stripped of his economic influence, Wallace was confirmed.[25]

Wallace's short career directing the Commerce Department was racked with controversy. Eighty-two days after Wallace left office as vice president, Franklin Roosevelt died, making Harry Truman president. Truman's administration took a decidedly hard-line turn against the Soviet Union, a policy that, coupled with the increasing influence of conservatives in Truman's cabinet, confounded and alienated Wallace. Expressing his disapproval of Truman's foreign policy, Wallace wrote a twelve-page letter urging the United States to exercise caution in abandoning its powerful wartime ally. Wallace firmly believed that the only way to end the spread of communism was to raise the world's standards of living. In a speech at Madison Square Garden in September 1946, Wallace warned that American foreign policy towards Russia could lead to a third world war. Although Wallace had previously cleared his remarks with Truman, his speech occurred at the very time Secretary of State James Byrnes was negotiating with Soviet authorities in Paris. Byrnes charged that Wallace's speech had undermined U.S. policy and suggested damaging disunity within the administration. Shortly thereafter, Truman fired Wallace as secretary of commerce.[26]

Later Years

Wallace's final public action was a failed bid for the presidency in 1948. Still commanding a modest following from left-wing groups, he ran on the Progressive ticket, campaigning against Truman, the Republican candidate Thomas E. Dewey, and the Dixiecrat candidate Strom Thurmond. Support from the Communist party damaged Wallace's campaign by alienating many liberals and other voters. The aggressive actions of the Soviets in Berlin and Czechoslovakia also turned voters against Wallace. The former vice president had little impact on the election, except by capturing enough votes in New York to throw that state to Dewey. Rather than present himself as the liberal, internationalist alternative to the cold warriors, Wallace had bolted to a third party. This action, combined with the walkout of conservative southern Democrats over the issue of civil rights, made Truman appear to be the centrist candidate carrying on the traditions of Roosevelt and the New Deal, thus enabling him to win the upset victory of the century.

Following his defeat in 1948, Henry Wallace retired from official political life. He still believed in his concept of world peace and worked for social justice in Latin America, travelling there on numerous occasions and persuading foundations to support the region's developing nations. In retirement, Wallace continued his genetic experimentation on various strains of corn and other crops, a scientific inquiry that provided him with the satisfaction his political career had lacked. At the end of his life, as he suffered from Lou Gehrig's Disease, Wallace continued to reflect on international issues and worried about the United States' deepening involvement in Vietnam. He traced the origins of that war back to the beginning of the cold war, "when I was getting the hell kicked out of me for suggesting that we were taking on more than we could chew." Wallace died on November 18, 1965, in Danbury, Connecticut.[27]

Henry Wallace will be remembered as an unusual vice president because of the circumstances of his rise and fall from power and because of his unprecedented executive responsibilities. His foreign travels also forged new political paths that later vice presidents would follow. Clearly Wallace's personal eccentricities contributed to his political failure in Washington politics. Yet, viewed in retrospect from after the end of the cold war, his visionary social liberalism—so radically different from the politics of Harry Truman—raises the question of how world events might have been different had the vote for vice president at the 1944 Democratic convention not been delayed overnight.

NOTES

[1] Jules Witcover, *Crapshoot: Rolling the Dice on the Vice Presidency* (New York, 1992), pp. 405–6; Allen Drury, A Senate Journal, 1943–1945 (New York, 1963), pp. 137–38.

[2] J. Samuel Walker, *Henry A. Wallace and American Foreign Policy* (Westport, CT, 1976.), pp. 3–8.

[3] Witcover, pp. 77–78.

[4] Norman D. Markowitz, *The Rise and Fall of the People's Century: Henry A. Wallace and American Liberalism, 1941–1948* (New York, 1973), pp. 15–27; Witcover, p. 77.

[5] Markowitz, pp. 28–31; Doris Kearns Goodwin, *No Ordinary Time: Eleanor and Franklin Roosevelt: The Home Front in World War II* (New York, 1994), pp. 128–33.

[6] Walker, pp. 50–60; Charles J. Errico and J. Samuel Walker, "The New Deal and the Guru," *American Heritage* (March 1989), pp. 92–99.

[7] John Morton Blum, ed., *The Price of Vision: The Diary of Henry A. Wallace, 1942–1946* (Boston, 1973), pp. 23–24; Richard J. Walton, *Henry Wallace, Harry Truman, and the Cold War* (New York, 1976), p. 8; Edward L. and Frederick H. Schapsmeier, *Prophet in Politics: Henry A. Wallace and the War Years, 1940–1965* (Ames, IA, 1970), p. 22.

[8] Walton, pp. 8–10; Schapsmeier and Schapsmeier, pp. 50–71.

[9] Blum, pp. 53–229.

[10] Schapsmeier and Schapsmeier, p. 20; Markowitz, pp. 65–70.

[11] Markowitz, pp. 70–73; Moley quoted in Donald Young, *American Roulette: The History and Dilemma of the Vice Presidency* (New York, 1972), p. 194.

[12] Blum, p. 22; Schapsmeier and Schapsmeier, p. 7; Richard Langham Riedel, *Halls of the Mighty: My 47 Years at the Senate* (Washington, 1969), p. 193.

[13] Blum, pp. 22–23; Riedel, p. 193.

[14] Drury, p. 121.

[15] Schapsmeier and Schapsmeier, pp. 38–49; Drury, pp. 137–38.

[16] Walton, pp. 15–16; Schapsmeier and Schapsmeier, p. 91.

[17] Blum, pp. 335–48; Schapsmeier and Schapsmeier, pp. 85–91.

[18] Blum, pp. 349–60; Schapsmeier and Schapsmeier, pp. 91–98.

[19] Witcover, p. 82.

[20] Walker, pp. 83–97; Schapsmeier and Schapsmeier, pp. 30–37; Blum, pp. 13–15.

[21] Walton, pp. 22–23; Witcover, pp. 84–87.

[22] Blum, pp. 361–62.

[23] Witcover, pp. 84–87; Schapsmeier and Schapsmeier, pp. 102–3.

[24] Schapsmeier and Schapsmeier, pp. 104–9; Markowitz, p. 91; David McCullough, *Truman* (New York, 1992), pp. 292–323.

[25] Schapsmeier and Schapsmeier, pp. 114–19; Drury, pp. 345–55; U.S., Congress, Senate, *Congressional Record*, 79th Cong., 1st sess., pp. 694–95, 1163–67.

[26] Walker, pp. 133–63; McCullough, pp. 513–18.

[27] Schapsmeier and Schapsmeier, pp. 224–39; Walker, p. 212.

Chapter 34

HARRY S. TRUMAN
1945

HARRY S. TRUMAN

Chapter 34

HARRY S. TRUMAN

34th Vice President: 1945

I enjoyed my new position as Vice-President, but it took me a while to get used to the fact that I no longer had the voting privileges I had enjoyed for ten years as a senator.

—HARRY S. TRUMAN

When Democratic party leaders determined to dump Vice President Henry Wallace from the ticket in 1944, they looked for a suitable replacement. They considered Wallace too unpredictable to serve another term under Roosevelt, whose health had visibly declined during the Second World War. There was no shortage of candidates: Majority Leader Alben Barkley, presidential assistant James F. Byrnes, Supreme Court Justice William O. Douglas, and others advertised their availability. But the nomination went to someone who did not want it. Missouri Senator Harry S. Truman had committed himself to nominating Byrnes. When a reporter asked why he did not become a candidate himself, considering that the next vice president might likely "succeed to the throne," Truman shook his head and replied, "Hell, I don't want to be President." Harry Truman felt content to stay in the Senate, where he had spent ten happy years.[1]

A Farm Boy at Heart

Despite a long record of public service, the always underestimated Truman made an unlikely candidate for national office. He was at heart a farm boy, born in the rural village of Lamar, Missouri, on May 8, 1884. His father, John Truman, was a farmer and livestock dealer. For much of their childhood, Harry and his brother and sister lived on their grandmother's six hundred-acre farm near Grandview, Missouri. Poor eyesight corrected by thick glasses kept him from playing

sports but failed to hamper his love of books. When the children were old enough for schooling, the Truman family moved to Independence. Then, in 1903, after John Truman went bankrupt speculating in grain futures, the family moved to Kansas City, where John Truman took a job as night watchman at a grain elevator. Harry applied to West Point but was rejected because of his poor eyesight. Instead of attending college, he worked as a timekeeper on a railroad construction crew, a newspaper wrapper, and a bank teller. In 1905 the parents returned to the Grandview farm, and Harry and his brother followed the next year. After John Truman died in 1914, Harry Truman assumed the supervision of the farm, plowing, sowing, harvesting, and repairing equipment himself. For the rest of his life, Truman always enjoyed returning to the family's farm (now subdivided into suburban housing, although the farmhouse stands as part of the Harry S. Truman National Historical Site). As president, he later asserted: "I always give my occupation as farmer. I spent the best years of my life trying to run a 600-acre farm successfully, and I know what the problems are."[2]

Farming meant hard work and isolation. Nor did it produce sufficient income for Harry to marry his childhood sweetheart Elizabeth (Bess) Wallace. Truman proposed in 1911, but Bess turned him down. Undaunted, he pursued the courtship for another eight years. After long days on the farm, Harry devoted his evenings to practicing the piano and reading history. He had other dreams as well: as a boy, he and his father had attended the Democratic National Convention in Kansas City in 1900 and watched William Jennings Bryan be nominated a second time for president. The "Great Commoner" always remained one of his heroes. Truman's father loved politics. "Politics is all he ever advises me to neglect the farm for," Harry wrote to Bess.[3]

The United States entered the First World War in 1917. At thirty-three, Truman was two years over the age limit for the draft and would also have been exempted as a farmer. But he turned the farm over to his mother and sister and enlisted, overcoming his poor eyesight by memorizing the eye chart. Having served in the National Guard, Truman helped organize a regiment from a National Guard company in Kansas City and was elected first lieutenant. When the 129th Field Artillery went overseas, he was promoted to captain and placed in command of Battery D. The "Dizzy D" had a wild and unruly reputation, but Captain Harry whipped them into line. They encountered heavy fighting in the Meuse-Argonne offensive, from which Truman emerged with the undying respect of his troops and increased confidence in his own abilities. His exploits also lifted him in the eyes of Bess Wallace, who at last married him after the war, in June 1919.[4]

Machine Politics

Truman temporarily moved into his in-laws' house in Independence, Missouri, an arrangement that lasted for the rest of his life. Instead of returning to the farm, he started a haberdasher's shop in Kansas City with his Battery D sergeant, Eddie Jacobson. When Truman & Jacobson failed during the recession of 1922, bankruptcy turned Harry Truman from business to politics. Another army buddy, Jimmy Pendergast, introduced Truman to his uncle Thomas Pendergast, the Democratic political boss of Kansas City. In 1922 the Pendergast machine endorsed Truman for county judge in Jackson County, which was an administrative rather than a judicial function. After narrowly winning the primary, he sailed easily to election as the Democratic candidate that fall. In this and all future elections, Truman could count on the loyal support of the veterans of the 129th, most of whom lived in the Kansas City vicinity. In 1924, the year his only daughter, Margaret, was born, Truman lost his bid for reelection when the anti-Pendergast faction of the Democratic party split away and swung its support to the Republicans. He then sold memberships in the Kansas City Automobile Club until he won reelection in 1926. During the next twenty-six years of uninterrupted public service, he never lost another election—to the surprise of everyone except Harry Truman.[5]

Like most political machines, the Pendergast organization depended upon patronage and government contracts. Pendergast owned the Ready-Mix Concrete Company and held interests in a variety of construction, paving, pipe, and oil companies that built roads, courthouses, and other public works in and around Kansas City. As an activist administrator, Truman sought to build roads and public buildings, but he held out against funneling county projects to corrupt contractors. Pendergast's interests got county contracts only when they were the lowest bidders. "Three things ruin a man," Truman later said. "Power, money, and women. I never wanted power. I never had any money, and the only woman in my life is up at the house right now." Once, when Truman discovered that an associate had taken money to cut a deal with a road builder, he kept silent to ensure that the construction went forward. In frustration, Truman poured out his feelings privately on paper:

> I had to compromise in order to get the voted road system carried out . . . I had to let a former saloonkeeper and murderer, a friend of the Boss's, steal about $10,000 from the general revenues of the county to satisfy my ideal associate and keep the crooks from getting a million or more out of the bond issue. Was I right or did I compound a felony? I don't know.[6]

Despite his machine connections, Truman developed a progressive reputation as county judge. In 1934 he wanted to run for the U.S. House of Representatives, but Pendergast had already picked another candidate. Instead, to Truman's astonishment, the boss wanted him to run for the Senate. In fact, Pendergast's first four choices had turned him down. Few gave Truman much of a chance. Missouri's anti-Pendergast Senator Bennett Champ Clark mocked Truman's assertion that if elected he would not attempt to boss or dictate to anyone. "Why, bless Harry's good kind heart—no one has ever accused him of being a boss or wanting to be a boss and nobody will ever suspect him of trying to dictate to anybody in his own right as long as a certain eminent citizen of Jackson County remains alive." But, in the Democratic primary, Truman waged a vigorous campaign over the entire state and won the three-way race by a wide margin. Since Missouri was a Democratic state, he coasted to victory in November. As Truman left for Washington, Tom Pendergast gave him some parting advice: "Work hard, keep your mouth shut, and answer your mail." [7]

A Workhorse in the Senate

Reversing historical trends, the Democrats gained ten Senate seats during the congressional midterm elections of 1934. The new class of Democrats included James Murray of Montana, Joseph Guffey of Pennsylvania, Francis Maloney of Connecticut, Sherman Minton of Indiana, and Lewis Schwellenbach of Washington. In contrast to these liberal Democrats, Harry Truman was more conservative and less known. "I was as timid as a country boy arriving on the campus of a great university for his first year," he later admitted. Following Pendergast's advice, he kept his mouth shut and his eye on his new colleagues. Before long he had separated out the "workhorses" from the "showhorses" and concluded that the real business of the Senate was conducted by conscientious senators who usually attracted the least publicity. Having also discovered that "the real work" of the Senate took place in committee rooms rather than on the floor, he devoted himself to committee work, through research, correspondence, and hearings. He made it his business "to master all of the details" of the legislation that came before his committees. "My ten years in the Senate had now begun," he wrote two decades later, "—years which were to be filled with hard work but which were also to be the happiest ten years of

my life." The only painful memories were of the scorn that some journalists continued to heap on him as Pendergast's errand boy. [8]

As a new senator, Truman relied on the veteran Democratic secretary, Leslie Biffle, to counsel him on how to act, when to speak, what committees to request, and other practical advice. Truman's down-home, poker-playing style soon won him friendships with many senators as well as with Vice President John Nance Garner—who invited Truman to join those who met at the "doghouse," his hideaway office, to "strike a blow for liberty" with shots of bourbon. Accepted as an insider, Truman had nothing but contempt for the Senate's most famous outsider, Huey Long. The Louisiana senator's flamboyant style and long-winded filibusters represented the entirely opposite route from the one Truman took in the Senate. [9]

Appointed to the Interstate Commerce Committee, Truman and its chairman, Montana Senator Burton K. Wheeler, began a long, detailed investigation of the nation's transportation system. Their efforts resulted in the Wheeler-Truman Transportation Act of 1940, which established new standards of federal regulation for the nation's railroad, trucking and shipping industries. It was the signal accomplishment of his first term. Most Washington observers doubted that Truman would have a second term. The U.S. district attorney in Kansas City, Maurice Milligan, was prosecuting Tom Pendergast for vote fraud and income tax evasion. Loyally standing by the boss, Truman delivered a blistering attack in the Senate chamber accusing the president, Milligan, and the federal courts of playing politics with Pendergast. But Pendergast was convicted and sent to the federal penitentiary in 1939. Seeing Truman as just an extension of the machine, Milligan then ran for the Democratic nomination for the Senate in 1940, as did Missouri Governor Lloyd Stark, who previously had sought Pendergast's endorsement but now presented himself as a reformer. President Roosevelt leaned toward Stark, and Truman seemed doomed to defeat, but Milligan and Stark split the anti-Pendergast vote, enabling Truman to squeak through to a victory in the Democratic primary, which "virtually guaranteed" his re-election in November.[10]

The Truman Committee

Returning to Washington his own man, Truman moved for the creation of a special committee to investigate the national defense preparations on the eve of World War II. He had heard of waste and extravagance and contractors overcharging the government at Missouri military bases, and he believed that a watchdog committee would be essential as the government pumped massive amounts of money into its defense industries. With the help of party secretary Les Biffle, Truman was appointed chair of the Special Committee to Investigate the National Defense Program, which became nationally known as the Truman Committee. As an avid student of history, Truman knew what havoc the Joint Committee on the Conduct of the War had created for President Abraham Lincoln, and he was determined to assist rather than to combat President Roosevelt. The Truman Committee investigated business, labor, and government agencies, seeking ways to make all three cooperate. Whenever the Truman Committee concluded that reforms were needed in war agencies, Truman took care to inform the president first, before he talked to the press, giving Roosevelt the chance to institute the necessary changes before being pressured by negative publicity.[11]

Harry Truman was fifty-seven when he assumed the chairmanship of the special committee and rose to national prominence. Of average height and appearance, speaking with a midwestern twang, and earthy in his expressions, he was known in Washington as diligent and unprepossessing. Over time, his voting record had increasingly conformed to Roosevelt administration policies, and he remained a loyal Democrat, more likely to complain in private than in public about any differences with the New Deal. The Truman Committee won its chairman favorable press notices for saving the taxpayers millions of dollars and the Roosevelt administration much potential embarrassment. "I have had considerable experience in letting public contracts," Truman said, recalling his Jackson County days,

"and I have never yet found a contractor who, if not watched, would not leave the Government holding the bag." The public agreed. As *Harper's Magazine* concluded in June 1945, before the war Truman had been "just another obscure junior Senator," but three years later "he had made himself known, and respected, as the chairman of a special committee investigating war production and, in consequence, the almost inevitable choice of his party as a compromise candidate for the Vice Presidency."[12]

Choosing Truman for Vice President

While it later seemed inevitable, there was nothing predictable about Truman's selection for vice president in 1944. Vice President Henry Wallace's unpopularity among party leaders had set off a monumental contest for the second spot at the Chicago convention. Senator Alben Barkley wanted the job, but his hot-tempered resignation and swift reelection as majority leader in protest over President Roosevelt's veto of a revenue bill in February 1944 eliminated him as an acceptable choice to the president. Barkley and "Assistant President" James Byrnes—a former senator and former Supreme Court Justice—each asked Truman to nominate him at the convention. Byrnes asked first, and Truman readily agreed. Senator Truman consistently told everyone—even his daughter Margaret—that he was not a candidate himself. The only race in his mind was for his reelection to the Senate in 1946.[13]

The pivotal person at the convention was Bob Hannegan, a St. Louis political leader serving as commissioner of internal revenue and tapped as the next Democratic National Committee chairman. During the heated Senate campaign of 1940, Hannegan had switched his support from Governor Stark to Truman as the better man, and he delivered enough St. Louis votes to help Truman win. Hannegan, Bronx boss Ed Flynn, Chicago mayor Ed Kelly, key labor leaders, and other party movers and shakers viewed Wallace as a liability for his leftist leanings. Byrnes was equally vulnerable for his segregationist record and his conversion from Catholicism. When these party leaders expressed their opposition to Wallace and Byrnes, Roosevelt suggested Supreme Court Justice William O. Douglas. The group then countered with Harry Truman, whom Roosevelt agreed had been loyal and "wise to the ways of politics." After much discussion, Roosevelt turned to Hannegan and conceded, "Bob, I think you and everyone else here want Truman." [14]

Hating to disappoint and alienate any of the potential candidates, Roosevelt kept them all guessing. At lunch with Vice President Wallace, Roosevelt informed him that the professional politicians preferred Truman as "the only one who had no enemies and might add a little independent strength to the ticket." Roosevelt promised Wallace that he would not endorse another candidate, but would notify the convention that if he were a delegate he would vote for Wallace. At the same time, the president held out hope to Byrnes that he was "the best qualified man in the whole outfit," and urged him to stay in the race. "After all, Jimmy," you're close to me personally," Roosevelt said. "I hardly know Truman." (Roosevelt, whose own health was growing precarious, did not even know Truman's age—which was sixty.) Despite encouraging Wallace and Byrnes, the president had written a letter for Hannegan to carry to the convention:

Dear Bob: You have written me about Harry Truman and Bill Douglas. I should, of course, be very glad to run with either of them and believe that either one of them would bring real strength to the ticket. [15]

Meanwhile, Senator Truman continued to deny any interest in the vice-presidency. In an off-the-record interview, he explained to a reporter that if he ran for vice president the Republicans would raise charges of bossism against him. He did not want to subject his family to the attacks and negative publicity of a national campaign. Bess Truman was against it, and so was Truman's ninety-one-year-old mother, who told him to stay in the Senate. "The Vice President simply presides over the Senate and sits around hoping for a funeral," Truman protested. "It is a very high office which consists entirely of honor and I don't have any ambition to hold an office like that." His secret ambition, admitted on a visit to the Senate chamber twenty years later,

was to occupy the front row seat of the majority leader. [16]

In an overheated hotel room, the politicians leaned heavily on Truman to run. They placed a call to Roosevelt, and as Truman sat nearby, Hannegan held the phone so that he could hear. "Bob, have you got that fellow lined up yet?" Roosevelt asked. "No. He is the contrariest Missouri mule I've ever dealt with," Hannegan replied. "Well, you tell him that if he wants to break up the Democratic party in the middle of the war, that's his responsibility," Roosevelt declared and hung up the phone. Stunned, Truman agreed to run, but added: "why the hell didn't he tell me in the first place?" [17]

Henry Wallace appeared personally at the convention to seek renomination, stimulating an enthusiastic reception from the galleries. On the first ballot, Wallace led Truman 429 to 319. But the party's leaders swung their delegations and put Truman over the top on the second ballot. In a speech that lasted less than a minute, Truman accepted the nomination. Democratic liberals bemoaned the choice, while Republicans mocked the "little man from Missouri." Newspapers charged him with being a member of the Ku Klux Klan, when in fact he had vigorously fought the Klan in Jackson County. Critics also noted that Truman had placed his wife on his Senate payroll, but Truman rejoined that hiring her had been legal and that she had earned every penny. (Truman's sister Mary Jane had also been on his Senate payroll since 1943.) None of these controversies mattered much. On election day, a majority of voters did not want to change leaders in wartime and cast their ballots for Roosevelt regardless of who ran with him. Eleanor Roosevelt, who had preferred Wallace and distrusted Byrnes, reflected the prevailing sentiment that the vice-presidential candidate had been a safe choice. She wrote that while she did not know Truman, "from all I hear, he is a good man." [18]

Roosevelt and Truman

After his nomination, Truman had gone to the White House for lunch with Roosevelt and had been shocked at the president's gaunt appearance and trembling hands. Only to his most intimate friends did Truman confide his fears that Roosevelt would never survive his fourth term. On a cold January 20, 1945, Truman stood with Roosevelt on the South Portico of the White House to take the oath as vice president. The ceremonies had been moved from their traditional location at the Capitol as a concession to the war and Roosevelt's health. After the post-inaugural luncheon, the new vice president slipped away and telephoned his mother who had heard the inauguration over the radio at Grandview. "Now you behave yourself," she instructed.[19]

Truman's vice-presidency was practically a continuation of his years in the Senate. The Trumans kept their same apartment at 4701 Connecticut Avenue, and he retained the same office in Room 240 of the Senate office building. He spent most of his time presiding over the Senate, whose rules and procedures he had already mastered, and whose members he already knew. "I enjoyed my new position as Vice-President," he late wrote, "but it took me a while to get used to the fact that I no longer had the voting privileges I had enjoyed for ten years as a senator." During his eighty-two days as vice president, Truman had only one opportunity to vote, on an amendment to limit the extension of Lend-Lease. The vice president voted against the amendment. As the United Press reporter Allen Drury observed: "Harry Truman, with all the brisk eagerness of someone who is bored to death, seized his first chance to vote in the Senate today and made the most of it. The vote wasn't necessary, for under the rules a tie kills a proposal, but he cast it anyway, with obvious satisfaction."[20]

During Truman's vice-presidency, critical decisions were being made regarding ending the war and planning for the future peace, but the president neither advised nor consulted him. Roosevelt left Washington for his long journey to Yalta two days after the inauguration and did not return for almost a month. Even then, he saw the vice president only twice more, on March 8 and March 19, before he left for a rest at the "Little White House" in Warm Springs, Georgia. Roosevelt assumed there would be time to educate his vice president later.[21]

Truman's major assignment was to help his predecessor, Henry Wallace, win confirmation as secretary of commerce. Roosevelt had appointed Wallace as a gesture of consolation to his former vice president, and enlisted Truman to win support from recalcitrant senators. To pacify Wallace's critics, the Democratic leadership cut a deal to remove the Federal Loan Agency from the Commerce Department. The House passed the measure first, and when it reached the Senate, Majority Leader Barkley planned to call it up for immediate consideration, to clear the way for Wallace's confirmation. Barkley, however, was not paying attention when Ohio Republican Senator Robert Taft sought recognition to move Wallace's confirmation vote first. Truman looked to the majority leader. "Finally, Barkley woke up and I recognized him," Truman commented, believing that his action saved Wallace from defeat. Ironically, as president, Truman would fire Henry Wallace from his own cabinet a year later.[22]

As vice president, Truman aspired to mend fences between Congress and the Roosevelt administration. During the depression, Roosevelt had ridden Congress like a rodeo cowboy, but he had been badly bucked during the "Court packing" fight in 1937. Despite large Democratic majorities, Congress not only rejected Roosevelt's efforts to add several new liberal justices to the Supreme Court, but also turned down his requests to reorganize the executive branch and to expand New Deal economic programs. The legislative and executive branches finally reconciled on the eve of the Second World War, when the president and Congress joined together to suspend American neutrality and aid the Allies. The war relegated Congress to a back seat behind the president as commander in chief, causing resentment, suspicion, and hostility toward the administration to simmer on Capitol Hill. During the war, a coalition of Republicans and conservative southern Democrats pruned many New Deal programs. Truman thought that he could help reestablish some common ground. Although recognizing that a vice president could never exert open influence in the Senate, Truman believed that "if he is respected personally and if he maintains good relations with the members of the Senate, he can have considerable power behind the scenes."[23]

A week after the January 1945 inauguration, Truman's political mentor, Tom Pendergast, died in Kansas City. Released from prison, Pendergast had spent his last years estranged from his family and old friends. Truman had not seen the boss in years, but he determined to go to Pendergast's funeral. He owed his rise in politics to Pendergast, who, he insisted, "never asked me to do a dishonest deed. He knew I wouldn't do it if he asked me. He was always honest with me, and when he made a promise he kept it." Although Truman meant this as an act of friendship and loyalty, many considered it disgraceful for a vice president to pay homage to a convicted criminal and interpreted the incident as evidence that Truman remained a parochial machine politician. The vice president earned more bad publicity a few weeks later when he played the piano at the Washington Press Club's canteen for servicemen. As Truman played, the movie actress Lauren Bacall posed seductively atop the piano, allowing photographers to snap some decidedly undignified pictures.[24]

The vice president spent most of his time around the Senate chamber, talking with senators and listening to tedious speeches as he presided. Watching him from the press gallery on April 12, 1945, Associated Press reporter Tony Vaccaro commented, "You know, Roosevelt has an awfully good man in that Truman when it comes to dealing with the Senate if he'll only make use of him." Then he added, "He doesn't make use of him though. Truman doesn't know what's going on. Roosevelt won't tell him anything." That day, Truman used his time while presiding to keep in contact with his mother and sister in Missouri. "I am trying to write you a letter today from the desk of the President of the Senate," he wrote, "while a windy Senator from Wisconsin [Alexander Wiley] is making a speech on a subject with which he is in no way familiar." He reminded them to turn on their radios the next evening to hear him make a Jefferson Day speech to the nation and to introduce the president. While Truman was presiding that after-

noon, Roosevelt collapsed and died of a cerebral hemorrhage in Warm Springs.[25]

Unaware of his impending fate, Truman recessed the Senate at five that afternoon and strolled through the Capitol, without his Secret Service agent. He was the first vice president to be assigned a regular Secret Service agent, after his military aide, Harry Vaughn, pointed out to Treasury Secretary Henry Morgenthau how odd it was to have scores of agents guarding the president and no one protecting the vice president. But the protection was somewhat erratic, enabling Truman to saunter unaccompanied through the Capitol to House Speaker Sam Rayburn's hideaway office, the "Board of Education." There he planned to mix a drink and spend some time talking politics with the Speaker and a handful of congressional cronies. When Truman arrived, Rayburn relayed a message that the president's press secretary wanted him to call right away. Truman called and was told to come to the White House as "quickly and quietly" as possible. "Holy General Jackson!" he exclaimed, the color drained from his face. Still not knowing exactly what had happened, Truman hurried back the length of the Capitol, still alone. At his office he grabbed his hat and his driver. They headed straight to the North Portico of the White House, where Truman was ushered up to the family quarters. There Eleanor Roosevelt told him that the president was dead.[26]

President Truman

That evening, Harry Truman took the oath as president in a somber ceremony in the Cabinet Room. He placed his first call from the Oval Office to Secretary of the Senate Leslie Biffle, asking him to arrange for the congressional leadership to attend the ceremony and to set up a luncheon at the Senate the next day. As Republican Senator Arthur Vandenberg noted in his diary:

Truman came back to the Senate this noon for lunch with a few of us. It shattered all tradition. But it was both wise and smart. It means that the days of executive contempt for Congress are ended; that we are returning to a government in which Congress will take its rightful place.

After Roosevelt's funeral, Truman returned to address a joint session of Congress. "Now

Harry—Mr. President—we are going to stand by you," Speaker Rayburn assured him. "I think you will," Truman replied. Majority Leader Alben Barkley further urged Truman to have confidence in himself. "If you do not, the people will lose confidence in you." [27]

Three months in the vice-presidency had given Truman no preparation for the nation's highest post. He was thrust into the role of commander in chief while war was still underway in Europe and the Pacific. He knew little about the development of the atomic bomb, yet within months he would be called upon to decide whether to use this weapon against Japan. Nor did he know much about the agreements Roosevelt had reached with the Russians and British at Yalta. Truman talked with everyone who had accompanied Roosevelt to learn as much as possible about what Roosevelt had agreed to and what he intended to do in foreign policy. Truman's inexperience in international matters contrasted sharply with his abundant knowledge of domestic affairs, gained from ten years in local government and another ten in the Senate. [28]

Truman's assets were his firm personal principles, his honesty, humility, and homespun character, and his ability to speak plain truths. Regardless of his lack of preparation, these qualities enabled him to face the challenges of the cold war, make portentous decisions, and retain the respect of the electorate, who accepted him as one of them. He could be magnanimous, as in his gesture of consulting with former President Herbert Hoover, long barred from the Roosevelt White House. He could be intrepid, as in his determination to remove General Douglas MacArthur from command in Korea, in order to preserve the superiority of the civilian government over the military. In 1948 Truman won the most unexpected election upset of the century. Although he left the presidency in 1953 at a low ebb in his popularity, his standing rose again over the years. After his death on December 26, 1972, he achieved the status of folk hero. Songs proclaimed: "America Needs You Harry Truman." A Broadway play, "Give 'Em Hell, Harry," was based on his life story, and biographies of him became best sellers. Presidential candidates from both parties claimed Truman rather than Roosevelt as their model. In retrospect, his selection for vice president had been a wise move by the party leaders. [29]

NOTES

[1] Edward A. Harris, "Harry S. Truman: 'I Don't Want to be President,'" in J.T. Salter, ed., *Public Men: In and Out of Office* (Chapel Hill, NC, 1946), pp. 4–5; Robert H. Ferrell, *Choosing Truman: The Democratic Convention of 1944* (Columbia, MO, 1994), pp. 1–34.

[2] Robert H. Ferrell, ed., *The Autobiography of Harry S. Truman* (Boulder, CO, 1980), pp. 17–20; Margaret Truman, *Harry S. Truman* (New York, 1973), p. 47; U.S., Congress, House, *Congressional Record*, 103d Cong., 1st sess., pp. H10918–20.

[3] David McCullough, *Truman* (New York, 1992), pp. 63, 88–90.

[4] Ibid., pp. 102–44; Richard Lawrence Miller, *Truman: The Rise to Power* (New York, 1986), pp. 103–48; Jhan Robbins, *Bess & Harry: An American Love Story* (New York, 1980), pp. 23–37.

[5] Margaret Truman, pp. 59–82; Ferrell, ed., *The Autobiography of Harry S. Truman*, pp. 81–84.

[6] Robert H. Ferrell, *Harry S. Truman: A Life* (Columbia, MO, 1994), pp. 91–116; McCullough, pp. 181–86.

[7] Margaret Truman, pp. 83–89; Ferrell, *Truman: A Life*, pp. 124–32; McCullough, pp. 202–13.

[8] Harry S. Truman, *Memoirs by Harry S. Truman*, vol. 1, *Year of Decisions* (Garden City, NY, 1955), pp. 142–43, 149; Alonzo L. Hamby, *Man of the People: A Life of Harry S. Truman* (New York, 1995) pp. 200–212; Harris, p. 9; Margaret Truman, p. 91.

[9] Ernest Barcella, "They Call Him Mr. Baffle," *Colliers* (January 29, 1949), pp. 27, 61–62; Margaret Truman, pp. 100–102.

[10] Truman, *Memoirs*, 1:159–63; McCullough, pp. 234–52; Hamby, pp. 213–47.

[11] Ferrell, *Truman: A Life*, pp. 153–61.

[12] Theodore Wilson, "The Truman Committee, 1941," in Arthur M. Schlesinger, Jr., and Roger Bruns, eds., *Congress Investigates: A Documented History, 1792–1974* (New York, 1975), 4:3115–3262; Hamby, pp. 248–60.

[13] Margaret Truman, p. 167; Miller, pp. 381–85.

[14] McCullough, pp. 292–301; Ferrell, *Choosing Truman*, pp. 35–50.

[15] McCullough, pp. 299–306; David Robertson, *Sly and Able: A Political Biography of James F. Byrnes* (New York, 1994), pp. 8–9; Robert H. Ferrell, *Ill-Advised: Presidential Health and Public Trust* (Columbia, MO, 1992), p. 44.

[16] McCullough, pp. 298–99, 317–318; Harris, pp. 4–5; *Remarks by Former President Harry S. Truman and Responses by Members of the Senate Thereto in the United States Senate on May 8, 1964* (Washington, 1964), p. 3.

[17] Truman, *Memoirs*, 1:192–93; Hamby, pp. 274–84.

[18] Miller, pp. 381–87; McCullough, pp. 324–33; Ferrell, *Choosing Truman*, pp. 57–61; Harris, pp. 5–6; Doris Kearns Goodwin, *No Ordinary Time: Franklin and Eleanor Roosevelt: The Home Front in World War II* (New York, 1994), p. 530.

[19] Jonathan Daniels, *The Man of Independence* (Port Washington, NY, 1971; reprint of 1950 edition), p. 255; Truman, *Memoirs*, 1:1–4, 194–95.

[20] Truman, *Memoirs*, 1:195–96; Allen Drury, *A Senate Journal, 1943–1945* (New York, 1963), p. 409.

[21] Margaret Truman, pp. 203–5.

[22] Truman, *Memoirs*, 1:195; Daniels, p. 257.

[23] Truman, *Memoirs*, 1:196–97; McCullough, pp. 335–36; see also James T. Patterson, *Congressional Conservatism and the New Deal: The Growth of the Conservative Coalition in Congress, 1933–1939* (Lexington, KY, 1967).

[24] Harris, p. 18; McCullough, pp. 336–37.

[25] Drury, p. 410; McCullough, p. 340.

[26] Margaret Truman, pp. 201–3; McCullough, pp. 335–42; Ferrell, *Truman: A Life*, pp. 174–76. Others have reported Truman's April 12, 1945, exclamation as "Jesus Christ and General Jackson!" (McCullough, p. 341; Robert J. Donovan, *Conflict and Crisis: The Presidency of Harry S. Truman, 1945–1948* (New York, 1977), p. 4.

[27] Arthur H. Vandenberg, Jr., ed., *The Private Papers of Senate Vandenberg* (Boston, 1952), p. 167; H.G. Dulaney, Edward Hake Phillips, and MacPhelan Reese, eds., *Speak Mr. Speaker* (Bonham, TX, 1978), p. 120; McCullough, p. 356.

[28] Marie D. Natoli, "Harry S. Truman and the Contemporary Vice Presidency," *Presidential Studies Quarterly* 14 (Winter 1988): 81–84.

[29] Ferrell, *Choosing Truman*, pp. 89–95. On Truman's presidency see Robert J. Donovan, *Conflict and Crisis: The Presidency of Harry S. Truman, 1945–1948* (New York, 1977), and *Tumultuous Years: The Presidency of Harry S. Truman, 1949–1953* (New York, 1977).

Chapter 35

ALBEN W. BARKLEY
1949–1953

ALBEN W. BARKLEY

Chapter 35

ALBEN W. BARKLEY

35th Vice President: 1949–1953

Barkley, as Vice President, was in a class by himself. He had the complete confidence of both the President and the Senate.

—HARRY S. TRUMAN

Alben W. Barkley, who served as vice president of the United States from 1949 to 1953, was popularly known as the "Veep." His young grandson had suggested this abbreviated alternative to the cumbersome "Mr. Vice President." When Barkley told the story at a press conference, the newspapers printed it, and the title stuck. Barkley's successor as vice president, Richard Nixon, declined to continue the nickname, saying that it had been bestowed on Barkley affectionately and belonged to him. While commentators may occasionally use "veep" as a generic term for vice presidents, historically the term is Barkley's alone.[1]

A storyteller of great repute, Alben Barkley frequently poked fun at himself and his office. He was especially fond of telling about the mother who had two sons. One went to sea; the other became vice president; and neither was heard from again. In Barkley's case, the story was not at all true. He made sure that the public heard from him, and about him, as often as possible. And what the public heard, they liked, for Alben Barkley performed admirably as vice president of the United States.

Seventy years old when he was sworn in as vice president, Alben Barkley was a genial grandfatherly figure—but with enough life left in him to court and marry a widow half his age and to captivate national attention with their May-December romance. In many ways, Barkley was the last of the old-time vice presidents, the

last to preside regularly over the Senate, the last not to have an office in or near the White House, the last to identify more with the legislative than the executive branch. He was an old warhorse, the veteran of many political battles, the perpetual keynote speaker of his party who could rouse delegates from their lethargy to shout and cheer for the party's leaders and platform. His stump-speaker's lungs enabled him to bellow out a speech without need for a microphone. He was partisan to the marrow, but with a sense of humor and a gift of storytelling that defused partisan and personal animosities.[2]

Campaigning on Horseback

Ever the politician, Alben Barkley loved to point out that he had been born in a log house, in Graves County, Kentucky, on November 24, 1877. The baby was named Willie Alben, a name that always embarrassed him, and as soon as he was old enough to have a say about it, he reversed the order and formalized the name to Alben William. "Just imagine the tribulations I would have had," he later commented, "a robust, active boy, going through a Kentucky childhood with the name of 'Willie,' and later trying to get into politics!"[3]

Barkley worked his way through Marvin College, a Methodist institution in Clinton, Kentucky. He also briefly attended Emory College and the University of Virginia law school. As did most lawyers in those days, he learned his trade mainly by "reading" law, in a Paducah law office, before hanging out his own shingle. In 1903 he married and began to raise a family. Two years later, Alben Barkley ran for prosecuting attorney of McCracken County. Later he would deny the stories that he campaigned on a mule. "This story is a base canard, and, here and now, I wish to spike it for all time," he wrote in his memoirs, *That Reminds Me*. "It was not a mule—it was a horse." [4]

From prosecuting attorney, Barkley ran for county judge, and in 1912, at the age of thirty-five, he won a seat in the U.S. House of Representatives. His victory began a forty-two-year career in national politics that would take him from the House to the Senate to the vice-presidency. Barkley entered politics as a Democrat in the mold of Jefferson, Jackson, and William Jennings Bryan, but in Congress he came under the powerful influence of President Woodrow Wilson. As a Wilsonian, Barkley came to define flexibility of government and a willingness to experiment with social and economic programs as the policies of "a true Liberal." Although he was later closely identified with the New Deal, Barkley asserted: "I was a liberal and a progressive long before I ever heard of Franklin D. Roosevelt." [5]

In 1923, Representative Barkley made an unsuccessful run for the Democratic nomination as governor of Kentucky. That sole electoral defeat actually helped propel him into the Senate, because the race gave him name recognition throughout Kentucky and won him the title "iron man," for his ability to give as many as sixteen speeches a day on the campaign trail. In 1926 Barkley won the nomination for the United States Senate and defeated an incumbent Republican to win the seat. By the 1930s he had moved into the Senate Democratic leadership as an assistant to Majority Leader Joseph T. Robinson. He also received national attention as the keynote speaker at the 1932 Democratic convention that first nominated Franklin D. Roosevelt for president. [6]

The Struggle for the Majority Leadership

During the early New Deal, Barkley served shoulder to shoulder with Majority Leader Robinson. Rarely were two leaders so starkly different in nature, which perhaps explains the effectiveness of their combined efforts. Joe Robinson of Arkansas, who had led the Democratic minority in the 1920s and became majority leader in 1933, gave the impression "of brute, animal strength, and a willingness to use it." He ran the Senate by a mix of threats, favors, and parliamentary skill. Robinson had no patience to cajole, and left such tasks to trusted aides like Barkley, South Carolina's James F. Byrnes, and Mississippi's Pat Harrison. "Scrappy Joe" could annihilate an opponent in debate, but for the most part he preferred to leave the oratory to Barkley, who could talk on any subject for any amount of time. Unlike Robinson, Barkley had no ability when it came to threatening and domineering. He succeeded through the art of compromise, and through his convivial personality and gift of storytelling. [7]

When Robinson died during the fierce legislative battle to enact President Roosevelt's "Court packing" plan in 1937, a contest developed between Senators Barkley and Harrison to become majority leader. Pat Harrison was chairman of the influential Finance Committee, and a beloved figure in the Senate who held the loyalty of many members. It appeared that Harrison would win the race—much to President Roosevelt's dismay. Although Harrison had worked for enactment of much New Deal legislation, he was too conservative and too independent for Roosevelt's taste. Moreover, most of the opponents of Roosevelt's Court plan stood with Harrison, who had refrained from speaking out on that controversial issue. Although professing neutrality, Roosevelt privately threw his support behind Barkley, pressing state Democratic leaders to lobby their senators in Barkley's behalf. Roosevelt also addressed a public letter to "My dear Alben," implying his endorsement of the Kentucky senator. When Barkley won the majority leadership by a single vote, many senators—including his own supporters—interpreted his election as a victory for the president rather than for Barkley. For many years thereafter his colleagues assumed that he spoke primarily for the White House to the Senate, rather than for the Senate to the White House.[8]

After the forceful leadership of Joe Robinson, any successor would suffer by comparison, and the press soon began to taunt "bumbling Barkley." On paper he led an enormous majority of 76 Democrats against 16 Republicans and a handful of independents. But in fact the Democratic party was seriously divided between its liberal and conservative wings, and Barkley could not guarantee a majority behind any of the administration's domestic programs. Not until World War II forged a new cohesiveness in the Senate did Barkley truly have a majority behind him. Without question, he grew in office, gaining respect from both senators and journalists for his dogged hard work and persistent good nature.

The Majority Leader Resigns

Senator Barkley was part of the "Big Four" that included Vice President Henry Wallace, House Speaker Sam Rayburn, and House Majority Leader John McCormack. The Big Four met regularly with President Roosevelt to map the administration's legislative strategy. Barkley saw himself as the leader of the president's forces, out to enact the president's program. But in 1944 even Barkley's loyalty was stretched to the breaking point. Relations between the administration and Congress had grown strained during the war, as the chief executive was preoccupied by military and diplomatic affairs. In February 1944, Roosevelt became the first president to veto a revenue bill, rejecting a two-billion-dollar tax increase as insufficient and declaring it a relief measure "not for the needy but for the greedy." Senator Barkley, who had worked out the compromises within the Senate Finance Committee, of which he was a member, and who believed it was the best bill he could get passed, felt incensed over the president's accusations. He rose in the Senate to urge his colleagues to override the president's veto. Then he resigned as majority leader.[9]

The next day, the Senate Democrats unanimously reelected Barkley as their leader, and from then on it was clear that Barkley spoke *for* the Senate *to* the White House. The dramatic resignation and reelection elevated Barkley's re-

spect and standing as a leader but also dampened his relations with President Roosevelt. That summer, when the Democratic convention met and it became clear that the unpopular Henry Wallace would need to be replaced as vice president, the mood of the convention favored Barkley for the job, but Roosevelt would not tolerate one who had so recently rebelled against him. Instead he chose the less-known Missouri Senator Harry Truman. The Roosevelt-Truman ticket won election in the fall, and in April 1945 it was Vice President Truman, not Alben Barkley, who inherited the presidency upon Roosevelt's death.[10]

Whatever bitterness Barkley might have felt he put aside, transferring his loyalty completely to Truman. During Truman's short vice-presidency, they enjoyed what Barkley called a "catcher-pitcher" relationship, with the majority leader calling the signals. They continued to work together closely after Truman moved to the White House. These were rough years for the Democrats. In the 1946 elections voters sent Republican majorities to the Senate and House for the first time since the Great Depression. Barkley became minority leader during the Eightieth Congress in 1947 and 1948. It was a foregone conclusion that the Republicans would also win the presidency in 1948, and the smart money was on New York Governor Thomas E. Dewey to become the next president.

A Remarkable Upset

A dispirited Democratic convention met in Philadelphia in 1948. Yet, once again, Alben Barkley was able to lift his party's spirits and get the delegates cheering with an old-fashioned, rip-roaring, Republican-bashing keynote address. The demonstration that followed his speech was so long and so enthusiastic that Barkley became the obvious choice for vice president. President Truman, suspicious that Barkley, who had mentioned him only once in the hour-long speech, was trying to replace him at the top of the ticket, was not eager to have the senator as his running mate. "Old man Barkley," as Truman called him, was seventy years old, and their neighboring states were too similar to balance the ticket regionally. But since others—like Supreme Court Justice William O. Douglas—had turned him down, Truman agreed to accept Barkley for his running mate if the delegates wanted him. "It will have to come quick," Barkley said of his selection. "I don't want it passed along so long it is like a cold biscuit." When offered the second place on the ticket, Barkley, so often the bridesmaid in the past, accepted with pleasure and set out on a grueling speaking tour that showed he was still an "iron man" at age seventy.[11]

While the president whistle-stopped by train, Barkley made the first "prop stop" campaign by air. He had come a long way since the days when he first campaigned for office on horseback. In six weeks he toured thirty-six states and gave more than 250 speeches. He spoke to so many small audiences that the press dubbed him "the poor man's candidate." But his strength and stamina refuted the charges that he had been too old to run.[12]

The election of 1948 proved to be the most dramatic upset of all time. It is doubtful whether there is a single American history textbook in the schools today that fails to include the famous picture of a smiling Harry Truman holding up the *Chicago Tribune's* erroneous headline: "Dewey Defeats Truman." So in January 1949 Alben Barkley stepped down again as Senate Democratic leader, this time to become president of the Senate. As vice president, Barkley buried whatever differences he had with Truman and the two men got along well, although some mutual suspicions lingered on. For years in the Senate it had been Truman who called Barkley "boss." And Barkley must surely have thought of President Truman: "There but for the spite of Franklin Roosevelt, go I." Yet in every respect, politically, ideologically, and socially, the two men were remarkably alike and worked together harmoniously.

The Delicate Nature of the Vice-Presidency

Having served in the job, even if briefly, Harry Truman understood the delicate nature of the vice-presidency, which he noted fell between the legislative and executive branches without being responsible to either. "The Vice-President cannot become completely acquainted with the policies of the President, while the senators, for their part, look on him as a presiding officer only, who is outside the pale as far as the senatorial club is concerned." Despite being presiding officer, the vice president was "hardly ever" consulted about legislative matters. Although he could lobby for the president's legislation, he had nothing to trade for votes. Truman noted that the status of John Nance Garner had rested more on his position within the Democratic party than on the vice-presidency, while Henry Wallace was a party outsider who had little influence within the Senate. Alben Barkley, by contrast, "was in a class by himself," declared Truman. "He had the complete confidence of both the President and the Senate."[13]

Although new in the job, Barkley had long experience in dealing with vice presidents. He recalled how as a freshman senator in 1927 he had gone to the rostrum in the Senate chamber to chat with Vice President Charles Dawes, who said, "Barkley, this is a helluva job I have as Vice-President." "What is the matter with it?" Barkley asked, to which Dawes replied: "I can do only two things here. One of them is to sit up here on this rostrum and listen to you birds talk without the ability to reply. The other is to look at the newspapers every morning to see how the President's health is."[14]

As party leader in the Senate, Alben Barkley had assessed the influence of several vice presidents over legislation and decided that the degree of influence depended on the person who held the office. Vice presidents with experience in the House or Senate could occasionally exercise some leverage on legislation. As an example, Barkley cited former House Speaker John Nance Garner as the vice president who "exercised larger influence in the passage of legislation than any other occupant of the Office." Garner assisted the passage of early New Deal legislation "in an informal and entirely proper way," helping to speed emergency bills through the Senate. Barkley therefore declared that "a Vice-President who is well liked by members of the Senate and by the corresponding members of the House in charge of legislation can exercise considerable power in the shaping of the program of legislation which every administration seeks to enact."

Unlike some of his predecessors, Barkley was determined not to enter into a "four-year period of silence." He accepted hundreds of invitations to speak at meetings, conventions, banquets, and other partisan and nonpartisan programs. "I like to do it," he explained. "I like people and I enjoy the thrill of crowds. I have always believed it to be the duty of those who are elected to high office by the people to take government to them whenever and by whatever legitimate means possible." Traveling almost exclusively by air, Barkley claimed to have spent more time in the air than all his predecessors combined. Having served twenty-two years as a member of the House and Senate, and the past twelve as Democratic leader, he missed taking an active part in the debates and piloting legislation through to passage. He found that the office did not consume all his energies. Barkley constantly sought other activities to occupy his time, attending meetings of the Senate Democratic Policy Committee, legislative conferences with the president, and cabinet meetings. He was the first vice president to become a member of the National Security Council, as provided by the National Security Act of 1947. "All these conferences I attend regularly," he said in 1952, noting that he enjoyed them and engaged freely in the discussions.[15]

Proud to be the Presiding Officer

Nevertheless, Alben Barkley was also the last vice president to preside regularly over the Senate. Senate Parliamentarian Floyd Riddick estimated that Barkley presided between 50 and 75 percent of the time, a figure that seems incredibly high today, but which reflected the traditional concept of the vice president's constitutional responsibility. As one who presided routinely, Barkley also used the Vice President's Room, outside the chamber, as his working office. He was proud to occupy that historic room, and liked to keep a wood fire burning in its fireplace, the smell of wood smoke reminding him of the open hearth in his childhood home. He also took pleasure in the furnishings and art works of the room that were associated with famous names from the past.[16]

In the Eighty-first Congress, which began in January 1949, the Democrats enjoyed a 54-to-42 majority in the Senate. By the Eighty-second Congress, their margin had shrunk to 49 to 47. But in both of those congresses the real majority belonged to a coalition of conservative Democrats and Republicans. This conservative coalition had emerged out of the opposition to FDR's Court packing plan in 1937 and predominated in the Senate at least until the liberal Democratic sweep of Senate elections in 1958. During the Second World War and throughout the Truman administration, this conservative coalition frequently frustrated administration efforts to enact domestic reform legislation.[17]

President Truman had proposed an ambitious Fair Deal program to deal with national health insurance, farm supports, labor-management relations, and civil rights, but the conservative coalition repeatedly derailed his legislative initiatives, often through the use of filibusters. In the field of civil rights, for instance, the president desegregated the armed forces through executive order but had no luck in winning congressional approval of bills to outlaw the poll tax, make lynching a federal crime, or prohibit segregation and discrimination in interstate commerce. More typical of congressional attitudes at the time was the passage of a bill to authorize segregated schools on federal property—a bill which President Truman vetoed. "Step by step we are discarding old discriminations," he declared, "we must not adopt new ones."[18]

The Senate overturned some of Vice President Barkley's rulings. Charles Watkins, who served as parliamentarian during Barkley's vice-presidency, observed that, while Barkley was well acquainted with the Senate's rules, he would sometimes get them mixed up or become obstinate about how a rule should be applied. On a few occasions, Barkley persisted in his own interpretations of the rules in spite of Watkins' advice, only to have the Senate reverse his rulings—which dealt with efforts to enact civil rights legislation. Early in 1949, Barkley's successor as majority leader, Senator Scott Lucas of Illinois, attempted to amend the rules to make cloture easier to obtain as a way of ending a filibuster. Georgia Senator Richard Russell led the opposition to any rules changes that might favor civil rights legislation. In a procedural move—and against the parliamentarian's advice—Barkley ruled against Russell's point of order, but the Senate, by a vote of 41 yeas to 46 nays, failed to sustain the chair's ruling. Barkley was apparently willing to take the risk of defeat both because of his support for the administration's civil rights program and because of his own frustration at the Senate's inability to invoke cloture and end debate during his years as majority leader.[19]

As vice president, Barkley did what he could to help his successors as majority leader, Scott Lucas (who served from 1949 to 1951) and Ernest McFarland (who held the leadership from 1951 to 1953). Barkley continued to interpret the relationship between the vice president and the floor leader as that of catcher and pitcher. With the divisions inside the ranks of the Democratic party, however, as well as the rapidly diminishing popularity of the Truman administration, Barkley often watched his successors' pitches go wild. Lucas and McFarland were more legislative mechanics than floor leaders, and neither achieved Barkley's status or prestige in the post. As one journalist observed, they made the job of majority leader "misery without splendor." Despite their leadership roles, Lucas and McFarland were each in turn defeated when they ran for reelection. Perhaps the sight of their increasing discomfort and distress may have added to Barkley's own comfort and pleasure in his position as presiding officer rather than floor leader.[20]

An Activist Vice President

As vice president, Alben Barkley tried to be as much of an activist as his office would allow. He was assisted by a sympathetic president, who not only had held the job, but was a student of American government and history and thought seriously about how to enhance the vice-presidency. By executive order, President Truman proclaimed a new coat of arms, seal, and flag for the vice president. "You can make 'em step aside now," Truman assured Barkley when the new symbols of office were unveiled. Truman also supported a raise in the vice president's salary and expenses.[21] When Barkley celebrated his

thirty-eighth anniversary of service in the legislative branch, President Truman paid a surprise visit to the Senate chamber to present to the vice president a gavel made from timber taken from the White House during its reconstruction. Barkley was deeply touched by the gesture. In accepting the gift, Barkley noted that President Truman frequently said that no president and vice president got along together as well as they did. "The reason for this," Barkley told the Senate, "is that I have let him have his way about everything."[22]

During the 1950 congressional campaign, which occurred after the United States had entered the Korean War, President Truman left the job of campaigning for Democratic candidates to Vice President Barkley, who barnstormed the nation. Although Barkley's party suffered losses, the Democrats retained their majorities in both houses of Congress.[23] Yet, despite his vigorous campaigning, it became evident that age was beginning to catch up with Alben Barkley. In 1950, the columnist Drew Pearson attended a dinner for the vice president, at which the president, chief justice, and Speaker of the House were present. Barkley gave a brief speech and "seemed a little old and tired," Pearson recorded in his private diary. "It was about the first time that his speech wasn't all it usually is."[24]

Even though he was exempted from the Twenty-second Amendment to the Constitution, ratified in 1951, that limited future presidents to two terms, Truman announced his decision not to seek a third term. Vice President Barkley then sought the Democratic nomination for president, but his age and failing eyesight defeated his candidacy. Organized labor, which exerted great influence within the Democratic party organization, openly opposed his nomination because he was too old. Although deeply hurt, Barkley accepted the decision and withdrew from the race. He was invited to deliver a farewell address to the convention and did so with characteristic grace and style, celebrating the Democratic "crusade" that he had helped to lead to ensure a "happier and fuller life to all mankind in the years that lie before us." When he bid the convention good-by, the delegates awarded him a forty-five-minute ovation, demonstrating the enormous affection that the party felt for him, even as they denied him his heart's desire.[25]

Return from Retirement

Alben Barkley retired to Kentucky but could not stay retired for long. In 1954 he ran once again for a seat in the Senate against the incumbent Republican Senator John Sherman Cooper. Campaigning always seemed to invigorate him, and he swept back into office by a comfortable margin. His victory helped return the Senate Democrats to a one-vote majority and made Lyndon Johnson majority leader. Two years later, in 1956, students at Washington and Lee University invited Senator Alben Barkley to deliver the keynote address at their mock convention. He accepted and gave one of his classic rip-snorting, Republican-bashing, Democratic-praising orations. At its conclusion he reminded his audience that after all of his years in national politics he had become a freshman once again, but that he had declined an offer of a front row seat with other senior senators. "I'm glad to sit on the back row," he declared, "for I would rather be a servant in the House of the Lord than to sit in the seats of the mighty." Then, with the applause of the crowd in his ears, Alben Barkley collapsed and died from a massive heart attack. For an old-fashioned orator, there could have been no more appropriate final exit from the stage.[26]

Clearly, Alben Barkley enjoyed being vice president of the United States. Although he missed the opportunity to speak out, maneuver, and vote on bills as he had as senator and majority leader, he enjoyed promoting the president's legislative program. He also savored the thrill of the crowds that a vice president can attract, relished performing the ceremonial duties, and delighted in the prestige of national office. "I hope the Vice-Presidency continues to hold the respect of the American people," he said. "The qualifications for it are the same as for the Presidency itself. They have to be; for he may become the President in case of a death or disability." The best way for vice presidents to retain respect, he concluded, was to deserve it. "I have always felt that public officers should lean backwards in the performance of their official duties because, to a larger extent than many people realize, they are looked upon as examples of probity and propriety in dealing with public matters. It will be a sad day for this country and its institutions if and when the people lose confidence in their public servants." For his part, Alben Barkley retained public confidence—even public affection—throughout his long career in the legislative branch and for four years cast the vice presidency in a highly positive light.

NOTES

[1] Alben W. Barkley, *That Reminds Me* (Garden City, NY, 1954), pp. 21–22.

[2] For Barkley's life and career, see James K. Libbey, *Dear Alben: Mr. Barkley of Kentucky* (Lexington, KY, 1976), and Polly Ann Davis, *Alben Barkley: Senate Majority Leader and Vice President* (New York, 1979).

[3] Barkley, *That Reminds Me*, p. 27.

[4] Ibid., p. 77.

[5] Donald A. Ritchie, "Alben W. Barkley: The President's Man," in Richard A. Baker and Roger H. Davidson, eds., *First Among Equals: Outstanding Senate Leaders of the Twentieth Century* (Washington, 1991), pp. 130, 146.

[6] Ibid., pp. 129–31.

[7] Donald C. Bacon, "Joseph Taylor Robinson: The Good Soldier," in Baker and Davidson, eds., *First Among Equals*, pp. 63–66.

[8] Ritchie, pp. 127–29.

[9] The events surrounding Barkley's resignation are dramatically recounted in Allen Drury's *A Senate Journal, 1943–1945* (New York, 1963), pp. 85–97.

[10] Barkley, *That Reminds Me*, pp. 169–94.

[11] Alonzo L. Hamby, *Man of the People: A Life of Harry S. Truman* (New York, 1995), pp. 448–51; Robert J. Donovan, *Conflict and Crisis: The Presidency of Harry S Truman, 1945–1948* (New York, 1977), pp. 405–6; Margaret Truman, *Harry S. Truman* (New York, 1973), pp. 9–11; David McCullough, *Truman* (New York, 1992), pp. 637–38.

[12] Barkley, *That Reminds Me*, pp. 195–204.

[13] Harry S. Truman, *Memoirs by Harry S. Truman*, vol. 1, *Year of Decisions* (Garden City, NY, 1955), p. 57.

[14] Alben W. Barkley, "The Vice-Presidency," May 1952, pp. 7–8, Alben W. Barkley Papers, University of Kentucky.

[15] Ibid., pp. 12–14.

[16] *Floyd M. Riddick: Senate Parliamentarian*, Oral History Interviews, June 26, 1978 to February 15, 1979 (U.S. Senate Historical Office, Washington, DC), p. 66; Barkley, *That Reminds Me*, p. 210.

[17] See James T. Patterson, *Congressional Conservatism and the New Deal: The Growth of the Conservative Coalition in Congress, 1933–1939* (Lexington, KY, 1967).

[18] Harold F. Gosnell, *Truman's Crises: A Political Biography of Harry S. Truman* (Westport, CT, 1980), pp. 439–49, 481–90.

[19] *Floyd M. Riddick*, pp. 67, 126–28, 144–46; U.S., Congress, Senate, *Congressional Record*, 81st Cong, 1st sess., p. 2274; Gilbert C. Fite, *Richard B. Russell, Jr.: Senator From Georgia* (Chapel Hill, NC, 1991), pp. 245–46.

[20] Ritchie, pp. 156–57.

[21] Davis, pp. 280–81.

[22] *Congressional Record*, 82d Cong., 1st sess, p. 1710.

[23] Gosnell, pp. 453–54.

[24] Tyler Abell, ed., *Drew Pearson, Diaries, 1949–1959* (New York, 1974), pp. 128–29.

[25] Barkley, *That Reminds Me*, pp. 231–51.

[26] Ibid., pp. 312–14.

Chapter 36

RICHARD MILHOUS NIXON
1953–1961

RICHARD M. NIXON

Chapter 36

RICHARD MILHOUS NIXON

36th Vice President: 1953–1961

[I]t just is not possible in politics for a Vice President to "chart out his own course".
—RICHARD M. NIXON [1]

On the morning of April 16, 1956, Vice President Richard Nixon served notice that the vice-presidency had finally become an office to be sought after by ambitious politicians rather than a position in which to gain four years of rest. After weeks of speculation that Nixon would be dropped from the Republican ticket in the coming presidential race, fueled by President Dwight Eisenhower's comment that the vice president had to "chart his own course," Nixon decided to force Ike's hand. The young politician walked into the Oval Office and said, "Mr. President, I would be honored to continue as Vice President under you." [2] Eisenhower now had to either accept his running mate or reject him openly. Not willing to risk a party squabble during what promised to be a successful reelection bid, Eisenhower told the press he was "delighted by the news." Richard Nixon had defied pressure to leave office voluntarily that came from within the White House, the press, and some segments of the party. In the process, he had been offered a major cabinet position and had been urged to run for a seat in the Senate. Instead, this ambitious young politician fought to remain in what had once been considered a meaningless office. Over the previous four years, Nixon had not only worked hard to promote the policies of the Eisenhower administration but had used the vice-presidency to build a foundation of support among the regulars of the Republican party that made him the early favorite for the presidential nomination in 1960. He had fought hard for the

office in 1952 and was not about to let anyone but Eisenhower take it from him.

From Whittier to Congress

Richard Nixon's career seems best described as a series of fierce political battles. Every campaign was bruising, and he never occupied a "safe" seat, perhaps only fitting for a man who had come so far, so fast. Born on January 9, 1913, to a Quaker family in Yorba Linda, California, Richard Milhous Nixon spent his childhood reading and working in the various family enterprises. As a teenager in Whittier, California, he split his time between the family grocery store and the high school debating team, where he received numerous awards. He went on to Whittier College, a small Quaker school not far from home, and then received a scholarship to attend law school at Duke University. Nixon's academic performance was characterized by perseverance and a determination to work harder than any of his classmates. That determination pushed him to finish third in his class at Duke in 1937 but did not result in any job offers from well-known firms in New York City, as Nixon had hoped. Disappointed, he returned to Whittier, joined a small firm, and began dabbling in local politics. In 1940 he married Thelma "Pat" Ryan, after wooing her persistently for more than two years.

As was the case for so many men of his generation, World War II interrupted Richard Nixon's plans. His Quaker background made Nixon reluctant to volunteer for duty in the armed services, but in 1942, he obtained a job with the Office of Price Administration in Washington that allowed him to contribute to the war effort and gain valuable government experience. Soon, however, the call to arms became too great to resist, and in August of 1942 he joined the navy. He served in the South Pacific Air Transport Command, operating airfields during General Douglas MacArthur's island-hopping campaign. While the war unexpectedly altered Nixon's career path, his service record made him an even more attractive political candidate than he had been previously. Even before his discharge was official, the Committee of 100, a group of southern California business and professional leaders looking for a promising Republican candidate to sponsor against incumbent Democratic Representative Jerry Voorhis, asked if Nixon was available as a congressional candidate. After brief interviews to determine that this returning young veteran held acceptably Republican views, the group helped launch a career that was more promising than they could have foreseen. Despite this impressive backing, however, the campaign against Voorhis was a hard-nosed affair that gained Nixon both ardent admirers and fierce enemies. Nothing ever came easily for Dick Nixon.[3]

That first campaign in 1946 gave Richard Nixon the issue that would catapult him to prominence. He vigorously attacked Representative Voorhis for being dominated by Communist-controlled labor unions. Like many Republican candidates across the country, Nixon accused the Democrats of allowing Communists to enter important positions in the federal government, thus undermining American security and threatening to "socialize" the United States. As the cold war began to heat up in Europe and Asia, the American public reacted positively to Republican appeals to throw the Communists out of government, as well as to calls for cutting back on the New and Fair Deals. Republicans swept to victory in congressional elections across the country, winning majorities in the House and Senate for the first time since 1928. Nixon rode this wave of protest, receiving a whopping 57 percent of the vote in his district. The

anticommunism that won him a seat in Congress became his trademark issue on Capitol Hill when he gained appointment to the House Committee on Un-American Activities (HUAC).[4]

Formed in the 1930s to investigate the activities of Nazi and Communist organizations in the United States, HUAC had also served as a forum for attacks on Jews, civil libertarians, and labor union activists. By the late 1940s, the committee had a tarnished reputation as an ineffective and irresponsible group that was more dedicated to attracting publicity than to preserving American security. But, with public anxiety on the rise, HUAC members had the opportunity to lead the fight against domestic communism. Nixon took little part in the committee's investigations of Hollywood during 1947, but he became the leading figure in its highly publicized investigation of Alger Hiss.

In 1948, Whittaker Chambers, an editor for *Time* and a former Communist, testified that Hiss, a former State Department official and adviser to President Roosevelt at Yalta, had been a Communist agent. Hiss denied the charge, but over the next year and a half, the attempt to uncover the real story thrust Richard Nixon into the spotlight. Nixon led the investigation that eventually sent Hiss to prison for perjury. The case gave Nixon a national reputation as a diligent hunter of Communists and established him as a rising, if controversial, young star in the GOP.[5]

Nixon was not content to remain in the House of Representatives. After only four years in the House, he set his sights on the Senate seat held by Democrat Sheridan Downey. Facing a primary challenge from Representative Helen Gahagan Douglas, an aggressive opponent, Downey decided to retire and to endorse another Democrat, Chester Boddy. While Douglas and Boddy engaged in a vicious primary battle, Nixon watched and waited. When Douglas, a former actress, narrowly won the nomination, one of the nastier senatorial campaigns in U.S. history began. Nixon attacked Douglas for having voted against appropriations for HUAC and insinuated that she was a Communist sympathizer, charges that Boddy had used during the primaries. The Nixon campaign distributed pink leaflets comparing Douglas' House voting record with that of Labor party member Vito Marcantonio of New York, while the candidate and others referred to her as "the Pink Lady." Douglas fought just as hard, implying that Nixon had fascist tendencies and was controlled by oil interests. She even pinned on him the label that would haunt him for years, "Tricky Dick." When the smoke cleared, Nixon emerged with an overwhelming victory, garnering 59 percent of the vote. Nixon ran well throughout the state, exhibiting an ability to win votes in traditional Democratic areas and gaining continued attention from Republican leaders nationwide. The campaign also brought harsh criticism. For years afterward, his opponents would point to the 1950 race as an example of the mean streak they considered so much a part of Richard Nixon's character. The victory brought him increased prestige within the Republican party and among conservatives generally, but it also formed the foundation for his reputation as an unscrupulous campaigner.[6]

Even a seat in the United States Senate, however, could not entirely satisfy the restless Californian. In 1951, he embarked on a national speaking tour, delivering forty-nine speeches in twenty-two states. His travels boosted his already rising popularity with Republicans, and he was soon regarded as the party's most popular speaker.[7] During these speeches, Nixon also showed his dexterity at reaching out to the different factions within the party. In the early 1950s, Republicans were deeply divided between the conservative party regulars, usually known as the Old Guard and personified by Ohio Senator Robert Taft, and the more liberal eastern wing of the party, led by Thomas Dewey of New York. Nixon's anticommunism appealed to conservatives, but his firm internationalism and moderate views on domestic policy also made him popular with more liberal audiences. This ability to appeal to the party as a whole would serve him well in the future. By 1952, people were already thinking of him as a national candidate. Any Republican presidential nominee would be under tremendous pressure to "balance" the ticket by finding a vice-presidential candidate who would be acceptable in both the East and the Midwest. Richard Nixon's consensus approach to Republican politics positioned him to fill that role.

Campaigning for the Vice-Presidency

In 1952 the campaign for the Republican presidential nomination centered around Taft and General Dwight D. Eisenhower. Senator Taft had been an influential force in the party for more than a decade, leading the opposition to President Harry Truman's "Fair Deal." Eisenhower, the commander of Allied forces in Europe during World War II, had been sought by both parties as a nominee ever since the end of the war. In 1952, he announced that he was a Republican and that he was willing to run. Widely, though not always accurately, considered more liberal than Taft, Eisenhower was primarily concerned that the Republicans were in danger of rejecting internationalism. After failing to convince Taft to support an internationalist program, Ike threw his hat in the ring.

The contest threatened to polarize the party, and a number of darkhorse candidates entered the Republican national convention hoping for a deadlock. The most prominent of these hopefuls was Governor Earl Warren of California. As a member of the California delegation, Senator Nixon was obligated to support Warren's candidacy until the governor gave up the race. Nixon, however, used the train ride to the convention in Chicago to lobby his fellow delegates on behalf of Eisenhower. He argued that, when (rather than if) Warren released his delegates, they should throw their support to Eisenhower, because Taft could not win the general election. Many Taft supporters later referred to Nixon's efforts as "the Great Train Robbery," claiming he sold out both Taft and Warren in exchange for the vice-presidential nomination. Nixon's support for Eisenhower was sincere, but both Thomas Dewey and Ike's campaign manager, Henry Cabot Lodge, Jr., had told Nixon weeks earlier that he was the probable choice if Eisenhower should win. These promises, coupled with Taft's preference for Nixon's California colleague Senator William Knowland, undoubtedly spurred his efforts. After Eisenhower won the nomination, he put together a list of potential running mates with Senator Nixon's name at the top. Party leaders had already decided that Nixon was their man.[8]

Richard Nixon was, in many ways, the ideal running mate for Dwight Eisenhower. The general indicated that he wanted someone "who was young, vigorous, ready to learn, and of good reputation."[9] Only on the last of these criteria was Nixon suspect, and the most outspoken critics of Nixon's tactics were liberal Democrats who probably would not have voted for the Republican ticket in any event. Aside from providing a youthful counter to the sixty-two-year-old Eisenhower, Nixon balanced the ticket geographically, since Eisenhower's campaign relied heavily on New Yorkers. His nomination also indicated that California was becoming increasingly vital in presidential politics. Perhaps most important, Nixon was one of only a very few Republicans of national stature acceptable to both the Eisenhower camp and the Old Guard.[10] His selection was intended to foster unity within the party and to calm the strife that could lead to another electoral disaster like that of 1948. Calm, however, was seldom to be associated with Richard Nixon.

On September 18, 1952, barely two months after the Republican convention and just as the campaign was beginning to heat up, the front page of the New York Post ran the headline, "Secret Nixon Fund!" The story reported that Nixon had established a "millionaire's club" to help pay his political expenses. About seventy California businessmen contributed $100 to $500 each to pay the senator's travel and postage bills and prepare for future campaigns. Unconcerned by the article at first, Nixon argued that the fund was hardly secret and was intended as a means of saving public funds that would otherwise have been applied to his Senate expense account. He apparently forgot that such uses of his account would have been illegal. The Truman administration had been rocked by a series of scandals over the previous two years, and one of the keys to the Republican campaign was Eisenhower's pledge to clean the "crooks and cronies" out of Washington. The Democrats charged the Republicans with hypocritically attacking the administration when the GOP's vice-presidential nominee was taking money from business interests. Democratic leaders called on Nixon to resign, and public pressure began to build for the Republicans to come clean about the "secret fund." The Washington Post and New York Herald Tribune joined the call for Nixon's resignation. His candidacy was in jeopardy before it could even get started.[11]

Eisenhower, meanwhile, remained cautious. He asserted his belief that his running mate was an honest man and that the facts would vindicate him. But Ike did not dismiss the possibility of Nixon's resignation, saying only that he would talk with Nixon about the situation as soon as possible. When Eisenhower later told the press that the Republican campaign must be "clean as a hound's tooth," Nixon advisers took it as a sign that their man was in trouble with the boss. Relations between the two camps had been strained from the beginning. Some of Eisenhower's advisers were uncomfortable with Nixon on the ticket, because they mistakenly viewed him as a tool of the Old Guard, and they would have been more than happy to see him go. For their part, Nixon's supporters resented the disdain they felt coming from Eisenhower's people and were angry that Ike was leaving Nixon to fend for himself.[12] Finally, Nixon decided to force a decision by appearing on national television to explain his actions. On September 23, just hours before he went on the air, he received a call from Tom Dewey, who explained that Eisenhower's "top advisers" had decided that it would be best if Nixon ended his speech by offering his resignation. Nixon was momentarily stunned, but when Dewey asked what he was going to do, he replied, "Just tell them I haven't the slightest idea as to what I am going to do and if they want to find out they'd better listen to the broadcast. And tell them I know something about politics too!"[13]

What Nixon did that night saved his candidacy. From a studio in Los Angeles, Nixon gave the nation a detailed report of his financial history, everything from the mortgage on his house to the one political gift he said he intended to keep, a little dog his daughters named "Checkers." While this reference to his dog provided the popular name for one of the twentieth century's most significant political speeches, Nixon did much more than create a colorful image. He effectively refuted the ridiculous charge that he used the fund to live a life of luxury, while deflecting the more fundamental questions involving the influence gained by its contributors—questions that the Democrats seemed to lose sight of in their haste to sensationalize the story. Nixon also challenged the other candidates to make a full disclosure of their assets, knowing that Democratic presidential nominee Adlai Stevenson had problems with a fund of his own. Finally, he urged viewers to write to the Republican National Committee to state whether Nixon should leave or remain on the ticket. He presented himself as a common American, struggling to pay the bills, doing his part to clean up "the mess in Washington," and suffering the attacks of vicious foes.

Many observers found Nixon's "Checkers" speech repulsive. Journalist Walter Lippmann called it "the most demeaning experience my country has ever had to bear," and Eisenhower's close friend, General Lucius Clay, thought it was "corny." But the speech seemed to touch a chord in what is often called "Middle America" that elite observers failed to understand. Historian Herbert Parmet has argued that the appeal was like that of a Frank Capra movie, with Nixon playing the role of "Mr. Smith." Nearly sixty million people watched the telecast (a record audience that would not be broken until Nixon debated John F. Kennedy in the 1960 presidential race), and the response was overwhelming. Over 160,000 telegrams poured into Republican national headquarters, and switchboards around the country were jammed with calls to local and state party officials urging Nixon to stay on the ticket. There was little Eisenhower could do but consent. In a bold stroke, Nixon had effectively taken the decision away from Eisenhower by appealing to the party faithful. Nixon remained on the ticket, and "Ike and Dick" cruised to a comfortable victory in November.[14]

The Eisenhower Team

Over the next eight years, Richard Nixon elevated the office of vice president to a position of importance never before seen. No previous vice president was ever as active within the administration or enjoyed as much responsibility, partly because of Nixon's own energetic habits. He was always looking for something to do and took a keen interest in almost every aspect of government. Circumstances also played a part because of Eisenhower's occasional health problems. Believing that Franklin Roosevelt's failure to keep Vice President Harry S. Truman informed of government initiatives like the Manhattan Project had been dangerous, Eisenhower was determined that his own vice president would be as well informed as anyone in the administration.[15] But the primary reason for Nixon's activist status was that Eisenhower provided him with unique opportunities. Apart from the vice president's constitutional role as presiding officer of the Senate, the occupant of that office can only safely take up the activities that the president indicates are appropriate. Most presidents made little use of their vice presidents. Eisenhower, however, with his military experience confirming the value of a well-trained subordinate officer, found that Nixon could be an important part of his "team" concept of presidential administration, especially since Nixon possessed many of the political skills that were lacking in some of Eisenhower's other key advisers. Also, unlike some other vice presidents, Nixon did not represent a former or potential challenger to Eisenhower. Ike was, therefore, willing to use his youthful vice president for important tasks, and Nixon was willing to be so used. When they differed on questions of policy, there was never any question that Nixon would follow the president's lead. Because Nixon could perform smoothly in the several roles that Eisenhower needed filled, he was able to cultivate the image of an active and important vice president.

Party Liaison

Nixon's most important function in the administration was to link Eisenhower with the party leadership, especially in Congress. Nixon and Henry Cabot Lodge, Jr., were the only former congressmen in the Eisenhower cabinet, and no one else had Nixon's connections with the Senate. Although the Republicans held a slim majority in Congress, it was not certain that the Old

Guard, many of whom were influential committee chairmen, would rally to Eisenhower's legislative agenda. If the president was going to push through his program of "modern Republicanism" and stave off unwanted legislation, he needed a former member who could "work the Hill" on his behalf. Nixon advised Eisenhower to go to Congress "only in dramatic circumstances," because "Truman came so often there were occasions when he didn't have a full House," but he need not have worried. Eisenhower had no intention of trying to dominate Congress the way his predecessors had. Eisenhower and Nixon held regular meetings with the Republican congressional leadership, but the president had little contact with other GOP members of Congress, and he seldom tried to harness public pressure against Congress to support his legislation. This approach suited Eisenhower's "hidden hand" style of leadership, but to be effective, someone had to serve as the administration's political broker with the rest of the Republicans. Nixon was the obvious candidate.[16]

One of the more immediate tasks for the new vice president was to help the administration defeat the Bricker amendment. In 1951, Republican Senator John W. Bricker of Ohio had introduced a constitutional amendment that would have drastically curtailed the ability of the president to obtain treaties and executive agreements with other nations. Bricker's immediate purpose was to prohibit President Truman from entering into agreements such as the United Nations Convention on the Prevention and Punishment of Genocide, for fear that it would compromise the sovereignty of the United States. More generally, the Bricker amendment aimed to increase the influence of Congress in making foreign policy. Even with a Republican in the White House, Bricker refused to back away from his amendment, offering it as the first order of business in the new Congress, with the support of almost every Republican senator. Eisenhower, however, believed the amendment would severely restrict the necessary powers of the president and make the nation "helpless in world affairs." Rather than confront his own party leadership, he hoped to delay action on the measure in order to gradually

chip away at its support. He sent Nixon and others to work with Bricker on compromises and suggested a "study committee," with Bricker as its chair, to come up with an agreeable alternative.[17] Bricker, however, would not yield on the substance of his amendment. Finally, in 1954, after much wrangling, the administration convinced Democrat Walter George of Georgia to offer a much less stringent substitute. On the crucial roll call, the substitute received a vote of 60 to 31, falling one short of the two-thirds majority necessary for passage of a constitutional amendment. Bricker tried to revive his amendment, but too many Republicans had changed sides.[18] Vice President Nixon had been one of the administration's most active lobbyists in defeating the amendment without splitting the party. His other primary assignment as party intermediary proved more demanding.

Senator Joseph R. McCarthy (R-WI) shot to fame in 1950 by brazenly claiming that the State Department was full of "known Communists." Over the next two years, he waged a running battle with the Truman administration over its conduct of foreign policy and the loyalty of its appointees. Many Republicans and some conservative Democrats joined in this anticommunist "crusade." They averred that the nation had been betrayed at Yalta and that Truman had "lost China." McCarthy promised to clean the Communists out of government and to end "twenty years of treason."

When Dwight Eisenhower entered the White House, he and his advisers hoped that Vice President Nixon could keep McCarthy in line if the senator continued his attacks. The results of this strategy were mixed. Nixon was certainly the right man for the job. As historian David Oshinsky writes, "Only Taft and Nixon seemed able to reach him [McCarthy], and Taft was now too sick to try."[19] Nixon was also one of the few people in the nation who could safely deal with the "McCarthy problem," because, as Eisenhower put it, "Anybody who takes it on runs the risk of being called a pink. Dick has had experience in the communist field, and therefore he would not be subject to criticism."[20] Nixon succeeded in convincing McCarthy not to pursue an investigation of the CIA, but the senator was soon talking about "twenty-one years of treason," implying that Eisenhower had not stemmed the tide. Neither Nixon nor anyone else could convince McCarthy not to investigate the U.S. Army. As chairman of the Committee on Government Operations' Permanent Investigations Subcommittee, McCarthy had wide discretion to conduct investigations, but Eisenhower publicly claimed that he would not allow members of the executive branch to testify about private conversations. He also supported army officers who refused to appear before the subcommittee. As the president did what he could to divert the hearings, he had Nixon make a national speech emphasizing the need to be "fair" in the pursuit of Communists. In the end, McCarthy went too far. The televised Army-McCarthy hearings revealed to the public a bellicose senator viciously attacking the army and the administration. As the president refused to give executive information to the committee, and as McCarthy's public support waned, his Senate colleagues finally decided they had seen enough. On December 2, 1954, with Vice President Nixon presiding, the Senate voted 67 to 22 to condemn McCarthy's behavior. Republicans split 22 to 22 on the vote, with Democrats unanimously in favor. Thus, after Eisenhower's attempt to use Nixon to contain McCarthy failed, the administration had resorted instead to quiet resistance, allowing McCarthy himself to bring about his own downfall.[21]

Adviser and Campaigner

Apart from his specific assignments, Nixon also served as the administration's general political expert. No one in the administration had a more thorough knowledge of the way Congress worked and how to get legislation passed. He always attended cabinet meetings and contributed his insight by pointing out the political implications of any decision. He urged cabinet members to get to know the chairmen of the committees that had jurisdiction over their departments. Eisenhower's speech writer, Emmett Hughes, described Nixon as "crisp and practical and logical: never proposing major objectives, but quick and shrewd in suggesting or refining methods."[22] Nixon also emphasized the need to sell "modern Republicanism" to the public. Cabinet members, he said, should not be afraid to make partisan speeches and should concentrate them in competitive congressional districts. He even suggested that they should welcome the chance to appear on such television interview shows as *Meet the Press*.[23] Meanwhile, both Eisenhower and Secretary of State John Foster Dulles used Nixon to publicly explore policy options and propose ideas that they were wary of advocating themselves. As Ike put it, "He [Nixon] can sometimes take positions which are more political than it would be expected that I take."[24]

Nowhere was this approach more in evidence than on the campaign trail. The Republican strategy in 1952 had been simple. While Eisenhower ran a positive campaign that emphasized his appeal to citizens of all parties, Nixon's job was to "hammer away at our opponents." He quickly gained a reputation as the Republican "hatchet man," an image that would be captured by *Washington Post* cartoonist "Herblock's" portrayal of him as a mud-slinging sewer dweller, an image that Nixon deeply resented. Nixon's campaign was a hard-hitting anticommunist assault, charging that Truman's secretary of state, Dean Acheson, "had lost China, much of Eastern Europe, and had invited the Communists to begin the Korean War," and calling Democratic presidential candidate Adlai Stevenson a graduate of Acheson's "Cowardly College of Communist Containment."[25] But Nixon's campaigning was hardly over after 1952. In fact, it seemed as though he were campaigning throughout his vice-presidency. In 1954 he hit the campaign trail once more on behalf of congressional Republicans.

In many ways, Nixon emerged as the party's spokesman during these years because Eisenhower was unwilling to take on that role. Eisenhower was determined to be president of "all the people," and did not "intend to make of the presidency an agency to use in partisan elections."[26] Apparently, he had no such qualms about the vice-presidency, and who better to rally the party faithful than Nixon, the man a contemporary observer called the "scientific pitchman of politics."[27] While Eisenhower would not go after the Democrats, he was quite willing to let Nixon do so. According to White House Chief of Staff Sherman Adams, "[Ike] told Nixon and others, including myself, that he was well aware that somebody had to do the hard-hitting infighting, and he had no objection to it as long as no one expected him to do it."[28] Nixon therefore conducted another aggressive campaign for the midterm election, covering nearly 26,000 miles to ninety-five cities in thirty states on behalf of Republican candidates. The outcome was not favorable for the GOP, which lost two Senate seats and sixteen House seats, and Nixon received little public credit for his efforts.[29]

Eisenhower's ambivalence about Nixon's attacking campaign style emerged forcefully two years later in their 1956 reelection campaign. Eisenhower told Nixon that he should try to elevate the level of his speeches and that he should avoid "the exaggerations of partisan political talk." Unlike Harry Truman's "give 'em hell" campaign of 1948, Ike wanted Nixon to "give 'em heaven." This more dignified campaign style led to discussions of a "new Nixon." He talked about "Republican prosperity" and Eisenhower's positive accomplishments as president. It seemed that Nixon had finally decided to put away his rhetorical boxing gloves. But it was a false impression. Nixon was uncomfortable with this approach. Republican crowds did not react with the same vigor as when he ripped into the Democrats, and he found it hard to suppress his "normal partisan instincts," and to "campaign with one arm tied behind [his] back."[30] Yet this was not entirely his campaign, and he had to abide by Eisenhower's wishes. Ike, however, soon remembered why he had chosen Nixon in the first place. As the campaign intensified and Stevenson (running once more) and the Democrats stepped up their attacks on the administration, Eisenhower decided to give his aggressive vice president a bit more rope. He told him, "Look, Dick, we've agreed that your speeches generally in this campaign ought to be on a higher level than in the past. Still I think it's perfectly all right for you to pick up on some of these wild charges and throw them back at the other fellow."[31] Eisenhower, of course, did not intend to follow this course himself. So, while Eisen-

hower's staff privately worried about Nixon "running loose through the country," the "old Nixon" reemerged with Eisenhower's blessing and once more provided Democrats with their favorite target.

Two years later, many of Nixon's friends advised him to stay away from the 1958 congressional elections. Despite Eisenhower's continued popularity and his comfortable victory in 1956, Republicans had lost ground in Congress in 1954 and again in 1956. Most observers predicted further losses in 1958. Many of Nixon's friends in the party, anticipating that he would run for president in 1960, thought that being associated with the certain disaster of 1958 would only get in the way. As Tom Dewey told him, "I know that all those party wheelhorses will tell you stories that will pluck your heartstrings, but you're toying with your chance to be President. Don't do it, Dick. You've already done enough, and 1960 is what counts now."[32]

If Nixon did not carry the banner for the party, who would? Eisenhower was not willing to do so, and no one else could. In the end, Nixon could not resist, and he took to the campaign trail once more. He was more disenchanted with the party's organization than ever, and the results of the elections confirmed his pessimism. (He reported to the cabinet, "There were just too many turkeys running on the Republican ticket.")[33] The GOP lost 13 seats in the Senate and 47 in the House while losing 13 of 21 gubernatorial races. The only really impressive victories for the Republicans were for governors Nelson Rockefeller in New York and Mark Hatfield in Oregon, and Senator Barry Goldwater in Arizona. The press proclaimed that the big winner was Rockefeller, while the big loser was Nixon. Years later, Nixon would lament, "Perhaps Dewey had been right: I should have sat it out."[34] Despite the immediate disaster, Eisenhower was not the only beneficiary of Nixon's campaigning. Rank-and-file Republicans did not forget that Nixon had tried to help, and party leaders throughout the nation owed the vice president a significant political debt. He would collect in 1960.

RICHARD M. NIXON

Goodwill Ambassador

While Nixon's roles as political adviser and campaigner were the most important ones in defining his place in the administration, it was his role as international goodwill ambassador that brought him the most praise. Henry Wallace had been the first vice president to travel abroad, but no one either before or since did so with greater fanfare than Nixon. On most occasions his visits were intended only as gestures of American friendship. Nixon's 1958 trip to Argentina for the inauguration of that nation's first democratically elected leader was one such visit. Sometimes, however, the vice president's travels had a more substantive purpose. On his first trip abroad, to Asia in 1953, Nixon took with him a note from Eisenhower to South Korean leader Syngman Rhee. The letter made it clear that the United States would not support a South Korean invasion of the North, and Nixon was sent to obtain a promise from Rhee that such an action would not take place.[35] Nixon visited a number of countries in Asia from Japan to Pakistan, travelling 38,000 miles. He established a practice of meeting with students, workers, and opposition leaders as well as with government officials. His openness seemed popular in most of these nations, and he developed an abiding interest in the continent and its politics. His travels gave him a reputation at home as an expert on Asian affairs that would remain with him throughout his life. He also travelled to Austria in 1956 to meet with Hungarian refugees and to Africa a year later.

But Nixon's most famous trips were still to come. When he set off for South America in 1958, he anticipated an uneventful tour that would merely distract him from his attempts to talk the administration into cutting taxes at home. He was unprepared for the vehemence of the anti-American demonstrations he would encounter from those opposing U.S. policy toward Latin America. In Peru, Nixon was blocked from visiting San Marcos University by a crowd of demonstrators chanting "Go Home Nixon!" He was met in Venezuela by hostile crowds that spat at him as he left his plane. In the capital, Caracas, the scene turned violent. A mob surrounded his car and began rocking it back and forth, trying to turn it over and chanting "Death to Nixon." Protected by only twelve Secret Service agents, the procession was forced to wait for the Venezuelan military to clear a path of escape. But by that time, the car had been nearly demolished and the vice president had seen his fill of South America. President Eisenhower sent a naval squadron to the Venezuelan coast in case they needed to rescue the vice president, but Nixon quietly left the country the next day. He returned to Washington to a hero's welcome. Over 15,000 people met him at the airport, including President Eisenhower and the entire cabinet. Over the next few days, politicians of both parties throughout the nation praised Nixon's courage, and congratulations poured in by the thousands. It was Nixon's shining moment, but the respect was more the result of Americans rallying behind their vice president than any change in Nixon's standing.[36]

Nixon's final trip abroad brought him more favorable reviews. In 1959, he travelled to the Soviet Union to open the United States Exhibition in Sokolniki Park in Moscow, part of a new cultural exchange program. As he and Soviet Premier Nikita Khrushchev toured the exhibit, they engaged in a lengthy and sometimes heated debate on the merits of capitalism versus communism. Much of this debate was captured by American television, which transmitted an image of the nation's vice president standing in a model American kitchen defending American progress against a belligerent Khrushchev. The encounter became known as "The Kitchen Debate," and the nation once more took pride in its feisty vice president. Nixon concluded his trip with a thirty-minute speech on Soviet television, becoming the first American official to address the Soviet Union in a live broadcast. He stressed "peaceful competition" between the East and West and expressed hope that the "Spirit of Geneva" would include a freer exchange of information. On his return, Nixon stopped in Warsaw, Poland, and was given a remarkable and touching reception by the people of that city, who crowded the streets, throwing roses and shouting "Long Live Nixon." While the trip contained little of real substance, it showed Americans an energetic young leader acting on the world stage, an impressive image and one that Nixon would try to cultivate for the future. In all, Nixon visited fifty-four countries and met forty-five heads of state during his eight years as vice president, setting a standard difficult for his successors to match and his opponents to discount.[37]

The vice president, of course, did not travel alone. Pat Nixon always accompanied her husband overseas and established her own role in spreading American "goodwill." She had vigorously campaigned with him for Congress in 1946 and 1950, but by 1952 she had grown weary of politics. Still, when her husband received the vice-presidential nomination, she took up campaigning with him once again. She seemed resigned to being married to a politician and concentrated on raising their two daughters, Tricia and Julie, with minimal privacy at their home on Tilden Street in Washington's Spring Valley section. However, as Nixon biographer Jonathan Aitken puts it, "Pat longed for that peace which the world of politics cannot give." She did, however, enjoy travelling and developed a reputation as an ambassador in her own right. While the vice president met with political leaders, Mrs. Nixon visited hospitals and schools, mixing with people wherever she went. She gave the first press conference exclusively for women reporters in Japan and dined in a previously all-male club in Kuala Lumpur. Everywhere she went, she was extremely popular and only added to the positive image of her husband. If anyone deserved the title "goodwill ambassador," it was Pat Nixon.[38]

Constitutional Roles

Apart from the jobs Eisenhower gave him, Nixon was also the presiding officer of the Senate, as provided in the Constitution. Like many of his predecessors, Nixon did not find this task to be particularly interesting. He was too energetic and ambitious to sit and listen to Senate speeches without being able either to vote or to intervene and was therefore seldom present in the Senate chamber. After the 1952 elections, Republicans held a one-vote majority in the Senate, with 48 members; the Democrats had 47; and

Wayne Morse (OR) had just left the Republican party and intended to vote as an Independent. But when Senate Republican Leader Robert Taft died in July 1953, Ohio's governor replaced him with a Democrat, Thomas A. Burke, shifting the one-vote majority to the Democrats. Wayne Morse made it clear, however, that he would vote with his former Republican colleagues on organizational matters, giving the Republicans exactly half the votes of the ninety-six-member Senate, with Vice President Nixon available to break a tied vote in the Republicans' favor. The Democrats therefore realized it would be futile to offer the resolutions necessary to give them control of the Senate's committee chairmanships and majority floor leadership offices. For the remainder of that Congress, Nixon occasionally appeared if he thought it would be necessary to break a tie, but otherwise he customarily left after the opening prayer and majority leader's announcements, turning over the chair to a junior member.[39]

As the Democratic majority grew during the 1950s, Nixon spent even less time in the Senate. Because Nixon had never been known as a legislative tactician or parliamentarian, and his one constitutionally mandated job did not provide any real opportunities to use his political skills, he avoided his duties in the Senate whenever possible.

The vice president did try to take a more active role in the Senate's deliberations on one occasion, but his effort failed. In 1957, the Eisenhower administration decided to push for a civil rights bill and anticipated that opponents of the bill would use a filibuster to kill it if necessary. Senate Rule XXII provided that cloture could not be invoked on a rules change, making it impossible to stop such a filibuster. At the opening of the first session of the Eighty-fifth Congress in 1957, Senator Clinton Anderson (D-NM), in a strategy intended to make cloture easier to obtain, moved that the Senate consider new rules. Nixon—over the objections of the Republican leadership, which supported the existing cloture provisions—stated that "in the opinion of the Chair," the membership after each election composed a new Senate rather than a continuing body. As a result, he ruled, the Senate could change the rules at the beginning of each Congress by vote of a simple majority. The Senate, however, tabled Anderson's motion the next day by a vote of 55 to 38. Later that year, after repeated attempts to change the cloture rule in order to pass the Civil Rights Act of 1957, Senate Majority Leader Lyndon Johnson engineered a compromise that applied cloture to debate on motions for changes in rules, but declared that "the rules of the Senate shall continue from one Congress to the next Congress unless they be changed as provided in these rules." [40]

The other task that is inherent in the vice president's job is, as Charles Dawes put it, "to check the morning's newspaper as to the President's health." [41] For Richard Nixon, that was not just an idle activity. On September 24, 1955, Nixon received a call informing him that the president had suffered a coronary attack. Nixon was placed in a very delicate situation. While the president was ill, Nixon needed to show that the nation's business was being handled effectively so as not to seem weak, but if he attempted to take too much control it would arouse fears of a power grab by an overly ambitious understudy. He recognized that "even the slightest misstep could be interpreted as an attempt to assume power." [42] Nixon and other members of the cabinet decided to emphasize that Eisenhower's team concept would ensure the government could operate without difficulty until the president recovered. The vice president would preside at cabinet and National Security Council meetings, just as he had done numerous times when the president had been away. White House Chief of Staff Sherman Adams flew to Denver, where Eisenhower was hospitalized, to assist the president, and when Ike was feeling better Nixon was one of the first to visit him. Still, Nixon was careful to observe proper protocol. He presided over cabinet meetings from the vice president's chair and conducted business from his office in the Capitol. He even made sure to visit cabinet members rather than having them come to see him. As he put it, he had "to provide leadership without appearing to lead." [43] Nixon handled this ambiguous situation with considerable skill,

leading Emmett Hughes, a frequent critic, to call it his "finest official hour." [44]

But while the vice president's actions, and inactions, brought widespread praise, they also raised fears that the Eisenhower administration could suddenly become the Nixon administration, especially when the president underwent an operation for ileitis in June of 1956. Eisenhower's health would become a primary issue in the 1956 election, as Democrats reminded voters that a vote for Eisenhower was also a vote for Nixon. Ike's health would continue to be a subject of concern during his second term, and after Eisenhower suffered a stroke in 1957 he decided that it was time to set out procedures for how Nixon should proceed if the president were to become incapacitated. He drafted a letter stating that, if he were unable to perform his duties, Nixon would serve as "acting president" until he recovered. Eisenhower would determine when he was sufficiently able to take control once more. The agreement was strictly between Eisenhower and Nixon and therefore amounted only to a shaky precedent (although Kennedy and Johnson copied it later).[45] Not until passage of the Twenty-fifth Amendment in 1967 was the issue of presidential incapacity officially dealt with.

Nixon and Eisenhower

In the end, Richard Nixon filled with considerable skill the roles that President Eisenhower gave him. So why did Eisenhower come close to dropping him from the ticket in 1956? Eisenhower's opinion of his vice president was most ambiguous. The president appreciated Nixon's efforts in carrying out his assigned tasks. He told associates, "it would be difficult to find a better Vice President" and publicly repeated such praises on a regular basis. He also "believed Nixon to be the best prepared man in government to take over [his] duties in any emergency." [46] This was more than just public flattery for a subordinate. Because of his wide-ranging interests and Eisenhower's willingness, Nixon was perhaps the most informed member of the administration. Secretary of State John Foster Dulles kept him briefed on State Department affairs, and even the CIA was willing to provide outlines of its current activities.[47]

For Eisenhower, this faith in Nixon as vice president did not translate into confidence about Nixon's potential for the presidency. He saw Nixon as a dedicated junior officer who performed his duties with skill but had not developed into a true leader. He worried constantly that his young vice president had not "matured." Eisenhower saw the presidency as the office of a statesman rather than a partisan politician. The 1960s image of Eisenhower as being naive or nonpolitical is inaccurate, but he did believe that presidential politics was different from congressional or statewide politics. The office required a person who could rise above unseemly partisan bickering (at least in public) to represent the national interest, and he did not believe that Richard Nixon had shown that kind of potential. This was partially an unfair assessment, since Nixon's public image as a fierce partisan was magnified by Eisenhower's insistence on using him to conduct the president's public political battles. Still, Nixon's "natural partisan instincts," as Nixon called them, were never far from the surface, and they made Eisenhower uncomfortable. In the end, Eisenhower decided that Nixon just had not "grown," and that he was not "presidential timber."[48]

When Eisenhower decided to run for reelection in 1956, he also began to feel uneasy about not having established a "logical successor."[49] He would have liked to run with Robert Anderson, his treasury secretary, but Anderson, a Democrat, knew the GOP would never accept him. The president hoped to find a way to get Nixon off the ticket without seeming to "dump" him. As a result, when he announced his own candidacy and the press asked him about Nixon, he dodged by claiming it was "traditional . . . to wait and see who the Republican Convention nominates."[50] Since this was a "tradition" that had been broken by Franklin Roosevelt and had not been observed by Eisenhower himself in 1952, it was obvious that Eisenhower was being disingenuous. No one saw this more clearly than Richard Nixon.

Eisenhower hoped to avoid a decision by convincing Nixon to leave the ticket voluntarily. He offered to appoint Nixon secretary of defense in a new administration. He argued that Nixon's low poll numbers might be a drag on the ticket and that Nixon needed to gain executive experience in order to improve his future prospects. Nixon replied that he would do whatever Eisenhower decided was best for the campaign, but that was exactly the decision the president was trying to avoid. He told the press that Nixon would have "to chart out his own course." Eisenhower's evasions infuriated Nixon, and after days of dangling on Ike's hook, he decided to force the issue by telling the president that he wanted to run again. Eisenhower, finally forced to choose, relented.[51]

There was one more "dump Nixon" attempt in 1956, led by Harold Stassen, Eisenhower's "secretary of peace" and foreign policy adviser, after Eisenhower's ileitis operation, but, by that time, Nixon already had the support of the party leadership and the convention delegates. Since Nixon had used the vice-presidency to build a strong base of support within the party and to gain tremendous press coverage, the argument that he would be better off in the cabinet was simply not credible. He realized that the rest of the nation would see it as a replay of the 1944 "demotion" of Henry Wallace rather than as a move into a more responsible position.[52] While it was not wise to say so, he also realized that he was only one uncertain heartbeat away from the presidency, and that was a chance worth taking.

Nixon, however, would have to deal with Eisenhower's ambivalence again in 1960. Nixon was clearly the favorite for the Republican presidential nomination that year, but he faced a significant challenge from New York Governor Nelson Rockefeller. Eisenhower did not openly endorse Nixon even though he certainly preferred Nixon and was furious with Rockefeller for attacks he had made on the administration. While Nixon managed to hold off Rockefeller, the governor's criticisms pointed out what would become an essential problem for Nixon during the general election: while Eisenhower personally maintained immense popularity, his administration did not. Nixon's campaign stressed his experience. In contrast to his Democratic opponent,

Massachusetts Senator John F. Kennedy, Nixon had met with world leaders, led sessions of the cabinet, and had better presidential "credentials" than any man in America. But this approach put Nixon in the difficult position of defending an administration for which he was not responsible. For two years he had privately urged a tax cut to stimulate the economy, but Ike would not unbalance the budget. Nixon had also urged increases in defense expenditures and an invasion of Cuba, but the president said they were unnecessary. These criticisms would be taken up by the Democrats in 1960, and Nixon had to defend the administration, even while privately agreeing with the critics. He refused campaign help from the White House staff but could not assemble a full staff to generate innovative policy ideas for fear of offending Ike.[53] It seemed he was boxed in.

Eisenhower himself exacerbated the problem. While Nixon campaigned as an experienced leader, the press asked Eisenhower what policy suggestions Nixon had made that had been implemented. Eisenhower replied, "If you give me a week, I might think of one."[54] This was hardly the sort of endorsement Nixon needed—and it was not entirely fair. Elliot Richardson, who served during Eisenhower's second term as an assistant secretary of the Department of Health, Education, and Welfare, tells the story of a 1959 cabinet meeting at which Nixon stood against a majority opposed to a higher education subsidy proposal. This followed a typical pattern of cabinet disinterest in the electoral value of its decisions. Richardson reported, "Time and again I would see Nixon get up from the table after Cabinet meetings so tense that beads of sweat were standing out on his brow." At the 1959 meeting, Nixon realized that a record of support for this legislation would be highly desirable in his 1960 presidential campaign. Consequently, he structured that day's discussion so that the opponents had to acknowledge that the bill would have little immediate budgetary impact, that it established no new precedent for federal support of education, and that it indeed met an important national priority. Eisenhower reluctantly added his support.[55]

Eisenhower mostly stayed out of the campaign until the last weeks, when he made several speeches on Nixon's behalf. His reluctance was due as much to Nixon's determination to run his own campaign as to Ike's ill health or indifference. The race itself was one of the closest in American history. It featured two bright young candidates who evinced an unbounded optimism about the nation's future squaring off in the historic television debates that captured the attention of the nation. In the end, Kennedy won by the narrowest of margins, but Nixon had run a highly competent campaign in spite of the handicaps of representing a minority party, being tied to an unpopular administration, and facing a charismatic opponent. He also was attempting to become the first sitting vice president to be elected president since Martin Van Buren. In light of these obstacles, it is amazing that he came as close as he did to winning, but he had been campaigning almost continuously since 1946, developing an ability to discern voters' concerns. He also devised innovative campaign techniques, using television and advertising, that allowed him to address those concerns. Only the magical charm of Jack Kennedy could finally defeat him.[56]

Most of Nixon's opponents hoped that his career was over, but more perceptive observers knew better. As Republican Congressional Campaign Committee Chairman William Miller said, "Any man who, at 47, comes within 300,000 [sic] votes of winning the presidency—for a party that is greatly outnumbered—has to be reckoned with. It's far too early to bury Dick Nixon."[57]

Nixon, however, soon walked into another disaster. He returned to California and challenged Democratic Governor Edmund G. (Pat) Brown in the 1962 gubernatorial race. Amid speculation that he only wanted the office as a step toward another presidential race, Nixon was defeated soundly and responded with a vitriolic "last" press conference in which he blamed the media for his defeat and declared, "You won't have Nixon to kick around anymore." But his retirement proved temporary, as he staged a remarkable comeback to gain the GOP nomination in 1968 and to win the presidency amid the national turmoil over the Vietnam War. Nixon's presidency would be marked by a new spirit of detente with the Soviet Union and by the establishment of diplomatic relations with the People's Republic of China, but all would be overshadowed by the tragedy of Watergate.

President Nixon was accused of using his office to cover up crimes in his reelection campaign, including a break-in at Democratic national headquarters in the Watergate office building, and misusing federal funds to influence government witnesses. Under threat of impeachment, Richard Nixon, in 1974, became the only president in American history to resign from office. This time, his retirement was permanent, but he remained in the public eye as a prolific author and one of the nation's most cogent commentators on international politics. He even served as an informal adviser to many of his successors. Richard Nixon died on April 22, 1994, at the age of 81.[58]

Nixon's opinion of the vice-presidency changed with his situation. Early on, he declared, "I like it much better than service in the House or Senate. In the vice-presidency you have an opportunity to see the whole operation of the government and participate in its decisions."[59] But at other times he was frustrated about being Eisenhower's "hatchet man."[60] Appropriately, his opinion of his chief also fluctuated. Nixon admired Eisenhower's political savvy, calling him a "far more complex and devious man than most people realize, and in the best sense of those words."[61] But, Nixon was also deeply hurt by Eisenhower's unwillingness to come to his support in the 1952 fund crisis, the "dump Nixon" movement of 1956, or his own election bid in 1960.[62] As a Nixon aide put it, the vice president's opinion of Eisenhower went from "hero worship, to resentment, to hero worship, to disenchantment."[63]

Yet Nixon's fortunes were intimately tied to Eisenhower's coattails. Years later, in 1968, Nixon would remind crowds that he "had a good teacher," and could still exhort crowds, "Let's win this one for Ike!" One of his first acts as president-elect would be a public visit to the dying general.[64] But it was never a comfortable situation. When reporters in 1960 asked Nixon what president best fit his idea of being "good for the coun-

try," Nixon praised Woodrow Wilson but settled on Theodore Roosevelt. Significantly, he did not mention Dwight D. Eisenhower.[65]

Franklin Roosevelt had briefly envisaged expanding the vice-presidency by making it a kind of "assistant presidency," with greater executive responsibilities. This is not the role that Eisenhower intended for Nixon. In fact, in 1959 Eisenhower proposed to his cabinet that he recommend legislation to create an office of assistant president. He envisioned perhaps two assistants, one dealing with foreign policy, the other with domestic matters. Nixon was horrified, arguing that the change would make the vice-presidency even more superfluous than it already was. More important, Secretary of State Dulles was equally mortified, and the plan was quickly dropped. Eisenhower's suggestion revealed that he never really considered Nixon a potential executive assistant.[66]

Nixon did expand the visibility and duties of the vice-presidency as none of his predecessors had, but those new duties were of a personal nature rather than an inherent part of the office, because they resulted more from the particular needs of President Eisenhower than from a reconstructed vision of the vice-presidency. As a result, the changes in the office were limited and unique to the situation. Nixon's new jobs were overwhelmingly political, as party liaison, campaigner, and goodwill ambassador, although he did have a few executive functions. He established an important precedent by presiding over nineteen cabinet meetings and twenty-six meetings of the National Security Council.[67] He also chaired the President's Committee on Government Contracts and the Cabinet Committee on Price Stability, but these jobs were minor, because it was Nixon's political role that mattered to the president. Not many presidents would need this kind of political troubleshooter, because Eisenhower was unusual in his lack of connections with his own party. Only the role of goodwill ambassador was really the kind of task future vice presidents could be expected to fill with regularity. The vice-presidency had become more visible, but whether it would continue to be more important would depend on the needs of future presidents.

When Eisenhower hoped Nixon would take a cabinet spot, he had worried that "Nixon can't always be the understudy to the star."[68] But Nixon was not even really the understudy. He was one part of Eisenhower's "team." His position on that team was one to which he was well suited, thus his determination to stay. He was constantly campaigning for Eisenhower and for other Republicans, but he realized that he was also campaigning for Richard Nixon. He had discovered how to turn the vice-presidency into a platform for greater ambitions, but he was always dependent on Eisenhower's needs. Nixon was right that he could not truly chart his own course. Luckily for him, the course laid out by Eisenhower was one Nixon wanted to follow, because it pointed toward the White House.

NOTES

[1] Richard M. Nixon, *RN: The Memoirs of Richard Nixon* (New York, 1978), p. 170.

[2] Ibid., p. 172.

[3] The two most comprehensive works on Nixon's early life and career are Roger Morris, *Richard Milhous Nixon: The Rise of an American Politician* (New York, 1990) and Jonathan Aitken, *Nixon: A Life* (Washington, DC, 1993).

[4] Morris, pp. 257–337.

[5] For the history of HUAC, see Walter Goodman, *The Committee: The Extraordinary Career of the House Committee on Un-American Activities* (New York, 1968). The most thorough work on the Hiss case is Allen Weinstein, *Perjury: The Hiss-Chambers Case* (New York, 1978).

[6] Morris, pp. 515–624.

[7] Ibid., pp. 628–29; Stephen E. Ambrose, *Nixon: The Education of a Politician, 1913–1962* (New York, 1987), p. 225; Aitken, pp. 193–94.

[8] For the details on the 1952 race, see George H. Mayer, *The Republican Party, 1854–1962* (New York, 1964), pp. 482–95; James T. Patterson, *Mr. Republican: A Biography of Robert A. Taft* (Boston, 1972), pp. 499–568; Stephen E. Ambrose, *Eisenhower: Soldier, General of the Army, President-Elect, 1890–1952* (New York, 1983), pp. 529–72. For Nixon's selection, see Dwight D. Eisenhower, *Mandate For Change, 1953–1956* (New York, 1963), p. 46; Morris, pp. 625–736; and Aitken, pp. 201–6.

[9] Eisenhower, p. 46.

[10] Ambrose, *Nixon*, p. 262. On Nixon's relationship with the Old Guard, see David W. Reinhard, *The Republican Right Since 1945* (Lexington, KY, 1983), pp. 131–32.

[11] Richard Nixon, *Six Crises* (New York, 1962), pp. 78–88; Ambrose, *Nixon*, pp. 256–58; Morris, pp. 757–850.

[12] Ambrose, *Nixon*, pp. 281–83. For his part, Eisenhower said privately that if he was still in the army and Nixon was a junior officer, Nixon would have been dismissed immediately, but politics was run by different norms. See Elmo Richardson, *The Presidency of Dwight D. Eisenhower* (Lawrence, KS, 1979), p. 20; Aitken, pp. 208–13.

[13] Nixon, *Six Crises*, p. 110.

[14] Herbert S. Parmet, *Richard Nixon and His America* (Boston, 1990), pp. 238, 248–49; Nixon, *Six Crises*, pp. 117–19. Nixon's appeal to "Middle America" would continue to astound his critics in the future, see Nicol C. Rae, *The Decline and Fall of the Liberal Republicans: From 1952 to the Present* (New York, 1989), p. 41; Aitken, pp. 213–20.

[15] Ambrose, *Nixon*, p. 309; Parmet, p. 316.

[16] Ambrose, *Nixon*, pp. 304–6, 309; Gary W. Reichard, *The Reaffirmation of Republicanism: Eisenhower and the Eighty-Third Congress* (Knoxville, TN, 1975), p. 219. The seminal work on Eisenhower's leadership style is Fred I. Greenstein, *The Hidden-Hand Presidency: Eisenhower as Leader* (New York, 1982).

[17] Reichard, *The Reaffirmation of Republicanism*, p. 62.

[18] Duane Tananbaum, *The Bricker Amendment Controversy: A Test of Eisenhower's Political Leadership* (Ithaca, NY, 1988), pp. 72, 157–215.

[19] David M. Oshinsky, *A Conspiracy So Immense: The World of Joe McCarthy* (New York, 1983), p. 317.

[20] Nixon, *RN*, p. 144.

[21] Oshinsky, pp. 416–95; Gary W. Reichard, *Politics as Usual: The Age of Truman and Eisenhower* (Arlington Heights, IL, 1988), pp. 98–109. For McCarthy and the Senate, see also Robert Griffith, *The Politics of Fear: Joseph R. McCarthy and the Senate* (Lexington, KY, 1970).

[22] Emmet John Hughes, *The Ordeal of Power: A Political Memoir of the Eisenhower Years* (New York, 1962, 1963), p. 117.

[23] Ibid., p. 103; Ambrose, *Nixon*, p. 309; Irving G. Williams, *The Rise of the Vice Presidency* (Washington, 1956), p. 247.

[24] Nixon, *RN*, p. 144. See also, Parmet, pp. 333–36.

[25] Nixon, *Six Crises*, p. 77; Nixon, *RN*, p. 110.

[26] Quoted in Jules Witcover, *Crapshoot: Rolling the Dice on the Vice Presidency* (New York, 1992), p. 125.

[27] Philip Potter, "Political Pitchman—Richard M. Nixon," in Eric Sevareid, ed., *Candidates 1960: Behind the Headlines in the Presidential Race* (New York, 1959), p. 69.

[28] Sherman Adams, *Firsthand Report: The Story of the Eisenhower Administration* (New York, 1961), p. 167.

[29] Nixon, *RN*, pp. 161–62.

[30] Ibid., pp. 177–78. For the "new Nixon," see Witcover, p. 133.

[31] Hughes, p. 161.

[32] Nixon, *RN*, p. 199.

[33] Ibid., p. 163.

[34] Ibid., p. 200; Nixon, *Six Crises*, pp. 233–34.

[35] Ambrose, *Nixon*, pp. 322–23.

[36] See Ambrose, *Nixon*, pp. 462–82; Nixon, *RN*, pp. 185–93; and Aitken, pp. 250–54.

[37] Ambrose, *Nixon*, pp. 509–34, 569; Aitken, pp. 258–65.

[38] Ambrose, *Nixon*, pp. 326, 621; Aitken, p. 235.

[39] Ambrose, *Nixon*, p. 308.

[40] Jacob K. Javits with Rafael Steinberg, *Javits: The Autobiography of a Public Man* (Boston, 1981), pp. 256–59; U.S., Congress, Senate, *The Senate, 1789–1989: Addresses on the History of the United States Senate*, by Robert C. Byrd, S. Doc. 100–20, 100th Cong., 1st sess., vol. 2, 1991, p. 129; Ambrose, *Nixon*, p. 609.

[41] Quoted in Nixon, *Six Crises*, p. 131.

[42] Ibid., p. 134.

[43] Ibid., pp. 144, 148.

[44] Hughes, p. 275.

[45] Nixon, *Six Crises*, pp. 177–79. For a provocative discussion of Eisenhower's health and of presidential health gen-

erally, see Robert H. Ferrell, *Ill-Advised: Presidential Health and Public Trust* (Columbia, MO, 1992).

[46] Dwight D. Eisenhower, *Waging Peace, 1956–1961* (New York, 1965), p. 8; Ambrose, *Nixon*, p. 387.

[47] Parmet, pp. 316–25.

[48] Richardson, p. 35; Stephen E. Ambrose, *Eisenhower: The President* (New York, 1984), pp. 319–20; Hughes, p. 152.

[49] Reichard, *Politics as Usual*, p. 120.

[50] Quoted in Ambrose, *Eisenhower: The President*, p. 296.

[51] Nixon, *RN*, pp. 166–73.

[52] Ambrose, *Nixon*, p. 381.

[53] Hughes, p. 277; Theodore H. White, *The Making of the President, 1960* (New York, 1961), p. 201. It is possible that Nixon would not have assembled such a group anyway. Even in Congress, Nixon did not have any legislative assistants, relying only on secretaries to deal with constituent services and dealing with all policy matters himself. Len Hall, his campaign manager in 1960, complained that Nixon insisted on running even the most minute details of the campaign himself. (See Garry Wills, *Nixon Agonistes: The Crisis of the Self-Made Man* (Boston, 1970), p. 16.) This pattern of personal control would persist even in his presidency.

[54] Quoted in Aitken, p. 284.

[55] Aitken, pp. 265–66.

[56] For the election of 1960, see White, *The Making of the President, 1960*.

[57] Quoted in Reichard, *Politics as Usual*, p. 166.

[58] For Nixon's later life and career, see Stephen E. Ambrose, *Nixon: The Triumph of a Politician, 1962–1972* (New York, 1989) and Ambrose, *Nixon: Ruin and Recovery, 1973–1990* (New York, 1991). For his presidency, see Joan Hoff, *Nixon Reconsidered* (New York, 1994) and Theodore H. White, *Breach of Faith: The Fall of Richard Nixon* (New York, 1975).

[59] Quoted in Donald Young, *American Roulette: The History and Dilemma of the Vice Presidency* (New York, 1965, 1972), p. 260.

[60] Ambrose, *Nixon*, p. 360.

[61] Nixon, *Six Crises*, p. 161.

[62] See Ambrose, *Nixon*, pp. 618–20.

[63] Potter, p. 88.

[64] Wills, pp. 116, 138.

[65] Potter, pp. 77–78.

[66] See Ambrose, *Nixon*, pp. 511–13.

[67] Interestingly, one of the most fervent advocates of Nixon's responsibility to preside in the president's absence was John Foster Dulles. As the nephew of Robert Lansing, Dulles vividly remembered Wilson's rage when Secretary of State Lansing presided over the cabinet while the president was disabled. Dulles wanted no confusion about where responsibility resided. See Chapter 28 of this volume, ''Thomas R. Marshall,'' p. 342.

[68] Quoted in Ambrose, *Nixon*, p. 392.

Chapter 37

LYNDON BAINES JOHNSON
1961–1963

LYNDON B. JOHNSON

Chapter 37

LYNDON BAINES JOHNSON

37th Vice President: 1961–1963

I think a fair assessment would be that there was a big sigh of relief when Johnson departed the Senate. Not that they didn't like Johnson . . . but he was so strong, and so difficult, and so tough, that it was a relief to get him over to the vice president's office.

—GEORGE A. SMATHERS

The only thing that astonished politicians and the press more than John F. Kennedy's offer of the vice-presidential nomination to Lyndon B. Johnson was Johnson's acceptance. Neither man particularly liked the other, and their styles contrasted starkly. Kennedy cultivated a smooth, sophisticated and self-deprecating image, while Johnson often appeared boorish, bullying and boastful. In the U.S. Senate, Johnson, as majority leader, for years had stood second only to the president of the United States in power and influence, whereas Kennedy was an unimpressive back bencher. Although Kennedy's choice for the second spot on the ticket dismayed his liberal supporters, the candidate recognized that Johnson could help him carry Texas and the South and that he would undoubtedly be easier to deal with as vice president than as majority leader. Johnson's reasons for accepting were more enigmatic, for he was trading a powerful job for a powerless one.

From Farm to Congress

Johnson reached the dubious pinnacle of the vice-presidency after a remarkable climb to power in Washington. It started on a farm near Stonewall, Texas, where he was born on August 27, 1908, the son of the Texas politico, Sam Ealy Johnson, and his refined and demanding wife, Rebecca Baines Johnson. Sam Ealy Johnson served six terms in the Texas House of Rep-

resentatives, faithfully supporting the interests of his constituents, until his various real estate, insurance brokering, and ranching ventures began to drag him into debt. Throughout his life, Lyndon Johnson never forgot the impact his father's economic disgrace had on his family.[1]

Graduating from high school in 1924, Johnson escaped both his family and the rugged Texas Hill Country by heading toward California in search of work. When nothing but hard labor turned up, Johnson returned home a year later and attended Southwest Texas State Teacher's College in San Marcos. Depleted funds forced him to leave college and spend a year as principal and teacher at a Mexican-American school in Cotulla, Texas, near the Mexican border. Years later he asserted, "You never forget what poverty and hatred can do when you see its scars in the face of a young child."[2]

When a candidate for governor failed to appear at a rally in 1930, Johnson delivered an impromptu campaign speech for him. This speech so impressed a candidate for the state senate, Welly Hopkins, that he recruited Johnson to manage his own successful campaign. Later, while Johnson was teaching high school in Houston, Hopkins recommended him to the newly elected Representative Richard Kleberg. Hired as Kleberg's secretary, Johnson arrived in Washington with a congressman more interested in golf than in legislating, a situation that gave the young aide the opportunity to take charge and make himself known. Directing Kleberg's staff, Johnson learned how Washington worked and also got himself elected Speaker of the Little Congress, an association of House staff members. In 1934, after he courted and married Claudia Alta "Lady Bird" Taylor, Johnson sought wider career horizons and was soon appointed Texas state director of the National Youth Administration, a New Deal agency designed to help students afford to stay in school. Success in that job propelled him into a special election for Congress in 1937, campaigning under banners that proclaimed "Franklin D. and Lyndon B." [3]

A New Deal Congressman

Johnson's victory began a thirty-two-year political career that would end in the White House. After the election, President Franklin D. Roosevelt visited Galveston, Texas, and warmly greeted the new congressman. FDR admired Johnson's vitality and predicted that someday he would become the "first Southern President" since the Civil War. Johnson had also become a protégé of his fellow Texan, Sam Rayburn, the future House Speaker, who guided much of his career. An active congressman, Johnson used his New Deal connections to bring rural electrification and other federal projects into his district, then, ambitious and in a hurry, he ran in a special election for the U.S. Senate in 1941. On election night, Johnson held a lead but announced his vote tallies too soon, allowing the opponent to "find" enough votes to defeat him. When America entered the Second World War, Johnson briefly served in uniform as a navy lieutenant commander. He received a silver star from General Douglas MacArthur for having flown as a passenger in a bomber that was attacked by Japanese planes (none of the others on board received a medal). When President Roosevelt called on members of Congress to choose between military and legislative service, Johnson returned to the House for the duration of the war. In 1948 he again ran for the Senate and fought a celebrated campaign for the Democratic nomination against the popular Governor Coke Stevenson. Having learned his lesson from the previous Senate race, Johnson held back on announcing his vote tallies

and with the help of some friendly political machines eked out an 87-vote victory for which he was dubbed "Landslide Lyndon." [4]

A Southern Moderate

Johnson rode into the Senate in 1949 on the political wave that returned Harry Truman to the White House and Democratic majorities to both houses of Congress. His class of freshmen senators included Democrats Hubert Humphrey of Minnesota, Robert Kerr of Oklahoma, Clinton Anderson of New Mexico, Estes Kefauver of Tennessee, and Paul Douglas of Illinois. Seeking to establish himself quickly against this formidable competition, Senator-elect Johnson called in the Senate's twenty-year-old chief telephone page, Bobby Baker, who had already gained a reputation as a head counter. "Mr. Baker, I understand you know where the bodies are buried in the Senate," he began their critical relationship by remarking. "I gotta tell you, Mr. Baker, that my state is much more conservative than the national Democratic party. I got elected by just eighty-seven votes and I ran against a caveman." [5]

Johnson sought to move to a middle ground that would enable him to rise in the national ranks of his party without losing his base in Texas. Just as Sam Rayburn had promoted Johnson's career in the House, Georgia Senator Richard Russell became the Senate mentor for the young Texan. Russell, a powerful, highly respected "senator's senator," might have served as Democratic floor leader in the Senate, except that he could not follow the Truman administration's lead on civil rights. He therefore preferred to exercise his influence as chairman of the Armed Services Committee and of the Southern Caucus. Johnson won the affection of the bachelor senator by adopting Russell as part of his family, inviting the Georgian to his Washington home on lonely Sundays and to Texas for Thanksgiving. Russell not only placed Johnson on the Armed Services Committee but made him chairman of its Preparedness Subcommittee. In 1952 Russell formally entered the race for the Democratic nomination for president, in part to prevent another "Dixiecrat" boycott of the party like the one that had occurred in 1948. Russell's defense of racial segregation, however, doomed his nomination—and served as a vivid example to Johnson of the need to rise above the image of a southern senator if he wished to realize his national ambitions.[6]

Turmoil in the Democratic ranks elevated Johnson swiftly in the Senate. In 1950 the Democratic majority leader and whip were both defeated for reelection. Democrats then chose Arizona Senator Ernest McFarland for leader and the freshman Johnson as their new whip. Two years later, MacFarland was himself defeated. At first Johnson urged Russell to take the leadership, already knowing that the Georgia senator did not want the job. When Russell declined, Johnson asked his support for his own bid, arguing that the prestige of the office would help his reelection in Texas. Although a handful of liberal Democrats backed Montana Senator James Murray for the post, Johnson with Russell's backing was overwhelmingly elected Democratic floor leader. He was still serving in his first senatorial term.[7]

Democratic Leader

Johnson led Senate Democrats during the entire eight years of the Republican Eisenhower administration, as minority leader for the first two years and as majority leader for the last six. The two parties were so evenly balanced that during Johnson's minority leadership the death and replacement of senators occasionally gave the Democrats a majority of the senators. After the 1954 election, the switch of Oregon Senator Wayne Morse from independent status helped give the Democrats a slim majority, but the party faced a deep internal division between southern conservatives, who opposed civil rights legislation, and northern liberals, who advocated racial integration. As Johnson moved to the center of his party, he worked to prevent an open split, commenting that his major concern was to keep Senator Russell and other southern conservatives "from walking across the aisle and embracing [Republican leader] Everett Dirksen."[8]

As majority leader, Lyndon Johnson demonstrated unrelenting energy, ambition, attention to detail, and an overwhelming personality.

His close aide John Connally described Johnson as alternately

cruel and kind, generous and greedy, sensitive and insensitive, crafty and naive, ruthless and thoughtful, simple in many ways yet extremely complex, caring and totally not caring; he could overwhelm people with kindness and turn around and be cruel and petty towards those same people; he knew how to use people in politics in the way nobody else could that I know of.

Above all, Johnson was a compromiser, a broker, and a master of the art of the deal. His hands-on method of persuading other senators, with its sweet talk, threats, and exaggerated facial expressions and body language, became widely known as "the treatment."[9]

Other politicians, regardless of party, admired Johnson as a virtuoso at their craft. Republican Representative Gerald Ford met Johnson in 1957 when they served on a bipartisan House-Senate committee to draft new legislation on space policy. "Johnson elected himself chairman," Ford recalled, "and boy, did he operate." The Senate leader did not twist arms, but "the pressure of his presence and the strength of his voice and the movement of his body made it hard to say no." A keen judge of people, Johnson knew how far to push and when to coax. "Any compromise that Lyndon made," Ford concluded, "he got better than fifty percent." Johnson insisted that his only power as majority leader was the power to persuade. But his friend George Smathers, senator from Florida, noted that "persuasion" often meant doing favors: putting senators on desired committees, sending them on trips, arranging for campaign contributions, and even getting them honorary college degrees. "He was a consummate artist," said Smathers. "How he did it, a color here, a little red here, a little purple there, beautiful."[10]

Senator Smathers was with Johnson on the weekend in 1955 when the majority leader suffered his first heart attack. When doctors advised Johnson that it would take weeks of recuperation before he could return to the Senate, Johnson delegated Smathers to stand in for him as floor leader. "We never saw Johnson again for some forty days, although he began to call us on the telephone in about a week," Smathers recalled. "Just ran us crazy talking to him on the phone, getting things done. He was the most hard-driving guy I ever saw in my life." The heart attack made Johnson pace himself differently than before. Periodically, he would leave Washington to spend time on his ranch in the Texas Hill Country. Typically, however, Johnson could not relinquish control and made the Senate adjust to his schedule. Whenever Johnson was absent, little could take place. Although the Democratic whip, Montana Senator Mike Mansfield, tried to move legislation along, Democratic Secretary Bobby Baker would circulate through the chamber advising senators to stall because "Johnson wants this kept on the burner for a while." When Johnson returned he would insist on passing things in a rush: "We've got to get this damn thing done tonight!" By letting measures pile up, sufficient pressure would have built up to pass everything in short order. "Who can remember," asked one journalist, "when one legislator so dominated Congress?" [11]

Civil Rights

The majority leader's signal achievement was the passage in 1957 of the first civil rights bill since Reconstruction. It served as a large step in his transformation from southerner to national figure. His patron, Richard Russell, had given Johnson "elbowroom" to move toward the center, protecting him from attack on the right and exempting him from signing "The Southern Manifesto" against the Supreme Court's ruling in *Brown* v. *Board of Education*. Although Johnson's move may have had an element of cynical maneuvering, those closest to him believed that he also felt genuine compassion for African Americans, for the poor, and for the disadvantaged. He spoke often of the hardships of his own childhood, and those memories seemed to inspire him to achieve something significant with his life. "Nobody needed to talk to him about why it's important to get ahead," George Smathers commented. "He was preaching that all the time to everybody." [12]

Although the civil rights bill had been proposed by the Eisenhower administration and was ostensibly managed by Republican leader

William Knowland, it was Lyndon Johnson who fashioned the compromises that led to its passage. In return for significant modifications in the bill, he persuaded southern conservatives not to filibuster, and he advised northern liberals to accept his deal as the best they could get. The fact that Congress passed any civil rights bill held symbolic significance, but angry liberals felt that the watered-down bill simply elevated "symbol over substance." Liberals pointed out that the bill provided southern blacks with little protection for either civil or voting rights. Criticism came from the right as well. One columnist in Dallas wrote that "Johnson did his party a great favor by his engineering of the Civil Rights Bill of 1957, but he did himself no good at all in Texas." [13]

During those congresses when the Senate was almost evenly divided, Johnson perfected his role as cautious broker. Then a severe economic recession triggered a Democratic landslide in the congressional elections of 1958. The Senate Democratic majority of 49 to 47 in the Eighty-fifth Congress swelled to 65 to 35 in the Eighty-sixth Congress, with the added margin of four Democratic seats from the newly admitted states of Alaska and Hawaii. Liberals who entered in the new class quickly became impatient with Johnson's moderate approach. While the majority leader sought to appease the newcomers with appointments to major committees, he found himself attacked as a dictator by mavericks like Pennsylvania's Joseph Clark and Wisconsin's William Proxmire. They demanded more meetings of the Democratic Conference so that other senators could have a say in setting the party's agenda. Johnson held his own, telling Proxmire that "it does not take much courage, I may say, to make the leadership a punching bag." But he faced a quandary, as his aide Harry McPherson noted, since "he had enough Democrats behind him to create major expectations, but not enough to override the President's vetoes." [14]

Johnson found it harder to control the larger majority but still retained his firm hand on the leadership and enjoyed the "perks" of office. When the New Senate Office Building (later named the Dirksen Building) opened in 1958, it allowed many committees to move out of the

Capitol. Johnson took over the District of Columbia Committee's two-room suite just outside the Senate chamber, turning it into his leadership office. The larger of the two rooms—dubbed the "Taj Mahal" by reporters—with its elegant frescoed ceilings, crystal chandelier, and marble fireplace, symbolized the preeminence of the majority leader. "Behind his desk in his imperial suite," wrote one journalist, "Johnson is the nerve center of the whole legislative process." [15] (Later, during Johnson's vice-presidency, the Senate named the room in his honor.)

As the election of 1960 approached, several senators jumped into the presidential race, but Lyndon Johnson held back. Some joked that, as Democratic leader under Eisenhower, Johnson had already served eight years as president and was constitutionally ineligible to run. Despite the power and prestige of his office, however, its duties kept him from stumping the country as did Massachusetts Senator John F. Kennedy. Rather than enter the primaries and challenge Kennedy (whom he privately derided as "Sonny Boy"), Johnson chose to wage his presidential campaign through House Speaker Rayburn and other powerful congressional leaders, confident that they could corral their state delegations at the Democratic National Convention in support of his candidacy. "He thought that national politics were the same as Senate politics," said Howard Shuman, a Senate staff member who observed Johnson at the time. "He tried to get the nomination by calling himself a Westerner and combining the southern and mountain states to give him the nomination. That is the way he dominated the Senate." But Johnson was caught off-guard by Kennedy's savvy and sophisticated campaign, with advanced polling techniques identifying those issues that would strengthen or weaken the candidate in every state. As Johnson later told Bobby Baker, if he learned anything from the campaign it was "that Jack Kennedy's a lot tougher, and maybe a lot smarter, than I thought he was." [16]

Johnson waited until July 5, 1960, to announce his formal candidacy and then fought a bitter fight against the front-running Kennedy. When the two met at the convention on July 12 to address a joint session of the Texas and Minnesota delegations, Johnson portrayed himself as the diligent legislator who had fought the good fight, dutifully answering every quorum call on the recent civil rights bill, in contrast to Kennedy, who had missed all of the quorum calls while out campaigning. Kennedy refused to be baited. He wittily commended Johnson's perfect record on quorum calls and strongly endorsed him—for majority leader. [17]

The 1960 Election

The next day, Kennedy won the Democratic nomination on the first ballot and then had twenty-four hours to select a vice president. He had given no indication of having made up his mind in advance. The party's pragmatists urged Kennedy to choose Johnson in order to carry Texas and the South, but conservatives like Richard Russell urged Johnson to stay off the liberal-leaning ticket. Still recalling the bitter experience of "Cactus Jack" Garner, who traded the House speakership for the vice-presidency with Franklin D. Roosevelt, Rayburn and the Texas delegation adamantly opposed the notion that Johnson should give up the majority leadership for the hollow status of being vice president. Liberal Democrats reacted negatively to Johnson as a wheeler-dealer, and Robert Kennedy, as the campaign manager, had given his word to labor leaders and civil rights groups that Johnson would never be the vice-presidential candidate. When John Kennedy reported that he would offer the second spot to Johnson, his brother interpreted the move as only a token gesture of party solidarity, since Johnson had told people he would never accept the second spot. Then Johnson astonished both brothers by accepting. Considering the choice a terrible mistake, Robert Kennedy was delegated to talk the Texan out of running. Going to Johnson's suite, he proposed that the Texas become instead the Democratic party's national chairman. But a tearful Johnson declared, "I want to be Vice President, and, if the President will have me, I'll join him in making a fight for it." John Kennedy chose to retain him on the ticket, but the animosity between Johnson and Robert Kennedy never diminished. [18]

Pondering why Johnson had accepted, some of his aides thought that he saw no future in being

Kennedy's majority leader. If he succeeded in enacting the party platform, the credit would have gone to the president. If he failed, the blame would have been his. Since the Texas state legislature had passed a law permitting Johnson to run for reelection to the Senate at the same time that he sought national office, Johnson may also have been gambling that Kennedy would lose to Richard Nixon, leaving Johnson as majority leader with a Republican in the White House. Another factor, mentioned by Johnson's friends, was that Lady Bird Johnson had influenced his decision by reasoning that, after his heart attack, the vice-presidency would be less strenuous than the majority leadership. Johnson offered his own reason when he called Richard Russell and explained that, if he had declined the vice-presidency, he would have been "left out" of party affairs in the future.[19]

Before the campaign could begin, the Kennedy-Johnson ticket had to return to Washington for a post-convention session of the Senate. On the assumption that he would be the party's standard bearer, Johnson had devised this session to demonstrate his legislative prowess and launch his fall campaign. Instead, he found himself playing second fiddle. Republican senators mocked the majority leader, asking if he had cleared moves in advance with "your leader." When the Democratic Policy Committee met for its regular luncheon, everyone waited to see whether Kennedy would bounce Johnson from his usual place at the head of the table. Kennedy dodged the issue by not showing up. With the Republican presidential candidate, Richard Nixon, presiding over the Senate as vice president, Senate Republicans were not likely to hand Kennedy any victories. The session failed dismally.[20]

In the fall, Johnson campaigned intensely, conducting a memorable train ride through the South. He also pressed for a joint appearance of the Democratic candidates somewhere in Texas. They arranged the meeting at the airport in Amarillo, where campaign advance men stopped all air traffic during the brief ceremonies so that the candidates could address the crowd. But they had not counted on the Republican-leaning airline pilots, who deliberately ran the engines of their planes in order to drown out the speakers. At the close of the ruined appearance, a photographer snapped a concerned Kennedy placing his hand on Johnson's shoulder, trying to calm his angry, gesticulating running mate. Then, just before the election, Lyndon and Lady Bird Johnson were jeered and jostled by a hostile crowd of right-wingers in Dallas, Texas. Dismayed over this event, Senator Richard Russell cut short a tour of Europe and flew to Texas to campaign for Johnson. News of Russell's endorsement was carried in newspapers throughout Dixie, helping to solidify the Democratic ticket's hold on the increasingly unsolid South.[21]

Vice President Johnson

Those who spent election night with Johnson later observed that he showed no signs of jubilation at the narrow victory over Richard Nixon and gave every impression of not wanting to become vice president. After the election, he used his influence to recommend candidates for cabinet appointment—especially Arkansas Senator J. William Fulbright to be secretary of state, but Fulbright withdrew his name from consideration. The chief of staff of the Senate Foreign Relations Committee, Carl Marcy, recalled an encounter in the Democratic cloakroom where Johnson grabbed him by the lapels, breathed in his face and said: "What's wrong with Bill Fulbright? I had it set for him to be Secretary of State and he turned it down." Johnson helped to assure Senate approval of Robert Kennedy's nomination for attorney general by persuading conservative opponents to drop their request for a recorded vote, but when Johnson promoted his supporter Sarah T. Hughes for federal judge, Robert Kennedy rejected the sixty-four-year old Dallas lawyer as too old. Later, when Johnson was out of the country, House Speaker Sam Rayburn traded passage of an administration bill in return for Hughes' appointment. It was an object lesson in the power of the Speakership versus the powerlessness of the vice-presidency.[22]

Not intending to become an inactive vice president, Johnson retained the "Taj Mahal" as his office and anticipated keeping the rest of his authority as majority leader. He proposed that, as vice president, he continue to chair the meetings of the Democratic Conference. Although the new majority leader, Montana Senator Mike Mansfield, did not object, other senators warned him that the scheme would never work. As Hubert Humphrey observed, Johnson "was not an easy man to tell that you can't do something." When the Democratic Conference met on January 3, 1961, senator after senator stood to denounce the proposal, including some whom Johnson had considered his supporters. Although the conference voted 46 to 17 to permit the vice president to preside, it was clear that he could not play the role of "super majority leader." Afterwards, Johnson pulled back and seemed reluctant to approach senators and lobby for their votes. "I think a fair assessment would be that there was a big sigh of relief when Johnson departed the Senate," his friend George Smathers concluded. "Not that they didn't like Johnson . . . but he was so strong, and so difficult, and so tough, that it was a relief to get him over to the vice president's office." The Senate now shifted from "the benevolent dictatorship" of Lyndon Johnson to the more democratic leadership of Mike Mansfield. On the occasions when Johnson presided over the Senate, he habitually appeared bored.[23]

Facing constraints in his legislative role, Johnson sought to expand his activities within the executive branch. In addition to the Taj Mahal at the Capitol, he occupied a large suite in the Executive Office Building next to the White House. Johnson's staff prepared a draft of an executive order making the vice president in effect a deputy president, giving him "general supervision" over most space and defense programs. The proposal went to President Kennedy and never returned, although the president did appoint Johnson to chair the Space Council and the White House Committee on Equal Employment. These posts were not sufficient to halt the vice president's shrinking status. When Johnson entered the Democratic cloakroom, senators treated him courteously, but since he was no longer in a position to court their votes or distribute coveted committee assignments, he was no longer the center of their attention.[24]

Johnson grumbled in private but kept his silence in public and at White House meetings.

President Kennedy always treated his vice president cordially, but the president's young aides, mostly ivy leaguers, snickered about "Uncle Cornpone." Acutely aware of their contempt, Johnson attended National Security Council and other policy-making sessions but said nothing unless questioned directly. He felt insecure and ignored and wore his feelings openly. "I cannot stand Johnson's damn long face," John Kennedy once complained to George Smathers. "He comes in, sits at the cabinet meetings, with his face all screwed up, never says anything. He looks so sad."[25]

Seeking to boost the vice president's spirits by giving him some public exposure, Kennedy sent Johnson on a string of foreign missions and goodwill tours. The elixir worked. Johnson attracted enthusiastic crowds and reveled in the press attention. Traveling in Pakistan in 1961, Johnson repeated a line that he often used while campaigning: "You-all come to Washington and see us sometime." To his surprise, an impoverished camel driver, Bashir Ahmed, took the invitation literally and set out for America. When the press mocked the story, Johnson arranged for the People-to-People program to pay the camel driver's costs, personally met him at the airport in New York and flew him to his Texas ranch, turning a potential joke into a public relations coup. On the negative side, Johnson's taste for hyperbole led him to proclaim South Vietnam's ill-fated President Ngo Dinh Diem to be the "Winston Churchill of Asia." These persistent journeys prompted *The Reporter* magazine to define the vice president as someone "who chases around continents in search of the duties of his office."[26]

The press attention garnered on foreign visits tended to evaporate as soon as Johnson returned to the Capitol. One reporter who had covered his years as majority leader spent an hour in the vice president's office and noticed a striking difference: not one other visitor appeared and the phone rang only once. Late in the afternoons, Johnson's aides would invite reporters from the Senate press gallery down for a drink with the vice president. "When a vice president calls he might have something to say," United Press reporter Roy McGhee reasoned. "Generally, he didn't, except blowing his own horn." Little substantive news ever came out of the meetings, and sometimes the press would leave with nothing to write about at all. The press considered Johnson no longer a significant player in Washington events. The television program "Candid Camera" exploited his growing obscurity by asking: who is Lyndon Johnson? People guessed a baseball player, an astronaut, anything but vice president of the United States.[27]

Where Johnson most logically might have played a constructive role in helping pass the president's legislative agenda, he seemed to abdicate responsibility. John F. Kennedy had promised a vigorous administration, but his proposals on issues from Medicare to civil rights had stalled in Congress. The power of conservative southern Democratic committee chairmen, the death in November 1961 of Speaker Sam Rayburn, and the passive leadership style of Senator Mansfield combined to deadlock the legislative process. As part of the Kennedy administration, Johnson was moving leftward away from his former power base of southern conservatives, and this further reduced his effectiveness in planning legislative strategy. Harry McPherson noted that by mid-1963 the vice president seemed to share in the "general malaise" of the time, and that he "had grown heavy and looked miserable." Rumors persisted that he would be dropped from the Democratic ticket in 1964.

A Scandal

Johnson saw Attorney General Robert Kennedy as his chief adversary, but rather than Bobby Kennedy, it was Democratic Majority Secretary Bobby Baker who most threatened his political survival. For years, Bobby Baker had been Johnson's alter ego, known as "Little Lyndon." Baker combined unlimited energy and ambition with poor judgment. While Johnson served as majority leader he dominated Baker's activities, telling him exactly what he wanted done. "Get so and so on the telephone," Johnson would snap his fingers, sending Baker off to relay the leader's wishes. Senator Mansfield retained Baker as the Democratic secretary, but left him to his own devices. During the 1960s, Baker de-

voted as much time to his own finances as he did to Senate business.[28]

Dabbling in everything from vending machines to motels and real estate ventures, Bobby Baker was sued by one of his partners in August 1963. This event triggered press inquiries into Baker's financial dealings and reports of his influence peddling. As the story unfolded, Johnson's name surfaced in connection with an insurance agent close to Baker who charged that he had given the vice president kickbacks in the form of gifts and advertising on the Johnson family television and radio stations as conditions for selling him an expensive life insurance policy. Republican senators demanded a full-fledged investigation, and on October 7, Baker resigned his Senate position. "I knew Johnson was petrified that he'd be dragged down," Baker later wrote; "he would show this by attempting to make light of our former relationship and saying that I had been more the Senate's employee than his own." One day, when Senator Russell rose to pay tribute to Harry McPherson, who was leaving to take a post at the Pentagon, Johnson as presiding officer called over one of the Democratic cloakroom staff and muttered:

> Now here's a boy—Harry McPherson—from Tyler, Texas. I brought him up here. I put him on the policy committee. . . . Now here is Senator Russell down there on the floor saying what a great man he is. . . . On the other hand, when I came here Bobby Baker was working here. . . . Then he gets in trouble. Everybody says he's *my* boy. But they don't say anything about Harry McPherson being my boy.[29]

Despite the negative publicity, John Kennedy gave every indication of keeping Lyndon Johnson as vice president during his second term. Late in 1963, reporter Charles Bartlett privately asked why he did not get another vice president. Kennedy replied that dumping Johnson would only hurt the Democratic ticket's chances in Texas. It was to mend political fences between Democratic factions in Texas that Kennedy traveled to Dallas in November 1963. Johnson met the official party and planned to entertain them at his ranch. The vice president was riding in a car behind Kennedy's limousine when shots were fired. When the motorcade rushed to the hospital, Johnson learned that Kennedy was dead. Taking the oath of office from Judge Sarah T. Hughes—herself a symbol of his limited influence as vice president—Johnson returned to Washington as president of the United States. Half of Kennedy's cabinet had been flying to a meeting in Tokyo when they received the news. As the plane changed course for home, someone spoke what they were all thinking: "I wonder what kind of a president Johnson will make?" [30]

Suddenly President

Lyndon Johnson underwent a remarkable transformation. The disaffected vice president grew into a remarkably active and determined president. He set out to heal a shocked nation, to enact Kennedy's legislative program, and to leave his own mark on the presidency. Freed from his obligations to the southern conservatives in the Senate, Johnson won passage of the most significant civil rights and voting rights legislation of the century. Following his landslide reelection in 1964, Johnson enacted the most sweeping domestic reforms since the New Deal. Few areas of American social and economic life were left untouched by his "Great Society" programs. Commented the liberal Democratic Senator Paul Douglas, "Had I been told in 1956 that ten years later I would be one of Lyndon Johnson's strongest supporters, I would have thought the seer was out of his mind." [31]

As president, Johnson played the ultimate majority leader, although as the chief executive he found there were some areas where he could not cut a deal. His civil rights triumphs could not stop racial turmoil and riots in American cities. Nor could his ability to ram the Gulf of Tonkin Resolution through Congress ensure a military victory in Southeast Asia. There his efforts to fortify the shaky government of South Vietnam led to America's longest and most unpopular war and ultimately to his withdrawal as a candidate for reelection in 1968. Returning to his Texas ranch a rejected and deeply wounded man, Lyndon Johnson died on January 23, 1973, just as the peace accords in Vietnam were being finalized. Recalling his old friend's career, George Smathers asserted that of all the people with whom he served Johnson "was far and away the man who accomplished the most, by far. He deserves to be remembered for the good things that he did, and not just to be remembered as sort of a lumbering, overbearing, sometimes crude individual who tried to dominate everybody he was with." [32]

NOTES

[1] Robert A. Caro, *The Years of Lyndon Johnson: The Path to Power* (New York, 1982), pp. 79–137.

[2] Bruce J. Schulman, *Lyndon B. Johnson and American Liberalism: A Brief Biography with Documents* (Boston, 1995), p. 9.

[3] Ibid., p. 18; Caro, *The Path to Power*, pp. 217–40, 261–68.

[4] Schulman, p. 19; Robert A. Caro, *The Years of Lyndon Johnson: Means of Ascent* (New York, 1990).

[5] Bobby Baker, *Wheeling and Dealing: Confessions of a Capitol Hill Operator* (New York, 1978), pp. 34, 40.

[6] John A. Goldsmith, *Colleagues: Richard B. Russell and His Apprentice, Lyndon B. Johnson* (Washington, 1993), pp. 9–30; Robert Dallek, *Lone Star Rising: Lyndon Johnson and His Times, 1908–1960* (New York, 1991), pp. 378–80.

[7] Dallek, pp. 421–23; Bobby Baker, pp. 59–63.

[8] Goldsmith, p. 73.

[9] Merle Miller, *Lyndon: An Oral Biography* (New York, 1980), p. xvi; Harry McPherson, *A Political Education* (Boston, 1972), p. 159; Robert L. Riggs, ''The South Could Rise Again: Lyndon Johnson and Others,'' in Eric Sevareid, ed., *Candidates 1960; Behind the Headlines in the Presidential Race* (New York, 1959), pp. 299–300; Rowland Evans and Robert Novak, *Lyndon B. Johnson: The Exercise of Power* (New York, 1966), p. 104.

[10] James Cannon, *Time and Chance: Gerald Ford's Appointment with History* (New York, 1994), p. 67; *George A. Smathers, United States Senator from Florida*, Oral History Interviews, 1989, (U.S. Senate Historical Office, Washington, DC), pp. 45, 74–75.

[11] Smathers oral history, p. 22; *Darrell St. Claire: Assistant Secretary of the Senate*, Oral History Interviews, 1976–1978 (U.S. Senate Historical Office, Washington, DC), pp. 134, 214–15; Riggs, p. 295.

[12] George Reedy, *The U.S. Senate: Paralysis or a Search for Consensus?* (New York, 1986), p. 107; Smathers oral history, pp. 57, 70.

[13] Howard E. Shuman, ''Lyndon B. Johnson: The Senate's Powerful Persuader,'' Richard A. Baker and Roger H. Davidson, eds., *First Among Equals: Outstanding Senate Leaders of the Twentieth Century* (Washington, 1991), pp. 222–29; Dallek, pp. 517–27.

[14] McPherson, pp. 159, 168; Jay G. Sykes, *Proxmire* (Washington, 1972), pp. 109–20.

[15] Riggs, p. 301.

[16] McPherson, p. 171; Dallek, p. 569; *Howard E. Shuman,, Legislative and Administrative Assistant to Senators Paul Douglas and William Proxmire, 1955–1982*, Oral History Interviews, 1987 (U.S. Senate Historical Office, Washington, DC), pp. 116–17; Bobby Baker, p. 138.

[17] Evans and Novak, p. 273.

[18] Arthur Schlesinger, Jr., *Robert Kennedy and His Times* (Boston, 1978), 1: 209–21; Dallek, pp. 574–81.

[19] McPherson, pp. 178–79; Smathers oral history, p. 88; Goldsmith, p. 77.

[20] McPherson, p. 179; *Dorothye G. Scott, Administrative Assistant to the Senate Democratic Secretary and the Secretary of the Senate, 1945–1977*, Oral History Interviews, 1992 (U.S. Senate Historical Office, Washington, DC), pp. 140–41.

[21] Goldsmith, p. 81; *Rein J. Vander Zee, Assistant to the Senate Democratic Whip and Assistant Secretary of the Majority, 1961–1964*, Oral History Interviews, 1992 (U.S. Senate Historical Office, Washington, DC,) p. 65. The photograph is included in Susan Kismaric, *American Politicians: Photographs from 1843 to 1993* (New York, 1994), p. 166.

[22] Miller, pp. 272–73; *Carl Marcy, Chief of Staff, Foreign Relations Committee, 1953–1973*, Oral History Interviews, 1983 (U.S. Senate Historical Office, Washington, DC), p. 128; Goldsmith, p. 86; Evans and Novak, pp. 314–15.

[23] Goldsmith, pp. 83–84; Leonard Baker, *The Johnson Eclipse: A President's Vice Presidency* (New York, 1966), pp. 22–28, 32; Smathers oral history, pp. 89, 121; Shuman oral history, p. 239.

[24] Goldsmith, p. 86; McPherson, pp. 184–85.

[25] William S. White, *The Professional: Lyndon B. Johnson* (Boston, 1964), pp. 227–46; Goldsmith, p. 87; Leonard Baker, pp. 42–48; Smathers oral history, pp. 86, 89.

[26] Leonard Baker, pp. 62–67, 167; Paul Conkin, *Big Daddy from the Pedernales: Lyndon Baines Johnson* (Boston, 1986), pp. 167–69.

[27] Booth Mooney, *LBJ: An Irreverent Chronicle* (New York, 1976), p. 141; *Roy L. McGhee, Superintendent of the Senate Periodical Press Gallery, 1973–1991*, Oral History Interviews, 1992 (U.S. Senate Historical Office, Washington, DC), pp. 22–23.

[28] Evans and Novak, pp. 311–13; Goldsmith, p. 91; McPherson, p. 200; Smathers oral history, pp. 61–62.

[29] Bobby Baker, pp. 172–91; Vander Zee oral history, pp. 87–88.

[30] Miller, pp. 308, 316.

[31] Paul H. Douglas, *In the Fullness of Time: The Memoirs of Paul H. Douglas*. New York, 1972), p. 233.

[32] Smathers oral history, pp. 165–66.

Chapter 38

HUBERT H. HUMPHREY
1965–1969

HUBERT H. HUMPHREY

Chapter 38

HUBERT H. HUMPHREY

38th Vice President: 1965–1969

I did not become vice president with Lyndon Johnson to cause him trouble.
—HUBERT H. HUMPHREY, 1965

As vice president during 1968—arguably the United States' most politically turbulent post-World War II year—Hubert Humphrey faced an excruciating test of statesmanship. During a time of war in Southeast Asia when the stakes for this nation were great, Humphrey confronted an agonizing choice: whether to remain loyal to his president or to the dictates of his conscience. His failure to reconcile these powerful claims cost him the presidency. Yet few men, placed in his position, could have walked so agonizing a tightrope over so polarized a nation.

Near the end of his long career, an Associated Press poll of one thousand congressional administrative assistants cited Hubert Humphrey as the most effective senator of the preceding fifty years.[1] A biographer pronounced him "the premier lawmaker of his generation."[2] Widely recognized during his career as the leading progressive in American public life, the Minnesota senator was often ahead of public opinion—which eventually caught up with him. When it did, he was able to become one of Congress' most constructive legislators and a "trail blazer for civil rights and social justice."[3] His story is one of rich accomplishment and shattering frustration.

Hubert Humphrey's oratorical talents, foremost among his abundant personal and political qualities, powered his rapid ascent to national prominence.[4] Lyndon Johnson remarked that "Hubert has the greatest coordination of mind and tongue of anybody I know,"[5] although Harry Truman was one among many who recog-

nized that this "Rembrandt with words" frequently talked too much.[6] Dubbed "Minnesota Chats,"[7] by Johnny Carson, Humphrey often left himself open to the charge that he was "a gabby extremist of the Left," a label that stuck with him despite his moves towards moderation.[8] Any lapses of caution may have been the result of Humphrey the orator being an "incandescent improviser,"[9] with overstatement being the price he paid for his dazzling eloquence.

Humphrey drew his oratorical power from his emotional temperament, which sometimes left him in tears on the stump, undoubtedly moving many in his audience. He would say that he had a "zealous righteousness burning within him," yet his ultimate legislative accomplishments were achieved when he moderated the firebrand and willingly compromised with his opponents.[10] In fact, Humphrey learned to combine his rhetorical talents effectively with his substantive goals by developing into a persuader and for the most part foregoing intimidation, unlike his colleague and mentor Lyndon Johnson. It is not surprising that, while Johnson hated the powerlessness of the vice-presidency, Humphrey relished the national podium it offered.

A Prairie Progressive

The origins of the Minnesotan's "zealous righteousness" can be found in his home state's tradition of agrarian reformism that tenaciously promoted "the disinherited" underdogs at the expense of "the interests."[11] Humphrey personally was a warm, sincere, even "corny" populist, an old-time prairie progressive politically descended from the likes of William Jennings Bryan, George Norris, and Robert La Follette, Sr.

Born in South Dakota in 1911, Humphrey learned his ideology first hand in the persistent agricultural depression of the Midwest during the 1920s and 1930s. He and his family were victims, like so many others, of the Dust Bowl and the Great Depression that had evicted them from their home and business. Humphrey's poor, rural upbringing stirred both him and his pharmacist father to become politically conscious, ardent New Dealers. Thus Humphrey was "permanently marked by the Depression," which in turn stimulated him to study and teach college political science in the employ of the New Deal's Works Progress Administration.[12] After Humphrey became an administrator in that agency, the Minnesota Democratic party recognized his oratorical talents and, in their search for "new blood," tapped him as candidate for mayor of Minneapolis.[13] Although he lost his first race in 1943, he succeeded in 1945. This post would prove to be Humphrey's sole executive experience until the time of his vice-presidency. He made the most of it, successfully impressing his reformist principles on organized crime by stretching his mayoral powers to their limit on the strength of his personality and his ability to control the city's various factions.

Hubert Humphrey's mayoral success and visibility propelled him directly into the Senate for a career that would encompass five terms. He was first elected in 1948 after gaining national attention at the Democratic National Convention with his historic plea for civil rights legislation. Although no strong constituency existed for this issue in Minnesota, the position was in line with Humphrey's championing of others among his state's underdogs, including farmers, labor, and small business. In hammering his civil rights plank into the platform, Humphrey helped to bring the breakaway progressive supporters of Henry Wallace back into the Democratic fold, while simultaneously prompting the Dixiecrats to walk out of the convention hall and the party.

In the Senate

Humphrey's headline-grabbing civil rights speech appealed to Minneapolis' liberal community, and his stand in favor of the Marshall Plan and against the Taft-Hartley labor-management relations law attracted the support of farmers and labor. As a result, Minnesota elected a Democrat to the Senate for the first time since 1901. In his first feisty days in the Senate, Humphrey immediately moved to the cutting edge of liberalism by introducing dozens of bills in support of programs to increase aid to schools, expand the Labor Department, rescind corporate tax loopholes, and establish a health insurance program that was eventually enacted a decade and a half later as Medicare. In addition, Humphrey spoke as a freshman senator on hundreds of topics with the ardor of a moralizing reformer. Accustomed to discussing candidly and openly policy matters that disturbed him, the junior senator quickly ran afoul of the Senate's conservative establishment. He found that many senators snubbed him for his support of the Democratic party's 1948 civil rights plank and, as Senator Robert C. Byrd has written, Humphrey "chose his first battles poorly, once rising to demand the abolition of the Joint Committee on the Reduction of Nonessential Federal Expenditures as a nonessential expenditure." Committee chairman Harry Byrd, Sr., happened to be away from the Senate floor at the time, but he and other powerful senior senators punished this breach of decorum by further isolating Humphrey.[14]

Yet Humphrey, under the guidance of Democratic leader Lyndon Johnson, soon moderated his ways, if not his goals. As *New York Times* congressional correspondent William S. White observed in his classic study of the early 1950s Senate, Humphrey's

> slow ascent to grace was [due to] the clear, but far from simple, fact that he had in him so many *latently* Senatorial qualities. Not long had he been around before it became evident that, notwithstanding his regrettable past, he had a tactile sense of the moods and the habits and the mind of the place.[15]

By the mid-1950s, Humphrey had moved into the ranks of the Senate's "Inner Club."

It is hardly surprising that a politician so filled with energy and vision had presidential ambitions dating from the time of his mayoral election. Indeed, on six occasions during his career Humphrey sought either the presidency or the vice-presidency. His first foray into the vice-presidential race was 1952, but it was the 1956 contest that revealed the essential Humphrey, as he campaigned vigorously for that office after presidential nominee Adlai Stevenson threw open the nomination. Undaunted by his failure in that contest, Humphrey continued his advocacy role in the Senate. Then, in 1958, during a visit to the Soviet Union as part of a fact-finding trip to Europe, Humphrey engaged in a historic eight-and-a-half-hour impromptu conversation on disarmament with Soviet Premier Nikita Khrushchev. This event thrust him into the international spotlight, and the publicity he gained made him an instant presidential candidate for 1960. Yet Humphrey, a longtime proponent of disarmament, then paradoxically exploited this publicity to criticize President Dwight Eisenhower for allowing a "missile gap" to develop.

In 1960 a defense issue of a more personal stripe helped to undermine Humphrey's presidential bid. More than in any other of his many election years, his World War II draft deferment—first as a father and then for a medical condition identified as a right scrotal hernia [16]—was used against him in the primaries. Although Humphrey's draft status seemed to invite exploitation by his political opponents, his chronic lack of campaign funds and organization, as well as his moderate liberal image, actually lost him the nomination.

Out of defeat, the irrepressible Minnesotan snatched senatorial victory by becoming the choice of departing Majority Leader and Vice President-elect Lyndon Johnson for Senate majority whip. Humphrey used his new post to become a driving force in the Senate. Johnson had promoted Humphrey for this leadership position as a reward for his cooperation in the Senate and to solidify a relationship for the benefit of the Kennedy administration. Newly elected Majority Leader Mike Mansfield noted Humphrey's "vibrant personality and phenomenal energy." These traits, coupled with a new-found prag-matism, gained him appointment to the Appropriations Committee and a solid record of legislative accomplishment.[17] Humphrey went on to become a major congressional supporter of a number of New Frontier programs, many of which had been originally outlined in his own bills in the 1950s. Chief among these were the Job Corps, the Peace Corps, an extension of the Food for Peace program, and "a score of progressive measures" pertaining to health, education, and welfare.[18]

Humphrey's role in pressing for the landmark 1963 Limited Nuclear Test Ban Treaty with the Soviet Union ranks as one of his greatest triumphs. A supporter of disarmament since the 1950s, he helped persuade President Eisenhower to follow the Soviets into a voluntary testing moratorium. Humphrey was a follower of George Kennan's geo-strategic analysis, which counselled a moderate course designed selectively and nonprovocatively to contain Soviet probes into areas vital to the United States. This middle way between provocation and disarmament also encouraged pragmatic negotiations, and Humphrey continued to prod President John F. Kennedy into the more permanent test ban treaty and the establishment of a U.S. Arms Control and Disarmament Agency. At the treaty-signing ceremony, President Kennedy recognized Humphrey's years of often lonely efforts, commenting, "Hubert, this is your treaty—and it had better work."[19]

The principal items on Humphrey's longstanding domestic legislative agenda failed to advance significantly until the so-called "Great Society" period that followed Kennedy's death. The first, and perhaps biggest, breakthrough came with passage of the 1964 Civil Rights Act, which he managed in a Senate obstructed by southern filibusterers. In working for that legislation, Humphrey skilfully combined his talent as a soft-spoken, behind-the-scenes negotiator with a rhetorical hard sell focused on the media. Humphrey's subsequent record of legislative achievement was remarkable. With his support, federal aid to farmers and rural areas increased, as did the new food stamp program and foreign-aid food exports that benefitted the farms. Congress authorized scholarships, scientific research grants, aid to schools, rehabilitation of dropouts, and vocational guidance. Legislation promoted public power projects, mass transportation, public housing, and greater unemployment benefits.

While the Minnesota senator could claim credit for helping to create millions of jobs, he also reaped the scorn of critics fearful of deficit spending. Humphrey replied that "a balanced budget is a futile dream," which could not be attained anyway until "the world is in balance." Dismissing those "Scrooges" who harbored a "bookkeeper's mentality," Humphrey, a self-proclaimed "jolly Santa," reiterated his priority, people's "needs and desires." [20]

Campaigning for Vice President

Hubert Humphrey was convinced he could fulfill these "needs and desires" only by becoming president. He saw the vice-presidency as the major stepping stone to this objective, reasoning that, as vice president, he would also have greater access to the president than he did as Senate whip. Humphrey believed he would need the national prominence of the vice-presidential office to secure the presidency because he lacked the requisite financial base to run such a large national campaign. Since 1945 the vice-presidency had come to be viewed as a viable springboard to the presidency—a notion furthered by the near success of Vice President Nixon in the 1960 presidential contest. Yet Humphrey recognized that the vice-presidential office itself was "awkward" and "unnatural" for an energetic politician.[21]

Humphrey realized that he would have to pay the price for his greater access to power by compromising some of his principles, because, above all, Johnson demanded loyalty from his vice president. But in 1964, the cost did not appear to be substantial, since Johnson needed Humphrey and the entrée he provided to the Democratic party's liberal wing. There was, however, never any question as to who was boss. Even when both men served together in the Senate, their relationship was "one of domination-subordination."[22] Humphrey had been Johnson's protégé, his "faithful lieutenant" and go-between with the liberals.[23] It is ironic that when Humphrey actually became Johnson's vice president, one of the closest political relationships in Congress eventually turned into one of the most mutually frustrating presidential-vice-presidential relationships in history. This conflict occurred even though the new vice president sought to accommodate the chief executive by adopting a more conservative stance on both domestic and foreign policy issues, with the resulting erosion of his former liberal credentials.

Johnson succeeded in effectively manipulating Humphrey by running hot and cold, alternately favoring and punishing him. Such behavior modification began early in the political season of 1964, when Johnson played Humphrey off against rivals for the vice-presidency, encouraging all the potential candidates to campaign publicly for popular support. Humphrey's political adroitness in arranging a compromise solution for the racially divided Mississippi delegation at the Democratic National Convention impressed Johnson and finally clinched the nomination for the Minnesotan. Humphrey augmented his popularity by delivering a speech at the convention with a famous refrain attacking right-wing opposition to the Great Society programs that many Republicans had indeed voted for: "But not Senator Goldwater."[24] The charges by the Republican vice-presidential candidate William Miller during the fall campaign that Humphrey was a "radical," on the "left bank . . . of the Democratic Party"[25] had little impact on the voters. Humphrey campaigned persuasively, dispelling his past reputation as a "flaming radical" by explaining that, although he retained his old goals, he was now willing to take an incremental approach and "make what progress is available at the moment."[26]

Lobbying for the Administration

After the landslide mandate of the 1964 election, Humphrey enthusiastically reverted to type and became, according to biographer Albert Eisele, "the busiest vice president in history during his first year in office."[27] An active vice-presidential lobbyist, he sought to trade on his former status as "one of the most well-liked members of the Senate."[28] Concentrating on selling Congress and the nation on the domestic measures to bring about the Great Society, Humphrey maintained a degree of involvement that was unprecedented for a vice president. No previous vice president had been so intimately associated with crafting such a body of legislation. The "legislation long dear to his heart" included the 1965 Voting Rights Act, Medicare, establishment of the Department of Housing and Urban Development and the Office of Economic Opportunity, and creation of the Head Start program.[29] Humphrey's vision for the Great Society included providing federal funds for the National Endowment for the Arts, the Public Broadcasting Service, and solar energy research. Instrumental in passage of the Food Stamp Act of 1964, Humphrey was also the White House's most vigorous salesman in persuading farmers to accept the Model Cities program, African-Americans to abide the draft, and conservatives to tolerate the expanded welfare state.[30]

The president assigned Humphrey his primary job inside the halls of Congress, where his knowledge and contacts would be invaluable. After presiding in the Senate chamber, Humphrey took his campaign for the administration's agenda into the adjacent cloakrooms—the most effective legislative venue, as his long years of experience had taught him. Humphrey's tenure as a member also made him acutely aware of the Senate's unwritten codes of behavior. The vice president understood that as Senate president he must never forget the difference between its chamber and its cloakrooms: now that he was no longer a regular member of the "club," he must confine his political dealings to the cloakrooms, while limiting his chamber activities to the strictly procedural.

After Johnson announced in 1965 that his Great Society programs and the mission in Vietnam could be accomplished simultaneously, Humphrey worked the Senate on a daily basis, encouraging the sale of some raw materials from the U.S. strategic stockpile to pay for the rapidly escalating costs of military involvement, since the administration did not propose to increase taxes.

Humphrey's lobbying activity on Capitol Hill reflected his style of perpetual exertion. Senate Majority Leader Mike Mansfield utilized the vice president's consensus-gathering talents when he asked him to mediate between contentious factions supporting the 1965 Voting Rights bill. The next year, the vice president dealt directly with congressional leaders to push the administration's version of the Model Cities bill.[31] Humphrey understood that he no longer had any legislative authority, but in his capacity as the president's "field marshal on Capitol Hill," he "collect[ed]" debts that were "due" him from his past accumulation of goodwill. In 1965, Humphrey spent far more time in his chandeliered office a few steps from the Senate chamber than he did across town in the Old Executive Office Building. On Capitol Hill he exercised his skills as a "legislative troubleshooter" and "intermediary" between factions. "Time and again," the vice president "delivered votes from lawmakers who seemed immune to blandishments from any other quarter." According to *Newsweek*'s Charles Roberts, Humphrey sometimes cautioned senators in the cloakroom that he would be obligated to make unflattering speeches about them in their districts if they did not vote his way.[32]

By 1966, however, Great Society programs began to stall in Congress and racial tensions mounted, prompting Humphrey to increase the pressure for summer jobs for inner city youth. In frustration, the vice president blurted out one day that, if he were a slum dweller, immersed in rats and garbage, he himself might "revolt."[33] When riots broke out a week later, Humphrey, under fire from both critics and the White House, qualified his earlier statement by adding that "we cannot condone violence."[34] And when urban riots flared again in the summer of 1967, while the administration's agenda remained in limbo, Humphrey called for a "Marshall Plan" for the cities.[35] Johnson, burdened by soaring inflation, interest rates, and government debt, immediately rebuked his vice president, who did not mention his plan again.

On the domestic front Humphrey was motivated by the disparity in standards of living he observed in the richest country on earth. He constantly pressed for increases in Aid to Families with Dependent Children, Social Security, and welfare benefits.[36] The glory of the Great Society was its future-oriented generosity, yet as the economic consequences became apparent, President Johnson grew more fiscally conservative. As a result, Vice President Humphrey felt doubly cheated, not only because his long-held vision was being constrained, but also because, despite his continuous congressional lobbying efforts, the more parsimonious president—and not he—received all the credit for the successes that were achieved.[37] Nevertheless, Humphrey could hardly be dissatisfied with the results of the domestic policy labors that he so enjoyed.

A Varied Role

Although domestic legislation consumed most of Humphrey's energies early in his term, his vice-presidential role can be divided into roughly three separate functions. He was, at various times, the executive branch's representative in the Senate, the chief of numerous executive councils, and the president's spokesman-at-large. Among the statutory duties assigned to the vice-presidency were the administration of oceanography and the space race. As the chairman of councils on topics ranging from Native Americans to the environment, youth, and tourism, Humphrey served as titular head of a wide variety of executive branch enterprises.

But Humphrey soon abandoned most of these White House duties when he realized that the president personally controlled everything of significance. He did, however, maintain his role as liaison to the country's mayors, a duty that dovetailed nicely with his assignment as civil rights coordinator and liaison to the country's African American leaders. These activities were all part of Humphrey's political mission to reduce racial inequities and conflicts by instituting just governance.

In 1966, with the Great Society's remaining legislation stalled in Congress, Humphrey used his vice-presidential platform to support Democrats seeking congressional seats in the coming midterm elections. To that end, Humphrey campaigned in almost every state as party cheerleader and presidential surrogate. He also used his liaison duties to channel political information back to the president, thereby influencing the aid many candidates would receive and gaining a substantial hand in overall campaign strategy.

Humphrey proved to be a vigorous campaigner. As the escalating war in Vietnam slowly smothered domestic legislative initiatives, he advised campaigners to "Run on Vietnam" and became the administration's "chief spear carrier."[38]

Despite Humphrey's energetic Senate lobbying, by 1966 events had shifted the focus of his vice-presidency from Capitol Hill to the White House. Indeed, he became the most active White House spokesman, and his nationwide speaking tours were geared to a "frantic pace."[39] Humphrey's frenzy may be traced in part to the insecurity that his mercurial and manipulative boss engendered. Johnson had a "routine of slapping Humphrey one day and stroking him the next."[40] The president would publicly praise his vice president and then, shortly afterward, exclude him from the inner councils, chiefly because Humphrey talked too much and too freely in public. Johnson, inordinately concerned with leaks and their relationship to loquacity, ended up giving Humphrey little opportunity to contribute to administration policy decisions. The more Humphrey was shut out, the more he became a mere "political spokesman," as he put it, falling back on his formidable rhetorical talents.[41] This choice reflected not only his pledge of loyalty to the president, but also his inclination to seek compromise.

With the situation in Vietnam heating up, Johnson made Humphrey his primary spokesman on war policy. The vice president duly visited university campuses to answer questions and reiterate the administration's policy line. But his new, more conservative stance began to alienate liberal supporters as he uttered such hawkish assertions as, "only the Viet Cong commit atrocities."[42]

Anticommunist and Internationalist

The president also sent Humphrey to Europe to gather support for the administration's war policy, along with a nuclear nonproliferation treaty, increased East-West trade, and international monetary reform. Although many considered the vice president's efforts on his European trip a diplomatic success, he encountered antiwar demonstrators everywhere he went. Humphrey handily dismissed these Europeans as "Communist led," [43] an assessment in keeping with his political record, since he had supported United States cold war policy since 1950. Even as mayor, Humphrey had battled Communists and pro-Soviet leftists for control of his Democratic-Farmer-Labor party. In the Senate, Humphrey had joined the anticommunist crusade in the interest of protecting his noncommunist friends in labor unions. Ideologically, he had always been an internationalist, a Wilsonian, committed to worldwide free trade and open markets, which would, "coincidentally," benefit his Minnesota farm constituents.

The Minnesota Democrat was not always consistent in his internationalist motivations and foreign policy views. For example, although he was a longtime advocate of disarmament, chairman of the Senate disarmament subcommittee, and later father of the Limited Nuclear Test Ban Treaty of 1963, Humphrey had also attacked the Eisenhower administration's "missile gap" in 1960. Even though he may have indulged in a measure of political inconsistency, his views were fundamentally moderate. He never espoused unilateral disarmament but rather supported an active policy of negotiating mutual nuclear and conventional cutbacks with the Soviets. While he advocated outright independence for the "captive nations" of Eastern Europe, he denounced Secretary of State John Foster Dulles' "brinksmanship" over Vietnam, Taiwan, and Korea as a dangerous game of threatening to use massive nuclear force.

Humphrey's record on the cold war at home was even more complex. He had voted for the McCarran Internal Security Act of 1950 and had introduced the Communist Control Act of 1954, both of which severely repressed those identified as American Communists. Humphrey later regretted his participation in the latter act and called for its repeal. Yet, at the time, he was silent regarding the actions of Senator Joseph McCarthy, even though he did deplore the "psychosis of fear" and "this madness of know-nothingness." [44] In the 1950s Humphrey supported the generally held view that agents of foreign governments committed to the overthrow of the U.S. government were not entitled to civil liberties. Yet, this stance could also be explained as a cynical attempt to save the Democrats from the "soft on communism" label, especially during the election year of 1954, the apogee of McCarthyism.

While Humphrey's staunch anticommunism became even more pronounced as he progressed into the upper echelons of the "Establishment," he struggled to maintain his position as a moderate, shifting nimbly to the right and left of center as the circumstances warranted—the so-called "Humphrey duality." [45] By the time of the 1964 presidential campaign, Humphrey labeled Goldwater and his faction as "reactionary," predicting that, if Goldwater were elected, he would institute a "nuclear reign of terror." [46] In spite of his strong anticommunism, Humphrey feared that an East-West confrontation could escalate into nuclear warfare. Thus, his conservative detractors were able to label him "soft on communism" when the compromiser in him proposed, for instance, the solution of coalition governments in Southeast Asia. [47] Humphrey believed that, if the native Communist and anticommunist elements could pragmatically combine in a parliamentary forum, the local military conflict would be less likely to engender an eventual superpower confrontation.

The Vietnam War I: Opposition

As early as 1954, Humphrey had opposed any continuance of the French war in Vietnam by the United States. On that issue, his pre-vice-presidential foreign policy can generally be described as "dovish," despite the often precarious balance he sought to strike. Humphrey did lead the effort to ratify the SEATO treaty in 1955 and asserted in 1960 that, "I happen to believe that the most dangerous, aggressive force in the world today is Communist China." [48] But for Vietnam, he advocated the counterinsurgency techniques of General Edward Lansdale that, rather than a conventional military strategy, emphasized an unconventional and, above all, a political solution incorporating a "rural reconstruction" program. [49] In the 1964 campaign, although Humphrey endorsed a "free civilization" resisting the "expansion of Communist power," he remained a relatively consistent moderate as the campaign's political rhetoric focused more on do-

HUBERT H. HUMPHREY

mestic affairs and the larger cold war, in which the Democrats appeared more moderate than the saber-rattling Goldwater and his running mate, William Miller.[50]

Just a few weeks after the newly elected Johnson administration took office, however, the Viet Cong attacked and killed American troops in South Vietnam, spurring the president to retaliate by bombing the North. Humphrey, virtually alone among Johnson's inner circle, immediately opposed this "Operation Rolling Thunder" with several arguments. The first was drawn from the advice of Undersecretary of State George Ball. A former member of the U.S. Strategic Bombing Survey after World War II, Ball understood the limited capabilities of the U.S. Air Force. Humphrey himself reminded the cabinet that the United States' experience in Korea demonstrated the pitfalls of the nation engaging in a land war in Asia, even though that earlier conflict had indeed represented a clearer case of a conventional invasion. Citing that precedent, Humphrey warned that U.S. escalation in Vietnam could provoke an intervention by the Chinese or even by the Soviets, with potential nuclear consequences. The vice president asked what good reason the United States could have to interject itself into "that faraway conflict" when "no lasting solution can be imposed by a foreign army."[51]

In 1965 Humphrey pushed for a political resolution as the only hope to save not only the unstable government of South Vietnam, but also the full funding of the Great Society programs. The vice president included these points in both verbal counsel and memos to the president, also reminding him that direct bombing by the United States had been Goldwater's position during the campaign. Humphrey predicted that the president would eventually be opposed not by the Republicans, but more dangerously, from within his own party. Johnson's response was increasingly to freeze the vice president out of the Vietnam councils, forcing him to concentrate on Great Society issues. Although Humphrey lost access to the president because of a variety of injudicious public comments, the gulf over Vietnam was the principal cause of his year-long executive exile. This period proved to be the turning point not only of his vice-presidency, but also of his political career.

The Vietnam War II: A Change of Position

As Humphrey's legislative and executive opportunities dwindled, the penitent vice president eventually became only too happy to carry out the new role Johnson had assigned him, that of special envoy. The president sent him on propaganda and fact-finding trips to Southeast Asia to gather evidence of Chinese aggression. On his first trip in early 1966, Humphrey was strongly influenced by the hawkish views of Ambassador Henry Cabot Lodge and General William Westmoreland. So eager was Humphrey to regain the good graces of the president that, even as early as November 1965, he had reported back from his visits to college campuses, which were now holding "teach-ins" against the war, that students were increasingly supporting the Vietnam policy. As Humphrey found that his hopes for compromise were not always attainable, he began to make his irrevocable political choice between loyalty to his lifelong conscience and loyalty to Lyndon Johnson. "I did not become vice president with Lyndon Johnson to cause him trouble," he declared in 1965.[52] The president may have somewhat appeased Humphrey just before his February 1966 conversion with the Christmas 1965 bombing pause of which Johnson said that he was now trying "Hubert's way."[53]

Humphrey departed on his extended peace offensive throughout Indochina and South Asia, which even included some impromptu, and ultimately fruitless, negotiations with Soviet Premier Alexei Kosygin in India. At the end of this publicity-laden circuit, Johnson continued his pattern of molding Humphrey's behavior. The president rewarded—or exploited—depending on one's perspective, Humphrey's demonstration of renewed loyalty by permitting him to announce ambitious plans "to export the Great Society to Asian countries," like South Vietnam.[54] Humphrey instinctively responded to the idea of extending the war on poverty and injustice to other nations.

During the vice president's grand tour of South and Southeast Asian capitals, the local leaders easily persuaded him that the Red Chinese menace and its advance "agent North Vietnam" necessitated U.S. military aid to their countries.[55] Humphrey returned to the United States convinced that Chinese "imperialism and expansion" threatened to topple Asian dominos as far as Australia.[56] He dismissed Senator Mike Mansfield and other skeptical senators as having missed the "big picture" regarding the Communist "master plan" and the Chinese "epidemic [that] we must stop" before they come "closer to home" and all the way to Honolulu and San Francisco.[57] When Senator Robert F. Kennedy suggested the possibility of a coalition government for South Vietnam, a position Humphrey himself had espoused in his pre-vice-presidential days, the vice president retorted that would be like "putting a fox in a chicken coop."[58] Humphrey soon came to regret the memorable quality of some of his more strident statements, as he lost the support of many liberals and midwestern progressives who now characterized him as being "more royalist than the crown."[59] *Newsweek* magazine observed that Humphrey was "the scrappiest warrior in the White House phalanx."[60]

The Vietnam War III: Public Support and Private Doubts

Johnson again tapped Humphrey's inherent exuberance in a successful campaign to persuade Congress to vote more money for the war. As one Democratic liberal commented, the vice president was "one hell of a salesman."[61] Humphrey declared that his new position was born out of "conscience"[62] and that the war was "a matter of survival." He pointed out that "Vietnam today is as close to the U.S. as London was in 1940" and would require the same kind of long-term U.S. commitment.[63] Such statements were more than enough to get Humphrey readmitted to the administration's inner circle of Vietnam advisers. Having done his duty, the vice president was rewarded with a second trip to Southeast Asia in 1967. There, shortly after hearing another of General William Westmoreland's optimistic estimates, he publicly hailed the Vietnam war as "our great adventure," which was making the world freer and better.[64]

Humphrey's closest foreign policy adviser, George Ball, recognized that the vice president "could never do anything half heartedly." Yet as a genuine intimate, Ball also knew that "Humphrey's loyal and excessively exuberant support" masked a vice president who "was personally revolted by the war."[65] Ball believed that a Humphrey administration would pull out of Vietnam quickly. Although Humphrey had no input into the Johnson administration's Vietnam policy, as Defense Secretary Clark Clifford was well aware, the vice president did join Clifford's faction in the White House, which advocated a more dovish diplomacy. This group pushed for a pause in bombing North Vietnam without precondition as an inducement to the Communists to reciprocate. The more hawkish faction demanded advance concessions by the North Vietnamese. Humphrey was caught between loyally supporting the hawks in public and actually being antiwar, "in his heart."[66]

Humphrey had already begun to rediscover the doubts in his heart during his second trip to Southeast Asia. He observed the continuing indifference of South Vietnamese Generals Nguyen Van Thieu and Nguyen Cao Ky to their own forces and their apparently unlimited demands on the United States at the very time the war was supposedly being "de-Americanized." After that second trip, Humphrey implied to his close friend, Dr. Edgar Berman, that he identified with Republican presidential candidate George Romney, who had destroyed his political future by admitting in 1967 that he had been "brainwashed" by American officials into believing the United States was winning the war.[67] Berman later related that Humphrey had told him privately that the United States was "throwing lives and money down a corrupt rat hole" in South Vietnam.[68] When Humphrey sent a confidential memo suggesting this to Johnson, who was beginning to have private doubts of his own, the president typically became infuriated by the dissent. In fact, the vice president was the associate on whom Johnson took out most of his anger, remaining rigid in his insistence that it was the North Vietnamese who had to yield a concession first before U.S. deescalation could occur.

Neither the president nor the vice president, however, could ignore for long the fact that their administration was publicly backing a seemingly losing cause that was also undermining Humphrey's homegrown American Great Society. When the U.S. bombing neither forced North Vietnam to the negotiating table nor did much strategic damage, since that country had little infrastructure, Humphrey in the spring of 1968 strongly advised a halt. This action was Humphrey's first serious divergence from Johnson's policy since 1965.

The 1968 Election

This vice-presidential advice, delivered just days before the end of March 1968, was not the only instance of a prominent Democrat dissenting from Johnson's policy. As Humphrey had predicted three years earlier, the president's own party was now sharply divided, resulting in a strong showing by the peace candidate, Senator Eugene McCarthy, in the New Hampshire and Wisconsin presidential primaries. When Johnson on March 31 announced his decision not to run for reelection, Humphrey was in Mexico City initialing a nuclear nonproliferation treaty. The vice president immediately became the Democratic frontrunner, although he declined to enter any primaries. Robert Kennedy's assassination in June, after winning the California primary, assured Humphrey the nomination by default but left the Democratic party in serious disarray. The path to the November election was strewn with other obstacles, as well, not the least of which was Humphrey's late start due to Johnson's last-minute surprise withdrawal. As a result, Humphrey lacked either sufficient campaign funds or a mature organization to apply them. Moreover, the vice president contributed to his own organizational inefficiency by decentralizing his campaign structure.

The Democrats projected an image of disorganization and chaos to the nation that year, as the party at one time or another split as many as four ways into factions supporting Humphrey, Johnson, Eugene McCarthy, and George Wallace. The raucous Chicago convention—with nationally televised images of police beating young antiwar protesters in the parks—further weakened Humphrey's standing in the polls, and the extreme polarization within the party prevented him from achieving his trademark unifying compromise. The vice president struggled to avoid either being too closely identified with the unpopular president, or dissociating himself so far that he would lose his Democratic party support and Johnson-controlled campaign funds. Even though Johnson had withdrawn from the race in March, the possibility remained that the president might reenter the campaign if circumstances allowed him to be drafted at the August convention. With this sword hanging over Humphrey's head, he did not feel secure enough to risk provoking Johnson into such a move by openly opposing the president's policy. As a result, the vice president had publicly associated himself with the president's policy for so long that a post-convention switch would lack credibility with the voters.

Johnson not only intimidated Humphrey, but he also cajoled the vice president into supporting the administration's line on the war in order to avoid jeopardizing the delicate Paris peace talks. Since Republican nominee Richard Nixon had adopted the patriotic stance of not criticizing Johnson's current handling of the war, Humphrey could not differentiate himself from his Republican opponent on that score without being perceived as disloyal either to the president, to the country, or to his own vice-presidential record. In classic fashion, Humphrey presented ambiguous scenarios for a bombing halt and troop withdrawal. These proposals were directly rejected by Johnson, who thus appeared to move closer to Nixon! In the face of the national crisis, both candidates chose to divert their attention to the domestic problems of law and order and inflation.[69] As these issues, too, were inextricably bound to the war itself, all topics seemed to associate the party in power with the general chaos. Humphrey refused to repudiate either the positions taken during his vice-presidency or his belief that there would be a breakthrough at Paris. Johnson had convinced Humphrey that the latter was imminent, even while denying his vice president detailed information from those negotiations.[70]

Badly behind in the polls, Humphrey took to television in late September to try to solve the dilemma of his private opposition to the war and his public pledge to bring it to an "honorable conclusion." [71] For the first time, he publicly proposed halting the bombing as an inducement to North Vietnamese reciprocity once he became president. As a result, his popularity rebounded in the final month of the campaign. When the election returns came in, Humphrey had collected 42.7 percent of the popular vote to Richard Nixon's 43.4 percent, although the Republican had 301 electoral votes to Humphrey's 191. Too many voters had remembered the vice president's overselling of the war and distrusted his recent apparent conversion.[72]

After the election, Humphrey blamed the loss on his failure to break with Johnson but contended that he could not have proceeded differently. A more dovish or hawkish approach might not have secured Humphrey the presidency, but it is probable that a less ambivalent, less inconsistent message might have satisfied enough of the electorate. In the end, perhaps Humphrey could not have overcome the profound irony inherent in the fact that the war that gave him his presidential chance also took it away.

Back in the Senate

Humphrey's electoral defeat finally removed the constraints of his office, allowing him to express his personal political opinions. He did so in his newspaper column, his memoirs, and as a college political science teacher, along with other educational ventures. Humphrey almost immediately began to seek the Minnesota Senate seat that Eugene McCarthy planned to vacate in 1970. Easily winning on his old populist platform and underplaying the Vietnam issue, Humphrey resumed his prior senatorial pattern of introducing an abundance of bills that were mostly domestic in content. As in his early Senate career, most of his new legislative proposals were stymied. Returning as a new senator without seniority or important committee assignments, Humphrey also had lost many of his valuable former contacts, who had left the Senate. The times had passed him by.

But the irrepressible warrior already had his eye on the 1972 presidential contest, believing he could successfully challenge Richard Nixon on economic issues. Humphrey also criticized the administration's rough handling of dissidents, asserting that "you can't have civil order without civil justice." [73] Still, he remained vulnerable on Vietnam, especially after the 1971 publication of the Pentagon Papers, which revealed that a deceitful Johnson had decided before the 1964 election to bomb North Vietnam and thus escalate the war. These disclosures resuscitated Humphrey's image as Johnson's dupe or shill and convinced many citizens that the former vice president could not be trusted. Although leading in the national polls in December 1971, Humphrey was soon accused of waffling even on domestic issues, and another poll that same year found that he was viewed as "too talkative, too willing to take both sides of an issue." [74] Too many Democrats saw the former vice president as part of the "Establishment" and turned to his Senate colleague George McGovern as the agent of change. Despite failing to win the 1972 nomination, Humphrey tried unsuccessfully once more in 1976.

During his typically active Senate term, Humphrey resumed his seat on the powerful Appropriations Committee and by 1975 was chairman of the Joint Economic Committee. In 1974 he introduced the highly ambitious Humphrey-Hawkins Full Employment and National Growth bill, which eventually passed after his death in 1978. This final legislative monument symbolizes Humphrey's entire career, which was committed to "the humanitarian goals of the New Deal." [75] Humphrey realistically understood that his core constituency comprised those Americans from the lower social and economic classes—the disadvantaged underdogs—a positioning that flowed from what journalist Murray Kempton called Humphrey's "overabundance of feeling for humanity." [76] Although this instinct lit his way onto the public stage in 1948 when he made his singular stand for civil rights, his historical vision became blinded by his failure to recognize that the Vietnam war could destroy his hopes for the Great Society. Humphrey's digression into self-delusion had prompted him in 1968 to stump for "the politics of joy," a slogan that many viewed as entirely inappropriate in the midst of wartime and civil disorder.[77] Humphrey's greatest asset, his enthusiasm, paradoxically may have also been his greatest liability. In the course of pragmatically compromising on the chief issue of the day, Vietnam, he allowed himself to become the administration's loudest proponent of the war.

Although Humphrey's tactics may have sometimes veered off course, he understood the profound value of the strategy of compromise, without which, he said, the Great Society legislation would not have been possible. In 1971 Humphrey called himself a gradualist, the soundest course by which one can make "steady progress if we don't bite off too much."[78] In 1973, former Secretary of State Dean Rusk echoed Humphrey's self-assessment by characterizing him as "a liberal with common sense."[79] Humphrey was able to realize the difference between campaigning, where it was constructive to be partisan, and governing, where to hold grudges would be, in his words, "Neanderthal."[80] While this generosity of spirit made him incapable of being ruthless, a trait probably essential to a presidential aspirant, it also made him an ideal senator or vice president, an advocate and deal maker who "was a terrific fighter but no killer."[81] As a result, the "Happy Warrior" in the public service knew enough defeats to ensure that his "name had become synonymous with cheerfulness in the face of adversity."[82] Humphrey's behavior during his last days testifies to his awe-inspiring strength of character. Terminally ill and in great physical discomfort, he continued his senatorial workload with the same intensity and affability as always. He died on January 13, 1978.

Perhaps the key to Humphrey's indefatigable essence was that he placed personal political ambition below his support of a larger agenda. The innumerable bills that he introduced and shepherded through Congress demonstrate that, with Humphrey, the people and their issues came first.

NOTES

[1] Edgar Berman, *Hubert, the Triumph and the Tragedy of the Humphrey I Knew*, (New York, 1979), p. 23.

[2] Carl Solberg, *Hubert Humphrey: A Biography*, (New York, 1984), p. 214.

[3] Jules Witcover, *Crapshoot: Rolling the Dice on the Vice Presidency*, (New York, 1992), p. 182.

[4] Solberg, p. 387.

[5] Ibid., p. 12.

[6] Ibid., p. 167.

[7] Hays Gorey, "I'm a Born Optimist," *American Heritage*, December 1977, p. 63.

[8] Allan H. Ryskind, *Hubert, An Unauthorized Biography of the Vice President*, (New York, 1968), p. 234.

[9] Solberg, p. 91.

[10] Ryskind, p. 300.

[11] Ibid., p. 231.

[12] Berman, p. 17.

[13] Solberg, p. 89.

[14] U.S., Congress, Senate, *The Senate, 1789–1989: Addresses on the History of the United States Senate*, by Robert C. Byrd, S. Doc. 100–20, 100th Cong., 1st sess., vol. 1, 1989, p. 606.

[15] William S. White, *Citadel: The Story of the Senate* (New York, 1957), pp. 112–13.

[16] Solberg, pp. 99, 209.

[17] Albert Eisele, *Almost to the Presidency, a Biography of Two American Politicians* (Blue Earth, MN, 1972), p. 179.

[18] Ibid., p. 181.

[19] Ibid., p. 185.

[20] Ryskind, pp. 280, 281.

[21] Berman, p. 87.

[22] Marie D. Natoli, "The Humphrey Vice Presidency in Retrospect," *Presidential Studies Quarterly* 12 (Fall 1982): 604.

[23] Ryskind, p. 319.

[24] Solberg, p. 258.

[25] Joel K. Goldstein, *The Modern American Vice Presidency*, (Princeton, NJ, 1982), pp. 121, 122.

[26] Eisele, pp. 206, 212.

[27] Ibid., p. 235.

[28] Natoli, p. 604.

[29] Witcover, p. 197.

[30] Solberg, pp. 462–63; Berman, p. 97.

[31] *Congressional Quarterly Almanac*, 89th Cong., First sess., 1965, vol. 21 (Washington DC, 1966), pp. 547, 821, 829; vol. 22, p. 226.

[32] Charles Roberts, *LBJ's Inner Circle*, (New York, 1965), pp. 190–91.

[33] Ryskind, p. 324; Eisele, p. 249.

[34] Eisele, p. 249.

[35] Solberg, p. 309.

[36] Berman, pp. 27, 31.

[37] Goldstein, p. 181.

[38] Solberg, p. 297; Eisele, pp. 249–50.

[39] Ibid., p. 236.

[40] Witcover, p. 199.

[41] Natoli, p. 605.

[42] Solberg, p. 301.

[43] Ibid., p. 304.

[44] Eisele, p. 99.

[45] Gorey, p. 62; Eisele, p. 99; Solberg pp. 157–59, 468.

[46] Ryskind, p. 266.

[47] Ibid., p. 275.

[48] Eisele, p. 229.

[49] Ibid., p. 230; Solberg, p. 276.

[50] Witcover, p. 195.

[51] Berman, p. 102.

[52] Eisele, p. 224.

[53] Solberg, p. 284.

[54] Eisele, p. 243.

[55] Solberg, p. 291.

[56] Eisele, p. 243.

[57] Solberg, p. 289; Goldstein, p. 194; Eisele, p. 243.

[58] Ryskind, p. 303.

[59] Solberg, p. 290.

[60] Goldstein, p. 194.

[61] Eisele, p. 246.

[62] Ibid., p. 246.

[63] Solberg, p. 291.

[64] Ibid., p. 312.

[65] George Ball, *The Past has Another Pattern: Memoirs* (New York, 1982), pp. 445, 409.

[66] Clark Clifford, with Richard Holbrooke, *Counsel to the President: Memoirs* (New York, 1991), pp. 527, 570.

[67] Berman, p. 111.

[68] Ibid., p. 115.

[69] Eisele, p. 369.

[70] Solberg, pp. 347–48, 350.

[71] Eisele, p. 379; Berman, p. 215.

[72] Solberg, p. 407.

[73] Eisele, p. 432.

[74] Ibid., p. 440.

[75] Ibid., p. 445.

[76] Berman, p. 40.

[77] Solberg, p. 332.

[78] *LBJ Oral History Collection*, Joe B. Frantz interview with Hubert Humphrey, 1971, University of Texas Oral History Project, p. 17.

[79] Natoli, p. 604.

[80] Berman, p. 60.

[81] Solberg, p. 469.

[82] Eisele, p. 393.

Chapter 39

SPIRO THEODORE AGNEW
1969–1973

SPIRO T. AGNEW

Chapter 39

SPIRO THEODORE AGNEW

39th Vice President: 1969–1973

A little over a week ago, I took a rather unusual step for a Vice President . . . I said something.
—SPIRO AGNEW

On November 13, 1969, Vice President Spiro Agnew became a household word when he vehemently denounced television news broadcasters as a biased "unelected elite" who subjected President Richard M. Nixon's speeches to instant analysis. The president had a right to communicate directly with the people, Agnew asserted, without having his words "characterized through the prejudices of hostile critics." Agnew raised the possibility of greater government regulation of this "virtual monopoly," a suggestion that the veteran television newscaster Walter Cronkite took as "an implied threat to freedom of speech in this country." But Agnew's words rang true to those whom Nixon called the Silent Majority. From then until he resigned in 1973, Agnew remained an outspoken and controversial figure, who played traveling salesman for the administration. In this role, Spiro Agnew was both the creation of Richard Nixon and a reflection of his administration's siege mentality.[1]

Early Years

The son of a Greek immigrant whose name originally was Anagnostopoulos, Spiro Theodore Agnew was born in Baltimore, Maryland, on November 9, 1918. He attended public schools and went to Johns Hopkins University in 1937 to study chemistry, before transferring to the University of Baltimore Law School, where he studied law at night while working at a grocery and an insurance company during the day. In 1942 he married a fellow insurance company employee, Elinor Isabel Judefind, known to all as Judy. Drafted into the army during World War II, he won a Bronze Star for his service in France and Germany. He returned to school on the GI Bill of Rights, received his law degree in 1947, practiced law in a Baltimore firm, and eventually set up his own law practice in the Baltimore suburb of Towson.

Remaking His Image

Moving from city to suburb, Agnew remade his own image. When he recalled the ethnic slurs he suffered about "Spiro" while a school boy, he now called himself "Ted" and vowed that none of his children would have Greek names. Agnew similarly changed party affiliations. Although his father was a Baltimore Democratic ward leader and Agnew had first registered as a Democrat, his law partners were Republicans and he joined their party. In 1957 the Democratic county executive of Baltimore County appointed him to the board of zoning appeals. In 1960 Agnew made his first race for elective office, running for associate circuit judge, and coming in fifth in a five-person contest. In 1961, when a new county executive dropped him from the zoning board, Agnew protested vigorously and in so doing built his name recognition in the county. The following year he ran for county executive. A bitter split in the Democratic party helped make him the first Republican elected Baltimore County executive in the twentieth century. In office he established a relatively progressive record, and in

1966, when nominated as the Republican candidate for governor of Maryland, Agnew positioned himself to the left of his Democratic challenger, George Mahoney. An arch segregationist, Mahoney adopted the campaign slogan, "Your Home Is Your Castle—Protect It," which only drove liberal Democrats into Agnew's camp. Charging Mahoney with racial bigotry, Agnew captured the liberal suburbs around Washington and was elected governor.[2]

It came as a shock to Agnew's liberal supporters when as governor he took a more hard-line conservative stance on racial matters than he had during the campaign. Early in 1968, students at the predominantly African American Bowie State College occupied the administration building to protest the run-down condition of their campus—at a time when Maryland essentially ran separate college systems for black and white students. Instead of negotiating, Agnew sent the state police to take back the administration building. When the students went to Annapolis to protest, Agnew ordered their arrest and had the college temporarily closed down. Then in April, when riots broke out in Baltimore following the assassination of Dr. Martin Luther King, Jr., Governor Agnew summoned black leaders to his office. Rather than appeal for their help, he castigated them for capitulating to radical agitators. "You were intimidated by veiled threats," Agnew charged, "you were stung by . . . epithets like 'Uncle Tom.'" Half of the black leaders walked out before he finished speaking. "He talked to us like we were children," one state senator complained. The incident dramatically reversed Agnew's public image, alienating his liberal supporters and raising his standing among conservatives.[3]

Spiro Who?

On the national scene, Agnew formed a committee to draft New York Governor Nelson Rockefeller for president in 1968. In March, during his weekly press conference, Agnew watched on television what he expected would be Rockefeller's declaration of candidacy. Without warning, Rockefeller withdrew from the contest, humiliating Agnew in front of the press corps. Rockefeller later jumped back into the race, but

by then Agnew had moved toward the frontrunner, Richard Nixon. When polls showed none of the better-known Republicans adding much as Nixon's running mate, Nixon surprised everyone—as he liked to do—by selecting the relatively unknown Agnew. "Spiro who?" asked the pundits, who considered Agnew unqualified for national office. Despite such doubts, Nixon saw much promise in his choice. "There can be a mystique about the man," Nixon assured reporters. "You can look him in the eyes and know he's got it."[4]

Nixon expected Agnew to appeal to white southerners and others troubled by the civil rights movement and recent rioting in the cities. Attention shifted from this issue during the campaign, however, when Agnew made a number of gaffes, including some ethnic slurs and an accusation that Vice President Hubert Humphrey, the Democratic candidate, was soft on communism. Agnew also encountered allegations of having profited financially from his public office, charges that he flatly denied. Agnew's biggest problem was that he seemed so ordinary and unremarkable. A tall, stiff, bullet-headed man and the sort of fastidious dresser who never removed his tie in public, he tended to speak in a deadening monotone. Whether he helped or hurt the campaign is not clear, but in November the Nixon-Agnew ticket won a razor-thin victory over the Democratic candidate Hubert Humphrey and the independent candidacy of Alabama Governor George Wallace.[5]

Learning the Constraints of the Office

Although Nixon had chosen a running mate who would not outshine him, he had pledged to give his vice president a significant policy-making role and—for the first time—an office in the West Wing of the White House. Nixon also encouraged Agnew to use his position as presiding officer of the Senate to get to know the members of Congress in order to serve as their liaison with the White House, and Agnew enthusiastically charged up Capitol Hill. Having had no previous legislative experience, he wanted to master the techniques of presiding over the Senate. For the first months of his vice-presidency, he met each morning with the Senate parliamentarian, Floyd

Riddick, to discuss parliamentary procedures and precedents. "He took pride in administering the oath to the new senators by never having to refer to a note," Riddick observed. "He would study and memorize these things so that he could perform without reading." According to Riddick, at first Agnew presided more frequently than had any vice president since Alben Barkley.[6]

"I was prepared to go in there and do a job as the President's representative in the Senate," said Agnew, who busily learned to identify the senators by name and face. Yet he quickly discovered the severe constraints on his role as presiding officer. Agnew had prepared a four-minute speech to give in response to a formal welcome from Majority Leader Mike Mansfield. When Mansfield moved that the vice president be given only two minutes to reply, Agnew felt "it was like a slap in the face." The vice president also unwittingly broke precedent by trying to lobby on the Senate floor. During the debate over the ABM (Anti-Ballistic-Missile) Treaty, Agnew approached Idaho Republican Senator Len Jordan and asked how he was going to vote. "You can't tell me how to vote!" said the shocked senator. "You can't twist my arm!" At the next luncheon of Republican senators, Jordan accused Agnew of breaking the separation of powers by lobbying on the Senate floor, and announced the "Jordan Rule," whereby if the vice president tried to lobby him on anything, he would automatically vote the other way. "And so," Agnew concluded from the experience, "after trying for a while to get along with the Senate, I decided I would go down to the other end of Pennsylvania Avenue and try playing the Executive game."[7]

The vice president fit in no better at the White House than at the Capitol. Nixon's highly protective staff concluded that Agnew had no concept of his role, especially in relation to the president. Nixon found their few private meetings dismaying because of Agnew's "constant self-aggrandizement." Nixon told his staff that as vice president he rarely had made any requests of President Dwight Eisenhower. "But Agnew's visits always included demands for more staff, better facilities, more prerogatives and perquisites." The

anticipated use of Agnew as a conduit to the nation's mayors and governors floundered when it became apparent that Agnew did nothing more than pass their gripes along to the president. When Agnew protested that Nixon did not see enough of his cabinet, Nixon grumbled that his vice president had become an advocate for all the "crybabies" in the cabinet who wanted to plead their special causes. Nixon's chief of staff H.R. Haldeman took Agnew aside and advised him that "the President does not like you to take an opposite view at a cabinet meeting, or say anything that can be construed to be mildly not in accord with his thinking."[8]

Nixon appointed Agnew head of the National Aeronautics and Space Council but again found the vice president more irritant than asset. In April 1969, while at Camp David, Nixon summoned Haldeman to complain that the vice president had telephoned him simply to lobby for a candidate for director of the Space Council. "He just has no sensitivity, or judgment about his relationship" with the president, Haldeman noted. After Agnew publicly advocated a space shot to Mars, Nixon's chief domestic advisor, John Ehrlichman, tried to explain to him the facts of fiscal life:

> Look, Mr. Vice President, we have to be practical. There is no money for a Mars trip. The President has already decided that. So the President does not want such a trip in the [Space Council's] recommendations. It's your job . . . to make absolutely certain that the Mars trip is not in there.

From such experiences, the White House staff concluded that Agnew was not a "Nixon team player."[9]

Unleashing Agnew

Throughout his first term, President Nixon was preoccupied with the war in Vietnam. By the fall of 1969, Nixon came to the unhappy conclusion that there would be no quick solution in Vietnam and that it would steadily become his war rather than Lyndon Johnson's. On November 3, Nixon delivered a television address to the nation in which he called for public support for the war until the Communists negotiated an honorable peace. Public reaction to the speech was generally positive, but the Nixon family was "livid with anger" over the critical commentary by various network broadcasters. Nixon feared that the "constant pounding from the media and our critics in Congress" would eventually undermine his public support. As president he wanted to follow the Eisenhower model of remaining above the fray and to use Agnew for the kind of hatchet work that he himself had done for Ike. When his speech writer Pat Buchanan proposed that the vice president give a speech attacking network commentators, Nixon liked the idea. H.R. Haldeman went to discuss the proposed speech with the vice president, who was interested "but felt it was a bit abrasive." Nevertheless, the White House staff believed the message needed to be delivered, "and he's the one to do it." [10]

Agnew already had some hard-hitting speeches under his belt. On October 20, 1969, at a dinner in Jackson, Mississippi, he had attacked "liberal intellectuals" for their "masochistic compulsion to destroy their country's strength." On October 30 in Harrisburg, Pennsylvania, he called student radicals and other critics of the war "impudent snobs." On November 11 in Philadelphia he decried the "intolerant clamor and cacophony" that raged in society. Then, on November 13 in Des Moines, Iowa, he gave Buchanan's blast at the network news media. Haldeman recorded in his diary that, as the debate on Agnew mounted, the president was "fully convinced he's right and that the majority will agree." The White House sent word for the vice president "to keep up the offensive, and to keep speaking," noting that he was now a "major figure in his own right." The vice president had become "Nixon's Nixon." [11]

Agnew relished the attention showered upon him. He had been frustrated with his assignment as liaison with the governors and mayors, and dealing with taxation, health, and other substantive issues had required tedious study. By contrast, he found speechmaking much more gratifying. As John Ehrlichman sourly noted, Agnew "could take the texts prepared in the President's speechwriting shop, change a phrase here and there, and hit the road to attack the effete corps of impudent snobs." His colorful phrases, like "nattering nabobs of negativism,"

and "radiclibs" (for radical liberals) were compiled and published as "commonsense quotations." "I have refused to 'cool it'—to use the vernacular," Agnew declared, "until the self-righteous lower their voice a few decibels. . . . I intend to be heard over the din even if it means raising my voice." [12]

The Agnew Upsurge

The "Agnew upsurge" fascinated President Nixon, who took it as evidence that a new conservative coalition could be built between blue-collar ethnic voters and white-collar suburbanites. Nixon believed that Agnew was receiving increasing press coverage because his attacks on the media "forced them to pay attention." When some of his advisers wanted to put Agnew out in front in opposition to expanded school desegregation, Nixon hesitated because he did not want to "dilute or waste the great asset he has become." By March 1970, the relationship between the president and vice president reached its apex when the two appeared for an amusing piano duet at the Gridiron Club. No matter what tunes Nixon tried to play, Agnew would drown him out with "Dixie," until they both joined in "God Bless America" as a finale. [13]

As the strains of their duet faded, Nixon began having second thoughts and concluded that he needed to "change the Agnew approach." He informed Haldeman that the vice president had become a better salesman for himself than for the administration, emerging as "too much of an issue and a personality himself." That month, when the Apollo XIII astronauts had to abort their mission and return to earth, Haldeman worked frantically to keep Agnew from flying to Houston and upstaging the president. Agnew sat in his plane on the runway for over an hour until Nixon finally canceled the trip. "VP mad as hell," Haldeman noted, "but agreed to follow orders." In May 1970, after National Guardsmen shot and killed four students at Kent State University, Nixon cautioned Agnew not to say anything provocative about students. Word leaked out that the president was trying to muzzle his vice president. The next time Buchanan prepared "a hot new Agnew speech," Nixon felt more leery than before. [14]

By the summer of 1970, Nixon pondered how best to use Agnew in that fall's congressional elections. The president himself wanted to remain remote from partisanship and limit his speaking to foreign policy issues while Agnew stumped for candidates. Nixon worried that, if Agnew continued to appear an unreasonable figure, using highly charged rhetoric, he might hurt rather than help the candidates for whom he campaigned. "Do you think Agnew's too rough?" Nixon asked John Ehrlichman one day. "His style isn't the problem, it's the content of what he says. He's got to be more positive. He must avoid all personal attacks on people; he can take on Congress as a unit, not as individuals." Some Republican candidates even asked Agnew to stay out of their states. As the campaign progressed, Agnew's droning on about law and order diminished his impact. Nixon felt compelled to abandon his presidential aloofness and enter the campaign himself, barnstorming around the country, as Attorney General John Mitchell complained, like a man "running for sheriff." The disappointing results of the midterm elections—Republicans gained two seats in the Senate but lost a dozen in the House—further shook Nixon's confidence in Agnew.[15]

The Number One Hawk

In 1971 the president devoted most of his attention to foreign policy, planning his historic visit to China, a summit in Moscow, and continued peace talks with the North Vietnamese in Paris. The vice president went abroad for a series of good-will tours and ached for more involvement in foreign policy—an area that Nixon reserved exclusively for himself and National Security Adviser Henry Kissinger. Nixon preferred that Agnew limit himself to attacking the media to "soften the press" for his foreign policy initiatives. He decided to keep the vice president out of all substantive policy decisions, since Agnew seemed incapable of grasping the big picture. For his part, Agnew complained that he was "never allowed to come close enough" to Nixon to participate in any policy discussions. "Every time I went to see him and raised a subject for discussion," the vice president later wrote, "he would begin a rambling, time-consuming monologue."[16]

Agnew, who described himself as the "number-one hawk," went so far as to criticize Nixon's "Ping-Pong Diplomacy" with the People's Republic of China. The dismayed president considered Agnew "a bull in the . . . diplomatic China shop." Nixon had H.R. Haldeman lecture the vice president on the importance of using the China thaw to "get the Russians shook." "It is beyond my understanding," Nixon told Ehrlichman. "Twice Agnew has proposed that he go to China! Now he tells the world it's a bad idea for me to go! What am I going to do about him?"[17]

The Connally Alternative

By mid-1971, Nixon concluded that Spiro Agnew was not "broad-gauged" enough for the vice-presidency. He constructed a scenario by which Agnew would resign, enabling Nixon to appoint Treasury Secretary John Connally as vice president under the provisions of the Twenty-fifth Amendment. By appealing to southern Democrats, Connally would help Nixon create a political realignment, perhaps even replacing the Republican party with a new party that could unite all conservatives. Nixon rejoiced at news that the vice president, feeling sorry for himself, had talked about resigning to accept a lucrative offer in the private sector. Yet while Nixon excelled in daring, unexpected moves, he encountered some major obstacles to implementing this scheme. John Connally was a Democrat, and his selection might offend both parties in Congress, which under the Twenty-fifth Amendment had to ratify the appointment of a new vice president. Even more problematic, John Connally did not want to be vice president. He considered it a "useless" job and felt he could be more effective as a cabinet member. Nixon responded that the relationship between the president and vice president depended entirely on the personalities of whoever held those positions, and he promised Connally they would make it a more meaningful job than ever in its history, even to the point of being "an alternate President." But Connally declined, never dreaming that the post would have made him president when Nixon was later forced to resign during the Watergate scandal.[18]

Nixon concluded that he would not only have to keep Agnew on the ticket but must publicly demonstrate his confidence in the vice president. He recalled that Eisenhower had tried to drop him in 1956 and believed the move had only made Ike look bad. Nixon viewed Agnew as a general liability, but backing him could mute criticism from "the extreme right." Attorney General John Mitchell, who was to head the re-election campaign, argued that Agnew had become "almost a folk hero" in the South and warned that party workers might see his removal as a breach of loyalty. As it turned out, Nixon won reelection in 1972 by a margin wide enough to make his vice-presidential candidate irrelevant.[19]

Immediately after his reelection, however, Nixon made it clear that Agnew should not become his eventual successor. The president had no desire to slip into lame-duck status by allowing Agnew to seize attention as the frontrunner in the next election. "By any criteria he falls short," the president told Ehrlichman:

"Energy? He doesn't work hard; he likes to play golf. Leadership?" Nixon laughed. "Consistency? He's all over the place. He's not really a conservative, you know."

Nixon considered placing the vice president in charge of the American Revolution Bicentennial as a way of sidetracking him. But Agnew declined the post, arguing that the Bicentennial was "a loser." Because everyone would have a different idea about how to celebrate the Bicentennial, its director would have to disappoint too many people. "A potential presidential candidate," Agnew insisted, "doesn't want to make any enemies."[20]

Impeachment Insurance

Unbeknownst to both Nixon and Agnew, time was running out for both men's political careers. Since the previous June, the White House had been preoccupied with containing the political repercussions of the Watergate burglary, in which individuals connected with the president's reelection committee had been arrested while breaking into the Democratic National Committee headquarters. Although Watergate did not influence the election, persistent stories in the media and the launching of a Senate investigation spelled trouble for the president. Innocent of any connection to Watergate, Agnew spoke out in Nixon's defense.

Then, on April 10, 1973, the vice president called Haldeman to his office to report a problem of his own. The U.S. attorney in Maryland, investigating illegal campaign contributions and kickbacks, had questioned Jerome Wolff, Agnew's former aide. Wolff had kept verbatim accounts of meetings during which Agnew discussed raising funds from those who had received state contracts. Agnew swore that "it wasn't shakedown stuff, it was merely going back to get support from those who had benefitted from the Administration." Since prosecutor George Beall was the brother of Maryland Republican Senator J. Glenn Beall, Agnew wanted Haldeman to have Senator Beall intercede with his brother—a request that Haldeman wisely declined.[21]

President Nixon was not at all shocked to learn that his vice president had become enmeshed in a bribery scandal in Maryland. At first, Nixon took the matter lightly, remarking that taking campaign contributions from contractors was "a common practice" in Maryland and other states. "Thank God I was never elected governor of California," Nixon joked with Haldeman. But events began to move quickly, and on April 30, 1973, Nixon asked Haldeman and Ehrlichman to resign because of their role in the Watergate coverup. Then, that summer, the Justice Department reported that the allegations against Agnew had grown more serious. Even as vice president, Agnew had continued to take money for past favors, and he had received some of the payments in his White House office.[22]

Nixon had quipped that Agnew was his insurance against impeachment, arguing that no one wanted to remove him if it meant elevating Agnew to the presidency. The joke took on reality when Agnew asked House Speaker Carl Albert to request that the House conduct a full inquiry into the charges against him. Agnew reasoned that a vice president could be impeached but not indicted. That line of reasoning, however, also jeopardized the president. For over a century since the failed impeachment of President Andrew Johnson, it had been commonly accepted reasoning that impeachment was an impractical and inappropriate congressional tool against the presidency. Agnew's impeachment would set a precedent that could be turned against Nixon. A brief from the solicitor general argued that, while the president was immune from indictment, the vice president was not, since his conviction would not disrupt the workings of the executive branch. Agnew, a proud man filled with moral indignation, reacted to these arguments by digging in his heels and taking a stance that journalists described as "aggressively defensive." He refused the initial suggestions from the White House that he resign voluntarily, after which Agnew believed that high-level officials "launched a campaign to drive me out by leaking anti-Agnew stories to the media." [23]

"I Will Not Resign If Indicted!"

By September, it was a more desperate, less confident-looking man who informed Nixon that he would consider resignation if granted immunity from prosecution. Nixon noted that "in a sad and gentle voice he asked for my assurance that I would not turn my back on him if he were out of office." Believing that for Agnew to resign would be the most honorable course of action, Nixon felt confident that, when the vice president left for California shortly after their meeting, he was going away to think matters over and to prepare his family for his resignation. But in Los Angeles, fired up by an enthusiastic gathering of the National Federation of Republican Women, Agnew defiantly shouted, "I will not resign if indicted!" As Agnew later explained, he had spent the previous evening at the home of the singer Frank Sinatra, who had urged him to fight back. [24]

Nixon's new chief of staff and "crisis manager," General Alexander M. Haig, Jr., was haunted by the specter of a double impeachment of the president and vice president, which could turn the presidency over to congressional Democrats. General Haig therefore took the initiative in forcing Agnew out of office. He instructed Agnew's staff that the president wanted no more speeches like the one in Los Angeles. He further advised that the Justice Department would prosecute Agnew on the charge of failing to record on his income tax returns the cash contributions he had received. Haig assured Agnew's staff that, if the vice president resigned and pleaded guilty on the tax charge, the government would settle the other charges against him and he would serve no jail sentence. But if Agnew continued to fight, "it can and will get nasty and dirty." From this report, Agnew concluded that the president had abandoned him. The vice president even feared for his life, reading into Haig's message: "go quietly—or else." General Haig similarly found Agnew menacing enough to alert Mrs. Haig that should he disappear she "might want to look inside any recently poured concrete bridge pilings in Maryland." [25]

A Plea of Nolo Contendere

Meanwhile, Agnew's attorneys had entered into plea bargaining with the federal prosecutors. In return for pleading nolo contendere, or no contest, to the tax charge and paying $160,000 in back taxes (with the help of a loan from Frank Sinatra), he would receive a suspended sentence and a $10,000 fine. On October 10, 1973, while Spiro T. Agnew appeared in federal court in Baltimore, his letter of resignation was delivered to Secretary of State Henry Kissinger. Agnew was only the second vice president to resign the office (John C. Calhoun had been the first). Prior to resigning, Agnew paid a last visit to President Nixon, who assured him that what he was doing was best for his family and his country. When he later recalled the president's gaunt appearance, Agnew wrote: "It was hard to believe he was not genuinely sorry about the course of events. Within two days, this consummate actor would be celebrating his appointment of a new Vice-President with never a thought of me." [26]

Nixon still wanted to name John Connally as vice president, but Senate Majority Leader Mike Mansfield intimated that Congress would never confirm him. On October 12—even as pictures of Agnew were being removed from federal offices around the country—Nixon appointed House Republican Leader Gerald R. Ford as the first vice president to be selected under the Twenty-fifth Amendment. Agnew was stunned by the laughter and gaiety of the televised event that seemed "like the celebration of a great election victory—not the aftermath of a stunning tragedy." [27]

The coda to the Agnew saga occurred the following year, as Nixon's presidency came to an end. In June 1974, the besieged president dictated an entry in his diary in which he confronted the real possibility of impeachment. Nixon reviewed a series of decisions that now seemed to him mistakes, such as asking Haldeman and Ehrlichman to resign, appointing Elliot Richardson attorney general, and not destroying the secret tape recordings of his White House conversations. "The Agnew resignation was necessary although a very serious blow," Nixon added,

> because while some thought that his stepping aside would take some of the pressure off the effort to get the President, all it did was to open the way to put pressure on the President to resign as well. This is something we have to realize: that any accommodation with opponents in this kind of a fight does not satisfy—it only brings on demands for more.

On August 9, 1974, Richard Nixon joined Spiro Agnew in making theirs the first presidential and vice-presidential team in history to resign from office.[28]

Following his resignation, the vice president who had made himself a household word faded quickly into obscurity. Agnew moved to Rancho Mirage, California, where he became an international business consultant, tapping many of the contacts he had made with foreign governments on travels abroad as vice president. He published his memoir, ominously entitled *Go Quietly . . . or else*, and a novel, *The Canfield Decision*, whose protagonist was a wheeling and dealing American vice president "destroyed by his own ambition." For the rest of his life, Agnew remained largely aloof from the news media and cut off from Washington political circles. Feeling "totally abandoned," he refused to accept any telephone calls from former President Nixon. When Nixon died in 1994, however, Agnew chose to attend his funeral. "I decided after twenty years of resentment to put it aside," he explained. The next year, Spiro Agnew's bust was at last installed with those of other vice presidents in the halls of the U.S. Capitol. "I'm not blind or deaf to the fact that there are those who feel this is a ceremony that should not take place," he acknowledged. Agnew died of leukemia on September 17, 1996, in his home state of Maryland.[29]

NOTES

[1] John R. Coyne, Jr., *The Impudent Snobs: Agnew vs. the Intellectual Establishment* (New Rochelle, NY, 1972), pp. 7–18, 265–70.

[2] Jim G. Lucas, *Agnew: Profile in Conflict* (New York, 1970), pp. 9–37.

[3] Ibid., pp. 37–62.

[4] Jules Witcover, *White Knight: The Rise of Spiro Agnew* (New York, 1972), pp. 4–10, 180–99; Robert W. Peterson, ed., *Agnew: The Coining of a Household Word* (New York, 1972), pp. 1–25; Dan Rather and Gary Paul Gates, *The Palace Guard* (New York, 1974), p. 295.

[5] Witcover, pp. 234–82; Lucas, pp. 19, 63–100; Richard Nixon, *RN: The Memoirs of Richard Nixon* (New York, 1978), 311–13.

[6] Tom Wicker, *One of Us: Richard Nixon and the American Dream* (New York, 1991), p. 344; Peterson, ed., p. 9; Nixon, p. 340; Allen Drury, *Courage and Hesitation* (Garden City, NY, 1971), p. 98; *Floyd M. Riddick: Senate Parliamentarian,* Oral History Interviews, 1978–1979 (U.S. Senate Historical Office, Washington, DC), p. 68.

[7] Drury, pp. 98–100; Witcover, p. 293.

[8] H.R. Haldeman, *The Haldeman Diaries; Inside the Nixon White House* (New York, 1994), p. 27; John Ehrlichman, *Witness to Power: The Nixon Years* (New York, 1982), pp. 106, 111, 145–46; Spiro T. Agnew, *Go Quietly. . . or else* (New York, 1980), pp. 31–32.

[9] Haldeman, p. 53; Ehrlichman, pp. 144–45, 152.

[10] Nixon, pp. 409–12; Haldeman, pp. 99, 106; Witcover, pp. 296–97, 449.

[11] Coyne, pp. 253–70; Haldeman, p. 109; Rather and Gates, p. 296.

[12] Ehrlichman, p. 146; James Calhoun, *The Real Spiro Agnew: Commonsense Quotations of a Household Word* (Greta, LA, 1970), p. 45.

[13] Haldeman, pp. 118, 127–28.

[14] Ibid., pp. 147, 150, 161–62, 169.

[15] Ibid., pp. 179–80; Ehrlichman, p. 103; Rather and Gates, pp. 300–302.

[16] Haldeman, pp. 240–41; Agnew, p. 34.

[17] Nixon, p. 549; Haldeman, p. 247; Ehrlichman, pp. 154–55; Agnew, p. 23.

[18] Haldeman, pp. 275, 296, 306–7, 317, 327; Witcover, pp. 432–33; Agnew, pp. 38–40.

[19] Nixon, pp. 674–75; Haldeman, pp. 356–57.

[20] Ehrlichman, p. 142; Haldeman, p. 534; Agnew, pp. 37–38.

[21] Haldeman, p. 629; Agnew, pp. 50–51, 57–58; Richard M. Cohen and Jules Witcover, *A Heartbeat Away: The Investigation and Resignation of Vice President Spiro T. Agnew* (New York, 1974), pp. 3–16.

[22] Jonathan Aitken, *Nixon: A Life* (Washington, 1993), pp. 356–57, 503–4; Nixon, p. 823; Ehrlichman, pp. 142–43; Agnew, pp. 98–99.

[23] Agnew, pp. 100–103, 130–32; Cohen and Witcover, pp. 149, 190–216.

[24] Nixon, pp. 912–18; Agnew, p. 178.

[25] Agnew, pp. 182–83, 186–90; Alexander M. Haig, Jr., *Inner Circles: How America Changed the World: A Memoir* (New York, 1992), pp. 350–67.

[26] Agnew, pp. 192–99.

[27] Ibid., pp. 201–2, 220–21; Haig, pp. 367–70.

[28] Nixon, pp. 1002–5.

[29] *Washington Post*, September 19, 1996.

Chapter 40

GERALD RUDOLPH FORD
1973–1974

GERALD R. FORD

(Addressing a joint session of Congress after his swearing in
as vice president on December 6, 1973)

Chapter 40

GERALD RUDOLPH FORD

40th Vice President: 1973–1974

Life plays some funny tricks on people. Here I have been trying . . . for 25 years to become Speaker of the House. Suddenly, I am a candidate for President of the Senate, where I could hardly ever vote, and where I will never get a chance to speak.

—GERALD R. FORD

The assassination of President John F. Kennedy in November 1963 placed Lyndon Johnson in the White House and—for the sixteenth time in American history—left the vice-presidency unoccupied. Just months later, former Vice President Richard M. Nixon, his political career seemingly terminated by his loss to Kennedy in the presidential election of 1960 and his subsequent defeat for governor of California in 1962, appeared before the Senate Judiciary Subcommittee on Constitutional Amendments to discuss means of filling vice-presidential vacancies. The existing order of succession that placed the Speaker of the House and president pro tempore of the Senate next in line to the presidency troubled Nixon. He pointed out that there were no guarantees that either of these legislative officials would be ideologically compatible with the president or even of the same party. He similarly disliked proposals for the president to nominate a vice president subject to confirmation by Congress, since a Congress controlled by the opposition party might unduly influence the president's choice. Nixon proposed that the Electoral College elect the new vice president. Not only would this method guarantee that the same electors who chose the president would choose the vice president, but having been elected by the people the electors would give additional legitimacy to the new vice president.[1]

Chairman Birch Bayh, an Indiana Democrat, and other subcommittee members listened respectfully to Nixon's arguments but were unpersuaded. They considered the Electoral College "too much of a historical curiosity," too cumbersome, and too far removed from public awareness to make such an important decision. Instead, the subcommittee reported an amendment that provided:

> Whenever there is a vacancy in the office of Vice President, the President shall nominate a Vice President who shall take the office upon confirmation by a majority vote of both houses of Congress.

The Twenty-fifth Amendment, which also included provisions for the vice president to take charge during a president's disability, was passed by Congress and ratified by the required three-quarters of the states in 1967.

Six years later the amendment was implemented by none other than President Richard Nixon. Following Spiro Agnew's resignation, Nixon nominated Gerald R. Ford as his new vice president. Confronting the scenario that he had described in his earlier testimony, Nixon could not choose the candidate he preferred, John Connally. Because the Democratic majorities in both houses of Congress opposed Connally, the president was forced to settle for someone more likely to win confirmation. For the Democrats, there was also some irony involved. Less than a year later, when Nixon himself resigned, it was the former Republican leader of the House who succeeded him. Had the Twenty-fifth Amendment not been adopted, the resignations—or impeachments—of Nixon and Agnew would have handed the presidency to the Speaker of the House, a Democrat.[2]

An Uncomplicated Man

The amendment's first beneficiary, Gerald Rudolph Ford, was an uncomplicated man who traveled a complex path to become vice president. He was born Leslie Lynch King, Jr. in Omaha, Nebraska, on July 14, 1913. His mother, after having been physically abused by his father, obtained a divorce and moved to her parents' home in Grand Rapids, Michigan. There she met and married Gerald R. Ford, a paint salesman, who formally adopted her son and renamed him. The novelist John Updike has observed that Ford therefore became "the only President to preside with a name completely different from the one he was given at birth," which was just as well, since 'President King' "would have been an awkward oxymoron."[3]

After this uncertain start, Jerry Ford lived a normal Middle American childhood in what he described as a "strait-laced, highly conservative town." He attended public schools, excelled in athletics, and worked lunch times grilling hamburgers. His mother was an active member of her church, garden clubs, and various civic organizations, and his stepfather was a Mason, Shriner, and Elk. Jerry became an Eagle Scout. The family fortunes alternated between prosperous and strapped, more often the latter; some football boosters arranged for Ford to receive scholarships and part-time jobs to help him attend the University of Michigan, where he became a star football player. The Green Bay Packers and Detroit Lions offered to sign him as a professional player, but Ford chose instead to attend the Yale Law School. To support himself, he coached Yale's freshman football squad, two of whose members—William Proxmire and Robert Taft, Jr.—would one day as senators vote for his confirmation as vice president.[4]

A "B" student among Phi Beta Kappas, Ford found the academic competition as tough as anything he had experienced on a football field. His classmates at Yale included Cyrus Vance, Potter Stewart, and Sargent Shriver. Yet Ford managed to rank in the top third of his class. "How that happened," he later commented, "I can't explain." He completed course work in 1941 and went back to Michigan to take the bar exam and start a law practice. After Pearl Harbor he enlisted in the navy and spent the war in the Pacific. Discharged in 1946, he returned to Grand Rapids, moved to a larger law firm, and joined the American Legion and Veterans of Foreign Wars. In 1947 Ford began dating Elizabeth (Betty) Bloomer Warren, the fashion coordinator for a local department store, who was in the process of obtaining a divorce.

Politics also attracted him. At Yale he had supported the Republican presidential candidate Wendell Willkie in 1940 and had become involved in the isolationist group America First. Ford would remain a Republican, but Pearl Harbor and the Second World War converted him to an internationalist foreign policy. He modeled himself after his state's senior senator, Republican Arthur Vandenberg, who had similarly reversed his position on America's role in world affairs. In 1948, the thirty-four-year-old Ford decided to challenge the renomination of Republican Representative Barney Jonkman, an outspoken isolationist and critic of Senator Vandenberg. Conventional wisdom pictured Jonkman as unbeatable, but when President Harry Truman called the Eightieth Congress back into special session that summer, Ford had the district to himself for campaigning, while the incumbent was busy in Washington. He drew support from internationalists in both parties—since Democrats knew they had no chance of electing a Democrat in that district. In the primary, Ford beat Jonkman 2 to 1. On October 15, 1948, shortly before the general election, Ford married Betty Warren. He had been campaigning just minutes before the ceremony, and the next day the newly married couple attended a political rally. "I was very unprepared to be a political wife," Betty Ford later observed, "but I didn't worry because

I really didn't think he was going to win." She was wrong. Although Truman and the Democrats carried the election of 1948, Gerald Ford won election to Congress with 61 percent of the vote.[5]

Rising in the House Leadership

When Ford entered the House of Representatives in the Eighty-first Congress, an oldtimer on the Michigan delegation advised him that he could either spend his time in committee, mastering one area of legislation, or on the floor, learning the rules, parliamentary procedure and debating tactics. Ford chose the latter. It was on the House floor that he first met Richard Nixon, who had already achieved notoriety during the House Un-American Activities Committee's investigation of the Alger Hiss-Whittaker Chambers controversy. Impressed with Nixon's performance, Ford tried to be present whenever the Californian spoke in the House. The two men shared similar backgrounds and outlooks on foreign and domestic politics and liked to talk about football and baseball. In 1951, Ford invited the newly elected Senator Nixon to speak at a Lincoln Day banquet in Grand Rapids.[6] The next year, when Nixon delivered his famous "Checkers" televised speech to save his vice-presidential candidacy, Ford wired him:

> Over radio and newspapers I am in your corner 100 percent. Fight it to the finish as you did the smears by Communists when you were proving charges against Alger Hiss. . . . I will personally welcome you in Grand Rapids or any other part of Michigan.[7]

As Nixon's horizons expanded, Ford retained his seat in the House, slowly amassing seniority and respect. Ford had joined with Nixon and other new members of the House to organize the Chowder and Marching Society, an informal caucus of Republican veterans of the Second World War, which became his first stepping stone to leadership. In 1960, Ford's name surfaced as a possible vice-presidential candidate to run with Nixon. In 1963, Lyndon Johnson appointed him a member of the Warren Commission to investigate the assassination of John F. Kennedy. But Ford focused his ambition principally on the House, where he hoped someday to become Speaker. Elected chairman of the Republican Conference in 1963, Ford was also moving up in seniority on the powerful Appropriations Committee. In 1965, after his party suffered a thirty-six-seat loss and had its ranks reduced to the lowest level since the Great Depression, a group of dissatisfied Republicans known as Young Turks promoted Ford as their candidate to replace the incumbent Charles Halleck as minority leader. Ford attributed his narrow victory over Halleck to the help of Representative Bob Dole, who delivered the support of the Kansas delegation to him as a bloc.[8]

President Johnson, having worked closely with Halleck, deplored Ford's elevation to the Republican leadership. Expecting Ford to be more partisan than Halleck and less cooperative, Johnson made wisecracks that the trouble with Ford was that "he used to play football without a helmet" and that he was "too stupid to walk and chew gum at the same time." Johnson also told reporters that Ford had violated national security by leaking stories told to him in confidence. These charges were untrue, and reporters backed Ford's denial, but the incident revealed the depth of Johnson's animosity toward the new Republican leader. Ford's friend and supporter, New York Representative Charles Goodell, believed that "Johnson thought Ford was stupid because he was predictable." Goodell saw Ford as a solid fellow who had no instinct for the kind of political manipulation upon which men like Johnson and Nixon thrived.[9]

In September 1965, at a time when Ford's star was on the rise and Richard Nixon's had gone into political eclipse, the two men met for breakfast at the Mayflower Hotel to discuss rebuilding their damaged party. Nixon, who still harbored presidential ambitions, pledged to campaign for House Republican candidates, admitting that he was motivated by "pragmatism more than altruism." Thereafter, Nixon maintained close ties with Ford, calling him sometimes from pay phones during his political journeys around the country. "Many people in politics respected Richard Nixon's abilities," the journalist Richard Reeves observed, "but Ford was one of the few who talked about liking Nixon."[10]

Ford also spent much of the time between 1965 and 1968 traveling from state to state to speak for Republican candidates and reinforce his political base in the House. During his first six months as leader, Ford visited thirty-two states. When reporters asked if he was running for something, he replied: "I'm running for House Speaker." Given that the Republicans held only 140 out of 435 House seats, this was an extravagant ambition, but in 1966 his efforts helped House Republicans make a remarkable rebound with a gain of 47 seats. Ford's long hours on Capitol Hill and frequent absences from home for political speaking engagements, however, took their toll on his family, especially on his wife Betty, who turned to alcohol and pain-killers to compensate for her loneliness. "I'd felt as though I were doing everything for everyone else, and I was not getting any attention at all," she lamented.[11]

The Ultimate Nixon Loyalist

In 1968, a "new Nixon" won the Republican presidential nomination, and Ford was again mentioned as a vice-presidential candidate. Ford, the permanent chairman of the convention, had been an unequivocal Nixon supporter from the beginning of the campaign. At a strategy session, Nixon turned to him and said, "I know that in the past, Jerry, you have thought about being Vice President. Would you take it this year?" Ford replied that, if the Republicans did as well in 1968 as they had two years earlier, they might take the majority in the House, and he would prefer to become Speaker. He endorsed New York Mayor John Lindsay for vice president. But in fact, Nixon had already decided on Maryland Governor Spiro Agnew as his running mate—even before asking Ford. Ford shook his head in disbelief at that choice.[12]

During Nixon's first term, House Republican leader Gerald Ford was the ultimate Nixon loyalist in Congress. In May 1971, when the House voted to restore funds for the Supersonic Transport (SST) project, but not enough votes could be found in the Senate, President Nixon ruminated to his aide, H.R. Haldeman, on the "lack of leadership" in Congress, "making the point that Gerry Ford really is the only leader we've

got on either side in either house." Ford annoyed conservative Republicans by his support for Nixon's Family Assistance Plan and angered liberals by his efforts to impeach Supreme Court Justice William O. Douglas—an action widely interpreted as a response to the defeat of two of Nixon's Supreme Court nominations.[13]

For all these efforts, Ford and his Republican counterparts in the Senate "had trouble finding anyone on the White House staff dealing with policy who was interested in consulting with us on domestic legislative priorities." Whenever the Republican congressional leadership met with Nixon at the White House, the members received promises that his aides would work with them, "but they never did." Ford attributed this unresponsiveness to the "us versus them" mentality of Nixon's staff. He also regretted Vice President Agnew's intemperate attacks on the news media, which Ford believed would only reopen old wounds. Nevertheless, Ford felt confident that Nixon's coattails in 1972 would carry a Republican majority into the House and finally make him Speaker. On election night, he was deeply disappointed with the results. "If we can't get a majority [in the House] against McGovern, with a Republican President winning virtually every state, when can we?" Ford complained to his wife. "Maybe it's time for us to get out of politics and have another life." He began to think seriously of retiring as House leader when Nixon's second term was over in 1976.[14]

The First Appointed Vice President

Unforseen events during the next year completely changed Gerald Ford's life. When stories broke that Vice President Agnew had taken kickbacks from Maryland contractors, the vice president visited Ford to swear to his innocence. Although Ford professed not to doubt Agnew's word, after that meeting he made certain that someone else was always present whenever he saw the vice president. On October 10, 1973, Nixon called Ford to his hideaway office at the Executive Office Building and told him that there was evidence that Agnew had received illegal payments in his office in the West Wing of the White House and that the matter was going to court. Ford returned to the House chamber, where just minutes later the word was passed: "Agnew has resigned." The next day, Nixon met with Ford and Senate Republican leader Hugh Scott at the White House to discuss filling the vacancy under the Twenty-fifth Amendment and asked them to have their Republican colleagues each send him their top three choices for the office.[15]

Nixon knew that Democrats felt apprehensive about confirming someone who might be a strong contender for the presidency in 1976 and that they preferred "a caretaker Vice President who would simply fill out Agnew's unexpired term." Nixon wanted to appoint his Treasury Secretary, John Connally, but after meeting with the Democratic congressional leadership he concluded that Connally would have a difficult time being confirmed. At Camp David, Nixon prepared an announcement speech with four endings, one each for Nelson Rockefeller, Ronald Reagan, Connally, and Ford. Looking through the names that Republican party leaders had suggested, he found that Rockefeller and Reagan had tied, Connally was third, and Ford last. However, among members of Congress, including such Democrats as Senate Majority Leader Mike Mansfield and House Speaker Carl Albert, Ford's name came in first and, as Nixon noted, "they were the ones who would have to approve the man I nominated." As Speaker Albert later asserted, "We gave Nixon no choice but Ford."[16]

The Watergate scandal had so preoccupied and weakened Nixon that he could not win a fight over Connally. Choosing either Rockefeller or Reagan would likely split the Republican party. That left Ford. Nixon reasoned that, not only were Ford's views on foreign and domestic policy practically identical with his, but that the House leader would be the easiest to confirm. He had also received assurances that Ford "had no ambitions to hold office after January 1977," which would clear the path for Connally to seek the Republican presidential nomination. On the morning of October 12, 1973, Nixon called Ford to a private meeting. While he intended to nominate Ford for vice president, Nixon explained, he planned to campaign for Connally for president in 1976. Ford raised no objections to that arrange-

ment, and that evening, Nixon announced the news publicly from the East Room.[17]

Ford's nomination was subject to confirmation in both the Senate and House, where Democrats held commanding majorities. Because of the Watergate scandal, congressional Democrats were concerned that the individual they confirmed as vice president might well become president before Nixon's term was completed. Liberals expressed displeasure with Ford's conservative voting record on social welfare and other domestic issues and his undeviating loyalty to President Nixon's foreign policies but did not believe they could withhold confirmation merely because of policy disagreements. A few liberals, led by New York Representative Bella Abzug, tried to block action on Ford's nomination, anticipating that Nixon's eventual removal would make House Speaker Albert president. Albert, however, pushed for Ford's speedy confirmation. Then, on October 20, Nixon fired Special Prosecutor Archibald Cox in defiance of his attempts to subpoena the White House tape recordings, an event the press dubbed the "Saturday Night Massacre." Both Democrats and Republicans now felt it legitimate to ask what position Ford would take as president on such questions as executive privilege and the independent jurisdictions of the legislative and judicial branches. Congress appeared to hold Ford's nomination hostage until Nixon complied with the subpoenas of his tapes.[18]

White House chief of staff Alexander Haig worried that, if Nixon were impeached before Ford became vice president, Democrats might delay his confirmation in order to make Speaker Albert president. Haig therefore helped break the logjam by pressing Nixon to move on the appointment of a new special prosecutor and a new attorney general (since Elliot Richardson had resigned rather than fire Cox), as well as to guarantee some compliance on the matter of the tapes. On November 27 the Senate voted 92 to 3 to confirm Ford, and on December 6, the House agreed, 387 to 35 (with Ford voting "present"). President Nixon wanted Ford to take the oath of office in the East Room of the White House, but Ford thought it more appropriate to hold the ceremony in the Capitol, where he had served for a quarter of a century. Nixon had little desire to appear in a House chamber where impeachment motions were being filed against him, and where he might be booed, but at last he relented. Addressing his enthusiastic former colleagues, the new vice president modestly identified himself as "a Ford, not a Lincoln." General Haig complained about the atmosphere in the House chamber: "Ford was treated throughout the ceremony and afterwards as a President-in-waiting, especially by Republicans, and there can be little question that Richard Nixon's presidency was over, in their minds, from the moment his successor took the oath." [19]

A Catalyst to Bind the National Wounds

Although warmly cheered in Congress, the new vice president received only a lukewarm reception in the press. Many journalists did not believe Ford measured up to the job. The *New York Times* dismissed him as a "routine partisan of narrow views," and the *Washington Post* regarded him as "the very model of a second-level party man." The columnist David Broder thought that Nixon did not want "a partner in policy-making or an apprentice President." The harshest criticism came from the conservative *Wall Street Journal*, which pronounced, "The nomination of Mr. Ford caters to all the worst instincts on Capitol Hill—the clubbiness that made him the choice of Congress, the partisanship that threatened a bruising fight if a prominent Republican presidential contender were named, the small-mindedness that thinks in terms of those who should be rewarded rather than who could best fill the job." [20]

During the confirmation process, Republican Senator Mark Hatfield of Oregon asked Ford whether his role might be that of "a catalyst to bind up some of these deep-seated wounds, political and otherwise?" Ford replied that he expected to make speeches around the country. "I would maximize my efforts not to do it in an abrasive way," he promised, "but rather to calm the waters." Ford carried out that promise so well that President Nixon discovered he had a new political weapon: an honest, believable, and congenial vice president. Although some skeptics regarded Ford, in the words of the columnist

Nicholas von Hoffman, as just "Agnew without alliteration," the public generally accepted the new vice president as trustworthy, forthright and unpretentious if not particularly brilliant. Ford spent most of his eight months as vice president on the road rather than in the Senate chamber, delivering an almost continuous stream of speeches, holding fifty-two press conferences, and giving eighty-five formal interviews, in an effort to demonstrate a new openness in government. [21]

Vice President Ford balanced precariously between supporting the president and maintaining some distance from the Watergate scandal. "I am my own man," he proclaimed. The Nixon White House thought differently. Ford's top aide, Robert Hartmann, a crusty former newspaper correspondent, was summoned by General Haig's staff secretary to receive a lengthy list of priorities for the new vice president. Included were congressional relations, speaking engagements outside of Washington, serving as the administration's point man during the 1974 campaign, and being available for foreign travel. If Ford needed assistance in speech writing, scheduling, and advance personnel, the White House would provide it. Hartmann concluded that Nixon's staff "intended to integrate [Ford's] supporting staff so completely with the White House that it would be impossible for him to assert even the little independence Agnew had managed." At the meeting's end, the staff secretary shook Hartmann's hand and declared, "What we want to do is to make the Vice President as much as possible a part of the White House staff." [22]

The Smoking Gun and the President's Resignation

Although Ford steadfastly defended Nixon throughout the Watergate crisis, he could never understand why the president did not simply release the tapes to clear his name and end the controversy, if he was as innocent as he professed. The longer Nixon stonewalled, the more pressure mounted from members of his own party on Capitol Hill for the president to resign before the midterm elections of 1974. Where Nixon and Ford had once hoped to achieve Republican majorities in Congress, they now faced the prospect of massive losses of seats. In the first few months of 1974, Republicans lost four of five special elections—including Ford's old Grand Rapids district. In May 1974, when Nixon released the first, highly edited transcripts of his secret tapes, public opinion turned even further against him. Senate Republican leader Hugh Scott called the language and contents of the transcripts "deplorable, shabby, disgusting, and immoral." Ford also admitted that the tapes "don't exactly confer sainthood on anyone." The vice president attended a Senate Republican Policy Committee luncheon where Arizona Senator Barry Goldwater rose and said: "I'm not yelling at you, Mr. Vice President, but I'm just getting something off my chest. The president ought to resign. It's not in the best interest of everybody to have to face an impeachment trial." Ford immediately excused himself and left.[23]

The release of the additional tapes finally produced the "smoking gun" that demonstrated beyond question that Nixon—despite his protestations to the contrary—had personally directed the cover-up of the Watergate scandal. By the beginning of August, Nixon realized that he would have to resign to avoid impeachment, and he instructed General Haig to tell Ford to be prepared to take over the presidency within a matter of days. Nixon noted that, while Ford was not experienced in foreign affairs, "he's a good and decent man, and the country needs that now." General Haig went to Ford's office, but finding Ford's aide Robert Hartmann there, Haig hesitated to give Ford a list of options prepared by the president's legal counsels that included the power of the incoming president to pardon his predecessor (the legal counsels had gone so far as to draft a pardon in Ford's name, dated August 6, 1974). After the first meeting concluded, Haig called Ford at his Capitol office to set up another meeting—alone—where he could be more candid. Ford seemed receptive, but the next time they talked, Haig observed that Ford's voice had grown more formal and that he called him "General" rather than "Al." "I want you to understand," Ford said, "that I have no intention of recommending what the President should do about resigning or not resigning, and nothing we talked about yesterday afternoon should be given any consideration in whatever decision the President may wish to make." Haig concluded that Ford was trying to protect himself from potential charges that he had made a deal to get the presidency. Haig insisted that Nixon had never known of the list of options, and that his own actions had not been Machiavellian.[24]

On August 8, Nixon called Ford to the Oval Office and told him that he was resigning. "Jerry," he added, "I know you'll do a good job." He recommended that Ford keep Henry Kissinger as secretary of state, because if Kissinger were to leave along with Nixon "our foreign policy would soon be in disarray." He also urged him to retain Haig as chief of staff during the transition, to handle the inevitable "scramble for power" within the staff and cabinet. Ford accepted both recommendations. Nixon noted that he would be gone by noon the next day so that Ford could take the oath of office at the White House as Truman had done. A tearful Nixon closed the conversation by thanking Ford for his long loyal support.[25]

The First Nonelected President

The next morning, Nixon departed from the White House lawn by helicopter while Gerald Ford waved goodbye. The first nonelected vice president was then sworn in as president of the United States. In his inaugural address, Ford proclaimed that "our long national nightmare is over." The nation agreed, and Ford entered office on the crest of favorable public opinion. Within a month, however, the good will dissipated when Ford pardoned Richard Nixon. Although deeply dismayed when the tapes showed that Nixon had lied to him, Ford felt personally concerned about Nixon's mental and physical health and politically concerned about the national impact of a trial of a former president. He decided that Nixon's resignation and the sentence of having to live with the humiliation was as severe a punishment as a jail term. "You can't pull a bandage off slowly," he concluded, "and I was convinced that the sooner I issued the pardon the better it would be for the country."[26]

Although Ford pardoned Nixon, he declined to pardon Nixon's coconspirators, many of whom served jail terms for obstruction of justice;

he also declined advice to issue a general amnesty for Vietnam-era draft evaders. The Nixon pardon proved more unpopular than Ford expected and forced him to spend the rest of his presidency explaining and justifying the action to a suspicious public. Adverse reaction to the pardon precipitated a Democratic landslide in the congressional elections of 1974, with House Democrats gaining forty-eight seats.

A man of Congress, who had wanted to restore a sense of cooperation and conciliation between the executive and legislative branches, President Ford confronted a hostile legislature that turned his presidency into a clash of vetoes and veto overrides. During his term, Congress further trimmed the powers of the "imperial presidency" and challenged executive authority in foreign and domestic affairs. Ford fought back, becoming an outspoken critic of Congress. The veteran Washington correspondent Sarah McClendon interpreted Ford's aggressiveness as his response to all those frustrating years of serving in the House without becoming Speaker. She imagined him thinking: "Now that I am president, I can finally be Speaker of the House, too. I am going to make up for all those years by driving those Democrats out of their seats, and out of their minds, if I can." She concluded that he almost did.[27]

Ford sought reelection to the presidency in 1976 but was challenged in the primaries by former California governor Ronald Reagan. Once having secured the nomination, Ford chose as his running mate Senator Robert J. Dole of Kansas. In the first presidential race under the new Federal Election Campaign Act that provided partial public funding to presidential candidates, Ford and Dole faced former Georgia governor Jimmy Carter and Minnesota Senator Walter F. Mondale. The candidates engaged in the first televised presidential campaign debates since 1960. Although Ford stressed his many years of government experience, Carter, the outsider, won a narrow victory, denying Ford election to a full term in the office he had held for two years.

NOTES

[1] U.S., Congress, Senate, Judiciary Committee, Subcommittee on Constitutional Amendments, *Presidential Inability and Vacancies in the Office of Vice President* (Washington, 1964), pp. 234–50.

[2] U.S., Congress, Senate, Committee on Rules and Administration, *Nomination of Gerald R. Ford of Michigan to be Vice President of the United States* (Washington, 1973), pp. 4, 144–64.

[3] John Updike, *Memories of the Ford Administration: A Novel* (New York, 1992), p. 354.

[4] Gerald R. Ford, *A Time to Heal: The Autobiography of Gerald R. Ford* (New York, 1979), pp. 42–56; James Cannon, *Time and Chance: Gerald Ford's Appointment with History* (New York, 1994), pp. 1–38.

[5] Ford, pp. 57–68; Cannon, pp. 32–52.

[6] Ford, pp. 68–70; Cannon, pp. 54–55.

[7] Richard Nixon, *RN: The Memoirs of Richard Nixon* (New York, 1978), pp. 101–2.

[8] Ford, pp. 72–78; Cannon, pp. 53–55; Nixon, pp. 215–16.

[9] Ford, pp. 78–79; Samuel Shaffer, *On and Off the Floor: Thirty years as a Correspondent on Capitol Hill* (New York, 1980), pp. 264–65; Richard Reeves, *A Ford, Not a Lincoln* (New York, 1975), p. 26.

[10] Cannon, pp. 89–90; Reeves, p. 115.

[11] Clark R. Mollenhoff, *The Man Who Pardoned Nixon* (New York, 1976), p. 13; Jerald F. terHorst, *Gerald Ford and the Future of the Presidency* (New York, 1974), p. 97; Cannon, p. 88.

[12] Ford, pp. 85–86; Cannon, p. 95.

[13] H.R. Haldeman, *The Haldeman Diaries: Inside the Nixon White House* (New York, 1994), pp. 286, 288; Mollenhoff, p. 14; Nixon, pp. 427, 438.

[14] Ford, pp. 89–90; Cannon, p. xv.

[15] Robert T. Hartmann, *Palace Politics: An Inside Account of the Ford Years* (New York, 1980), pp. 14–17.

[16] Nixon, p. 925; Cannon, p. 205.

[17] Nixon and Ford tell different versions of the event in their memoirs: Nixon, pp. 926–27; and Ford, pp. 104–6; see also Cannon, pp. 210–11.

[18] Committee on Rules and Administration, *Nomination of Gerald R. Ford*, p. 5.

[19] Alexander M. Haig, Jr., *Inner Circles: How America Changed the World: A Memoir* (New York, 1992), pp. 427, 439–41; Hartmann, p. 87.

[20] Mark J. Rozell, *The Press and the Ford Presidency* (Ann Arbor, MI, 1992), pp. 15–16.

[21] Ibid., p. 19; Ford, p. 127; Cannon, p. 273.

[22] Stanley I. Kutler, *The Wars of Watergate: The Last Crisis of Richard Nixon* (New York, 1990), p. 420; Hartmann, p. 82.

[23] Nixon, pp. 988–89, 996–97, 1001; Shaffer, p. 293.

[24] Nixon, pp. 1057–58; Haig, pp. 481–86; Kutler, p. 555; Ford, pp. 4–6.

[25] Nixon, pp. 1078–79.

[26] Ford, pp. 157–82; Hartmann, p. 255.

[27] Haig, pp. 512–15; Cannon, pp. 359–91, 414–15; Sarah McClendon, *My Eight Presidents* (New York, 1978), pp. 186–87.

Chapter 41

NELSON ALDRICH
ROCKEFELLER
1974–1977

NELSON A. ROCKEFELLER

Chapter 41

NELSON ALDRICH ROCKEFELLER

41st Vice President: 1974–1977

I've known all the Vice Presidents since Henry Wallace. They were all frustrated, and some were pretty bitter.

—NELSON ROCKEFELLER

Television cameras that had been installed in the Senate chamber to cover the expected impeachment trial of President Richard M. Nixon were used instead to broadcast the swearing-in of Nelson A. Rockefeller as vice president on December 19, 1974. A year earlier, Gerald Ford had chosen to take his oath as vice president in the House chamber, where he had served as Republican floor leader. Rockefeller might have opted for a White House ceremony but decided to take the oath in the chamber where he would preside as president of the Senate. With President Gerald Ford attending and Chief Justice Warren Burger administering the oath, Rockefeller became the nation's second appointed vice president. After the brief ceremony, the cameras were switched off. Not until 1986 would Senate proceedings be televised on a regular basis.[1]

A Family of Wealth and Power

Nelson Aldrich Rockefeller came to the vice-presidency boasting a remarkable pedigree. His maternal grandfather, Rhode Island Senator Nelson Aldrich, had been the Senate's most powerful member at the turn of the century. Aldrich chaired the Senate Finance Committee and played the key role in passage of tariffs that influenced every industry and agricultural product. In 1901, Aldrich's daughter Abby married John D. Rockefeller, Jr., son of the nation's

wealthiest man, the founder of Standard Oil. Although they combined political power and corporate wealth, the reputations of Nelson Aldrich and John D. Rockefeller, Sr. were less than stellar. In a series of articles for *Cosmopolitan* magazine during 1906, muckraking journalist David Graham Phillips portrayed Aldrich as a corrupt boss who contributed to the "Treason of the Senate." Similarly, writer Ida Tarbell exposed the senior Rockefeller as a ruthless robber baron, and President Theodore Roosevelt included him among the "malefactors of great wealth." At the time of Nelson Rockefeller's birth, on July 8, 1908, both of his grandfathers were afflicted by negative publicity. Senator Aldrich withdrew from politics in 1911, while John D. Rockefeller, Sr., hired one of the first public relations specialists to reshape his public image into that of a kindly old gentleman handing shiny dimes to children.[2]

Nelson Aldrich Rockefeller inherited both a vast family fortune and a family image that he had to live down in order to achieve his political ambitions—because even as a little boy he wanted to be president of the United States. "After all," he reasoned, "when you think of what I had, what else was there to aspire to?" The third of five brothers, Nelson was the energetic, outgoing leader within his own family. He and his brothers grew up in the family home on West 54th Street in New York, which was so filled with art that his parents bought the town house next door just to house their collection. Eventually the Rockefellers gave the property to the Museum of Modern Art. Nelson attended the progressive Lincoln School of Teachers College at Columbia University, but dyslexia hindered his schooling and prevented him from attending Princeton. With the help of tutors he graduated Phi Beta Kappa from Dartmouth in 1930. Shortly thereafter, he married Mary Todhunter Clark, known as Tod, whose calm reserve seemed to balance his boundless enthusiasms. After a round-the-world honeymoon, they settled in New York and Nelson went to work for the family business.[3]

Nelson Rockefeller proved so successful in renting out space in the newly constructed Rockefeller Center that his father made him president of the Center. He earned negative publicity after he ordered the removal from Rockefeller Center of murals painted by the noted Mexican artist Diego Rivera, which contained a heroic Lenin and a villainous-looking J.P. Morgan. Otherwise, Rockefeller won high praise for his executive abilities. He became a director of the Creole Petroleum Company, a Rockefeller subsidiary in Venezuela. He learned Spanish and began a lifelong interest in Latin-American affairs. Art was another of his passions, and during the depression he served as treasurer of the Museum of Modern Art. In 1939 he became the museum's president, encountering such intense infighting that he boasted, "I learned my politics at the Museum of Modern Art."[4]

In 1940, President Franklin Roosevelt appointed the thirty-two-year-old Rockefeller to the new post of coordinator of the Office of Inter-American Affairs. It was a shrewd move on Roosevelt's part, designed to mute the Rockefeller family's support of Wendell Willkie for president that year. Although his brothers served in uniform, Nelson held civilian posts throughout World War II, becoming assistant secretary of state for American republics affairs in 1944. He played a key role in hemispheric policy at the United Nations Conference held in San Francisco, developing consensus for regional pacts (such as the Rio Pact and NATO) within the UN's framework. Although President Roosevelt tried to lure Rockefeller into the Democratic party, he remained loyal to his family's Republican ties. When Roosevelt died, his successor showed less appreciation for Rockefeller's talents. In August 1945 the failed haberdasher Harry Truman fired the multimillionaire Rockefeller, in order to settle a dispute within the State Department.[5]

Reputation as a Spender

Rockefeller returned to government during Dwight Eisenhower's administration, where he chaired a committee on government organization, became under secretary of the new Department of Health, Education and Welfare, served as special assistant to the president for cold war strategy, and headed the secret "Forty Committee," a group of high government officials who were charged with overseeing the CIA's clandestine operations. He was slated for a high-level post in the Department of Defense until fiscally conservative Secretary of the Treasury George Humphrey vetoed Rockefeller as a "spender."[6]

Rockefeller returned to New York determined to establish his own political career. In 1958 he challenged the popular and prestigious governor Averell Harriman, in what the press dubbed the "battle of the millionaires." Rockefeller campaigned as a man of the people, appearing in shirtsleeves and eating his way through the ethnic foods of New York neighborhoods. His victory in a year when Republicans lost badly elsewhere made him an overnight contender for the Republican presidential nomination in 1960. Republicans who distrusted Vice President Richard Nixon rallied to Rockefeller, and Democrats like Senator John F. Kennedy considered him the most formidable candidate that the Republicans might nominate. Because Rockefeller's advisers were reluctant to have him enter the party primaries, however, he was never able to demonstrate his popular appeal or overcome Nixon's lead among party loyalists. Instead, Rockefeller used his clout to summon Nixon to his Fifth Avenue apartment and dictate terms for a more liberal party platform. Arizona Senator Barry Goldwater denounced this event as "the Munich of the Republican Party," the beginning of a long estrangement between Rockefeller and the Republican right.[7]

Nixon's defeat in 1960 made Rockefeller the frontrunner for the Republican nomination in 1964. But between the two elections he stunned the nation by divorcing his wife of thirty-two years and marrying a younger woman, Margaretta Fitler Murphy, better known as "Happy." She was the recently divorced wife of an executive in the Rockefeller Medical Institute. The birth of their son, Nelson, Jr., on the eve of the Republican primary in California reminded voters of the remarriage and contributed to Rockefeller's loss to Goldwater. At the party's convention in San Francisco, Goldwater's delegates loudly booed Rockefeller when he tried to speak. To them, he embodied the hated "Eastern liberal establishment." Rockefeller sat out the election, an act that further branded him as a spoiler.[8]

An Impressive Record as Governor

Unsuccessful in his presidential bids, Rockefeller achieved a more impressive record as governor. He was a master builder, overseeing highway construction, the expansion of the state university system, and the erection of a vast new complex of state office buildings in Albany. Although New Yorkers joked about their governor's "edifice complex," they elected him to four terms. To pay for his many projects without raising taxes excessively, Rockefeller consulted the prominent municipal bond specialist John Mitchell (later attorney general under Richard Nixon) who advised the creation of quasi-independent agencies that could issue bonds. The State University Construction Fund would repay its bonds through tuition and fees, while other agencies would build roads, public housing, and hospitals. As a result, control of a large part of the budget and of state operations shifted from the legislature to the governor. It was later revealed during Rockefeller's vice-presidential confirmation hearings that he had also made personal financial contributions to the chairmen of these independent agencies, thereby reinforcing their loyalty to the governor.[9]

In perpetual motion, Governor Rockefeller tackled one project after another. He waded into campaigning with similar gusto, shaking hands and giving his famous greeting: "Hiya, fella!" He laced his speeches with superlatives and platitudes and so often repeated the phrase, "the brotherhood of man under the fatherhood of God," that reporters shortened it to create the acronym BOMFOG. Although he campaigned as a man of the people, he lived in a different world. When aides proposed a plan for the state to take over state employee contributions to Social Security, in order to increase their take-home pay, Rockefeller asked, "What is take-home pay?"[10]

A staunch anticommunist, Rockefeller never opposed the war in Vietnam, explaining that he did not want to offend President Lyndon Johnson and risk cuts in federal aid to New York. In 1968 Johnson tried to convince Rockefeller to run for president. "He told me he could not sleep at night if Nixon was president, and he wasn't all that sure about Hubert [Humphrey] either," Rockefeller later revealed. The governor responded that he had promised his wife not to run again, but Johnson insisted, "Let me talk to Happy," and took her off in the White House to apply some of his famed personal persuasion. "They came back a half hour later," Rockefeller recalled, "and Lyndon said, 'I've talked her into letting you run.'" Rockefeller announced his candidacy, but Nixon's powerful campaign apparatus rolled over him. When Humphrey became the Democratic nominee, he invited Rockefeller to run as his vice president. "I turned him down," Rockefeller said. "Franklin Roosevelt wanted me to be a Democrat (back in the 1940s). It was too late."[11]

Despite an inability to hide his personal disdain for Richard Nixon, Rockefeller campaigned for Nixon in both 1968 and 1972. He admired Nixon's tough stands in Vietnam and Cambodia—shaped by National Security Adviser Henry Kissinger, who originally had served as Rockefeller's foreign policy adviser. Nixon appointed Rockefeller to serve on the Foreign Intelligence Advisory Board to oversee CIA activities. Meanwhile, Rockefeller's own politics were shifting toward the right, partly to make peace with conservative Republicans who had vilified him, and partly in response to the so-called "conservative backlash" of the late 1960s. Rockefeller's tough "law and order" stand during the Attica prison riots in 1971 further diminished his liberal image. The governor refused demands of rioting prisoners at the state penitentiary that he negotiate with them in person and instead sent in state troops, resulting in the deaths of many inmates and their captives. At the Republican convention in 1972, Rockefeller nominated Nixon. After the election, as Nixon sank into the Watergate scandal, Rockefeller steadfastly resisted attacking him while he was down.[12]

Broadening the Ticket's Electoral Appeal

When Vice President Spiro Agnew resigned in October 1973, Rockefeller let it be known that he would not turn down a vice-presidential nomination, as he had done in 1960 and 1968. But Nixon, believing that choosing Rockefeller would offend Republican conservatives, instead selected the more centrist Gerald Ford. Happy Rockefeller said she never expected Nixon to pick her husband because "weakness never turns to strength." That December, Rockefeller resigned after fourteen years as governor, to give his long-serving lieutenant governor, Malcolm Wilson, a chance to run for the office as the incumbent. Rockefeller then devoted his attention to the newly created Commission on Critical Choices for America, which many expected he would use as a vehicle to run for the presidency in 1976.[13]

Rockefeller was firmly convinced that Nixon would never resign, but events proved him wrong. In August 1974, when Gerald Ford assumed the presidency and prepared to appoint his own vice president, Rockefeller and George Bush headed his list of candidates. Bush, a former Texas congressman and chairman of the Republican National Committee, was the safer, more comfortable choice. But Ford believed in a balanced ticket (in 1968 Ford had urged Nixon to select New York City's liberal Republican mayor John Lindsay as his running mate). Weighing the assets and deficits, Ford acknowledged that Rockefeller was still anathema to many conservatives. Still, the new president believed that the New Yorker was well qualified to be president, would add executive expertise to the administration, and would broaden the

ticket's electoral appeal if they ran in 1976. Also, by selecting as strong a man as Rockefeller, Ford would demonstrate his own self-confidence as president.[14]

Robert Hartmann, one of Ford's closest aides, asked Rockefeller why he had accepted the vice-presidency now after turning it down before. "It was entirely a question of there being a Constitutional crisis and a crisis of confidence on the part of the American people," Rockefeller replied. "I felt there was a duty incumbent on any American who could do anything that would contribute to a restoration of confidence in the democratic process and in the integrity of government." Rockefeller also reasoned that, while Ford as a former member of Congress understood the "Congressional-legislative side" of the issues, he as governor had mastered the "Executive-administrative side," and that together they could make an effective team. Although fully aware of the limitations of his office, and recognizing that he was "just not built for standby equipment," Rockefeller had accepted because Ford promised to make him a "partner" in his presidency.[15]

Number One Achievement

The media applauded the selection. After berating Nixon for picking Ford, reporters praised Ford's appointment of "a man of national stature." The *New York Times* called it a "masterly political act," and *Newsweek* congratulated Ford for adding a "dollop of high style" to his "homespun Presidency." *Time* observed that President Ford felt secure enough to name a dynamic personality as vice president. Ford basked in his accomplishment. In November, when reporters asked him what he considered the top achievements of his first hundred days as president, Ford replied: "Number one, nominating Nelson Rockefeller."[16]

Yet nomination was only half the process, for the Twenty-fifth Amendment to the Constitution required confirmation by both houses of Congress. Democrats and some conservative Republicans relished the prospect of opening the books on the private finances of one of the nation's wealthiest families. Even President Ford expressed fascination with the details as they emerged. "Can you imagine," he said privately, "Nelson lost $30 million in one year and it didn't make any difference." After the shocks of Watergate and the revelations that Agnew had taken kickbacks, it was reassuring to have a vice president too rich to be bought. But the confirmation hearings revealed that Rockefeller had been making personal contributions to government officials, including Henry Kissinger and the administrators of New York's supposedly independent commissions. Since state law had prohibited making large financial gifts to state appointees, Rockefeller had given the money as "loans" that he never expected to be repaid.[17]

Rockefeller's confirmation hearings dragged on for months, and House and Senate leaders talked of delaying his confirmation until the new Congress convened in January. "You just can't do that to the country," President Ford complained to House Speaker Carl Albert and Senate Majority Leader Mike Mansfield. "You can't do it to Nelson Rockefeller, and you can't do it to me. It's in the national interest that you confirm Rockefeller, and I'm asking you to move as soon as possible." The Senate finally acted on December 10, and the House on December 19. That evening, Rockefeller took the oath in the Senate chamber.[18]

The secretary of the Senate found it amusing to give Rockefeller the standard orientation, signing him up for health insurance and other benefits he did not need. Ironically, Rockefeller was also the first vice president eligible to occupy the new vice-presidential mansion—formerly the residence of the chief of Naval Operations—on Massachusetts Avenue. "Congress has finally determined to give the Vice President a home in Washington," Ford told Rockefeller. "It's up on Admiral's Hill, and you'll have to live in it." Rockefeller grimaced but nodded in agreement. He already had a home in Washington that he purchased during the Second World War, a colonial-era farmhouse situated on twenty-seven acres of land, one of the most expensive properties in the District of Columbia. Rockefeller spent only a single night in the vice-presidential mansion, but he stimulated some publicity by installing a mink-covered bed designed by Max Ernst that was valued at $35,000. Press criticism

later resulted in the bed being loaned to a museum. Years after, when Happy Rockefeller visited George and Barbara Bush at the vice-presidential mansion, she offered to return the bed to the mansion. Barbara Bush insisted that Mrs. Rockefeller was always welcome to spend the night and did not need to bring her own bed.[19]

Less Than a Full Partner

Gerald Ford told the nation that he wanted his vice president to be "a full partner," especially in domestic policy. "Nelson, I think, has a particular and maybe peculiar capability of balancing the pros and cons in many social programs, and I think he has a reputation and the leadership capability," Ford explained. "I want him to be very active in the Domestic Council, even to the extent of being chairman of the Domestic Council." But during the months while Rockefeller's nomination stalled in Congress, Ford's new White House staff established its control of the executive branch and had no intention of sharing power with the vice president and his staff. One Rockefeller aide lamented that the "first four month shakedown was critical and he wasn't involved. That was when the relationship evolved and we were on Capitol Hill fighting for confirmation."[20]

Rockefeller envisioned taking charge of domestic policies the same way that Henry Kissinger ran foreign policy in the Ford administration. Gerald Ford seemed to acquiesce, but chief of staff Donald Rumsfeld objected to the vice president preempting the president. When Rockefeller tried to implement Ford's promise that domestic policymakers would report to the president via the vice president, Rumsfeld intervened with various objections. Rockefeller shifted gears and had one of his trusted assistants, James Cannon, appointed chief of the Domestic Council. Rumsfeld responded by cutting the Council's budget to the bone. Rockefeller then moved to develop his own policies independent of the Domestic Council. Tapping the scientist Edward Teller, who had worked for Rockefeller's Commission on Critical Choices, he proposed a $100 billion Energy Independence Authority. Although Ford endorsed the energy plan, the president's economic and environmental advisers lined up solidly against it.[21]

Usually, Ford and Rockefeller met once a week. Ford noted that Rockefeller "would sit down, stir his coffee with the stem of his horn-rimmed glasses and fidget in his chair as he leaped from one subject to another." Nothing, Ford observed, was too small or too grandiose for Rockefeller's imagination. Beyond the substantive issues, the two men also spent much time talking over national politics. Yet Ford and his staff shut Rockefeller out of key policy debates. In October 1975, when Ford proposed large cuts in federal taxes and spending, the vice president complained, "This is the most important move the president has made, and I wasn't even consulted." Someone asked what he did as vice president, and Rockefeller replied: "I go to funerals. I go to earthquakes." Rockefeller had disliked the vice-presidential seal, with its drooping wings and single arrow in its claw. He had a new seal designed with the eagle's wings outspread and multiple arrows in its clutch. As one of his aides recalled, "One day after a particularly long series of defeats, I walked into the Governor's office [Rockefeller's staff always referred to him as "Governor"] with yet another piece of bad news. The Governor turned to me and pointed at the new seal and flag, sighing, 'See that goddamn seal? That's the most important thing I've done all year.'"[22]

An Impervious Senate

Vice President Rockefeller found the Senate equally impervious to his desire to exert leadership. In January 1975, when the post-Watergate Congress met, the expanded liberal ranks in the Senate moved to amend Rule 22 to reduce from two-thirds to three-fifths of the senators the number of votes needed to invoke cloture and end a filibuster. Minnesota Democratic Senator Walter Mondale introduced the amendment, and Kansas Republican James Pearson moved that the chair place before the Senate a motion to change the cloture rule by a majority vote. When the Senate took up the matter in February, Senate Democratic Majority Leader Mike Mansfield raised a point of order that the motion violated Senate rules by permitting a simple majority vote

to end debate. Instead of ruling on the point of order, Vice President Rockefeller submitted it to the Senate for a vote, stating that, if the body tabled the point of order, he "would be compelled to interpret that action as an expression by the Senate of its judgment that the motion offered by the Senator from Kansas to end debate is a proper motion." The Senate voted 51 to 42 to table Mansfield's motion, in effect agreeing that Senate rules could be changed by a simple majority vote at the beginning of a Congress. The Senate, however, adjourned for the day without actually voting on the resolution to take up the cloture rule change. The leaders of both parties then met and determined that they disagreed with this procedure, which they felt had set a dangerous precedent. The leadership therefore devised a plan to void the rulings of the chair and revise the cloture rule in a more traditional manner. More than a week later, in early March, the Senate voted to reconsider the vote by which the Mansfield point of order had been tabled and then agreed to Mansfield's point of order by a majority vote. A cloture motion was then filed and agreed to, 73 to 21, after which the Senate adopted a substitute amendment introduced by Senator Robert C. Byrd, which specified that cloture could be invoked by a three-fifths vote on all issues except changes in the rules, which would still require a two-thirds vote. [23]

In making his controversial ruling, Rockefeller had notified the Senate parliamentarian that he was making the decision on his own, contrary to the parliamentarian's advice. As parliamentarian emeritus Floyd Riddick observed,

> Certainly it was contrary to the practices and precedents of the Senate, and I think that is why the leadership, under Mr. Mansfield as majority leader, wanted to vitiate in effect all of the statements made by the vice president and come back and do it under the rules, practices, and precedents of the Senate.[24]

On another occasion as presiding officer, Rockefeller tried to break a filibuster by declining to recognize Senators James Allen of Alabama and William Brock of Tennessee and instead ordering the roll call to proceed. Senator Barry Goldwater challenged him, but Rockefeller replied, "It says right here in the precedents of the Senate, 'The Chair may decline to respond; the chair may decline to answer a parliamentary inquiry.'" "That is correct," Goldwater countered. "That is what it says, but I never thought I would see the day when the chair would take advantage of it." Later, Rockefeller apologized for any "discourtesy" he may have shown the Senate by this incident. "If I make a mistake I like to say so." [25]

Investigating the CIA

President Ford also sought to use Rockefeller to head off a Senate investigation of the Central Intelligence Agency. In December 1974, the *New York Times'* reporter Seymour Hersh published an exposé of CIA spying on antiwar activists that constituted domestic activities in violation of the CIA's charter. When Democrats called for an investigation, Ford appointed a blue-ribbon Commission on CIA Activities and made Rockefeller its chairman. But the Senate went ahead and established its own Select Committee on Intelligence Activities, chaired by Frank Church of Idaho. When Senator Church asked for materials from the White House, he was told that the papers had been given to the Rockefeller Commission. When the senator demanded the papers from Rockefeller, the vice president declined to provide them on the grounds that only the president could grant access to the papers. One Church aide called Rockefeller "absolutely brilliant" in denying them access in a friendly manner. "He winked and smiled and said, 'Gee, I want to help you but, of course I can't—not until we've finished our work and the president approves it.'" Said Senator John Tower, vice chair of the committee, "We were very skillfully finessed." [26]

The CIA assignment put Rockefeller in the crossfire between critics and defenders of the agency. Whether his report was critical or lenient, it was sure to draw fire. Rockefeller himself had a long involvement in CIA matters, dating back to the Eisenhower and Nixon administrations, when he served on panels that oversaw the highly secret agency. Yet even Rockefeller seemed unprepared for the revelations that the intelligence agency had plotted the assassinations of foreign leaders. To the surprise of both Senator Church and President Ford, the Rockefeller Commission chose to adhere to its original mandate and not investigate the assassinations. The panel turned those records over to the Senate committee, allowing Rockefeller to extricate himself from a difficult situation. [27]

Ford's Biggest Political Mistake

In the fall of 1975, President Ford determined to run for election and appointed Howard "Bo" Callaway of Georgia as his campaign manager. Ford did not consult Rockefeller until the day he announced the choice. Callaway immediately began spreading the word that Rockefeller was too old, and too liberal, and too much of a detriment to the ticket. Some administration officials believed that Donald Rumsfeld wanted the vice-presidential nomination for himself and hoped that this humiliation would encourage Rockefeller to remove himself from contention. President Ford was given opinion polls that showed twenty-five percent of all Republicans would not vote for him if Rockefeller remained on the ticket. Ford's advisers complained that Rockefeller was not a "team player," and that he had been a "commuting" vice president, flying weekly to New York where his wife and sons had remained. Still, Rockefeller hung on doggedly, patching up his difference with Barry Goldwater and making public appearances in the South—to prove, as he said, that he did not have horns. After one rally in South Carolina, a Republican leader conceded that the vice president had changed some minds from "hell no," to "no." [28]

When it became clear that former California Governor Ronald Reagan would challenge Ford for the Republican nomination, Ford reluctantly resolved to jettison Rockefeller. Putting the situation to him, Ford insisted that he was just telling him the facts, not what to do. Rockefeller, however, had been in politics long enough to know that he was being asked to leave gracefully. He announced that he would not be a candidate for vice president the following year. Although he publicly insisted that he jumped without having been shoved, privately he told friends, "I didn't take myself off the ticket, you know—he asked me to do it." [29]

Rockefeller's withdrawal, along with Ford's clumsy firing of Defense Secretary James Schlesinger—replacing him with Donald Rumsfeld—became known as the "Halloween Massacre." It resulted in a plunge in Ford's popularity and polls that showed Reagan leading him for the Republican nomination. Southern Republicans largely deserted the president for Reagan, causing Rockefeller to comment that he had made a mistake in withdrawing when he did. "I should have said in that letter . . . when Bo Callaway delivered to you the Southern delegates, then I'm off the ticket." Ford responded, "You didn't make the mistake. We made the mistake." Dumping Rockefeller embarrassed Ford as much as it did Rockefeller. "It was the biggest political mistake of my life," Ford confessed. "And it was one of the few cowardly things I did in my life." [30]

Despite being dropped, Rockefeller still wanted to be a major player. Before the Republican convention in 1976, he even proposed taking over as White House chief of staff, to help boost morale and public confidence. At the convention, Rockefeller delivered the large New York state delegation to Ford, participated in the choice of Senator Robert Dole as Ford's running mate, and placed Dole's name in nomination. He campaigned hard for the Republican ticket in the fall. At one stop in Birmingham, New York, hecklers provoked the vice president into making an obscene gesture back at them. Photographs of the vice president "giving the finger" were widely reprinted as a symbolic act of signing out of politics.[31]

Leaving office in January 1977, Rockefeller retired from politics and devoted his last two years (he died on January 26, 1979) to other interests, primarily in the arts. He always insisted that he had understood full well what he was getting into when Ford offered him the vice-presidency. "I've known all the Vice Presidents since Henry Wallace," he said. "They were all frustrated, and some were pretty bitter. So I was totally prepared." Rockefeller expressed thanks for the respectful way in which Ford had treated him. "I was never told to make a speech or to clear a speech with the President," he noted. But he regretted not having had more responsibilities in the administration and not being able to make a greater contribution to public policy. "The Vice-Presidency is not much of a job," he concluded. "But at least Washington is where the action is."[32]

NOTES

[1] *Floyd M. Riddick: Senate Parliamentarian*, Oral History Interviews, June 16, 1978 to February 15, 1979 (U.S. Senate Historical Office, Washington, DC), pp. 255–65.

[2] For Aldrich, see Horace Samuel Merrill and Marion Galbraith Merrill, *The Republican Command, 1897–1913* (Lexington, KY, 1971); for Rockefeller see Allan Nevins, *John D. Rockefeller: The Heroic Age of American Enterprise* (New York, 1940), 2 vols.

[3] *Memorial Addresses and Other Tributes in the Congress of the United States on the Life and Contributions of Nelson A. Rockefeller*, S. Doc. 96–20 (Washington, 1979), p. 16.

[4] Joseph E. Persico, *The Imperial Rockefeller: A Biography of Nelson A. Rockefeller* (New York, 1982), pp. 25–32; Peter Collier and David Horowitz, *The Rockefellers: An American Dynasty* (New York, 1976), pp. 206–10.

[5] Collier and Horowitz, pp. 214, 237, 242–43.

[6] Ibid., pp. 272–76; Michael Kramer and Sam Roberts, *"I Never Wanted to Be Vice-President of Anything!" An Investigative Biography of Nelson Rockefeller* (New York, 1976), p. 373.

[7] Collier and Horowitz, p. 342.

[8] See Theodore H. White, *The Making of the President, 1964* (New York, 1965).

[9] Ibid., pp. 469–77.

[10] Persico, p. 227; *Memorial Addresses*, p. 229.

[11] Richard Reeves, *A Ford, Not a Lincoln* (New York, 1975), p. 150; *Memorial Addresses*, p. 237.

[12] Persico, p. 241.

[13] Robert T. Hartmann, *Palace Politics: An Inside Account of the Ford Years* (New York, 1980), p. 238.

[14] Reeves, p. 149; Gerald R. Ford, *A Time to Heal: The Autobiography of Gerald R. Ford* (New York, 1979), pp. 143–44.

[15] Hartmann, pp. 230–36; Persico, p. 245.

[16] Mark Rozell, *The Press and the Ford Presidency* (Ann Arbor, MI, 1992), pp. 45–46; Reeves, p. 147.

[17] Reeves, p. 147; Kramer and Roberts, pp. 369–70.

[18] Ford, p. 224.

[19] *Dorothye G. Scott: Administrative Assistant to the Senate Democratic Secretary and the Secretary of the Senate, 1945–1977*, Oral History Interviews, 1992 (U.S. Senate Historical Office, Washington, DC), p. 174; Ford, p. 145; Persico, pp. 262–63.

[20] "How It Looks to Ford," *Newsweek* (December 9, 1974), p. 37; Paul C. Light, "The Institutional Vice Presidency," *Presidential Studies Quarterly* 13 (Spring 1983): 210; Paul C. Light, *Vice-Presidential Power: Advice and influence in the White House* (Baltimore, Press, 1984), pp. 180–83.

[21] Hartmann, pp. 304–10; Kramer & Roberts, pp. 372–73.

[22] Ford, p. 327; Persico, p. 262; Light, "The Institutional Vice Presidency," p. 211.

[23] Riddick Oral History, pp. 212–219; U.S., Congress, Senate, Committee on Rules and Administration, *Senate Cloture Rule*, by Congressional Research Service, S. Print 99–95, 99th Cong., 1st sess., 1985, pp. 30–31.

[24] Riddick Oral History, pp. 218–19; U.S., Congress, Senate, *Congressional Record*, 94th Cong., 1st sess., p. 3841.

[25] Kramer and Roberts, p. 371.

[26] Loch K. Johnson, *A Season of Inquiry: The Senate Intelligence Investigation* (Lexington, KY, 1985), pp. 30–31, 41–43.

[27] Ibid., p. 48; Light, *Vice-Presidential Power*, pp. 184–87.

[28] Light, *Vice-Presidential Power*, pp. 183, 189–90; Hartmann, p. 354; Persico, p. 272; Kramer and Roberts, p. 375.

[29] Ford, p. 328; Hartmann, pp. 357, 365–66.

[30] Ford, p. 331; Hartmann, p. 367; James Cannon, *Time and Chance* (New York, 1994), p. 407.

[31] Hartmann, p. 400; Persico, pp. 274–75.

[32] Ford, p. 437; Hartmann, p. 231; Persico, pp. 245, 277.

Chapter 42

WALTER F. MONDALE
1977–1981

WALTER F. MONDALE

Chapter 42

WALTER F. MONDALE

42nd Vice President: 1977–1981

We understood each other's needs. We respected each other's opinions. We kept each other's confidence. Our relationship in the White House held up under the searing pressure of that place because we entered our offices understanding—perhaps for the first time in the history of those offices—that each of us could do a better job if we maintained the trust of the other. And for four years, that trust endured.

—WALTER F. MONDALE

The wisest decision Walter Mondale ever made was not to run for president in 1976. For two years, the Minnesota senator tested the waters for a presidential campaign, conducting an extensive fund-raising and public relations tour of the country. Concluding that he had neglected both his family and his senatorial responsibilities, that he had little taste for mass media image making, and that his standing in the polls had not risen, he dropped out of the race in November 1974. At the time, he explained that he lacked "the overwhelming desire to be President" and dreaded spending another year "sleeping in Holiday Inns." A number of Democratic senators announced for president in 1976, but the candidate who won the nomination was the little-known former governor of Georgia, Jimmy Carter, who showed the determination to conduct precisely the kind of campaigning that Mondale had rejected. Carter then bypassed the senators who had run against him and tapped Mondale for his running mate. Although he would never become president, Walter Mondale proved himself one of the more successful vice presidents in American history, in terms of shaping administration policies and exercising influence over cabinet appointments.[1]

Being selected by Carter for the vice-presidential nomination followed a familiar pattern for Mondale, in which he was admired, trusted, and promoted by other politicians. His career progressed as much by selection as by election. As a college student in the 1940s he organized a "Diaper Brigade" of student volunteers to help Hubert Humphrey, Orville Freeman, and Karl Rolvaag take control of the Minnesota Democratic-Farmer-Labor party, and each of those leaders later fostered his career. Mondale was twenty-one when he first went to Washington as a protégé of Senator Humphrey; at thirty-two Governor Freeman appointed him state attorney general; and at thirty-six Governor Rolvaag appointed him to fill Humphrey's vacant seat in the United States Senate. Despite his youth when he entered the Senate, Mondale held values closer to those of the older generation of Democrats—forged by the Great Depression and the New Deal and influenced by the liberalism of Franklin D. Roosevelt—than they were to the new generation of postwar politicians of the era of John F. Kennedy. As a senator, vice president, and presidential candidate, Mondale played a transitional role in the Democratic party, seeking to bridge the generational and ideological divisions that racked the party during and after the 1960s.[2]

"Crazy Legs" from Elmore

A small-town, midwestern preacher's son, Walter Frederick "Fritz" Mondale was born in Ceylon, Minnesota, on January 25, 1928. His father Theodore Sigvaard Mondale was a Methodist minister and his mother Claribel Hope Mondale taught music. The family's Norwegian surname originally had been Mundal. As a child, Fritz moved with his family when his father was reassigned to a church in Elmore, Minnesota, in 1937. A strong believer in the social gospel of helping the poor and needy, who feared the concentration of wealth in the hands of the few, Mondale's father regularly talked politics with his family at mealtimes. The family's heroes were Franklin Roosevelt and Minnesota's radical governor Floyd Olson.[3]

Fritz was an ambitious youth, eager to make a name for himself. Showing more interest in sports than religion, Mondale excelled at basketball and track in high school, and won the nickname "Crazy Legs" as a star football player. He also showed an interest in politics, founding the "Republicrats," a student political organization and winning election as president of the junior class (although he lost his race for senior class president). Once, on a summer job, his wisecracks caused a fellow worker to lose his temper. "I'm sorry, George, I didn't mean any harm," Mondale apologized. "But I'm planning to go into politics someday, and I've gotta learn how to get people's hackles up." In 1946 he enrolled in Macalester College in St. Paul, working at odd jobs to pay his way.[4]

As a college freshman in the days of the cold war, Mondale encountered political science professors who warned against the extremes of both the right and left and called for liberals to seek the middle ground. In October 1946, Mondale heard the left-leaning former Vice President Henry Wallace speak at the campus. A few months later he was more impressed when he heard Minneapolis Mayor Hubert H. Humphrey. A political science professor had taken Mondale to a rally that aimed at merging the Democratic party with the Farmer-Labor party to support Humphrey's reelection as mayor. Captivated by the thirty-five-year-old mayor's energy and rhetoric, Mondale volunteered his services to Humphrey's campaign. Campaign manager Orville Freeman enlisted him to put up signs and hand out leaflets. Humphrey and other liberal Democrats were attempting to steer the leadership of the Democratic-Farmer-Labor party away from

the Communists and other radical groups of the type that had coalesced around Wallace. In 1948, Mondale again volunteered to help Humphrey win first the Democratic nomination for the U.S. Senate against the radical Elmer Benson and then the Senate seat from the Republican incumbent Joseph Ball.[5] Humphrey had helped organize the Americans for Democratic Action (ADA), and Mondale became active in its campus offshoot, Students for Democratic Action (SDA). After his father died in 1948, Mondale dropped out of college. Too excited by politics to sit passively in college lectures, he followed Humphrey to Washington to become national secretary of the SDA. Writing to his mother, he described the post as placing him "in an excellent position to meet and know national figures in the liberal movement" and that he was "exploiting this advantage to its fullest." Labor unions, however, withheld funding from the ADA, which they dismissed as comprised of college professors and visionaries. Mondale therefore spent his time raising money and shuffling paperwork rather than pursuing politics, which left him disillusioned. An SDA colleague, Norma Dinnerstein, to whom he was briefly engaged, diagnosed his discontent: "because you were moving so very fast and seeking so very much, you found corruption and a certain defeat in every victory," she wrote. "And worst of all, you figured out that 'Crazy Legs' from Elmore wasn't worth so very much in the big wide world."[6]

A Rising Young Politician

In January 1950, Mondale returned to college at the less-expensive University of Minnesota, graduating in the summer of 1951, *cum laude*. With the United States fighting a war against Communist North Korea, Mondale enlisted in the army. Stationed at Fort Knox, Kentucky, he was a corporal in education programs at the time of his discharge in 1952. Armed with the GI Bill, he entered the University of Minnesota Law School and received his law degree in 1956. He then practiced law in Minneapolis until 1960. A blind date during the summer of 1955 introduced him to Macalester student Joan Adams. He did not know her, but she had heard of him, since "he was well known on campus." Although more interested in art than politics, she, too, was the child of a small-town minister, and the two found they had much in common. They married on December 27, 1955.[7]

In 1958, Mondale managed Orville Freeman's gubernatorial race and became the Democratic-Farmer-Labor party's finance director, as well as a special assistant to the state attorney general on interstate trade matters. The next year, the Mondales moved into a house located in a newly created state senate district, because he planned to run for office. Before he could announce, however, he received an appointment from Governor Freeman to be state attorney general—making him the youngest state attorney general in the nation.[8]

Mondale catapulted to national attention by investigating the celebrated Sister Elizabeth Kenny Foundation, a Minneapolis-based charity that advertised nationally in its crusade to help the handicapped. When allegations arose that the Foundation's directors had been diverting millions of dollars from the donations to their private use, Mondale investigated and found that only 1.5 percent of the money raised actually supported medical services. The resulting press attention kept him on the front pages and assured his election to the attorney general post. Mondale won by 246,000 votes, while Freeman lost his bid for reelection as governor. In office, Mondale solidified his reputation as an active "people's lawyer," pursuing consumer protection and civil rights cases. Rather than running for governor in 1962, as many had expected, Mondale deferred to Lieutenant Governor Karl Rolvaag, who defeated the incumbent Republican Governor Elmer Anderson by only ninety-one votes. Meanwhile, Mondale won reelection as attorney general with more votes than any other candidate on the ballot. In 1963 he persuaded twenty-three other state attorney generals to sign a brief in favor of the indigent prisoner Clarence Earl Gideon, who was urging the U.S. Supreme Court to establish the right to free counsel for those charged with major crimes but unable to hire their own attorneys.[9]

The Great Society and the Vietnam War

In the presidential election of 1964, Lyndon Johnson chose Hubert Humphrey as his running mate. With their landslide victory, Humphrey's Senate seat became available. Governor Rolvaag appointed Mondale to the vacancy over several more senior Democrats—because he considered Mondale the most likely to win reelection. The appointment sent Fritz Mondale to Washington at an auspicious moment for Democratic liberals. Following the Johnson landslide, the Senate of the Eighty-ninth Congress opened with 68 Democrats facing 32 Republicans and a similarly lopsided margin in the House. So many Democrats crowded the Senate chamber, in fact, that an extra fifth row of desks was set up to accommodate Mondale, Robert Kennedy of New York, Joseph Tydings of Maryland, and Fred Harris of Oklahoma. The younger, more liberal senators were eager to help Johnson build his "Great Society." In 1966 Mondale sponsored the Fair Warning Act, requiring automotive manufacturers to notify owners of any defects in their cars. He then surprised everyone by forging the legislative compromise that led to the enactment of an open housing amendment to the Civil Rights Act of 1968. Mondale steadfastly endorsed Lyndon Johnson's handling of both domestic and foreign policy issues and stuck with the president even when the Democratic party began to divide over the Vietnam War.[10]

As a senator, Mondale labored long hours and demanded similar stamina from his staff. He revealed little of Hubert Humphrey's passionate political style. Cool, deliberate, and rarely emotional, Mondale wore a coat and tie even to the most informal gatherings, refused to be photographed smoking the cigars he loved, sported bad haircuts, and tended to look wooden and formal. Although he attracted respectful notice from the press, he was uncomfortable speaking on television, unable to adopt the more relaxed and natural style that medium favored. Balancing these shortcomings were Mondale's natural decency and seriousness. "The thing that is most evident about Mondale," Hubert Humphrey once observed, "is that he's nonabrasive.

He is not a polarizer." These were not attributes that drew public attention or acclaim. Mondale could walk through any airport in the country, he joked, "and not a head will turn." Nevertheless, when he stood for election to his Senate seat in 1966, a year that favored Republican candidates, he won by a comfortable margin.[11]

When Johnson withdrew from the presidential campaign of 1968, Mondale cochaired Hubert Humphrey's bid for the Democratic nomination. That tragic campaign year was marred by the assassination of Senator Robert F. Kennedy and by riots at the Democratic convention in Chicago. Humphrey gained the nomination but also a badly tattered party. "I didn't leave Chicago," Mondale later recalled, "I escaped it." During the campaign, he urged Humphrey to support a bombing halt over North Vietnam, a position that Humphrey finally embraced in late September. The Democratic ticket then gained in the polls and in the end lost the election to the Republican candidate Richard Nixon by less than one percent of the popular vote.[12]

Nixon's entrance into the White House gave Walter Mondale and other liberal Democrats an opportunity to reevaluate their views about the war and the "imperial presidency." In a speech at Macalester College in October 1969, Mondale reversed his position on the Vietnam War. He called the war "a military, a political and a moral disaster" and declared that the United States government could not impose a solution on Vietnam's essentially internal conflict. As a liberal, Mondale also feared that the war was draining financial resources that should be applied to domestic problems. In 1971 he voted for the McGovern-Hatfield Amendment to stop American military actions in Cambodia and to set a timetable for withdrawing American troops from Vietnam. In 1973 he cosponsored the War Powers Resolution. Mondale had come to the Senate sharing the conventional view that "we had to rely greatly on the President of the United States." But the events had showed him "the consequences of having a President who is largely unaccountable to Congress, to the law or to the American people."[13]

The Nixon administration provided a natural foil for Mondale's liberalism. As chairman of the Senate Select Committee on Equal Educational Opportunity, Mondale fought Nixon's proposed antibusing legislation. He similarly opposed the administration's plans to build costly antiballistic missile systems and supersonic transport aircraft. But, facing reelection in 1972, Mondale was careful to avoid unpopular causes that might alienate him from his middle-class constituency. "I don't like wasting my time slaying windmills," he insisted. When Senator George McGovern emerged as the frontrunner for the Democratic presidential nomination that year, he sent his campaign manager Gary Hart and the Hollywood actor Warren Beatty to ask whether Mondale would be a vice-presidential candidate. The Minnesotan declined to give up his Senate seat to join a losing campaign, headed by a candidate with whom he often disagreed. Although Mondale's opponent in his Senate race tried to paint him as a "McGovern liberal," Mondale won by an even greater margin than in his previous race.[14]

Running for President—and for Vice President

After 1972 the Watergate scandal inverted the political landscape. Democratic chances looked brighter with Nixon crippled by a string of devastating revelations about illegal activities, combined with public concerns over a weakened economy. Early in 1973, Mondale began constructing a campaign for the next presidential nomination. To gain more depth in foreign policy issues, he toured foreign capitals from London to Jerusalem. In order to raise both funds and his public visibility, he logged some 200,000 miles, visiting thirty states, campaigning for Democratic candidates for Congress, meeting with local party organizers, and engaging in as many radio and television interviews as possible. Mondale and his legislative assistant, Roger Colloff, also wrote a book, *The Accountability of Power: Toward a Responsible Presidency*, discussing ways to keep the presidency strong and yet fully accountable to the Congress and the people. But before the book was published in 1975, Mondale had already dropped out of the race.[15]

Mondale found the road to the nomination tortuous and unendurable. "It is a process which involves assembling an experienced and qualified core staff, raising funds in staggering quantities, and traveling to every corner of the nation in preparation for a series of delegate selections each of which is unique." The time required to campaign kept a candidate away from his family, his job, and his rest. For all the agony, Mondale's standing in the polls never rose. On November 21, 1974, he surprised everyone by announcing his withdrawal from the race. Many lamented his decision as a sign that only someone "single-mindedly obsessed" with pursuing the presidency could achieve it.[16]

Free of the campaign, Mondale returned to his Senate duties. With civil rights legislation primarily in mind, he led a movement in 1975 to change the Senate cloture rule in order to make ending a filibuster easier, by reducing the votes needed from two-thirds to three-fifths of the senators. He also won recognition for his diligent work as a member of the select committee, chaired by Senator Frank Church, that investigated the covert activities of the CIA and FBI. Having done the necessary background research to ask incisive questions, Mondale regularly upstaged Church, who was still actively campaigning for president. Church, Henry Jackson, Birch Bayh, and other senators appeared to be the leading contenders for the nomination until a surprise candidate claimed victory in the Iowa caucuses. Former Georgia Governor Jimmy Carter campaigned as an "outsider," removed from the Washington political scene that had produced the Vietnam War, the Watergate scandal and other policies that dismayed and disillusioned American voters. Carter's freshness, down-to-earth style, and promise of a government that would be honest, fair, and compassionate seemed a welcome antidote to the "imperial presidency." By June, Carter had the nomination sufficiently locked up and could take time to interview potential vice-presidential candidates.[17]

The pundits predicted that Frank Church would be tapped to provide balance as an experienced senator with strong liberal credentials. Church promoted himself, persuading friends to intervene with Carter in his behalf. If a quick choice had been required as in past conventions, Carter later recalled, he would probably have chosen Church. But the longer period for deliberation gave Carter time to worry about his compatibility with the publicity-seeking Church, who had a tendency to be long-winded. Instead, Carter invited Senators Edmund Muskie, John Glenn, and Walter Mondale to visit his home in Plains, Georgia, for personal interviews, while Church, Henry Jackson, and Adlai Stevenson III would be interviewed at the convention in New York.[18]

When Mondale arrived in Plains, it was evident that he had studied for the interview. He had researched Carter's positions on every issue to identify their similarities and differences. He read Carter's book, *Why Not the Best?* and talked to those who knew the Georgia governor. Carter found him "extremely well prepared" and was also impressed by Mondale's assertion that he would not trade in his Senate seat for a purely ceremonial office. He was only interested in being vice president if the position became "a useful instrument of government." There were many similarities in the two men's lives, both having grown up in small towns with strong religious influences. Of all the potential candidates, Carter found Mondale the most compatible. When reporters asked why the Minnesotan wanted to get back into a race he had already dropped out of and spend more nights in Holiday Inns, he replied wryly, "I've checked and found out they've all been redecorated."[19]

Mondale's longtime mentor Hubert Humphrey strongly advised him to accept the second spot. "My vice presidential years were tough years but I am a better man for it and I would have made a better President," he counseled. "I learned more about the world and the presidency than I could have ever learned in the Senate." To provide some suspense for the convention, Carter waited until the last moment to announce his choice. When the offer finally came, Mondale accepted instantly. The press dubbed the ticket "Fritz and Grits." After the convention, Mondale set off on a rigorous campaign that emphasized economic issues. The high point of the campaign for him came during his televised debate with the Republican vice-presidential candidate, Senator Robert Dole. Carter's advisers felt so certain that Mondale had won the debate that they featured it in televised advertisements, asking, "When you know that four of the last six vice presidents have wound up as president, who would you like to see a heartbeat away from the presidency?" [20]

Teamwork in the Carter White House

A close election put Carter in the White House and made the Mondales the first family to settle into the vice-presidential mansion on Massachusetts Avenue. That twenty-room Victorian house, previously occupied by the chief of Naval Operations, was, Mondale observed, "the best house we've ever had." No longer did American vice presidents have to provide their own lodging. Joan Mondale won the nickname "Joan of Art" for her elaborate presentations of artworks in the vice president's mansion and her promotion of American artists. She also expanded the role of "second lady" by reviving, and serving as honorary chair of, the Federal Council on the Arts and Humanities.[21]

Carter and Mondale formed a remarkably close team. Carter was conscious that previous "forced marriages" of presidents and vice presidents had not worked, that White House staff had shut out vice presidents, and that strong men like Hubert Humphrey and Nelson Rockefeller had been frustrated in the job. Determined to make Mondale more of a partner, Carter directed that Mondale be given an office inside the West Wing—the first since Spiro Agnew—and instructed that the presidential and vice-presidential staffs be integrated "as a working team" (Mondale had a vice presidential staff that ranged from fifty-five to sixty members). The office space proved critical, since as one vice-presidential aide commented, "Mondale didn't have to beg anyone to visit him in the West Wing." Not everyone was happy with this arrangement, especially the Georgians who had accompanied Carter to power. Attorney General Griffin Bell thought that moving the vice president into the White House had been a mistake, noting that, even though Carter was a more conservative Democrat than Mondale, the vice president had shaped much of the administration's program to his own liking. "He managed to do this because of his physical location in the West Wing of the

White House," Bell concluded, "and because of placing some close aides in crucial posts in the policy-making apparatus." [22]

Famous as a politician who always did his homework, Mondale studied the vice-presidency to determine why so many of his predecessors had failed. He had not paid much attention to the subject previously; his book on the presidency, *Accountability of Power*, had mentioned the vice-presidency only in terms of succession. Mondale identified Nelson Rockefeller's chairing of the Domestic Council as a mistake and observed that vice presidents too often took minor functions "in order to appear that their role was significant." Instead of specific assignments, he preferred to remain a generalist and a troubleshooter, someone consulted on all issues. At one point he even turned down Carter's suggestion that the vice president become the chief of staff. "If I had taken on that assignment," Mondale reasoned, "it would have consumed vast amounts of my time with staff work." The vice president also planned to avoid being shunted into such ceremonial functions as attending state funerals. The chief exception that he made was to travel to Yugoslav President Tito's funeral in 1980, because high-level diplomatic contact was required.[23]

From the start, Carter invited Mondale to every meeting that he scheduled and gave him the opportunity to pick and choose those he wished to attend. Carter and Mondale also held private luncheons each Monday to discuss any matters that either wanted to bring up. Mondale received the same daily intelligence information that Carter got and met regularly with the senior staff and the National Security Council. Yet the vice president usually kept silent in group meetings, knowing that he would later have an opportunity to talk with Carter alone. Having played junior partner to men like Hubert Humphrey and Orville Freeman, Mondale instinctively understood his role as vice president. In groups of any size he automatically deferred to Carter. The president responded by threatening to fire any staff member who assailed the vice president. Hamilton Jordan, Carter's eventual chief of staff, also made sure that Mondale and his staff were never isolated from current policy discussions. "I consider I work for Mondale," Jordan insisted. "He's my second boss, the way Carter is my first boss." Jordan, whose office was located next to Mondale's, liked the vice president, whom he considered shrewd. "In the White House, he played his cards wisely," Jordan reflected.[24]

"We understood each other's needs," Mondale later said of his relationship with Carter. "We respected each other's opinions. We kept each other's confidence. Our relationship in the White House held up under the searing pressure of that place because we entered our offices understanding—perhaps for the first time in the history of those offices—that each of us could do a better job if we maintained the trust of the other. And for four years, that trust endured." The vice president's free access to the Oval Office gave him considerable leverage over the administration's agenda. Unlike many of his predecessors, he could bring ideas to the table and win recognition for them. When Mondale took a position, Carter usually listened. In 1978, when Congress passed a defense authorization bill that provided $2 billion for a new aircraft carrier that Carter opposed, Mondale advocated a veto. Carter's top aides believed that a veto would surely be overridden, embarrassing the president, but Mondale went to Carter and argued that he had to take a stand against unnecessary spending, saying, "If you don't do it now, you'll never get control." Carter vetoed the bill, and Congress upheld his veto.[25]

A Crisis of Confidence

At the same time, Mondale cringed at Carter's inept handling of Congress and tried unsuccessfully to stop actions that might alienate the administration from its erstwhile supporters on Capitol Hill. Mondale watched Carter squander the initial good will afforded his administration by pursuing a legislative agenda that was much too ambitious and complicated, rather than focusing on a few major issues. In one instance, however, Mondale himself became the object of congressional ire. In 1977 Senate liberals led by Howard Metzenbaum of Ohio and James Abourezk of South Dakota filibustered against Carter's proposal to deregulate natural gas.

Using the recently devised tactics of the "post-cloture filibuster," they filed more than five hundred amendments to the bill. After the Senate debate had dragged on for twelve days, including an all-night session, Majority Leader Robert C. Byrd persuaded Mondale to cooperate in a daring strategy to cut off the filibuster. On the floor, Byrd raised points of order that many of the amendments should be ruled out of order as incorrectly drawn or not germane. As presiding officer, Mondale ruled thirty-three amendments out of order in a matter of minutes. The Senate erupted into angry protest, with even senators who had not filibustered denouncing the tactic. The vice president was lectured by many senators, including some of his longtime friends, for abusing the powers of the presiding officer. In his defense, Senator Byrd pointed out that the vice president was not there to "pull the rug out" from under the Senate. "The Vice President is here to get the ox out of the ditch." Although the strategy worked and the bill was enacted, "the struggle had left some deep wounds," Byrd later concluded.[26]

Repeatedly, Mondale urged President Carter to make clear his goals for the nation and the reasons the public should follow his lead. Neither a New Deal nor a Great Society liberal, nor a traditional conservative, Carter seemed to straddle the issues and avoid choosing sides. Ironically, when Carter finally did attempt to define his presidential identity, he left Mondale in despair. During the summer of 1979, Carter abruptly canceled a planned televised address on energy policy and closeted himself at Camp David with groups of citizen advisers to help him rethink his administration's aims. Pollster Patrick Caddell wanted the president to address the "malaise" that seemed to have settled on America. Mondale thought Caddell's analysis "crazy" and warned that if the president made such a negative speech he would sound like "an old scold and a grouch." Although Carter's other advisers reluctantly came around, Mondale could not reconcile himself to Carter's position. "I thought it would destroy Carter and me with him," Mondale later noted. He felt so strongly about this issue that he contemplated resigning if Carter gave Caddell's speech. The president took Mondale for a long walk at Camp David and tried to calm him down. "I had only partial success," Carter recorded, "convincing him to support my decision even though he could not agree with it." Carter went on to deliver a televised speech warning of a "crisis of confidence" and to charge that Americans were suffering from a national malaise. He followed that speech with a drastic overhaul of his cabinet, giving the impression that his administration was falling to pieces. The negative public reaction proved Mondale's concerns fully justified.[27]

The Carter administration's standing in the public opinion polls slipped steadily. In November 1978, Republicans had made considerable gains in the congressional elections, including winning both Senate seats in Minnesota. The "malaise" speech and cabinet shake-ups further disenchanted the voters. Exhausted staff members, pessimistic about the president's reelection chances, began making plans for themselves after the 1980 election. The Georgians in the president's inner circle grew increasingly protective of him and complained about the lack of loyalty in the cabinet, and some also criticized the vice president. Reporters noted that Mondale no longer attended the White House weekly staff sessions on congressional relations.[28]

One crisis after another eroded public confidence in the president's abilities. The nation sustained gasoline shortages, double-digit inflation, and a serious recession. Carter's decision to impose an austerity budget to cut inflation, rather than stimulating the economy to end the recession, offended Democratic liberals, who urged Massachusetts Senator Edward M. Kennedy to challenge the president for renomination. As matters grew worse, Mondale took a less visible and active role. "I thought there was not much I could do to change things," he later explained, "so why break my health trying." In November 1979, militant Iranians seized the American embassy in Teheran and took sixty-three hostages. In December, Soviet troops invaded Afghanistan. Initially, these foreign policy crises boosted Carter's popularity and were enough to help Carter and Mondale win renomination. But as the months wore on with no solutions, Carter

again slipped in the polls. The Republican candidate, Ronald Reagan, portrayed the Carter administration as weak abroad and in disarray at home. Mondale campaigned vigorously for the Democratic ticket, but as vice president he drew little media attention. "I'd have to set my hair on fire to get on the news," he complained.[29]

Titular Leader and Presidential Candidate

Reagan's election discredited Carter and left Mondale as the titular leader of the Democratic party. Although he returned to private law practice in Minnesota, Mondale had determined, even before he left the vice-presidency, to run for president in 1984. As a private citizen, he traveled abroad to meet with foreign leaders, consulted with leading American economists, and sought to build bridges to reunite the Democratic party. During the 1982 congressional elections, Mondale campaigned far and wide for Democratic candidates. A deep recession swung many voters back to the Democratic party and made Reagan vulnerable as a candidate for reelection, but in 1983 the economy began to revive, for which "Reaganomics" took full credit. Surprise contenders for the Democratic nomination also appeared, among them the Reverend Jesse Jackson and Colorado Senator Gary Hart. Although Mondale had the support of labor and other traditional elements of the Democratic coalition, he was more reserved, less charismatic, and less telegenic than his competitors. Hart campaigned as the candidate of "new ideas," but Mondale countered with a parody of a popular television commercial, asking: "Where's the beef?" He won the nomination but then faced Ronald Reagan in the general election campaign.[30]

The 1984 race between Walter Mondale and Ronald Reagan offered a clear-cut choice between liberal and conservative candidates and philosophies. While running against one of the best-loved presidents, Mondale won credit for being one of the best-informed candidates ever to run for the presidency. He also added some spark to his campaign by selecting the first woman candidate for vice president on a major party ticket, Representative Geraldine Ferraro, a liberal who also appealed to many conservatives in her Queens, New York, district. During the first television debate of the campaign, Reagan seemed to appear distracted and show his age. In a later debate, however, the seasoned performer bounced back by promising not to make an issue of Mondale's "youth and inexperience." With the nation facing huge deficits, Mondale told the voters that a raise in taxes was inevitable. "Mr. Reagan will raise taxes, and so will I," he said. "He won't tell you, I just did." It was a disastrous strategy. Reagan promised prosperity, a strong defense, and balanced budgets without raising taxes. Mondale ended his campaign in Minneapolis, telling the crowd, "You have given me, a small-town boy from Elmore, a chance to shape our country and to shape our times," but on election day, he lost forty-nine states and carried only Minnesota and the District of Columbia. Assessing the results, Mondale commented, "Reagan was promising them 'morning in America,' and I was promising a root canal." [31]

In later years, many anticipated that Mondale would challenge Minnesota Republican Rudy Boschwitz for his Senate seat in 1990. Polls showed Mondale running ahead, but at age sixty-two he chose not to reenter politics. "I believe it's time for other candidates to step forward," he said, admitting that it had been a difficult decision to make. When Bill Clinton won the presidency in 1992, he offered Mondale the ambassadorship to Japan, which he accepted. The Mondales had frequently visited that country, and Joan had considerable knowledge of Japanese pottery and art. The Japanese dubbed Fritz Mondale an *Oh-mono*, which roughly translates, "big wheel," or "big cheese." As reporter T.R. Reid commented, "Mondale brings to the Tokyo embassy everything Japan wanted in a U.S. ambassador: political clout, personal access to the president and a genuine appreciation for Japanese culture and traditions." One Japanese newspaper described him as "A man with real power in Congress and the Democratic Party!!" Mondale professed to be "glad to be back in public life" with such "an exciting, challenging undertaking." He was sworn in as ambassador by Vice President Al Gore, who declared that Mondale's experiences as a senator had prepared him for a diplomatic life "full of tribal feuds and strange languages." Responding in kind, Mondale insisted that "Nothing could be more ennobling that to be sworn in by a Democratic vice president." [32]

NOTES

[1] Finlay Lewis, *Mondale: Portrait of a Politician* (New York, 1984), pp. 160–61; Paul C. Light, *Vice-Presidential Power: Advice and Influence in the White House* (Baltimore, 1984), p. 1.

[2] Steven M. Gillon, *The Democrats' Dilemma: Walter F. Mondale and the Liberal Legacy* (New York, 1992), pp. x-xiv.

[3] Ibid., pp. 1–15; Lewis, pp. 9–11.

[4] Lewis, p. 15.

[5] Ibid., pp. 20–34; Gillon, pp. 17–21.

[6] Gillon, pp. 21–40.

[7] Ibid., pp. 41–52; Lewis, pp. 49–52.

[8] Gillon, pp. 51–54.

[9] Ibid., pp. 56–66; Lewis, pp. 62–75.

[10] Gillon, pp. 69–97; Lewis, pp. 76–84.

[11] Gillon, pp. 99–111, 146–47; Lewis, p. 43.

[12] Gillon, pp 111–22.

[13] Ibid., pp. 123–30; Walter F. Mondale, *The Accountability of Power: Toward a Responsible Presidency* (New York, 1975), pp. vii-ix.

[14] Gillon, pp. 130–41.

[15] Ibid., pp. 143–53; Mondale, pp. ix-xv.

[16] Mondale, pp. 23–30; Gillon, p. 152.

[17] Gillon, pp. 153–62; Loch K. Johnson, *A Season of Inquiry: The Senate Intelligence Investigation* (Lexington, KY, 1985), pp. 105, 153–56.

[18] LeRoy Ashby and Rod Gramer, *Fighting the Odds: The Life of Senator Frank Church* (Pullman, WA, 1994), pp. 522–26; Jimmy Carter, *Keeping Faith: Memoirs of a President* (New York, 1982), pp. 35–36.

[19] Gillon, pp. 163–67; Carter, p. 37.

[20] Gillon, pp. 163–85.

[21] *Washington Post*, August 14, 1993; Lewis, pp. 230–40.

[22] Carter, pp. 39–40; Light, pp. 75, 164–65, 207.

[23] Mondale, pp. 72–76; Light, pp. 29, 47, 206.

[24] Light, pp. 49–50, 141, 146, 208–9, 212–15, 229.

[25] Ibid., pp. 42, 213, 251.

[26] U.S., Congress, Senate, *The Senate, 1789–1989: Addresses on the History of the United States Senate*, by Robert C. Byrd, S. Doc. 100–20, 100th Cong., 1st sess., vol. 2, 1991, pp. 154–56; Gillon, pp. 187–93.

[27] Gillon, pp. 200–203, 260–66; Lewis, pp. 214–15; Light, p. 255; Carter, pp. 115–16; Garland A. Haas, *Jimmy Carter and the Politics of Frustration* (Jefferson, NC, 1992), pp. 83–85.

[28] Light, p. 216; Haynes Johnson, *In the Absence of Power: Governing America* (New York, 1980), p. 287.

[29] Gillon, pp. 251–57, 267–76, 289; Lewis, pp. 208–10.

[30] Lewis, p. 245; Gillon, pp. 301–32.

[31] Gillon, pp. 365–90, 394; Elizabeth Drew, *Campaign Journal: The Political Events of 1983–1984* (New York, 1985), pp. 555–57, 619–22.

[32] *Roll Call*, June 4, 1989; *Washington Post*, August 14, September 15, 1993.

Chapter 43

GEORGE H.W. BUSH
1981–1989

GEORGE H.W. BUSH

(Presiding in old Senate chamber)

Chapter 43

GEORGE H.W. BUSH

43rd Vice President: 1981–1989

Only the President lands on the south lawn.

—VICE PRESIDENT GEORGE BUSH, MARCH 30, 1981

Rarely had a vice president come to the office so eminently qualified as George Bush. He had been a businessman, United States representative, United Nations ambassador, chairman of the Republican National Committee, chief U.S. liaison officer to the People's Republic of China, Central Intelligence Agency director, and presidential contender. Yet while his vice-presidential predecessors had struggled to show they were part of the president's inner circle of policymakers, Bush found himself having to insist that he was "out of the loop." While he occupied the vice-presidency, he kept his profile low, avoided doing anything that might upstage his president, and remained ever loyal and never threatening. That strategy made him the first vice president in more than 150 years to move directly to the presidency by election.

A Tradition of Public Service

Bush dedicated his vice-presidential memoirs, *Looking Forward*, to his mother and father, "whose values lit the way." "Dad taught us about duty and service," he said of Senator Prescott S. Bush. The son of an Ohio steel company president, Prescott Bush had attended Yale, where he sang with the Whiffenpoofs and excelled in athletics. After military service in the First World War, he married Dorothy Walker in 1921 and produced a family of five children. In 1923 Prescott Bush moved east to take a managerial position in Massachusetts, and two years later shifted to New York City, establishing his

family in suburban Greenwich, Connecticut. In 1926 he became vice president of W.A. Harriman and Company, an investment firm, later Brown Brothers, Harriman. In addition to his Wall Street activities, Prescott Bush served as president of the United States Golf Association during the 1930s. During World War II, he helped to establish the United Service Organization (USO). Prescott Bush also sought elected office. From 1947 to 1950 he was finance chairman of the Connecticut Republican party. He lost a race for the Senate in 1950 by just a thousand votes, and in 1952 defeated Representative Abraham Ribicoff for a vacant seat in the Senate. Tapping his golf skills, Prescott Bush became a frequent golfing partner with President Dwight Eisenhower. After two terms in the Senate, he retired in 1962, an exemplar of the eastern, internationalist wing of the Republican party.[1]

As much as George Bush physically resembled his tall, lean, athletic father and followed his footsteps in business and politics, he was raised primarily by his mother, Dorothy. An athletic woman herself (she was runner-up in the national girls' tennis tournament of 1918), Dorothy Bush brought up her large family while her husband absented himself to devote long hours to business and public service. She taught her children kindness, charity, and modesty—and rebuked them for any signs of self-importance. George Bush's closest associates attributed his difficulty in talking about himself to his mother's admonitions. Once when he was vice president,

Dorothy complained that her son had been reading while President Ronald Reagan delivered his State of the Union address. Bush explained that he was simply following the text of the speech, but she still thought it showed poor manners.[2]

George Herbert Walker Bush was born on June 12, 1924, at Milton, Massachusetts, where his father was then working. His mother named him for her father, George Herbert Walker, and since Walker's children had called him "Pop," his namesake won the unfortunate diminutive "Poppy." George grew up in Greenwich and spent his summers at his grandfather's vacation home in Kennebunkport, Maine. At twelve he went off to the prestigious Phillips Academy in Andover, Massachusetts, in preparation for entering his father's alma mater, Yale. When the Japanese bombed Pearl Harbor, on December 7, 1941, George Bush determined to enlist. Secretary of War Henry Stimson delivered the commencement address at Andover, urging the graduating class to get a college eduction before putting on a uniform. "George, did the Secretary say anything to change your mind?" his father asked. "No, sir. I'm going in," Bush replied. He was sworn into the navy on his eighteenth birthday.[3]

The youngest aviator in the navy, Bush was sent to the Pacific and flew missions over Wake Island, Guam, and Saipan. On September 2, 1944, his plane was hit by antiaircraft fire. Bush managed to drop his cargo of bombs (winning the navy's Distinguished Flying Cross for completing his mission under fire) before he flew out to sea to give his crew a chance to parachute. However, one crew member was trapped on the plane and the other's chute failed to open. Bush ejected, drifted alone at sea on a raft, and was rescued by the American submarine, *U.S.S. Finback*. Rejoining his squadron, he saw further action over the Philippines, flying a total of fifty-eight combat missions before he was finally ordered home in December 1944.[4]

Two weeks later he married Barbara Pierce in her home town of Rye, New York. They had met as teenagers at a Christmas dance and become engaged in 1943 (in the Pacific he had nicknamed his plane "Barbara"). The newlyweds headed to New Haven, where George Bush enrolled at

Yale. Their first child—a future governor of Texas—was born there in July 1946. Having a wife and child to support deterred Bush neither from his education nor from his extracurricular activities. He graduated Phi Beta Kappa, captained the Yale baseball team, and was admitted to the prestigious Skull and Bones Club. Unlike fellow student William F. Buckley, Bush was not offended by the liberal humanism of Yale in the 1940s. Neither a political activist nor an aggrieved conservative, Bush concerned himself primarily with winning a national baseball championship at the College World Series.[5]

A Shift to the Sunbelt

Having graduated in two and a half years with honors and won two letters in sports, Bush considered applying for a Rhodes scholarship but concluded that he could not afford to bring his wife and son with him to England. He turned instead to a career in business and accepted an offer from a close family friend, Neil Mallon, to work in the Texas oil fields. Bush started as an equipment clerk at Odessa, Texas. The company then transferred him to California as a salesman and then called him back to Midland, Texas. George and Barbara Bush moved frequently and calculated that they had lived in twenty-eight different houses before eventually reaching the White House. During these years their family increased to four sons and two daughters, although, tragically, their first daughter, Robin, died of leukemia as a child. Bush coached Little League and was less an absentee father than his own father had been, but it was Barbara Bush who served as the disciplinarian and kept the growing family in line.[6]

Once back in Texas, George Bush decided to go independent. He and a neighbor, John Overby, formed the Bush-Overby Oil Development Company, which benefitted from Bush family connections on Wall Street that financed its operations. His uncle Herbert Walker invested nearly a half million dollars, for instance. Others, including *Washington Post* owner Eugene Meyer, were willing to invest in a "sure-fire" business headed by Senator Prescott Bush's son. By 1953 Bush-Overby had merged with another independent oil company to form Zapata Petroleum—picking the name from the Mexican revolutionary and Marlon Brando film, *Viva Zapata!* In 1959 the company split its operations between inland and offshore oil and gas, and Bush moved to Houston as president of Zapata Offshore.[7]

The moving force for Bush's energetic business career was a desire to amass sufficient capital to enter politics. His father had been elected to the Senate in 1952 from Connecticut, but the son, born and raised a Yankee, staked his claim instead in the "Solid South." In 1952 Democrats held almost every House and Senate seat in the southeastern and southwestern states, a vast expanse sweeping from Virginia to Southern California. Yet dramatic change was already underway. In 1948 southern delegates had walked out of the Democratic convention in protest over including a civil rights plank in the platform and had run South Carolina Governor J. Strom Thurmond as the "Dixiecrat" candidate for president. In 1952 Republican presidential candidate Dwight D. Eisenhower made inroads into the states of the old Confederacy, carrying Virginia, Tennessee, Florida, and his birth state of Texas. Texas' conservative governor Allan Shivers led a "Democrats for Eisenhower" movement, and in 1961 a political science professor named John Tower won Vice President Lyndon Johnson's vacated Senate seat, becoming the first Texas Republican senator since Reconstruction.[8]

George Bush reflected a significant political power shift in post-World War II America. Young veterans like himself sought a fresh start by moving from inner cities into new suburbs and from the Rust Belt to the Sunbelt. Throughout the South, military bases established or expanded during the Second World War continued to grow during the cold war. In Texas, the postwar demand for energy sources brought boom times to the oil fields. The state attracted eager young entrepreneurs not bound by old party loyalties. In 1962, a group of Republicans fearful that the reactionary John Birch Society might take over the local party operations invited Bush to head Houston's Harris County Republican party organization. "This was the challenge I'd been waiting for," he said, "—an opening into politics at the ground level, where it all starts." [9]

Bush did not plan to stay at the ground level for long. In 1963 he announced his candidacy for the Republican nomination for the Senate to oust the incumbent liberal Democrat Ralph Yarborough. Bush won the primary with 67 percent of the vote. Although the Texas electorate was lopsidedly Democratic, Bush believed he could appeal to its conservative majority. But in 1964 he ran on a ticket headed by Barry Goldwater, while Yarborough had the coattails of Texas' own Lyndon B. Johnson. LBJ took 63 percent of the state's votes, while Bush managed to pare Yarborough's winning margin to 56 percent. It was a creditable first race for a novice politician.[10]

The national population shift also added new members to the Texas delegation in the House of Representatives. In 1963, as Harris County chairman, Bush had filed suit under the Supreme Court's one-man-one-vote ruling for a congressional redistricting in Houston. Victory in court led to the creation of a new Seventh Congressional District, for which Bush ran in 1966. To finance his campaign, he resigned from Zapata, selling his share for more than a million dollars. His opponent, the Democratic district attorney of Houston, portrayed Bush as a carpetbagger, but Bush knew that three-fourths of the district's residents were also newcomers. It was a "silkstocking" district—white, wealthy, and with only a small Hispanic and African American population. Cashing in on the name recognition he had gained from his Senate bid, Bush took the House seat with 57 percent of the vote.[11]

Congressman Bush

The 1966 election provided a midterm rebound for Republicans after the disaster two years earlier. Former Vice President Richard Nixon canvassed the nation for Republican congressional candidates, building a base for his own political comeback. Nixon toured Houston for Bush, as did House Republican leader Gerald Ford in his bid to become Speaker. Both Nixon and Ford had known Prescott Bush in Washington. Due to his father's prominence and his own well-publicized race for the Senate, George Bush arrived in the House better known than most of the forty-six other freshmen Republicans. As a freshman he won a coveted seat on the Ways and Means Committee (which put the Bushes on everyone's "list" of social invitations). He paid diligent attention to constituent affairs and in 1968 was reelected without opposition. That year, after a single term in Congress, his name surfaced on the short list of candidates whom Nixon considered as running mates. Holding a safe seat and fitting comfortably into the camaraderie of the House, Bush might have made his career there, except for his greater ambitions and for the urging of two presidents of the United States that he run for the Senate.[12]

Neither Lyndon Johnson nor Richard Nixon cared for the liberal Democratic senator Ralph Yarborough, and both appealed to Bush to challenge him again. Nixon added a particular inducement by promising Bush a high-level post in his administration should he lose the race. Calculating the conservative mood of his state, Bush concluded that he could unseat Yarborough in a rematch. In 1970 he easily won the Republican nomination but was distressed when Yarborough lost the Democratic primary to the more conservative Lloyd Bentsen. Rather than campaigning from the right of his opponent, Bush found himself situated on the left. Democrats portrayed him as a liberal, Ivy League carpetbagger. (At a Gridiron dinner years later, Texas Representative Jim Wright was still teasing Bush as "the only Texan I know who eats lobster with his chili. . . . He and Barbara had a little down-home quiche cook off.") Bush lost the race with 46 percent of the vote. It would take him eighteen years to even the score with Bentsen.[13]

Politics and Foreign Policy

Bush reminded President Nixon of his offer of a job but did not want anything in the White House, where he might be under the thumb of Nixon's "praetorian guard," H.R. Haldeman and John Ehrlichman. He volunteered instead for the post of United Nations ambassador, arguing that it would position him within New York's social circles, where Nixon lacked a strong political base. That argument appealed to Nixon, who was very concerned about his own reelection in 1972. Bush's appointment raised complaints that he was a Texas oilman-politician with no pre-

vious experience in foreign affairs. He retorted that his experience as a salesman would make him "the American salesman in the world marketplace for ideas."[14]

Nixon won a landslide reelection in 1972 and went to Camp David to reorganize his administration, determined to put absolute loyalists in every top position. In his memoirs, Bush later recalled that he hoped for a cabinet appointment, but when he received his summons to the president's mountain retreat it was to take over the Republican National Committee from Senator Bob Dole. Bush reluctantly agreed to take the job but only if he could attend cabinet meetings. At the time, he had no notion that the Watergate break-in of June 1972 would erupt into a postelection scandal and destroy Nixon's presidency. But from the moment he took office, Bush recalled, "little else took up my time as national committee chairman." Throughout the storm, Bush defended the president against all charges. Finally, the release of the "smoking gun" tape revealed that Nixon had participated in the Watergate cover-up, eroded what was left of the president's support on Capitol Hill, and changed Bush's mind.[15]

On Tuesday, August 6, 1974, Nixon called a cabinet meeting to dispel rumors of his impending resignation. He announced that had decided not to resign because it would weaken the presidency and because he did not believe he had committed an impeachable offense. As Nixon then tried to steer the discussion onto economic issues, White House chief of staff Alexander Haig heard a stir from the group sitting away from the cabinet table:

It was George Bush, who as a guest of the President occupied one of the straight chairs along the wall. He seemed to be asking for the floor. When Nixon failed to recognize him, he spoke anyway. Watergate was the vital question, he said. It was sapping public confidence. Until it was settled, the economy and the country as whole would suffer. Nixon should resign.

Surely it was unprecedented, Haig observed, for the chairman of the Republican National Committee to advise a Republican president to resign from office at a cabinet meeting. The cabinet sat in shocked silence as all realized that Nixon's resignation was inevitable. Bush, who thought that Nixon had looked "beleaguered, worn down by stress, detached from reality," felt that the issue needed to be addressed squarely. In a letter the next day he reiterated that Nixon should resign, adding that his view was "held by most Republican leaders across the country."[16]

Nixon's resignation on August 9 made Gerald Ford president and opened a vacancy in the vice-presidency. Bush let Ford know that he was available for the post. A poll of Republican officeholders put Bush at the top of the list, but he was passed over for New York Governor Nelson Rockefeller, who carried more independent stature. To soften the blow, Ford offered Bush a choice of ambassadorships to London or Paris. Instead, Bush asked to be sent to China. There he thought he could both broaden his foreign policy expertise and remain politically visible. Nixon's initiatives in 1971 had drawn great public attention and put China back on the American political map. During his year in Beijing, China attracted a steady stream of American visitors, from President Ford and Secretary of State Henry Kissinger to members of Congress and countless delegations of prominent American citizens.[17]

When he made the appointment, Ford told Bush to expect to stay in China for two years, but after a year Bush wrote the president that he wanted to return to the United States. His letter arrived while Ford was preoccupied with congressional scrutiny of the Central Intelligence Agency. Considering Bush an able administrator and a savvy politician, Ford telegraphed him to come home to be CIA director. The "for eyes only" cable came as a shock to Bush, who had expected a cabinet appointment. He never anticipated taking charge of an agency that was under investigation for everything "from lawbreaking to simple incompetence." Since the post had traditionally been nonpolitical, Bush suspected his rivals within the administration wanted to bury him there. Yet he felt he had no choice but to accept. His confirmation was stalled when congressional Democrats demanded that Bush promise not to run for vice president in 1976. "If I wanted to be Vice President," Bush demurred, "I wouldn't be here asking you to confirm me for the CIA." He refused to renounce his "political birthright" for the price of confirmation. The senators persisted until Bush finally asked Ford to exclude him from consideration for the second spot. "I know it's unfair," he told the president, "but you don't have much of a choice if we are to get on with the job of rebuilding and strengthening the agency." After Ford notified the Senate Armed Services Committee that Bush would not be considered for vice president, the CIA confirmation followed speedily.[18]

Although he briefed the president each week on intelligence matters, Bush found that the CIA directorship was not a policy-making position. It also kept him on the fringe of politics. From his offices in Langley, Virginia, Bush watched the 1976 presidential race take place in the distance. Challenged from the right by former California Governor Ronald Reagan, Ford dropped Rockefeller and selected Kansas Senator Bob Dole for vice president. An even more unexpected political saga was unfolding on the Democratic side, where a pack of senior Democratic senators vying for the nomination were eliminated by an obscure political "outsider," former Georgia Governor Jimmy Carter. In Iowa, Carter scored an upset by persistent personal campaigning and by promising to create a less "imperial" presidency. As CIA director, Bush briefed candidate Carter, then later returned to Plains, Georgia, to brief him as president-elect. Bush informed Carter that if the president wanted to name his own director he would resign from the CIA.[19]

Running for President—and Vice President

Back in private life in Houston for the first time in a decade, Bush laid the groundwork for a presidential campaign in 1980. As with the Democrats, Republican party reforms had shifted control of the delegate-selection process from state party organizations to primary elections. In 1979, Bush logged more than 250,000 miles to attend 850 political events. Like Carter, he intended to make his mark in the Iowa caucuses. The field of Republican contenders included Senators Howard Baker and Bob Dole, Representatives John Anderson and Philip Crane, and former Texas Governor John Connally, but the man to beat was Ronald Reagan. After narrowly losing the nomination in 1976, Reagan made it clear that despite his age he planned to run again. As the frontrunner, Reagan initially pursued a more traditional campaign, spending most of his time in New Hampshire and the northeast, while Bush devoted nearly every day to Iowa. A week before the Republican caucuses, Bush's organization sent a million pieces of mail to party members across the state. When the caucuses met on January 21, 1980, Bush won 31.5 percent to Reagan's 29.4 percent. The margin was slim but enough to enable Bush to claim momentum—or as he called it "the Big Mo." [20]

The news from Iowa jolted Ronald Reagan, who learned the result while watching an old movie. Rather than become unnerved, however, Reagan found the loss reinvigorating. He reorganized his staff, replaced his campaign manager, and concentrated his fire on Bush in New Hampshire. Reagan and Bush agreed to meet at a head-to-head debate sponsored by the *Nashua Telegraph*. When four other Republican candidates objected to the two-person format, Bush opposed opening the debate, while Reagan dramatically appeared at the debate trailed by the four excluded candidates. As Bush sat stiffly, Reagan started to explain why he had brought the others. The debate moderator, *Nashua Telegraph* editor Jon Breen, ordered Reagan's microphone turned off. Reagan replied, "I am paying for this microphone." No matter that he had swiped the line from an old Spencer Tracy movie, *State of the Union*, Reagan had given a memorable performance. Leaving the debate, Reagan's staff told him that "the parking lot was littered with Bush-for-President badges." Having regained command of the race, Reagan remained in the state until election night, convincingly beating Bush by 50 to 23 percent.[21]

Bush was frustrated at the way the public perceived him and his opponent. Bush had been a combat pilot in the Second World War, but Reagan was widely known for his war movies. Bush had actually "met a payroll" as an independent oil company executive, while Reagan had simply preached the free-enterprise system to appreciative audiences. Bush was a devoted family man, while Reagan won attention for defending family values, despite being divorced and estranged from his children. Bush looked and sounded awkward and inarticulate on television, while Reagan mastered the medium. Bush's media advisers warned him about his "preppy" and "elitist" appearance, but when he asked why the public had never held Ivy League attendance against the Roosevelts, Tafts, and Kennedys, they had no explanation. He concluded that his image was "just something I'd have to live with." [22]

The New Hampshire primary effectively ended Bush's presidential campaign well before he formally dropped out of the race in May. It was during this interregnum, when his political future seemed doubtful, that Bush sold his home in Houston and purchased his grandfather's old estate, Walker's Point, at Kennebunkport, Maine. This move further blurred his identity: was he a Texan or a Yankee? In July, he went to the Republican convention in Detroit with a slim hope for the vice-presidential nomination but encountered a boom for Gerald Ford. With a good chance of defeating the incumbent President Jimmy Carter and the divided Democrats, Reagan wanted to unify the Republican party. At Henry Kissinger's suggestion, Reagan approached Ford with the novel idea that the former president run for vice president. Ford indicated he might accept if assured a meaningful role in the administration.

Word of this "dream ticket" sparked considerable enthusiasm at the Republican convention. Then Ford visited the CBS booth to be interviewed by Walter Cronkite. The veteran broadcaster pressed Ford about the details of how a former president might accept the second spot, prompting Ford to elaborate on his ideas for a co-presidency. From his hotel room, Bush watched the interview with the sinking feeling that Ford would never talk so freely unless all of the arrangements for his candidacy had been completed. But Ronald and Nancy Reagan also watched Ford's interview, with mounting dismay. "*Wait a minute*" Reagan later recalled thinking, "*this is really two presidents he's talking about.*" Later that night, Reagan called Ford to his hotel suite, where the two men met behind closed doors. When they emerged after ten minutes alone together, the "dream ticket" had evaporated. "The answer was no," Reagan told his staff. "He didn't think it was right for him or for me. And now I am inclined to agree." Reagan knew he needed to make a prompt decision about a replacement, since any delay would cause a letdown among the delegates and raise questions about his decision-making abilities. As Michael Deaver described the scene, Reagan "picked up the phone and said, to the amazement of everyone in the room, 'I'm calling George Bush. I want to get this settled. Anyone have any objections?'" Recognizing the need to broaden the ticket ideologically, no one could offer an alternative. Reagan placed the call, telling Bush that he wanted to announce his selection right away, if he had no objection. Surprised and delighted, Bush had none.[23]

Joining the Reagan Team

Reagan had not been impressed by Bush during the primaries. During their contest, Bush had leveled the charge of "voodoo economics" against Reagan's programs, a taunt that still stung. Reagan thought Bush lacked "spunk" and became too easily rattled by political criticism. "He just melts under pressure," Reagan complained. Thus when Reagan won the presidency in 1980, there were indications that Bush would remain an outsider from the Reagan team. Washington observers commented that the Reagans and the Bushes rarely socialized. Yet Bush had several advantages as vice president. His personality and his long experience in appointed offices made him naturally deferential to the president. He avoided criticizing or differing with Reagan in any way. He also had the good fortune of seeing his campaign manager, James A. Baker III, appointed chief of staff in the Reagan White House. While other vice presidents had to combat protective chiefs of staff, the longtime friendship of Bush and Baker continued throughout Reagan's administration. Although Baker served Reagan foremost, he made sure nothing would jeopardize Bush's eventual succession to the presidency.[24]

George and Barbara Bush moved into the vice-presidential mansion at the Naval Observatory and thrived on the many social duties of the office. Bush's attendance at a string of state funerals became a common joke for comedians. Barbara Bush felt such criticism was shortsighted, since "George met with many current or future heads of state at the funerals he attended, enabling him to forge personal relationships that were important to President Reagan—and later, President Bush." From the start, Bush recognized the constitutional limits of the office. He would not be the decision maker, since that was the president's job. His position would be meaningful therefore only if the president trusted him enough to delegate significant responsibilities to him. He determined to be a loyal team player and not to separate himself when things got tough. As president of the Senate, he also tried to stay in close touch with the senators and to keep the president informed of what was happening on the Hill. Respecting the limitations on his legislative role, however, he avoided trying to intervene in Senate deliberations.[25]

That attitude served Bush well during the first crisis of his vice-presidency. Touring Texas, where he had unveiled a historical marker at the hotel where John Kennedy spent his last night before Dallas, Bush received word that President Reagan had been shot and seriously wounded. He immediately flew to Washington. When his plane landed at Andrews Air Force Base, aides wanted him to proceed directly to the White House by helicopter. They thought it would make dramatic television footage and demonstrate that the government was still functioning. Bush vetoed the idea, declaring that "only the President lands on the south lawn." His helicopter instead flew to the vice-presidential residence, from which he drove to the White House. The gesture was not lost on Ronald Reagan, who slowly warmed to his vice president.[26]

Over time, Reagan grew comfortable with his vice president. The genial Reagan especially appreciated Bush's effort to start staff meetings with a "joke of the day." The two men had lunch together every Thursday and their discussions, according to Bush, were "wide-ranging, from affairs of state to small talk." The vice president made a point of never divulging publicly the advice he gave the president in private, and Reagan clearly appreciated his loyalty and discretion.[27]

As vice president, Bush devoted much attention to two special projects the president assigned to him. One was to chair a special task force on federal deregulation. The task force reviewed hundreds of rules and regulations, making specific recommendations on which ones to revise or eliminate in order to cut red tape. Bush chaired another task force on international drug smuggling, to coordinate federal efforts to stem the flow of drugs into the United States. Not coincidentally, both efforts—against big government and illegal drugs—were popular issues with Republican conservatives. Having joined the Reagan ticket as a representative of the moderate wing of his party, Vice President Bush courted conservatives to erase their suspicions. His conspicuous efforts to befriend the likes of New Hampshire publisher William Loeb and Moral Majority leader Jerry Falwell drove the newspaper columnist George Will to comment: "The unpleasant sound Bush is emitting as he traipses from one conservative gathering to another is a thin, tinny arf—the sound of a lap dog." [28]

A Troubled Second Term

Bush so solidified his position by 1984 that there was no question of replacing him when Reagan ran for a second term. By then, Barbara Bush had also become a national figure in her own right. The public enjoyed her direct, warm, and casual style. In 1984 she published a popular children's book, *C. Fred's Story*, about the family's basset hound—a forerunner of the best-selling *Millie's Book* by C. Fred's replacement. Yet George and Barbara Bush found the reelection campaign far more trying than the race four years earlier. The Democratic candidate, Walter Mondale, had made history by choosing the first woman candidate for vice president on a major national ticket. New York Representative Geraldine Ferraro was an attractive and aggressive candidate. Although a millionaire herself, she represented a blue-collar district in Queens that placed her in sharp contrast to Bush's Ivy League image. While Ferraro encountered significant problems of her own, she brought color to an otherwise dull and packaged campaign. Many reporters, especially women members of the press, cheered her campaign, leaving Bush at a decided disadvantage. As his anger flared after his televised debate with Ferraro, Bush was quoted as saying that he had "tried to kick a little ass last night." Despite Reagan's landslide reelection, the campaign left Bush feeling depressed and wondering if he still had a future in politics.[29]

Bush's friends Jim Baker and Nicholas Brady quickly helped revive his optimism and enthusiasm, and by that Christmas they were already planning strategy for his run for the presidency in 1988. From the Reagan camp, Bush hired Craig Fuller as his vice-presidential chief of staff, and from Reagan's campaign team he selected Lee Atwater as his chief campaign strategist. Before the end of 1985, Atwater had set up a political action committee, the Fund for America, that had raised more than two million dollars. Well in advance of the election, Bush became the conceded frontrunner to replace Reagan. The strategy, however, depended upon Reagan retaining his phenomenal popularity. Then news of the Iran-Contra scandal shook the Reagan administration.[30]

The press and public were astonished in the fall of 1986 to learn that the Reagan administration had secretly reversed its declared intention not to sell arms to Iran. Designed to free American hostages, the arms sales had produced revenue that administration officials had diverted to support anticommunist rebels in Nicaragua, in direct violation of the law. These revelations implicated President Reagan's national security advisers, Robert McFarland and John Poindexter, and a National Security Council aide, Oliver North. When Secretary of State George Shultz and Secretary of Defense Caspar Weinberger made it clear that they had opposed the Iran-Contra plan, they left open the question of the vice president's position. Either way, whether he had supported the illegal plan or been kept in the dark about it, Bush stood to lose. Alexander Haig, one of his opponents for the Republican nomination, asked: "Where was George Bush during the story? Was he the copilot in the cockpit, or was he back in economy class?" [31]

The vice president maintained that those who ran the operation had "compartmentalized" it, so that he knew of only some parts of the plan and had been "deliberately excluded" from others. Despite his claims of being "out of the loop," public opinion polls indicated that people had trouble believing Bush was an innocent bystander. The issue burst open in a live television encounter between Bush and CBS anchorman Dan Rather on January 25, 1988. Lee Atwater and Roger Ailes, Bush's campaign director and media adviser, worried much over the vice president's image as a "wimp." Before the interview, they convinced Bush that the broadcaster was setting a trap for him and planned to "sandbag" him over the Iran-Contra affair. Rather prefaced the interview by suggesting that Bush had been present at numerous White House meetings on Iran-Contra and then devoted his first question to the scandal. Bush angrily charged that CBS had misrepresented the purpose of the interview. Rather replied that he did not want to be argumentative, but Bush retorted, "You do, Dan. . . . I don't think it's fair to judge a whole career . . . by a rehash on Iran." Atwater, and Ailes were delighted. Bush's obvious fury had put "the wimp issue" to rest.[32]

Winning the Presidency in His Own Right

By the time Bush had officially declared his candidacy for president, his campaign had already raised ten million dollars, but he was by no means assured of the nomination. No vice president since Martin Van Buren in 1836 had won election on his own immediately following the term of the president with whom he had served. While Reagan was still personally popular, the Iran-Contra scandal had hobbled his administration. Senate Republican Leader Bob Dole was pressing a hard campaign against Bush, as was televangelist Pat Robertson. Returning to an economically depressed Iowa, Bush campaigned surrounded by Secret Service agents and rode in a motorcade of official limousines that looked like "the caravan of an Eastern potentate." The results of the Iowa caucuses relegated Bush to a dismal third place behind Dole and Robertson.[33]

As it did for Ronald Reagan eight years earlier, the embarrassing loss in Iowa forced Bush to re-vamp his strategy. The Bushes flew to New Hampshire, where Governor John Sununu assured Barbara: "Don't worry. He'll win in New Hampshire. 'Mr. Fix-it' will see to it." Bush followed the advice of his "handlers"—Sununu, Baker, Atwater, and Ailes. He abandoned his set speeches in favor of meeting voters at factories and shopping malls and drove an eighteen-wheel truck, trying to shed his "preppy" image and show a more down-to-earth personal side. He also went on the attack, pledging that he would never raise taxes as president, while claiming that Senator Dole had straddled the tax issue. The New Hampshire campaign saw the beginning of the negative attack advertisements that would mark the Bush campaign for the rest of the year. The decent, affable, self-effacing Bush, who had trouble boasting about his own impressive resume, had fewer compunctions about attacking his opponents. Bush defeated Dole and Robertson in New Hampshire and went on to take the Republican nomination.

Although he started well behind in the polls at the outset, he waged a vigorous general election campaign against Massachusetts Governor Michael Dukakis and his running mate, Lloyd Bentsen (who had defeated Bush for the Senate in 1970). Atwater and Ailes crafted a campaign of direct attacks on the Democratic candidate for refusing to sign a bill making the Pledge of Allegiance mandatory for school children, for allowing a weekend parole system that released convict Willie Horton from prison, and for not having cleaned up a badly polluted Boston harbor. Never appreciating the impact of the negative ads, Dukakis responded to them inadequately. Bush won an impressive victory in November, portraying himself as proudly patriotic, tough on crime, opposed to taxes, and sympathetic to educational and environmental issues.[34]

The chief circumstance in which candidate Bush ignored the advice of his "handlers" concerned the choice of his own vice-presidential candidate. Neither James Baker nor Lee Atwater was impressed with the qualifications of Indiana Senator Dan Quayle, although Roger Ailes and Craig Fuller saw Quayle's potential to attract younger and more conservative voters. Quayle had also been conducting his own "sub rosa" campaign to bring his availability to Bush's attention. Bush viewed Quayle as a young, good-looking, successful politician who was likely to play the same appreciative and deferential role that Bush had as vice president. Whatever Quayle's merits, the Bush campaign's strategy of keeping his choice secret until the last moment to add some drama to an otherwise predetermined convention, proved to be a mistake. Quayle was so little known to the nation—even to the media—that his public image became shaped entirely by initial perceptions, which were not favorable. One 1988 Democratic campaign button read simply, "Quayle—A Heartbeat Away."[35]

George Bush served one term as president of the United States. His years of experience in foreign policy prepared him well to serve as the nation's first post-cold war president. When the Iraqi army under Saddam Hussein invaded Iraq's oil-rich neighbor Kuwait, Bush responded promptly and boldly on both the diplomatic and military fronts. The lightning-quick Persian Gulf war lifted his public approval rating to an astonishing 91 percent. On the domestic front, his administration fared less well, diminished by a persistent economic recession, mounting federal deficits, and his broken campaign pledge not to raise taxes. Bush also suffered from his lack of what he called "the vision thing," a clarity of ideas and principles that could shape public opinion and influence Congress. "He does not say why he wants to be there," complained columnist George Will, "so the public does not know why it should care if he gets his way." Standing for reelection, Bush faced a "New Democrat," Arkansas Governor Bill Clinton, and a scrappy Texas billionaire independent candidate, Ross Perot. In November 1992, President Bush finished second with 38 percent of the vote to Clinton's 43 percent and Perot's 19 percent.[36]

In retrospect, George Bush lost in 1992 for the same reason he had won in 1988. Having served as Reagan's vice president, he personified a continuation of the previous policies. By 1992, Barbara Bush concluded that "we lost because people really wanted a change. We had had twelve years of a Republican presidency." Seen in those terms, Bush's defeat represented the vice-presidential conundrum: once having achieved the office, one never escapes it.[37]

NOTES

[1] George Bush with Victor Gold, *Looking Forward* (New York, 1987), p. 26; Leonard Schlup, "Prescott Bush and the Foundations of Modern Republicanism," *Research Journal of Philosophy and Social Sciences* (1992), pp. 1–16; Garry Wills, "Father Knows Best," *New York Review of Books* (November 5, 1992), pp. 36–40.

[2] George Bush, pp. 26–27; *Washington Post*, November 20, 1992.

[3] George Bush, pp. 30.

[4] Ibid., pp. 32–40; Fitzhugh Green, *George Bush: An Intimate Portrait* (New York, 1989), pp. 27–40.

[5] George Bush, pp. 41–45; Barbara Bush, *Barbara Bush: A Memoir* (New York, 1994), pp. 16–29; see William F. Buckley, *God and Man at Yale: The Superstitions of Academic Freedom* (Chicago, 1951).

[6] George Bush, pp. 46–58; Green, pp. 55–58, Barbara Bush, pp. 30–49.

[7] Green, pp. 59–74; George Bush, pp. 61–68.

[8] See Dewey W. Grantham, *The Life and Death of the Solid South: A Political History* (Lexington, KY, 1988).

[9] Green, pp. 75–81.

[10] Ibid., pp. 81–87; George Bush, pp. 77–89.

[11] Barbara Bush, pp. 57–63; George Bush, pp. 89–93.

[12] George Bush, pp. 93–98; Barbara Bush, p. 67; Richard Nixon, *RN: The Memoirs of Richard Nixon* (New York, 1978), p. 312.

[13] George Bush, pp. 99–103; Bob Schieffer and Gary Paul Gates, *The Acting President* (New York, 1989), p. 317; *Washington Times*, March 24, 1986.

[14] Schieffer and Gates, p. 317; Barbara Bush, p. 79; Green, pp. 115–17; George Bush, pp. 107–20; H.R. Haldeman, *The Haldeman Diaries: Inside the Nixon White House* (New York, 1994), p. 217.

[15] George Bush, pp. 120–25; Haldeman, pp. 540, 545, 553.

[16] Alexander M. Haig, Jr., with Charles McCarry, *Inner Circles: How America Changed the World: A Memoir* (New York, 1992), pp. 492–93; George Bush, pp. 122–25.

[17] George Bush, pp. 129–49.

[18] Barbara Bush, pp. 108, 130–31; George Bush, pp. 153–59; Gerald Ford, *A Time to Heal: The Autobiography of Gerald R. Ford* (New York, 1979), pp. 325–26, 337–38; Loch K. Johnson, *A Season of Inquiry: The Senate Intelligence Investigation* (Lexington, KY, 1985), pp. 158–59.

[19] George Bush, pp. 164–79.

[20] Ibid., pp. 184–85; Lou Cannon, *Reagan* (New York, 1982), pp. 229, 247–48.

[21] Cannon, pp. 249–54; Ronald Reagan, *An American Life* (New York, 1990), pp. 212–13.

[22] Schieffer and Gates, p. 341; George Bush, p. 203.

[23] Marie D. Natoli, "The Vice Presidency: Gerald Ford as Healer?" *Presidential Studies Quarterly* 10 (Fall 1980): 662–64; Schieffer and Gates, pp. 313–14; Cannon, pp. 265–67; Reagan, pp. 214–16; Michael Deaver, *Behind the Scenes* (New York, 1987), pp. 96–97; Barbara Bush, p. 169.

[24] Cannon, pp. 262–63; Schieffer and Gates, p. 125.

[25] Barbara Bush, p. 182; Green, pp. 185–96; George Bush to Senator Mark Hatfield, April 14, 1995, Senate Historical Office files.

[26] George Bush, pp. 217–32.

[27] Schieffer and Gates, p. 318.

[28] George Bush, p. 233; Schieffer and Gates, p. 320.

[29] Barbara Bush, pp. 194–97; Schieffer and Gates, p. 318.

[30] Schieffer and Gates, p. 319.

[31] William S. Cohen and George J. Mitchell, *Men of Zeal: A Candid Inside Story of the Iran-Contra Hearings* (New York, 1989), p. 268; see also Theodore Draper, *A Very Thin Line: The Iran-Contra Affairs* (New York, 1991).

[32] George Bush, pp. 240–41; Green, pp. 216–18; Cohen and Mitchell, p. 264; Schieffer and Gates, pp. 347–50; Jack W. Germond and Jules Witcover, *Whose Bright Stripes and Bright Stars? The Trivial Pursuit of the Presidency, 1988* (New York, 1989), pp. 118–30.

[33] Schieffer and Gates, pp. 321–23, 342–45; Germond and Witcover, pp. 65–80, 101–18.

[34] Barbara Bush, pp. 224–25; Schieffer and Gates, pp. 353–55, 373; Germond and Witcover, pp. 399–467.

[35] Schieffer and Gates, pp. 365–67; Germond and Witcover, pp. 375–95; David S. Broder and Bob Woodward, *The Man Who Would be President: Dan Quayle* (New York, 1992), p. 15.

[36] George F. Will, *The Leveling Wind: Politics, the Culture and Other News, 1990–1994* (New York, 1994), pp. 282–94; on Bush and the Persian Gulf War, see Bob Woodward, *The Commanders* (New York, 1991).

[37] Barbara Bush, p. 498.

Chapter 44

J. DANFORTH QUAYLE

1989–1993

J. DANFORTH QUAYLE

Chapter 44

J. DANFORTH QUAYLE

44th Vice President: 1989–1993

The essence of the vice presidency is preparedness.

—VICE PRESIDENT DAN QUAYLE

New Orleans' Spanish Plaza, on a hot August day in 1988, teemed with people waiting for the SS *Natchez* to steam down the Mississippi River. On board the riverboat was Vice President George Bush, soon to become the Republican nominee for president of the United States. Frantically pushing their way through the mob on the plaza were Indiana Senator Dan Quayle and his wife Marilyn. Those who had been standing in the broiling sun for hours understandably were not anxious to make way for the late arrivals. Only the Quayles knew that he was to join Bush on deck to be announced as the vice-presidential candidate. Bush had insisted that the choice remain secret to add drama to the event. "This was not the best-planned episode in political history," Quayle lamented. The Quayles waved vainly at Bush's staff members on the boat but went unnoticed until South Carolina Senator Strom Thurmond and a few others on board pointed them out in the crowd, and the Secret Service parted the way for the Quayles to board. Barbara Bush later commented that "Dan and Marilyn had trouble getting to the platform because they looked too young and no one realized why they needed to be up there."[1]

More of a problem for Quayle than reaching the boat was being taken seriously once he got there. Bush's tactic of not revealing his vice-presidential choice until the last moment added suspense to an otherwise predictable convention but did a disservice to Quayle. Little known to the national media and to the public outside of his own state, the forty-one-year-old senator found his public identity shaped by some unfortunate first impressions. Jacketless on the sweltering deck, Quayle grabbed Bush's arm and shouted "Let's go get 'em!" He reminded reporters less of a vice-presidential candidate than an elated game show contestant who had just won a car. Even Bush's own staff had to order speedy background research to find out about their nominee. When keen observers like journalists David Broder and Bob Woodward and political scientist Richard Fenno examined his background and positions closely, Quayle appeared fairly substantial. Yet his initial image as a lightweight made his selection seem so inappropriate that the entire vice-presidency, in the metaphor of journalist Jules Witcover, appeared to be a "crapshoot."[2]

The media legitimately wanted to know what credentials Quayle possessed for the nation's second-highest job. Could he confirm reports that he had been a poor student? What was his family's financial standing? Had he dodged the Vietnam War? Quayle did not handle these initial inquiries well. He seemed tongue-tied and flustered, wearing a stunned expression that Bush's media adviser Roger Ailes described as "that deer-in-the-headlights look." Campaign managers made things worse by staging Quayle's first formal news conference in his home town of Huntington, Indiana, among a crowd of supporters so protective of their candidate and hostile to the reporters that the event soured Quayle's relations with the press from the start.[3]

A Problem of Perception

Quayle perceived himself quite differently from the image he saw in the general media. The press pictured him as wealthy, because his grandfather Eugene Pulliam owned radio stations and such newspapers as the *Indianapolis Star* and the *Arizona Republic*. But Quayle argued that his own family had lived a much more modest, middle-class life. His grandfather had actually left his money in a series of trusts designed to protect the financial security of his newspapers rather than to enrich his family.

Born on February 4, 1947, in Indianapolis, the son of Corrine Pulliam Quayle and James C. Quayle, he was named James Danforth Quayle after a college friend of his father who was killed in World War II. James Quayle, a manager for the Pulliam newspapers, moved the family to Scottsdale, Arizona, in the mid-1950s and then back to Huntington, Indiana, in 1963, where he published the *Huntington Herald-Press*. Dan Quayle grew up in a Republican family—he recalled once walking behind his grandfather and his golfing partner Dwight Eisenhower—and the family newspapers were staunchly conservative. But Dan Quayle "was never much of a student government type," and at DePauw University his prime interests were golf and the Delta Kappa Epsilon fraternity. He described himself as a "late bloomer," and admitted that he enjoyed the movie *Ferris Bueller's Day Off* because it reminded him of his own lackadaisical schooldays.[4]

Intending to go to law school, Quayle realized that his draft deferment would expire when he graduated from DePauw in 1969. He therefore chose to join the Indiana National Guard, which would most likely keep him out of the Vietnam War. Countless other young men of his generation were making similar decisions, but this act would have serious consequences when Quayle was selected to run for vice president. Grilled by Bush's staff regarding whether he had any regrets about going into the Guard rather than to Vietnam, he replied, "I did not know in 1969 that I would be in this room today, I'll confess." A

related question was whether Quayle's family pulled any strings to get him into the Guard. Interviewed during the convention, Quayle could not recall any special connections but speculated that "phone calls were made." Identification with his family's newspaper had further helped gain him assignment as an information officer with the Guard's public relations unit.[5]

After his six months in the National Guard, Quayle applied to Indiana University Law School. His poor college grades kept him out of the main law school in Bloomington, but he was admitted to the night school in Indianapolis. Quayle studied harder in law school, finding time also to work as a research assistant for the state attorney general, as an administrative assistant in the governor's office, and as director of inheritance taxes for the state department of revenue. A joint project on a capital punishment brief introduced him to fellow law student Marilyn Tucker, and a short courtship led to their marriage ten weeks later in 1972. Two years later, after they both passed the bar exam on the same day (and in the same month that their first child was born) the Quayles moved back to Huntington. They set up a law practice, Quayle and Quayle, in the building that housed his father's newspaper. Marilyn handled most of the legal business, while Dan spent his time as an associate publisher of the paper. His real career objective, however, was politics rather than journalism. They chose a house in a district represented in the state legislature by a Democrat, whom Quayle planned to challenge in 1976.[6]

Upset Victories

Unexpectedly, in February 1976, Republican county chairman Orvas Beers approached the twenty-nine-year-old Quayle and asked him to run for Congress. "You mean now?" the astonished Quayle asked, thinking of his plan to start in the state legislature. Beers explained that no one else wanted to run for the House seat against eight-term Democrat Ed Roush. After consulting with his wife and his father, and obtaining promises from Beers to provide enough money to mount a creditable campaign, Quayle announced his candidacy. Copying Jimmy Carter's style, Quayle ran as a Washington "outsider," attacking the Democratic Congress and Roush's liberal voting record. While he went out campaigning, Marilyn Quayle set up a headquarters in a back room of Mother's Restaurant in Fort Wayne, where she "met with the county chairmen and stroked everybody and made everybody fall into place." Rather than rely on the party organization, Quayle developed his own cadre of volunteers, drawn especially, as he noted, from "the Christian community." Roush failed to take his challenger seriously and agreed to a series of debates that gave the newcomer much-needed exposure. Election day provided ample Republican coattails, as Indianans cast their votes for Republicans Gerald Ford for president, Otis Bowen for governor, and Richard Lugar for senator. Dan Quayle upset Ed Roush with 54 percent of the vote. In the wake of the victory, both Dan and Marilyn Quayle suspended their law practice.[7]

Congressman Quayle began his term by introducing a term-limit bill that would restrict himself and his colleagues to no more than twelve years' service. He identified himself as a critic of "the old ways" and as an opponent of pork barrel politics, congressional pay raises, and government bureaucracy. Yet Quayle had a lackluster attendance record in the House, often skipping committee meetings and missing votes to play golf. People referred to him as a "wet head," because he always seemed to be coming from the House gymnasium. The House never engaged his interest. "Almost as soon as I was in, I wanted out—or up," he admitted. Since, as a freshman member of the minority party, Quayle would have little influence over legislation, he devoted most of his attention to constituent services and building a strong base back home, spending most of his second year running for reelection. For years Quayle's district had been considered marginal, with only a few percentage points dividing the two parties. But in 1978 he won reelection by a smashing two-to-one margin, causing people to talk about him challenging Birch Bayh for the Senate.[8]

Quayle approached "Doc" Bowen, the popular governor of Indiana, offering to support Bowen for the Senate in 1980 but stating that, if Bowen chose not to run, then Quayle would declare his own candidacy. He repeated that message to Republican leaders across the state. Bowen's decision in 1979 not to make the Senate race cleared the way for Quayle. As a thirty-three-year-old challenger, Quayle reversed the tables on the veteran Bayh, who himself had challenged and upset a three-term incumbent while still in his thirties. It was a classic race of a liberal versus a conservative, with the two men differing on every issue from abortion to welfare. The political scientist Richard Fenno joined Quayle on the campaign trail while the candidate was still the decided underdog. "He struck me as a remarkably handsome kid, but more kid even than handsome," Fenno noted. "As a campaigner, he was a natural—vigorous (but not polished) in speech, attentive in personal contact, open in dialogue and undaunted by potentially unfriendly audiences." The National Conservative Political Action Committee (NCPAC) and the Moral Majority ran ads attacking Bayh, but, even more significantly, double-digit inflation and unemployment in the state undermined the incumbent. Ronald Reagan's 1980 challenge to Jimmy Carter provided a further boost to Republican senatorial candidates. Carter dragged down to defeat with him such senior Democratic senators as George McGovern, Frank Church, Warren Magnuson, and Birch Bayh. For the first time since 1952, Republicans won control of the Senate.[9]

Quayle found it both a curse and a blessing to be so constantly underestimated. Like Roush, Bayh had agreed to a series of debates, assuming that he could easily outshine his opponent. By the end of the campaign, Bayh regretted the decision. Although not particularly articulate as a debater, Quayle exuded confidence and demonstrated his highly competitive nature. Even after this second impressive upset, however, Quayle arrived in the Senate identified as a "golden boy" who had led a "charmed life." Reinforcing this image, his name surfaced in a scandal in March 1981, when it was revealed that he and two representatives on a golfing weekend in Florida had shared a cottage with an attractive female lobbyist. Both representatives lost their seats in the next election, while Quayle lost face. He also found the transition to the Senate difficult, especially missing the afternoon basketball games in the House gym. "There aren't many senators under thirty-five with children under six," he observed (the Quayles by then had three small children). Sessions in the Senate ran late into the nights. Good advice, however, came from Senator Mark Hatfield, who took Quayle aside and said, "Look, you're young and you've got a family. Make time for them." Marilyn Quayle later commented that there was probably not another U.S. senator who rearranged his schedule to coach his sons' basketball teams.[10]

Building a Record in the Senate

In choosing committees, Quayle had hoped for Foreign Relations and Finance. Instead he was assigned to Armed Services, Budget, and Labor and Human Resources. Initially, Quayle showed no interest in the Labor Committee but took it when he determined that he could achieve seniority there faster than on any other committee. In the past, freshman senators had to bide their time before they could chair a committee, but Senate reforms in the 1970s had ensured that most new senators of the majority party would chair a subcommittee. Quayle had sought to chair the Labor Committee's subcommittee on Health, but committee chairman Orrin Hatch chose that spot for himself. Instead, Quayle chaired the Employment and Productivity Subcommittee, which would handle the reauthorization of the Comprehensive Employment and Training Act (CETA). During his campaign, Quayle had criticized CETA as one of the worst examples of big government programs, yet he recognized that any jobs program would impact on the high unemployment in Indiana.[11]

President Ronald Reagan was leading a concerted effort to trim government spending on domestic programs, particularly those identified with the welfare state. Quayle also wanted to cut government, but he had stepped up from representing a single, fairly prosperous district to serving a state with a severe unemployment crisis. "The scale of problems Gary has is so much greater than Fort Wayne," he commented. If CETA were abolished, who would help poor and unskilled workers retrain? Since the members of the slim Republican majority might not be united

on this issue, Quayle sought to build a bipartisan coalition. He sidestepped the subcommittee's cantankerous ranking Democrat, Ohio Senator Howard Metzenbaum, and forged an alliance instead with Massachusetts Senator Edward M. Kennedy. When reporters asked about this pragmatic union, which flew in the face of ideological differences, Quayle replied:

> They don't know who Dan Quayle is in Massachusetts. But they do know who Ted Kennedy is in Indiana. I don't think there will be any recall. Actually, the fact that the two of us would get together underscores the seriousness of the problem of unemployment, and it emphasizes our commitment.[12]

The Quayle-Kennedy alliance caught the Reagan administration off guard and disrupted its plan to let CETA expire. The administration countered with an alternative bill, but Quayle's bipartisan approach enabled him to negotiate between Kennedy, Hatch, and the Reagan administration. The eventual Quayle-Kennedy bill resulted in creation of the Jobs Training Partnership Act of 1982. Senator Kennedy congratulated Quayle for having worked hard to develop a common consensus while remaining consistent with his own principles. Both congressional Democrats and the Reagan administration claimed credit for the act, and to Quayle's dismay the White House scheduled the signing ceremony for a day when he would be out of town. Still, his success won considerable attention, gave him credibility as an effective senator, and provided him with ammunition for his Senate reelection campaign.[13]

In foreign affairs, Quayle was eclipsed by Indiana's senior senator, Richard Lugar, who chaired the Foreign Relations Committee. Yet Quayle involved himself in foreign policy issues through the Armed Services Committee. As a freshman, he took the lead in persuading other freshmen Republicans to reach a compromise on a Reagan administration plan to sell AWACS surveillance planes to Saudi Arabia. Quayle arranged for Reagan to sign a "letter of certification" that satisfied enough otherwise doubtful senators to win approval for the sale. Quayle was also willing to take positions independent of the administration. In 1987, as the Intermediate Nuclear Forces (INF) Treaty moved toward completion, Quayle joined a group of conservative Republican senators in opposition. When President Reagan accused them of accepting the inevitability of war, Quayle denounced the president's comments as "totally irresponsible." A question arose over whether the treaty covered such "futuristic" weapons as lasers, particle beams and microwaves. Both the State Department and the Soviets agreed they were covered, but Quayle insisted they were not. (Later it became evident that the economic deterioration of the Soviet Union severely hampered its ability to compete with the United States in developing such sophisticated space weapons.) "Senator Quayle came at me repeatedly with complaints about this issue," Secretary of State George Shultz recalled. At last the secretary begged, "Dan, you have to shut down! We can't have the president's achievement wrecked by Republicans!" The treaty was finally approved by a vote of 93 to 5, with Quayle voting in favor.[14]

Senate Republican Leader Howard Baker appointed Quayle in 1984 to chair a special committee to examine procedural chaos in the Senate. Quayle had impressed the leadership, as Alan Ehrenhalt noted, for "asking troublesome questions in a way that might lead to constructive answers." The Quayle Committee argued that too many committees and subcommittees stretched senators' time too thin. It recommended that senators serve on no more than two major committees and one secondary committee and chair no more than two committees or subcommittees. The panel urged that the number of committee slots be reduced and called for no more than five subcommittees per committee. Reviewing floor procedures in the Senate, the committee proposed limiting "nongermane" amendments and other dilatory tactics. None of these rules changes was adopted, but based on the report, seventeen senators gave up their extra committee seats, and one committee reduced its subcommittees. Secretary of the Senate William Hildenbrand, who had followed the process closely, called it remarkable that any senators gave up committee memberships, since they "had staff on those committees, and they didn't want to lose staff." Hildenbrand said Quayle succeeded "beyond my wildest expectations." Quayle, however, considered the achievements more modest than the recommendations. He was especially disappointed when the Democrats reversed several committee cutbacks after they won back control of the Senate in 1987.[15]

These accomplishments gave Quayle a strong record on which to campaign in 1986, and he defeated his opponent, Jill Long, by an impressive 61 percent of the vote. His reelection was more notable because, without Ronald Reagan heading the ticket, many other first-term Senate Republicans—including Mark Andrews of North Dakota, Jeremiah Denton of Alabama, Paula Hawkins of Florida, and Mack Mattingly of Georgia—went down to defeat when they ran on their own. As a result, Democrats won enough seats to regain the chamber's majority. Quayle's margin of victory was large enough to give him thoughts of running for president. But when Vice President George Bush survived the Iran-Contra scandal and reestablished himself as the Republican frontrunner, Quayle shifted his attention to the vice-presidency.[16]

The Unexpected Vice-Presidential Candidate

No one runs for vice president so much as making oneself strategically available for the selection. Quayle consciously began to give more Senate speeches, particularly on such high-profile issues as the INF Treaty. He issued more press releases and wrote more op-ed pieces to raise his name recognition. He made a point of dropping by George Bush's office at the Capitol for informal chats. He also maintained contact with Bush's campaign aides. He tried "as subtly as I could, to make it clear I was both qualified and available."[17]

Although some of Bush's top staff considered Quayle a lightweight, the sixty-four-year-old Bush had compelling reasons for picking the Indiana senator as his running mate. Youthful and photogenic, Quayle would appeal to a younger generation of voters. He had proven his ability to campaign by his upset victories for the House and Senate. He had applied himself seriously as a senator, building a strong conservative voting

J. DANFORTH QUAYLE

record and receiving high marks from conservative groups that were suspicious of Bush's moderation. As a midwesterner, Quayle would add regional balance to Bush's Texas-New England background. And especially since Quayle had not yet established a national identity, he would be likely to remain dependent and deferential toward Bush, in much the same manner that Bush had served Ronald Reagan. To maintain suspense about his choice, Bush kept his decision secret from everyone. Not until they were flying to the convention in New Orleans, did Bush whisper to his wife Barbara that he had chosen Quayle for vice president, because he felt Quayle was respected as a senator, was bright, and "the right age."[18]

Neither Bush nor Quayle anticipated the incredulity and negative publicity that the selection would trigger. The press felt blindsided by the choice of Quayle, and reporters scrambled to collect information about him. As the first person named to a national ticket who had been born after World War II and who had come of age during the Vietnam War, Quayle found that his background was scrutinized differently than it had been during his previous campaigns. Initial reports also distorted Quayle's family finances and connections. The candidate himself had trouble perceiving himself the way others did. What seemed to him a normal, middle-class upbringing appeared more affluent to others. Dan Coats, who served on his staff and succeeded him in the House and Senate, observed: "standing back and looking at the surface of his life, almost everyone would say it was fairly sheltered, some would say privileged. Plenty of opportunities to play golf; enough money in the family to live a comfortable lifestyle."[19]

Quayle blamed Bush's aides for not making available to the press more background material about his record and for allowing a hostile caricature to develop. With a sickening feeling, Quayle realized that "the stories and the jokes and the contempt were going to keep coming." Bush's aides blamed Quayle's inexperience in dealing with the national press. He had a habit of not reading prepared texts that led him to make offhand remarks, and the resulting incoherent expressions and nonsequiturs fed the monologues of late-night television comedians. Bush's staff took over Quayle's campaign and designed it to avoid drawing any attention away from the presidential candidate. Quayle's "handlers" prevented him from talking directly to the press and arranged his schedule to skirt major cities or other areas where the ticket was in trouble.[20]

The lowest point of the campaign occurred on October 6, 1988, during his nationally televised vice-presidential debate with the Democratic candidate, Lloyd Bentsen. Quayle had promised the debate would give viewers "a much better impression" of him. Because the press painted him as a juvenile, unseasoned for national office, he had often responded that he had as much experience in Congress as Jack Kennedy had when he sought the presidency. His advisers warned that a Kennedy analogy could backfire, but during the debate a nervous Quayle fell back on the line. When he did, Bentsen had a well-prepared response: "Senator, I served with Jack Kennedy. I knew Jack Kennedy. Jack Kennedy was a friend of mine. Senator, you are no Jack Kennedy." The audience laughed and applauded, and the next day Michael Dukakis' campaign ran an ad featuring pictures of Bentsen and Quayle, with the message: "This is the first presidential decision that George Bush and I had to make. Judge us by how we made it and who we chose." But voters rarely cast a ballot for or against a vice-presidential candidate. Despite bad publicity and negative public opinion polls, Quayle was not enough of a liability to prevent George Bush's election. On inauguration day, in January 1989, it was Senator Quayle not Senator Bentsen who took the oath of office as vice president.[21]

Inside the Bush Administration

Bush's staff described his White House as "smaller, more collegial—intimate even" than it had been under Reagan. The informal tone suited Vice President Quayle well, and he enjoyed regular access to the president. Still, Quayle lacked the standing of such strong-minded officials as Secretary of State James A. Baker, Office of Management and Budget director Richard Darman, and White House Chief of Staff John

Sununu. The top staff preferred that Quayle keep occupied with "the traditional busywork of the No. 2 job." Marilyn Quayle, always her husband's closest and most candid adviser, complained that the vice president's overcrowded schedule prevented him from focusing on specific issues. Quayle countered by forming a smart, young staff (six of whom held Ph.D.s), headed by William Kristol, known as "the Great Reaganite Hope" in the Bush White House for arguing for conservative positions with Bush's more moderate advisers. His staff—larger than Mondale or Bush's vice-presidential staffs—worked to carve an independent identity for Quayle within the confines of the president's agenda.[22]

Several former vice presidents offered Quayle solicitous advice. Richard Nixon emphasized the need for loyalty to the president. Walter Mondale counseled him not accept any "line item authority," meaning responsibility for particular programs, since the vice-presidency did not provide the authority to carry out such tasks and he would only be blocked by cabinet members and other centers of power within the administration. George Bush, who had held the job for the previous eight years, suggested that he travel a lot to get some seasoning. Bush also encouraged Quayle to "say some things that the President cannot say," particularly on ideological themes popular with conservative groups. The president invited his vice president to attend all significant meetings to become fully informed about every aspect of the presidency.[23]

Shortly after the election, Quayle asked: "How am I going to spend my day?" He seriously considered taking a more activist role as presiding officer of the Senate. "The gavel is a very important instrument," he insisted, ". . . an instrument of power. An instrument that establishes the agenda." The problem was that the Democrats controlled the Senate, and the rules of the Senate, which allowed any ruling of the chair to be overturned by a majority vote, made presiding more a responsibility than a power. Quayle soon lapsed back into the traditional legislative role of the vice-presidency. He visited Capitol Hill weekly for the regular luncheon meetings of Republican senators and stood ready when needed to break a tie vote (although he never had an opportunity to do so). He argued the administration's case on legislation and unsuccessfully tried to persuade senators to confirm John Tower as secretary of defense. Steadily he felt himself becoming more a part of the executive than the legislative branch. "When I was in the Senate, I thought it was disorganized but manageable," he mused. "From the viewpoint of the Executive Branch, I found the Senate disorganized and unmanageable."[24]

Marilyn Quayle faced similar problems in defining her new role. The governor of Indiana asked if she would be interested in being appointed to fill Dan's Senate seat. The Quayles briefly considered the office but concluded that it would not work, since the press would pounce upon the slightest disagreement between herself and the Bush administration. She thought of resuming her law career, but concluded that it raised the appearances of conflict of interest. She chose instead to play a more traditional role as hostess and unofficial adviser. On the side, she and her sister wrote and published *Embrace the Serpent*, a novel about politics, intrigue and a vice president's wife.[25]

The vice-presidency was, in Quayle's words, an "awkward job," far more confining than his years in the House and Senate when he could determine for himself what he supported and what he would say. Not only did the president set the program, but others in the administration held jurisdiction for carrying it out and jealously guarded their territory. Quayle, who met early each weekday morning with the president and his national security adviser and lunched with the president weekly, felt free to argue his positions in any meeting. Once a decision was made, however, he loyally fell in behind, even if he had opposed it. "Anyone who thinks cheerleading for a policy you don't believe in amounts to hypocrisy doesn't really understand the way government has to work," he insisted.[26]

Following the lead of his predecessors, Quayle traveled widely, giving speeches for the administration, raising funds for the Republican party, and introducing himself in foreign capitals. At the White House he chaired the White House Council on Competitiveness, which aimed at reducing burdensome regulations. Quayle received relatively little publicity for his efforts on the council, in part because he thought deregulation could be achieved more easily if the council worked behind the scenes and avoided clashing with Congress. He received more press attention for chairing the National Space Council, which coordinated policy for the space program.[27]

On Capitol Hill, the vice president played a liaison role with the conservative wing of the Republican party. His services proved most useful in 1990, when a "budget summit" with congressional Democrats led Bush to break his "no-new-taxes" pledge. House Republicans revolted and voted down the initial budget compromise. Georgia Representative Newt Gingrich commented that for several days conservatives in the House were no longer talking to budget director Richard Darman or chief of staff John Sununu, leaving vice president Quayle as "the primary source of information between the most active wing of the House Republican Party" and the Bush administration. "Oddly enough," Quayle concluded, "I came out of the debacle somewhat enhanced within the party and the West Wing." He did not talk down to House Republicans in the manner of Darman and Sununu, and he demonstrated that in private he could play a role as broker and peacemaker. By contrast, his public position of blaming tax increases on the Democrats drove his ratings down further in the opinion polls.[28]

A similar gap between Quayle's backstage activity and the public perception of him developed in foreign policy matters. In late 1989, when President Bush and Secretary of State Baker were flying to a meeting with Mikhail Gorbachev at Malta, an attempted coup took place in the Philippines. Quayle presided over the White House Situation Room, coordinating American efforts to ensure the survival of Philippine President Corazon Aquino's government. When those in the Situation Room had reached a consensus to provide air power to keep rebel planes from taking off, rather than to bomb them as Aquino had requested, Quayle called Air Force One and had Bush awakened to present their recommendation. Quayle prided himself on his crisis management, but since the activity took place away from

public view, and since he could not publicly brag about his role, only "a small spate of welcome stories" appeared.[29]

In other matters of foreign policy, George Bush remained very much in command, leaving little room for his vice president other than to attend the meetings and offer the president his support. In January 1991, just before "Operation Desert Shield" changed to "Desert Storm," Bush sent Quayle to the Middle East to meet with Saudi Arabian leaders. On his own, Quayle determined to visit American troops. He realized that the gesture might rekindle press ridicule of his National Guard service but decided that he had no other choice. "The fact is I had to do it," he later explained. "The essence of the vice-presidency is preparedness, and if I ever had to take over from President Bush—especially at a time like this—I would not be able to function if I felt I couldn't visit the troops who would be under my command."[30]

The "Dump Quayle" Movement

Victory in the Persian Gulf War lifted President Bush's standing in the public opinion polls to unprecedented heights. As leading Democrats took themselves out of contention, Bush seemed certain of reelection in 1992. Quayle's position on the ticket received a boost from a seven-part series of respectful articles by the prominent journalists David Broder and Bob Woodward that appeared in January 1992 on the front pages of the *Washington Post*. These were later published as a book, *The Man Who Would Be President*. Broder and Woodward argued that "serious assessments of Quayle have taken a back seat to jokes about him." After his "gaffe-ridden performance" in 1988, he had been "saddled with a reputation as a lightweight and treated as a figure of fun." The press had focused on the vice president only when he did something that lived down to their expectations. But Broder and Woodward concluded that "all jokes aside—Dan Quayle has proved himself to be a skillful player of the political game, with a competitive drive that has been underestimated repeatedly by his rivals."[31]

The election, however, turned out differently than expected. A persistent recession held the economy stagnant, and the Bush administration mustered none of the decisiveness on economic issues that it had demonstrated in winning the Gulf War. The president's health also revived worries about Quayle's ability to succeed him. While jogging in May 1991, Bush suffered heart fibrillations, and plans were made for Quayle to take over presidential powers if Bush needed to be anesthetized to regulate his heart beat. This news inspired a tee-shirt featuring the Edvard Munch painting of "The Scream," with the caption: President Quayle?[32]

The vice president still suffered from gaffes. To his dismay he heard that even Republican members of Congress were telling Quayle jokes, most of them apocryphal, such as his comment that his Latin American travels made him wish he had studied Latin harder in school. The conservative magazine American Spectator ran a cover story on "Why Danny Can't Read." In May 1992, Quayle delivered a speech on family values in which he criticized the popular television program Murphy Brown for "mocking the importance of fathers, by bearing a child alone." Although even his critics conceded that the rise of single-parent families was a cause for alarm, the vice president's example of a fictional television character seemed to trivialize his issue. The next month brought an even more embarrassing flap when Quayle visited a school in Trenton, New Jersey, for a "little photo op," helping students prepare for a spelling bee. The word was "potato." The student at the blackboard spelled it correctly, but the card Quayle had been handed read "potatoe." Television pictures of the vice president coaxing the puzzled student to misspell "potato" confirmed everyone's worst suspicions. "Boy, I hope this doesn't hurt his credibility," mocked comedian Jay Leno.[33]

During the summer of 1992, the Bush administration seemed increasingly vulnerable, and nervous Republicans urged the president to dump Quayle from the ticket. Public opinion polls showed him to be the least popular vice president in forty years, scoring even lower than Spiro Agnew. The televised Persian Gulf War had also raised public awareness of other players in the Bush administration, among them Secretary of Defense Dick Cheney and Chairman of the Joint Chiefs of Staff Colin Powell, who began to be mentioned as replacements for Quayle. However, the White House staff concluded that changing running mates would be a sign of panic, would make Bush appear disloyal, and would serve as an admission that his original choice had been a mistake. Bush made it clear he would stick with Quayle, while Quayle in a television interview said that he had Bush's complete confidence and added, "Believe me, if I thought I was hurting the ticket, I'd be gone."[34]

Now four years older, slightly grayer, and more seasoned in the job, Quayle hoped that the reelection race would cast him in a more favorable light. This time his own staff ran his campaign. Having been the first member of the postwar generation on a national ticket, Quayle this time faced two more "baby boomers," Arkansas Governor Bill Clinton for president and Tennessee Senator Al Gore for vice president. Quayle and Gore both had come to the House in 1977 and had played basketball together in the House gym. The orderly announcement of the Democratic vice-presidential selection caused Quayle some envy: "It was hard for me to watch Gore's unveiling without thinking back to the chaos of Spanish Plaza in New Orleans and shaking my head." Most of all, he anticipated that a debate with Gore could wipe the slate clean, erasing his faltering performance against Bentsen four years earlier. It was a scrappy debate, with neither vice-presidential candidate conceding any points to the other. This time it was Admiral James Stockdale, running mate of third-party candidate Ross Perot, who seemed clearly out of his depth. Although critics declared the debate a draw, Quayle won by not losing. Columnist Charles Krauthammer described his performance as nervy: "His party facing annihilation, his colleagues deserting, his ammunition gone, Quayle seemed determined to go down fighting. It was a display of frantic combativeness that verged on courage."[35]

Returning to Huntington, Indiana, to vote on election day, Quayle by chance encountered Ed Roush, the man he had beaten for Congress in his first race. The incident seemed a forewarning that his decade and a half in politics "was coming full circle." That night the Bush-Quayle ticket lost with 38 percent of the vote to Clinton-Gore's 43 percent and Perot-Stockdale's 19 percent. Dan Quayle retired from the vice-presidency to write a popular memoir, *Standing Firm*, to appear in a Frito-Lay potato chip commercial, and to contemplate his own race for president in 1996. Although he moved back to Indiana, he made it clear that he would not run for governor. "If I ever run for public office again," he promised, "it will be for president." His every step seemed to point to a return to the national political arena, but serious illnesses, including blood clots in the lungs and a benign tumor on his appendix, convinced him to withdraw from the race. He announced that he planned to put his family first "and to forgo the disruption to our lives that a third straight national campaign would create." [36]

"No Vice President took as many shots—unfair shots—as Dan Quayle," declared Senate Republican Leader Bob Dole. "And no Vice President withstood those shots with as much grace, good humor, and commitment to not back down." Barbara Bush similarly saluted Quayle for being "a superb vice president." He was loyal and smart, she insisted. "There is no question that he had a perception problem, and it was politically chic to kick Dan around. It was darned unfair." Admitting that he had been bruised by the experience, the former vice president kept his sense of humor. When asked about his handicap in golf, Quayle quipped: "My handicap is the same as it has been ever since I became vice president: the news media." [37]

NOTES

[1] Dan Quayle, *Standing Firm: A Vice-Presidential Memoir* (New York, 1994), pp. 3–9; Barbara Bush, *Barbara Bush: A Memoir* (New York, 1994), p. 226.

[2] David S. Broder and Bob Woodward, *The Man Who Would Be President: Dan Quayle* (New York, 1992), pp. 57, 62; Richard F. Fenno, Jr., *The Making of a Senator: Dan Quayle* (Washington, 1989), pp. vii-viii; Jules Witcover, *Crapshoot: Rolling the Dice on the Vice Presidency* (New York, 1992), pp. 4–11.

[3] Witcover, p. 343; Broder and Woodward, p. 65; *New York Times*, August 17, 25, 1988.

[4] Broder and Woodward, pp. 37, 84–87; Quayle, p. 43; Maureen Dowd, "The Education of Dan Quayle," *New York Times Magazine*, (June 25, 1989), p. 20; *Washington Post*, October 2, 1988.

[5] Quayle, pp. 30–41; *New York Times*, August 26, 1988.

[6] Quayle, pp. 11–12; Fenno, pp. 3–4.

[7] Quayle, pp. 12–14; Broder and Woodward, pp. 33–46.

[8] Fenno, pp. 6–12, 30; Quayle, p. 14.

[9] Quayle, pp. 14–15; Broder and Woodward, pp. 47–51; Fenno, p. 13.

[10] Fenno, pp. 21–22; Quayle, pp. 15–16; *Washington Post*, August 18, 1988.

[11] Fenno, pp. 23–24, 35–36.

[12] Ibid., pp. 35–51, 61; Quayle, pp. 16–17.

[13] Fenno, pp. 69–118.

[14] Ibid., pp. 24–31; George P. Shultz, *Turmoil and Triumph: My Years as Secretary of State* (New York, 1993), pp. 1007, 1084–85.

[15] Alan Ehrenhalt, *Politics in America: Members of Congress in Washington and at Home* (Washington, 1985), p. 498; William F. Hildenbrand, *Secretary of the Senate,* Oral History Interviews, 1985 (U.S. Senate Historical Office, Washington, DC), p. 331; Dan Quayle, "The New Senate: Two Steps Backwards," *Congressional Record*, 100th Cong., 1st sess., January 13, 1987, pp. 1215–17; Temporary Select Committee to Study the Senate Committee System, *Report Together with Proposed Resolutions*, 98th Cong., 2d sess., S. Prt. 98–254.

[16] Quayle, *Standing Firm*, p. 18.

[17] Ibid., pp. 18–19; Broder and Woodward, pp. 15–21.

[18] Quayle, *Standing Firm*, p. 18; Bush, pp. 225–26; Bob Schieffer and Gary Paul Gates, *The Acting President* (New York, 1989), pp. 365–67.

[19] Broder and Woodward, p. 36.

[20] Quayle, *Standing Firm*, pp. 26–58; Schieffer and Gates, p. 366.

[21] *Washington Post*, October 2, 1988; Quayle, *Standing Firm*, pp. 59–67; Jack W. Germond and Jules Witcover, *Whose Broad Stripes and Bright Stars? The Trivial Pursuit of the Presidency, 1988* (New York, 1989), pp. 435–44; Fitzhugh Green, *George Bush: An Intimate Portrait* (New York, 1989), p. 238.

[22] John Podhoretz, *Hell of a Ride: Backstage at the White House Follies, 1989–1993* (New York, 1993), pp. 165, 219; Broder and Woodward, pp. 18–19, 120; *Roll Call*, September 17, 1992.

[23] Quayle, *Standing Firm*, pp. 74–76, 91–92; Dowd, p. 36; Dan Quayle to Senator Mark O. Hatfield, June 1995, Senate Historical Office files.

[24] *Washington Post*, December 3, 1988; Quayle to Hatfield, June 1995.

[25] Quayle, *Standing Firm*, pp. 77–78; Broder and Woodward, pp. 155–74; Marilyn T. Quayle and Nancy T. Northcott, *Embrace the Serpent* (New York, 1992).

[26] Broder and Woodward, pp. 90–91; Quayle, *Standing Firm*, p. 105.

[27] Broder and Woodward, pp. 91–92, 125–52; Quayle, *Standing Firm*, pp. 177–90.

[28] Broder and Woodward, p. 101; Quayle, *Standing Firm*, pp. 189–203.

[29] Quayle, *Standing Firm*, pp. 145–239; Bob Woodward, *The Commanders* (New York, 1991), pp. 146–53.

[30] Quayle, *Standing Firm*, p. 219; see also Paul G. Kengor, "The Role of the Vice President During the Crisis in the Persian Gulf," *Presidential Studies Quarterly* 24 (Fall 1994).

[31] Broder and Woodward, p. 10.

[32] *Washington Post*, May 6, 1991; Quayle, *Standing Firm*, pp. 251–63.

[33] Quayle, *Standing Firm*, pp. 131–32, 315–36; Dan Quayle, "Restoring Basic Values," *Vital Speeches of the Day* 58 (June 15, 1992), pp. 517–20.

[34] Quayle, *Standing Firm*, pp. 255–56; 337–46; *Washington Post*, July 2, August 19, 1992.

[35] Quayle, *Standing Firm*, pp. 337–38, 351–53; *Washington Post*, October 15, 1992.

[36] Quayle, *Standing Firm*, p. 356; *Washington Post*, January 13, 1993, February 10, 1995.

[37] U.S., Congress, Senate, *Congressional Record*, 103d Cong., 1st sess., January 27, 1993, p. S771; Bush, p. 447.

APPENDIX

Major Party Presidential and Vice-Presidential Candidates

Election Year	Winners/Party	Losers/Party
1788	George Washington (Federalist) John Adams	
1792	George Washington (Federalist) John Adams	
1796	John Adams (Federalist) Thomas Jefferson	Thomas Jefferson (Republican) [1]
1800	Thomas Jefferson (Republican) Aaron Burr [2]	John Adams (Federalist) Charles C. Pinckney
1804	Thomas Jefferson (Republican) George Clinton	Charles C. Pinckney (Federalist) Rufus King
1808	James Madison (Republican) George Clinton	Charles C. Pinckney (Federalist) Rufus King
1812	James Madison (Republican) Elbridge Gerry	DeWitt Clinton (Federalist) Jared Ingersoll
1816	James Monroe (Republican) Daniel Tompkins	Rufus King (Federalist) John E. Howard
1820	James Monroe (Republican) Daniel Tompkins	J. Q. Adams (Republican) [3] Richard Stockton
1824	J.Q. Adams (National Republican) [4] John C. Calhoun	Andrew Jackson (Republican) John C. Calhoun
1828	Andrew Jackson (Democrat) [5] John C. Calhoun	J.Q. Adams (National Republican) Richard Rush
1832	Andrew Jackson (Democrat) Martin Van Buren	Henry Clay (National Republican) John Sergeant
1836	Martin Van Buren (Democrat) Richard M. Johnson [6]	W. H. Harrison/Daniel Webster/H.L. White (Whig—regional candidates) [7] Francis Granger/John Tyler
1840	W.H. Harrison (Whig) John Tyler [8]	Martin Van Buren (Democrat) Richard M. Johnson [9]

Election Year	Winners/Party	Losers/Party
1844	James K. Polk (Democrat) George M. Dallas	Henry Clay (Whig) Theodore Frelinghuysen
1848	Zachary Taylor (Whig) Millard Fillmore	Lewis Cass (Democrat) William O. Butler
1852	Franklin Pierce (Democrat) William R. King	Winfield Scott (Whig) William A. Graham
1856	James Buchanan (Democrat) John C. Breckinridge	John C. Frémont (Republican) William L. Dayton
1860	Abraham Lincoln (Republican) Hannibal Hamlin	Stephen A. Douglas (Democrat)[10] Herschel V. Johnson
1864	Abraham Lincoln (Republican) Andrew Johnson[11]	George B. McClellan (Democrat) G. H. Pendleton
1868	Ulysses S. Grant (Republican) Schuyler Colfax	Horatio Seymour (Democrat) Francis P. Blair, Jr.
1872	Ulysses S. Grant (Republican) Henry Wilson	Horace Greeley (Democrat)[12] B. Gratz Brown
1876	Rutherford B. Hayes (Republican) William A. Wheeler	Samuel J. Tilden (Democrat) Thomas Hendricks
1880	James Garfield (Republican) Chester A. Arthur	Winfield S. Hancock (Democrat) William H. English
1884	Grover Cleveland (Democrat) Thomas A. Hendricks	James G. Blaine (Republican) John A. Logan
1888	Benjamin Harrison (Republican) Levi P. Morton	Grover Cleveland (Democrat) Allen G. Thurman
1892	Grover Cleveland (Democrat) Adlai E. Stevenson	Benjamin Harrison (Republican) Whitelaw Reid
1896	William McKinley (Republican) Garret A. Hobart	William J. Bryan (Democrat) Arthur Sewall
1900	William McKinley (Republican) Theodore Roosevelt	William J. Bryan (Democrat) Adlai E. Stevenson
1904	Theodore Roosevelt (Republican) Charles W. Fairbanks	Alton B. Parker (Democrat) Henry G. Davis
1908	William H. Taft (Republican) James S. Sherman	William J. Bryan (Democrat) John W. Kern

APPENDIX

Election Year	Winners/Party	Losers/Party
1912	Woodrow Wilson (Democrat) Thomas R. Marshall	Theodore Roosevelt (Progressive) [13] Hiram W. Johnson
1916	Woodrow Wilson (Democrat) Thomas R. Marshall	Charles E. Hughes (Republican) Charles W. Fairbanks
1920	Warren G. Harding (Republican) Calvin Coolidge	James M. Cox (Democrat) Franklin D. Roosevelt
1924	Calvin Coolidge (Republican) Charles G. Dawes	John W. Davis (Democrat) [14] Charles W. Bryan
1928	Herbert C. Hoover (Republican) Charles Curtis	Alfred E. Smith (Democrat) Joseph T. Robinson
1932	Franklin D. Roosevelt (Democrat) John N. Garner	Herbert C. Hoover (Republican) Charles Curtis
1936	Franklin D. Roosevelt (Democrat) John N. Garner	Alfred M. Landon (Republican) Frank Knox
1940	Franklin D. Roosevelt (Democrat) Henry A. Wallace	Wendell L. Willkie (Republican) Charles L. McNary
1944	Franklin D. Roosevelt (Democrat) Harry S. Truman	Thomas E. Dewey (Republican) John W. Bricker
1948	Harry S. Truman (Democrat) Alben W. Barkley	Thomas E. Dewey (Republican) [15] Earl Warren
1952	Dwight D. Eisenhower (Repub.) Richard M. Nixon	Adlai E. Stevenson (Democrat) John J. Sparkman
1956	Dwight D. Eisenhower (Repub.) Richard M. Nixon	Adlai E. Stevenson (Democrat) Estes Kefauver
1960	John F. Kennedy (Democrat) Lyndon B. Johnson	Richard M. Nixon (Republican) Henry Cabot Lodge, Jr.
1964	Lyndon B. Johnson (Democrat) Hubert H. Humphrey	Barry M. Goldwater (Republican) William E. Miller
1968	Richard M. Nixon (Republican) Spiro T. Agnew	Hubert H. Humphrey (Democrat) Edmund S. Muskie
1972	Richard M. Nixon (Republican) Spiro T. Agnew	George S. McGovern (Democrat) R. Sargent Shriver [16]
1976	Jimmy Carter (Democrat) Walter F. Mondale	Gerald R. Ford (Republican) Robert J. Dole

APPENDIX

Election Year	Winners/Party	Losers/Party
1980	Ronald Reagan (Republican) George Bush	Jimmy Carter (Democrat) Walter F. Mondale
1984	Ronald Reagan (Republican) George Bush	Walter F. Mondale Geraldine Ferraro
1988	George Bush (Republican) Dan Quayle	Michael S. Dukakis (Democrat) Lloyd Bentsen
1992	Bill Clinton (Democrat) Al Gore, Jr.	George Bush (Republican) Dan Quayle

NOTES

[1] Jefferson ran against Adams for president. Since he received the second highest electoral vote, he automatically became vice president under the system that existed at the time. (See note 2.) "Republican" refers to two different parties widely separated in time: Jeffersonian Republicans of the late eighteenth and early nineteenth centuries, and the present Republican party, which was founded in the 1850s. The election dates should make clear which of the two parties is intended.

[2] In the nation's early years, electors did not differentiate between their votes for president and vice president, and the runner-up for president became vice president. In 1800 Jefferson and Burr each received 73 electoral votes, thus sending the election to the House of Representatives, which selected Jefferson as president. Burr automatically became vice president. This stalemate led to ratification of the Twelfth Amendment to the Constitution in 1804.

[3] By 1820 the Federalist party was defunct, and a period of party realignment began that continued until 1840 when the Whig and Democratic parties became established. In the interim, party affiliations underwent considerable flux. For much of that time, the split fell between the supporters and opponents of Andrew Jackson. The pro-Jackson forces evolved into the Democratic party, while those opposing Jackson eventually coalesced into the Whig party.

[4] All the presidential candidates in 1824 were Republicans—although of varying persuasions—and Calhoun had support for the vice-presidency from both the Adams and Jackson camps. As no presidential candidate received the necessary majority of electoral votes, the House of Representatives made the decision. Calhoun, however, received a clear majority (182 of 260) of the vice-presidential electoral votes.

[5] The Democratic party was not yet formally created during Jackson's two terms as president but developed later from his supporters. (See note 3.)

[6] As no vice-presidential candidate received a majority of electoral votes in 1836, the Senate for the only time in its history selected the vice president.

[7] For a discussion of the early origins of the Whig party in the 1836 election, see Chapter 9, "Richard Mentor Johnson," p. 127, and Chapter 10, "John Tyler," p. 139.

[8] Although Tyler ran on the Whig ticket, he remained a Democrat throughout his life.

[9] The Democratic party initially failed to nominate a vice-presidential candidate in 1840 but ultimately backed Johnson. (See Chapter 9, p. 130.)

[10] John C. Breckinridge and Joseph Lane were the presidential and vice-presidential nominees of the Southern Democratic party that year. John Bell and Edward Everett ran on the Constitutional Union party ticket.

[11] Johnson was a War Democrat, who ran on a fusion ticket with Republican President Abraham Lincoln. (See Chapter 16, p. 215.)

[12] Also the candidates of the Liberal Republican party.

[13] William Howard Taft and James S. Sherman were the Republican presidential and vice-presidential candidates.

[14] Robert M. La Follette and Burton K. Wheeler were the presidential and vice-presidential nominees of the Progressive party that year.

[15] J. Strom Thurmond and Fielding L. Wright were the presidential and vice-presidential nominees of the States' Rights Democratic party that year.

[16] Added to the ticket on August 8, 1972, after the resignation of Thomas Eagleton.

SELECTED BIBLIOGRAPHY

This selected bibliography includes general works dealing with the history of the vice-presidency as well as studies and published works of the individuals who have served as vice president from 1789 to 1993. "Campaign biographies" are not included, except for those vice presidents who lack more scholarly biographies. Period histories are omitted, but presidential histories likely to provide useful background information are listed as appropriate. The voluminous literature dealing with the Twenty-fifth Amendment is not included.

GENERAL REFERENCES

Bayh, Birch. *One Heartbeat Away: Presidential Disability and Succession*. Indianapolis, 1968.

Cantor, Joseph E. "The Vice Presidency and the Vice Presidents: A Selected Annotated Bibliography." Congressional Research Service Report No. 84–124 L, October 1, 1976. Revised July 31, 1984 by George H. Walser.

David, Paul D. "The Vice Presidency: Its Institutional Evolution and Contemporary Status." *Journal of Politics* 29 (November 1967): 721–48.

Dorman, Michael. *The Second Man: The Changing Role of the Vice Presidency*. New York, 1968.

Feerick, John. *From Failing Hands*. New York, 1965.

———. "The Problem of Presidential Inability—Will Congress Ever Solve It." *Fordham Law Review* 32 (1963): 73–134.

———. *The Twenty-Fifth Amendment*. New York, 1976.

Ferrell, Robert H. *Ill Advised: Presidential Health and Public Trust*. Columbia, MO, 1992.

Goldstein, Joel L. *The Modern American Vice Presidency: The Transformation of a Political Institution*. Princeton, NJ, 1982.

Graf, Henry F. "A Heartbeat Away." *American Heritage* 15 (August 1964).

Hatch, Louis C., and Shoup, Earl L. *A History of the Vice-Presidency of the United States*. New York, 1934.

Kiser, George C. "Presidential Primaries: Stepping-Stones to the Vice Presidential Nomination?" *Presidential Studies Quarterly* 22 (Summer 1992): 493–517.

Learned, Henry B. "Casting Votes of the Vice Presidents, 1789–1915." *American Historical Review* 20 (April 1915): 571–76.

———. "Some Aspects of the Vice Presidency." *American Political Science Review* 7 (February 1913 supp.): 162–77.

Medina, J. Michael. "The American Vice President: Toward a More Utilized Institution." *George Mason University Law Review* 13 (Fall 1990): 77–111.

Paullin, Charles O. "The Vice President and the Cabinet." *American Historical Review* 29 (April 1924): 496–500.

Tompkins, Dorothy C. *The Office of Vice President: A Selected Bibliography*. Berkeley, CA, 1957.

Waugh, Edgar Wiggins. *Second Consul: The Vice-Presidency: Our Greatest Political Problem*. Indianapolis, 1956.

Wilhelm, Stephen J. "The Origins of the Office of the Vice Presidency." *Presidential Studies Quarterly* 7 (Fall 1977): 208–14.

Williams, Irving G. *The American Vice-Presidency: New Look*. Garden City, NY, 1954.

———. "Senators, Rules, and Vice-Presidents." *Thought Patterns* 5 (1957): 21–35.

———. *The Rise of the Vice Presidency*. Washington, 1956.

Witcover, Jules. *Crapshoot: Rolling the Dice on the Vice-presidency*. New York, 1992.

Young, Donald. *American Roulette: The History and Dilemma of the Vice Presidency*. New York, 1974.

Young, Klyde, and Lamar Middleton. *Heirs Apparent: The Vice Presidents of the United States*. 1948. Reprint. Freeport, NY, 1969.

JOHN ADAMS (Chapter 1)

Adams, John. *Diary and Autobiography*. Edited by Lyman H. Butterfield. 4 vols. Cambridge, MA, 1961.

Adams, John. *Papers of John Adams*. Edited by Robert J. Taylor, Mary-Jo Kline, Gregg L. Lint, et al. 8 vols. Cambridge, MA, 1977–1989.

Bowling, Kenneth R., and Veit, Helen E. *The Diary of William Maclay and Other Notes on Senate Debates. Documentary History of the First Federal Congress, 1789–1791*, vol. 9. Baltimore, 1988.

Dauer, Manning J. *The Adams Federalists*. 1953. Reprint. Baltimore, 1968.

Ellis, Joseph J. *Passionate Sage: The Character and Legacy of John Adams*. New York, 1993.

Ferling, John. *John Adams: A Life*. Knoxville, TN, 1992.

Guerrero, Linda Dudik. "John Adams' Vice Presidency, 1789–1797: The Neglected Man in the Forgotten Office."

SELECTED BIBLIOGRAPHY

Ph.D. dissertation, University of California, Santa Barbara, 1978.

Howe, John R., Jr. *The Changing Political Thought of John Adams*. Princeton, NJ, 1966.

Hutson, James H. "John Adams' Titles Campaign." *New England Quarterly* 41 (1968): 34–41.

Shaw, Peter. *The Character of John Adams*. Chapel Hill, NC, 1976.

Smith, Page. *John Adams*. 2 vols. 1962–1963. Reprint. Norwalk, CT, 1988.

THOMAS JEFFERSON (Chapter 2)

Brown, Ralph Adams. *The Presidency of John Adams*. Lawrence, KS, 1975.

Cunningham, Noble E., Jr. *The Jeffersonian Republicans: The Formation of Party Organization, 1789–1801*. Chapel Hill, NC, 1957.

Gibbs, George. *Memoirs of the Administrations of Washington and John Adams*. 2 vols. New York, 1846.

U.S. Congress. Senate. *A Manual of Parliamentary Practice*, by Thomas Jefferson. 1801. Reprint. S. Doc., 103–8, 102d Cong., 2d sess., 1993.

Jefferson, Thomas. *The Life and Selected Writings of Thomas Jefferson*. Edited, and with an introduction by Adrienne Koch and William Peden. New York, 1944.

————. *The Writings of Thomas Jefferson*. Edited by Paul Leicester Ford. 10 vols. New York, 1892–1899.

Kurtz, Stephen G. *The Presidency of John Adams: The Collapse of Federalism, 1795–1800*. Philadelphia, 1975.

Malone, Dumas. *Jefferson and the Ordeal of Liberty. Jefferson and His Time*, vol. 3. Boston, 1962.

Peterson, Merrill D. *Thomas Jefferson and the New Nation: A Biography*. 1970. Reprint. Norwalk, CT, 1987.

AARON BURR (Chapter 3)

Abernethy, Thomas Perkins. *The Burr Conspiracy*. 1954. Reprint. Gloucester, MA, 1968.

Alexander, Holmes Moss. *Aaron Burr, the Proud Pretender*. 1937. Reprint. Westport, CT, 1973.

Burr, Aaron. *Memoirs of Aaron Burr*. 2 vols. 1836–1837. Reprint. New York, 1971.

Cunningham, Noble E., Jr. *The Jeffersonian Republicans in Power: Party Operations, 1801–1809*. Chapel Hill, NC, 1963.

————. *The Process of Government Under Jefferson*. Princeton, NJ, 1978.

Harrison, Lowell. "John Breckinridge and the Vice-Presidency, 1804: A Poltical Episode." *Filson Club History Quarterly* 26 (April 1952): 155–65.

Kline, Mary-Jo, and Joanne Wood Ryan, eds. *Papers of Aaron Burr*. Ann Arbor, MI, 1978–1981. Microfilm, 27 reels and guide, 1 supplemental reel.

————. *The Political Correspondence and Public Papers of Aaron Burr*. 2 vols. Princeton, NJ, 1983.

Lomask, Milton. *Aaron Burr*. 2 vols. New York, 1979–1982.

Malone, Dumas. *Jefferson the President: First Term, 1801–1805. Jefferson and His Time*, vol. 4. Boston, 1970.

Mitchill, Samuel Latham. "Dr. Mitchill's Letters from Washington, 1801–1813." *Harper's New Monthly Magazine* 58 (April 1879): 740–55.

Pancake, John S. "Aaron Burr: Would-Be Usurper." *William and Mary Quarterly* 8 (April 1951).

Parmet, Herbert S., and Marie B. Hecht. *Aaron Burr: Portrait of An Ambitious Man*. New York, 1967.

Plumer, William. *William Plumer's Memorandum of Proceedings in the United States Senate, 1803–1807*. Edited by Everett S. Brown. 1923. Reprint. New York, 1969.

Reports of the Trials of Colonel Aaron Burr. David Robertson, Reporter. 1808. Reprint. New York, 1969.

Slaughter, Thomas P. "Conspiratorial Politics: The Public Life of Aaron Burr." *New Jersey History* 103 (Spring/Summer 1985): 69–81.

Thomas, Gordon L. "Aaron Burr's Farewell Address." *Quarterly Journal of Speech* 39 (1953).

GEORGE CLINTON (Chapter 4)

Cunningham, Noble E., Jr. *The Jeffersonian Republicans in Power: Party Operations, 1801–1809*. Chapel Hill, NC, 1963.

————. *The Process of Government Under Jefferson*. Princeton, NJ, 1978.

Kaminski, John P. *George Clinton: Yeoman Politician of the New Republic*. Madison, WI, 1993.

Malone, Dumas. *Jefferson the President: Second Term, 1805–1809. Jefferson and His Time*, vol. 5. Boston, 1974.

Plumer, William. *William Plumer's Memorandum of Proceedings in the United States Senate,1803–1807*. Edited by Everett S. Brown. 1923. Reprint. New York, 1969.

Rutland, Robert Allen. *The Presidency of James Madison*. Lawrence, KS, 1990.

Spaulding, Ernest Wilder. *His Excellency George Clinton, Critic of the Constitution*. 1938. Reprint. Port Washington, NY, 1964.

ELBRIDGE GERRY (Chapter 5)

Austin, James T. *The Life of Elbridge Gerry*. 2 vols. 1828–1829. Reprint. New York, 1970.

Billias, George Athan. *Elbridge Gerry, Founding Father and Republican Statesman*. New York, 1976.

Learned, Henry B. "Gerry and the Presidential Succession in 1813." *American Historical Review* 22 (October, 1916): 94–97.

Rutland, Robert Allen. *The Presidency of James Madison*. Lawrence, KS, 1990.

SELECTED BIBLIOGRAPHY

DANIEL D. TOMPKINS (Chapter 6)

Ammon, Harry. *James Monroe: The Quest for National Identity*. 1971. Reprint. Charlottesville, VA, 1990.

Irwin, Ray W. *Daniel D. Tompkins: Governor of New York and Vice President of the UnitedStates*. New York, 1968.

Jenkins, John S. *Lives of the Governors of New York*. Auburn, NY, 1852.

Mooney, Chase C. *William Crawford, 1772–1834*. Lexington, KY, 1974.

Rayback, Joseph G. "A Myth Re-examined: Martin Van Buren's Roles in the Presidential Election of 1816." *Proceedings of the American Philosophical Society* 124 (April 29, 1980): 106–18.

Remini, Robert V. "New York and the Presidential Election of 1816." *New York History* 31 (1950).

Tompkins, Daniel D. *Public Papers of Daniel D. Tompkins, Governor of New York, 1807–1817*. 3 vols. New York, 1898–1902.

JOHN CALDWELL CALHOUN (Chapter 7)

Capers, Gerald M. *John C. Calhoun, Opportunist: A Re-Appraisal*. Gainesville, FL, 1960.

Coit, Margaret L. *John C. Calhoun: American Portrait*. 1950. Reprint, with new introduction by Clyde N. Wilson. Columbia, SC, 1991.

Cole, Donald B. *The Presidency of Andrew Jackson*. Lawrence, KS, 1993.

Ewing, Gretchen Garst. "Duff Green, John C. Calhoun, and the Election of 1828." *South Carolina Historical Magazine* 79 (April 1978): 126–37.

Hay, Robert P. "The Pillorying of Albert Gallatin: The Public Response to His 1824 Vice-Presidential Nomination." *Western Pennsylvania Historical Magazine* 65 (June 1982): 181–202.

Hay, Thomas R. "John C. Calhoun and the Presidential Campaign of 1824." *North Carolina Historical Review* 12 (1935): 20–44.

Meriwether, Robert M., W. Edwin Hemphill, and Clyde N. Wilson, eds. *The Papers of John C. Calhoun*. 22 vols. to date. Columbia, SC, 1987.

Niven, John. *John C. Calhoun and the Price of Union*. Baton Rouge, LA, 1988.

Peterson, Merrill D. *The Great Triumvirate: Webster, Clay and Calhoun*. New York, 1987.

"Sketch of the Life of J.C. Calhoun, Vice-President of the United States." *The Casket* 3 (March 1827): 81–82.

Stenberg, Richard R. "The Jefferson Birthday Dinner, 1830." *Journal of Southern History* 4 (1938): 334–46.

————. "A Note on the Jackson-Calhoun Breach of 1830–1831." *Tyler's Quarterly Historical and Genealogical Magazine* 21 (1939): 480–96.

Wiltse, Charles M. *John C. Calhoun*. 3 vols. 1944–1951. Reprint. New York, 1968.

MARTIN VAN BUREN (Chapter 8)

Cole, Donald B. *Martin Van Buren and the American Political System*. Princeton, NJ, 1984.

————. *The Presidency of Andrew Jackson*. Lawrence, KS, 1993.

Curtis, James C. "In the Shadow of Old Hickory: The Political Travail of Martin Van Buren." *Journal of the Early Republic* 1 (Fall 1981): 249–68.

Fitzpatrick, John C., ed. *The Autobiography of Martin Van Buren*. 2 vols. 1920. Reprint. New York, 1973. Originally published as *American Historical Association Annual Report for the Year 1918*, vol. 2.

Gammon, Samuel Rhea, Jr. *The Presidential Campaign of 1832*. Baltimore, 1922.

Mintz, Max M. "The Political Ideas of Martin Van Buren." *New York History* 30 (October 1949): 422–48.

Moody, Robert D. "The Influence of Martin Van Buren on the Career and Acts of Andrew Jackson." *Papers of the Michigan Academy of Science, Arts and Letters* 7 (1926): 225–40.

Niven, John. *Martin Van Buren: The Romantic Age in American Politics*. New York, 1983.

Remini, Robert V. *Andrew Jackson and the Course of American Democracy, 1833–1845*. New York, 1984.

————. *Martin Van Buren and the Making of the Democratic Party*. New York, 1959.

RICHARD MENTOR JOHNSON (Chapter 9)

Bolt, Robert. "Vice-President Richard M. Johnson of Kentucky: Hero of the Thames—or the Great Amalgamator?" *Register of the Kentucky Historical Society* 74 (July 1977): 191–203.

Brown, Thomas. "The Miscegenation of Richard Mentor Johnson as an Issue in the National Election Campaign of 1835–1836." *Civil War History* 29 (1993): 5–30.

Curtis, James C. *The Fox at Bay: Martin Van Buren and the Presidency, 1837–1841*. Lexington, KY, 1970.

Meyer, Leland Winfield. *The Life and Times of Colonel Richard M. Johnson of Kentucky*. 1932. Reprint. New York, 1967.

Niven, John. *Martin Van Buren: The Romantic Age of American Politics*. New York, 1983.

Padgett, James A., ed. "The Letters of Colonel Richard M. Johnson of Kentucky." *Register of the Kentucky Historical Society* 38 (1940): 186–201, 323–39; 39 (1941): 22–46, 172–88, 260–74, 358–67; 40 (1942): 69–91.

Schlesinger, Arthur M., Jr. *The Age of Jackson*. Boston, 1945.

Sprague, Stuart S. "The Death of Tecumseh and the Rise of Rumpsey Dumpsey: The Making of a Vice President." *Filson Club History Quarterly* 59 (October 1985): 455–61.

Williams, Major L. *The Presidency of Martin Van Buren*. Lawrence, KS, 1984.

SELECTED BIBLIOGRAPHY

JOHN TYLER (Chapter 10)

Adams, John Quincy. *The Diary of John Quincy Adams, 1794–1845: American Diplomacy, and Political, Social and Intellectual Life from Washington to Polk.* Edited by Alan Nevins. 1928. Reprint of 1951 ed. New York, 1969.

Chitwood, Oliver P. *John Tyler, Champion of the Old South.* 1939. Reprint. New York, 1964.

Leigh, Benjamin Watkins. "John Tyler and the Vice Presidency." *Tyler's Quarterly Historical and Genealogical Magazine* 9 (July 1927).

Seager, Robert. *And Tyler Too: A Biography of John & Julia Gardner Tyler.* New York, 1963.

Shelley, Fred, ed. "The Vice President Receives Bad News in Williamsburg: A Letter of James Lyons to John Tyler." *Virginia Magazine of History and Biography* 76 (1968): 337–39.

Stathis, Stephen W. "John Tyler's Presidential Succession: A Reappraisal." *Prologue* 8 (Winter, 1976): 223–36.

Tyler, Lyon Gardner, ed. *The Letters and Times of the Tylers.* 3 vols. 1884–1886. Reprint. New York, 1970.

GEORGE MIFFLIN DALLAS (Chapter 11)

Ambacher, Bruce I. "George M. Dallas: Leader of the 'Family' Party." Ph.D. dissertation, Temple University, 1971.

————. "George M. Dallas and the Bank War." *Pennsylvania History* 42 (April 1975): 117–35.

Belohlavek, John M. *George Mifflin Dallas: Jacksonian Patrician.* University Park, PA, 1977.

Bergeron, Paul H. *The Presidency of James K. Polk.* Lawrence, KS, 1987.

Burt, Struthers. "George Mifflin Dallas [1792–1864]: The Other Vice-President from Princeton." In *The Lives of Eighteen from Princeton,* edited by Willard Thorp, pp. 178–91. 1946. Reprint. Freeport, NY, 1968.

Dallas, George Mifflin. *Diary of George Mifflin Dallas, United States Minister to Russia, 1837–1839.* 1892. Reprint. New York, 1970.

Nichols, Roy, ed. "The Library: The Mystery of the Dallas Papers." *Pennsylvania Magazine of History and Biography* 73: 349–92, 475–517.

MILLARD FILLMORE (Chapter 12)

Barre, W. L. *The Life and Public Services of Millard Fillmore.* 1856. Reprint. New York, 1971.

Dix, Dorothea Lynde. *The Lady and the President: The Letters of Dorothea Dix & Millard Fillmore.* Lexington, KY, 1975.

Fillmore, Millard. *Millard Fillmore Papers.* Edited by Frank Hayward Severence. 2 vols. Buffalo, NY, 1907.

————. *Millard Fillmore Papers.* Edited by Lester W. Smith. Buffalo, NY, 1975. Microfilm. 68 reels and guide.

Rayback, Robert J. *Millard Fillmore: Biography of a President.* Buffalo, NY, 1959.

WILLIAM RUFUS KING (Chapter 13)

Martin, John M. "William R. King and the Vice Presidency." *Alabama Review* 16 (January 1963): 35–54.

Martin, John M. "William Rufus King: Southern Moderate." Ph.D. dissertation, University of North Carolina, 1955.

————. "William R. King: Jacksonian Senator." *Alabama Review* 18 (October 1985).

U.S. Congress. *Obituary Addresses.* 33d Congress, 1st session, 1853–1854. Washington, 1854.

JOHN CABELL BRECKINRIDGE (Chapter 14)

Davis, William C. *Breckinridge: Statesman, Soldier, Symbol.* Baton Rouge, LA, 1974.

Harrison, Lowell H. "John C. Breckinridge: Nationalist, Confederate, Kentuckian." *Filson Club History Quarterly* 47 (April 1973): 125–44.

Heck, Frank H. "John C. Breckinridge in the Crisis of 1860–1861." *Journal of Southern History* 21 (August 1955): 316–46.

————. *Proud Kentuckian, John C. Breckinridge, 1821–1875.* Lexington, KY, 1976.

O'Connor, John R. "John Cabell Breckinridge's Personal Secession: A Rhetorical Insight." *Filson Club History Quarterly* 43 (October 1969): 345–52.

Stillwell, Lucille. *Born to Be a Statesman: John Cabell Breckinridge.* Caldwell, ID, 1936.

HANNIBAL HAMLIN (Chapter 15)

Fite, Emerson David. *The Presidential Campaign of 1860.* 1911. Reprint. Port Washington, NY, 1967.

Hamlin, Charles Eugene. *The Life and Times of Hannibal Hamlin.* 2 vols. 1899. Reprint. Port Washington, NY, 1971.

Hunt, H. Draper. *Hannibal Hamlin of Maine: Lincoln's First Vice-President.* Syracuse, NY, 1969.

————. "President Lincoln's First Vice President: Hannibal Hamlin of Maine." *Lincoln Herald* 88 (Winter 1986): 137–44.

Luthin, Reinhard H. *The First Lincoln Campaign.* 1944. Reprint. Gloucester, MA, 1964.

Scroggins, Mark. *Hannibal: The Life of Abraham Lincoln's First Vice President.* Lanham, MD, 1993.

ANDREW JOHNSON (Chapter 16)

Benedict, Michael Les. *The Impeachment and Trial of Andrew Johnson.* New York, 1972.

DeWitt, David M. "Vice President Andrew Johnson." *Publications of the Southern History Association* 8 (November 1904): 437–42; 9 (January 1905): 1–23, (March 1905): 71–86, (May 1905): 151–59, (July 1905): 213–25.

Glonek, James F. "Lincoln, Johnson, and the Baltimore Ticket." *Abraham Lincoln Quarterly* 6 (March 1951): 255–71.

Graf, LeRoy P., Ralph W. Haskins, Paul H. Bergeron, eds. *The Papers of Andrew Johnson.* 12 vols. to date. Knoxville, TN, 1967– .

SELECTED BIBLIOGRAPHY

Hardison, Edwin T. "In the Toils of War: Andrew Johnson and the Federal Occupation of Tennessee." Ph.D. dissertation, University of North Carolina, 1981.

Harris, William C. "Andrew Johnson's First 'Swing Around the Circle': His Northern Campaign of 1863." *Civil War History* 35 (June 1989): 153–71.

McCulloch, Hugh. *Men and Measures of Half a Century: Sketches and Comments.* New York, 1888.

Trefousse, Hans L. *Andrew Johnson: A Biography.* New York, 1989.

SCHUYLER COLFAX (Chapter 17)
Hesseltine, William Best. *Ulysses S. Grant, Politician.* 1935. Reprint. New York, 1957.

Hollister, Ovando J. *Life of Schuyler Colfax.* New York, 1886.

McFeely, William S. *Grant: A Biography.* New York, 1981.

Smith, Willard H. *Schuyler Colfax: The Changing Fortunes of a Political Idol.* Indianapolis, 1952.

HENRY WILSON (Chapter 18)
Abbott, Richard. *Cobbler in Congress: The Life of Henry Wilson, 1812–1875.* Lexington, KY, 1972.

Hesseltine, William Best. *Ulysses S. Grant, Politician.* 1935. Reprint. New York, 1957.

McFeely, William S. *Grant: A Biography.* New York, 1981.

McKay, Ernest. *Henry Wilson: Practical Radical; A Portrait of a Politician.* Port Washington, NY, 1971.

———. "Henry Wilson and the Coalition of 1851." *New England Quarterly* 36 (1963): 338–57.

Nason, Elias, and Thomas Russell. *The Life and Public Services of Henry Wilson, Late Vice-President of the United States.* 1876. Reprint. New York, 1969.

U.S. Congress. *Memorial Addresses.* 44th Congress, 1st session, 1875–1876. Washington, 1876.

Wilson, Henry. *History of the Rise and Fall of the Slave Power in America.* 3 vols. 1872–1877. Reprint. New York, 1969.

WILLIAM ALMON WHEELER (Chapter 19)
Davison, Kenneth E. *The Presidency of Rutherford B. Hayes.* Westport, CT, 1972.

Hoogenboom, Ari Arthur. *The Presidency of Rutherford B. Hayes.* Lawrence, KS, 1988.

Howells, William Dean. *Sketch of the Life and Character of Rutherford B. Hayes: Also A Biographical Sketch of William A. Wheeler.* 1876. Reprint. Folcroft, PA, 1977.

Otten, James T. "Grand Old Partyman: William A. Wheeler and the Republican Party, 1850–1880." Ph.D. dissertation, University of South Carolina, 1976.

CHESTER ALAN ARTHUR (Chapter 20)
Arthur, Chester Alan. *Chester A. Arthur Papers.* Microfilm. 3 reels. Washington, 1959.

Doenecke, Justus D. *The Presidencies of James A. Garfield and Chester A. Arthur.* Lawrence, KS, 1981.

Howe, George Frederick. *Chester A. Arthur, A Quarter-Century of Machine Politics.* 1935. Reprint. New York, 1957.

Memorial Sketch of Lafayette S. Foster, United States Senator from Connecticut, and Acting Vice-President of the United States. Boston, 1881.

Reeves, Thomas C. *Gentleman Boss: The Life of Chester Alan Arthur.* New York, 1975.

Schwartz, Sybil. "In Defense of Chester Arthur." *Wilson Quarterly* 2 (Autumn 1978): 180–84.

THOMAS ANDREWS HENDRICKS (Chapter 21)
Gray, Ralph D. "Thomas A. Hendricks: Spokesman for the Democracy." In *Gentlemen from Indiana: National Party Candidates, 1836–1940,* edited by Ralph D. Gray, pp. 117–39. Indianapolis, 1977.

Hensel, William. "A Biographical Sketch of Thomas A. Hendricks, Nominee for the Vice-Presidency of the United States." In *Life and Public Services of Hon. Grover Cleveland,* by William Dorshimer. Philadelphia, 1884.

Holcombe, John Walker, and Hubert Marshall Skinner. *Life and Public Services of Thomas A. Hendricks, With Selected Speeches and Writings.* Indianapolis, 1886.

U.S. Congress. *Memorial Addresses.* 49th Congress, 1st session, 1885–1886. Washington, 1886.

LEVI PARSONS MORTON (Chapter 22)
Harney, Gilbert L. *The Lives of Benjamin Harrison and Levi P. Morton.* Providence, RI, 1888.

Katz, Irving. "Investment Bankers in American Government and Politics: The Political Activities of William C. Corcoran, August Belmont, Sr., Levi P. Morton, and Henry Lee Higginson." Ph.D. dissertation, New York University, 1964.

McElroy, Robert McNutt. *Levi Parsons Morton: Banker, Diplomat, and Statesman.* 1930. Reprint. New York, 1975.

Testimonial to Vice-President Levi P. Morton, Upon His Retirement from Office on March 4, 1893. Concord, NH, 1893.

ADLAI EWING STEVENSON (Chapter 23)
Baker, Jean H. *The Stevensons: A Biography of an American Family.* New York, 1996.

Schlup, Leonard. "The Political Career of the First Adlai E. Stevenson." Ph.D. dissertation, University of Illinois at Urbana-Champaign, 1973.

———. "The Congressional Career of the First Adlai E. Stevenson." *Illinois Quarterly* 38 (Winter 1975): 5–19.

———. "Vilas, Stevenson, and Democratic Politics, 1883–1892." *North Dakota Quarterly* 44 (Winter 1976): 44–52.

———. "Adlai E. Stevenson and the 1892 Campaign in Alabama." *Alabama Review* 29 (January 1976): 3–15.

———. "Adlai E. Stevenson's Campaign Visits to West Virginia." *West Virginia History* 38 (January 1977): 126–35.

————. "Adlai E. Stevenson and the Presidential Election of 1896." *Social Science Journal* 14 (April 1977): 117–28.

————. "Grover Cleveland and His 1892 Running Mate." *Studies in History and Society* 2 (Fall 1977): 60–74.

————. "Adlai E. Stevenson's Campaign Visits to Kentucky in 1892." *Register of the Kentucky Historical Society* 75 (April 1977): 112–20.

————. "Adlai E. Stevenson and the 1892 Campaign in Virginia." *Virginia Magazine of History and Biography* 86 (July 1978): 345–54.

————. "Democratic Talleyrand: Adlai E. Stevenson and Politics in the Gilded Age and Progressive Era." *South Atlantic Quarterly* 78 (Spring 1979): 182–94.

————. "Presidential Disability: The Case of Cleveland and Stevenson." *Presidential Studies Quarterly* 9 (Summer 1979): 303–10.

————. "Vice-President Stevenson and the Politics of Accommodation." *Journal of Political Science* 7 (Fall 1979): 30–39.

————. "Adlai E. Stevenson and the Southern Campaign of 1892." *Quarterly Review of Historical Studies* 17 (August 1977): 7–14.

————. "Adlai E. Stevenson and Presidential Politics in the Cleveland Era." *International Review of History and Political Science* 16 (August 1979): 1–10.

————. "Gilded Age Politician: Adlai E. Stevenson of Illinois and His Times." *Illinois Historical Journal* 82 (Winter 1989): 219–30.

————. "An American Chameleon: Adlai E. Stevenson and the Quest for the Vice Presidency in Gilded Age Politics." *Presidential Studies Quarterly* 21 (Summer 1991): 511–29.

————. "Adlai E. Stevenson and the 1892 Campaign in North Carolina: A Bourbon Response to Southern Populism." *Southern Studies*, New ser. 2 (Summer 1991): 131–49.

Stevenson, Adlai E. *Something of the Men I have Known: With Some Papers of A General Nature, Political, Historical, and Retrospective.* Chicago, 1909.

GARRET AUGUSTUS HOBART (Chapter 24)

Glynn, Martin H. *In Memoriam. Garret A. Hobart, Vice-President of the United States.* Washington, 1900.

Hobart, Jennie Tuttle (Mrs. Garret A. Hobart). *Memories.* Patterson, NJ, 1930.

Magie, David. *Life of Garret Augustus Hobart, Twenty-fourth Vice President of the United States.* New York, 1910.

Roosevelt, Theodore. "The Three Vice-Presidential Candidates and What They Represent." *Review of Reviews* 14 (September 1896): 289–97.

Russell, Henry Benajah. *The Lives of William McKinley and Garret A. Hobart, Republican Presidential Candidates of 1896.* Hartford, CT, 1896.

U.S. Congress. *Memorial Addresses.* 56th Congress, 1st session, 1899–1900. Washington, 1900.

THEODORE ROOSEVELT (Chapter 25)

Blum, John Morton. *The Republican Roosevelt.* Cambridge, MA, 1954.

Chessman, G. Wallace. *Theodore Roosevelt and the Politics of Power.* Boston, 1969.

————. "Theodore Roosevelt's Campaign Against the Vice-Presidency." *Historian* 14 (Spring 1952).

Gould, Lewis L. "Charles Warren Fairbanks and the Republican National Convention of 1900." *Indiana Magazine of History* 77 (December 1981): 358–72.

Grantham, Dewey W., comp. *Theodore Roosevelt.* Englewood Cliffs, NJ, 1971.

Harbaugh, William Henry. *Power and Responsibility: The Life and Times of Theodore Roosevelt.* New York, 1961.

Lodge, Henry Cabot, and Charles Redmond, eds. *Selections from the Correspondence of Theodore Roosevelt and Henry Cabot Lodge, 1884–1918.* 2 vols. 1925. Reprint. New York, 1971.

Morris, Edmund. *The Rise of Theodore Roosevelt.* New York, 1979.

Pringle, Henry F. *Theodore Roosevelt: A Biography.* 1931. Revised ed. New York, 1954.

Roosevelt, Theodore. *The Letters of Theodore Roosevelt.* Edited by Elting E. Morison and John Blum. 8 vols. Cambridge, MA, 1951–1954.

————. *Theodore Roosevelt, An Autobiography.* 1913. Reprint, with new introduction by Elting Morison. New York, 1985.

————. *The Works of Theodore Roosevelt.* National ed. Edited by Hermann Hagedorn. 20 vols. New York, 1927.

Schlup, Leonard. "Theodore Roosevelt and Adlai Stevenson: An Examination of Differences in 1900." *Theodore Roosevelt Association Journal* (Spring 1989): 2–7.

CHARLES WARREN FAIRBANKS (Chapter 26)

Gould, Lewis L. "Charles Warren Fairbanks and the Republican National Convention of 1900: A Memoir." *Indiana Magazine of History* 77 (December 1981): 358–72.

————. *The Presidency of Theodore Roosevelt.* Lawrence, KS, 1991.

Madison, James H. "Charles Warren Fairbanks and Indiana Republicanism." In *Gentlemen from Indiana: National Party Candidates, 1836–1940,* edited by Ralph Gray. Indianapolis, 1977.

Rissler, Herbert J. "Charles Warren Fairbanks: Conservative Hoosier." Ph.D. dissertation, Indiana University, 1961.

Shipp, Thomas R. "Charles Warren Fairbanks, Republican Candidate for Vice President." *American Monthly Review of Reviews* 30 (August 1904): 176–81.

Slaydon, Ellen Maury. *Washington Wife: Journal of Ellen Maury Slaydon from 1897–1919.* New York, 1963.

Smith, William Henry. *The Life and Speeches of Hon. Charles W. Fairbanks, Republican Candidate for Vice-President.* Indianapolis, 1904.

JAMES SCHOOLCRAFT SHERMAN (Chapter 27)

Coletta, Paolo E. *The Presidency of William Howard Taft.* Lawrence, KS, 1973.

Schlup, Leonard. "The Pulse of Old Guard Politics: James S. Sherman and the 1908 Republican Ticket." *Social Science Quest* 5 (Summer 1988): 9–22.

U.S. Congress. *Memorial Addresses.* 62d Congress, 3d session, 1912–1913. Washington, 1913.

THOMAS RILEY MARSHALL (Chapter 28)

Brown, John R. "Woodrow Wilson's Vice-President: Thomas R. Marshall and the Wilson Administration, 1913–1921." Ph.D. dissertation, Ball State University, 1970.

Canfield, Leon Hardy. *The Presidency of Woodrow Wilson: Prelude to a World in Crisis.* Rutherford, NJ, 1966.

Lincoln, A. "Theodore Roosevelt, Hiram Johnson, and the Vice Presidential Nomination of 1912." *Pacific Historical Review* 28 (August 1959): 267–83.

Marshall, Thomas R. *Recollections of Thomas R. Marshall, Vice-President and Hoosier Philosopher: A Hoosier Salad.* Indianapolis, 1925.

Smith, Gene. *When the Cheering Stopped: The Last Years of Woodrow Wilson.* 1964. Reprint with introduction by Allan Nevins. Alexandria, VA, 1982.

Thomas, Charles M. *Thomas Riley Marshall: Hoosier Statesman.* Oxford, OH, 1939.

CALVIN COOLIDGE (Chapter 29)

Bagby, Wesley M. *The Road to Normalcy: The Presidential Campaign and Election of 1920.* Baltimore, 1962.

———. "The 'Smoke-Filled Room' and the Nomination of Warren G. Harding." *Mississippi Valley Historical Review* 41 (March 1955).

Coolidge, Calvin. *The Autobiography of Calvin Coolidge.* 1929. Reprint. Rutland, VT, 1984.

———. *The Price of Freedom: Speeches and Addresses.* New York, 1924.

Fuess, Claude M. *Calvin Coolidge, The Man From Vermont.* 1940. Reprint of 1965 ed. Westport, CT, 1976.

Margulies, Herbert F. "Senator Irvine Lenroot and the Republican Vice Presidential Nomination of 1920." *Wisconsin Magazine of History* 61 (Autumn 1977): 21–31.

McCoy, Donald R. *Calvin Coolidge: The Quiet President.* 1967. Reprint, with new preface. Lawrence, KS, 1988.

White, William Allen. *A Puritan in Babylon: The Story of Calvin Coolidge.* 1938. Reprint. Gloucester, MA, 1973.

CHARLES GATES DAWES (Chapter 30)

Ackerman, Carl W. *Dawes—The Doer!* New York, 1924.

Dawes, Charles G. *A Journal of the McKinley Years.* Chicago, 1950.

———. *Essays and Speeches.* Boston, 1915.

———. *Notes as Vice President, 1928–1929.* Boston, 1935.

Gilbert, Clinton Wallace. *"You Takes Your Choice."* New York, 1924.

Leach, Paul Roscoe. *That Man Dawes.* Chicago, 1930.

Fixton, John E., Jr. "The Early Career of Charles G. Dawes." Ph.D. dissertation, University of Chicago, 1953.

Timmons, Bascom N. *Charles G. Dawes, Portrait of An American.* New York, 1979.

CHARLES CURTIS (Chapter 31)

Ewy, Marvin. *Charles Curtis of Kansas: Vice-President of the United States, 1929–1933.* Emporia, KS, 1961.

Fausold, Martin L. *The Presidency of Herbert Hoover.* Lawrence, KS, 1985.

Schlup, Leonard. "Charles Curtis: The Vice-President from Kansas." *Manuscripts* 35 (Summer 1983): 183–201.

Unrau, William E. *Mixed-Bloods and Tribal Dissolution: Charles Curtis and the Quest for Indian Identity.* Lawrence, KS, 1989.

JOHN NANCE GARNER (Chapter 32)

Fisher, Ovie C. *Cactus Jack.* Waco, TX, 1978.

Garner, John Nance. "This Job of Mine." *American Magazine* 118 (July 1934): 23, 96.

James, Marquis. *Mr. Garner of Texas.* Indianapolis, 1939.

Patenaude, Lionel V. "John Nance Gardner." In *Profiles in Power: Twentieth-Century Texans in Washington,* edited by Kenneth E. Hendrickson, Jr., and Michael L. Collins. Arlington Heights, IL, 1993.

Romano, Michael J. "The Emergence of John Nance Garner as a Figure in American National Politics, 1924–1941." Ph.D. dissertation, St. John's University, 1974.

Timmons, Bascom N. *Garner of Texas: A Personal History.* New York, 1948.

HENRY AGARD WALLACE (Chapter 33)

Markowitz, Norman D. *The Rise and Fall of the People's Century: Henry A. Wallace and American Liberalism, 1941–1948.* New York, 1973.

Schapsmeier, Edward L., and Frederick H. Schapsmeier. *Henry A. Wallace of Iowa: the Agrarian Years, 1910–1940.* Ames, IA, 1968.

———. *Prophet in Politics: Henry A. Wallace and the War Years, 1940–1965.* Ames, IA, 1973.

Wallace, Henry Agard. *Democracy Reborn. Selected from Public Papers and Edited with an Introduction and Notes by Russell Lord.* 1944. Reprint. New York, 1973.

———. *Henry A. Wallace Papers at the University of Iowa.* Edited by Earl M. Rogers. Iowa City, IA, 1974. Microfilm. 67 reels and guide.

———. *The Price of Vision: The Diary of Henry A. Wallace, 1942–1946.* Edited by John Morton Blum. Boston, 1973.

SELECTED BIBLIOGRAPHY

————. *The Reminiscences of Henry Agard Wallace.* Columbia University Oral History Program Collection, part 3, no. 40. Glen Rock, NJ, 1977. Microfilm. 2 reels.

————. *Whose Constitution? An Inquiry into the General Welfare.* 1936. Reprint. Westport, CT, 1971.

HARRY S. TRUMAN (Chapter 34)

Asbell, Bernard. *When F.D.R. Died.* New York, 1961.

Bishop, Jim. *FDR's Last Year: April 1944–April 1945.* New York, 1974.

Daniels, Jonathan. *The Man of Independence.* 1950. Reprint. Port Washington, NY, 1971.

Donovan, Robert J. *Conflict and Crisis: The Presidency of Harry S Truman, 1945–1948.* New York, 1977.

Ferrell, Robert H. *Choosing Truman: The Democratic Convention of 1944.* Columbia, MO, 1994.

————. *Harry S. Truman: A Life.* Columbia, MO, 1994.

————, ed. *The Autobiography of Harry S Truman.* Boulder, CO, 1980.

Flynn, Edward J. *You're the Boss.* New York, 1947.

Goldman, Elliot. "Justice William O. Douglas: The 1944 Vice Presidential Nomination and His Relationship with Roosevelt, an Historical Perspective." *Presidential Studies Quarterly* 12 (Summer 1982): 377–85.

Hamby, Alonzo L. *Man of the People: A Life of Harry S. Truman.* New York, 1995.

Heaster, Brenda L. "Who's on Second: The 1944 Democratic Presidential Nomination." *Missouri Historical Review* (January 1986).

Helm, William P. *Harry Truman, A Political Biography.* New York, 1947.

Kirkendall, Richard S. "Truman's Path to Power." *Social Science* 43 (1968): 67–73.

McClure, Arthur F., and Donna Costigan. "The Truman Vice Presidency: Constructive Apprenticeship or Brief Interlude?" *Missouri Historical Review* 65 (April 1971): 318–41.

McCullough, David G. " 'I Hardly Know Truman'." *American Heritage* 43 (July/August 1992): 46–64.

————. *Truman.* New York, 1992.

Parker, Daniel F. "The Political and Social Views of Harry S Truman." Ph.D. dissertation, University of Pennsylvania, 1951.

Partin, John W. "Roosevelt, Byrnes, and the 1944 Vice-Presidential Nomination." *Historian* 42 (1979): 85–100.

Rovin, Fern R. "Politics and the Presidential Election of 1944." Ph.D. dissertation, Indiana University, 1973.

Steinberg, Alfred. *The Man from Missouri: The Life and Times of Harry S Truman.* New York, 1962.

Truman, Harry S. *Memoirs.* 2 vols., Garden City, NY, 1955–1956.

Tugwell, Rexford Guy. *How They Became President: Thirty-five Ways to the White House.* New York, 1964.

ALBEN W. BARKLEY (Chapter 35)

Barkley, Alben W. *That Reminds Me.* Garden City, NY, 1954.

Barkley, Jane R. and Francis Spatz Leighton. *I Married the Veep.* New York, 1958.

Claussen, E. Neal. "Alben Barkley's Rhetorical Victory in 1948." *Southern Speech Communications Journal* 45 (1979): 79–92.

Davis, Polly Ann. *Alben W. Barkley, Senate Majority Leader and Vice President.* New York, 1979.

————. "Alben W. Barkley: Vice President." *Register of the Kentucky Historical Society* 76 (April 1978): 112–32.

Libbey, James K. *Dear Alben. Mr. Barkley of Kentucky.* Lexington, KY, 1979.

Wallace, H. Lew. "Alben Barkley and the Democratic Convention of 1948." *Filson Club History Quarterly* 55 (July 1981): 231–52.

RICHARD MILHOUS NIXON (Chapter 36)

Aitken, Jonathan. *Nixon—A Life.* Washington, 1993.

Ambrose, Stephen E. *Nixon.* 2 vols. to date. New York, 1987–1989.

Casper, Dale C. *Richard M. Nixon: A Bibliographic Exploration.* New York, 1988.

De Toledano, Ralph. *Nixon.* Rev. and expanded ed. New York, 1960.

Goldstein, Joel K. "The American Vice-Presidency, 1953–1978." Ph.D. dissertation, Oxford University (London), 1978.

Mazo, Earl and Stephen Hess. *Nixon: A Political Portrait.* New York, 1968.

Nixon, Richard M. *RN: The Memoirs of Richard Nixon.* New York, 1978.

————. *Six Crises.* 1962. Reprint, with new introduction. New York, 1990.

"Nixon's Own Story of Seven Years in the Vice-Presidency." *U.S. News and World Report* 48 (May 16, 1960): 98–106.

Pach, Chester J., Jr., and Elmo Richardson. *The Presidency of Dwight D. Eisenhower.* 1979. Rev. ed. Lawrence, KS, 1991.

Rovere, Robert H. "Letter from Washington: National Security Council and Cabinet Under Direction of Mr. Nixon." *New Yorker* 31 (October 8, 1955): 179–86.

LYNDON BAINES JOHNSON (Chapter 37)

Baker, Leonard. *The Johnson Eclipse: A President's Vice Presidency.* New York, 1966.

Caro, Robert A. *The Years of Lyndon Johnson.* 2 vols. to date. New York, 1982-.

Dalleck, Robert. *Lone Star Rising: Lyndon Johnson and His Times, 1908–1960.* 1 vol. to date. New York, 1991.

SELECTED BIBLIOGRAPHY

Evans, Rowland and Robert Novak. *Lyndon B. Johnson: The Exercise of Power, A Political Biography*. New York, 1966.

Goldstein, Joel K. "The American Vice-Presidency, 1953–1978." Ph.D. dissertation, Oxford University (London), 1978.

Johnson, Lyndon B. *The Vantage Point: Perspectives of the Presidency, 1963–1969*. New York, 1971.

Kearns, Doris. *Lyndon Johnson and the American Dream*. New York, 1976.

Lester, Robert Leon. "Developments in Presidential-Congressional Relations: FDR-JFK." Ph.D. dissertation, University of Virginia, 1969.

Light, Paul C. "The Institutional Vice Presidency." *Presidential Studies Quarterly* 13 (Spring 1983): 198–211.

Riccards, Michael P. "Rare Counsel: Kennedy, Johnson and the Civil Rights Bill of 1963." *Presidential Studies Quarterly* 11 (1981): 395–98.

White, William S. *The Professional: Lyndon B. Johnson*. Boston, 1964.

HUBERT HORATIO HUMPHREY (Chapter 38)

Broder, David. "Triple H Brand of Vice Presidency." *New York Times Magazine* (December 6, 1964).

Eisele, Albert. *Almost to the Presidency: A Biography of Two American Politicians*. Blue Earth, MN, 1972.

Garrettson, Charles Lloyd, III. *Hubert H. Humphrey: The Politics of Joy*. New Brunswick, NJ, 1993.

Goldstein, Joel K. "The American Vice-Presidency, 1963–1978." Ph.D. dissertation, Oxford University (London), 1978.

Humphrey, Hubert H. "Changes in the Vice Presidency." *Current History* 67 (August, 1974): 58–59, 89–90.

Humphrey, Hubert H. *The Education of a Public Man: My Life and Politics*. Edited by Norman Sherman. 1976. New ed. Minneapolis, 1991.

Natoli, Marie D. "The Humphrey Vice Presidency in Retrospect." *Presidential Studies Quarterly* 12 (Fall 1982): 603–9.

Pomper, Gerald. "The Nomination of Hubert Humphrey for Vice-President." *Journal of Politics* 28 (August 1966).

Ryskind, Allan H. *Hubert: An Unauthorized Biography of the Vice President*. New York, 1968.

U.S. Congress. *Memorial Addresses*. 95th Congress, 2d session, 1978. Washington, 1978.

SPIRO THEODORE AGNEW (Chapter 39)

Agnew, Spiro T. *Addresses and State Papers of Spiro T. Agnew, Governor of Maryland, 1967–1969*. Edited by Franklin L. Burdett. 2 vols. Annapolis, MD, 1975.

Agnew, Spiro T. *Collected Speeches of Spiro Agnew*. New York, 1971.

———. *Go Quietly . . . Or Else*. New York, 1980.

———. *The Canfield Decision*. Chicago, 1976.

———. *Where He Stands*. New York, 1968.

Aiken, George D. *Aiken: Senate Diary, January 1972-January 1975*. Brattleboro, VT, 1976.

Albright, Joseph. *What Makes Spiro Run: The Life and Times of Spiro Agnew*. New York, 1972.

Cohen, Richard M., and Jules Witcover. *A Heartbeat Away: The Investigation and Resignation of Vice President Spiro T. Agnew*. New York, 1974.

Coyne, John R., Jr. *The Impudent Snobs: Agnew vs. the Intellectual Establishment*. New Rochelle, NY, 1972.

Goldstein, Joel K. "The American Vice-Presidency, 1953–1978." Ph.D. dissertation, Oxford University (London), 1978.

Witcover, Jules. *White Knight: The Rise of Spiro Agnew*. New York, 1972.

GERALD R. FORD (Chapter 40)

Firestone, Bernard, and Alexej Ugrinsky, eds. *Gerald R. Ford and the Politics of Post-Watergate America*. 2 vols. Westport, CT, 1993.

Ford, Betty, with Chris Chase. *The Times of My Life*. New York, 1978.

Ford, Gerald R. *A Time to Heal: The Autobiography of Gerald R. Ford*. 1979. Reprint. Norwalk, CT, 1987.

———. *Selected Speeches*. Edited by Michael V. Doyle. Arlington, VA, 1973.

Ford, Gerald R., et al. "On the Threshold of the White House." *Atlantic Monthly* 234 (July, 1974): 63–72.

"Gerald R. Ford: Close Scrutiny Before Confirmation." *Congressional Quarterly* 31 (20 October 1973): 2759–72.

Goldstein, Joel K. "The American Vice-Presidency, 1953–1978." Ph.D. dissertation, Oxford University, 1978.

"Michigan Congressman GOP Vice Presidential Possibility." *Congresssional Quarterly* 22 (10 July 1964): 1445–48.

Mollenhoff, Clark R. *The Man Who Pardoned Nixon*. New York, 1976.

Natoli, Marie D. "The Vice Presidency: Gerald Ford as Healer?" *Presidential Studies Quarterly* 10 (Fall 1980): 662–64.

Reeves, Richard. *A Ford, Not a Lincoln*. New York, 1975.

Schapsmeier, Edward L., and Frederick H. Schapsmeier. *Gerald R. Ford's Date With Destiny: A Political Biography*. New York, 1989.

Syers, William A. "The Political Beginnings of Gerald R. Ford: Anti-Bossism, Internationalism, and the Congressional Campaign of 1948." *Presidential Studies Quarterly* 20 (Winter 1990): 127–42.

Sidey, Hugh. *Portrait of a President*. New York, 1975.

TerHorst, Jerald F. *Gerald Ford and the Future of the Presidency*. New York, 1974.

U.S. Congress. House. Committee on the Judiciary. *Nomination of Gerald R. Ford to the Vice Presidency of the United States*.

SELECTED BIBLIOGRAPHY

Hearings, 93rd Cong., 1st sess. November 15–26, 1973. Washington, 1973.

U.S. Congress. Senate. Committee on Rules and Administration. *Nomination of Gerald R. Ford of Michigan to be Vice President of the United States.* Hearings, 93rd Cong., 1st sess. November 1–14, 1973. Washington, 1993.

U.S. Congress. *Tributes to Honorable Gerald R. Ford, President of the United States.* 95th Cong., 1st sess., 1977. Washington, 1977.

NELSON ALDRICH ROCKEFELLER (Chapter 41)

Bales, Peter Relyea. "Nelson Rockefeller and His Quest for Inter-American Unity." Ph.D. dissertation, State University of New York, Stony Brook, 1992.

Connery, Robert H., and Gerald Benjamin. *Rockefeller of New York: Executive Power in the Statehouse.* Ithaca, NY, 1979.

Desmond, James. *Rockefeller.* New York, 1964.

Firestone, Bernard, and Alexej Ugrinsky, eds. *Gerald R. Ford and the Politics of Post-Watergate America.* 2 vols. Westport, CT, 1993.

Goldstein, Joel K. "The American Vice-Presidency, 1953–1978." Ph.D. dissertation, Oxford University (London), 1978.

Kramer, Michael S., and Sam Roberts. *"I Never Wanted to be Vice-President of Anything": An Investigative Biography of Nelson Rockefeller.* New York, 1976.

Library of Congress. Congressional Research Service. *Analysis of the Philosophy and Public Record of Nelson A. Rockefeller, Nominee for Vice President of the United States.* 93rd Cong., 2d sess. House. Committee Print. Washington, 1974.

Light, Paul C. "Vice-Presidential Influence Under Rockefeller and Mondale." *Political Science Quarterly* 98 (Winter 1983–1984): 617–40.

————. *Vice-Presidential Power: Advice and Influence in the White House.* Baltimore, 1984.

Morris, Joe Alex. *Nelson Rockefeller, A Biography.* New York, 1960.

Persico, Joseph E. *The Imperial Rockefeller: A Biography of Nelson A. Rockefeller.* New York, 1982.

Rockefeller, Nelson A. *The Future of Freedom: A Bicentennial Series of Speeches.* Washington, 1976.

Turner, Michael. *The Vice President as Policy Maker: Rockefeller in the Ford White House.* Westport, CT, 1982.

Underwood, James E., and William J. Daniels. *Governor Rockefeller in New York: The Apex of Pragmatic Liberalism in the United States.* Westport, CT, 1982.

U.S. Congress. House. Committee on the Judiciary. *Nomination of Nelson A. Rockefeller to be Vice President of the United States.* Hearings, 93rd Cong., 2d sess. November 21-December 5, 1974. Washington, 1974.

————. *Selected Issues and the Positions of Nelson A. Rockefeller, Nominee for Vice President of theUnited States: An Analysis.* 93rd Cong., 2d sess. Committee Print. Washington, 1974.

U.S. Congress. Senate. Committee on Rules and Administration. *Nomination of Nelson A. Rockefeller of New York to be Vice President of the United States.* Hearings, 93rd Cong., 2d sess. September 23-November 18, 1974. Washington, 1974.

U.S. Congress. *Memorial Addresses.* 96th Cong., 1st sess., 1979. Washington, 1979.

WALTER F. MONDALE (Chapter 42)

Carter, Jimmy. *Keeping Faith: Memoirs of a President.* New York, 1982.

Eisele, Albert. *Almost to the Presidency: A Biography of Two American Politicians.* Blue Earth, MN, 1972.

Gillon, Steven M. *The Democrats' Dilemma: Walter F. Mondale and the Liberal Legacy.* New York, 1992.

Goldstein, Joel K. "The American Vice-Presidency, 1953–1978." Ph.D. dissertation, Oxford University (London), 1978.

Lewis, Finlay. *Mondale: Portrait of An American Politician.* New York, 1980.

Light, Paul C. "Vice-Presidential Influence Under Rockefeller and Mondale." *Political Science Quarterly* 98 (Winter 1983–1984): 617–40.

Mondale, Walter F. *The Accountability of Power: Toward a Responsible Presidency.* New York, 1975.

————. *Vice-Presidential Power: Advice and Influence in the White House.* Baltimore, 1984.

Natoli, Marie D. "The Vice Presidency: Walter Mondale in the Lion's Den." *Presidential Studies Quarterly* 8 (Winter 1978): 100–102.

"Vice Presidential Campaign Debate: Mondale-Dole Meet in Houston." In *The Presidential Campaign 1976.* Vol. 3, *The Debates,* pp. 154–79. Washington, 1979.

GEORGE BUSH (Chapter 43)

Bush, George, with Victor Gold. *Looking Forward.* Garden City, NY, 1987.

Bush, George. *The Wit & Wisdom of George Bush: With Some Reflections from Dan Quayle.* Edited by Ken Brady and Jeremy Solomon. New York, 1989.

Ide, Arthur Frederick. *Bush-Quayle: The Reagan Legacy.* Irving, TX, 1989. King, Nicholas. *George Bush: A Biography.* New York, 1980.

Kirschten, Dick. "George Bush—Keeping His Profile Low So He Can Keep His Influence High."*National Journal* 13 (June 20, 1981): 1096–1100.

U.S. Congress. Senate. Committee on Armed Services. *Nomination of George Bush to be Director of Central Intelligence.* Hearing, 94th Cong., 1st sess. December 15–16, 1975. Washington, 1975.

J. DANFORTH QUAYLE (Chapter 44)

Broder, David S. *The Man Who Would be President: Dan Quayle.* New York, 1992.

Campbell, Colin S.J., and Bert A. Rockman, eds. *The Bush Presidency: First Appraisals.* Chatham, NJ, 1991.

SELECTED BIBLIOGRAPHY

DeMoss, Dorothy. "George Bush." In *Profiles in Power: Twentieth-Century Texans in Washington*, edited by Kenneth E. Hendrickson, Jr., and Michael L. Collins. Arlington Heights, IL, 1993.

Duffy, Michael, and Dan Goodgame. *Marching in Place: The Status Quo Presidency of George Bush*. New York, 1992.

Fenno, Richard F., Jr. *The Making of a Senator: Dan Quayle*. Washington, 1989.

Ide, Arthur Frederick. *Bush-Quayle: The Reagan Legacy*. Irving, TX, 1989.

Mullins, Kerry, and Aaron Wildavsky. "The Procedural Presidency of George Bush." *Political Science Quarterly* 107 (Spring 1992): 31–62.

Quayle, Dan. *Standing Firm: A Vice-Presidential Memoir*. New York, 1994.

CREDITS FOR ILLUSTRATIONS

Cover illustration: *Prints and Photographs Division, Library of Congress, LC–USZ62– 116624*

Frontispiece: *AP/WideWorld Photo*

John Adams: *The Harvard University Art Museums, Acc. No. H073*

Thomas Jefferson: *Office of the Curator, The White House*

Aaron Burr: *Prints and Photographs Division, Library of Congress, LC–USZ62–16737*

George Clinton: *The National Portrait Gallery, Smithsonian Institution, NPG 84.172*

Elbridge Gerry: *Prints and Photographs Division, Library of Congress, LC–USZ62–74104*

Daniel D. Tompkins: *Collection of the City of New York, City Hall*

John C. Calhoun: *The National Portrait Gallery, Smithsonian Institution, NPG 78.64*

Martin Van Buren: *Prints and Photographs Division, Library of Congress, LC–USZ62–19608*

Richard Mentor Johnson: *Prints and Photographs Division, Library of Congress, LC–USZ62–1887*

John Tyler: *Prints and Photographs Division, Library of Congress, LC–USZ62–96919*

George M. Dallas: *Prints and Photographs Division, Library of Congress, LC–USZ62–10549*

Millard Fillmore: *Prints and Photographs Division, Library of Congress, LC–USZ62–13013*

Willam R. King: *Prints and Photographs Division, Library of Congress*

John C. Breckinridge: *Prints and Photographs Division, Library of Congress, LC–USZ62–9895*

Hannibal Hamlin: *Prints and Photographs Division, Library of Congress, LC–BH82–3882*

Andrew Johnson: *Prints and Photographs Division, Library of Congress, LC–B8184–10690*

Schuyler Colfax: *Prints and Photographs Division, Library of Congress, LC–USZ62–116494*

Henry Wilson: *Prints and Photographs Division, Library of Congress, LC–BH83–3701*

William A. Wheeler: *Prints and Photographs Division, Library of Congress, LC–BH832–29130*

Chester A. Arthur: *Prints and Photographs Division, Library of Congress, LC–USZ62–13021*

Thomas A. Hendricks: *Prints and Photographs Division, Library of Congress*

Levi P. Morton: *Prints and Photographs Division, Library of Congress, LC–USZ62–10566*

Adlai E. Stevenson: *Prints and Photographs Division, Library of Congress, LC–USZ62–108489*

Garret Augustus Hobart: *Prints and Photographs Division, Library of Congress, LC–USZ62–10553*

Theodore Roosevelt: *Prints and Photographs Division, Library of Congress, LC–USZ62–12095*

Charles W. Fairbanks: *Prints and Photographs Division, Library of Congress, LC–USZ61–445*

James Schoolcraft Sherman: *Prints and Photographs Division, Library of Congress, LC–USZ62–85213*

Thomas R. Marshall: *Prints and Photographs Division, Library of Congress, LC–USZ62–116554*

Calvin Coolidge: *Prints and Photographs Division, Library of Congress, LC–B2–5253–4*

Charles G. Dawes: *Prints and Photographs Division, Library of Congress, LC–USZ62–08528*

Charles Curtis: *Prints and Photographs Division, Library of Congress, LC–USZ62–11655*

John Nance Garner: *Prints and Photographs Division, Library of Congress, LC–USZ62–116737*

Henry A. Wallace: *Prints and Photographs Division, Library of Congress, LC–USW3–6470–D*

Harry S. Truman: *Harry S. Truman Presidential Library*

CREDITS FOR ILLUSTRATIONS

INDEX

[This index generally includes individuals mentioned in the book only if they play a sufficient role in the story or appear in more than one chapter. But major party presidential and vice-presidential candidates are included even if they are only mentioned in passing. Wives of vice presidents are indexed but rarely parents.]

INDEX

INDEX

INDEX

INDEX